Parkways: Past, Present, and Future

The Appalachian Consortium

The Appalachian Consortium is a non-profit educational organization comprised of institutions and agencies located in the Southern Highlands. Our members are volunteers who plan and execute projects which serve 156 mountain counties in seven states. Among our goals are:

- *Preserving the cultural heritage of Southern Appalachia*
- *Protecting the mountain environment*
- *Improving the educational opportunities for area students and teachers*
- *Conducting scientific, social, and economic research*
- *Promoting a positive image of Appalachia*
- *Encouraging regional cooperation*

The Member Institutions of the Appalachian Consortium are:

Appalachian State University
Blue Ridge Parkway
East Tennessee State University
Gardner-Webb College
Great Smoky Mountains Natural History Association
John C. Campbell Folk School
Lees-McRae College
Mayland Community College
Mountain Regional Library
North Carolina Division of Archives and History
Southern Appalachian Highlands Conservancy
Southern Highlands Handicraft Guild
U. S. Forest Service
Warren Wilson College
Western Carolina University
Western North Carolina Historical Society

Parkways: Past, Present, and Future

Proceedings of the Second Biennial
Linear Parks Conference
1987

Appalachian Consortium Press
Boone, North Carolina 28608

The Appalachian Consortium was a non-profit educational organization composed of institutions and agencies located in Southern Appalachia. From 1973 to 2004, its members published pioneering works in Appalachian studies documenting the history and cultural heritage of the region. The Appalachian Consortium Press was the first publisher devoted solely to the region and many of the works it published remain seminal in the field to this day.

With funding from the Andrew W. Mellon Foundation and the National Endowment for the Humanities through the Humanities Open Book Program, Appalachian State University has published new paperback and open access digital editions of works from the Appalachian Consortium Press.

www.collections.library.appstate.edu/appconsortiumbooks

ISBN (pbk.: alk. Paper): 978-1-4696-4202-4
ISBN (ebook): 978-1-4696-4205-5

Distributed by the University of North Carolina Press
www.uncpress.org

Table of Contents

The Blue Ridge Parkway: Eight Visions

A photographic exhibition entitled "The Blue Ridge Parkway: Eight Visions" was created specifically for the 1987 conference "Parkways: Past, Present, and Future," whose proceedings are published herein. The Appalachian Environmental Arts Center, a program of the University of North Carolina at the Highlands Biological Station, organized and curated the exhibition.

Eight regionally and nationally known photographic artists were invited to submit work concerning the theme "Personal Vision/The Blue Ridge Parkway." They were encouraged to keep a strong personal perspective of the area.

Exhibiting artists were William Bake, Gil Leebrick, Jay Phyfer, Benjamin Porter, John Scarlata, Michael Schultz, Sam Wang, and Merry Moor Winnett. Each artist worked with the medium of photography, his or her own combinations and techniques, and his or her personal vision to reflect the diverse manner in which each of us sees the unique area of the Blue Ridge Parkway.

Although space does not allow for all the photographs from the exhibit to be reproduced in this book, a very small sampling can be found on the pages dividing the text into sections (e.g. "Keynote Addresses," "Design and Planning," etc.), along with comments by or about the photographers.

Gilbert W. Leebrick
Associate Director
Appalachian Environmental Arts Center

Introduction

"Parkways: Past, Present, Future," is the second in a series of biennial conferences focusing on linear parks around the world. The first conference, held at Appalachian State University in 1985, examined the impact of the Blue Ridge Parkway as an agent of transition during the first fifty years.

The resounding success of the first conference promoted a suggestion by participants that the conference format be expanded in future years to include an examination of parkways around the world. As devised by the conference steering committee, the stated purpose was to "examine the history of parkways, their conceptual foundations, current contributions as a part of our transportation system, and alternative roles they may play in our future." It was the hope of the steering committee that the conference would be truly interdisciplinary and attract broad representation. I think you will agree after reviewing the table of contents that the committee succeeded in meeting this objective. Presenters representing a wide variety of disciplines attended from Europe, Canada, Asia, and thirty of the lower forty-eight states.

This second biennial conference represented a coordinated effort of several organizations which are interested in focusing international attention on the importance of linear parks. The two primary sponsors of the initial conference, the Appalachian Consortium and the Blue Ridge Parkway, were again instrumental in the Roanoke gathering. The River Foundation, leaders of Project EXPLORE on the Roanoke river in Virginia, joined the conference as the third major sponsor in 1987. As was the case with the 1985 gathering, a large portion of the success of "Parkways: Past, Present, Future," can be attributed to the support and involvement of the American Society of Landscape Architects.

Parkways: Past, Present, Future features keynote addresses by Harrold Eidsvik on parkways in Canada's National Park System and by John B. Slater on the American Society of Landscape Architects' view of parkways. Also highlighting the conference were Gary Everhardt's presentation "Blue Ridge Parkway: Sensitivity, Vision, and Design" and H. Bern Ewert's discussion of the 5,000 acre river greenway and parkway in Roanoke, Virginia called EXPLORE.

For the purpose of this proceedings, the remaining presentations have been divided into four broad categories: "Design and Planning," "Historical Perspectives," "Environmental and Economic Perspectives," and "Management." The first broad category, "Design and Planning," contains presentations which reflect the geographic variety which was evident throughout the entire conference. Parkways, or plans for parkways, in Mississippi, Arizona, Virginia, Canada, Washington, North Carolina, and Missouri are featured. The "Historical Perspectives" section includes a variety of papers but is strongly colored by analysis of eastern systems in New York and Washington. The theme expressed most often in the "Environmental and Economic Perspectives" section is the problem of encroachment and preserving the scenic landscape associated with parkways. Finally, the "Management" portion of these proceedings looks at such themes as visitor expectations, visual preferences, alternative information management systems, land acquisition, and citizen involvement.

We invite you to join us in future linear park conferences. Through these biennial events we have established an important forum for the exchange of knowledge and information about parkways and have fostered a sense of "shared community" between practitioners from diverse cultural and professional backgrounds. We believe that those participating come away from the conferences with a renewed commitment to preserving the natural landscape around the world.

Barry M. Buxton
Conference Chairman

"ZERO DUSK" WILLIAM BAKE

I. Keynote Addresses

William Bake is no stranger to us or the Parkway. He has had much of his vision of this land published for all of us to enjoy. His images give us the sense of grandeur while retaining the magic of the Blue Ridge Parkway.—Gilbert W. Leebrick

Welcoming Remarks

Douglas Cruickshanks, Jr., President, The River Foundation

On behalf of The River Foundation, I would like to welcome you to PARKWAYS: PAST, PRESENT, FUTURE. It is exciting for The Foundation to be a part of bringing together professionals from across this country and from around the world to see and experience one of the finest examples of parkways in the world, the Blue Ridge Parkway, and to stimulate thinking about the future role of parkways in transportation, conservation, history and the environment.

As part of the program, you have an opportunity to learn more about The River Foundation's plans to create a 5,000 acre conservation area, including a Roanoke River Greenway and Parkway, and the EXPLORE Park. EXPLORE will be an American adventure, relating our past in a unique way. We look forward to sharing that with you.

While you are here in the Roanoke Valley, I hope you will enjoy the scenic beauty which abounds. Now as we turn our attention to Parkways and the values they represent to us in protecting the landscape, I am reminded of old man McCaslin's remarks in William Faulkner's short story, "The Bear." To paraphrase if I may, from his conversation about the land, he said: We can never own the land, it is a gift. We are only its stewards and this stewardship demands that the land is preserved for those who follow us.

Blue Ridge Parkway: Sensitivity, Vision, and Design

Gary Everhardt, Superintendent, Blue Ridge Parkway

This international conference provides a focus and an opportunity to share valuable information, and, in the process, promotes a camaraderie between all of us who support parkways.

None of us exists as an island and meeting together like this not only facilitates the work of all of us, but also promotes a spirit of cooperation that benefits us all. I hope that in months and years to come we will continue to meet to exchange ideas and renew friendships.

Some 54 years ago, a young (he was 25 at the time) landscape architect, Stanley Abbott, received the somewhat unenviable task of designing a parkway nearly 500 miles in length. As he himself said, "It is no simple matter to define irrevocably what a national parkway should be. We have no precedent, as far as I know of, in the world."

But having precedent was not Abbott's only concern. The young man not only had to design the parkway, he had to do so by coordinating the efforts of a multitude of local state and federal agencies.

And the terrain over which the parkway was to pass was certainly far from pristine. In some cases the land was clear cut; erosion was prevalent. The countryside was far from "unspoiled." Yet, Stan Abbott and his assistant, Edward Abbuehl, were not deterred. They were sensitive to the parkway landscape and saw potential that they translated into a vision. They followed this vision with admirable zeal.

As Abbott saw it, the job meant "fitting the parkway into the mountains as if nature had put it there." He saw that like any work of art, "the Parkway must carry its justification throughout its entire composition," for in his words, "it can't have its dead areas, its neglected detail. All elements must compose as to please."

The road itself was to be built "in a manner that equals the magnificence of the countryside." Structures were to be characterized by "simplicity and informality in order that they might harmonize with the natural environment." In his vision, the parkway was to be built so as to "reveal the charm and interest of the native American countryside."

This obvious sensitivity took its physical expression in a design with distinct features. There would be generous buffer zones. Abbott reasoned that parkway vistas should reveal nothing offensive to the visitor "as far as the eye can see."

This included eliminating road crossings and acquiring right-of-way of sufficient width to preclude billboards and strip development. The road, for the most part, would follow the crest of the Blue Ridge, although even here were constraints dictated by topography, by the various states and federal agencies involved, and by available funds.

Now, more than a half-century later, we have inherited that farseeing vision from the past. It is as modern as the day it was conceived, even though we live in a world far different from that of the Depression years.

In 1986, the Blue Ridge Parkway accommodated more than 21 million visits, a number that surely would have staggered its designers. Visitation has steadily climbed at a rate of about five per cent per year for the past decade. The end is nowhere in sight.

Yet, we not only are able to accommodate that number, we are able to provide quality experiences. I suggest to you that this affection for the Parkway is the result of a combination of several things: The natural beauty of the area, its cultural history and artifacts, and the sensitivity and the vision that led to the ultimate design, management and operation.

Over the years, others have followed Abbott's pattern - Sam Weems, Jim Eden, Granville Liles, Joe Brown and many others. But, it is not enough to applaud the work of our predecessors; we must follow through.

Our operations must reflect attention to detail and strict adherence to the highest standards. Our new facilities must be in keeping with the structures and design concepts that are, by now, well established. In this respect, we must strive not merely to "live up to" those who came before us, but to carry out the dream. And dreams, after all, are what capture the imagination and motivate us to do our best.

On September 11, 1987, we completed the final section of the Parkway. I can't help but think that our founders would be pleased with the product. Surely nothing could have gone more "lightly upon the land," could have been built in more harmony or with more consistency with the natural environment than the Linn Cove Viaduct, a structure on that final section. It is, in my opinion, not only a continuation of the high principles that were set years ago, but is, in fact, an outstanding example of those principles. While the technology that built the Viaduct is a product of the late 20th century, the concepts it embodies are as old as the parkway itself.

EXPLORE: An American Adventure

H. B. Ewert, EXPLORE Project Director

It is a pleasure for me to join you today. It is an honor for our community to host, in this one room, such an outstanding collection of knowledge and interest in parkways. Those of us who live here share with you a deep devotion to the parkway concept—our own Blue Ridge Parkway stands for preservation, conservation, scenic beauty, and environmental protection. And, in the years ahead in our Roanoke Valley region, the parkway will have even greater significance.

Our region is planning a bold and innovative project called "EXPLORE"—a multi-faceted undertaking that forever will enhance our beautiful and historic part of the Commonwealth. The Blue Ridge Parkway had a part in the development of the EXPLORE concept, and the parkway will be an integral part of the completed project.

Three years ago, as the City Manager of Roanoke, I was visited by Gary Everhardt, Superintendent of the Parkway. He reminded me that Roanoke is the largest urban area along the parkway path, and he was interested in the role the city would play in the parkway's upcoming fiftieth anniversary. At about the same time, I was visited by the board of our Mill Mountain Zoo, a local facility that has a direct spur off the parkway into Roanoke. The board was concerned that the zoo had too little space on the mountain for expansion. A third, but significant factor in my story is the situation and condition of the Roanoke Valley economy, whose growth rate is not as healthy as that of other regions in Virginia and neighboring states.

These three factors became the impetus for EXPLORE. For me, they served to reinforce the realization that our natural beauty, environment, and rich heritage were value assets that deserved protection. Simultaneously, I recognized that in order to insure regional growth and vitality, to create and maintain employment for current and future generations, and to stimulate business growth and expansion, something *big* had to be done. Thus, the idea of EXPLORE. So, it is only fitting that Explore and the Blue Ridge Parkway will be so closely linked.

What is EXPLORE? It will be a five thousand acre conservation area and education-history project—a family destination that will combine four features into one: an American Indian Park showing authentic Indian heritage and culture, a Blue Ridge Town that replicates an eighteenth century pioneer village and tells of continental frontier expansion, an American Wilderness Park that features continental flora and fauna, and a 25-mile Roanoke River greenway with a scenic roadway, a bicycle path, and a ten-mile extension of the Blue Ridge Parkway into the Explore Park site. Explore will be a national historical zoological park that combines a "living museum" with lodging, restaurants, and a variety of visitor services.

Expected to attract one million annual visitors from the Blue Ridge Parkway and Interstate 81, EXPLORE will be designed to create the equivalent of nineteen hundred full time and over twelve hundred indirect jobs, not to mention an additional two thousand construction jobs over our seven year construction period. It will provide a 16 million dollar payroll, while generating local tax revenues of 1.8 million dollars annually and state tax revenues of 2.2 million annually.

The principal force behind the EXPLORE project is The River Foundation, a non-profit organization with a number of regional concerns and interests: promoting the scenic quality, initiating positive regional economic growth, providing an education of our rich heritage, preserving our natural beauty, protecting the Roanoke River corridor, and establishing closer connections with other existing resources that include the Blue Ridge Parkway, Smith Mountain Lake, and Virginia Tech.

Here is how the Foundation's purposes will be accomplished through EXPLORE:

- through a concerted, regional approach with local, state, and federal assistance in partnership with the private sector;
- through expert planning and design, by the most qualified and experienced persons;
- through a combination of funding sources that includes Commonwealth planning funds, in-kind land and water resources by the Town of Vinton, private contributions, federal funding this spring in the Highway Bill for the extension of the Blue Ridge Parkway to our site, and access funds from Roanoke County to initiate parkway funds from the state. Further funding is anticipated in the state's 1988 biennium budget that will be used for matching federal road funds, purchasing land for the state park, engineering, and flood control.

As you can see, EXPLORE is designed to be a major part of the region's economic development. When combined with other regional efforts—airport expansion, a better connector to Blacksburg, flood control, a convention center, and our arts center expansion—EXPLORE will enable western Virginia to enjoy the benefits of tourism as a clean, vital industry.

Further, by creating this destination in the vicinity of the Blue Ridge Parkway and I-81, western Virginia will enhance its position as the third part of a statewide triangle of tourism that also includes Tidewater and northern Virginia. Our region will benefit from EXPLORE—and all of Virginia will benefit from the visitors we direct to other destinations.

EXPLORE will be a state park that is served by an extension of the Blue Ridge Parkway. Without a doubt, EXPLORE—like the parkway—will endure for years to come.

Ours is an ambitious project. And it has its share of risk. But EXPLORE is no greater a risk than the experiences of the three hundred thousand Americans—roughly ten percent of our nation's population in the late 1700s—who flooded over and beyond these great Blue Ridge to the Cumberland Gap, pushing the nation's frontier ultimately across the continent.

These pioneers are the symbol of our American spirit. The vision we have in western Virginia today is a legacy to their efforts.

Thank you very much for being here, and for recognizing the importance to our Blue Ridge Mountains and its timeless parkway.

The American Society of Landscape Architects' View of Parkways

John B. Slater, Vice President, ASLA

Thank you very much for the opportunity to be here with you today. The American Society of Landscape Architects (ASLA) is both pleased and proud to be supporting this most worthwhile conference on Parkways: Past, Present, Future. The title of my talk is "The American Society of Landscape Architects' View of Parkways." That's a rather formidable topic. I hope I'll be able to keep your attention.

While researching background material for this talk I came across many references to the Westchester Parkway System and more specifically the Bronx River Parkway. This struck an interesting chord with me since part of my youth was spent within walking distance of the Bronx River Parkway. I can remember snow days when we would hike over to the ponds along the parkway to go ice skating and stopping to climb the rocks on the way back from the movies. They are fond memories for me and I sense the Bronx River Parkway taught me very early on that roads do not have to be a harsh intrusion in our environment. As Dr. Jolley mentioned earlier, "there is a way more beautiful."

The message I would like to leave with you from the American Society of Landscape Architects is one of Vision and Value, the theme of our Annual Meeting in Baltimore this year. Vision and value is another way of saying, "there is a way more beautiful" and it takes vision to think of ways more beautiful.

Everyone tackles his own task based on his own perspective, training, education, and experience. Landscape architects are trained to constantly think in terms of the quality of life for the user. The user might might be walking through a site, driving into a park, or just sitting passively alongside a river. The important concerns deal with the means to make the experience as positive and pleasant as possible.

I am reminded of the time an architect (a building architect and friend) and I had the opportunity to visit a site to research a particular concept of office building. We were doing this because we would soon be working on a similar type project. Unable to debrief immediately we met three or four days later to review our observations Interestingly enough he was able to describe in the most minute detail features of the building. He could describe the structural system, the roof and parapet dimensions, the fenestration of the windows - all of the features of the building. On the other hand his memory of the "site" conditions was extremely vague. He could not tell me the things that were of interest to me, the site features I had noticed: How was access to the site handled? What was the orientation of the parking? How and where did they deal with the dumpster? How was the entry area of the building handled?

Two simple conclusions. One is that you observe better those things you are instinctively interested in, and two is that if you spend your time day in and day out solving a particular sort of problem then the odds are when you have an opportunity to see something you've not seen before your observations relate back to your day to day experiences. Landscape architects spend their days analyzing and designing sites constantly thinking of how to move the user from an arrival point through the site to his intended destination or use. We spend our time trying to choreograph the sequence of events and the "set design" to create a "way more beautiful." We design the "hole in the donut." Outdoor spaces or outdoor rooms replace "set design" and the donut might be many flavors. The space may be enclosed by trees and shrubs or by building walls or some other site elements.

It takes Vision to create Value. "Quality of life" is a popular phrase these days but it really translates into increased value for the site or the user. Stanley Abbott had the Vision to design a beautiful parkway. It was his concern that the Value of the park, The Blue Ridge Mountains, and the driving experience be enhanced. Olmsted had the Vision when he set out to work with the land to design parks and public institutions all over this fine country of ours. He has added immense value for a countless number of cities and people.

In Maryland the ASLA is currently working on a C.A.T. (Community Assistance Team) to raise the public awareness of the Olmsted Brothers' Vision for Baltimore - that is a series of wide green boulevards and parkways to connect the people with the parks and institutions throughout the city. Seventy-three years ago in Baltimore the Olmsted Brothers were in the business of creating value by enhancing outdoor spaces. I can imagine they were forced many times to argue against their client obtaining a couple more building lots and having to convince the client to spend a little more money to create a quality environment.

We all need to spend more time being concerned with our quality of life, with the quality of our environment. There is too much visual pollution, we have too many "Route Ones" with cluttered signage, messy looking intersections, and huge expansive uninterrupted parking lots.

Too often we all become numb and complacent when it comes to our surroundings. Landscape architects care about the quality of our environment and we need your help and expertise so we can work hand in hand to make this planet a better place to live.

Thank you.

Heritage Highways in Canada's National Parks

Harrold Eidsvik, Senior Policy Advisor, Chairman IUCN–Commission on National Parks & Protected Areas, Environment Canada–Parks, Les Terrasses de la Chaudiere, Ottowa

I welcome the opportunity to participate in this important conference. For you, it is a time of real celebration! The final chapter in the development of a pioneering concept in heritage preservation, the Blue Ridge Parkway, is now written: the completion of this innovative, intimate, scenic motor route along the mountain crests of Eastern America.

We, in Canada, share the spirit of celebrating heritage. Two years ago Canadians toasted the first hundred years of our National Parks System. That birthday party made Canadians focus closely upon the rich natural legacy we hold in trust for ourselves and the rest of the world. Our centennial events made all of us appreciate our natural park lands in a deeper, more complete fashion.

This evening, I would like to first introduce you to Canada's National Parks, and secondly share with you some of the special places found along our parkways. Canada has, along with the United States, one of the largest National Park Systems in the world yet it makes up only 1.8% of our country's land mass.

Environment Canada–Parks, the agency which administers our 34 National Parks, also has responsibility over more than 60 national historic parks and sites, and 9 canals. There are National Parks in all 10 provinces, and both territories; from Newfoundland on Canada's east coast to the western coast of Vancouver Island and now, westward still to the brooding magnificence of the Queen Charlotte Islands. From Canada's most southerly land form, Point Pelee on Lake Erie, to the northern vastness of Auyuittuq, Northern Yukon and, as of last year, Ellesmere Island National Park Reserve, an arctic wilderness on the very roof of our country —all across our wide and varied land—National Parks beckon the visitor: Wood Buffalo, Canada's largest National Park and the second largest in the world; Riding Mountain; The Bruce Peninsula, in Ontario, Canada's newest National Park and our first National Marine Component; farther east, on the tip of the rugged Gaspé Peninsula is the Forillon National Park Highland Peninsula which punctuates the Gulf of the St. Lawrence; and Kejimkujik, a prime example of Nova Scotia's quiet interior and a canoeist's heaven flavored with legends of early Indians.

It all began in Banff in 1885 with 10 square miles of national landscape dedicated to public benefit and education. Today Banff boasts 2,564 square miles of mountains, lakes, glaciers and valleys. Overwhelming land forms in the Icefields Parkway stretching north to neighboring Jasper National Park are linked by the most spectacular parkways in our entire parks system and indeed, one of the most breathtaking on the entire continent.

Just as our two countries are distinct, so are our parkways. The Blue Ridge, like the Natchez Trace, is a distinct unit of the U. S. Park Service. Environment Canada - Parks has no such specific designation for parkways. Our parkways are strictly access routes within established National Parks. Canada's parkways vary greatly in nature and length.

In Cape Breton Highlands National Park on our Atlantic Coast, the Cabot Trail skirts 85 miles of rocky coastline and uplands, offering the visitor a true highland adventure. Because parts of the Cabot Trail lie outside the Park, visitors can experience the neighboring region and communities as well as park features. In fact many Cabot Trail travellers fail to distinguish the park territory from its surrounding setting.

In Cape Breton the visitor's environmental experience does not end at the park boundary. Within the Park the visitor can sample all major park environments from the parkway, including two different coastlines, the only boreal forest in Nova Scotia, maple-filled valleys, and historical structures such as the Lone Shieling, a reconstructed Crofter's House modelled after those in the Scottish Highlands. Bus touring has grown in popularity and our Park interpreters have developed a successful self-guiding audio tape, so that bus tour groups can interpret the parkway features for themselves.

Brushing against the international boundary in the middle of the St. Lawrence River lies St. Lawrence Islands National Park served by the provincially owned Thousand Islands Parkway. Although not administered by Environment Canada, this parkway provides ready visitor access to our resources as well as to a host of heritage destinations along the river. At one time, during the war of 1812, this was a real zone of tension between our two nations. Now it is a heritage corridor managed by a series of cooperating agencies; a tourist haven for Americans, Canadians and visitors from abroad.

The province of Quebec boasts three Canadian National Parks. La Mauricie National Park between Montreal and Quebec City, a ten hour drive north of New York City, represents the definitive Canadian woodland

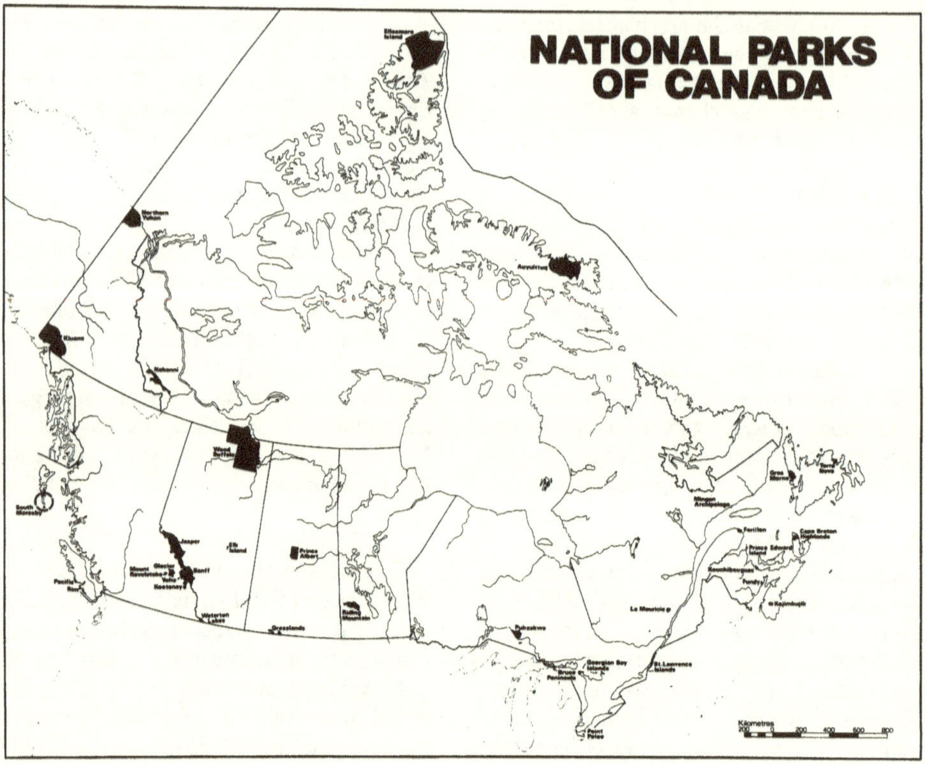

NATIONAL PARKS OF CANADA

Top: ***Fig. 1. National Parks of Canada.*** Bottom: ***Fig. 2. Banff-Jasper Highway.***
(Photo: Environment Canada–Parks, photo by T. Grant.)

landscape. Before park establishment, hunting and fishing clubs controlled access and use in this area. A modern parkway, following a u-shaped corridor, provides access to numerous visitor activity areas within the park, including picnic sites, hiking and walking trails, scenic lookouts, canoe portages, and such Laurentian landscape features as meandering lakes.

Thousands of miles west near Edmonton in Central Alberta, the parkway of Elk Island National Park invites visitors to examine this prairie environment on an intimate scale. This route provides direct access to park trails exploring lakeshores, marshlands, upland forests and open meadows. The design of the Elk Island Parkway encourages vehicle users to look closely at the park's heritage features as they slowly traverse this motor "nature trail."

Certain of our parks have parkways which do not lie lightly on the land, and do not help the visitor relate to park resources. Some of these roads date from a time when landscape planning did not have a high priority in design. Such is the case with Kejimkujik National Park in southwestern Nova Scotia. Here park managers have turned a design liability into a visitor attraction. Time, care and the green goodness of wild plants have healed the over-designed, wide shoulders, and the road surface now attracts increasing numbers of parkway cyclists. The parkway leads visitors to lakeland and wilderness canoe launching points, interpretation trails, a viewing tower, campgrounds and beaches.

National Parks have successfully recycled some older roadways into attractive parkways. Such is the case in Waterton Lakes National Park, the Canadian component of Waterton-Glacier International Peace Park. Here the Akimina and Red Rock Canyon Parkways traverse prehistoric migratory routes. Made available to the visitor are on-site exhibits, picnic areas, trailheads to mountain valleys and alpine lakes.

When parks professionals consider parkway planning and design they realize the important legacy the Blue Ridge Parkway has established for all of us. I have seen few parkways which match its standard of excellence. This splendid roadway displays a melding of landscape architecture and engineering that, above all, respects the landscape through which it passes. It is an uncommon access system; one that beckons and calms the visitor and provides a series of varied, personal interpretive opportunities; a true Appalachian mountain high!

Back home in Canada's national capitol, Ottawa, where I live, we enjoy a roadway inspired by the concept of the Blue Ridge Parkway. The Gatineau Parkway provides motorized access to the park of the same name, a park perched on the very doorstep of Canada's fourth largest metropolitan area. Although administered by a sister agency of Environment –Canada Parks, namely the National Capitol Commission, Gatineau Park fills the same regional niche as Maryland's Catoctin Mountain Park does for your national capitol (Washington and region).

In our two countries, efforts of enlightened engineers, landscape architects, interpreters and planners have built an enduring legacy. Canadians have learned much from your successes at the Blue Ridge and other parkways and applied them to our northern part of North America. Our experience with parkways shows that two factors are of critical importance to the visitor. One is the way we greet visitors, and the other is the manner in which we orient and present the visitor to the heritage features en route.

Two visitor sub-systems are critical to success. One is signage; the other relates to visitor reception facilities. We are a country with two official languages and many international visitors. We have adopted the international signage system throughout our national parks. Other park systems have copied our success. Some international symbols tend to confuse - i.e., the symbol "E" for exhibit is not understood by many park visitors. We are in the process of revising our prize winning sign manual.

Visitor reception centers have become more important with the increasing trend in group touring. We are proud of some visitor reception centers, like the one at the Cheticamp Entrance to Cape Breton Highlands National Park in

Nova Scotia. Not all sitings of visitor reception centers have been successful. We can share with you some of our experience through evaluations which we have made of them.

We have found the most successful siting criteria for visitor reception centers are similar to siting criteria for gas stations on roadways outside of parks; yet we have a tendency to want to hide our V. R. C.'s and conceal our message.

The current reality in Canada is that the public must increasingly pay for public amenities. Since 1984 we have increased total revenues collected by Environment Canada - Parks by about fifty percent in an attempt to reduce the shortfall between costs and revenues. Many revenues are collected through entrance fees to national parks. Because some park roadways provide linkages in transcontinental corridors, there are real problems in collecting revenues to cover costs of operations which are borne by national parks; yet rising road maintenance costs and particularly winter snow clearing costs are ever increasing cost components of national park operations. We are in the process of finding sources of revenue to offset these costs.

There are many more challenges associated with the management of parkways and I am certain they will be thoroughly aired and expertly discussed through this invigorating forum. At this time I wish to express sincere thanks for this opportunity to share with you some examples of what we have learned and adapted, and to express my appreciation for including me in the deliberations of this remarkable conference.

May I close with a warm welcome to you, to explore our heritage areas and discover the best of our geography along the parkways of Canada's National Parks.

MICHAEL SHULTZ

II. Design and Planning

Michael Shultz, a self-educated photographer living in North Carolina, says, "I think most people who have taken time along the Parkway realize it is a door into a special geographical area."

Urban Environments and the Mississippi River Corridor Parkway: A Design Critique

Professor Robert T. Mooney, AIA, School of Architecture, University of Illinois at Urbana-Champaign

INTRODUCTION

The Mississippi River is the mainstream of America. As it winds its way from near the northern border of the United States to the Gulf of Mexico, it is numbered among the great rivers of the world. In its magnificent journey to the sea, it offers the possibility for a dynamic studio without walls for the investigation of parkway design in the urban context the length of the river corridor. Within this framework, and from an architect's perceptions of the Mississippi River corridor, this paper will examine and investigate a number of major metropolitan areas and parkway advocacy as related to urban design-water environment interface. Urban design theory and parkway development often experience extreme tensions in major metropolitan areas. Numbered among generators of those tensions are forces such as acquisition of easements for land transportation systems, sight line loss, outdated zoning, industrial blight, inappropriate architectural density, insensitivity to vertical scale, flood control dynamics, lack of provision for pedestrian and public spaces, the absence of long range planning and the deadliest villain of all, disinterested municipal governments. Those same tensions affect design decisions, directly impact the quality of the natural environment of the waterway and, as a result, virtually ignore the idea of the grand potential of river edge parkways in urban settings. Minneapolis, Minnesota; Dubuque, Iowa; St. Louis, Missouri; Memphis, Tennessee; Baton Rouge, Louisiana; and New Orleans, Louisiana offer dynamic models for investigating the quality of the union of urban edge and river edge in major metropolitan sites. They represent the full spectrum of the good, the bad and the ugly. The environment of the metropolitan river edge the length of the river provides interesting contrasts and comparisons. Examination of those same contrasts and comparisons illustrates a range of cause and effect relating to parkway design, from protracted demise to that of an ebullient renaissance.

THE RIVER OVERVIEW

In examining the idea of parkway from the position of an architectural designer, I view the term in the first instance in the context of the entire Mississippi River corridor, both urban and rural. Ideally, a parkway in that corridor might be one long, continuous, landscaped thoroughfare which could provide, by its design, interface with the river and its panoramas appropriate to both vehicles and pedestrians. From my viewpoint, the ideal and the reality are far apart despite the years of noble effort behind the so called "Great River Road," which is not a parkway, even though it should be a handsome boulevard of international acclaim, designed to recognize the sweeping grandeur of the Mississippi.

With that in mind, and before I address urban parkways specifically, I would like to drop back in time for a moment to look at the Mississippi and its place in American history. I think this is very important, for the river has had a very important role in the development of the United States. The precedents which have emerged from that extremely complex role directly impact upon and are germane to our attitudes and philosophy concerning parkway development.

RIVER HISTORY

There is no place . . . no place on earth . . . quite like the Mississippi River. Indeed, there is no place among all of the nations of the world that so reflects in its historical image the personality of a nation, as the Mississippi River reflects the spirit of the richness of the freedom of America.

As the river corridor and its broader valley became settled, the Mississippi, as a lineal site, became the anvil on which the tide of immigrants paused to test their values, to seek the fulfillment of the dream of their place in this new land, and to steel and merge their cultures. It was indeed their destiny to forge into the American way of life the real meaning of those sacred documents authored by the founding fathers which assured the profoundly free qualities of life, in these United States, which we cherish so highly.

From the time of the earliest explorers traversing the American wilderness, waterways served first as glittering and swift pathways of discovery and later as meandering routes for networking, travel, commerce, and urban growth. Along their wooded and prairie banks, settlements formed among the grand vistas, representing a blending of diverse ethnic origins, cultures and social values. The shorelines of the Mississippi offered all along their length points of pause for arriving pioneers, and they served as well as the starting line to "tame the wild west." Its shifting moods were captured in the vibrance of the penetrating rhythm of the music associated with the river, the birth of the blues and dixieland. It was both in legend and in fact a rip-roaring place of explorers, wars, steamboats, cardsharps, river rats, Indians, lumber barons, plantation gentlemen, slaves, merchants, and among all of this, dramatic architectural statements. The Mississippi was the Grand Boulevard of the prairies and, by its majestic outreach across the land, that of the world as well. It was, and even seems to be today, the edge of the frontier.

The fertile flood plains and soaring bluffs of the Mississippi provided splendid sites for the development of the built form and cultural expression of the midlands of America. Though its towns and cities encompassed diversity in function and style, it is important to understand that the river did not lend itself as a palette for grouping architectural styles nor, for that matter, appropriate urban design. Many forces such as political dynamics, cultural values, shifts in the river channel, the great western migration, and time itself have, not by design, dictated a disarray of design thought along the length of the river. As the number of settlers and population density grew, as commerce increased, and as commitment to place became reconciled, the diversity in architectural and urban design and the significance of aesthetics, in a piece by piece way, took a higher place in the hierarchy of personal values. And in this whole process, what was virtually ignored was the development of appropriate urban pathways for vehicular traffic (and the railroads) which worked with the river. The importance of pedestrian access to the edge of the river in urban sites was ignored as well.

THE GREAT RIVER ROAD

"The Great River Road," the main vehicular pathway along the river, essentially follows the length of the river from Minnesota to Louisiana. At first glance, one might think that this is a carefully designed thoroughfare winding in and about the woodlands and soaring bluffs in the north and meandering with the great tide of the river as it spans the delta. A designed thoroughfare it is not, but it is rather a series of roads across the ten states contiguous to the river which have been diligently promoted under that name through years of dedicated interest by the Mississippi River Parkway Commission. "The Great River Road" is not what its name might imply. Its 2000-mile length was not designed with the intent of land-river interface but rather the title of the road was applied to a series of connecting highways after the fact. The idea of "parkway" quite simply does not exist along the length of the river in either rural or urban contexts. It would appear that there is greater potential for parkway development in rural areas rather than urban areas along the Mississippi but the political dynamics of accomplishing a uniform design throughout the ten Mississippi River states are at best staggering. This is particularly true when faced with the spector of meshing ten separate state budgetary formats linked with necessary federal assistance.

THE URBAN-RIVER EDGE

Historically, the romance associated with the river was, more often than not, associated with its towns and cities. They were once the ports of call for the steamboat trade of the nineteenth century, and today those major cities remain centers of business, industry and agriculture. The major urban areas such as Minneapolis, St. Louis, Memphis, Baton Rouge and New Orleans have grown helter-skelter beside the river and, with the exception of Minneapolis, have received little planning consideration until too late. A critical part of that planning was lack of recognition of appropriate vehicular and pedestrian access to and along the river in urban areas.

If one examines archival photographs of major cities along the Mississippi it is quite easy to discern how they were initially visually open to the river. Then, with the passage of time that special kind of urban-river interface which should be so much a part of river towns began to vanish. Abandonment of this interface began in earnest following the end of the steamboat era. The aesthetic value and visual excitement of the river was simply no longer recognized. Lack of appropriate zoning and timid planning accelerated the demise. Political expediencies generally disdained association with the river as something of value and so the river was ignored.

Movement of city vehicular traffic close by the river became a winding, tortuous experience and, more often than not, that movement came into direct visual conflict with warehouses and industrial walls lining the river's edge. The very idea of "park" for pedestrians and "lineal parks" or parkways for vehicles was somewhere out over the horizon in the zoning, design and planning process. Following World War II, shopping malls on the opposite side of towns from the river were *in*. The river was *out*. Indeed, the Mississippi river became passe, a sad commentary on one of the greatest waterways in the world which was, in the first instance, the very reason for the existence of its cities. In the decades following the 40's, vehicular traffic increased, the urban river became more and more hidden and road design in cities along the river, for the most part, failed to appropriately accommodate the visual excitement of the river.

As I discussed early on, the cities of the Mississippi River corridor offer a number of models for the examination of parkway design. There is a range of success but more directly there is, by the very absence of urban parkways, a range of overwhelming problems which dictate the conditions which seem to insure and exacerbate the continuation of that absence.

It is interesting that in parkway design there are no real common denominators along the river. The problems and the political and fiscal forces have similarities, but the physical problems are quite diversified. For example, Minneapolis is advanced in its parkway work while St. Louis faces a nearly insurmountable problem in parkway development. There are clear and basic reasons for this. There are other contrasts that fall in between and the difficulty varies from city to city.

I perceive the need for parkways along the river to be for both vehicles and pedestrians whether the site be rural or urban. This thesis then holds the expectation of a powerful physical, indeed sensory and tactile, link between vehicular man and pedestrian man and the water. In other words I see urban-river-parkways as people places with a real shoreline-water connection. For a number of very real reasons and very real conditions that relationship may be virtually an unachievable reality in the built environment of the 20th century along the Mississippi River corridor. I believe that this is all tied to education, awareness and values. There are no easy answers and, of even more concern, there isn't a compelling movement toward public enlightenment in this regard.

EXAMPLES OF URBAN PARKWAY POTENTIAL ON THE MISSISSIPPI RIVER, NEW ORLEANS, LOUISIANA

In examining the cities of the river, a candid look behind the scenes quickly zeros in on the problems but does not necessarily offer quick solutions. For example, New Orleans is the oldest city of the river and is composed of 18 distinct districts. It is one of the major seaports in the world. Once the Mississippi River was its grand boulevard. The business of the city and indeed the nation was often conducted, literally, at the edge of the water. Now, an industrial wall of warehouses separates the river from the city (fig.1). The magnificent and delicate scale of the French Quarter has given way to high-rise hotels and office buildings. New Orleans has the potential for one of the most dynamic waterfronts along the river. Indeed, it is one of the busiest waterfronts in the world. But it offers pedestrians access only by the Moon Walk at Jackson Square, at the Spanish Plaza and at the Audubon Park. It does not provide visual accommodation with the river from passing automobiles nor for pedestrians who wish to immerse themselves in the sites, sounds and smells of the port activities as they stroll nearby the river. There is virtually no serious landscape design nor areas for relaxation and observation.

New Orleans is tied up in the knots of political expediency and though it has, on paper, a highly structured planning organization, it lacks both the talent and vision for innovative parkway design. There is a well-entrenched "good old boy" syndrome at work that smacks of political intrigue which has little if any understanding of appropriate design. The slivers of urban-river interface which have been opened up have all too quickly become sites for hotels and shopping centers (fig.2). Traffic is congested and streets near the river are unappealing. It is impossible to draw the line between planning and design, and lack of planning and built chaos. Across the river from downtown New Orleans, historic Algiers languishes in slow deterioration. There is a wonderful opportunity here to develop a parkway on both sides which would play upon the magnificent elevations of the city. In this regard, New Orleans lacks visual conceptualization which captures the spirit of the river. The city has produced planning report after planning report full of statistics and land use information without utilizing those investigations to generate more productive use financially and more pleasing use aesthetically. There are physical barriers which may be difficult to overcome, but given the correct design momentum and political support, they could be. Perhaps, for example, considerably fewer docks and warehouses should be opposite the city center. Certainly selective removal would offer a broad spectrum of possibilities for parkway design which would open the city to the river. New Orleans needs a touch of class, a statement of elegance along its river banks. Certainly a parkway, handsomely landscaped with places to drive, play, sit, and walk along the river, could be designed in harmony with vehicular movement. It could be one of the most handsome parkways in America. The 1983 New Orleans Central Riverfront Study addressed this issue but the city has not come to grips with the problem. Lack of achievable priorities has left New Orleans wanting in just about all aspects of physical planning and design. The problem is massive, almost beyond comprehension, but nonetheless offers a magnificent and worthy challenge. A well designed parkway is probably the last thing that will happen in New Orleans. It is probably in the first order of magnitude in terms of what should happen.

BATON ROUGE, LOUISIANA

Moving up-river, Baton Rouge, the capitol of Louisiana, faces the same political problems as New Orleans but has begun to move on its city-river interface. A broad boulevard follows the shore of the river along the length of the city center but it has the visual image of a four lane street rather than a parkway. It lacks frequent and easy pedestrian access from downtown and automobile pullouts for viewing river activities. A master plan has been developed to enhance the several city districts but little has been conceptualized in the way of designing Route 61 along the river as a parkway (fig.3). The city is moving to bring more pedestrian activities to the edge of the river with museums and shopping. Louisiana has recently faced tremendous financial problems and it is unlikely that parkway development is very high among state priorities. However, with the strong city movement to interface with the river, park-

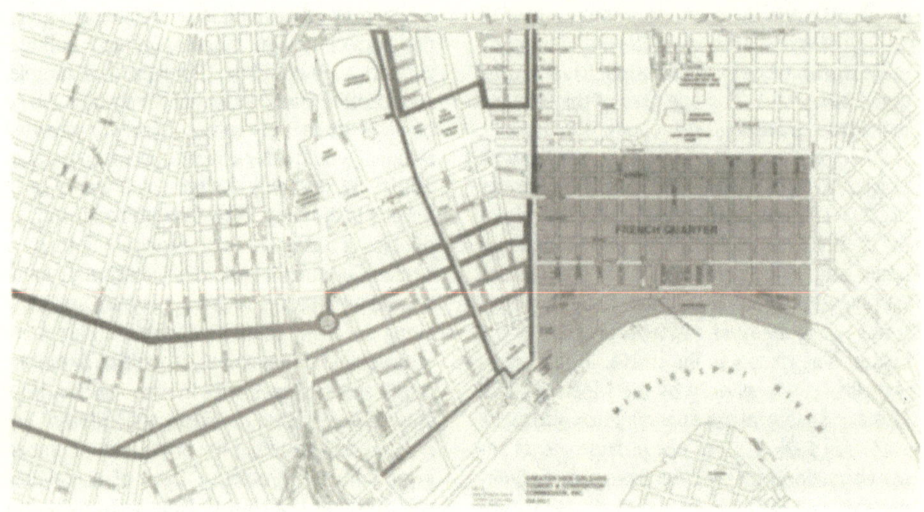

Top: *Fig.1. New Orleans, Louisiana, Docks at the City Center.*
Bottom: *Fig. 2. New Orleans, Louisiana, Overview.*

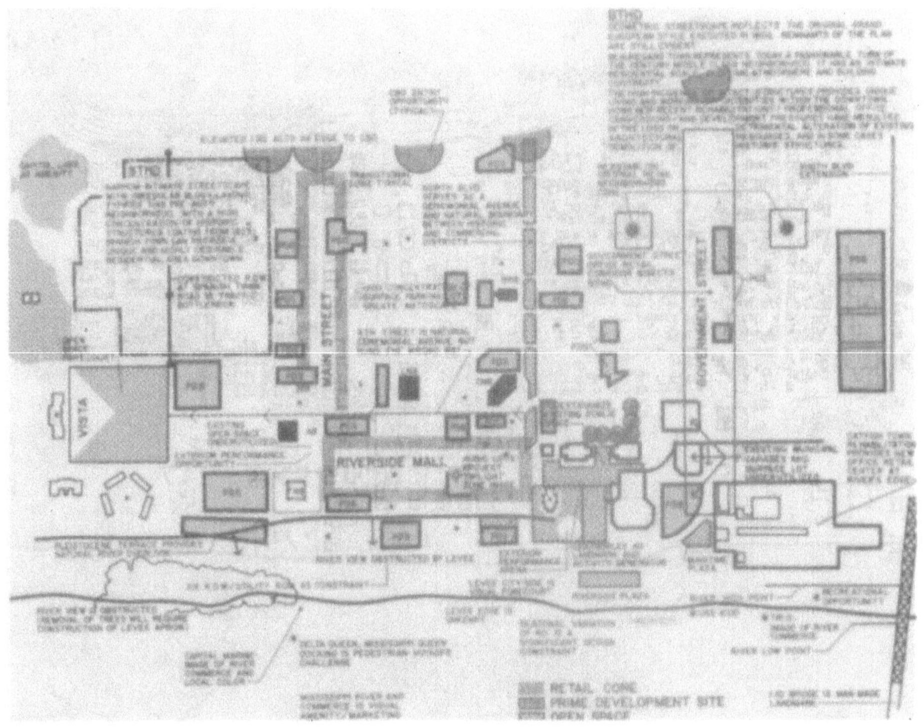

Fig. 3. Baton Rouge, Louisiana, Urban Design Issues.

way development in Baton Rouge is an achievable reality. Though Route 61 is a bland statement, examination of its lineal site indicates tremendous potential for a landscaped greenbelt which could bring the city center and the river together. The Baton Rouge Study for the year 2000 certainly supports this thesis and the ease of potential development is greater than that of New Orleans, Memphis or St. Louis.

MEMPHIS, TENNESSEE

The development of a parkway for Memphis, Tennessee, poses an extremely interesting problem. The city of Memphis is located high on a bluff overlooking the river. Access to the city from the west is via two interstate bridges (I-55 and I-40), which cross the Mississippi just north of and just south of the central business district. This introduces the mainstream of vehicular traffic into the city at right angles to the river and well into the city rather than at the edge of the Mississippi. Thus, traffic in Memphis parallel to the river tends to be more local. Memphis has a parkway of sorts below the bluffs of the city, separating the city from Mud Island which should be the focus for Memphis on the river with its excellent museum and pedestrian activities. The Memphis River Road is not really a parkway in the meandering sense or in an aesthetically designed sense for it injects vehicles too quickly on and exits them too quickly off and the traffic is excessively fast. Memphis is in an awkward situation for parkway development because of the close position of its two interstate bridges (I-55 and I-40). The west elevation of the city is not particularly long and the travel time element on

Fig. 4. Memphis, Tennessee, River Overview.

the existing River Drive is not conducive to casual viewing of the river (fig.4). A planned development spine of the city to the north and south and a more meandering design of the parkway with pedestrian access to the river is a reasonable expectation. There has been intense reliance on Mud Island for pedestrian use but access is too forced (through monorail) for casual use. Mud Island is one of the most important but most overlooked city attractions along the length of the Mississippi, and Mud Island as a design element could be nicely integrated into the parkway concept. A more relaxed parkway below the bluffs with the parks meandering up the bluffs to the city and incorporating Mud Island offers exciting possibilities. Memphis suffers from lack of conceptualizing. It has lost the vigor of its central business district and has somehow lost the dream of vitality. The time is ripe for strategic development of a city plan within strong physical planning as opposed to a socio-political planning framework. Landscape architecture is a lost art along the river at Memphis just as it is in all the major cities except Minneapolis. Memphis is prime for enhancement, and a redesigned parkway at the edge of the river or a totally new parkway on the bluffs linked to the river could be the catalyst that the city needs. Memphis needs a bold plan in the spirit of Daniel Burnham. It is important for the city to preserve its historic architecture near the river. However, it is also important that Memphis move, at the same time, into a very positive physical design effort and to plan for, and to zone for, the idea of a well designed parkway now, or it will never become a reality.

ST. LOUIS, MISSOURI

St. Louis is the "Gateway to the West" and it seems that it should also be regarded as the gateway to the north and the south along the river. St. Louis is in perhaps the most difficult position for the development of a well designed parkway because it has zoned itself in above and below the Arch and LaCledes Landing with an industrial wall. In so many ways St. Louis has been a visionary city in its planning but its city-river interface has been saved only by the Jefferson National Expansion Memorial (fig. 5). The idea of parkway along the river in St. Louis is in the magnitude of the problem in New Orleans. There is no simple solution and I am not at all sure that there is even a complex solution. The 1967 Saint Louis Riverfront Development Plan certainly acknowledges the problem but the reality of successfully addressing it seems light years away. The wholesale and historic lack of planning and visionary zoning along the river has allowed the St. Louis riverfront to become an industrial wasteland with aesthetic and environmental ramifications which are at once local, regional and national (fig.6). Perhaps the most expedient solution and one which would certainly showcase the image of the city is to develop the St. Louis parkway on the Illinois side of the river.

MINNEAPOLIS, MINNESOTA

Of all the cities along the river, the most elegant in its design and indeed in its philosophy of design as relating its whole metro area to the river, is Minneapolis (fig.7). The city of Minneapolis enjoys a highly structured and professional planning department which generates the best combination of physical and social planning. This is of the first order of importance in the process of successfully uniting the images of city and river. It has vitally active legislative interest at the city government level and serious involvement in the planning process by the city community. Since its beginning in the middle of the nineteenth century, Minneapolis has been sensitive to the river and its place in the city landscape and urban circulation. Its West River Parkway study done in 1985 is a model of analysis of city functions along the river including parks, recreational facilities, pedestrian movement, adaptive reuse of historic districts and vehicular circulation (fig.8). It is planned that the West River Parkway be all-weather and that is be a part of the Great River Road System. It includes new land acquisition in its plan and it also merges with the Minneapolis Park System in its design. The design of the parkway stresses protection of the

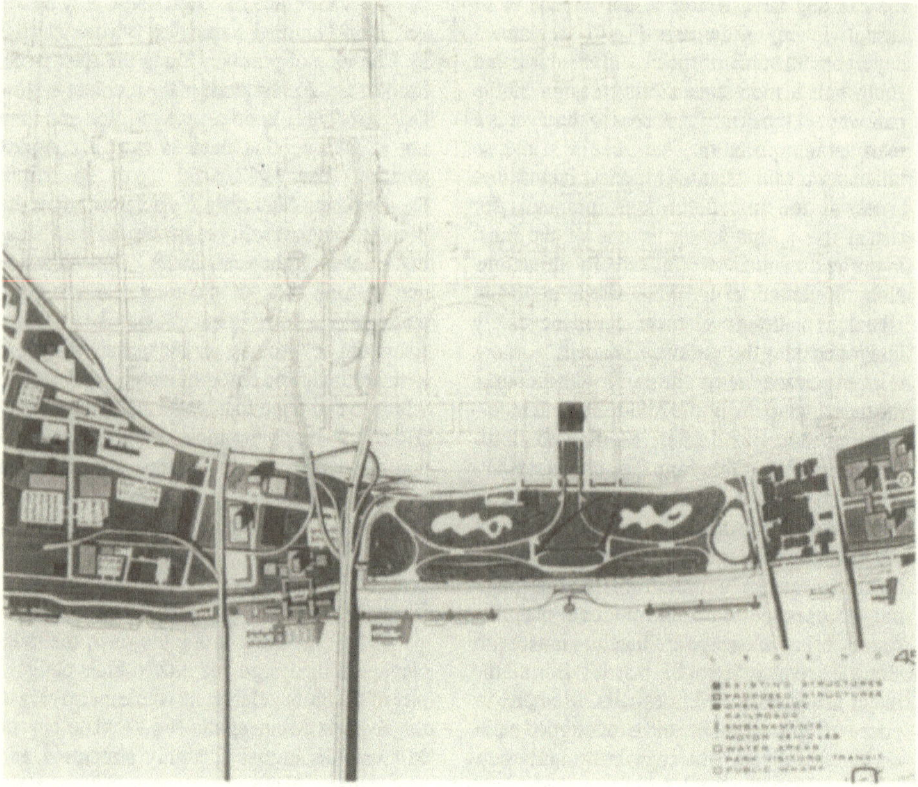

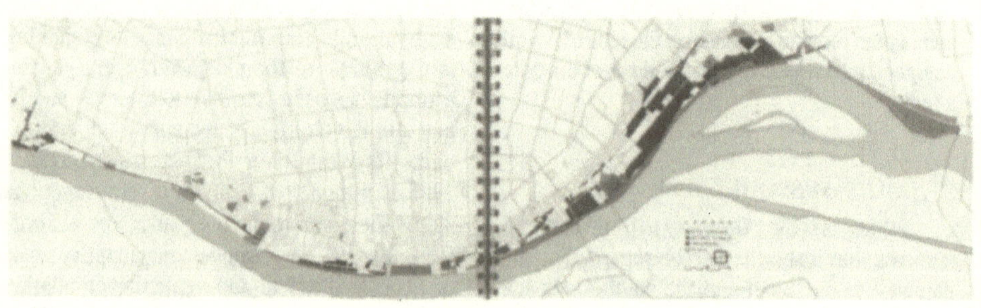

Top: *Fig. 5. St. Louis, Missouri, at the Arch.*
Bottom: *Fig. 6. St. Louis, Missouri, Industrial Wall.*

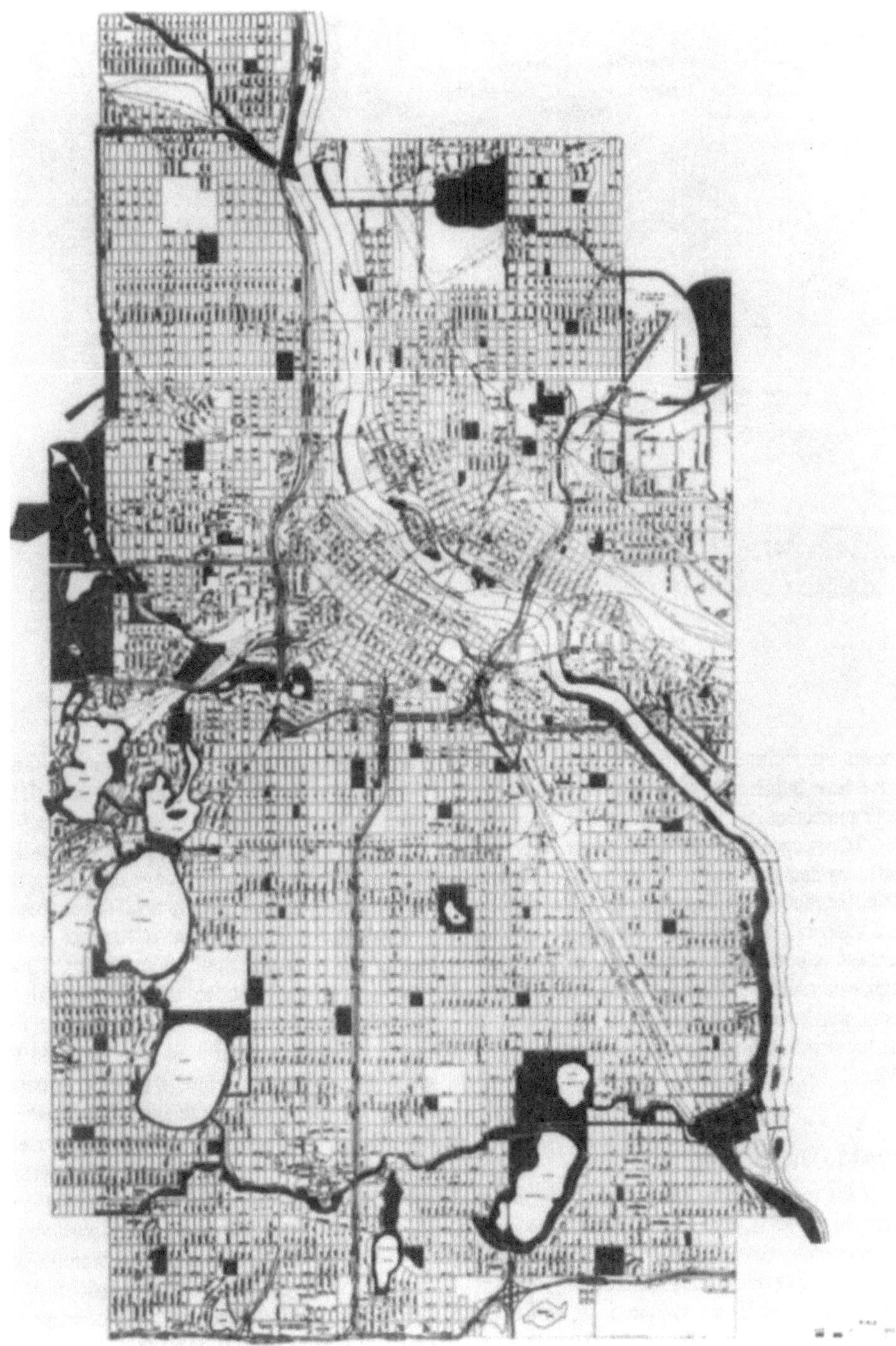

Fig. 7. Minneapolis, Minnesota, River Overview.

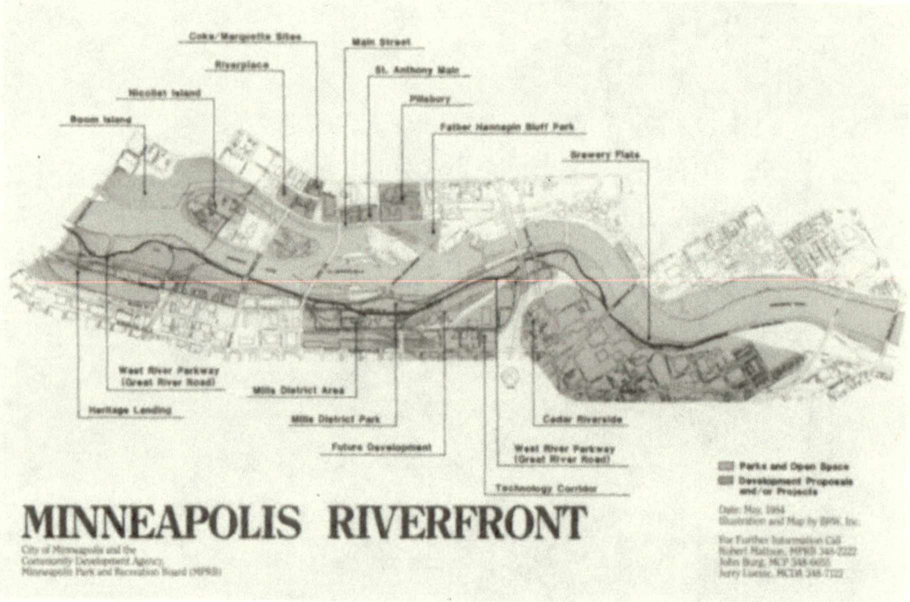

Fig. 8. Minneapolis, Minnesota, Riverfront.

natural environment of the river while at the same time handsomely provides for parkway-river interface.

Minneapolis is the role model city for parkway design in major urban areas along the length of the river. It has decades of experience and success. The primary ingredient for that success is community sensitivity to good design, community value of the natural environment, and strong and positive design structure in the administration and governance of the city.

CONCLUSION

With the exception of Minneapolis and more recently St. Paul, the cities of the Mississippi River corridor face an uphill battle in recognizing the importance of implementing design sensitivity in parkway planning. It would be delightful if the Great River Road could be a two thousand mile green belt from the lakes of Minnesota to the Gulf of Mexico incorporating both its urban and rural environments. The "Great River Road" is a magnificent idea. It is a proper direction and it is the only game in town. Though this paper addresses urban parkways, urban and rural parkways should not be considered separately. They need to become a unified whole. But the name of the road is not enough. It needs national "pride of place." That "pride of place" can be realized through a national effort to return to the Mississippi River the dignity of its natural environment and to enrich the lives of the people of the river through design excellence in the relationship between the urban and rural environments and the river. It will require at the urban scale specific interest in learning about and utilizing the role model of Minneapolis. At the scale of the full corridor, it will require the complete and total commitment of the ten contiguous states and the resources of the federal government. It is a concept of national worthiness. It holds the challenge of an American renaissance and an American achievement.

BIBLIOGRAPHY

1. NEW ORLEANS, LOUISIANA:
    a. Algres Riverfront Study 1985, the City Planning Commission, New Orleans, Louisiana.
    b. The City of New Orleans Development Guidebook 1981, The City Planning Commission, New Orleans, Louisiana.
    c. Annual Report 1984-1985, Edition 62, The City Planning Commission, New Orleans, Louisiana.
    d. New Orleans Historic Warehouse District Study, Charles Coplinger Planners, New Orleans, Louisiana.
    e. Urban Design Review Inventory 1980, The City Planning Commission, New Orleans, Louisiana.
2. BATON ROUGE, LOUISIANA:
    a. Baton Rouge 2000, An Economic Development Program for the Central Business District, Office of the Mayor-President, Baton Rouge, Louisiana.
3. MEMPHIS, TENNESSEE:
    a. Memphis Riverfront Study 1987, Memphis and Shelby County Office of Planning and Development, Memphis, Tennessee.
    b. Memphis 2000 Policy Plan 1981, Memphis and Shelby County Office of Planning and Development, Memphis, Tennessee.
    c. Memphis 2000, Annual Report 1983, Memphis and Shelby County Office of Planning and Development, Memphis, Tennessee.
    d. Riverfront Railroad Alternatives Analysis and Feasibility Study 1984, Memphis State University Transportation Studies Institute, Memphis, Tennessee.
4. ST. LOUIS, MISSOURI:
    a. St. Louis Riverfront Development Plan 1967, City Planning Commission of St. Louis, St. Louis, Missouri.
5. MINNEAPOLIS, MINNESOTA:
    a. West River Parkway Final Location/Design Report 1985, Minneapolis Park and Recreation Board.
    b. West River Parkway Engineering Feasibility Technical Report, Minneapolis Park and Recreation Board.
    c. West River Parkway Final Scoping Report, Minneapolis Park and Recreation Board.
    d. Minneapolis Metro Center Plan 1990, City of Minneapolis Planning Department.

Developing the Arroyo Concept for Tucson's First Urban Parkway

Walter E. Rogers, ASLA, APA

THE CHALLENGE

One: Design a 5-mile urban parkway through the heart of Tucson, Arizona—a growing sunbelt city with a hot arid climate and 12 inches of rainfall a year.

A serious problem of ground water depletion has caused public awareness of the need for water conservation and for significant limitations on plant species that require excessive amounts of irrigation Using turf, extensive ground cover, or trees and shrubs that are high water consumers is strictly out of the question. Visualizing a verdant parkway like those found in areas of the country where annual rainfall naturally supports huge shade trees and lush grasses is also not appropriate.

Two: Design a 5-mile urban parkway through the heart of Tucson, Arizona—a city, with an anti-freeway public sentiment.

The city's first proposed urban parkway, studied under a $1.2 million planning contract, was put to a public referendum vote in 1984 and soundly defeated.

Neighborhood coalitions have grown strong and have used the public meeting requirements of local government to stall, change or stop roadway projects.

Three: Design a 5-mile urban parkway through the heart of Tucson, Arizona — a western frontier city not known for outstanding visual quality of its built environment or the view from its roads.

Until recently, the pressure of rapid development has resulted in a prioritization of only the basic public roadway improvements with very small budgets, if any, for visual quality and aesthetics such as sensitive landform grading and landscaping. Until recently, few requirements were put on developers to control signage, landscaping and the visual impact of chaotic development. Indeed, Tucson's notorious Speedway Boulevard often has been referred to as one of the ugliest streets in the country.

BACKGROUND

In the late 1970's it was clear that a long range transportation plan would be one of the measures needed to deal with the growth experienced in Tucson and eastern Pima County and the anticipated future population in excess of one million people by 2005.

Population Statistics and Projections, Eastern Pima County[1]

	1985 Population	2005 Estimated	Increase 1985-2005
Pima County	624,347	1,062,792	438,445
City of Tucson	377,546	504,207	126,661
Unincorporated	235,132	532,210	297,078
Other Incorp.	11,669	26,375	14,706

One of the roadways recommended in the long range transportation plan was a controlled access parkway located along the glide path of the main runway at Davis Monthan Air Force Base — the Aviation Corridor. The route would connect Tucson's only interstate highway just north of the CBD to another major arterial providing for about 10 miles of unimpeded east-west traffic flow. (See Figure 1.)

In February, 1981, the Mayor and Council of the City of Tucson authorized Phase I of the Aviation Corridor Study in which a "No Build Alternative" was compared to three improvement alternatives. In December, 1982, the Mayor and City Council adopted the transportation alternative which recommended a new parkway in the Aviation Corridor. This recommendation was approved by the Arizona Department of Transportation (ADOT) and the Aviation Corridor was officially designated as State Route 210.

The 1981 Regional Long Range Transportation Plan intended to serve transportation needs of the Tucson Metropolitan area through the year 2005. In addition to the Aviation Corridor, another key feature of this plan was a major east-west connector — the Rillito Corridor — also to be planned as a parkway.

A strong coalition from the affluent neighborhoods in the foothills north of the proposed Rillito Parkway bitterly fought this highway. In spite of the plans, the Foothills Coalition argued that the highway would decrease property values, severely impact riparian habitat along the edge of the Rillito Wash, and be an intrusion in an area of high visual quality. They also did not trust the engineers and planners, not believing that adequate landscaping or park development would actually be provided for or that it would be properly funded for immediate implementation. The Rillito Parkway was defeated in a public referendum as mentioned above and was deleted from the Long Range Transportation Plan in 1985.

Because of the significance of the Rillito Parkway in accommodating regional travel, a new long range transportation plan was authorized and completed in June of 1986. This new plan for the year 2005 accommodated the estimated travel demand for the Rillito Corridor in large part by upgrading and enlarging arterial roads throughout the metropolitan area.

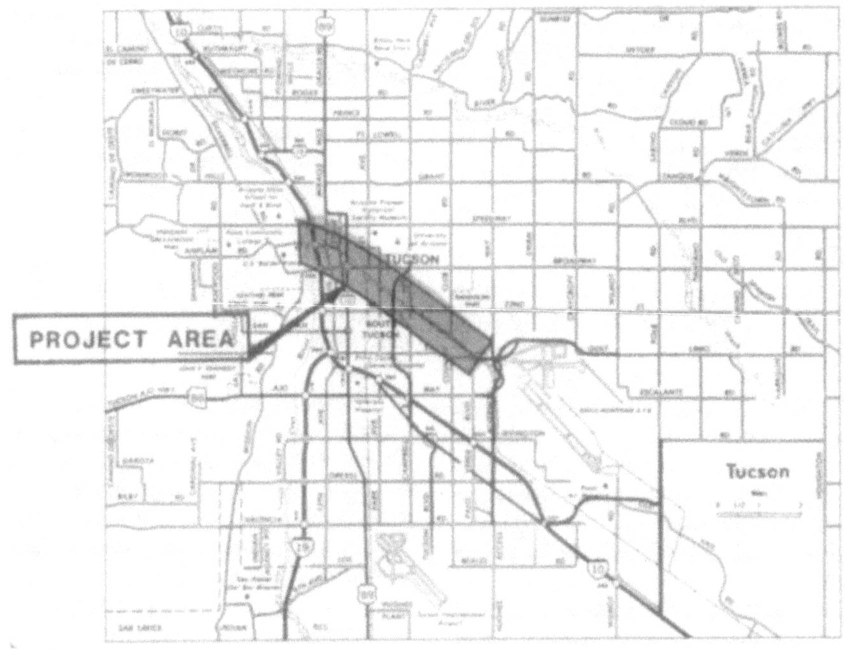

Fig. 1. Location Map.

The 1986 Long Range Transportation Plan also reaffirmed the Aviation Corridor, State Route 210, as a key component of satisfying travel needs.

Planning for the Aviation Corridor included a Concept Design Phase from 1983 to May of 1985. Authorized by Mayor and Council, the plan was prepared by Finical and Dombrowski of Tucson in a joint venture with Barton-Aschman Associates, Inc. This plan set the preliminary engineering criteria for the parkway and included participation of citizens and neighborhood groups. Its main goal was to establish the City of Tuscon's general design criteria.[2]

In 1986, Parsons, Brinckerhoff, Quade & Douglas, Inc. (PBQD) were selected by the ADOT to manage the design process, prepare the engineering designs for the parkway, establish a definitive right-of-way, and manage the preparation of construction documents. PBQD hired Rogers, Gladwin & Harmony, Inc. (RGH) to serve as project landscape architects. PBQD's formidable task was to develop final plans that would be acceptable to the ADOT, the City of Tuscons's Transportation Department, and a long list of special interest groups including the AIA, downtown business groups, neighborhood associations, various environmental groups, even a group sponsoring revival of Tuscon's early twentieth century trolley cars.

PBQD and the project's advocates did not want the Aviation Corridor to suffer the fate of the Rillito Corridor and they have taken careful measures to follow the qualitative planning and design criteria that had been established for the project. The input of RGH was essential to successful portrayal and design of the road as a parkway.

THE SETTING

By the year 2005, State Route 210, the 5-mile Aviation Parkway, is planned to carry 40,000 to 50,000 vehicles per day. The controlled access facility will slice through the heart of the City's incorporated area.

The western 1 1/2 miles abuts the northern edge of the city's Central Business District (CBD) including a historic neighborhood and bisects a warehouse and light industrial district. The CBD has declined severely as a retail center since 1970 and has been evolving as a government, office and cultural center for the metropolitan area. The northern edge of the CBD has physically existed since the late 19th century due to the alignment of the Southern Pacific Railroad (SPRR) tracks. Therefore, the new parkway will not break up or bisect existing land use patterns in the CBD area.

For the next mile, the parkway will travel through residential areas to the north and south of the right-of-way. These neighborhoods have developed differently and also have been separated by the SPRR tracks. Therefore, the integrity of the neighborhoods will not be greatly impacted.

The eastern half of the parkway runs along the northern edge of a very large Southern Pacific Freight Yard. The parkway actually will buffer the freight yard from the residential areas to the north.

The eastern 3 3/4 miles will include a continuous bike path. Screen walls will mitigate noise pollution and loss of privacy in all residential areas.

The western section through the CBD area will have significant vertical elevation changes of up to thirty-five (35) feet necessitating extensive retaining walls, drainage structures and even a tunnel at one point under the SPRR tracks. The parkway development will be designed compatibly with the historical character of the El Presidio Historic District.

An extensive site analysis an visual analysis was carried out by Rogers, Gladwin & Harmony, Inc. The goal of the visual analysis was to determine the extent that landscape treatment should occur to provide:

1. A parkway experience.
2. Mitigation of adverse visual effects of the project on adjacent land use.
3. Mitigation of adverse visual impacts on the parkway user.
4. Visibility of urban landmarks including the mountain ranges that enclose the City of Tucson on the north, east, west and south.
5. Aesthetic visual quality of the roadway structure, landscaping, and the view from the road.

The visual analysis was based on "Visual Impact Assessment for Highway Projects", prepared as a field guide by the American Society of Landscape Architects (ASLA) for the Federal Highway Administration. (See Figure 2.)

The most important conclusion of the visual analysis was that relative to other places in Tucson, the opportunities for interesting or beautiful views from this project are limited. The structural profile will be low, near, or below grade in most places, and opportunities for 360-degree panoramic views will be limited to one overpass. This minimal opportunity for panoramic views led the landscape architects to their concept of creating a parkway with an introverted landscape character and a strong sense of place.[3]

THE ARROYO CONCEPT

For as long as people have inhabited the hot dry desert region of Tucson, they have utilized the shady green landscape of the arroyo as a natural park. Even before human habitation of the region, arroyos were used as wildlife movement corridors.

The arroyo is an intermittent stream known as a wash to locals. Water often occurs in flash floods during the summer thunderstorm season and may run for days at at time during winter rains and spring runoff periods. The rest of the time the arroyo features a sandy bottom and heavily wooded side slopes or flood plain.

While there are many plants that make up the southwestern riparian plant community, the most ubiquitous and well known is the native mesquite, *Prosopis velutina*. The mesquite often looks like a large shrub when found in small arroyos at elevation of 4-5000 feet; however,

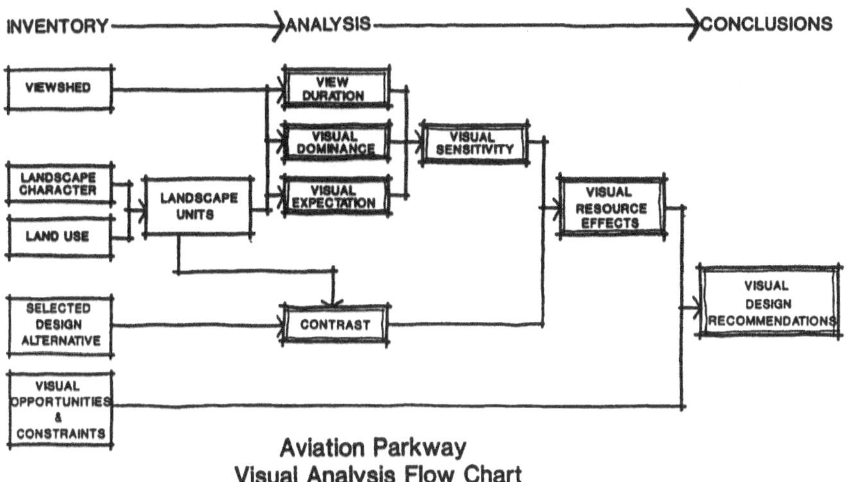

Fig. 2. Visual Analysis Flow Chart.

it can grow to a handsome tree with a large spreading canopy in large washes at valley floor elevations of about 2000 feet above sea level in Tucson.

The mesquite often grows in dense bosques that contrast sharply with the desert setting. The mesquite bosque is a compelling landscape that draws one to it for respite from the surrounding xeriscape. To those who live in this hot desert, the rivurine arroyo landscape is a natural park.

In brainstorming the landscape concept for the Aviation Parkway, we found no parkway model in an urban setting anywhere in the desert areas of the state. In fact, Arizona has miles of beautiful roadside and only one officially designated rural parkway that meets ADOT's standards.[4]

We observed that the Aviation Corridor sliced through the urban setting like a natural arroyo slices through the desert landscape; and we began to visualize the Aviation Parkway as an adaptation of the natural riparian corridor.

The Aviation Parkway could become a landscape metaphor for the natural processes of the Valley. The dense canopy of the mesquite trees, which would mature to a 40-foot height and a 50-foot spread, will provide a cool and shady environment for parkway users, reduce glare and pollution, provide psychological noise mitigation, and provide a buffer for adjacent residents. Planting excess right-of-way parcels wherever possible would undulate the edges of the corridor, further enhancing the rivurine character.

The concept was well received by the ADOT's Roadside Development Section because it emphasized drought tolerant trees, used virtually no groundcover, provided for water conservation by choice of plant material and utilization of a drip irrigation system, and accommodated maintenance concerns.

IMPLEMENTING THE CONCEPT

Dreaming up the concept for the Aviation Parkway was one thing. Implementing it was another.

Right-of-Way Width. Undulating the edges of the parkway planting to recreate a rivurine bosque of mesquite trees was one broad design goal. This, however, required obtaining excess right-of-way in which to plant. Excess right-of-way is very costly, especially when the main justification for its acquisition is to undulate the horizontal landscaped edge of a parkway. RGH

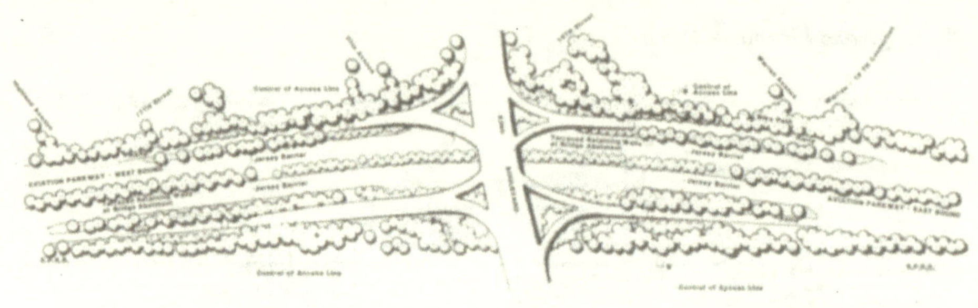

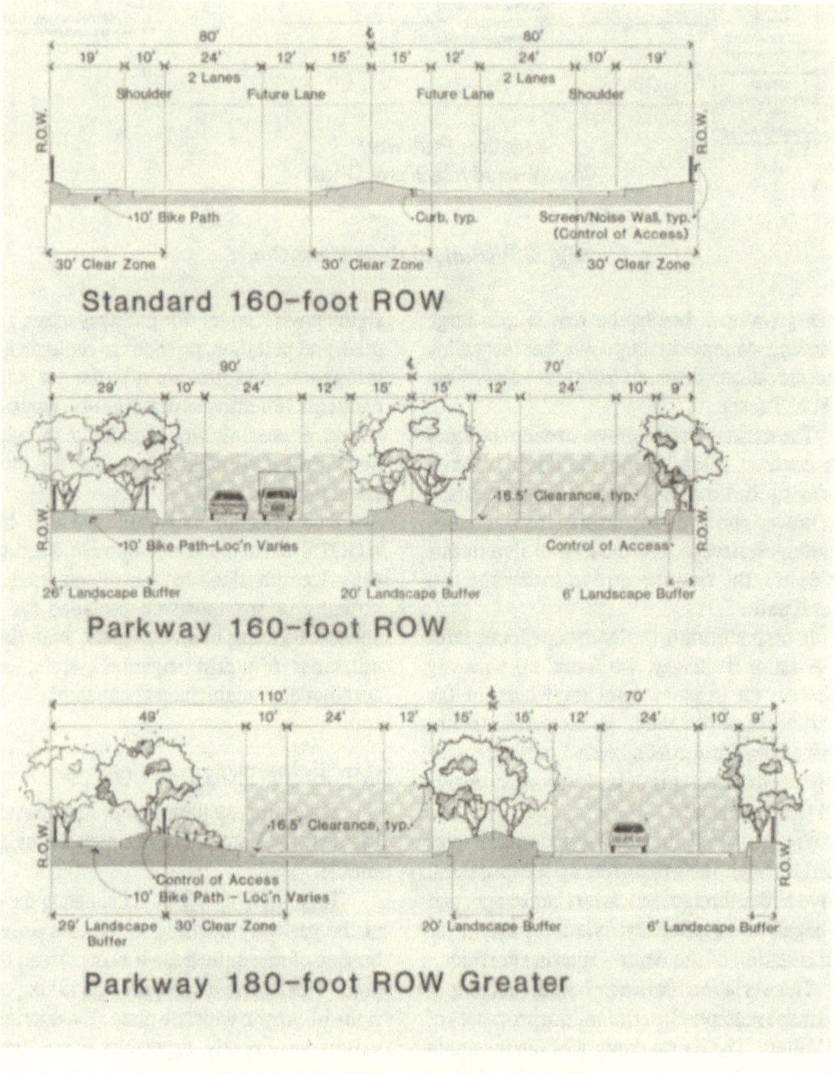

80' | 80'
19' 10' 24' 12' 15' | 15' 12' 24' 10' 19'
2 Lanes | 2 Lanes
Shoulder | Future Lane | Future Lane | Shoulder
R.O.W. | R.O.W.
10' Bike Path | Curb, typ. | Screen/Noise Wall, typ. (Control of Access)
30' Clear Zone | 30' Clear Zone | 30' Clear Zone

Standard 160-foot ROW

90' | 70'
29' 10' 24' 12' 15' | 15' 12' 24' 10' 9'
16.5' Clearance, typ.
R.O.W. | R.O.W.
10' Bike Path-Loc'n Varies | Control of Access
26' Landscape Buffer | 20' Landscape Buffer | 6' Landscape Buffer

Parkway 160-foot ROW

110' | 70'
49' 10' 24' 12' 15' | 15' 12' 24' 10' 9'
16.5' Clearance, typ.
R.O.W. | R.O.W.
Control of Access
10' Bike Path – Loc'n Varies
29' Landscape Buffer | 30' Clear Zone | 20' Landscape Buffer | 6' Landscape Buffer

Parkway 180-foot ROW Greater

Top: *Fig. 3. Typical parkway planting.*
Bottom: *Fig. 4. Basic right-of-way section, clear zone, and proposed R.O.W. treatment.*

has been successful, however, in a number of cases, and in other places we'll resourcefully rely on existing parks and open spaces to visually extend the parkway beyond the linear right-of-way. (See Figure 3.)

Clear Zones. The biggest challenge to creating a parkway with a shade tree canopy was the 30-foot clear zone—AASHTO's criteria for planting setbacks for safety reasons. In the standard 160-foot right-of-way, we were not allowed to plant a tree over 4" caliper within thirty feet of the travel lane.

When we examined the impact of the clear zone requirement on the basic 160-foot right-of-way we were working with, we concluded that we couldn't execute our planting concept. In fact, under this criteria, no trees over four (4) inch caliper would be permitted within the parkway right-of-way.

In order to solve this problem and allow us to achieve the desired mesquite tree canopy effect, we proposed the introduction of Jersey Barriers at the median edge and at each side of the right-of-way. We also proposed shifting the right-of-way off-center by 10 feet allowing the residential side of the right-of-way to carry the bike path. In places where a 180-foot right-of-way could be obtained, we found the Jersey Barrier on one side could be eliminated. (See Figure 4.)

Maintenance Access. Approval of the Jersey Barrier proposal also depended on coming up with a solution for safe maintenance access to the medians. An offset Jersey Barrier with a mountable curb was the acceptable solution we came up with. (See Figure 5.)

Downtown Segment. A real challenge was finding a way to continue the canopy tree effect through the western downtown portion. Much of this section of the Aviation Parkway will be depressed at depths up to thirty-five (35) feet.

Here we recommended stepped retaining walls to provide multi-level planting benches mitigating the height of the retaining walls and allowing the arroyo concept to be continued through downtown. (See Figures 6a and 6b.)

One objection to the stepped retaining walls was the difficulty of maintenance access. We proposed a gated stairway access which seems to have resolved the problem. Others suggested that the planting benches would create a nice place for Tuscon's homeless winter visitors to sleep in. We haven't yet found a solution for this problem; however, we wonder how well the fumes and noise of 40,000 vehicles per day as well as the bright highway lighting will induce sleep.

Continuity of Rustication. Not a new concept, continuity of rustication for walls and structures is an important feature of the Aviation Parkway. Split face and fluted CMU block and matching form liner finishes in a soft brown color will be used throughout. Treatment also includes specialty pavements and pedestrian amenities at intersections.

Signature Elements. A unique concept we recommended was using a signature medallion fashioned of copper — the State metal. The copper medallion has a southwest thematic design. We envisioned its use as a decorative element in overpass structures, wall cornices, bollards, and other design elements. (See Figure 7.)

Historic Neighborhood Buffer. To buffer the historic El Presidio Neighborhood a linear park alongside the right-of-way was proposed. The plan is a direct response to adjacent land uses and the neighborhood character. (See Figure 8.)

CONCLUSION

During the final design stages, the landscape architects have maintained a firm posture that the success of the project depends on the extensive and continuous planting of mesquite trees as the dominant theme plant. As each new issue occurs which could reduce the concept, we have found creative solutions to keep the concept in tact.

Our vision of the parkway as a shady arroyo enhancing the urban transportation experience is a strong one. (See Figure 9.) The growth rate of the mesquite tree is at least five (5) feet per year, so we'll know how effective the concept is in ten (10) years. We hope the idea will become a model for future urban parkways in hot arid climates.

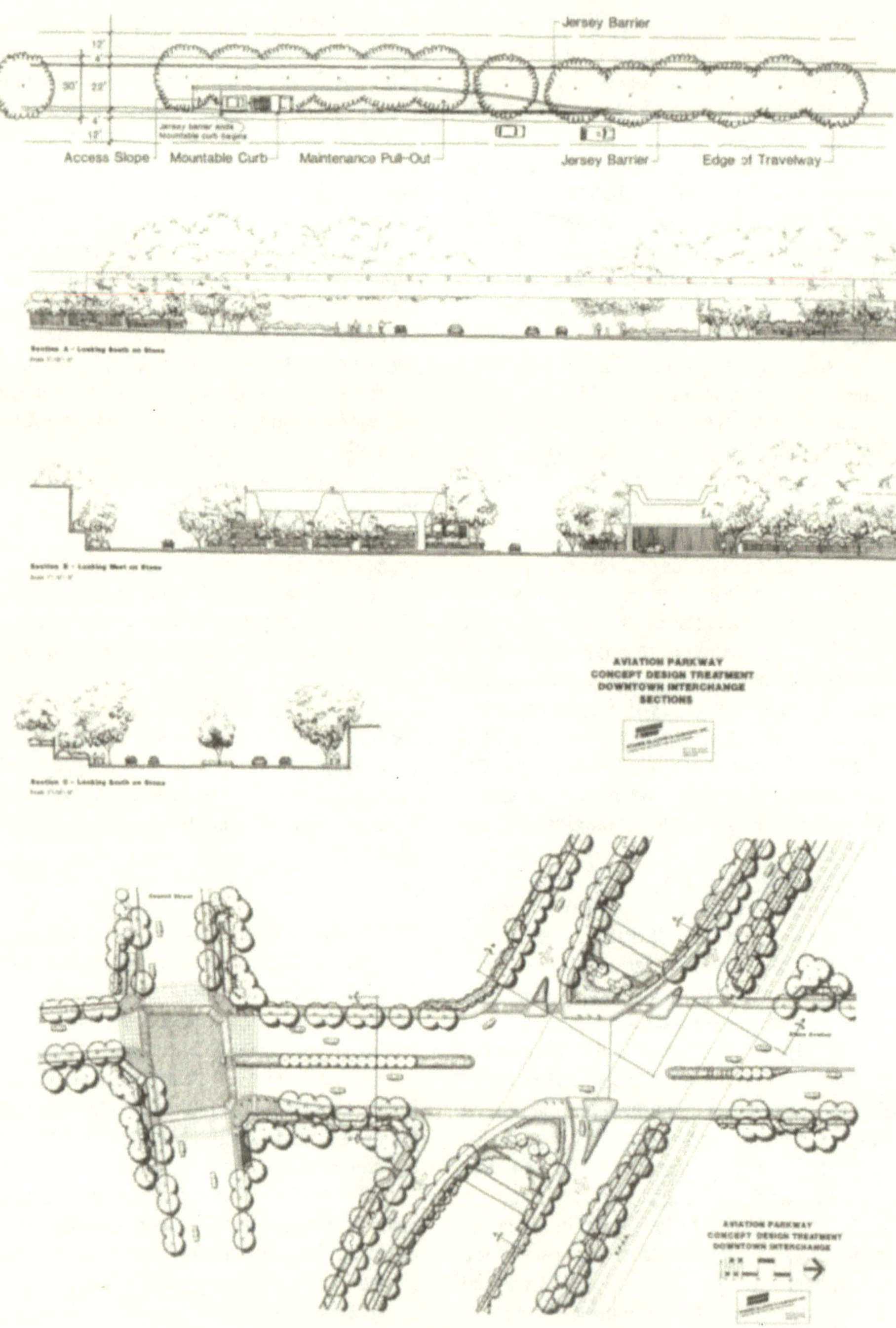

Top: ***Fig. 5. Maintenance access to medians.***
Center and Bottom: ***Fig. 6a and 6b. Downtown intersection and stepped planters.***

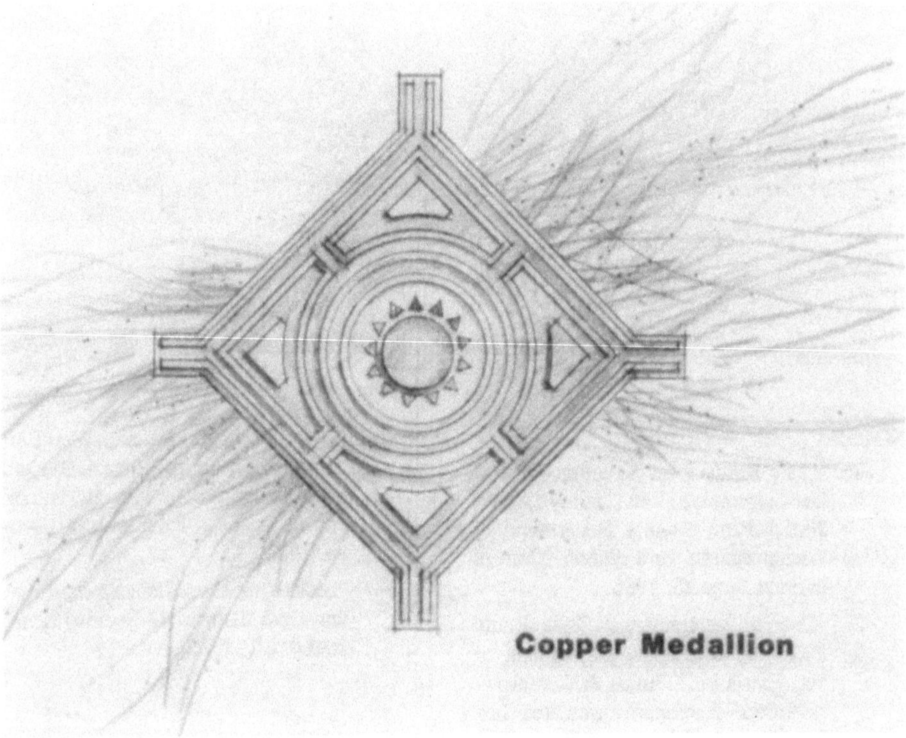

Copper Medallion

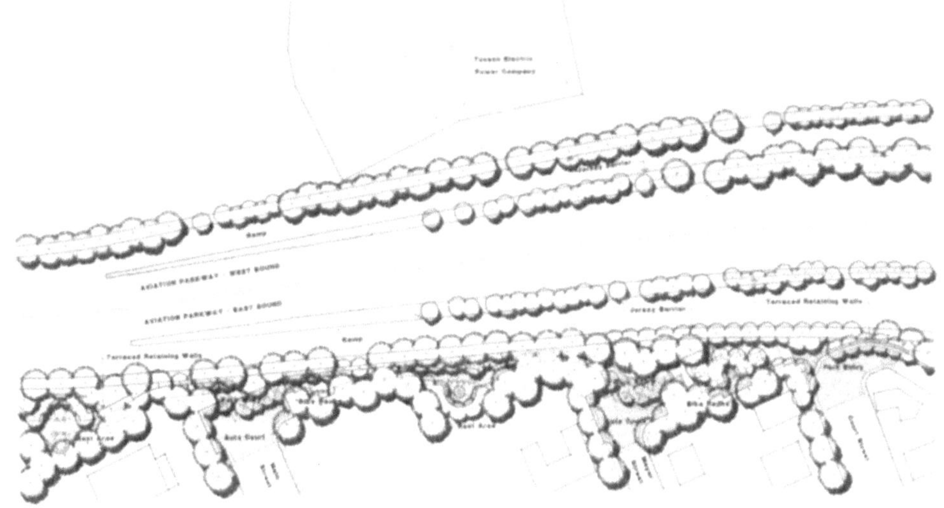

Top: ***Fig. 7. Signature medallion.***
Bottom: ***Fig. 8. El Presidio Linear Park.***

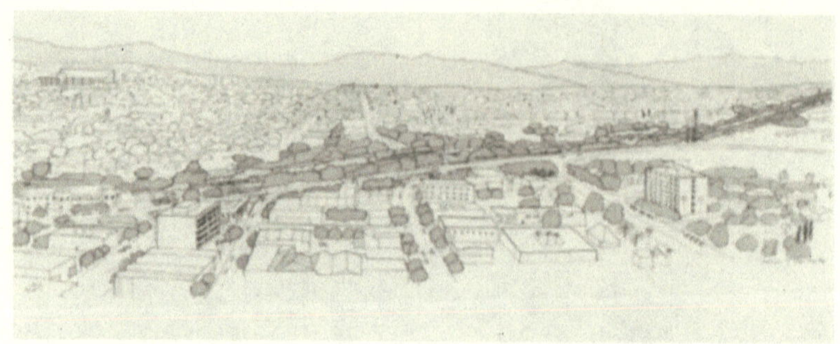

Fig. 9. The Arroyo Concept, birdseye perspective.

NOTES

1. "Long Range Transportation Plan for Unincorporated Pima County 1986 to 2005," Pima County Department of Transportation and Flood Control District, June 25, 1986.
2. "Concept Design Report, State Route 210, City of Tucson Department of Transportation," Finical & Dombrowski/Barton-Aschman Associates, Inc. Joint Venture, May 10, 1985.
3. "Aviation Parkway Landscape Concept Design Report," Rogers, Gladwin & Harmony, Inc. for Parsons, Brinckerhoff, Quade & Douglas, Inc., October 1986.
4. "Establishment and Designation of Parkways and Historic and Scenic Roads", ARS41-412 through 41-518.

Parkway Design

Gary L. Klinedinst, Eastern Direct Federal Division, Federal Highway Administration, Department of Transportation

INTRODUCTION

The design and construction of scenic Parkways in the Southeastern United States has historically had a large Federal Government presence. The two agencies most responsible throughout the years for Federal Parkways have been the National Park Service (NPS) and the Bureau of Public Roads (BPR), now the Federal Highway Administration (FHWA).

The cooperation between the two agencies can be traced to a 1926 "Memorandum of Agreement" between the NPS and Bureau of Public Roads, BPR (then in the Department of Agriculture), which provided for engineering and technical support for the survey, design, construction, and improvement of roads and trails in the National Parks and National Monuments by the BPR. This was the start of a long and close relationship between the two agencies which endures to this day and has produced Parkways on Federal lands throughout the eastern United States that give enjoyment to millions of visitors each year and have in their own right become national treasures.

The BPR office responsible for these engineering functions in the eastern United States today is known as Federal Highway Administration, Eastern Direct Federal Division (EDFD). This office, established in 1934 as Eastern Forest and Park District in Washington, D.C., has had many titles throughout the years such as: District 15, Division 15, Region 15, and EDFD since 1981.

The Federal Parkways that EDFD and its predecessors have participated in with the National Park Service are:

Mount Vernon Parkway, Virginia - authorized in 1928.

Skyline Drive, Virginia - authorized in 1930.

Colonial Parkway, Virginia - authorized in 1930.

George Washington Memorial Parkway, Virginia - authorized in 1930, which included the newly completed Mount Vernon Parkway.

Blue Ridge Parkway, Virginia & North Carolina - authorized in 1933 to connect Shenandoah Park with the Great Smoky Mountains.

Natchez Trace Parkway, Mississippi, Alabama & Tennessee - authorized in 1934 to connect Natchez, Mississippi, with Nashville, Tennessee.

Rock Creek Parkway, District of Columbia - authorized in 1913.

Suitland Parkway and Baltimore-Washington Parkway, District of Columbia & Maryland - which were wartime efforts to connect military installations and later converted to Parkways.

Foothills Parkway, Tennessee - authorized in 1944 for land acquisition to begin.

The development of these Parkways was a joint effort of the National Park Service landscape architects and the Bureau of Public Roads engineers which singly could not have accomplished the creation of these true Parkways. Without this joint effort, as many have found since, you may have a Parkway in name but in reality you have just another transportation facility.

PARKWAY DESIGN

From an engineering standpoint, designing a Parkway follows standard highway design practice with the exception that extra care needs to be exercised by the engineer in designing the roadway to fit the local terrain and geology. In conceiving and designing a roadway, typical highway design practice follows three major steps:

1. Corridor study
2. Location studies
3. Final design

During the corridor study, aerial photographs and large scale mapping are used to define an acceptable corridor through which the roadway is to traverse. Many preliminary alignment studies within a corridor may be made and field checked by a number of engineering specialists and the landscape architect. As the corridor study progresses more information is generated and more decisions are made which indicate the desired corridor and the location of the preferred general alignment within the corridor. At this point locations for scenic views, park facilities, and locations posing unique technical attention (such as tunnels, exceptional long or high bridges) are highlighted.

The location studies concentrate on further developing the decisions made in the corridor study, i.e., one acceptable alignment with possibly a few alternate alignments in controversial areas. At the conclusion of the location studies, a set of preliminary plans is produced that has an acceptable Parkway alignment along with other established criteria such as Parkway cross section, vertical alignment and special features requiring further detailed study or design. Constructability of the chosen alignment has also been considered with input from structural, geotechnical, hydraulic and construction engineers. Other professional specialties (from the NPS) are drawn upon at this point in time to consider archeology, history, and of course, landscape architecture. Outstanding features of a Parkway such as the Linn Cove structure on the Blue Ridge Parkway, where complex technical problems as well as ecological problems existed, required all the above specialties to bring the structure to reality. This team approach is not unique to highway design but the degree of team work and interagency involvement is considerably higher in Parkway design.

The last major step in conceiving a Parkway is the final design. During this step final details are pulled together to produce the plans and specifications that translate all previously made team decisions into a constructable roadway. Final plans and specifications also include other details such as parking area layouts, environmental mitigation measures, and the final contract documents detailing how the Parkway is to be constructed both administratively and technically.

As previously stated the above procedures are standard highway design practice. Parkway design deviates and improves on these standard procedures in five major areas. They are:

1. Teamwork
2. Alignment
3. Design Standards
4. Construction Sensitive to the Environment
5. Architectural and Landscape Details

TEAM WORK

The high degree of interdisciplinary teamwork required for Parkway design as discussed before is essential and unique. This close working relationship of specialists from many professions allows the Parkway to be in harmony with the terrain which is the secret of a good Parkway design.

Alignment of a Parkway is one of the most important elements. Parkway alignment is always curvilinear; meaning a flowing alignment from curve to tangent, thanks to the use of spirals. Spirals are a means to transition from a curve to a tangent section of roadway by gradually changing the curvature. This eases you from the curve to the tangent section of the Parkway. Spirals are frequently called easement curves. In many mountain Parkways, the transition from one curve to another is so close that little or no tangent sections of roadway are possible. Thus the alignment along with roadway widening through the curves allows driving along a Parkway to be easy in rough terrain and gives the appearance of a flowing ribbon of roadway.

Along with the use of spirals another important feature of Parkway alignment is minimizing cut and fill as much as possible. Retaining walls, structures and varying the degree of curvature are used as well as taking advantage of naturally occurring geologic phenomenon to minimize disturbance to the original terrain.

DESIGN STANDARDS

Another important area that makes Parkway design unique is the design standards used and their flexible application to the design. It is interesting to note that the first Memorandum of Agreement between the NPS and BPR called for a standardization of design not only among Park roads but between Park roads and roads of the Federal-aid Highway system. Since that time, the NPS and the FHWA have had continuing discussions concerning the standards for Park roads and Parkways. As caretaker of the Parks, the NPS sees Parkways as accesses to Parks or historic areas which should minimally disturb the natural terrain and emphasize landscape and aesthetic considerations. The FHWA due to its role in the Federal-aid Highway system emphasizes traffic and engineering considerations from the standpoint of safety and increased benefits to the user. In an effort to provide the safest and most aesthetic facilities possible, the EDFD and the NPS have worked closely on each Parkway to outline the design criteria appropriate to each Parkway's use. In fact, most of the Parkways were designed before the first general Park road standards were written in the 1940's. The present (1984) NPS Park Road Standards are a blend of past experience and accepted highway engineering practice, i.e., American Association of State Highway and Transportation Officials standards and landscape architectural considerations. The standards define such features as roadway width, side slopes, grades and degree of curvature. These standards are applied flexibly so that unique situations can be designed individually, balancing costs and aesthetics with safety. The blind application of standards whether they are NPS or the AASHTO is discouraged in Parkway design.

CONSTRUCTION SENSITIVITY TO THE ENVIRONMENT

Another unique aspect of Parkway design is the sensitive construction techniques needed to bring the plans and specifications to fruition. The construction personnel need more than "an all bulldozer ahead" mentality so common in highway construction. Construction personnel must enforce all environmental constraints in the specifications, insist on quality construction, and constantly be on the lookout for ways in which to adapt the roadway to the geologic conditions encountered in the field. This may entail small design changes during construction in such areas as erosion control, shifting of parking areas to enhance views, and alignment adjustments. Above all, the construction personnel have to have a good working relationship with the NPS Architect and know when to call on the specialists to solve field problems before they get out of control.

ARCHITECTURAL AND LANDSCAPE DETAILS

The remaining important unique aspect to creating a Parkway is the architectural and landscaping details which are by far one of the most important features that set a Parkway apart from any other roadway. These details are what allows each Parkway to have its unique character.

PARKWAY RECONSTRUCTION

As a number of the Parkways reach 50 years of age, they are in need of reconstruction. Time has taken its toll on them even though at their age you can't help marveling at how well they have withstood time. The challenge to the engineer in reconstruction of a Parkway is to blend new technology into the process in order to allow the Parkway to age more gracefully and to become safer for the traveling public but at the same time not destroy its well accepted character. Parkways presently under reconstruction are the Mount Vernon Memorial Parkway, Skyline Drive, the Colonial Parkway and Suitland Parkway.

During reconstruction, safety retrofitting becomes important in order to decrease the Government's liability from tort claims and to protect the Parkway visitor. This safety retrofitting must be accomplished in such a way as not to destroy the Parkway character. Examples of safety retrofitting without changing the character of the Parkway can be seen on both the reconstruction of the Mount Vernon Memorial Highway and the Skyline Drive.

On the Mount Vernon Highway safety improvements include intersection improvements and the addition of crashworthy guardrails where appropriate by current standards. The guardrails used are crash tested wood or masonry. An example of the masonry guardrail was used at the Alexander Street Overpass structure. The masonry facing on the guardrail matches the original masonry on the structure and provides a deterrent for errant vehicles. Vehicles can no longer crash into the abutments of the bridge which are located next to the roadway; instead, the vehicle would strike the aesthetic guardrail and be guided past the abutments saving life and decreasing property damage.

The Skyline Drive is also receiving crashworthy masonry guardrails in place of the original mortarless hand-placed rock walls. The original walls would allow errant vehicles to either go through them or be catapulted over them due to their type of construction and low height. The new wall has a reinforced concrete core with a 6-inch stone veneer facing. The new wall, although different in appearance (mortared masonry and 23 inches high) from the original wall, looks quite natural and keeps the character of the Drive when viewed in context with the finished roadway. The new wall also meets present day vehicle crash tests and the improved wall foundations will resist settling into the fill as had previously happened to the original wall.

INNOVATIVE SOLUTIONS

The design, construction, and reconstruction of a Parkway presents a special challenge to the engineer. Designing and constructing Parkways takes the innovativeness of today's design team. To illustrate this innovativeness, unique solutions to three areas will be discussed:

1. solutions to control cost,
2. solutions to aid the environment,
3. solutions to conquer the terrain.

SOLUTIONS TO CONTROL COST

Civil engineering is rooted in not only solving problems but solving problems in such a way that is affordable to the client. Although cost is generally not the basis for a decision on a parkway, the solution to that decision considers cost to a high degree. An example of this concept would be the decision to construct a retaining wall in place of constructing a fill or cut. This decision is usually dictated by environmental or aesthetic concerns and desired by the landscape architect. A retaining wall generally is by far a more costly solution to a problem than a cut or fill. Where cost becomes critical in the decision is in the actual design and construction of the retaining wall. New technology and good engineering will provide an affordable solution.

Costs through the years have escalated as has everything else in our society. A good example of the degree of escalation can be vividly seen by comparing the $30,000 per mile cost of the first section of the Blue Ridge Parkway constructed in 1935, to the $4 million per mile cost of the Grandfather Mountain section of the Parkway which has just been completed.

Many examples of innovative solutions to control cost are available, but one that also includes the use of new technology is the retaining wall around Rough Ridge on Grandfather Mountain on the Blue Ridge Parkway in North Carolina. The retaining wall was requested by the NPS to conserve the natural vegetation on Rough Ridge which would have been covered and destroyed by a fill. The wall would also be highly visible from other sections of the Parkway and thus would need a stone masonry facing to maintain the character of the Parkway. The retaining wall, due to its height of 40-plus feet, was a technical and cost control challenge using normal reinforced concrete technology. A wall constructed of only stone masonry would not only be a huge wall (due to height) but a very expensive one at today's $1,000 per cubic yard. The solution was a new technology called "Reinforced Earth" which was used as the basic retaining wall. A stone masonry veneer facing was provided to maintain Parkway character.

Reinforced Earth is a process of reinforcing a gravelly soil with steel strips so that the soil will support itself and retain the hillside. The "Reinforced Earth" readily solved the technical problems of building a retaining wall 40 plus feet high and at the same time was half the cost of a conventional retaining wall constructed of reinforced concrete.

Another example of innovation and cost control is the aforementioned Skyline Drive guardwalls. The wall uses reinforced concrete technology to provide stability and crash-worthiness and uses a stone masonry veneer for aesthetics. The savings in stone masonry cost is considerable as the wall is 75% reinforced concrete.

Other cost control technology, such as modern post tensioning of structural concrete, provides savings over conventional reinforced concrete. Post tensioning allows thinner, more cost efficient structures and enables the designers to create such spectacular structures as the Linn Cove Viaduct on the Blue Ridge Parkway.

SOLUTIONS TO AID ENVIRONMENT

Since most Parkways traverse areas of great beauty, there is great concern for protecting the environment from the construction of the Parkway. Over the last 10-15 years, great strides have been made in this area using new technology as it continues to be developed. The FHWA and EDFD, in particular, have been pioneers in the field of environmental control. Our specifications are stringent in this area. The use of textile fences to catch and retain sediments in runoff water was pioneered by EDFD. Strict enforcement of the maintenance of these so-called silt fences is performed.

A previous Gatlinburg, Tennessee Division Engineer pioneered the use of "stepped slopes" as a means to induce quick vegetative growth on shale slopes which otherwise would not naturally vegetate. This process constructs small steps into the cut slope so that vegetation can quickly establish itself on the steps. During a period of time the steps gradually erode into a uniform slope leaving little trace of their existence. From these experiments came the realization, universally used in highway construction today, that slopes (cut or fill) should no longer be smooth finished, if quick vegetation is desired in order to reduce erosion.

Another design aid that ultimately helps the environment is the use of photomontage during the planning stage. Photomontage is the computer projection of the Parkway alignment onto an oblique photograph. With artist enhancement, the result is a near accurate picture of what the completed Parkway section will look like. This enables study of the effects Parkway construction will have on the surrounding environment. This process was successfully used to gain support for the Linn Cove Viaduct on the Blue Ridge Parkway before its construction. Viewing these early photomontages of Linn Cove Viaduct, you couldn't help but feel it was going to be the spectacular structure it is today and that its presence would enhance rather than detract from the environment.

SOLUTIONS TO CONQUER TERRAIN

Due to the very nature of a scenic Parkway, the country through which it traverses may be rugged, desolate, extremely treacherous and sometimes unstable. Parkway design through such areas requires innovative engineering solutions. A case in point is the newly completed Grandfather Mountain section of the Blue Ridge Parkway in North Carolina. A large portion of this section of Parkway is through rugged talus (rock from above cliffs) and boulder strewn slopes that are inherently unstable and contain underground streams. To conquer the terrain throughout this section, cuts and fills had to be minimized so as to cause the least disturbance to existing marginally stable slopes. Retaining walls in some areas were made flexible since they were founded on talus material that over time will shift and move. Liberal use of structures to cross underground streams was necessary.

The Linn Cove Viaduct was an innovative solution to a tough problem. Conventional roadway construction was deemed unacceptable from an environmental damage point of view; thus was born the use of a structure on a hillside. The lack of good foundation locations caused by a boulder strewn terrain throughout the Linn Cove area required the structure be located at preselected foundation sites. The resulting span lengths plus the environmental restraints on the construction of the structure resulted in the necessity to seek a technique such as the match cast segmental construction which ultimately was used to construct this unusual structure.

This is not to say that all innovative and unique solutions are saved for the Blue Ridge Parkway. Other Parkways have also benefited from innovative and unique solutions such as the Natchez Trace which has the spectacular Tom Bigbee waterway crossing structure with an impressive 400 plus feet center span as well as the graceful arch structures on the newly completed Tennessee section.

CONCLUSION

Parkway design, whether it is in the lofty Blue Ridge Mountains, low lying Mississippi sediments, or in the urban Washington, D.C., area, is a challenge for the engineer. The teamwork with other disciplines and the close attention to detail, whether they be engineering, landscaping, or environmental, are what makes a Parkway design different from other transportation facilities.

The Skyline Drive: A Western Park Road in the East

Sarah Georgia Harrison, ASLA

INTRODUCTION

Skyline Drive from Front Royal to Rockfish Gap lies within the Shenandoah National Park in Virginia. It is distinct from the Blue Ridge Parkway, which begins at its southernmost tip and extends southward to Great Smoky Mountains National Park. Although both roads are within the National Park System, there are physical and administrative differences which demonstrate the different economic and historic conditions under which they were built.

The intention of this study is to show that the Skyline Drive, although not a parkway itself, was influential in the development of succeeding parkways - most notably and most directly, the Blue Ridge Parkway.

The scope of this study will encompass a brief history of the events surrounding the establishment of Shenandoah National Park; a study of the origin and significance of the design within its historical context; and a study of the experiential qualities of the Drive which are demonstrative of its background and its influence.

SHENANDOAH PARK HISTORY

A study of the history of Shenandoah National Park established it as the first major national park east of the Mississippi, as a precedent for later eastern park roads and parkways, and as a product of the difficult times in which it was created. First, this study will show how the joint interest of the National Park Service and the State of Virginia in preservation in the East led to establishment of the park. Second, the intent is to show how the process of the purchase of land and the sequence of construction for the Skyline Drive set precedents for succeeding national parks and parkways within the East. Third, the intent is to present the design of the Drive as a product of the "makework" projects of the Depression.

The movement for an eastern park began in late 1923 at the initiative of Stephen Mather, first Director of the National Park Service. A strong believer in the accessibility of the national treasures to the people, Mather regretted the distance which separated the great majority of Americans from the western parks. The only existing national park in the populated eastern states was the tiny Lafayette (now Acadia) National Park on the Maine coast. He persuaded the Secretary of the Interior, Hubert Work, to appoint a commission to study the possibility of establishing a park in the southern Appalachians. (1)

In December 1924 the Southern Appalachian National Park Commission recommended that "a portion of the northern 'Blue Ridge of Virginia'" and the Great Smokies of North Carolina and Tennessee be developed as national parks. Because of its accessibility to highly populated areas, the Blue Ridge site was considered the most attractive for initial concern, with development of the Smokies to follow later. The committee enthusiastically urged construction of a "skyline drive along the mountaintop" to present sweeping views of the Shenandoah Valley and the Piedmont. (2)

By 1925 it was clear that establishment of a national park in the East was to be quite different from the process in the West, where virtually untouched public lands were set aside for preservation. Most of the Blue Ridge was in private ownership and much of it was second growth forest. The holdings were generally rather small, and the inhabitants eked a poor living out of the wasted soils and dying chestnut forests. Establishment of a national park would involve purchase of the lands, removal of the inhabitants, and restoration of the natural processes to the forests. This was not to be an easy process. In spite of their poverty, the Appalachian people were reluctant to leave the mountains they loved, and bitterly contested efforts to remove them. In addition, Congress specified that no federal funding was to be available for the purchase. Creation of the park was entirely dependent upon transfer of title of the land from the state to the federal government. This left the burden of acquisition on the State of Virginia.

Under the influence of Governor Harry T. Byrd, the Commission for Conservation and Development, an unpaid state commission headed by William Carson, was appointed to solicit pledges of private individuals and organizations. The fundraising goal was 2.5 million dollars in order to purchase the chosen 400,000 acres. (3) In the eight years, 1926-1934, that passed before title was acquired, the movement might easily have faltered were it not for several factors. First, much credit is due to the personal dynamism of William Carson. (4) Second, Governor Byrd convinced the Virginia General Assembly to grant an appropriation of one million dollars to the fund. Third, Congress reduced the minimum required acreage two separate times, in 1928 and 1932, resulting in a more easily attainable 160,000 acres. (5) Fourth, a generous donation from John D. Rockfeller boosted the funds. (6) Fifth, President Herbert Hoover attempted to draw public attention to the prospective site by establishing his fishing camp on the Rapidan River (7) in an area that is today part of the park.

This camp was significant not only in that it brought needed publicity to fund the campaign, but also in that it provided the reason for the first National Park Service road to be built in the proposed park. For presidential security, a road was built in the summer of 1931 from the Rapidan Camp to Big Meadows and then north to intersect with the Lee Highway, now U.S. 211, at Thornton Gap. Since this was an area hard hit by depression and drought, Congress specified the use of Drought Relief funds and local labor for the construction. (8)

The segment from Skyland to Thornton Gap was the beginning of the fulfillment of that grand prediction made in 1924 by the Shenandoah National Park Commission for a skyline drive along the mountaintop. This was possibly the goal William Carson had in mind when he urged Congress to build the road for the more practical and urgent reasons of presidential security and local employment. Plans were quickly made to continue the road from Skyland south to the Spottswood Trail, now U.S. 33, at Swift Run Gap. (9) Then, in the last days of the Hoover administration, Congress approved a northern extension from Thornton Gap to Front Royal. (10)

The ultimate goal of a skyline drive stretching the length of the park was always in sight, but it was accomplished one piece at a time. The three eventual sections were completed in the following order: the middle section, 1934; the north section, 1936; and the south section, 1939. Each section was planned and designed independently; each section had a characteristic terrain to which it responded; each was built with different constraints of funding and time; each was divided into subsections, ten to twelve miles in length, which were contracted out for construction. To a certain extent the design reflects these variations; however, there is a characteristic unity throughout. This unity can be attributed to the landscape architects and engineers who first walked the alignment, striving to fit the topography, to minimize the impact, and to enhance the experience of being in a natural environment in the best tradition of those who struggled with the introduction of roads into the untouched park lands of the West.

The National Park Service was established to preserve the vast parks of the West. All of the parks prior to 1930 were carved out of the public domain, primarily untouched by the hand of man. In order to make the scenic and natural features accessible to the public, the Park Service constructed roads from which the parks could be experienced. These roads were potentially great threats to the preservation of the parks.

The early park road designers searched for a workable solution. Within the great variety of western parks the designers met with a diversity of conditions and terrains. They found that arbitrary standards were less useful than more flexible ones. (11) They relied on ideal concepts and tried to adapt within each situation. They maintained the following general principles:

1. They strove to fit the topography rather than conform to predetermined standards of alignment, curvature and grade. (12)
2. They considered the appearance of the road (13) and sought graceful curves whose horizontal and vertical components would flow together in easy rhythm.
3. To enhance the experience of being in a natural environment, they allowed the vegetation to come to the edge of the road where possible.
4. They designed low speed roads to better fit the topography and to allow for enjoyable recreational travel.
5. They wound the road between features in a manner that often increased the length of the road and in an order that presented the most logical interpretive sequence.
6. To heal the scars of construction and to protect the roadside from erosion they insured rounding and flattening of slopes and they replanted only indigenous plant species.
7. During the construction process, they were careful to protect large trees and to locate borrow pits out of sight of roads and features.
8. They developed maintenance plans with careful instructions for selective cutting and thinning of vegetation to open up views and vistas. (14)

Until the development of the master plan with its detailed graphic and narrative instructions, these design concepts were not recorded; instead, they were understood within a tight group of design professionals, composed of landscape architects and engineers.

In 1926 an Interbureau Agreement, authored by L.I. Hewes with Horace M. Albright (15) established a formal working relationship between engineers of the Bureau of Public Roads and landscape architects of the Park Service. It stated: "... the Bureau will instruct its District Engineer to proceed, in cooperation with the Landscape Engineer of the Park Service and the Superintendent of the Park, with the location survey, and to prepare plans, specifications, and estimates for the project." (16)

For the Skyline Drive the joint cooperation of the Bureau of Public Roads and the National Park Service brought to the Drive a quality equivalent to that of the western park roads. Two of the individual designers who worked on the Skyline Drive had prior experience on the western roads. Charles E. Peterson, a landscape architect who advised the engineers and other landscape architects on the middle and north sections of the Skyline Drive, worked on the General's Highway of the Sequoia National Park early in his career. (17) William Milnes Austin, engineer for the Bureau of Public Roads, who worked on the project from beginning to end, supervised construction of the General's Highway and later worked on the Blue Ridge Parkway. (18)

The designers were influenced by the western park roads, especially those built under the Interbureau Agreement. In addition, there were new developments in road design at the time that very likely made an impact on the design of the Skyline Drive. During the 1920's and 1930's the use of spiral easements was becoming more and more prevalent. More and more designers were concluding that the use of spirals was advantageous because of the resultant saving in distance, reduction in cost, ease and safety of travel, and the improved aesthetic appearance. (19) V.R. Ludgate cited Hickerson's Highway Curves and Earthwork, published in 1926, as the authoritative source on spirals used by field designers at the time. It defines a spiral thus: "A transition curve (or spiral) is an easement providing a gradual change of curvature from a straight line to a circular arc. The degree-of-curve changes directly as the distance along the curve." (20) It is perhaps indicative of the newness of the concept of spirals or perhaps the difference in western park roads and eastern parkways to note that the Skyline Drive was not initially laid out with spiral curves. Plain circular curves were used on the first section. (21) Spirals were added as the design progressed.

Many of the finest design intentions could not have been carried out were it not for an available labor force. Because of the support of President Franklin D. Roosevelt, six Civilian Conservation Corps camps were established in or near the park in 1933. (22) This provided a wealth of the needed manpower to refine and finish the design. The CCC was responsible for maintenance operations such as vista clearing, cutting and thinning of vegetation, and rounding and flattening of slopes. Under the direction of local masons they built dry stone guard walls. (23) Their work made invaluable additions to the beauty of the design.

At the time of the dedication of Shenandoah National Park on July 3, 1936, two-thirds of the Skyline Drive was complete. In his address at the ceremony President Roosevelt announced the proposal for an extension of the Drive to the Great Smoky Mountains National Park. This ultimately resulted in the building of the Blue Ridge Parkway. (24)

The conditions under which the Drive was built must be recognized for their uniqueness and for their consequent influence on the design. First, it is fortunate that the Drive was built at all, since construction began before establishment of the park. The need for sustaining the interest of the public in the park project was a part of the push for construction. Second, the funds and labor source for the construction were evidence of the times in which it was built. The Drought Relief money, the local labor force, and later the CCC were necessary for work to proceed. Third, the joint cooperation of the Bureau of Public Roads and the National Park Service continued the Park Service quality of road-building established in the western parks. Fourth, the process of constructing in sections resulted in slight variations in the design that responded to the conditions of the terrain, time and availability of funds. Fifth, the fact that construction was contracted out in subsequent units, each ten to twelve miles in length, set a precedent that was followed by the Blue Ridge Parkway and other later parkways. Sixth, the process by which the State of Virginia acquired and deeded the land to the federal government was an adaptation that the National Park Service was obliged to make in the move East; nevertheless, it set an important precedent for other potential national park lands in settled areas. A 1937 Park Service pamphlet entitled "Requirements and Procedure to Govern the Acquisition of land for National Parkways" establishes the following procedure: "...the states through which the parkway passes, acquire and deed to the United States the rights of way, and the federal government then assumes the responsibility for the construction and maintenance of the parkway road and adjoining recreational areas." (25) A reasonable conclusion is that the national parkways followed the example of the Skyline Drive in the process of the acquisition of land.

A study of the history, then, lends an understanding of the following points:

1. The Skyline Drive was a product of the depression, as demonstrated by the sources of funds and labor, and by the speed with which the design was completed.
2. The Drive was a product of the National Park Service of the West. It was built under the Interbureau Agreement by some of the same men who had worked on the earlier western national park roads.
3. The Skyline Drive was a precedent for the Blue Ridge Parkway. Construction for the Drive, and later the Parkway, was contracted out in units of 10-12 miles, and the acquisition of land was the responsibility of the State.

THE SKYLINE DRIVE

In the 1924 report to Secretary of Interior Hubert Work recommending establishment of Shenandoah National Park, the Southern Appalachian National Park Commission suggested that:

> *The greatest single feature, however, is a possible skyline drive along the mountain top, following a continuous ridge and looking westerly on the Shenandoah Valley, from 2,500 to 3,500 feet below, and also commanding a view of the Piedmont Plain stretching easterly to the Washington Monument, which landmark may be seen on a clear day. Few scenic drives in the world could surpass it.* (26)

From the very earliest days Shenandoah National Park was thought to be best presented as a driving experience. Seven years later when the planning and design was actually begun, the conception had matured into the idea of a one-day round trip drive from Washington, D.C. and vicinity. The key idea, as first expressed by Stephen Mather, was that of accessibility to a large segment of the population. The beautiful scenic views of the mountaintop were to be made accessible to the many, not just the hardy few.

Not only did the first park road in the east bring beautiful views to more people, but it also brought design techniques and traditions which became influential on later roads. A study of the experiential qualities of the road will help to demonstrate the physical manifestations of its historical context.

Alignment. The Skyline Drive was designed to follow the ridgetops in a manner that would reveal the best scenic views and cause the least amount of scar on the land. Views of the patchwork farms and towns of the Shenandoah Valley were alternated with the hazy views of the rolling Piedmont. The alignment was curved right, then left, in a graceful manner that was intended to be pleasing and restful to the eye. (27) Design along the ridge avoided many of the grading problems of a road cut through a side hill, yet the changing elevations of the peaks made it necessary to follow the gaps (28) and swing around the highest points. Design from gap to gap allowed for the alternation of views as each peak blocked one view to shift the focus to another.

Cross-Section. Along with the alignment, the cross-section and the extent of grading were considered. Heavy cuts and fills were avoided and a smooth line from shoulder to pavement to ditch slope (29) that blended with the natural topography was the ideal. Where possible, side hill construction balanced the cut and fill to reduce the scar and create a gentle natural line. (30)

Overlooks. Sixty-seven parking overlooks were provided along the drive for motorists to stop and view scenery of outstanding beauty. Although they were designed to fit the individual site, there are general characteristics which can describe all but a few minor variants. Designed to accommodate roughly twenty cars, the overlooks were usually structured with planting areas to direct the parking and flow of traffic. Dry stone walls were built by the CCC to edge the parking surface and mark the grade break.

Middle Section. Standards for gradients and curves varied as work on the Drive progressed. Each section had its own constraints of topography and the standards were responsive to them. In 1931 construction was begun on the middle section of the Drive. Since the park land had not yet been acquired, a 100-foot right of way strip, based on the preliminary road location, was obtained for construction to proceed. As a limited time was allowed for use of the Drought Relief funds, design and construction was rapid. Horizontal curves were initially laid out as circular rather than spiral curves. The minimum radii for curves was less than two hundred feet in order to save time and excavation costs. (31) The roadway width was thirty feet including shoulders. (32) An overlook on the middle section demonstrates the speed of the design of the section and the lack of development of some of the later standard design principles.

North Section. For the north section ample time was available to study the design and location of the route. If there were hasty decisions made on the middle section, the north section was designed with a greater care for flowing alignment. The gentle, slowly descending terrain was more adaptable to a good line. The roadway width increased to thirty-four feet and shoulders blended ever more gracefully with the land. The terrain permitted larger, more gracious overlooks.

South Section. The south section was the only one to be constructed after the establishment of the park in 1936. Time and funds were available, fortunately, because it was here that the ingenuity of the designers was the most taxed. The terrain was extremely rugged and required careful field study of alternate routes. Because of the quantity of excavation on the south section, the roadway was reduced to the thirty foot width used on the middle section. Although the design of overlooks had matured, in many cases they were difficult to locate without scar.

Visitor Section. From the campground and store at Loft Mountain, to the lodge at Big Meadows, visitor services were designed to enrich the experience of travellers. They were carefully situated to avoid encroachment on the scenic value of the road (33) and cause the least damage to the land. As in the national parks of the West, the park road led from feature to feature to visitor service.

Vegetation. During the initial design and construction phases, the vegetation was considered primarily from a preservationist rather that aesthetic viewpoint. Large trees were carefully protected during blasting operations and the roadway and overlooks were designed to preserve as much standing vegetation as possible. Valuable trees on fill sections were protected with tree wells. The only planting was to restore vegetation to the graded slopes. This was done with strictly indigenous plant materials. It is worthy of note that the chestnut blight and the cutting practices of past inhabitants in many places left denuded slopes. The Park Service intended for the vegetation to restore itself according to natural processes with very little reforestation. With the exception of Big Meadows, which is maintained by burning and cutting, the cleared areas were allowed to slowly recover.

Some work was done with the vegetation by the CCC after the road design and construction was complete. Thinning of dense trees, or vista clearing, allowed greater visibility of scenic views without exposing the roadway and cars to a distant observer. Trees at the overlooks were trimmed or removed as necessary to open and frame views.

The original design intent was to allow the vegetation to come to the edge of the road to keep the natural character as much as possible. Maintenance practices through the years have altered this considerably. Today the vegetation is mowed or scythed ten or more feet from the road in many places. Where tall trees remain close to the road, the arching branches sometimes meet, cathedral-like, with the trees of the other side.

Details. In some cases maintenance practices are different from the original design intentions. The surface of the roadway, when new, was composed of material from the blasting operation to maintain a natural color harmonious with the soil types. The original drainage structures, such as headwalls of pipes and culverts, were faced with hand-laid stones and modestly located. The newer drain types are more conspicuous. Stone guard walls were built by the CCC to define the overlooks and visually reinforce the sharpest curves. Originally these were two feet wide, two feet high (34) and made of local stone. A recent replacement for the now-crumbling original walls is a stonefaced concrete wall that is frequently three feet or more in height. The increased height of the wall can obscure views, especially on the outside of a superelevated curve, where the top of the wall may be equal to or above eye level.

Landscape Types. From the time of the first opening of the middle section, the Skyline Drive has been popular with the public. A visit to the Drive can be appreciated for the beauty and the excitement of achieving magnificent views so easily. Looking down from the mountain can create a sense of awe for the visitor. The experience of the Drive can be broken down into several landscape types which are recognized for their beauty and variety.

The first landscape type is achieved by the filtered views to the lower elevations as the visitor gradually ascends. With anticipation, he may view distant features, revealed through carefully thinned and controlled vegetation. At an overlook, he may stop to more closely examine the features, through filtered branches which frame and compose scenes within the view.

A second type of landscape is characterized by the openness of views. At many overlooks, especially on heavy fill sections, there are very few trees. In contrast to the feeling of security which the trees provide, these vast platforms may suddenly expose the visitor to the sun and wind as he steps out of his car. This may be positive or negative, depending on the season, but it is clearly a part of the perceptual experience. Another instance on the Drive where the vegetation opens to create feelings of expanse is at Big Meadows. This area is maintained by mowing and burning to remind the visitor of past land use practices on the Blue Ridge, but it also serves to create visual variety. Here the experience is one of travelling through a broad landscape where the sky meets the ground.

A third landscape type is the sense of enclosure that happens at several special moments along the Drive. Mary's Rock Tunnel creates the most absolute enclosure for six hundred and sixty feet of darkness. In places where the trees arch and touch creating the semblance of a vaulted cathedral, attention is focused within a restricted corridor. Another special instance of enclosure is created where the road has been cut through rocks which may perhaps be adorned with fragrant hemlock trees.

The Skyline Drive was not designed with careful consideration of the sequential experience. It could be criticized for its monotony. The Drive is completely on the skyline for one hundred and five miles, with virtually the same two views to the east and to the west. The sequence lacks enough variety in the landscape types to compensate for the distance travelled. After the first thrill of being on the mountaintop has abated, there is very little to sustain interest. Soon a rhythm is established as the road curves right, then left, and as the views open and close to the east and west. In one sense the rhythm itself may be enjoyed for the perilousness of the sharp, winding curves that give the fun one might expect in a mountain road. It can also, without relief, become mesmerizing and quickly become tiresome.

THE BLUE RIDGE PARKWAY

While many of the best moments of the Skyline Drive can be attributed to chance and to the innate beauty of the Blue Ridge Mountains, the sequence of the Blue Ridge Parkway was more carefully designed and planned. Stanley Abbott has been called an "innovator" (35) and even "the father of the Parkway Idea as we define parkways." (36) His ideas on design were descendants of the Westchester County Parkways and Gilmore Clarke. The parkway varied from the skyline to obtain views of special features such as rock outcroppings, streams and waterfalls. Mr. Abbott intended to open glimpses into the deepest woods to reveal such features. Also, native trees and shrubs were extensively planted with careful attention to massing of large quantities of similar species. In Stanley Abbott's words: "At focal points a concentration of flowering materials, the mountain laurel, rhododendron, azalea, and the dogwood will be introduced to heighten the interest of the drive." (37) In addition, large rocks were strategically placed to add to the variety. These are not only characteristics of the Blue Ridge Parkway, but they begin to demonstrate the innovations.

CONCLUSION

The Skyline Drive is a national park road in the tradition of the earlier western national park roads. Through its influence on the Blue Ridge Parkway, the parkway idea, as we now understand it, incorporates the tradition of the National Park Service with the design history of eastern parkways. The National Park Service, together with the Westchester County parkways, created the idea of the national parkways, which, from the Foothills Parkway to the Natchez Trace, enrich recreational travel today.

NOTES

(1) Dennis E. Simmons, "Conservation, Cooperation, and Controversy: The Establishment of Shenandoah National Park, 1924–1936," The Virginia Magazine of History and Biography 89, No. 4 (October 1981), p. 388.

(2) Ibid., p. 391.

(3) Ibid., p. 393.

(4) Carter Wormeley, "The Shenandoah National Park Will Be Established in Two Years" Broadside, 1927.

(5) Simmons, "Conservation, Cooperation, and Controversy," pp. 396, 398.

(6) Interview with Charles E. Peterson, FAIA, Architectural Historian, Restorationist, and Planner, Philadelphia, Pennsylvania, 26 February 1984.

(7) Simmons, "Conservation, Cooperation and Controversy," p. 397.

(8) Ibid., p. 397.

(9) Ibid., p. 397.

(10) Ibid., p. 398.

(11) U.S. Department of the Interior, National Park Service, "Policy and Guidelines for the Design and Construction of Park Roads," Memorandum to Director from Deputy Assistant Director, Design and Construction (7 December 1967), p. 5.

(12) Idem, Traffic Quarterly, "Planning Our National Park Roads and Our National Parkways," by Dudley C. Bayliss (1957), p. 419.

(13) H. J. Spelman, "Building Roads in Shenandoah National Park: Area in Virginia Blue Ridge Made Accessible by Recreational Parkway," Civil Engineering 5, No. 8 (August 1935), p. 483.

(14) U.S. Department of the Interior, NPS, Traffic Quarterly, pp. 419-420.

(15) Benjamin C. Howland, Park Roads and Parkways, L-l, p. 7.

(16) U.S. Department of the Interior and U.S. Department of Agriculture, "Memorandum of Agreement Between the National Park Service and the Bureau of Public Roads Relating to the Survey, Construction, and Improvement of Roads and Trails in the National Parks and National Monuments," No. 77562 (1926), p. 3.

(17) Interview with Peterson.

(18) Engineering News Record. Obituary of William Milnes Austin, 138, No. 19 (8 May 1947), p. 789.

(19) T. F. Hickerson, Highway Curves and Earthwork, 1st ed. (New York: McGraw-Hill Book Company Inc., 1926), p. 117.

(20) Ibid., p. 83.

(21) U.S. Department of the Interior, The Regional Review, p. 4.

(22) Simmons, "Conservation, Cooperation and Controversy," p. 398.

(23) H. J. Spelman, "Building Roads," p. 484.

(24) Simmons, "Conservation, Cooperation and Controversy," p. 398.

(25) U.S. Department of Interior, NPS, "Requirements and Procedure to Govern the Acquisition of Land for National Parkways," No. 9219, 9 November 1937.

(26) Idem, Region One, The Regional Review 4, No. 2, Richmond, Virginia, "The Skyline Drive: A Brief History of a Mountaintop Motorway," by Harvey P. Benson, February 1940, p. 4.

(27) Spelman, "Building Roads," p. 483.

(28) Interview with Peterson.

(29) Ibid.

(30) J. L. Harrison, "A New Standard for the Development of Highway Accessibility to Mountain Scenery," Roads and Streets 77, No. 12 (December 1934), p. 434.

(31) U.S. Department of the Interior, The Regional Review, p. 4.

(32) Ibid., p. 6.

(33) Ibid., p. 8.

(34) U.S. Department of Agriculture, Bureau of Public Roads, Final Construction Report, Shenandoah National Park, Skyline Drive Projects l-AB and l-BC.

(35) Interview with Ludgate.

(36) Benjamin C. Howland, List of Biographies, personal files of B. Howland.

(37) Stanley Abbott, "Shenandoah - Great Smoky Mountains National Parkway," 26 June 1935, p. 4., Collected Papers of Carter Glass, Box 332, Manuscript Collection, Alderman Library, University of Virginia.

BIBLIOGRAPHY

I. Books

Crowe, Sylvia. The Landscape of Roads. London: The Architectural Press, 1960.

Heatwole, Henry. Guide to Skyline Drive and Shenandoah National Park. Luray, Virginia: Shenandoah Natural History Association, 1978.

Hickerson, T.F. Highway Curves and Earthwork. 1st ed. New York: McGraw-Hill Book Company, Inc., 1926.

Lambert, Darwin. Illustrated Guide to Shenandoah National Park and Skyline Drive. Luray, Virginia: Lauck and Company, 1947.

Newton, Norman T. Design on the Land: The Development of Landscape Architecture. Cambridge, Massachusetts: The Belknap Press of Harvard University Press, 1978.

Pollock, George Freeman. Skyland: The Heart of the Shenandoah National Park. Washington, D.C.: Stuart E. Brown, Jr., 1960.

II. Articles and Periodicals

Albright, Horace M. "The National Park Policy." Western Architect: Current Architecture 39 (June 1930), pp. 93-96.

Bayliss, Dudley C. "Parkway Development Under the National Park Service." Parks and Recreation. February 1937, pp. 255-259.

Bell, J. Haslett. "New Road Construction in Western National Parks." Landscape Architecture 31, No. 2 (January 1941),pp.63-67.

Bugge, W.A., and Snow, W. Brewster. "The Complete Highway." The Highway and the Landscape. Ed. W. Brewster Snow. New Jersey: Rutgers University Press, 1959.

Clarke, Gilmore D. "The Parkway Idea." The Highway and the Landscape. Ed. W. Brewster Snow. New Jersey: Rutgers University Press, 1959.

Davidson, Arthur. "Skyline Drive and How It Came to Virginia." Conserving and Developing Virginia. Ed. State Commission on Conservation and Development, 1934, pp. 75-79.

Engineering News Record 138, No. 19. Obituary of William Milnes Austin (8 May 1947), p. 789.

Harrison, J.L. "A New Standard for the Development of Highway Accessibility to Mountain Scenery." Roads and Streets 77, No. 12 (December 1934), pp. 431-436.

Nichols, Arthur R. "Landscape Design in Highway Development." Landscape Architecture 30, No. 3 (April 1940), pp. 113-117.

Simmons, Dennis E. "Conservation, Cooperation, and Controversy: The Establishment of Shenandoah National Park, 1924-1936." The Virginia Magazine of History and Biography 89, No. 4 (October 1981), pp. 387-404.

Snow, W. Brewster, ed. "Contributors." The Highway and the Landscape. New Jersey: Rutgers University Press, 1959.

Spelman, H.J. "Building Roads in Shenandoah National Park: Area in Virginia Blue Ridge Made Accessible by Recreational Parkway." Civil Engineering 5, No. 8 (August 1935), pp. 482-484.

Vivian, C.H. "A 450-Mile Pleasure-Only Highway." Compressed Air Magazine (February 1935), pp. 4652-4657.

III. Government Documents

U.S. Department of Agriculture. Bureau of Public Roads. Final Construction Report. Shenandoah National Park, Skyline Drive Projects 1-AB and 1-BC.

___. Manual of Surveys, Design and Construction of Park Roads and Parkways. By H.J. Spelman. Washington, D.C., 1937.

U.S. Department of Commerce. "Scenic Roads and Parkways Study." Manual. Washington, D.C., 26 October 1964.

U.S. Department of Interior. National Park Service. "The 1937 Master Plan for Shenandoah National Park." Shenandoah National Park, Virginia, 1937.

___. "Park and Parkway Road Guidelines." Memorandum to Mr. Swem from Mr. Brown, 14 February 1967.

___. Parkways: A Manual of the Revised Requirements Instructions and Information Relating to National Parkways for Use in the National Park Service. No. 7806, 1937, "Parkways of the Future: A Radio Discussion between Mr. McDonald, Chief of the United States Bureau of Public Roads and Mr. Demaray, Associate Director of the National Park Service." 14 April 1935.

___. Ibid. "Discussion of Federal Parkways." By A. E. Damaray. No. 112585, 24 January 1936.

___. Ibid. "Requirements and Procedure to Govern the Acquisition of Land for National Parkways." No. 9219, 9 November 1937.

___. "Policy and Guidelines for the Design and Construction of Park Roads." Memorandum to Director from Deputy Assistant Director, Design and Construction, 7 December 1967.

U.S. Department of the Interior. National Park Service. Traffic Quarterly. "Planning Our National Park Roads and Our National Parkways." By Dudley C. Bayliss, 1957, pp. 417-440.

___. Region One. The Regional Review 4, No. 2, Richmond, Virginia. "The Skyline Drive: A Brief History of a Mountaintop Motorway." By Harvey P. Benson. February 1940, pp. 3-10.

U.S. Department of the Interior and U.S. Department of Agriculture. "Memorandum of Agreement Between the National Park Service and the Bureau of Public Roads Relating to the Survey, Construction, and Improvement of Roads and Trails in the National Parks and National Monuments." No. 77562, 1926.

IV. Unpublished Studies

Howland, Benjamin C. Park Roads and Parkways. Roads Class Notes, LAR 525, Landscape Architecture Division, School of Architecture, University of Virginia, 1982.

___. "Park Roads and Parkways." List of Biographies. Personal files of B. Howland.

___. "Roads." Personal files of B. Howland.

"Proposed Parkway Connecting Shenandoah and Great Smoky Mountains National Parks." Copy from Denver Service Center, National Park Service, 9 December 1933.

Simmons, Dennis E. "The Creation of Shenandoah National Park and the SkylineDrive, 1924-1926." Ph.D. Dissertation, University of Virginia, 1978.

V. Manuscript Collections

University of Virginia. Alderman Library. Manuscript Collection. Box 332. Collected Papers of Carter Glass. Stanley Abbott, " Shenandoah Great Smoky Mountains National Parkway." 26 June 1935.

Wormeley, Carter. "The Shenandoah National Park Will Be Established in TwoYears." Broadside, 1927.

VI. Interviews

Ludgate, V. Rosewell. Retired Regional Landscape Architect for the National Park Service. Richmond, Virginia. Interview, 4 March 1984.

Peterson, Charles E., FAIA, Architectural Historian, Restorationist and Planner. Philadelphia, Pennsylvania. Interview, 26 February 1984.

The Banff Highway: Pleasing the Park

Dr. Bruce F. Leeson, Chair, TCH Environmental Subcommittee, Environment Canada–Parks, and Geoff G. Allan, Senior Landscape Architectural Technologist, Public Works Canada

INTRODUCTION

The Trans Canada Highway (TCH) was first constructed in 1960 under the authority of the Trans Canada Highways Act. Public Works Canada, as the Canadian Federal Government's construction agency, designed and administered construction within Banff National Park. The TCH was first built as a two lane highway extending 80 km from the Park's East Gate near Canmore Alberta to Yoho National Park in British Columbia. The highway provides access to Jasper and Kootenay National Parks and most importantly is an integral part of the major east-west interprovincial highway route.

Banff National Park, a recently designated World Heritage Site, is Administered by Environment Canada–Parks under the authority of the National Parks Act. A road of national importance running through a National Park is an unusual situation whereby the road contravenes the basic dedication to leave the Park unimpaired for the enjoyment of future generations. Yet the National Park's policy accepts, as one of the facts of economic life, that transportation routes through the National Parks are required in the national interest. Thus, while proposed construction or modification of any major route through the park is the responsibility of Public Works Canada, Parks Canada reviews all such proposals as a matter of policy to ensure that the spirit of the National Parks Act is maintained.

Following completion of the TCH in 1960, traffic demand progressively increased and initial studies for twinning commenced as early as 1963. Further impetus to twinning was generated in 1968 with completion, by the Province of Alberta, of a four lane highway from Calgary to the Parks East Gate. Between 1963 and 1971, two proposals were submitted by Public works for twinning the TCH: one for 120 km through both Banff and Yoho National Parks, and a second for 75 km to the Icefields Parkway junction; however, neither proposal met with approval. It wasn't until 1978 that Public Works Canada formally presented an approved plan for review.

The proposal comprised three separate design and construction phases designated as Phases I, II, and III. These sections are 13, 14 and 50 km in length respectively. Phase I is complete, Phase II is to be completed in the fall of 1987 and the pre-engineering studies have begun on Phase III.

ENVIRONMENTAL REVIEW PROCESSES

In the intervening years between 1971 and 1978, environmental considerations began to play a greater role in the evaluation of all construction projects in Canada. In response to these concerns, the Canadian Government established the Environmental Assessment and Review Process (EARP) in 1973, to ensure:

- that environmental effects are taken into account early in the planning of new federal projects, programs and activities;
- that an environmental assessment is conducted for all projects which may have an adverse effect on the environment before commitments or irrevocable decisions are made, and those which may have significant adverse effects are referred to the Minister of Environment for formal review; and
- that the results of these assessments are used in planning, decision-making, and implementation.

After an Environmental Screening, if a proposed project requires further study to mitigate the environmental impacts, an Initial Environmental Evaluation (IEE), the second of the 4 levels of environmental assessment integral to EARP, is undertaken. This document provides further assessment of the significance of environmental effects so that a proponent can judge whether the project should be studied in complete detail to produce a full environmental analysis called the Environmental Impact Statement (EIS). Beyond that is a formal panel review of the project. The magnitude of public concern for the project is a vital criterion in assessing the need for full formal panel review.

Public Works Canada began environmental studies on the Trans Canada Highway proposal as early as 1971; however, in 1978, an IEE was completed for the section known as Phase I between km 0 and 13. On the basis of the IEE and significant public concern, Public Works Canada as both proponent and initiator of the project, with the concurrence of the Minister responsible for Parks Canada, submitted the twinning proposal to the Federal Environmental Assessment Review Office (FEARO) requesting a formal review.

Upon receipt of the request to review the project, FEARO immediately appointed a five member panel. Environmental Impact Statement guidelines were provided to PWC and public information meetings were held to explain the impending review process to interested parties. In February 1979, PWC submitted a completed EIS. Public information sessions were held in May 1979 and formal public meetings were held in June 1979. The culmination of all these activities was the release of the Panel Report in October 1979 in which the project was approved subject to specific environmental conditions. It was to the recommendations and conditions outlined in this report that PWC then directed its efforts in the detailed design stages of the project.

This process was repeated to gain approval for Phase II of the project. However, Phase III received approval to proceed after the submission of only the Initial Environmental Evaluation and a series of public information sessions. This is regarded to be a significant measure of the success of the project to date.

PROJECT DESCRIPTION

Phase I comprised 13 km of parallel roadway from the Banff Park East Gate to the Banff Townsite. The alignment traverses an existing side valley bench before dropping to the floor of the Lower Bow River Valley. The main structural features included three highway bridges, eight animal underpass structures, 26 km of animal fencing complete with pedestrian stiles, one way gates, vehicle gates and Texas Gates and the relocation and recreation of a major trout stream. Three median designs were utilized: a variable width treed median, a 13 metre wide grassed median, and a raised concrete barrier median.

Phase II comprises a further 14 km of divided highway with all but the last 5 km separated by a raised concrete median barrier. This section moves out of the valley floor and rises to traverse a narrow side bench constructed in rock above an aquatic preserve known as the

Vermilion Lakes. This section consists of construction of three minor traffic interchanges, 4 animal underpass structures, 9 Texas gates, and a further 28 km of fencing with the gates and access controls previously described. This section is to be completed in the fall of 1987.

Phase III will comprise 50 km of completely separate alignment, some cases with up to 500 metres of separation. Pre-engineering studies of aquatic, wildlife, visual, vegetative, geotechnical and alignment elements have been initiated to compile a sound data base for use in the ensuing engineering design.

ENVIRONMENTAL MANAGEMENT STRUCTURE

Although Parks Canada assumes in its mandate the responsibility for environmental protection, the Panel decided that a committee system was required to ensure that the highway design and construction meet with the high environmental and aesthetic standards necessary in the Park. To this end, PWC set up a management structure comprised of six committees. The management structure was composed of three levels: The Policy Committee, the Senior Committee and four working subgroups: the Design, Construction, Public Relations, and Environmental Subcommittees. These committees were composed of personnel from Parks Canada, Public Works Canada, Canadian Wildlife Service and the Environmental Protection Service. Of these working groups, the most active was the Environmental Subcommittee. This subcommittee was responsible for ensuring that the requirements as well as the spirit of the recommendations of the Environmental Review Panel were upheld and satisfied. The issues dealt with by this subcommittee meant the involvement of many different professions including biologists, archaeologists, palaeantologists, landscape architects and engineers.

A position of Environmental Coordinator was created to liaise with project management and act as the "eyes and ears" of the Environmental Subcommittee. This unique position had the responsibility of alerting both project management and environmental specialists of potential and existing impacts in order that solutions could be worked out in a timely fashion to prevent or reduce adverse impacts.

THE ENVIRONMENTAL ISSUES

The assessment of the possible environmental influence of the four laning projects addressed an unusually comprehensive scope of natural resource subjects because of the National Park setting. Several widely occurring situations and several site-specific conflicts were identified as subjects requiring special attention. These included wildlife/vehicle collisions, fish streams, archaeological resources, wildlife habits and habitat, terrain impact and biophysical restoration.

The project location in a major valley of the Front Range of the Canadian Rockies is an important habitat for an unusually diverse assemblage of wildlife. In addition to birds and small mammal populations, the valley is occupied by elk, mule and whitetailed deer, bighorn sheep, moose, grizzly and black bears, wolves, cougars and coyotes. All species have been tallied in the road kill statistics. Elk, with up to 1,000 head being present on winter ranges in the project area, were most commonly involved in vehicle collisions. Prior to the project, approximately one large animal was struck and killed or injured every second day.

Any increase in the wildlife collision rate which might be caused by upgrading the highway was unacceptable. Following a study of habits and habitat of the highly mobile and vulnerable wildlife species and an examination of potential mitigating techniques used elsewhere in the world, Public Works Canada and Parks Canada decided on a total exclusion policy. A 2.4 metre high page wire fence continuously enclosing both sides of the highway has been erected. Underpass structures of a conventional open span bridge design have been built approximately every two kilometres to facilitate wildlife access to both sides of the valley.

Minimizing the visibility of the fence for highway travellers and maximizing wildlife access to traditional habitat were the most important criteria in positioning the fence and bridge structures. Texas gates, jumpouts, railway crossings, one-way gates, stream barriers, pedestrian stiles, bicycle crossings, hiking trails, access roads and fence terminations were all first time challenges for dealing with the wide diversity of wildlife and recreational use requirements. The complexities of this element of the project and the completeness of dealing with them probably represents a unique undertaking.

Relocation of about one kilometre of stream, which was the only habitat for brown trout in Banff National Park, was necessary to maintain the preferred highway route alignment. A new, parallel streambed was constructed approximately 300 metres away with special attention to pool/riffle ratios, cutbanks, streambed material and preferred brown trout habitat features. The trout were captured by electro-shocking and, in a one week switchover procedure, held in separate ponds until the new channel could be flushed. Aquatic plants from the abandoned channel were also transplanted to act as nurse stock for eventual colonization of the new channel.

The loss of scarce montane ecotypes, which are highly valued ecosystem components in Banff National Park, created a special need for restoration and replacement where impact was unavoidable. Landscape recontouring was undertaken to extend terrain modulations such as gullies or convex slopes from adjacent undisturbed topography into the constructed landscape. Topsoil salvage strategies and selection of indigenous grass seed sources were efforts of precedential uniqueness.

Gravel sources were located and developed with special consideration for size, depth and configuration of extraction to enhance the disturbed landforms' subsequent attractiveness as grazing habitat for ungulates. Similarly, waste materials were used to restore earlier disturbed but unreclaimed sites to productive parklands. Exceptionally difficult rehabilitation situations involved experimentation and numerous product demonstration trials.

Visitor appreciation of views from and of the highway was an important element of design consideration for profile, viewscape opportunities, structural architecture, landform modulation, landscaping and safety.

Archaeological investigations revealed an unexpected treasure of prehistoric occupation of the Bow River Valley. These discoveries literally revolutionized previously held theories of post-glacial colonization of Western Canada's cordillera up to 11,000 years before present. Similarly, this information necessitated a substantial revision of current hypotheses of the duration and positions of the last glacial advances. More immediately pertinent was the absolute requirement to redesign and relocate portions of the new roadway to safeguard these cultural resources.

MONITORING AND ENVIRONMENTAL RESEARCH

In addition to the day-to-day attention performed by the Environmental Subcommittee, a substantial program of in-house, contracted and external research is under way. Investigations directed specifically to measuring the success of environmental protection measures are arranged and supervised by the Environmental Subcommittee. These studies reveal a highly successful reduction of the wildlife collision incidences in Phase I: four collisions in the year following fence installation compared to over one hundred collisions in the year prior to fencing.

Increasing acceptability of the bridge underpasses as movement corridors for wildlife is being demonstrated. There appear not to be any measurable influences which are negatively affecting wildlife in an enduring fashion.

The trout stream re-creation project has been so successful that more fish biomass is present in the new stream two years after construction than was recorded prior to disturbance.

Erosion prevention, slope stabilization, vegetative cover establishment and terrain modulation are all judged to be admirably successful. The success of blending reconstructed areas into the native vegetation cannot be evaluated for some years to come.

Ongoing research will focus on the long

term effects on the wildlife populations, their habits and the impacts on their habitat. To that end, 50 elk have been outfitted with radio telemeters and are relocated on a weekly basis. A surveillance recording camera system will shortly be installed to provide direct and continuous evidence of behaviour which may reveal stress induced by the highway facilities. Changes to existing and future projects will be implemented where improved methods can be devised. Possible habitat changes will be revealed by vegetation plot studies which were initiated several years before the highway project began.

New research initiatives will focus on the nearby railway as a negative influence on wildlife, carnivore predation strategies which employ the fence, and the requirement and possibilities for habitat enhancement. An unexpected and visually undesirable result of the successful rehabilitation of the fenced portion of the roadway, is lush ground cover growth. As this area is unavailable for ungulate grazing, the abundant growth looks out of place. We had not imagined the need to devise growth suppression strategies.

The administrative process of the bipartite arrangement, whereby Public Works Canada constructed a major project on Parks Canada's lands where environmental preservation is paramount, has been intriguing to numerous researchers. The successful and comparatively harmonious cooperation which facilitated the accomplishment of two such potentially conflicting objectives may be more noteworthy than the environmental successes. Good will and the desire to succeed clearly were critical to the favourable results achieved.

THE FUTURE

Twenty seven kilometres of the two-lane highway in Phases I and II have been twinned, fenced and reclaimed at a cost of 60 million Canadian dollars. In view of the demonstrated need to upgrade Phase III of the Trans Canada Highway route, environmental and predesign studies have been proceeding for two years. The reduced wildlife collision situation has created a new and demanding challenge: how to build an unfenced highway without aggravating and hopefully reducing the existing wildlife conflict. In place of small sensitive trout streams, large powerful rivers must be handled in a sensitive fashion which preserves their environment and recreational values.

The demonstration of good intent and environmental management capability in the first 27 kilometres has been so successful that the proponent, with Parks Canada's concurrence, has been excused from the rigorous public scrutiny applied to the early stage proposals. Rather, Public Works Canada is obliged to perform all the same preparations, but to present the information and proposals to concerned target populations. This may even provide an opportunity for more innovative ideas for the management of a high profile public treasure that is Banff National Park.

The Columbia River Shoreline: Highway or Parkway?

Sally Schauman, Associate Professor, and Mary Jorgensen, MLA Candidate, Department of Landscape Architecture, University of Washington, Seattle, Wash.

Ideally, one would think that most major American rivers are considered scenic resources and community open spaces. This is certainly true of the Mississippi River as many cities and towns along its path have created parks or open spaces at the river's edge. It is also true that interest groups have formed to conserve river resources, especially the scenic quality of many American rivers such as the Hudson, the Suwannee and the Willamette rivers. Unfortunately, the scenic quality and open space resources of one of America's largest rivers, the Columbia, has not received equal attention.

Of course, we have all heard of the recent designation of the Columbia River Gorge as a National Scenic Area. While this action is noteworthy, it only deals with a fraction of the Columbia River. The majority of the 1,200 mile long river has received almost no attention as a scenic and open space resource. Debate on the Columbia has mainly focused on other river uses such as hydroelectric power, fish habitat and irrigation supply. Almost no public discussion has occurred regarding the scenic and open space potential of the Columbia upriver from "The Gorge". The reasons for this are many.

One of the most obvious reasons is that the river is not visually accessible in many places upriver from "The Gorge" area. It flows in a deep crevasse for much of its distance, separated from the roads and towns high above on the plateau. One of the reasons "The Gorge" has received its conservation designation is because many were familiar with its beauty as it is one of the few places the roads and towns are on grade with the river. Other than "The Gorge," the Columbia is visible and accessible on grade only in a few places. One of these rare sites is nine miles of the river's shoreline in and near the small town of East Wenatchee, Washington (population 1,690).

This town shares the river with its neighbor, the more populous (17,980) town of Wenatchee. In both towns riparian vegetation grows along the river's edge providing a perch for eagles looking for salmon lunch and a path for hikers to enjoy the water views. Outside of the towns and back form the riparian edge are the rows of irrigated apple and peach trees. Both in and out of the town limits the landscape is level with the river and provides a sharp visual and ecological contrast to the surface arid mountainscape. Here is a special regional site.

Here also is the site of the rerouted corridor of Washington State Route 2 and 28 (SR2/28). First proposed in the mid 1950's when the land was purchased, this road was planned in the mid 1960's without regard for the visual and ecological features of the site and redesigned as a reaction to some wildlife and recreation concerns with only fleeting regard for the specialness of the site. Probably it is a highway that should not be built, possibly a highway that could have been a parkway. Looking back through the history of this site instructs us about what we should avoid, more than what directions we should take.

More than thirty years ago, the Washington State Department of Highways acquired a "water grade" right of way (ROW) for a 4-lane highway from East Wenatchee to Rocky Reach dam. In 1957/58, the final right of way was purchased using one million dollars of federal funds and twelve years later additional land that was needed for a realignment was purchased for $649,000. During this time the community value of the river edge was first formally recognized by a Riverfront Committee formed in 1966, to promote parks on the Wenatchee Area Shorelines. Later, this committee became the Columbia River Environmental Study Team (CREST), and in 1974, called for a park on both sides of the river thus connecting the shorelines by way of the bridges into a greater Wenatchee area open space system. This shoreline plan recognized the unusual open space opportunity on the undeveloped, accessible river edge landscape in Wenatchee and East Wenatchee.

Wenatchee did create a park on its side. The highway ROW not in orchards on the East Wenatchee side continued to be used on an ad hoc basis as community open space by joggers, fishermen, bikers, picnickers, and hikers. The fact that all these opportunities would be lost to a highway seemed remote until June, 1980, when the Washington State Department of Transportation (WSDOT) held a public meeting to discuss the future of the ROW land. One year later WSDOT made public a route study and their decision to retain the ROW for a future highway when funding became available. During this time there is no record of much citizen opposition to the highway, only a few local newspaper articles and a small group pleading for the preservation of the river edge. In 1983, WSDOT released an environmental assessment, but not an environmental impact statement (EIS). Since the Federal Highway Administration found that a highway built on this site constituted "no significant environmental impact", WSDOT stated a full environmental impact statement would not be needed. This action galvanized local attention, a Save the River Committee

(STRC) filed a lawsuit against WSDOT for failing to file an EIS, and a Build the Highway Committee joined WSDOT as a friend of the court. In 1985, WSDOT released a final EIS showing the river edge route as the preferred environmental design and the STRC sued again, challenging the adequacy of the EIS. In autumn of 1985, the University of Washington's Department of Landscape Architecture decided to use the site as a class project.

As an example of a stressed riparian area, the site provided a good learning laboratory for a graduate landscape architectural design studio the multiple resource values of this riparian edge. Simultaneously, but separately, another Landscape Architecture graduate studio, studying computer analysis techniques, was inventorying all of the state of Washington, evaluating natural and cultural features, population demands and recreational characteristics in order to identify lands with high recreation potential. Ranked statewide, the East Wenatchee site fell in the top 11% (Gibson et al., 1986). In other words, the onsite multiple resource values identified by the "riparian" studio were confirmed to have state-wide significance by the "computer" studio. Two questions then arose:

1. How should this site of state-wide importance be designed to enhance its open space value while conserving natural features?
2. How can the road design be modified to enhance the site's open space and natural values?

The nine students in the studio divided into two teams and attempted to answer these questions. The first team investigated the open space, habitat, commercial and recreational designs for the site assuming a road would not be built. Their hardest task was one of assigning priorities. For example, where is an animal access to the river's edge more important than human use? The second team looked at the possibilities of modifying the highway design to reduce its impact on wildlife habitat while simultaneously increasing human access, both visual and actual, to the river's shoreline. This group assumed a highway with limited access, perhaps one closed to commercial vehicles. None of the WSDOT alternatives proposed separating commercial and passenger vehicles. However, the proposed highway is a new route for an existing road and presumably, commercial traffic could be maintained on the existing road although WSDOT discounted this possibility by saying it was unsafe.

In answering the second question, the student team investigated the possibilities for a "parkway" design. They found it was possible to bridge over rather than to culvert the natural drainways, thus travelways for thirsty upland wildlife seeking the water's edge could be maintained.The students proposed the creation of additional wetlands using irrigation tail water thereby increasing the scant amount of this riparian habitat along the Columbia. The student design also provided a place for bald eagle perching, the only wildlife species to command any significant notice in the various agency reviews of the highway proposal. In the end, the student designed "Columbia River Parkway" had a much richer wildlife habitat than the WSDOT proposal. While habitat design was a class focus, the student proposal also dealt with human access, archaeological resources and commercial developments as an intergral part of the parkway design.. The pleasure of traveling along the river without distracting views, the ease of, but controlled access to the water's edge, the non-conflicting accommodation of bicycle and hiker within the corridor and site design of a visually compatible commercial node were all facets of the student parkway missing from the State's design.

In the beginning the WSDOT proposal had a single purpose: move more vehicles faster and more safely from one point to another. The agency considered no resource value for the highway other than its ability to carry traffic. Later, WSDOT conducted a visual assessment with no public input, still failed to consider wildlife habitat needs other than the eagles, and provided no human access to the water's edge. In an arid zone of precipitation, any water edge is especially valuable. This riparian/wetland edge is a perceptual and actual oasis. The WSDOT original and later plans ignored most of the resource values of this site resulting from its oasis aspect.

During litigation, the review process and public debate on the proposed road, input from local citizens and other agencies stimulated WSDOT to mitigate and change the design. A bike trail along part of the road was added, one half-acre less of wetlands were to be filled, parking lots for river access were added and additional plantings envisioned (WSDOT, 1986). According to WSDOT staff, changes were made to meet individual comments, but not to fit an overall goal (Littooy, 1987). In other words, the design of a single purpose highway was revised in a minor, piecemeal way to gain public acceptance; but in doing so, more and more resembled the parkway the students envisioned.

In July, 1987, review and legal activities continue. The court found for WSDOT in the matter of insufficient Environmental Impact Statements, but this action is under appeal. A hearing was held in March 1987 by the State Shoreline Board concerning the appropriateness of the locally issued shoreline permit. A decision from this hearing should be made this fall. The WSDOT is confident it will build a road, but the Save The River Committee believes this is not a certainty. While a resolution is not in sight, some lessons can be learned from this experience.

The first lesson is to remember that accessible edges to major rivers should be considered for their multiple resource value to the community and the region. No one should assume that public ad hoc access to any water edge will continue. These are precious public resources. In the future, convenient local open spaces will be ever more important, as reported in 1986 by the President's Commission on Americans Outdoors (PCAO). The PCAO recommended greenway corridors throughout urban areas, thereby providing more opportunity for public access to open spaces (Shands, 1987, and Clawson, 1987). Every attempt through government and institutional means should be made to conserve water edge open spaces for the public's future access. One good way is to form local land trusts and to devise creative public/private partnerships to acquire these edges for all our use in perpetuity. In the case of East Wenatchee the local open space was clearly recognized. Even the judge who found for WSDOT cited its indigenous scenic quality and lamented the ugliness of the proposed highway.

> *. . . the Court cannot refrain from commenting on its enjoyment of the Court's view of the proposed route from this office. Seeing the seasons change from pale greens and yellows of the budding foliage in spring to the dark and verdant greenery of summer, to the reds and oranges and yellows of autumn leaves, to the bleak but beautiful snow-covered scenes of winter helps keep the Court in tune with the seasons and with the beauty of our North Central Washington homeland. Changing this natural asset to one of two lanes (eventually four lanes) of concrete and guardrail and discarded beer cans and McDonald's wrappers does not meet with the personal favor of the Court . . .* (Superior Court, 1987, p.2).

Unfortunately no one acted until it was perhaps too late.

The second important lesson involves the question: how can we justify public expenditures on single purpose projects in landscapes with existing multiple resource values? This lesson is related to and is as important as the first one, but harder for public action to result in immediate change. During the 1970's pressure for interdisciplinary planning and design of projects in the landscape helped implement the mandate of the National Environmental Policy Act (NEPA). As a result, public works projects included open space planning, wildlife needs, visual resource considerations and recreation. Sometimes an agency's authority was broadened and sometimes agencies took action under the authority of NEPA. In this era, previously single purpose projects, such as water resource construction, began to recognize special landscape conditions of the proposed site and started to include design features for the visual resources, passive recreation, pedestrian traffic and wildlife needs. Even the most single purpose landscape imaginable, military use, was broadened. For example, the Department of

Defense recognizes resource conservation awards for bases that plan for the multiple resource value of the landscape.

The recent President's Commission recognized both the fiscal waste of single purpose use of landscape and the need for more open space (Shands, 1987, and Clawson, 1987). The Commission recommended further expansion and change in the mandates and actions of several federal agencies. Clearly the Commission has answered the question; they have said we can no longer afford single function design or management of public lands. If the question were directed to the Federal or State Departments of Transportation, what would be their answer? Most likely they would agree but plead no contest because of the fiscal and legal constraints. Certainly the Federal Highway Administration that declared the East Wenatchee project to have "no significant environmental impact" failed to even recognize the archaeological resources, wildlife habitat and urban waterfront value of this site. Most highways have single purpose designs - moving volumes of vehicles swiftly and safely. The inclusion, much less the design, of other functions such as bike paths, visual resources, wildlife habitat and open space is inconsistent at best.

While the Federal Highway Administration and WSDOT do employ specialists such as landscape architects, biologists and conservationists, neither agency includes multiple purpose planning and design as a routine matter. The input of these specialists to the engineered design is often to address environmental concerns and/or to pacify public opinion. For example, landscape architects in WSDOT mainly provide planting designs to cover cut slopes and screen highway sights and sounds. They are not involved routinely on every project with the teams of engineers for route selection, alignment within the right of way, connections to existing paths, or earth grading designs. While some WSDOT staff may believe parkway features such as smooth alignment, visual assessment and scenic enhancement are all standard in WSDOT designs, the actual constructed results fall significantly short of parkway quality and rarely are multiple purpose. For example, bicycling is a major recreational activity in Washington. Both individual trips and organized events move people around our state and stimulate local economies. Yet WSDOT does not routinely consider bicycles as vehicles and includes them only when the local citizen pressure for bicycle traffic is great.

It is easy to point to WSDOT as an agency wasting public funds on single purpose design. Yet the WSDOT staffs are competent professionals. They are following agency policy and the public at large has not sent sufficiently strong signals to stimulate agency change. The history of agency inertia resisting change, leadership and the funding directions given by the legislature are all responsible for wasteful single purpose highway designs in Washington. The East Wenatchee proposed highway is but another example of what happens when citizens do not demand that agencies routinely plan and design for multiple purposes on public work projects built with their tax dollars.

Finally, this case study forces us to think about the future. Should parkways again be considered? Is it time to redefine the concept? What should be new in their design? How should they differ from other roads? Let us first consider the past before we think about the future.

In this country, road design seems to have been the focus of national attention in several areas. First was the pre-World War II era in which major eastern parkways such as the Blue Ridge and others were constructed. The landscape architectural historian, Norman Newton, described these not as roads, but as strips of land dedicated to recreation and the movement of pleasure vehicles (1971). In other words, these corridor landscapes had both a transportation and a psychological function. Limited access was an important design feature. This, along with route selection and alignment sensitive to the landscape, meant the edges between the parkway and the surrounding landscapes were melds, not abrupt lines. The parkway borrowed the best visual features from the adjacent landscape and screened the worst. For example, while driving the Blue Ridge Parkway one is almost unaware of the extensive resort, urban and second home development in adjacent lands.

The interstate highway era began after WWII and continues today. These familiar corridors adopted the limited access and broad curve designs of the parkways, but in no way provided a healthy recreational experience nor a psychologically refreshing view of nature as did the parkways. Minimum right of way widths and grades were developed to move traffic faster and hopefully safer. Now we depend on these routes to move us quickly from place to place. The engineering lessons learned from the interstate experience have had profound effects in all land use. The experience has been translated into standards for all level of roads. Thus, curving, narrowing county lanes are now straighter and wider. In a recent national survey of highway design standards in 225 counties done by the Department of Landscape Architecture at the University of Washington, the results indicate that minimum allowable road dimensions have increased over time and the pressure for increased standardization continues (Hightower, 1987). Whether the standardization of all roadway design is truly necessary and desirable should be considered.

The last national focus on highway design occurred in the early 1960's during the administration of President Lyndon Johnson. From this period of concern for natural beauty came regulations on billboards, junkyards and unsightly adjacent landscapes and the new emphasis on landscape plantings. Most of the present results of this period are attempts to use planting design to beautify the graded and filled edges of the highway (often an impossible challenge) or to screen truly ugly sights in adjacent landscapes. Since we depend on the interstate system and since common road standards are increasing throughout the United States, are parkways needed or even possible?

In our judgment, modern versions of parkways are very much needed, but their possibility depends directly on changing the present transportation planning and exluding some roads from uniform highway standards. We should not think of nationally significant landscapes for these corridors for two reasons. First, any pristine nationally significant landscape should be preserved without the intrusion of travelways; second, greenways are desperately needed closer to home.

We suggest contemporary parkways need to be locally important and designed for a wide variety of noncommercial vehicles including bicycles, motorcycles and even boats. These corridors should include pedestrian paths, commercial nodes wildlife habitats and restful green open spaces. Not all open spaces should have travelways within them, but new open spaces should be created and enjoyed by designing a pleasurable travel route to convey citizens from one local special place to another. These travelways might even exclude cars altogether or during busy times. In other words, we should expand the original parkway concept of moving people through the landscape in a pleasurable way. We should create new parkways, perhaps even restore derelict areas, in order to connect locally important sites and provide an enhanced, easily accessible nearby green corridor.

The need is clear; the President's Commission held 18 public hearings throughout the United States and conducted a national survey over 12 months. Citizens and the survey told the President's Commission of the need to have nearby open spaces (Shands, 1987). The Commission's subsequent recommendation for open spaces recognized the present trend for shorter family vacations spent closer to home rather than long drives to distant places. But anyone who had studied American open spaces already knew what the President's Commission discovered. Witness the immense popularity of Rock Creek Parkway in Washington DC, Ruston Way along Puget Sound in Tacoma, Washington, the Burke-Gilman Trail in Seattle or the River Walkway in San Antonio, Texas. Each of these travelways traverse unspectacular, but extremely pleasurable and important local landscapes. Each is overcrowded.

The Columbia River corridor and East Wenatchee have more spectacular landscape scenery than any of these examples. In fact, the East Wenatchee site has state-wide importance as open space. Yet the likelihood of a road is great and the design of the proposed highway in no way enhances the community open space quality. The present traffic engineering standards accommodate no other purpose than moving automobiles, buses and trucks. If we are to have local parkways then we will need to creatively design these without the presently restrictive highway standards that force all designs to homogeneity. Most importantly, we need an informed public who will designate those special local landscapes that could become future open spaces parkways. We should remember that if the proposed road is completely halted and this site turned over to the community, some travelway within the site would be needed. Thus, citizens should not only be informed as to local open spaces, they should come armed with creative design alternatives for making these accessible.

BIBLIOGRAPHY

Clawson, Marion, 1987. Outdoor Recreation Report Travels a Bumpy Road. In "Resources," Resources for the Future, No. 88, Summer 1987, Washington, D.C.

Gibson, Liz, et al., 1986. An Analysis of DNR Lands: Phase One for State Park Potential. Department of Landscape Architecture, University of Washington, Seattle.

Hightower, Jacqueline, E., 1987. Private Roads in Residential Communities. Master of Landscape Architecture Thesis, University of Washington, Seattle.

Littooy, Hans, 1987. Personal communication, June 30.

Newton, Norman T., 1971. Design on the Land, The Development of Landscape Architecture. The Belknap Press of Harvard University Press, Cambridge.

Shands, William E., 1987. Commission Gives Recreation a Shot in the Arm. In Conservation Foundation Newsletter, No. 2, Washington, D.C.

Superior Court of the State of Washington, 1987. Court's Memorandum Opinion, No. 86-2-00105-8.

WSDOT, 1985. Final Environmental Impact Statement SR2/SR28 East Wenatchee Vicinity, Douglas County, Washington.

___, 1986. Wetland and Riparian Mitigation Plan. SR2/SR28 East Wenatchee Vicinity, March.

The Roanoke Parkway, Greenway, and River Road

William G. E. Blair, Principal, Jones & Jones, and Curtis A. Miller, Senior Associate, Jones & Jones

INTRODUCTION

The Roanoke Parkway, Greenway, and River Road are examples of a renewed American interest in parkways and greenways. They are also evidence of a renewed cooperative spirit and division of labor among federal, state, and local government agencies and non-profit groups for major recreation and conservation projects.

As reported in a companion paper presented at this conference, the National Park Service (NPS) has recently completed a Reconnaissance Survey of the Roanoke River Parkway Corridor to determine if it would be feasible to build a parkway to connect the western end of Roanoke Valley to the existing Blue Ridge Parkway via the Roanoke Gorge, and then continue on the Booker T. Washington National Monument. The NPS assessed feasibility by locating sample routes that would meet three different sets of parkway design standards and then by evaluating the relative merits and costs of these alternatives.

This paper summarizes the results of a subsequent study conducted by Jones & Jones that has culminated in the Roanoke River Greenway Master Plan. The greenway master plan builds on the preceding NPS reconnaissance study but acknowledges recent legislative action that has authorized a federal parkway through the Roanoke Gorge. The greenway master plan also broadens the planning focus to include resources conservation along the river and incorporates the results of an extensive community involvement program that has helped the planning team fashion a plan for the Roanoke River that meets the test of public acceptance.

Both the greenway master plan and the NPS reconnaissance study were commissioned by The River Foundation, a non-profit organization located in Roanoke, Virginia, with funds provided by private donors and the State of Virginia. The goals of The River Foundation are twofold: first, to improve the quality of life in the Roanoke Valley by conserving and enhancing the environment along the Roanoke River; second, to strengthen the regional economy of Southwestern Virginia by developing a tourism industry that capitalizes on Roanoke's location along the Blue Ridge Parkway and that also respects the integrity of that national treasure.

To advance these goals, The River Foundation is planning the EXPLORE Project, which will:

1) create a tourism destination that will illustrate Virginia's historic role in developing the American West; and
2) create a 5000-acre conservation area—the Roanoke Greenway—to preserve, protect, and enhance the environment along the Roanoke River and the Blue Ridge Parkway; and
3) to assist in preventing future flooding.

The Roanoke River Greenway Master Plan advocates the establishment of a 40-mile linear open space system to link the natural and urban areas along the river and establish conservation and development goals tailored to the diverse resource issues and opportunities that exist in each area. For example, the Roanoke Greenway would include the Roanoke Parkway in the river gorge, the Roanoke River Road in the urban areas of Salem, Roanoke, and Vinton, and a series of conservation and recreation areas along the river. Land ownership within the Roanoke Greenway would be held by a mix of private individuals, businesses, institutions, and government agencies, and all of these groups would have roles to play in implementing the greenway master plan.

AUTHORIZATION OF THE ROANOKE PARKWAY

The Roanoke Parkway was conceived as an integral element of the EXPLORE Project, both as a way to experience the Roanoke River and also as a means to protect and enhance the river's environment. The parkway was initially projected to extend from the Dixie Caverns interchange on I-81, west of the Roanoke Valley metropolitan area, to Booker T. Washington National Monument, some 40 miles to the east.

In 1986, The River Foundation asked the National Park Service to determine whether such a parkway would be feasible. The NPS concluded that the two goals appear to be compatible in the Roanoke Gorge, which is largely undeveloped. In this location, the parkway also matches well with the NPS mission, because of the existing visual quality of the landscape that it would traverse.

Upstream from the gorge, however, the riverbanks are heavily urbanized. While some riverside areas have been set aside for parks, many portions of the floodplain are occupied by the railroad and manufacturing industries that have provided the economic base for the Roanoke Valley over the last century. In these areas, the issue is not conservation, but rehabilitation, and even reclamation. Consequently, the NPS concluded that a parkway through the urban area would not be an appropriate addition to the National Park System.

Accepting this reasoning, The River Foundation and its Roanoke Valley supporters asked the Virginia Congressional delegation to introduce legislation that would authorize the creation of a shorter federal parkway through the Roanoke Gorge. They were successful in these efforts and the Roanoke Parkway was designated as a 10-mile extension of the Blue Ridge Parkway by the Surface Transportation & Uniform Relocation Act of 1987, which specifies that the new parkway will extend from the east edge of the Roanoke Valley to Smith Mountain Lake and provide a connection between the Parkway and the site of the EXPLORE Project. The Act is silent about the possibility of an extension to Booker T. Washington National Monument.

The 1987 Act assigns the responsibility for the design and construction of the parkway to the National Park Service and the Federal Highway Administration. These agencies will direct the preparation of an Environmental Impact Statement (EIS) that will consider the environmental effects of alternative routes for the new parkway. As an interested party, The River Foundation is conveying its planning work on the routing and design of the new parkway by means of the Roanoke River Greenway Master Plan.

MASTER PLAN PROCESS

The overall goals of the planning process employed by The River Foundation were to build a constituency for the Roanoke River, as well as to develop a feasible and acceptable master plan for its protection and rehabilitation. Consequently, The River Foundation assembled a greenway planning team that included not only consultants with expertise in environmental planning and landscape architecture (Jones & Jones) and engineering (Mattern & Craig), but also in community involvement (Thomas & Means).

The planning team divided the greenway planning process into five major steps: 1) identify important issues, 2) inventory opportunities, 3) develop alternatives, 4) propose a draft greenway master plan, and 5) prepare the final greenway master plan.

Next, the greenway planning team used the geography of the river itself to help facilitate public and local government participation in this planning process, by dividing the study area into five community planning areas that correspond to the five river reaches identified in the NPS reconnaissance study. These reaches and community planning areas also correspond to jurisdictional divisions along the river, as shown in Table 1.

Recognizing that local governments would play key roles in adopting and implementing the greenway master plan, the greenway planning team took the lead in organizing a Policy Advisory Group comprised of local government administrators and elected officials, as well as a parallel Technical Advisory Group comprised of key local government staff members. These committees conducted progress reviews on the plan at each step of the planning process.

The greenway planning team also organized an extensive public involvement program that included a public workshop for each of the river reaches during each of the planning steps. The workshops gave community members a chance to review the contents of the greenway master plan that pertained to their own geographic areas. Conversely, the workshops gave the greenway planning team repeated opportunities to incorporate local knowledge and values into the plan. Some of the organizational characteristics of the workshops that made them particularly effective included:

- Outreach efforts to ensure broad community participation
- Recruitment of volunteers to serve as neutral facilitators and recorders

Table 1: Land-use jurisdictions and landscape character along the study area river reaches.

River Reach	Jurisdiction	Landscape Character
West Roanoke County	Roanoke County	rural, residential
Salem	City of Salem	residential, industrial
Roanoke	City of Roanoke	residential, industrial, recreation
Vinton	Town of Vinton, Roanoke County	natural (gorge)
Smith Mountain Lake	Bedford County, Franklin County	rural, lakeside residential

- Participation of local government staff and representatives in the roles of hosts, not proponents of the plan
- Brief opening presentations that included responses to questions raised at preceding workshops
- Written summaries of previous workshops and small-group discussions
- Small-group discussion sessions that gave all workshop participants an opportunity to discuss their concerns, ask questions, and critique the plan

GREENWAY GOALS AND ELEMENTS

The final greenway master plan has been shaped and modified by the results of the local government review meetings and the community workshops, beginning with the goals for the Roanoke Greenway and the elements to be included in it. The following goals emerged over the course of the planning process as a consensus of community aspirations for the river and the lands along it:

- Protect the river, and conserve natural and agricultural lands along the river
- Beautify the river, and clean up and maintain the river corridor
- Raise awareness and appreciation of the river
- Provide recreation opportunities along the river and public access to the river
- Protect people and property, and reduce flood damage along the river

The community workshops also helped to identify specific elements to be included in the Roanoke Greenway. This was important, because the term "greenway" is an elastic concept that requires definition for each project and locality. The starting point for identifying greenway elements was to explain the greenway concept. Most workshop participants were unfamiliar with the greenway concept, but understood the parkway concept because of the presence of the Blue Ridge Parkway. Therefore, greenways were explained by comparison to parkways, using the following text and illustrations.

What is a Parkway?

A Parkway is a road that is designed especially for pleasure driving or to provide a scenic route from one place to another. Parkways can be the same size as an ordinary road, but because scenery is important for recreational driving, parkway roadsides may sometimes be wider than ordinary roadsides. For the same reason, parkway agencies may make special agreements with neighboring landowners to conserve or enhance the scenic character of their lands. Parkways can also include additional features such as recreation sites, lookouts, picnic areas, rest stops, and information centers.

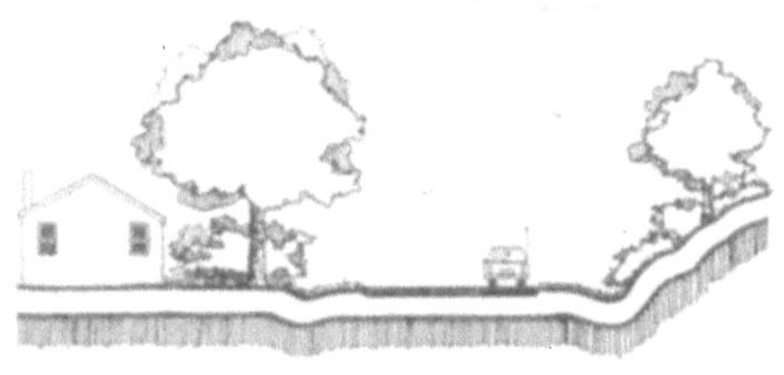

Fig. 1: A slice through a typical parkway.

What is a Greenway?

A Greenway is a connected series of lands that includes conservation and recreational areas, often along a river. Greenways can be located in natural areas. They can also be located in suburbs and cities, where they combine conservation and recreation areas with existing homes and businesses. Lands in a greenway can be owned by private individuals and businesses, local governments, or other institutions. Some areas in a greenway can be open to the public; other areas can be private. What is important is that the river and other natural resources in the greenway be protected. A wide variety of recreation features can be part of a greenway—for example, bike trails, sport fields, fishing spots, and nature preserves. A parkway can also be a part of a greenway. When planning a greenway, it is important to decide what kind of recreation is appropriate and where it should be located.

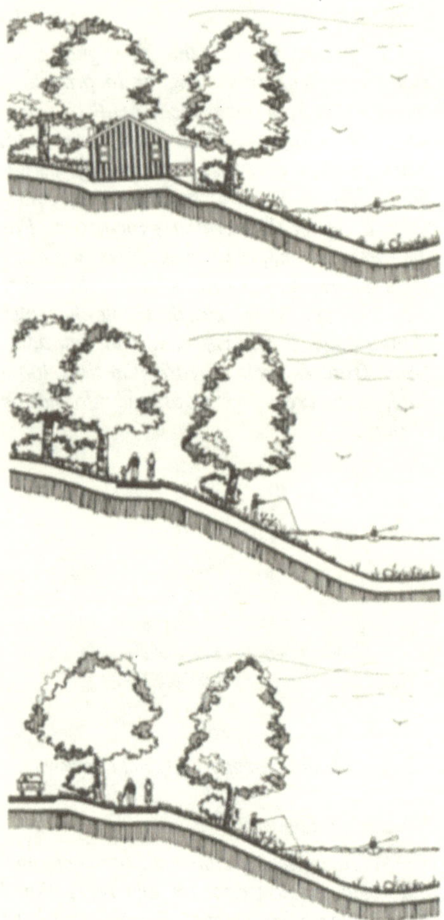

Fig. 2: A greenway could include a parkway, a bicycle trail, fishing areas, and more.

Fig. 3: Or greenway features could be limited to a trail and fishing areas, without a parkway.

Fig. 4: Or greenway features could be limited to river cleanup, flood damage reduction, and environmental protection, without public access.

Starting from this general definition of greenways, participants in the community meetings were asked to identify the elements they most wished to see included in their reach of the Roanoke Greenway. The tabulation of these results helped to establish priorities for the greenway as a whole and also helped to tailor the plan to the community values and desires that predominate within each reach. A summary of the results of all the community meetings is presented in Fig. 5.

Figure 5 demonstrates that the greenway elements with the highest level of preference are those related to river beautification and cleanup, conservation of natural areas, and the provision of path systems. While workshop participants also expressed support for other recreational elements, the overall level of support for these elements was considerably lower.

These results appear to reflect a significant difference in community attitudes among the rural and urban reaches of the river. Workshop participants from the urban reaches wanted the greenway to include both conservation and recreation elements in their areas. Participants from the rural reaches, on the other hand, generally wanted the greenway restricted to conservation elements. Many of the latter, particularly residents of West Roanoke County, expressed concerns about public access along the river. The survey team modified the greenway plan to emphasize conservation elements on the rural reaches and emphasize river cleanup and recreation elements in the urban reaches.

PROPOSED MASTER PLAN

A graphic summary of the resulting greenway master plan is presented in Figure 6. This figure indicates that the plan has been divided into three major components as a result of the reach-by-reach planning process: the Roanoke River Greenway and River Road, the Roanoke Parkway, and recommended highway improvements between Hardy Ford and Booker T. Washington National Monument. Proposed conservation areas along the river are indicated by boxes with a letter code, while recreation areas are indicated by a number code; both are explained in Table 2.

Roanoke River Greenway and River Road. The plan proposes a greenway and river road for the three western or upper reaches of the Roanoke River, beginning at the Roanoke County line. The continuous element in the Roanoke

What are some of the possible elements for a greenway?

Agricultural Lands
- 39 Farmland protection
- 20 Flower gardens
- 7 Garden plots

Cultural Sites
- 16 Archeological sites
- 2 Festival grounds
- 29 Historic sites

Environmental Protection
- 16 Conservation areas
- 27 Flood damage reduction facilities or areas
- 30 River cleanup areas

Facilities
- 10 Campgrounds
- 8 Canoe rental
- 4 Horse rings
- 8 Parking areas
- 24 Picnic areas
- 8 Playgrounds
- 23 Restrooms

Natural Areas
- 11 Arboretums
- 22 Bird sanctuaries and birdwatching areas
- 18 Duck feeding areas
- 28 Nature study areas and trails
- 30 Wildlife habitat improvement areas

Paths
- 29 Bicycle trails
- 7 Exercise courses
- 17 Horse trails
- 17 Parkways
- 38 Walking trails

Scenery
- 39 River beautification areas
- 32 Scenic view areas

Sports Fields
- 6 Ballfields
- 3 Basketball
- 7 Golf courses
- 5 Model airplane fields
- 3 Tennis

Water Recreation
- 13 Canoe & raft launches
- 24 Fishing access sites
- 15 River access sites
- 14 Swimming areas

Others
- 1 Cave exploration
- 4 Wildflower gardens
- 1 Spawning areas
- 1 Planned growth
- 3 Hunting preserve
- 2 Tubing rentals & tubing downriver
- 1 No elements, please

Fig. 5. Preferred Roanoke Greenway elements identified by community workshop participants.

River Greenway would be the river itself, with conservation and recreation areas sited along the river, much like beads on a necklace. A continuous pathway for non-motorized use - the Roanoke River Trail - would parallel the river through the Roanoke and Salem reaches. This would be a "Class I" trail, i.e., fully separated from motorized traffic. It would end at the east end of the West Roanoke County reach (conservation area "D"), where the trail would meet US 460. The plan proposes that the shoulders of US 460 be upgraded and improved as "Class II" bicycle lanes from this point on to Blacksburg.

A two-lane, urban "river road" would also follow the river through the Roanoke and Salem reaches, using existing streets such as Riverside Drive in Salem wherever possible. To preclude the development of heavy bypass traffic, however, the plan proposes a gap at either end of the Roanoke River Road. Thus, the eastern end of the river road would not connect directly to the Roanoke Parkway, but would connect to US 24 by means of 13th Street, an existing arterial. Similarly, to protect the undeveloped river run above Green Hill Park, the western end of the Roanoke River Road would tie into US 460 at the Salem city line, rather than continue along the river to the beginning of the West Roanoke County reach. Because of the restricted road rights-of-way along the river in the West Roanoke County reach and the concerns articulated by residents during the planning workshops, neither the river road nor the trail is proposed to follow the river through the narrow, steep-sided valley upstream to Dixie Caverns.

Within the Roanoke and Salem reaches, the greenway would also include several actions to reduce flood damage. In Salem, the most prominent of these actions would be to remove several buildings from an apartment complex that has been subjected to repeated severe flooding. These units would be replaced by a levee that would protect the remaining buildings and that would provide a right-of-way for a new section of the Roanoke River Road. In Roanoke, the greenway plan proposes a number of actions that would be coordinated with a Corps of Engineers plan to reduce flood damage by widening portions of the river floodway. The greenway plan suggests excavating bypass channels in locations where there is sufficient room, to create a series of islands that would help preserve existing riparian habitat and improve the appearance of Corps of Engineers project.

Roanoke Parkway. In keeping with the Surface Transportation & Uniform Relocation Assistance Act of 1987, the plan proposes that the Rke. Parkway extend from US 24 near the confluence of Tinker Creek to State Route 634

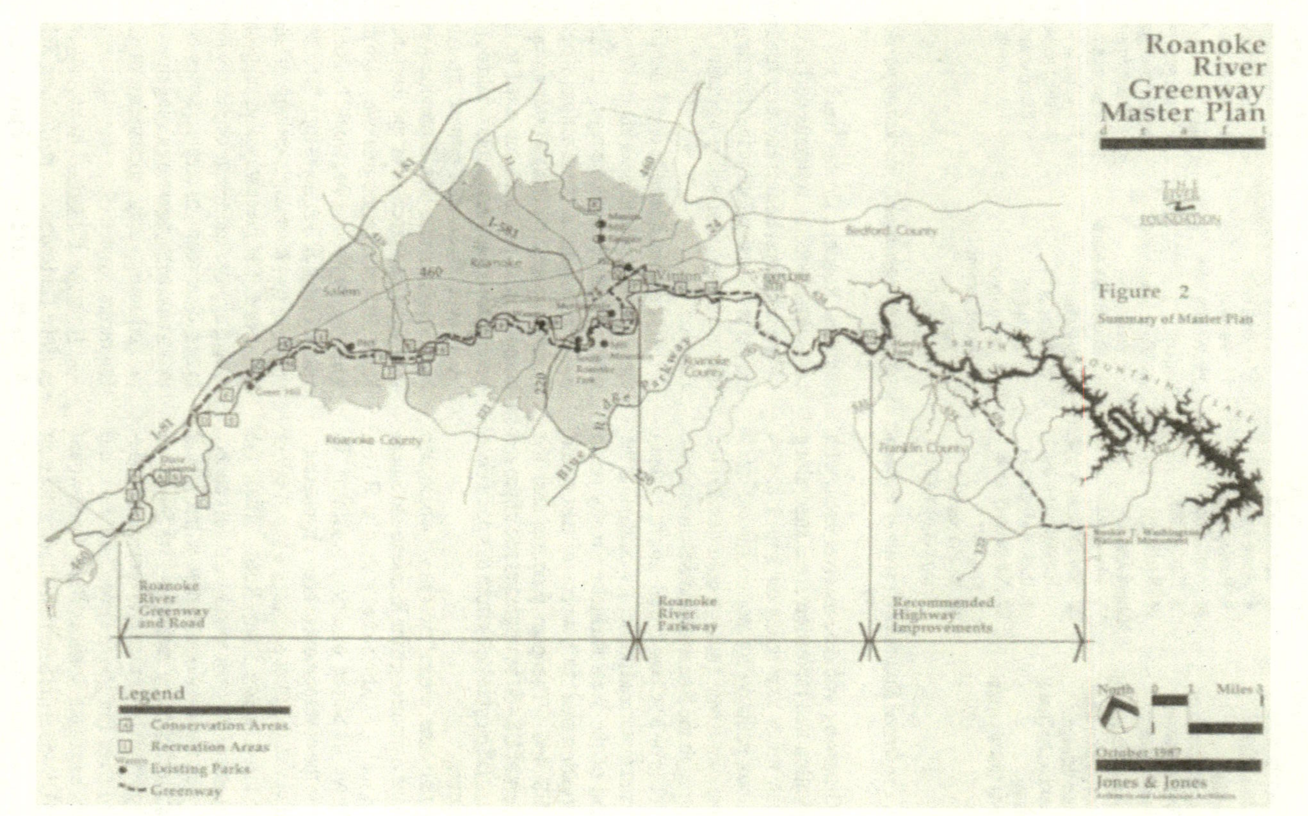

Roanoke
River
Greenway
Master Plan
draft
Figure 2
Summary of Master Plan
Bedford County
Roanoke County
Franklin County
Salem
Roanoke
Vinton
Green Hill
Blue Ridge Parkway
Smith Mountain Lake
Booker T. Washington National Monument
I-81
I-581
460
220
24
Roanoke River Greenway and Road
Roanoke River Parkway
Recommended Highway Improvements
Legend
Conservation Areas
Recreation Areas
Existing Parks
Greenway
North
Miles
October 1987
Jones & Jones

at Hardy Ford. The plan recommends a general alignment for this new parkway that appears to meet the tests of feasibility and public acceptability, and that would also integrate well with the planning for the EXPLORE Project. In making this plan, the River Foundation recognizes that the final alignment for the Roanoke Parkway will be determined by the National Park Service and the Federal Highway Administration, following the preparation of an EIS on alternate routes for the new parkway. As an interested party, however, The River Foundation believed it appropriate to try to identify a feasible location for the parkway in relation to the EXPLORE Project, to solicit public concerns regarding this location, and to carry forward their findings to the federal agencies for their independent consideration.

The proposed route for the parkway would start on the north side river in Vinton and would parallel an existing rail line through the Roanoke Gorge, under the Blue Ridge Parkway bridge, and into the site of the EXPLORE Project. The new parkway would provide an entrance both to the EXPLORE Project and to the Blue Ridge Parkway in this area. It would continue east, above the rail line, to the steep slopes of Pine Mountain, where it would cross the rail line and river to the south side of the gorge. Here the parkway would provide a second entrance to the EXPLORE Project, in the vicinity of the planned Blue Ridge Town. The parkway would then continue east and would cross back to the north side of the river. To avoid several residential enclaves, a number of alternatives have been investigated in this area; the most acceptable and feasible of these appears to be a route that avoids existing homes by means of a short tunnel through the neck of the river bend. The parkway route would then continue on the north side of the river to Hardy Ford. This area appears to provide a more suitable terminus for the parkway than any of the areas examined on the south side of the river, because of terrain and the geometry of existing highways.

Recommended Highway Improvements. The NPS reconnaissance study investigated several possibilities for continuing the Roanoke Parkway to Booker T. Washington National Monument. The Federal-Aid Highway Act of 1987 concluded debate on this issue for the immediate future by terminating the parkway at Hardy Ford. However, participants in the community workshops for the greenway planning process expressed the need for highway improvements beyond Hardy Ford.

The roads in this area serve as a travel corridor between the Roanoke Valley and the main portion of Smith Mountain Lake, which lies east of Booker T. Washington National Monument. Residents and other users of these roads are concerned about traffic safety problems on the existing roads. These problems appear due to deficient highway geometry and roadbed design; all of the roads are classified as secondary highways and most do not appear to have been designed in any formal sense. Although traffic volumes have been increasing steadily, the existing classifications of these roads effectively preclude state participation in their improvement, because state policies allow improvements to secondary highways only on the basis of existing traffic volumes.

The planning team examined the probable traffic impacts of the Roanoke Parkway and the EXPLORE Project in this area and concluded that these impacts would not be significant. Nevertheless, in recognition of the poor state of the existing roads and the increasing problems with traffic safety, The River Foundation has made a commitment to help the local residents in their efforts to secure improvements to the principal travel route in this area, shown on Figure 6 as a heavy dotted line. The first step in doing this would be to secure the designation of this route as a primary highway, which would make it eligible for improvement based on projected future traffic volumes. The planning team also identified the portions of this route that appear to exhibit serious design deficiencies, as a step toward determining the funding needs for improving this route.

These recommended highway improvements would also, of course, help improve

Opposite: ***Fig. 6. Summary of Master Plan.***

Table 2: Conservation and recreation elements included in the Roanoke River Greenway Master Plan (conservation elements are indicated on Figure 6 by letter codes; recreation elements are indicated by numbers).

Code	Recommended Action	River Reach
1	Provide US 460 bicycle lanes, roadside landscape	West Roanoke Co.
2	Provide Roanoke River Wayside improvements	West Roanoke Co.
3	Encourage Dixie Caverns improvements	West Roanoke Co.
A	Conserve scenic river bluffs	West Roanoke Co.
B	Conserve riparian woodland habitat	West Roanoke Co.
C	Conserve scenic river bluffs	West Roanoke Co.
D	Conserve farmland	West Roanoke Co.
E	Conserve scenic river bluffs	West Roanoke Co.
F	Conserve farmland	West Roanoke Co.
G	River cleanup, wooded buffer	Salem
H	River cleanup, wooded buffer	Salem
4	Provide Mill Lane historic site, river access	Salem
I	Conserve riparian woodland habitat	Salem
5	Provide Riverside Drive picnic area, river access	Salem
J	Conserve scenic river bluffs	Salem
K	River and tributary cleanup	Salem
L	Flood reduction, conserve scenic river bluffs	Salem
M	River and tributary cleanup	Salem
6	Provide VA Hospital river access, riparian habitat	Roanoke
7	Provide Railroad Ave. historic site, plant nursery	Roanoke
8	Provide Norwich river access, riparian habitat	Roanoke
9	Provide Wasena Park overlook, picnic area	Roanoke
10	Provide Riverview Park extension	Roanoke
N	Flood reduction, landscape buffer	Roanoke
O	Flood reduction, riparian habitat	Roanoke
P	River cleanup, conserve riparian habitat	Roanoke
Q	Tributary cleanup, conserve riparian habitat	Roanoke
R	Conserve farmland and historic landscape	Roanoke
11	Provide Tinker Creek parkway entrance	Vinton
S	Conserve riparian woodland habitat	Vinton
12	Provide Niagara dam interpretive center	Vinton
13	Provide B.R. Parkway & EXPLORE entrances	Vinton
14	Provide EXPLORE entrance at Blue Ridge Town	Vinton
T	Scenic overlook	Smith Mtn. Lake
U	View protection, landscape buffer	Smith Mtn. Lake
15	Provide Hardy Ford parkway entrance	Smith Mtn. Lake

access between the Roanoke Parkway and Booker T. Washington National Monument. In the long run, however, it may prove desirable to extend the Roanoke Parkway all the way to Booker T. Washington National Monument in order to separate regional tourism traffic from local recreational and residential commuter traffic between the Roanoke Valley and Smith Mountain Lake.

CONCLUSIONS

The River Foundation's Roanoke River Greenway Master Plan presents a vision for the future in which a cleaner and more beautiful Roanoke River would form the spine of a continuous system of open space that would traverse the urban Roanoke Valley and connect it to the scenic rural landscapes of the Blue Ridge. This vision of a regional greenway promises economic benefits, as well as environmental and recreational benefits, to the residents of the Roanoke Valley; the improvements to urban infrastructure that are necessary to revitalize declining industrial economics include improvements to the local quality of life as well as to streets and utilities.

The greenway vision is not limited to the Roanoke Valley. The President's Commission on Americans Outdoors articulates the vision of *"a living network of greenways"* for the entire nation in its report, Americans Outdoors: The Legacy, the Challenge (Island Press, 1987). As one of its principal action recommendations, the President's Commission urges, on page 142, that "*communities establish Greenways, corridors of private and public recreation lands and waters, to provide people with access to open spaces close to where they live, and to link together the rural and urban spaces in the American Landscape*." The benefits that the Roanoke Greenway offers the Roanoke Valley are precisely those that the President's Commission identifies, on page 146: "*Greenways will have significant environmental, conservation, and economic benefits. Innovative design and management could achieve the following:*

- *reduce flood damage;*
- *wildlife habitat protection, and plant and animal conservation;*
- *water table recharge in wetlands and healthy riparians;*
- *improved landscape aesthetics;*
- *enhanced community pride and identity;*
- *more effective use of limited land area for conservation;*
- *concurrent uses by compatible industries;*
- *enhanced awareness and appreciation for wildlands;*
- *more diverse local economies from tourism.*"

Again, the Roanoke River Greenway Master Plan presents a vision for the future. In delineating this vision, The River Foundation has been acting as an advocate for the natural and cultural heritage of the Roanoke Valley. The Foundation recognizes that adoption and implementation of this vision will require the cooperation of the many local, state, and federal agencies that share jurisdiction over the Roanoke River and its shorelands. The River Foundation also recognizes that private organizations, such as itself, also have direct roles to play in greenway implementation, such as land banking, land acquisition, and even some types of development. As the President's Commission on Americans Outdoors notes, "the focus of greenways creation should be local groups and individuals, local governments, and local chapters of regional and national organizations." Creation of the Roanoke Greenway will require partnership and The River Foundation is prepared to join that partnership.

BIBLIOGRAPHY

Jones & Jones, Explore Park Master Plan, The River Foundation, Roanoke, Virginia (1987).

Jones & Jones, Roanoke River Greenway Master Plan, The River Foundation, Roanoke, Virginia (1987).

Nolen, John, Comprehensive City Plan, Roanoke, Virginia, City Planning and Zoning Commissions, Roanoke, Virginia (1928).

The President's Commission on Americans Outdoors, Americans Outdoors: The Legacy, the Challenge, Island Press, Washington, D.C. (1987).

U.S. Army Corps of Engineers, Interim Feasibility Report and Environmental Impact Statement for Flood Damage Reduction, Wilmington, North Carolina (1984).

U.S. Department of the Interior, National Park Service, Reconnaissance Survey of the Roanoke River Parkway Corridor, Denver Service Center (1987).

The Development of the Geometric Design of Parkways

Frank B. Burggraf, FASLA, Professor of Landscape Architecture, University of Arkansas, Fayetteville

HISTORIC PERSPECTIVE

Until recently very few roads were located by engineering methods. Early rural roads which started as horse and wagon trails ran from farm to market with each landowner maintaining the road which passed along his property. Eventually this gave way to collective efforts to work on the roads at an appointed time in the common interest. Ultimately persons were hired by the county to work on the roads and the property owners paid taxes instead of giving their time. Often there was no right-of-way defined and when there was it was usually one chain or 66 feet. Roads followed the edge of properties, as no farmer wanted his fields cut in two by a public road. This often meant sharp corners at the end of a property, a reality still very much in evidence in the western U.S. at the junction of sections and quarter sections. Gradually the more important roads were improved, usually with surfacing, sometimes with improvements in the more troublesome alinements. Virtually all of our highways have grown out of successive improvements of existing roads, almost always within the existing right-of-ways.

In urban areas, streets were commonly plotted in rectangles or squares—the ubiquitous gridiron pattern, fashioned without regard for topography or natural features except for the most formidable of obstacles, and often ignoring existing trails which were located with more consideration of topography. Broadway in New York City is a classic example. It is in conspicuous nonconformance with the grid street pattern because it follows the Wickquasgeck trail of the Delaware Indians which predated even the Dutch settlement of New Amsterdam.

Modern highway location employs techniques of civil engineering and land surveying to fix the location and geometry of the road. These techniques are borrowed from earlier railroad engineering and also from early parkway siting experience.

PARKWAY GEOMETRICS

The basic geometric elements of a parkway are the curves (both horizontal and vertical), straightaways (tangents), ups and downs (grades) and cross sectional elements which locate the cartway in the landscape. Unlike the modern express highway which seeks the most direct and rapid location between two points, a parkway has as its objective the most pleasant location to be traveled at a pace appropriate to the enjoyment of the landscape.

Some parkways, by virtue of their controlled access and location, have become heavily used as expressways—the Cross County Parkway in Westchester, for example. Sometimes travel on the parkway seems as fast or faster than covering the same distance on an expressway. If you travel the Hudson River

Corridor between Albany and the outskirts of New York City as I have many times, you find a choice of routes. There are state highways like 9W which for the most part go through cities and towns and mix local and through traffic to the discomfort of both. There is the Thruway—a toll road which is designated a part of the Interstate system. It is controlled access with easy grades and curves, very direct and following an easy "water level route". There is the Taconic State Parkway which is controlled or limited access and which winds through more rugged highlands, mountains and rolling topography. My personal preference except in extreme time constraint is to drive the parkway. The absence of trucks to contend with and the pleasant and constantly changing landscape makes the drive much more enjoyable, less fatiguing, and while it is longer than the thruway, it actually seems to take less time.

EARLY PARKWAY PLANS

The parkway concept is generally considered to have its first expression with the construction of the Bronx River Parkway, although I have personally come across many references to parkways which predate it. In his book, Parks and Park Engineering, published in 1916 William T. Lyle writes:

> *The Parkway and Boulevard are connecting arteries which join the parks of a system. The Boulevard is the more formal of the two and is nothing more than a beautified avenue, while a Parkway is much broader, often about 400 feet wide, and may be laid out in a semi-informal manner.*[1]

John Nolen, a notable early landscape architect and planner, in his plan for the City of Little Rock, Arkansas, dated 1930, proposed, among other things,

> *Acquisition of land for a coordinated Park System which will provide playgrounds, athletic fields, neighborhood parks, for intensive use throughout the city, large scenic parks or reservations and connecting parkways.* (emphasis added) [2]

That Nolen already had a clear understanding of parkways at that time becomes evident by his definition in the report:

> *Parkways. Aside from the areas which are intensively used for recreation, there is the parkway, which performs a double function—the providing of scenic drives, and the connecting of the large parks and reservations. In this way the water courses, such as the creeks and portions of river banks, are made available for enjoyment, preventing them from falling into insanitary uses, and a means of seeing the city without traversing the crowded thoroughfares of the city.*[3]

Nolen went on to propose specific parkway routes including:

> *Circumferential Drive in the Surrounding Region, for example: a drive on the long ridge toward the Pinnacles, and Shindle Mountain, then leading south and east back to the city.*[4]

Russell Van Nest Black, a planning consultant and a member of both the American Society of Civil Engineers and the American Society of Landscape Architects, in a monograph for the public administration service published in 1933, not only lists parkways as a usual element of a physical plan for the average small city, but includes a photograph of a handsome grade separation structure on "Central Parkway Mt. Vernon, N.Y." credited to Gilmore Clarke, Landscape Architect and published courtesy of the Westchester County Park Commission. Included in Black's excellent monograph are two plans prepared by John Nolen.

One is entitled, "Mariemont: A New Town" subtitled, "An interpretation of Modern City Planning Principles applied to a Small Community to produce local Happiness." Dated July, 1921, the plan depicts tree lined boulevards and ribbon parks adjoining one of the major thoroughfares and the railroad. The other Nolen plan is for the City of Roanoke. It clearly depicts parkways following the watercourses and creating a ribbon of park linking the parks, the city and outlying areas.

As was often the case then and is still quite

common the excellence of the plan is no assurance of adoption. Funding such schemes obviously presented problems and although the authors of such plans clearly foresaw the growth in demand and the need for action before a rise in land costs, their clients did not share such concern—at least not enough to act on them.

Lyle makes an observation in his publication in 1916 which perhaps explains in part why there may have been a reluctance to expend public funds for parkways. In discussing the planning of parks he observes:

> *Parks should be planned with a distinct view of the requirements of the population to be benefited. The problem must be worked out for each individual case. The needs of the entire population must be considered with regard to wealth, culture, nationality, age, sex, density of population, etc. Drives, parkways and boulevards will principally benefit the wealthy.*[5]

The perception that parkways benefit the wealthy is understandable in 1916 as there were only about 4, 700,000 passenger cars and 400,000 trucks registered in the U.S. just before World War I. Ten years later the number of cars would have increased nearly five times and the number of trucks seven times. Not only was the common ownership of autos unforeseen but the impact upon the settlement and property development that was to be a consequence of such mobility was unimagined.

LOCATIONAL CONTROLS

In any highway location there are fixed objectives or termini which control the actual siting. For most highways the objective is to connect one community to another. This would be the primary control. Secondary controls would be elements that would have to be accommodated to reach the primary objectives, such as a river crossing, a mountain pass, an existing railroad overpass, a swamp or lake, etc. From our earlier observations we can see that parkways have different location controls. Parkways more often link parks and follow terrain features such as rivers, escarpments, etc. Secondary parkway controls might be desirable overlooks or unique views. Whereas highway engineers would usually avoid steep topography, some parkways are designed to engage and exploit mountainous terrain.

These days it is not uncommon for highways to be located entirely in the office from aerial photography and topographic maps. With the computer it is easy to do all the calculations and with modern earth moving equipment it is possible to disregard most topography, simply cutting and filling as necessary to achieve the desired grade and alinement. Parkways have traditionally been located in the field where it is possible to experience the landscape and to appreciate the views attainable and the landscape features too sensitive or valuable to disturb. This also requires collaboration of a high order among the surveyors, engineers and landscape architects.

PARKWAY ALINEMENT DESIGN

The parkway location will attempt to stay close to the natural earthforms and will minimize grade changes, particularly where grade change would result in extensive removal of vegetation or unnatural grades and slopes. Often the alinement will be compromised rather than the land disrupted.

When a vehicle goes around a curve, the resistance to centrifugal force tending to throw the car off the road is entirely a function of the resistance of the tires and any banking of the road which tends to deflect the car back. The larger the radius of a curve, the greater is the speed which the tire's road contact will permit as the less force is exerted by the turning action. Since parkways are often in rugged topography, there are a lot of curves and they are often of fairly small radii. Parkways are usually designed for lower speeds.

In cities, drivers are accustomed to driving at various speeds and stopping and going in response to traffic density, lights, changes in paving, intersections, etc. The geometry of curves of sight distances is less likely to determine speed.

> *Once clear of urban areas, the average driver tends to settle down to a steady speed which in his mind is as great as the traffic and the physical characteristics of the highway permit.* [6]

We all recognize that the modern vehicle can go faster than the speed limit or even the speed for which a curve is technically rated. Some drivers choose to drive closer to the practical limits of their equipment than others. It is important to design a road so there are no abrupt changes in the curvature, or if such changes are necessary they should become evident before the driver arrives at a curve which is too sharp for his rate of speed. Thus a road is designed to be balanced with the curves designed, as nearly as possible, for a uniform design speed.

Where curves follow the contour of the landscape there is often a sequence of curves first in one direction, then in the opposite. In between the curves there will be a straight stretch or tangent to the curves. In difficult topography there is little room for tangents between curves so the driver must quickly adjust from a turn in one direction to a turn in the opposite. The banking or superelevation of a curve which is necessary for safety and comfort must as quickly be added and subtracted and applied in the opposite direction. The shorter the radius the greater is the need for superelevation and the more quickly must the banking be added. However, a circular curve begins to curve at the point of tangency at the full rate of curvature. If the full rate of superelevation or banking is to occur at the start of the curve it must begin before and end after the curve. This warping can be drastic if curves in opposition occur close together. Conversely, there is little point in banking before the curve as it is not until the curve that it becomes necessary.

Transitions from tangents to horizontal curves were developed by the railroads and their use in road alinements was pioneered in parkway design. Transitions or spiral curves are curves of changing radius. They apply the curvature gradually. In other words, a transition curve is a curve of constantly changing radius. Since superelevation can thus be applied as the curvature develops, it makes for a smoother, gradual curve. The computations involved are much more complicated for the establishment of a spiral curve than for a circular curve; this has contributed to their lack of acceptance in highway design. Because of the quality of the resulting drive, particularly in steep topography where tighter curves are required, they have found favor in parkway alinement. The Mount Vernon Memorial Parkway built between 1929 and 1932 is reputed to have been designed entirely without any straight tangents. This accounts for the very liquid, comfortable driving experience where all the curves are so gradual as to be almost unnoticed.

The problem of difficult computations of transition alinements was solved in 1940 when the Bureau of Public Roads published Transition Curves for Highways, a book of tables of transition curves for various standard lengths and lengths of curve. Authored by Joseph Barnett, senior highway design engineer, they enabled significant improvement in the driving quality of roads employing the techniques set forth. In this short dissertation it is not possible to go into detail about the application of transition curves. Persons interested in exploring transition curves further are directed to the authoritative introduction in the beginning of that book. With today's modern computers such calculations are no longer of consequence. However, interstate standards are so generous (large radius curves) that there is slight need for transitions to be added.

A road must be designed to negotiate changes of direction not only right and left but up and down as well. Going up and down hills affects vehicle performance. Older roads often exceeded the 5 or 6% considered to be a practical grade for climbing without significant loss of speed and to be "free-wheeling" on the downgrade but without significant build up of speed because of gravity. As we all know, loaded trucks do not climb steep grades without losing speed. Modern interstates are therefore designed to keep grades to a maximum of 3%. At the top and bottom of grades there must be curves to transition from one slope to another. These curves are parabolic, effecting a smooth transition based on sight distances that permits safe passing or stopping maneuvers.

REFINEMENTS

Of course changes in grade and changes in direction often occur together and it is design judgments in this arena that constitute the "art" of alinement design.

> *The combination of profile and alignment is important for the landscape design as well as for traffic operation. The beauty of line may be lost if grade and line are not properly related. Lines "flowing with the country" with carefully placed profile changes are desired. Poorly placed grade changes can distort an otherwise beautiful curve. Thus a summit or hump in the profile of a concave curve, visible across a broad valley, may mar the entire line of the highway. Nor should a curve begin at a summit; it is better to suggest the change of direction before the road goes out of sight.*[7]

> *Some combinations which, to use engineer's parlance, are "statically and dynamically correct" may have an objectionable appearance. For example, where there is a small angular difference in direction between two long tangents, the horizontal curve connecting them should usually be very much longer for appearance's sake than the acceptable length dictated by design speed; otherwise the curve will appear as a sharp kink to the driver. Similarly, for appearance, longer vertical curves should be used at grade sags than might be required merely to effect the smooth transition from downgrade to upgrade motion.*[8]

THE PARKWAY CROSS SECTION

The early planners were aware of the need for a hierarchy of roads and streets to accommodate different traffic densities and kinds of use. Wider right-of-ways are determined to be necessary and early parkway designers soon determined the desirability of a median strip. The highway designers were learning that pavements only 16 feet wide were not safe for two lanes of traffic going 50 and 60 miles per hour. Indeed it is hard for us to imagine the three lane road which provided a central lane for passing from either direction. It is not surprising that this plan soon gave way to four lanes and then to the addition of a median strip.

> *The traffic accident rates between 1929 and 1939 were the highest ever recorded in this country. In 1929, 28,000 persons died in highway accidents, a number equivalent to 16.2 deaths for every 100 million miles of motor vehicle travel. In order to reduce the traffic hazard and make it easier to pass slow traffic, many highways were widened to include a third or "passing" lane. This was to prove disastrous. Since the passing lane was used by fast traffic moving in both directions, the frequency of head-on collisions increased and the accident rate on three-lane roads proved to be higher than on two-lane roads.*[9]

The Autobahn, Germany's new system of highways, also influenced American highway engineers. Designed as controlled-access highways built for high speed and with thick pavements, they were designed to provide mobility for the German War Machine. We would ourselves later finance highway construction as part of the "national defense". The Autobahn did have a 15 foot median strip, but it was the Merritt Parkway constructed across Connecticut between 1934 and 1940 that introduced the median strip of varying width, 20 feet at its width but narrowing to nothing at overpasses. The final step of two independent alinements for each direction with a variable median did not occur until later.

> *In 1934, California built its first rural divided highway, incorporating a median strip 20 feet in width. In June of that year, the Maryland Road Commission let grading contracts for a divided highway between Baltimore and Havre de Grace; it had a 30 foot median, although the com-*

mission expressed its conviction that a 50-foot-wide median would be preferable. California was probably the first state to build a divided highway with a 50-foot-wide median separating the roadways; this was in 1938.[10]

When right-of-ways were narrow, drainage ditches were at the edge of the cartway and backslopes were often quite steep. Shoulders were nonexistent. Gradually, with wider right-of-ways, shoulders were widened and slopes were eased. Again it was parkway designers concerned with the appearance of their creations that pioneered slope rounding and blending with the landscape. The concern for appearance even went beyond the limits of the right-of-way itself.

Regulations of the National Park Service, approved by the Secretary of the Interior Feb. 8, 1935, provide for acquisition by several states of rights of way and scenic easements for national parkways. Scenic easements are to be introduced for maximum protection without increasing the areas of land actually provided. A right of way of 100 acres or more per mile shall be provided. The 100-acre right of way would itself be equivalent to a strip of constant width of 800 feet but need not be uniform. Thus the acreage may be balanced to meet conditions, but at no point should it be less than 200 feet wide. Its variation in width will depend on topography and other natural conditions and on the requirements of the parkway design. Similarly, an additional requirement of the 50 acres per mile for scenic easement is a device to control future use of adjoining private land in order to maintain its values for the parkway. The requirements, among others attached to scenic easements, prohibit pole lines, dumps, etc. and structures other than farm buildings, also deny access to the roads and forbid the removal of trees or shrubs but permit government planting. Advertising signs are limited to owner advertisement by means of 18-by 24-inch signs.[11]

ACCESS

We are all familiar with the destruction of the capacity of a highway through unlimited access. No sooner would a highway be constructed than all manner of roadside business would locate along it, each with its own entry, each adding to the burden of traffic and conflict until yet another "by-pass" became necessary for expediting through traffic. The parkway designers, for the sake of their clients—the motoring public—limited access, making the road more pleasant to drive but also safer.

Some communities were concerned that highways would depreciate property as well as withdraw lands from taxation.

. . . as late as 1943, some residents of the Riverside section of Greenwich, Connecticut, most of them New York businessmen, were up in arms about the state's proposal to add a third highway to the Boston Post Road and the Merritt Parkway across Fairfield County. Said Town Assessor Clifford R. Wilmot, "if the road goes through Riverside, tax exemption on state-acquired property and depreciation of property along the route would reduce the Greenwich assessment list by $15,000,000."

In 1937, John Nolen and Henry V. Hubbard made a careful study of the trend of property values close to parkways in Boston, Kansas City, and Westchester County. Although the age and design criteria of each of these systems differed considerably, in each instance these authors showed that property close to landscaped parkways maintained or increased its value better or more than did comparison properties some distance away from the parkway. To obtain similar information about suburban and rural areas through which parkways and expressways had been built, the California Department of Highways, in 1949, set up a Land Economics Section within its Right-of-Way Department. All the published studies by this section confirm the Nolen and Hubbard findings.[12]

ROADSIDE PLANTING

While technically not a part of the parkway geometry, and worthy of a paper of this length in its own right, planting bears mention here. It relates to the geometry in a number of ways such as how it influences the choice of route for viewing or for protection of existing vegetation and in possible effects on sight distances. It also will influence the width of right-of-way.

Successful treatment of roadside and border growth begins with the acquisition of sufficient right of way. Scenic easement and abutting property control are also most desirable. A governing principle should be the preservation of natural growth and the avoidance of artificial effects. In many areas trees are the most important growth. In forested areas landscaping begins therefore with the clearing and grubbing, for it is necessary to preserve designated trees and even some shrubs. The landscape architect should be available and should mark clearly all trees to be left standing. He should work with the engineers and avoid designating trees that cannot survive grading work or that interfere with proper drainage or safety of future operation, including necessary sight distance and legal vertical clearance.

. . . To preserve certain groups of trees or specially fine single specimens the center line may require field changes that easily can be made, especially if provided for in the plans and specifications.[13]

Plantings also contribute to muffling traffic noise and provide screening between the highway and the community. Plantings can also be used to screen the headlights of oncoming traffic.

PARK SERVICE EXPERIENCE

The National Park Service and the Bureau of Public Roads have a long established partnership in the production of parkways and park roads. Despite the fact that they are housed in totally different departments, the collaboration has been effective and innovative.

While the aforementioned geometric considerations involve judicious application of standards during the "design" phase, there is more to the realization of a parkway design. As Conrad Wirth, then Director of the National Park Service, said in an address in 1955:

. . . The road systems providing access to these developments require the continuous attention of landscape architects from the time a road is proposed until it is completed. Even after the construction phase has been completed, certain activities and the possible needs for vista clearing, etc. are his responsibility.

Working with others, the landscape architect is responsible for creating a circulatory pattern which will serve the essential needs of preservation and protection and appropriate visitor use.

A road system of a park area may run a gamut of extremes. It may be a simple, short approach road terminating at its objective in a turnaround and parking area. Or a road system for a park area may be a network of roadways involving park roads, state roads, county roads, and private roads, perhaps requiring a number of different standards, and traversing difficult mountain terrain or extreme swamps or arid deserts.

The landscape architect charged with the problem of planning a roads and trails system for a park area must at all times balance scenic values against construction costs; he must locate a travel-way in such a manner that it will reveal and describe the splendors of an area—perhaps explain why the road was so located—and not develop traffic hazards or maintenance problems. In applying the forms of order to his composition—sequence, balance, repetition, as true of road location and design as of any landscape composition—he must apply certain corollary principles relating to areas in the National Park System in particular—principles such as conservation, preservation, public use an-

ticipation, and development restraint.

. . . A road may be primitive, relatively undeveloped, winding, narrow, with steep grades, leading to an accessible but seldom visited overlook of a breathtaking canyon view; or a road may be a multilane divided motorway complete with curbs, gutters, grade separations, and four-leaf interchanges. A primitive road may be used by only one venturesome motorist a day, or a primary may resound with 1,500 hurrying motorists per hour.

Taxing the ability of the landscape architect to cope with varying construction standards and practices is the variety of land forms over which the park roads pass. In Everglades National Park, Florida, the road must be built up from the swamps by a hydraulic and landfill road base of oolite and muck. A portion of Colonial Parkway in Colonial National Historical Park is being built up from tidewater land by a hydraulic silt fill. In Olympic National Park, Washington, the Heart o' the Hills Road, and in Glacier National Park, Montana, the Going-to-the-Sun Highway were literally carved along and through the mountains. In Death Valley National Monument, California, the park road is a sand fill, borrowed in place, generally, across a burning desert. At Cape Hatteras National Seashore, North Carolina, the road within the area is a long sand-and-bitumen ribbon along the sand dunes of an offshore barrier reef.[14]

The design of parkways is a challenging art and science. There are many fine examples of a high order of achievement throughout the United States and the influence of the design of other highways is also evident. Unfortunately it seems to be an art form that is out of favor. There are still many unique and deserving landscapes to be enjoyed, and the observation that pleasure driving is the number one recreation activity of Americans by the Outdoor Recreation Review Commission ought not to be ignored.

NOTES

1 Lyle, William T., Parks and Park Engineering, Wiley and Sons, London, 1916, p.7.

2 Nolen, John, City Plan, Little Rock Arkansas, John Nolen and Associates, Cambridge, Mass., 1930, p.4.

3 Ibid, p.11.

4 Ibid, p.12

5 Lyle, p.22

6 Barnett, Joseph, Transition Curves for Highways, Public Roads Admin., U.S. Govt. Print. Off., 1940, p.3.

7 Hewes, Laurence Ilsley, American Highway Practice, Wiley and Sons, London, 5th printing 1956, p.209.

8 Cron, F.W., "Fitting the Highway to the Landscape," The Highway and the Landscape, p.11.

9 Bugge, W.A., and Snow, Brewster, "The Complete Highway," The Highway and the Landscape, p.11.

10 Ibid, p.22.

11 Hewes, p.205.

12 Bugge and Snow, p.15.

13 Hewes, p.233.

14 Wirth, Conrad L. "The Landscape Architect in National Park Work," Landscape Architecture Quarterly, ASLA, 1955.

BIBLIOGRAPHY

American Association of State Highway Officials, A Policy On Geometric Design Of Rural Highways, AASHO, Washington, D.C., 1954.

Baylis, Dudley C., Planning our National Park Roads and Our National Parkways, U.S. Dept. of Interior, National Park Service, reprinted from July 1957 issue of Traffic Quarterly, ENO Foundation.

Barnett, Joseph, Transition Curves for Highways, Public Roads Administration, U.S. Government Printing Office, Washington D.C., 1940.

Black, Russell Van Nest, Planning for the Small American City, Public Administration Service, Chicago, Ill. 1936.

Hewes, Laurence Ilsley, American Highway Practice, Wiley and Sons, London, 5th printing 1956.

Lyle, William T., Parks and Park Engineering, Wiley and Sons, Inc., London, 1916.

McCluskey, Jim, Road Form and Townscape, Architectural Press, London, 1979.

Nolen, John, City Plan, Little Rock Arkansas, John Nolen and Associates, Cambridge, Mass., 1930.

Outdoor Recreation Review Commission, Outdoor Recreation for America, U.S. Government Printing Office, Washington, D.C., 1962.

Raymond, William G., The Elements of Railroad Engineering, Wiley and Sons, New York, 4th ed., 1923.

Snow, Brewster W., The Highway and the Landscape, Rutgers University Press, New Brunswick, N.J., 1959.

U.S. Commerce Dept., A Proposed Program for Roads and Parkways, U.S. Government Printing Office, Washington, D.C., 1968.

Urban Advisors to the Federal Highway Administration, The Freeway in the City, U.S. Government Printing Office, Washington, D.C., 1968.

The Mississippi River National Parkway

Lynn Miller, Pennsylvania State University

BACKGROUND AND CONCEPT

> *For sometime De Soto had been hearing of a great river to the west, a river called the* Mississippi. *He decided to find it. After a long and hard journey through forests and swamps the Spaniards came out of the woods and stood upon the banks of this mighty stream.*[1]

This is the typical fourth grade history book description of De Soto's discovery in the 16th century of the "Father of Waters" which had been used for millennia by the aboriginal Americans. The river became a world legend in the 19th century through the marvelous eyes and pen of Mark Twain, but it was not until the 20th century that it was ever studied and assessed as a significant American landscape.

The original idea for a parkway along the entire length of the Mississippi belongs to the late Albert P. Greensfelder of St. Louis, Missouri. In the 1930's he recommended that the proposed parkway along the Mississippi River in the state of Missouri be extended from Canada to the Gulf of Mexico. Explaining his concept, Greensfelder said:

> *Our Declaration of Independence 175 years ago pointed our way to the pursuit of happiness. Thomas Jefferson's phrase implies not merely personal but happy communities progressing and prospering.*
>
> *Our particular parkway can develop into a 'Happiness Highway' whereon you and I and those who follow us will seek and find happy days in pleasurable pursuits.*
>
> *A parkway is a way between parks and playlands. We, the people of mid America, must produce such a parkway commensurate with our potentialities. It will require vision, vigor and vitality. Who shall say we, the seven million people in the 118 river counties, lack them.*[2]

In 1938 planners from the ten Mississippi river states agreed to establish an interstate commission to be known as the Mississippi River Parkway Planning Commission.

Initial legislation was introduced in Congress in 1939 but action was delayed as the United States became involved in World War II. Following the end of the war, the Mississippi

River Parkway Planning Commission met with the National Park Service and the Bureau of Public Roads to discuss future parkway plans.

In August of 1949, the U.S. Congress authorized the National Park Service and the Bureau of Public Roads to study the feasibility of a national parkway along the entire length of the Mississippi River from Lake Itasca in Minnesota to the Gulf of Mexico. Stanley Abbott was called away from his work on the Blue Ridge Parkway to be the supervising landscape architect for the National Park System team working on this project.

Abbott, in describing the objectives and goals of this undertaking, said,

> *. . . we have all agreed that if this Parkway is to be simply another road with no claim to distinction, then the project has little reason for being. Our goal is higher. In words that are high sounding, but I think properly so, the job is to reveal for the visitor to this Valley every bit that we can of all that comes to mind with the word 'MISSISSIPPI'. . .*[3]

The feasibility study got underway at a time of "parkway fever." The National Park Service had achieved outstanding successes in the 1930's and 1940's with its parkways and especially with the "big daddy" of them all—The Blue Ridge Parkway. This fever or enthusiasm resulted in several studies being completed in the decade of the 1950's.

Although some of these proposed projects were challenged (as in the case of the C & 0 Canal Parkway when Associate Justice William O. Douglas of the U. S. Supreme Court argued that a parkway would destroy the uniqueness of the Canal and the project was abandoned), the study of the proposed Mississippi River Parkway resulted in the advancement of new ideas and techniques for the parkway concept. Although the parkway concept had been adapted to the conservation of mountain scenery and the preservation of historic trails and traces, no parkway had ever transversed a landscape comparable in scale or character to the Mississippi Valley.

THE STUDY

The study for the Mississippi River Parkway was one of immense proportions. It may very well be the largest single landscape architectural study ever undertaken. The river is 2,552 miles in length; its drainage basin encompasses 31 states. From its beginning at Lake Itasca in Minnesota, it passes through 10 states and 8 botanical/climatical zones; or, as Stanley Abbott described it,

> *. . . from the moose and caribou to the delta alligator . . .*[4]

In addition to its vast scale and its unique natural features, many of the events which shaped this country's history took place along the banks of this river. One must also consider the human life and cultures of prehistoric man, who existed along the river long before De Soto. Many of these cultures have never been studied or analyzed in any great detail by our archaeologists.

As with the Blue Ridge Parkway, this feasibility study was undertaken by a collaborative team from the Bureau of Public Roads and the National Park Service. The National Park Service team members provided the documentation and analysis of the historical, recreational and archeological aspects, along with the assessment of the scenic character of the region and its relationship to the proposed parkway. The Bureau of Public Roads team members completed the basic road survey data and the general determination of selected routes. Both of these agencies participated in the final selection of routes and prepared typical development plans and cost estimates. Collaboration was so successful that it was hard to tell where one team left off and the other started.

At the beginning of the study, the design team knew that the Mississippi did not have the awesomeness of the Grand Canyon or the scenic splendor of the Yosemite Valley, but it had the vistas and the magic places which had excited American writers such as Mark Twain to describe a sunset as . . .

> *. . . a broad expanse of river was turned to blood, in the middle distance the red hue brightened into gold through which a soli-*

tary log came floating black and conspicuous; . . .

. . . the shore on our left was densely wooded, and the somber shadow that fell from this forest was broken in one place by a long, ruffled trail that shone like silver; and above the forest wall a clean-stemmed dead tree waved a single leafy bough that glowed like a flame in the unobstructed splendor that was flowing from the sun. . .[5]

Any study of this size has its share of problems. First and foremost, was the magnitude of the study area. A proper study would require a complete analysis of a strip of land 15 to 25 miles in width along the entire length of the river or the equivalent of analyzing 90,000 square miles(57,600,000 acres) or something about the size of two Pennsylvanias.

At this point we see the influence of one of the advanced technologies resulting from World War II—aerial photography. This was one of the first projects to utilize aerial photography to any great extent. Over 22,000 aerial photos at the scale of 1:20,000 were studied which resulted in 10,000 miles of alternate routes being examined at the cost of only $25.00 per mile.

After evaluation of the basic data, three approaches were considered. The first was one which would satisfy the basic objectives of the Congressional authorization. This was to select a route for an all new parkway on both sides of the river from Minnesota to New Orleans and a single route from Lake Itasca to Minneapolis. The cost of this proposal was $1,450,000,000. A single route utilizing existing bridges would reduce the cost to $770,000,000. Since an all new parkway would most likely have to parallel existing roads, the economic feasibility of the approach was questioned.

The second approach was to build several shorter but disjointed sections of parkway. This was discarded because it would show preference to certain states and communities and it fell short of accomplishing the basic objective.

The third plan was to consider marking and designating existing highways on one or both sides of the river. The design team realized that this approach would not produce a meaningful solution since continuous pavements do not exist on favorable locations in proximity to the river.

It was realized that there was an opportunity for flexibility of parkway concepts rather than the simple duplication of past designs. Therefore, the logical and most successful approach would be to strike a happy medium between an all new parkway and the reclamation and upgrading of certain existing roads. This plan would result in a project which would cost only $81,000,000.

The joint report completed in 1951 concluded that developing a national parkway system on an entirely new location along the Mississippi was not advisable. The team recommended a plan for a scenic route to be developed and administered by the various state highway departments which would improve suitable existing highways to parkway standards with inter-connecting links of new parkway construction.

THE RECOMMENDED PLAN

Development of the recommended plan would begin with a careful selection of existing highways which would be officially designated "Mississippi River Parkway" when minimum land controls and agreements for future improvements would be obtained. As the existing highways would be "reclaimed," new sections of parkway would be built where the engineering, scenic and/or historic considerations had deemed them important. The plan estimated that 40% of the proposed route would be of new construction.

Several new ideas of parkway construction which could be incorporated into the planning emerged from the study. One was the construction of roadways from locally available and inexpensive hydraulic fill. The other was the opportunity to use the man-made levee as an elevated parkway (see figure 1). Levees had seldom been used in the past because they had predated the automobile. This unique man-made feature would give height to the parkway above the river flats and would enhance the view of the river and the landscape character. (see figure 2).

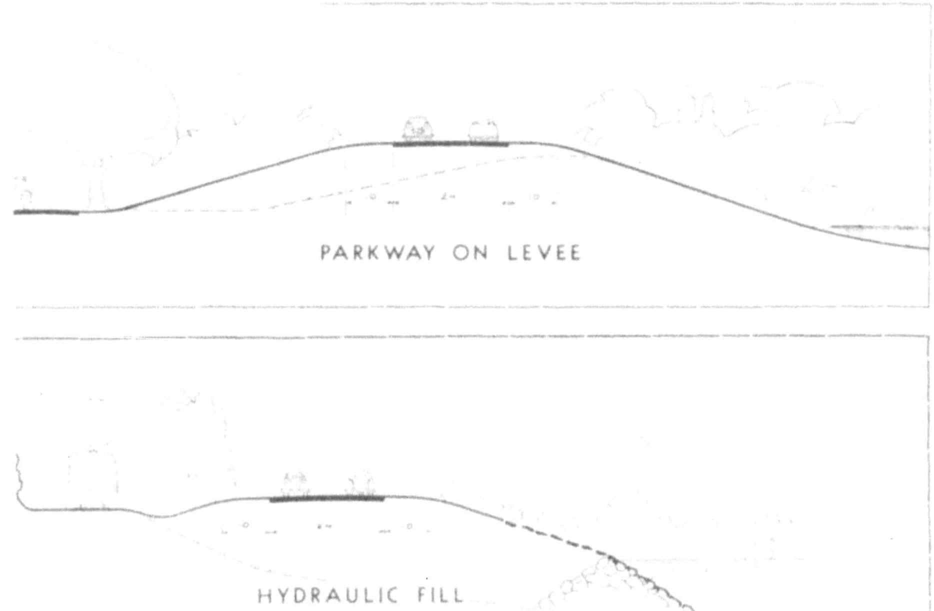

Top: ***Fig. 1.***
Bottom: ***Fig. 2***

The concept of utilizing existing highways with new parkway construction necessitated a detailed program of land controls to be considered. The following were considered to be absolutely essential:

1. Existing rights of way would have to be widened to the minimum of 220 feet for two lane and 250 feet for four lane.
2. Outright purchase of natural areas of marshland, bluffs, islands, etc.
3. Scenic easements 300 feet wide along both sides of the construction right of way to permanently attach the pastoral views to the parkway.
4. The acquisition of historic sites as well as scenic and recreational areas.

Another factor essential in the reclamation of existing roads would be the cleaning up of roadsides. The plan called for public pressure, using outright purchase and permanent zoning to accomplish this objective. A new approach to outdoor advertising was developed to supply needed information to the traveler. In lieu of billboards, the Mississippi River Parkway would have areas set aside along the main travel lanes where appropriate advertising agencies could lease space under strict supervision of the local and State Chambers of Commerce. Such facilities would be self supporting.

THE GREAT RIVER ROAD

In 1954 Congress responded to the recommendations of the feasibility study and authorized the development of the project along with additional studies. In 1964 new legislation was passed and the name was changed from the Mississippi River Parkway to The Great River Road.

At the present time all of the routes have been selected and designated by the river states except for about 20 miles of gravel roads in the state of Iowa. The Mississippi River Parkway Commission, which serves as the official representative of the Mississippi Parkway and The Great River Road, estimates that approximately 1/3 of the projected project as envisioned in the 1951 report has been completed.

THE ABBOTT PHILOSOPHY

In the present day analysis of this 1951 study, it is imperative that we look in detail at the philosophical input of Stanley Abbott. In a paper presented on February 8, 1951, Abbott expressed a philosophy for the successful development of this project (a philosophy still sound today):

> *The Mississippi River Parkway can be an efficient motorway and perhaps a pleasant one. . . . But the success of the project as a tourist facility will depend at least equally on the artistry which is put into the plans as they are finally drawn by the States and into the execution of those plans in every telling detail. . . .*
>
> *The Mississippi is a river. In the abstract the problem is to bring about a kind of* *marriage of the river and the road.*
>
> *. . . The parkway must court the river and the river views in every subtle way. . . .*[6]

In a comparative analysis of tourist facilities in Europe and America, Abbott pleaded:

> *. . . we should take a step beyond the forever hot dog, the ubiquitous hamburger. I think of the native dishes—as native as the trout to Minnesota, catfish to Arkansas, shrimp to the Gulf. Likewise, the gift shops should avoid the world's fair stamp and become, instead, the outlets for the native products of this Valley and its people. . . .*[7]

In a broader aspect, Abbott discussed the opportunity to really capture the vast sweep and content of the Valley's history. Sometimes the real history of a region goes by the board for sake of another "George Washington's teacup." In order to accomplish this objective, Abbott said:

> *. . . the minor detail of history and legend must not be overlooked. This is a colorful part of the River's lore, and a parkway roadside makes a good place for the telling. . . . During these days of high import one develops—or I find that I do—a certain tenderness for the unimportant things of history, such as the little red school-*

house which no one of prominence attended.[8]

With this sound philosophy in our minds, we can suddenly see in the distance, through the early morning mist, Huck and Jim floating down the stream in rhythm to the great river:

We catched fish, and talked, and we took a swim now and then to keep off sleepiness. It was kind of solemn drifting down the big still river, laying on our backs looking up at the stars, and we didn't ever feel like talking out loud. . . .[9]

NOTES

1. Kelty, Mary, The Story of the American People, New York, Ginn & Co., 1937, p.75.
2. Parkway for the Mississippi, A Report to Congress, Part II, prepared by the National Park Service and the Bureau of Public Public Roads, August 1952, p. 247.
3. Abbott, Stanley, "The Mississippi River National Parkway", Planning and Civic Comment, Vol. 17, #1, March 1951.
4. Parkway for the Mississippi, A Report to Congress, Part I, prepared by the National Park Service and the Bureau of Public Roads, 1951.
5. Marx, Leo, The Machine and the Garden, New York, 1964, Oxford University Press, p. 321.
6. Abbott, Stanley, Planning and Civic Comment, March 1951.
7. Ibid.
8. Ibid.
9. Marx, Leo, The Machine and the Garden, p. 327.

The Roanoke River Reclamation Project: Site Specific Planning for a Linear District

David P. Hill

Abstract. The most diverse riparian ecosystem on the entire Atlantic slope, the Roanoke River has been the victim of 200 years of civic neglect! The combination of unique and fragile qualities of the Roanoke River Corridor provides for a complex land use planning challenge. In 1984 the Roanoke River Reclamation Project was proposed for the linear district through Salem and western Roanoke County. The project proposes an alternative to the traditional land planning methods. Previous planning methods failed in river corridors because they simplify the synergism of riparian systems to one or several common bases. In traditional zoning, land uses become prescribed, exclusive, and the river corridor has the potential to become a jumble of inappropriate land uses. Realizing the natural and social complexities of the corridor, an innovative land planning methodology was composed to fit the multiple land uses into the corridor with minimum disturbance to the existing environment. The Site Signature Method of land planning was proposed as an alternative for the Roanoke River Corridor as a means of locating and constructing multiple land uses in the environmentally sensitive area. The Roanoke County planning office has been able to use this project as a catalyst to begin a performance zoning policy in environmentally sensitive areas.

The next decade presents a critical time for the Roanoke River corridor. During the next five to ten years, the U.S. Army Corps of Engineers plans to implement flood plain management strategies and the EXPLORE Project plans to use the river for its aesthetic resources. Several Roanoke Valley Governments intend to use water from a pump-storage reservoir to be created west of Salem in the next decade. Roanoke County plans to construct major infrastructure improvements in the western river corridor, including a sewer interceptor system. When implemented, all of these plans will bring about a major landscape change in the Roanoke River corridor. In a sense, we are discovering the Valley resources somewhat by default. Previously occupied generally by agricultural service and industrial uses, the River corridor now benefits from a shift in the public attention. For the first time in recent history the possibility exists for the river corridor to be enjoyed to its fullest potential by the public.

Some design professionals recognized the potential for the river long ago. In his 1928 Plan for Roanoke City, the preeminent landscape architect and city planner John Nolen discussed the potential resources of this linear district. Using explicit photographs, John Nolen declared, "The river banks are being used as dumps." He suggested that the Roanoke River near Salem presented a much more beautiful scene. A visual reconnaissance of Nolen's two sites sixty years later reveals that both sites have been the subject of civic neglect. The recent environmental history of the river corridor and the intensive plans scheduled for construction in the next decade frame quite a problem. The solution lies in whether it is possible to intensify development in the district, and by so doing actually improve the health of the Roanoke River corridor.

Historically insensitive land use coupled with the infrastructure for intensive new development calls for an aggressive land planning strategy. In order to solicit sensitive development in the river corridor greater potential for private profit must be created. By allowing greater flexibility in locational criteria of new land uses, development interests will be able to afford a better performance in the environmental criteria of their proposals. The result is a linear district used to the concerns of the business community and designed to the criteria established by the scientific community. By proposing a performance based linear district in west Salem and Roanoke County, the Roanoke River Reclamation Project intends to celebrate the unique resources of the river corridor. Sixty years after John Nolen's request, the Roanoke River Reclamation Project proposes to reclaim the resources of the Roanoke River for public enjoyment.

I. THE ROANOKE RIVER: ROANOKE VALLEY'S SECRET RESOURCE

Four critical dimensions of the Roanoke River Corridor make it a unique landscape within the Roanoke Valley. The physical, biological, cultural and aesthetic character of the linear district distinguishes it from others in the region. These dimensions were examined to set a stage for the guiding principles for river corridor development.

First, the river corridor has a PHYSICAL character that sets it apart from other parts of the Roanoke Valley, beginning with its geology. The Blue Ridge mountains are among the oldest on the North American continent. Beginning in the Cambrian Age, 225 million years ago, the mountains began to form, and since the Quaternary (and possibly the Tertiary) Period (Amato, 1974) the Roanoke River has broken through the Blue Ridge and sculpted the Roanoke Valley. The floor of the valley is composed of Cambrian carbonates (limestones and dolomites), overlain by quaternary unconsolidated sand, gravel, silt and clay. The characteristics of the geohydrologic formations combined with their position in the low area of the valley make the river corridor the most important ground water management area of the entire Upper Roanoke River Basin. This area has the highest potential for ground water production, and the highest potential to become polluted. Many Roanoke County and Salem residents rely on the quantity and quality of the aquifer.

In principle, no land use should be permitted in the river corridor maximum groundwater recharge zone which would damage the recharge potential of the aquifer by creation of excessive impervious surfaces; pollute the aquifer either from surface runoff or septic field pollution; or cause potentially hazardous sink holes from extensive use of large wells which cause cones of depression in the groundwater table.

Over the millennia, the Roanoke River

corridor has developed the best soils in the Roanoke Valley. The Captina-Taft-Elk-Robertsdale soil association is ranked by the USDA as category 1 for agricultural purposes. The same characteristics that make Captina among the best agricultural soils in the country are responsible for making it easy for lucrative development of other land uses. This is the classic land conflict: the prime land for agriculture is the prime land for development. The values of the community will determine the solution to the conflict. However, the relative scarcity of USDA category 1 soils in the region makes them an especially precious nonrenewable resource.

In principle, the Captina association, where other characteristics permit, should be kept open for agricultural use. Soil associations which have high potential for erodability, low potential for building foundations, or are unsuitable for septic percolation should be avoided.

Certain other physical characteristics, such as the floodplain and very steep slopes on the outside banks of the river, require exceptional care in construction methods. In principle, these unconventional sites, if they must be developed, must be developed in an unconventional manner which will neither be dangerous to its inhabitants, its neighbors, nor disturb the existing ecological balance of the river corridor.

BIOLOGICALLY, the river corridor is unique. The upper Roanoke River houses the most diverse riverine ecological community on the entire Atlantic slope (Burkhead, 1983). This situation has come about largely for two reasons. One reason has to do with its location and the other to do with its history. The Roanoke River shares both the characteristics of the northern and southern rivers on the Atlantic slope. It is in the middle, and the climate of the valley provides a niche for some of the species of both. Also significant is the fact that for about the last two million years, the Blue Ridge and the Alleghenies have protected the Roanoke Valley from rapid geologic disturbance. The result is the existence of endemic relics, time-trapped animals or "living dinosaurs (Burkhead, 1983)" inhabiting the river. Two such endemics are fishes. The Orange-Finned Madtom, Notorus Gilberti and the Roanoke Logperch, Percina Rex both inhabit the river, and the Roanoke Salamander and several rare plant species can be found on the banks.

The Roanoke River Basin is located in the eastern forest oak-hickory climax region. The vast majority of the land in the upper river basin has been logged and is now used for silvicultural, agricultural, residential, commercial and industrial purposes. About 70 percent of the land in the upper basin is mixed woods. The woods typically occupy steep slopes and the valley floor is generally clear for agricultural and other uses. The soils of the valley are excellent for wildlife, and these resources could be cultivated with proper development techniques.

In principle, river corridor development must not produce stream born silt which would endanger the habitat of the Madtom species. This is particularly important during the spring spawning months. Land uses should be discouraged when they will impinge on woodland habitats. Land uses shall be discouraged from occupying all of the existing open land habitat in the river corridor. New land uses will begin to develop the tremendous potential for a biologically diverse river corridor community.

There are certain SOCIAL systems that contribute to the value of the river corridor. It has been inhabited since the paleolithic period, possibly as early as 9500 B.C. The Paleo Indians were big game hunters in winter, they turned their attention to the river in the summer, and gathered nuts in the fall (Barber, 1980). An extensive woodland Indian society evolved in Southwestern Virginia beginning about 1000 B.C. and culminated about 950 A.D. In the woodland society a more centrally based settlement pattern arose, with emphasis on the floodplain's rich agricultural soils. There are several sites along the river which exhibit the characteristics of campsites, and at the time of the project (1984), the sites were all considered threshold level - they had not been investigated.

During the time of the great western migration of European and American immigrants, the Native American trail in the river corridor became the Wilderness Trail, taking the settlers to the land of opportunity beyond the Appalachians. Even though there are not any historical landmarks in the corridor, some culturally significant sites now occupy the lands adjacent to the river, including several log cabins and active farmsteads.

In principle, development of future land uses should avoid all archaeologically and culturally significant sites. In the case where this will not be avoided, development of archaeologically significant sites should be planned two years in advance of construction to allow professional organizations to recover the artifacts. Both structures and details of culturally significant features can be incorporated into new construction.

The Wilderness Trail is now roughly the course of U.S. Route 11. Commercial uses dominate the landscape of this strip. Between Route 11 and the river, industries have been developed on prime agricultural land. To the south of the river, the prime land uses are residential and agricultural. In principle, future land uses will be compatible with the existing land uses. Where existing land uses are appropriately sited, new development shall not impact their relationships with roads, river, or neighborhood. Where existing land uses are incompatible in their location, new land uses shall be utilized to moderate the relationship between existing land use and landscape.

There are myriad methods which can be used to assess the AESTHETIC character of the river corridor. The USFS and BLM methodologies work on a very large scale, and Jones and Jones have developed a method for assessing wilderness rivers. One of the most helpful methods for assessment of a developing corridor has been advanced by R. Burton Litton (1974). All of the methodologies discuss the importance both of water and topography in creating a sense of place. In the Roanoke Valley, the presence of the river provides the potential for an aesthetic experience. The Resources Group (1977) interviewed 85 riverside residents in the Roanoke Valley, and found specifically that the residents liked the natural rocks, ripples and old trees adjacent to the river. Residents also preferred parks and agricultural land uses in the corridor, liked residential uses and roads, and did not like industrial uses in the corridor.

The river occupies the low point of the valley, providing the greatest possible experience of the mountains. The variations in topography, landform, and vegetation, and the soothing presence of water contribute to the aesthetic appeal of the corridor. In principle, the visual significance of some places is too great to allow insensitive land development. The design of new structures along the river corridor should have minimal impact for such elements as rapids, pools, natural rocks, still water, and tall old trees along the river. Every attempt to emphasize these amenities should be made at the design phase of new projects.

With the realization that more intensive development is bound to happen, the unique case of the Roanoke River necessitates a unique method for land suitability planning: one that is intrinsically tuned to the physical, biological, social and aesthetic resources of each site in the corridor. The four dimensions begin to outline the rich resources of the river corridor. The challenge becomes one of fitting new land uses into the river corridor without sacrificing the resources there. In Virginia (Stats. 15. 1-863), there is an extension of the usual zoning powers that does not appear in the enabling legislation. "Cities are empowered to divide their jurisdictions into districts for the purpose of applying different building codes (Blair, 1969)." Conventional zoning will never adequately address the synergism of the characteristics in this diverse environment. This legislation provides the framework for a River Corridor District. The district would grant locational flexibility to developers in return for their ability to meet certain performance criteria on the chosen site of their project. In some instances, development of new facilities can be used to clean-up the problems associated with some sites, enhancing the potential biological, historical and aesthetic resources. A clear method for evaluation of proposed land uses is essential to the future health of the river.

Fig. 1. Roanoke Landscape, west of Salem, Virginia.

II. THE SITE SIGNATURE METHOD OF LAND PLANNING

There are two curt realities of the Roanoke River corridor which must be taken into consideration when proposing the establishment of a special zoning district. One is that in order for the plan to be politically successful, it would be a great boost to make the plan more lenient than the conventional zoning in place. The second reality is that the historical and biological resources, and to some extent the physical and aesthetic properties of the river corridor are absolutely nonrenewable. Based on the tenet that it is possible to align these frequently irreconcilable realities, the Site Signature Method asserts that in fragile and diverse environments, the issue of preserving and enhancing the intended resources is not so much a matter of regional location as a matter of local construction. Developers are given locational flexibility in exchange for meeting the land use performance criteria established by the scientific community. The result is a river corridor planned according to a free market but constructed to the specifications of the scientific community.

An early step of the process is the establishment of the District boundaries and the District sites. The ends of the river corridor are conveniently established at jurisdictional boundaries, or at changes in the existing land use. Normal determinants for the lateral boundaries include visibility of the river, existing land use patterns, floodplain and first order watershed.

Inside the study area, sites occur at about half-mile intervals. Sites vary in size depending on existing land use patterns such as property lines, roads, bridges and crests of hills. They are marked by the Army Corps of Engineers river mile number.

The Site Signature Method analyzes the landscape in two ways. The MAGNITUDE of the landscape is a quantitative statement about how much or how great site characteristics are. The CONDITION of the land is a qualitative assessment about the health of sites. The Site Signature Method uses MAGNITUDE to determine character for land use location.

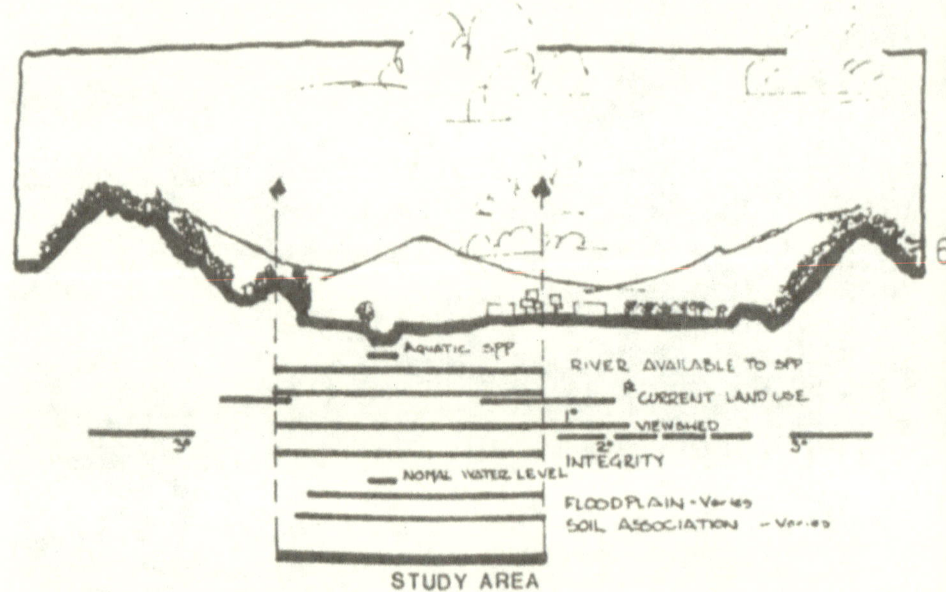

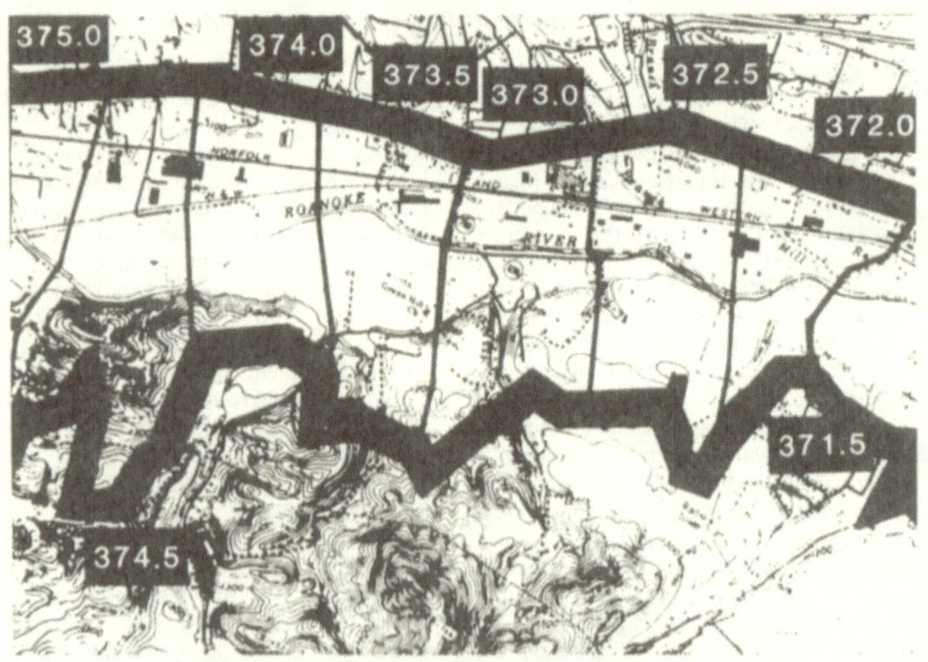

Top: ***Figure 2. Study for Establishment of a Lateral Boundary***
Bottom: ***Figure 3. Portion of the Roanoke River Corridor. Note the river miles, site boundaries at 1/2 mile intervals in the landscape.***

CONDITION is applied to establish site specific performance criteria.

The method documents the four critical dimensions of the landscape: biological, cultural, aesthetic and physical. A site sheet is the medium used to keep track of the character of each site. One has been developed for each site in the corridor. Magnitudes are totalled for each dimension and these totals are the basis for the site signature. The site signature represents the character of the site as a person's signature tells something about the character of the person. There is a pattern of larger site signatures upstream. These are more pristine sites, away from urbanized areas.

Currently there are 52 sites examined in the Roanoke River study covering both banks of the river along the 13 mile corridor. In order to find the sites appropriate for each proposed land use, a questionnaire was circulated to the planning and design community at Virginia Polytechnic Institute and State University. The instrument is planned so that there is a matrix of questions. The first asks the biological character of a site appropriate for each proposed land use category. The second asks the cultural character appropriate. Desirable aesthetic and physical character make up the third and fourth questions. The questionnaire is designed so questions are the ordinals which were used to establish the site signature grids. Modes of response are plotted on a grid congruent to the site signature grid. These are called Land Use Signatures.

The synthesis of questionnaire data and site data is a clear and simple process. To discover whether a site is appropriate for a particular land use, the Land Use Signature is overlaid with the Site Signature. If the corner points of the Site Signature fall within the shaded area of the Land Use Signature, the site is appropriate for the land use. If the proposed land use will be inappropriately sited, the incompatible dimensions are immediately visible. The decision can be traced in the score sheet to landscape characteristics. Traceability is a welcome benefit of the method.

A graphic synthesis is performed for the entire river corridor, crossing each Site Signature with Land Use Signature. Some sites will be appropriate for almost all land uses, some for one or two, some only for preservation. The product of this exercise is the flexible Land Suitability Plan.

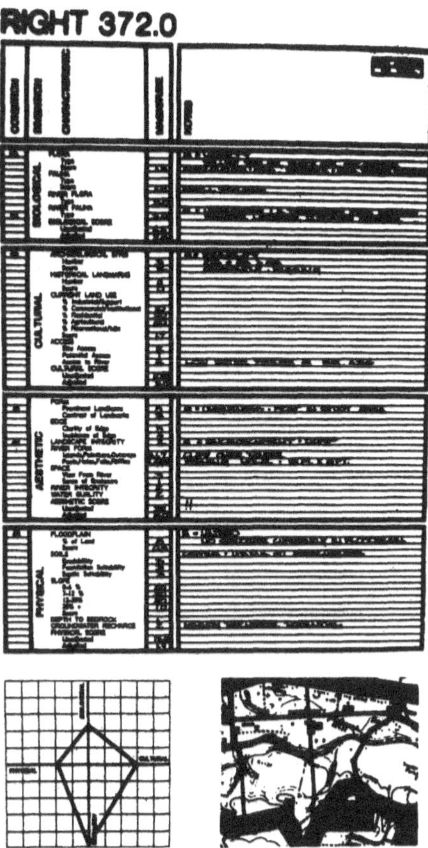

Fig. 4. Site sheet for the right bank site at mile 372.0. The site signature appears in the lower left corner of the site sheet.

The Land Suitability Plan is intended to allow locational flexibility for new land use proposals. A design evaluation process is proposed to insure quality development of the river corridor as development is put into place. When implemented, the flexible Land Suitability Plan alone is not sufficient control over the land use of the river corridor. Although a site is "zoned"

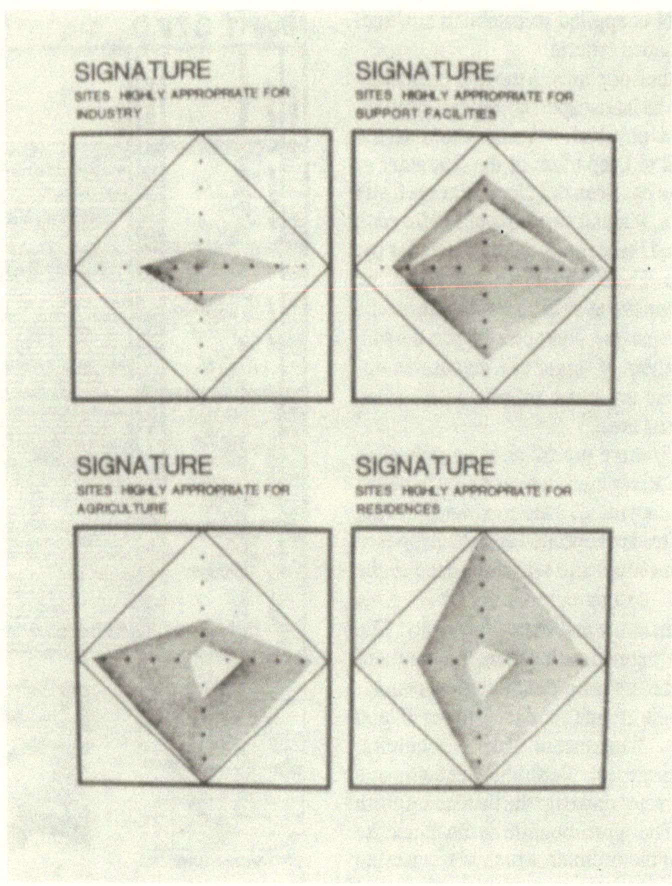

Fig. 5. Several land use signatures for the Roanoke River Project.

for any land use that appears on the LSP, in order to be built, the proposed land use must meet the performance criteria derived from the conditions of the desired site. By using site plan reviews, the Planning Commission requires a developer to sift his proposed development through the Land Suitability Plan (first, coarse sieve). The design evaluation is the second, fine mesh sieve a proposed development must pass before it can be built.

Conditions of the landscape are noted in each dimension of the study. They describe the health of sites. Unique features, the diversity of features, fragile features are noted, as well as all characteristics that have been encroached upon. For instance, a unique biological condition may be the "existence of a threatened species." A unique cultural condition may be "an historical landmark," etc. Each site has a distinct palette of different conditions. The conditions of the example site are noted with asterisks in figure 3.

According to the Land Suitability Plan, institutions, recreation and residences may be located in the example site. In order to be constructed, the chosen land use(s) must have minimum impact on the noted conditions. Given the incentive for higher potential profit, a developer can afford to invest in a sound design which will perform to these site specific standards.

Even though allowed by the LSP, the pros-

SIGNATURE
SITES HIGHLY APPROPRIATE FOR RESIDENCES

BIOLOGICAL
CULTURAL
PHYSICAL
AESTHETIC

SITE SIGNATURE Left 372.0

SIGNATURE
SITES HIGHLY APPROPRIATE FOR RESIDENCES

BIOLOGICAL
CULTURAL
PHYSICAL
AESTHETIC

SITE SIGNATURE Right 372.0

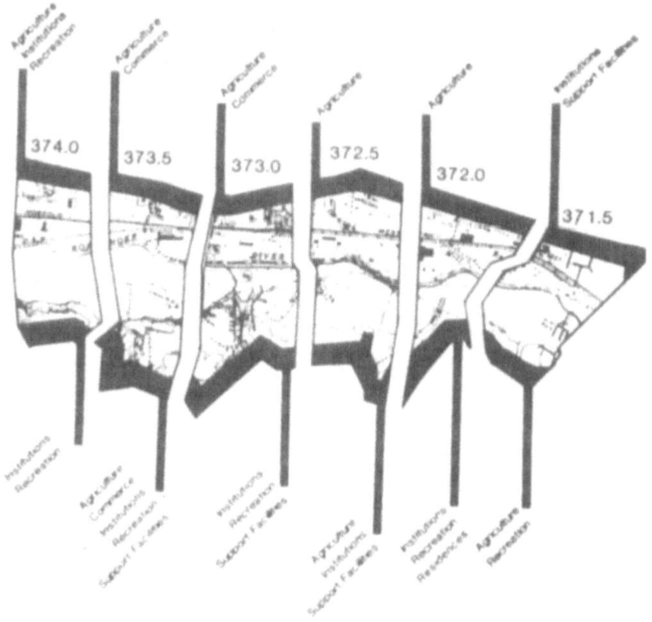

Top: ***Fig. 6. Site Right 372.0 is appropriate for residences. The physical character of the site across river rules it out for same land use.***
Bottom: ***Fig. 7. Portion of the Land Suitability Plan for the Roanoke River Corridor.***

PROPOSED LAND USE ______

SITE RIGHT BANK - 572.0

LOCATION RIVERSIDE DRIVE @ SR 694

APPROPRIATE LAND USES INSTITUTIONS, RECREATION, RESIDENCES

PROPOSAL ______

EVALUATOR ______

DATE ______

RIVER CORRIDOR DESIGN EVALUATION

	CHARACTERISTIC	CRITERIA	NOTES
*	UNIQUE HABITATS	No construction in delineated areas. Potential indirect impact is determined by expert at preliminary review.	
	RIVER & RIPARIAN STRIP	Only those activities which are inseparable from river water use are allowed within 100' of bank.	
	SWALES	Design must not interrupt established vegetative cover. Construction breaks are to be replanted in accordance with tree ordinance.	
	FRAGILE HABITATS	Erosion & Sedimentation Control Plan required. Zero Net Runoff Formula, Zero Net Non-point Source Pollution Formula required.	
	ACCESS TO RIVER	Public easement access required in 100' Riparian Strip.	
*	ARCHAEOLOGICAL SITES	Virginia Center for Archaeological Research is to be notified and allowed access to all threshold sites for 1 year interim period before site disturbance.	
	HISTORICAL/CULTURAL SITES	Options determined at preliminary site plan review.	
*	UNIQUE IMAGEABILITY	Design must perform to Imageability Formula.	
	FRAGILE VIEWS & VARIETY OF IMAGES	Noted landmarks shall not be blocked from the viewpoint of the riparian strip. Before/After impact sketches required at final review.	
*	ENCROACHMENT OF INTEGRITY	Encroaching elements are to be removed from the landscape before issuance of certificate of occupancy.	
	WATER QUALITY	All Projects--Zero Net Non-point Source Pollution Formula.	
*	FLOODPLAIN	Structures floodproofed to currents of 15f/s. Construction must leave No net change in flood elevation. No Habitable Floors Below 100 yr. Flood Elev.	
	ERODABILITY	All Projects--Executed in accordance with Virginia Erosion & Sedimentation Control Standards.	
	SEPTIC SUITABILITY	Septic fields prohibited above the major groundwater recharge zone.	
	FOUNDATION SUITABILITY	Refer to Soil Survey for preliminary performance predictions.	
	AQUIFER ZONE	Zero Net Runoff Formula.	

APPROVAL:

PRELIMINARY ______

FINAL ______

Fig. 8. A Design Evaluation Sheet set up for the conditions of the example site. The example site has five special requirements beyond those of the conventional code. They are highlighted with an (*) on the sheet.

pect of mitigating some potential land uses with the difficult conditions of some sites will be either physically or financially impossible, thus preserving them. Other sites will have few or no difficult constraints posed by site conditions, and can be developed intensively. Figure 8 shows how the method directly transfers "is" statements to "Thou shalt" statements. Proposed designs perform to existing stable amenities by passing impact formulae or by avoiding fragile areas.

Expert plan review is arranged for evaluation of rapidly changing or extremely fragile criteria. This will assist the developer, who sometimes has little knowledge of the requirements of the social and natural landscape, but has an ability to recognize the cost of dealing with the legislated constraints posed by some sites. More importantly, this will assist the local planning body, for discretionary controls require informed and defensible decisions. Of course, all site sheets and design requirements must be available to the public, so Site Signature Method assessments must be in a tight, implementable package. The studies are detailed, decisions are traceable, and the product can be reproduced.

III. DEVELOPING WITH THE RIVER

During the next decade, construction in the Upper Roanoke River Basin and especially in the Roanoke River Corridor, will determine the health of the natural and social environments for many decades to come. The current threshold state of the riparian landscape can go either toward a sensitively planned resource or an ecologically and visually dead nuisance. The difference in the future of the corridor lies in the communities' willingness to implement and enforce performance development standards. The answer is that simple. Conventional zoning is either unnecessarily prohibitive (hence politically undesirable) or an ineffective check on the crucial criteria of the district.

The first wave of construction in the Roanoke River Corridor will be the completion of public infrastructure. Site specific conditions will be of particular importance to roadway planning, water and sewer line construction, and park and parkway construction. The Roanoke Valley governments have both the background information and the methodology to put this information to meaningful use. It is especially important that public works projects set the example by employing site specific criteria for the upcoming multi-site projects.

It has been only in the last several years that we have seen a shift in attention to the Roanoke River Corridor as a popular issue. The new Roanoke County land use plans and zoning ordinance and the creation of the River Foundation have the potential to set milestones in the health of the river corridor. The Roanoke River Reclamation Project has been designed to be extended along the linear corridor from headwaters to the sea. There are several special concerns that surface when one plans an environmentally performance-based linear district. One in particular is that the multiple land uses proposed for the corridor may not be compatible with each other. This suitability concern has been incorporated as an addendum into the evaluation stage of proposed projects. To improve this method, adjacent land use compatibility needs to be considered in the inventory stage.

The Roanoke River Reclamation Project proposes a mediator between the developer, scientist and constituent by addressing the concerns of each. By employing the mediator, the landscape can be developed without loss of biological, cultural, aesthetic or physical resources. This "site specific zoning" results in an appropriately developed landscape which celebrates the character of the river corridor.

BIBLIOGRAPHY

Amato, Roger V. Geology of the Salem Quadrangle, Va. Charlottesville: Virginia Division of Mineral Resources, 1974.

Barber, Michael B. Personal Discussion. 1983. (Dr. Barber is archaeologist for Jefferson National Forest and teaches at Radford University.)

Burkhead, Noel M. and Rodney Jenkins. Personal Discussion. 1983. (Drs. Burkhead and Jenkins are faculty members, Department of Biology, Roanoke College, Salem, Virginia.)

Hill, David P. "The Site Signature Method of Land Suitability Planning in River Corridors." Ed. Roy Johnson. Riparian Ecosystems and Their Management. Tucson: University of Arizona Press. 1985.

Hill, David P. The Site Signature Method of Land Suitability Planning and the Roanoke River Reclamation Project. Blacksburg, Va.: David P. Hill, 1984.

Jones, Grant and R. Jones. 1973, Nooksack. Seatle, Wash.: Jones and Jones, Inc., 1973.

Litton, R. Burton, et al. Water and Landscape. Port Washington, New York. Water Information Center. 1974.

Nolen, John. "Comprehensive City Plan for Roanoke, Virginia." Cambridge, Massachusetts. 1928.

The Resources Group. Visual Analysis of the Roanoke River Corridor. (Research used for Environmental Impact Statement for Flood Damage Reduction, Roanoke River Upper Basin, Virginia.) Wilmington, N.C. U.S. Army Corps of Engineers, 1983.

Wilson's Creek National Battlefield

Allan B. Cooksey, A.S.L.A., and Peter A. Oppermann, A.S.L.A.[1]

The Battle of Wilson's Creek, named for the stream that crosses the area, was a bitter one fought between defending Union forces and invading Confederate forces for control of Missouri. The battle took place ten miles southwest of Springfield, Missouri, on August 10, 1861, the first year of the Civil War.

Although Union forces under the command of Brigadier General Nathaniel Lyon did not win the battle, they succeeded in keeping Missouri under Union control. Their success helped strengthen the position of Kentucky Unionists, who also kept much of their state loyal to the Union. Historians believe secession by Missouri and Kentucky would have strengthened chances of a Confederate victory in the Civil War.[2]

Brigadier General Lyon died in the Battle of Wilson's Creek. Public Law 86-434 established Wilson's Creek National Battlefield in 1960. Following the National Park Service's acquisition of 1,752 acres of the battlefield site, Public Law 91-554 provided $2,285,000 in 1970 for development of the battlefield.

Wilson's Creek National Battlefield is located 200 miles southwest of St. Louis, Missouri, 180 miles southeast of Kansas City, Missouri, and ten miles southwest of Springfield, Missouri. (Figure 1) It is the only national historic landmark in the surrounding ten-county region. The 1,752 acres of Wilson's Creek National Battlefield are typical of the Ozarks—rolling, hilly, and rocky. The area had changed little since the 1861 battle, and land was used primarily for farming until it was acquired by the National Park Service.

The first changes in the park area were minor site improvements to meet initial and short-term visitor needs. The Visitors' Center and the Tour Road followed.

The Visitors' Center, with its displays and fiberoptic interpretation of the battle, sets the stage for the struggle that was the Battle of Wilson's Creek and conveys Missouri's 1861 political and social climate. For many years before the Civil War, Missouri had been the scene of bitter conflict over the extension of slavery; the state was a microcosm of the nation. The Visitors' Center's interpretive program places the struggle in Missouri in the context of the Civil War as a whole and gives a sense of the conflict's fratricidal nature.

Interpretation of the Battle of Wilson's Creek takes place along the length of the 4.8-mile Tour Road. Using living history, recorded narrations, and the historic scene, interpretive areas help visitors understand not only what occurred on August 10, 1861, but also what it meant to the area and the nation.

The park has four major interpretive areas:

1. the hills and valley of Wilson's Creek,
2. the Ray House, from which John Ray observed the battle,
3. Sharp's Farm, which was Union Colonel Franz Sigel's third deployment of artillery, and
4. Bloody Hill, the scene of the fiercest fighting in the battle.

Our firm, Tuttle-Ayers-Woodward Co., which is a division of Shafer, Kline & Warren, P.A., was selected in 1978 to be a member of the consultant team that would design and develop the Visitor's Center and Tour Road according to the National Park Service Master Plan. (Figure 2) Our firm's planning and design responsibilities for the Visitors' Center were:

1. relocation of an intersection at the park entrance, plans for service drives, park access roads, and parking lot;
2. complete domestic water supply system including chlorinization from a deep-well source;
3. fire protection system with a 50,000-gallon underground reservoir;
4. physical/chemical sanitary treatment facility; and

70
WILSON'S
CREEK
NATIONAL
BATTLEFIELD
44

STATE OF MISSOURI
KANSAS
CITY
65
ST.
LOUIS
44
NORTH
60
WILSON'S
CREEK
WILSON'S CREEK
NATIONAL BATTLEFIELD
UNITED STATES DEPARTMENT OF
THE INTERIOR
NATIONAL PARK SERVICE
LEGEND
LAKES COUNTRY REGION
STATE PARK

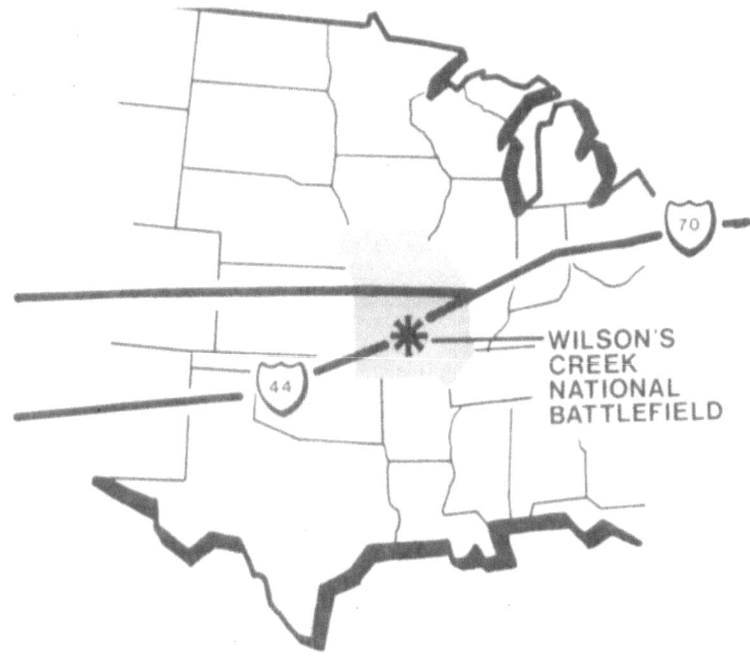

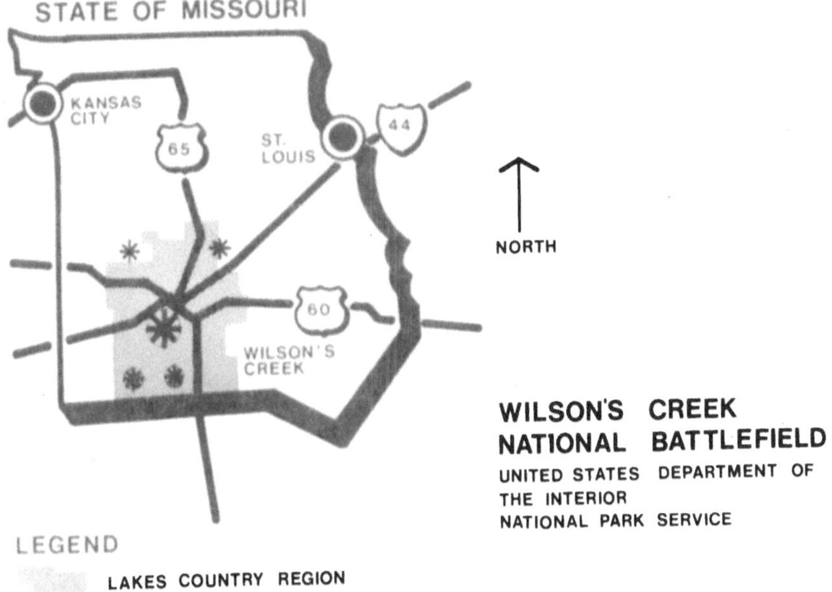

Fig. 1.

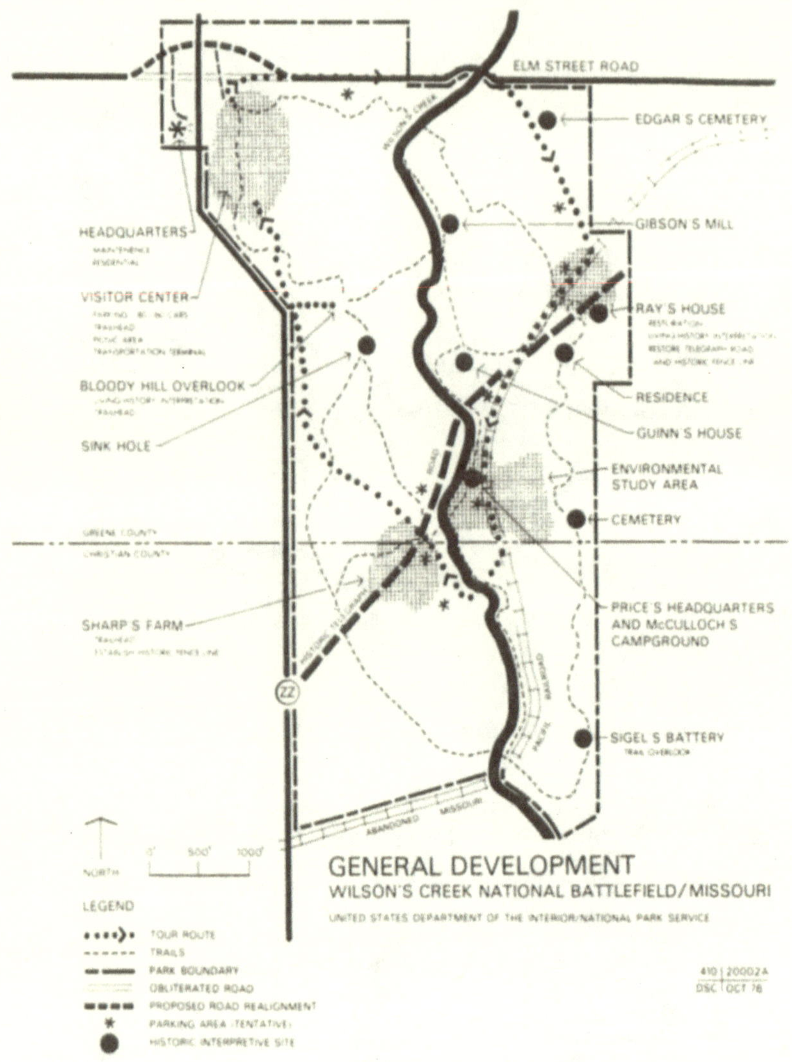

Fig. 2.

5. site grading, utilities layout, pavement design, construction details, and specifications.

Construction of the Visitors' Center was completed in 1983, and the Tour Road was completed in 1986.

THE TOUR ROAD

We included initial planning for the Tour Road in the Visitors' Center phase that began in 1978. Our responsibilities for the final design phase included civil engineering, landscape architecture, and land surveying for the 4.8-mile Road, which would include three bridges; seven historical turnouts with parking for cars,

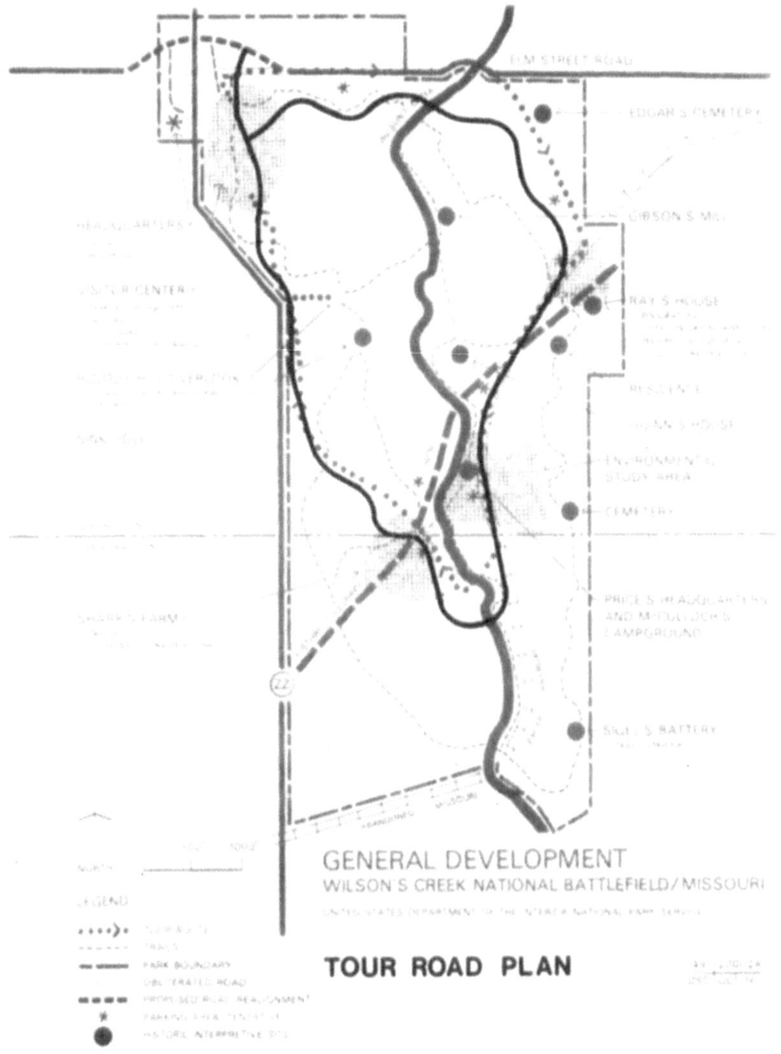

Fig. 3.

buses, recreation vehicles, and bicycles; four pullovers; three concrete box culverts; many roadway culverts; and revegetation plans. During construction we provided construction-related services that included shop drawing review, field change orders, center line staking, grade staking, slope staking, and plant material location staking.

We designed the Tour Road in accordance with the master plan under the supervision of the National Park Service Denver Service Center. Design criteria included the following interpretive requirements.

1. Provide vehicular routing sequential to the battle in a clockwise direction from the Visitors' Center. (Figure 3)

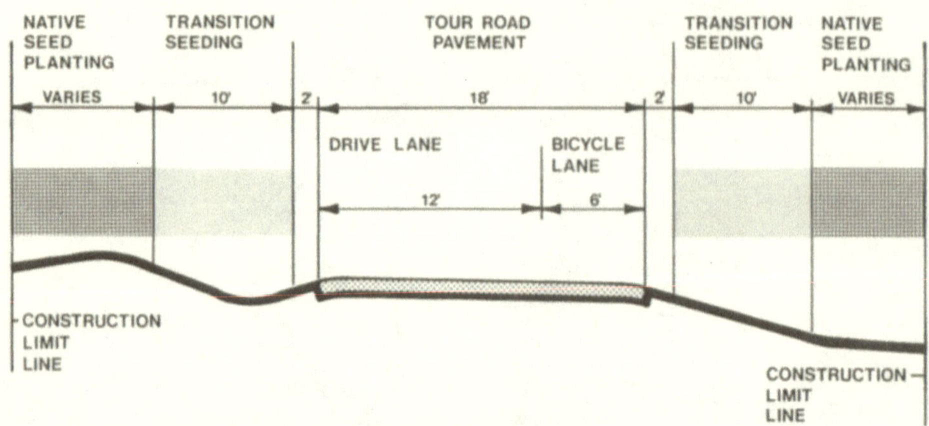

NATIVE SEED PLANTING
TRANSITION SEEDING
TOUR ROAD PAVEMENT
TRANSITION SEEDING
NATIVE SEED PLANTING
VARIES
10'
2'
18'
2'
10'
VARIES
DRIVE LANE
BICYCLE LANE
12'
6'
CONSTRUCTION LIMIT LINE
CONSTRUCTION LIMIT LINE
TYPICAL TOUR ROAD DETAIL - SECTION
NO SCALE

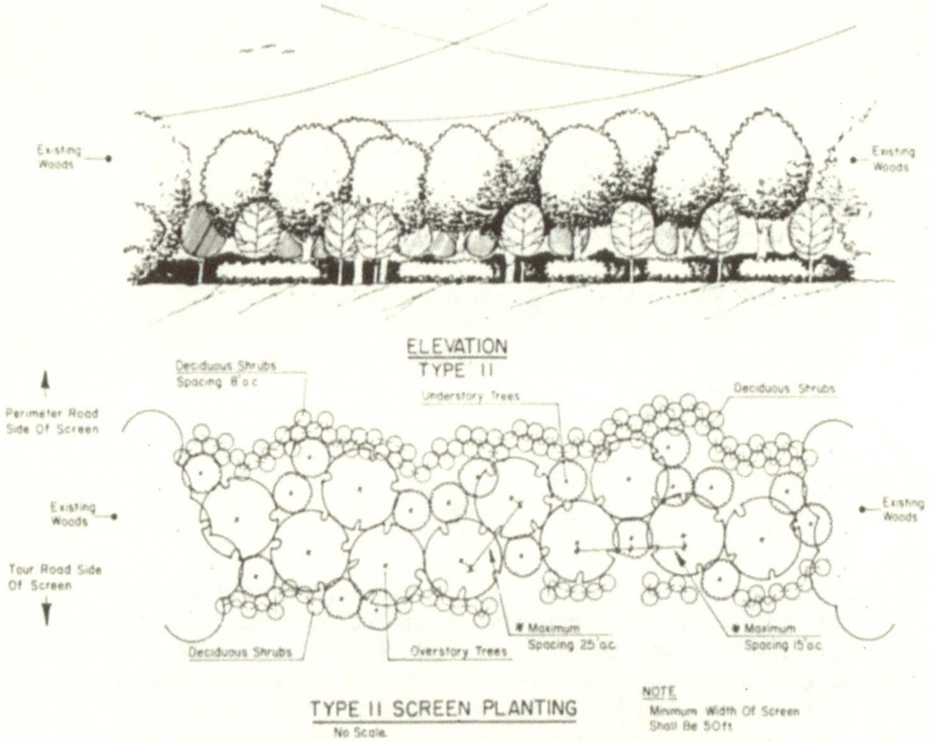

Existing Woods
Existing Woods
ELEVATION
TYPE II
Deciduous Shrubs Spacing 8' o.c.
Understory Trees
Deciduous Shrubs
Perimeter Road Side Of Screen
Existing Woods
Existing Woods
Tour Road Side Of Screen
* Maximum Spacing 25' o.c.
* Maximum Spacing 15' o.c.
Deciduous Shrubs
Overstory Trees
TYPE II SCREEN PLANTING
No Scale.
NOTE
Minimum Width Of Screen Shall Be 50ft.

Top: *Fig. 4.* Bottom: *Fig. 5.*

2. Design a one-way road 20+_ feet wide with shoulders to accommodate a speed of 20 miles per hour. (Figure 4)
3. Minimize the physical and visual effect of the road on the park and maximize the park's use and accessibility to interpretive areas.
4. Restore previous areas of resource disturbance to conditions that existed at the time of the battle. (Figure 5)

The Tour Road was initially planned for two-phased construction but was constructed in a single phase under supervision of the Federal Highway Administration and directed by the National Park Service. As part of our plans for the Road, bridges, and parking areas, we were to obliterate 11,000 feet of roadway, restore the natural contours and vegetation, emplace 6,900 feet of stabilized turf for walking trails, and revegetate nearly 40 acres disturbed during construction.

National Park Service staff members conducted an environmental assessment of the selected Tour Road alignment to evaluate the natural system, cultural environment, socioeconomic environment, and visitor use.

The Tour Road begins a few hundred feet southeast of the Visitors' Center and heads east. At its start, the Road descends gently through scattered woods with dense understory and passes the area at which Union forces entered the battlefield. The Road then skirts a small spring and breaks through the heavy vegetation. Continuing east, the Road crosses an intermittent Wilson's Creek tributary and passes an ancient Indian chipping area to the first of two bridges over Wilson's Creek.

The turnout for the Gibson's Mill trailhead is immediately past the bridge, and the interpretive display includes appurtenances we designed for all the turnouts—wheel stops, bicycle parking racks, and wooden bollards.

Leaving Gibson's Mill, the Tour Road undulates along the rolling terrain past Edgar Cemetery and through open meadows. As it approaches the Ray House from the north, the Tour Road passes over a large box culvert.

Although signs clearly mark the Ray House turnout, the ample parking area is concealed from visitors who choose to drive past. A stairway and continuing walkway provide access to the Ray House; a series of ramps and walks provide access for visitors who have disabilities.

South from the Ray House for nearly two miles, the Tour Road is built upon an abandoned railroad right-of-way and passes through heavy timber with steep, rocky slopes. Taking advantage of the railroad bed eliminates the need for large cuts in the wooded limestone ridge that parallels the east side of Wilson's Creek. A mile south of the Ray House, visitors find the turnout and short walk that lead to the location of the major Confederate artillery position during the battle.

The Tour Road continues south turning 180° in a long, sweeping curve with a bridge that crosses Wilson's Creek and heads north toward Sharp's Farm. Discovery and evaluation of an archeological site prompted relocation of the Wilson's Creek crossing 1,500 feet south of the original crossing location.

Approaching the Sharp's Farm turnout across a wide meadow, visitors can visualize Colonel Sigel's final artillery placement on the brow of a steep hill that overlooked the Confederate encampment during the battle.

The Tour Road descends steeply (12 percent slope) from Sharp's Farm, crosses Skegg's branch at the bottom of the hill, and proceeds north toward Bloody Hill. The terrain is rolling and has heavy understory. Parking areas at the Bloody Hill turnout are concealed from both the interpretive display and the trailhead several hundred feet to the east.

Past Bloody Hill, the Tour Road parallels the Union forces' entry into and retreat from the battlefield, passes through heavy timber and steep slopes, and returns to the Road's beginning.

Along its route, the Tour Road passes close to the battlefield boundary and adjacent roads. In order to preserve the experience for visitors and to prevent unauthorized access from adjacent roads, we designed plantings of native species in selected natural locations. With time, the screens will absorb into existing vegetative communities.

We introduced native grasses and forbs (nearly 50 species) in disturbed areas along the Tour Road to provide a revegetated base comparable to that at the time of the battle. In addition, plantings will provide a continuing source of native seed that can be used to revegetate other areas of the battlefield.

CONCLUSION

The development of Wilson's Creek National Battlefield is the result of the efforts of many dedicated individuals and organizations, ranging from local residents first concerned with the battle's significance to Missouri's state legislators to the U.S. Congress to the National Park Service and the Federal Highway Administration.

Our firm's multi-disciplined design team included professional engineers, landscape architects, and land surveyors with support staff in each area to prepare plans and specifications. During the design phase, we visited the site frequently to evaluate design plans in light of conditions at the battlefield. We walked the proposed sites, evaluated cut-and-fill needs, determined culvert locations and lengths, and examined the site effect and extent of revegetation required. We became intimately aware of site conditions and the need to minimize alterations of the resource.

An example of the care we took in our design is the relocation of a portion of the Tour Road. The center line was staked and evaluated when our design team walked the alignment with National Park Service personnel and decided to realign approximately three-fourths of a mile. We wanted to avoid disturbing the ancient Indian chipping area and removing a solitary red elm in the open meadow between the first two bridges. We redesigned the alignment of both bridges and their adjoining section of roadway.

In another instance, we lowered the Ray House turnout elevation two feet so that visitors to the Ray House would not have their view of the battlefield impeded by buses in the parking area. We realigned the Tour Road near the Sharp Farm to avoid affecting the location of the long since removed Sharp cabin.

We are grateful for the opportunity to participate in the development of Wilson's Creek National Battlefield, to be a part of the effort to preserve our past in the present for the future.

NOTES

1. Peter A. Oppermann, A.S.L.A., is land planning director for Shafer, Kline & Warren, P.A., Overland Park, Kansas; Allan B. Cooksey, A.S.L.A., is land planning director for the firm's division, Tuttle-Ayers-Woodward Co., Kansas City, Missouri.
2. Master Plan, Wilson's Creek National Battlefield, National Park Service, Denver Service Center, March 30, 1977.

BIBLIOGRAPHY

Archeological Survey and Testing, Tour Road Alternatives, A, B, and C. Wilson's Creek National Battlefield, Midwest Archeological Center, National Park Service, 1982

Environmental Assessment, Tour Road, Wilson's Creek National Battlefield, National Park Service, Midwest Region, 1982

Final Interpretive Prospectus, Wilson's Creek National Battlefield, National Park Service, Denver Service Center, 1975

Historic Base and Ground Cover Map Study, National Park Service, Denver Service Center, 1978

Master Plan, Wilson's Creek National Battlefield, National Park Service, Denver Service Center, March 30, 1977

Prairie Propagation Handbook, Boerner Botanical Gardens, Whitnall Park, Hales Corner, Wisconsin, 1975

Standard Specifications for Construction of Roads and Bridges on Federal Highway Projects, FP-79, U.S. Department of Transportation, Federal Highway Administration, 1979

"DR. MITCHELL'S RESTING PLACE" BENJAMIN PORTER

III. Historical Perspectives

Benjamin Porter: "If life in the mountains is a gift from God, then the Blue Ridge Parkway is the highway to heaven. . . . An exotic land lies outside my back door, and it's the Parkway that carries me there. No passports needed. And, Dr. Mitchell, I'd like to think you smile in the joy we tourists have travelling these mountains. For how can we help smiling when we find your resting place where your mountain meets the clouds?"

Appalachian Heroes as an Indicator of Appalachian Space: Changes in the Meaning of Appalachian Space and Time, 1858-1985

David P. Hill

ABSTRACT—The last one-hundred and thirty years mark an era of constant assault on the synergism of the man-land relationship unique in American experience. This paper will first discuss the events that distinguished the Southern Highlands and the rural land use patterns that were established and assaulted. Each assault came in the form of technological advances developed outside the region penetrating and saturating the Highlands. Each assault, even though it involved a product of industrial America, could be more precisely described as a conflict of values between the established Appalachian society and the outside American society. Having the technological achievements available to the region, and with the cultural and natural resource exploitation of the region, it is amazing that the patterns of Appalachian space held together as long as they did. Only since World War II has there finally been a breakdown in the rural land use pattern. This paper, through a history of sacred and profane iconography of the region, discusses the rise and fall of Appalachian space.

The Southern Highlands region of the United States has produced one of the most distinctive of American cultural landscapes. Within a century after colonization of the back mountain coves, the highland culture developed as one of the most isolated cultures in the history of the civilized world. This isolation provided the potential for an intense reliance on nature and natural phenomena, and fostered an intense commitment to religion. Despite assaults from all physiographical and sociological fronts during the second century of the culture, the conceptual rural farming patterns of the region remained steadfast, and it was not until the last four decades that the patterns of Appalachian space have begun to deteriorate.

Isolated development is one of the characteristics of rural agricultural areas in the Southern Highlands portion of the Appalachian Region. The western portions of Virginia and North Carolina are included in this province, as well as eastern portions of Kentucky, Tennessee, and West Virginia. The landscape of this region is marginally arable. Developing in isolation and having strong religious and individualistic ideals, the Appalachian farming families expressed these ideals in their crafts, land use patterns and folk songs. These form statements of democratic individualism and religious symbolism that are highly worthy of attention. In order to understand the changes in the cultural land use patterns, the first topic will be the role of the mountain as the primary determinant of Appalachian space. The historic roots of Appalachian attitudes toward mountains will be examined. These attitudes have specified the farming patterns of the region. After establishment of the historical pattern, this paper discusses the physiographic changes brought about by modernization of the mountain environment. Cultural changes can be detected by applying this simple ordering postulate: through a topographic slice, the relative cultural value of objects and issues can be determined by their relative elevation in the landscape.

By noticing the relative elevation of elements in the Highland landscape, it becomes apparent that the hero of Appalachian space has changed twice in the last one-hundred and thirty years. There have been two prominent changes in the ordering of Appalachian space. Spacial transformations have occurred as a result of changes in the travel industry from 1859 to 1986, and as changes have happened in the post-war era from 1945 to 1986. These "improvements" have shifted the primary determinant of land use patterns in the region. Modernization of the Southern Highlands has changed the way people have regarded mountains. With every technological advance, the mountains become a little less heroic, a little less sacred, and the natural environment becomes less meaningful.

I. HEROES IN A PROMISED LAND

SUBLIME HEROES

Since the beginning of American westward expansion the Mountains have been revered. The reverence takes many forms, but the mysterious qualities of the landscape are frequently present in writings, folksongs, in the paintings, and in land use. Thomas Jefferson, in a gesture of symbolism, perched his Monticello on a small knob at the eastern edge of the Appalachians and faced it west.[1] Jefferson certainly was not the average Appalachian of the time, but he gives incredible insight into settlement attitudes regarding mountain space and mountain sentiment. He gives us an example of eighteenth century reverence of the mountains with his commissioned descriptive passage about the Shenandoah. Query IV of his Notes on the State of Virginia (1785) is entitled simply "Mountains." While pursuing a descriptive passage, he suddenly is compelled to write:

> *The passage of the Patowmac through the Blue Ridge is one of the most stupendous scenes in nature. You stand on a very high point of land. On your right comes up the Shenandoah, having ranged along the foot of the Mountain an hundred miles to seek a vent. On your left approaches the Patowmac, in quest of a passage also. In the moment of their junction they rush together against the mountain, render it asunder, and pass off to the sea.... It is as placid and delightful, as is wild and tremendous...*

Jefferson not only admired the mountains, he bought them. With the land supplied to the U.S. by his Louisiana Purchase and the ideal of the pastoral farmer he professed, Jefferson created a land use system that has existed in the Southern Highlands until this date. (NOTE: Even though Jefferson's house occupied a knoll, it was carefully placed in a modest landscape position. Only in the last 20 years has someone built a house on the grassy hilltop behind Monticello, commanding a view over the place!)

ROOTS

The first permanent European settlement in the Highlands began in the 1730's with German settlers coming down the Shenandoah Valley from Philadelphia. The Scotch-Irish followed down the funnel in the 1740's, occupying the lands not inhabited by the Germans. The Scots hailed mainly from lowland Scottish areas, with soil and climate similar to the Valley. Most of the settlers were protestant, and the Scotch-Irish were aggressively independent. They made ideal frontiersmen, and stayed in the uplands as other groups went further west. The Germans settled in the bottomlands of the valleys, and the Scots moved beyond them into the coves of the mountains. There the cultural land use pattern was established.

For over 100 years, the mountaineers survived on the marginal landscape with independent, self-sufficient farms. The end of the French and Indian War of the 1760's opened the wilderness to travel, and over the next five decades an ethnic mixture of settlers poured through the region and onto the Great Plains beyond. Places off the beaten path developed in isolation from these corridors, and over a century established, as John Opie (1981) explains, from the Great Valley to the Midwestern Prairie, one of the world's great agricultural traditions. "Several features of this tradition were unique and gave the American society its distinctive coloration."

> *The frontier farmer labored through his days and nights in intense isolation. His degree of separation from the civilized world was unprecedented in human history and formed the backdrop for his thoughts and actions. More often than not the farmer and his family were literally "off the map," having settled on land that had not been explored, surveyed, or mapped. The impact of backwoods isolation is suggested by the intensity of frontier religion, especially highly emotional camp meeting revivalism* (Opie, 1981:62).

Human settlement and farming patterns in Appalachia were masterfully sewn to the land using religious beliefs as a thread. This can be seen at the regional scale, at the site scale with farm land use, and down to the smallest detail of the planting calendar.

AN APPALACHIAN PORTRAIT

The Highland Culture is distinguished by its capacity for non-discursive thought patterns (Wagner, 1981). Non-discursive thought patterns allow for more than one explanation to account for an occurrence. Frequently events are explained scientifically and with traditional sayings such as "If you don't cuss, you'll never raise gourds," or "If the bread's burnt the cook's mad." This harmony of myth and reason in Appalachia shows up in stories, folk song and land use patterns. "The superstitions are almost proverbs - they deal with social style as much as natural or supernatural occurrence (Whisnant, 1975)." The spiritual reasons for action are often tied to religious bases, and even though it may not have been the way the first Southern Highland farms were planned, religious belief grew to be associated with land use patterns.

In 1880, the average Appalachian farm consisted of 187 acres, of which 25 percent was cultivated, 20 percent was cleared pasture and the remainder was virgin forest (Eller, 1982). Within the typical farm, there was hierarchical organization of elements, based on the physical and the symbolic forms afforded by the topography. The farmhouses and outbuildings were typically sited in the valleys or on the lower slopes. There was a rationale for this. The houses benefit from their location near springs. There are symbolic reasons for it as well. The valleys feel protected between peaks, but more importantly the house in the valley is in the modest landscape location.

The dwelling area was surrounded on the slopes by the meadows, fields and orchards. The Appalachian husbandman worked God's fields in the day and then walked back down to Nature's protective valley at night. From the fields, the farmhouse in the valley was a safe and modest scene. From the farmhouse, the framework, rolling over the rising hills, appeared to have heightened importance. The successful farmer began to identify with his landscape. John Opie (1977) explains that, "the land was part of his own personal identity; conversely, he invented the place where he lived, creating it out of wilderness placelessness. This built landscape signalled to him his chances for survival."

Property lines ran back and forth along ridge-tops, cutting the farms into viewsheds. This was a very practical and safe way to divide land. The house was visible from the fields, and the surrounding fields were always in view from the house. Symbolically, this pattern created a sense of "one-ness" for each farm. The isolation created from the land use patterns fostered the mountaineer's independent attitude. Each bowl-shaped farm functioned as an independent organism. The daily life of the husbandman was a scene from Jefferson's picturesque painting of American agrarian life. The vernacular landscape designs had some symbolic meaning in the Southern Highlands; they provided the mountains as heroic monuments in an everyday landscape.

The picturesque farm scene and the sublime mountain scene composed the visual poetry of Appalachian Space. The higher the position of something, the more it was removed toward Heaven, and the more it was revered. Mountains themselves crowned the top of the order. Then came the ancestors of the husbandmen. The farmhouse typically occupied the valley in view from the hilltop family cemetery. The remains of immortal souls were silent on the timeless mountain. From the mountaintop, the house and fields in the valley below the cemetery were picturesque scenes. From the valley, the cemetery was in the realm of the sublime. Just as it conferred a kind of immortality on the dead, the cemetery determined descendants' actions for years to come. Children, of course, were born and raised in the valley, the most fertile area of the land. To construct a house in the valley, the farmer cut and dragged the logs from the surrounding woodlands down to the site where the cabin was assembled. The log house not only offered shelter from the environ-

Fig. 1. A Southwestern Virginia farm scene exhibiting traditional land use pattern.

ment, it quite literally was shelter constructed from the environment.

The mountains were the first heroes of Appalachia. All heroes have nicknames, and now maps of the mountains reveal the affection and territoriality within the terrain. Gender roles paralleled topographic contours. In North Carolina, for example, Grandmother Gap rests next to Grandfather Mountain. Communities named themselves to celebrate their ties with God and mountains. Mount Zion, Mount Olivet, and Mount Hope are all on the map of the region. Mountains created a framework for farm life, which in turn created a mountaineer's sense of place. The family identified with its farm in the cradle in the mountain. John Opie (1977) argues that the mountaineer's sense of place goes beyond family or even religious ties. He describes a solidarity with the homeplace as a "chthonic mystery," and in working the soil by manual means, the farmer has an intense personal, psychological and spiritual experience. "The rhythms of vegetation simultaneously reveal the mystery of life and creation and the mystery of youth, and immortality."

SACRED MOUNTAINS: APPALACHIA'S FIRST HERO

There are three cross-denominational religious consciousnesses in the Appalachian region: the zionistic, the evangelical and the mainstream Christian (Humphrey, 1984). The churches with a zionistic consciousness provide a case in point of the religious metaphor in the hills, for the tenets of these churches declare that Southern Appalachia is God's promised land. There is a sacred bond with one's geographic place and scripture is used to define planting and harvesting times.

An older woman from Watauga County, North Carolina powerfully describes this hold the land has on the people. "Our people are attached to the valleys and mountains all around us. It's been our home for generations. They have the land, the place . . . People offer us money for our land but we don't want to sell it. You just don't want to be cut off from the sacredness of your land."

Humphrey describes Psalms 121:1-2 as reference to the sacred nature of mountainous places. "I will lift up mine eyes unto the hills from whence cometh my help. My help cometh from the Lord which made Heaven and Earth." The passage from Psalms gives insight into the location of the house in the modest landscape position, and it also supports the family cemetery's traditional location on the hilltop.

The evangelical consciousness thrives on conversion and "rebirth" of its members, and professes that if people don't subdue nature it is at the expense of their own souls. Zionism helped to create the agricultural land use pattern, and during the time of mountain industrialization, evangelism provided an excuse for those who were forced by economic necessity to move to the milltowns and mining towns. Humphrey notes that evangelism "provided rationale for selling, leaving, changing, or destroying one's land and homeplace." Mainstream religion is also antagonistic to the zionistic consciousness. The wealthier professionals typify the mainstream consciousness. These are the people who manage the mines, or have the second homes in Appalachia.

Mainstream Christianity crept into the mountains just before the turn of the twentieth century, and the objective train of thought professed by these faiths runs contrary to the intense man-land emotional relationship which had evolved over the years. It is no accident that the mine managers (mainstream Christian) typically located their homes on the mountaintops, where the miners (zionist or evangelical) graciously occupied the houses in the camps in the Valleys below.

The establishment of mountains as heroes in a topographical order provided the possibility for several spatial phenomena: the importance of elevation and its vantage points, the importance of monuments, the importance of enclosure, and the relationship of these concepts to scale and time in the environment. However, the complexities of this system were not a concern of the outsider. By the one hundred and twentieth year after Appalachian settlement, the first challenge to the Appalachian hero was getting its finishing touches.

II. TECHNOLOGY: THE EMERGENT SUPER-HERO OF THE 19TH CENTURY

The first blow to the Mountain culture was the result of a conscious assault on the region from the outside. Beginning in the late 1850's and really thriving in the period following the Civil War was the period of mountain industrialization. The railroad companies of the 1850's and Uncle Sam's highways of the mid 1900's provided the figurative and the literal vehicles for exploitation of the mountain environment. Exploitation came in the form of the double bladed axe and the double bladed pick: while chopping the natural resources from the hills the new exploitative systems undercut the cultural patterns which had developed in the isolated mountains.

FIRE ON THE MOUNTAIN: RAILROAD AS HERO

The railroad changed the perception of Appalachian scale by the changes it made in the passage through Appalachian space. The railroad reduced mountains to objects which could be quickly surmounted. They became less sacred with easy travel through, over and under them. As the railroads sliced over, around and through the mountains, travelers' perceptions shifted from the mountains as sublime to technology as sublime.

Railroad technology and railroad advertising provided a change in the concept of Appalachian time. They brought to the Highlands a vast number of people who would seize this new development as an opportunity for exploitation of Appalachian resources - both natural and cultural. Cultural resources appeared to the mining and lumber barons as cheap labor, and when dealing with a culture that did not understand the meaning of the phrase "mineral rights," cultural exploitation was manifest by the acquisition of legal mineral rights to land almost free of charge.

Travel into the pioneer Southern Highlands had been along the early roads of the valley floors as they wove through mountain gaps. To the traveler, the Appalachians symbolized the great barrier to the Great Plains. The carriage roads along the valleys occupied the lowpoint of the landscape. With travel at a slow horse's pace, there can be no doubt that the traveler experienced the mountains to their utmost size and scale. The mountains in the earlier frontier represented the dark and dangerous qualities of the truly sublime. To the outlander, mountains held a special sense of reverence, and this was expressed in the humbling experiences while traveling through the region. Porte Crayon, one of Appalachia's well known travel artists of the 1800's, describes travel along the roadways to a spring in 1857 (from Fishwick, 1987):

> *The tired horses jogged on, fetlock-deep in dust. Deep forests grew taller and gloomier. There utter darkness closed her wing over all the land. . . . Mice, the driver was frightened. So were all the passengers. Nothing ahead but utter darkness. "We must trust the instinct of the horses," Mice said. . . .*

Instincts had to suffice in the dark. The outlander did not like to rely on what little providence can be found in these older methods, and industrial interests were bent on finding an alternative way to get into and through the "savage mountains." These days of slow and modest travel in the Southern Highlands were over when in 1858, after great expense, the Baltimore and Ohio Railroad opened its track from Baltimore to Charleston, West Virginia. As an advertising ploy, the B & O invited a group of prominent East Coast artists, journalists and politicos to a complimentary trip through the "wild and tremendous" scene Mr. Jefferson had described 73 years before as "worth a voyage across the Atlantic." Harper's Magazine (6/1859) reviewed the trip[2] and in the first paragraph of the article we get a vivid picture of the changed nature of travel in the mountains.

> *The ages of gold, and of silver, of brass, and iron, as described by the poets, are past. The present is the age of steam. . . . The real and the ideal have smoked pipes together. The iron horse and Pegasus have trotted side by side in double harness, puffing in unison, like a well-trained pair. What will be the result of this conjunction Heaven knows.*

The author of this passage was chiefly concerned with the social relationships that were to occur on the train, but the weight of his comments about scenery could not have been more appropriate. It is the author's later passages which indicate that the Appalachian Mountains were, in conjunction with steam power, capable of producing an experience of the technological sublime. "(The train) was composed of six cars, drawn by engine No. 232—a miracle of power, speed, and beauty, and much the same animal as Job had in his eye when he described Leviathon," he continues.

> *As we approached Harper's Ferry, suddenly a cry was raised on the foremost platform, which was repeated from car to car until the whole train resounded with the exultant shout, "The sun! the sun!" The dim clouds, broken and flying, hastened from the fields like a routed army, while the conquerer appeared in all his might and majesty. The heavens shone clear and blue as a baby's eye; the tender leafage of the mountains looked fresh as a budding girlhood; the swelling bosom of the river flashed with its jeweled foam. . . .*

(NOTE: Harper's artist was none other than Porte Crayon. In contrast to his miserable experience with horse travel one year previous, his illustrations in the Harper's article show an affection for the new steam power.)

The author has created a personality for the train, one of a conqueror. The personification of the train is important here, for the train was to replace the Mountain with its nicknames, and replace the Mountain as a symbol of power and omnipresence in the Appalachian environment. Another haunting significance in the above paragraph is that this journalist forecasts, with his tasteless description of the mountains, the attitude the East Coast was to take toward Appalachia in the subsequent fifty years. This

NISI PRO NOBIS.

ASCENDING THE ALLEGHANIES.

was an attitude of colonialist capitalism, and just as the author had lustily viewed the "tender leafage" of the sacred mountains, the lumber barons were to pick the fruits of this "girlhood" as soon as significant improvements to the railroad made harvest possible. The author goes on to describe Harper's Ferry:

> *The fact that it is the seat of a national armory, and has been described in glowing language by Jefferson, may have given it a wider notoriety than the comparative merits of its scenery would justify; and the tourist who only gives it a passing glance may experience a feeling of disappointment. But if, instead of four hours, he should have four days at his disposal, or even four weeks, to pass in exploring the town and its environs, he can be no lover of the sublime, the romantic, and beautiful, if he fails to acknowledge that his time has not been well spent, and that Harper's Ferry has justified her ancient renown.*

Here the author unintentionally reveals the difference between his new form of travel and the previous mode. The introduction of rapid travel into the mountains would kill the necessity to spend more than four hours in Harper's Ferry, or anywhere else for that matter. Iron horses do not need rest. Unless someone was especially seeking the sudden experience of the "Patowmac and the Shenandoah" by going through the woods at Jefferson's pace, he would never experience the full size and scale of the Appalachians.

The train could scale the mountains in a fraction of the time it took to walk them, and it carried its passengers inside a perceivably safe and effortless environment. This advancement eradicated the mountains as a terrorizing place, a place of the sublime. It replaced them however with the thrill of noise and speed, the technological sublime. The hero became the engineer who smote the former heroine turned villain; Nature. The author continues:

> *This system, when first proposed by the chief Engineer, B. H. Latrobe, was so far in advance of anything which had yet been attempted. . . . The result has been a splendid success. Thus, by one bold leap, the Alleghanies were scaled, and the Mountains of Difficulty which existed in the imaginations of the scientific world were dissipated. . . .*

Near the summit of the Alleghenies, the author describes the ladies riding on the shoulders of the engine and relaxing against "his brazen ribs as though he were a pet pony." Then the train arrives at the Cheat River Gorge:

> *From the high embankment that overlooks the river one may see the line of the road from some distance up and down; and nowhere else, perhaps, does the result of human labor lose so little in the immediate comparison to the grander works of nature. One wonders alternately at the vastness of the obstacles and the completeness of the achievement in surmounting them.*

The author concludes his query with uncharacteristic brevity. The "vastness of objects" in the course of one sentence was transformed into the "completeness of the achievement in surmounting them."

The railroad companies tried their best to insure the aesthetic experience occurred for all riders with the same clarity as the author's revelation. In fact, the artists' trip of 1858 on the B & O marked the beginning of a series of railroad advances which were to progressively conquer the Appalachian Chain. Each battle was celebrated by the railroad companies, and each advancement negated the Appalachians as a barrier, and in the mentality of the outsider, transformed any reverence for the mountains into reverence for technology. Lawrence Smith (1982) recalls the 1873 completion of a railroad from Huntington, W. Va. to the tidewater of Virginia:

> *The railroad was completed when the last*

Opposite: ***Fig. 2. Porte Crayon's illustrations of the new Hero of Appalachian Space. First the train Conquers time . . . then Space. Notice the ladies on the Cow-catcher.*** [Harper's New Monthly Magazine (6/1859).]

rails were joined and spikes driven near Hawks Nest on January 29, 1873, bringing to realization the dreams of Washington and many others after nearly a century. A train with Chief Engineer Whitcomb and many officials and dignitaries aboard steamed to Charleston where the historic occasion was celebrated with speeches and a display of fireworks. Later, at Huntington, the linking of the Tidewater with the Ohio was symbolized by pouring a barrel of water drawn from the James River into the Ohio. In a reciprocal gesture of symbolism, the train returned to Richmond with water from the Ohio and pulling several cars of coal.

Whether the media show caused the celebration of technology or vice versa, there was certainly something recklessly heroic about the railroad taking over the mountain and emerging as the new hero of the Southern Highlands. It seems only fitting that the railroad became the tool used by outlanders for exploitation of the regions' resources. Coal and timber rolled out of the highlands on the railroads, leaving barren lands in the mountains while reaping large profits for the non-resident timber and lumber barons. In an area where the people had been such a part and parcel of the landscape, it is not surprising that the cultural resources were stripped from the land as easily as the mineral resources.

Industrialization in the mountains brought about some of the greatest changes in economic life of the independent life of the family farm. Ron Eller (1978) cites the decades between 1880 and 1930 as the decades of major social changes in the mountains. The railroads were responsible for the change, as well as construction of company towns and the introduction of industrial employment. By the end of the 1920's, few farmers were left without at least some of the influence of mountain industrialization. Some of the effects of the cultural transition were drastic when viewed on the regional scale. Two statistics tell the tale of massive changes. First, during this half-century, over six hundred company towns were constructed in the Southern Highlands, and by the end of the period they outnumbered independent towns in coal mining regions five to one. To give a more detailed picture, we look at the health of the agricultural heritage: the average Appalachian farm in the 1880's included 187 acres. By the 1930's, the average size had dropped to 76 acres.

Railroadmen, lumbermen, and coalmen recruited unskilled mountain labor as a primary source of manpower in the filthy and dangerous business of construction and industrial operation. The farmers moved from the log cabin on the family farms in the upper valleys to the clapboard shacks in mill towns and coal towns. "By coming to a coal mining town, the miner had exchanged the independence and somewhat precarious self-sufficiency of the family farm for subordination to the coal company and dependence upon a wage income (Eller, 1978)."

The clapboard shack of the company town was clearly a poor substitute for the cabin on the family farm. This is not to point out that they were of atrociously poor quality, but rather that the land use pattern was incorrect for the culture. First, the houses were clustered in a group, which goes against the grain of the typical ownership patterns of independent coves or clan valleys of Appalachia. Built of imported materials, the company housing did not share the symbolism of the cabin, built literally from the local environment. The company houses were sited in the valleys, but they were typically located near the waste products of the industrial operations and the railroads. In contrast, the mine and mill superintendents' palatial houses were located (heroically!) on the hilltops. Rather than the previous experience of *lifting mine eyes to the hills from whence cometh my help*, the new experience revealed for the mountaineer *lifting mine eyes to the hills from whence cometh my oppression.* In fairness to the mine companies, the palatial homes on the hilltops were located there partially to create a sense of hope for the miners. After the complexity of the mountaineers' landscape symbolism, this certainly was not only a simple gesture, it was simple-minded. The palaces did incite emotion all right, and the indicated rewards served to broaden the mountaineer's economic repertoire to include materialistic covets and envies. The real profits of the businesses rolled out of the region on the same tracks to the same cities as rolled the resources.

The destruction of the agrarian society seemed eminent as farm sizes decreased and people began to move into the camps. It was no doubt difficult for the people to adjust to the drastic changes caused by a change in the economy from self-sufficient agriculture of industrial dependency. Such folk songs as "I Owe My Soul to the Company Store" reflect on the economic shift. It was also very difficult to leave the mountain coves, and to transfer some of the anguish about exemplary people or folk heroes emerged in the nascent industrial operations.

HAMMERIN' ON A REAL HERO

John Henry was such a folk hero. Although there is some disagreement about exactly who Henry really was, there is convergence on the point that he died in the hurried construction of the tunnels for the 1873 opening of the link between the James River and the Ohio. The popular song about his death gives insight into the displaced farmers' relationship to the mountains, and it shows the perceived need for man to out-perform the technology imported from the flatlands, even when it means the cost of his life. The overriding message of the spiritual is revealing in that even though John Henry proves more powerful than technology, he does not prove more powerful than the mountain . . . man over machine, but nature over man. In contrast to the popular American version of Engineer as hero, the song reminds us that the hierarchy of the zionist consciousness is clearly still in order with the Appalachian native:

D D
John Henry was a little baby,
A7
Sittin' on his daddy's knee,
G D
Said, "The Big Bend Tunnel on the C. and O. Road
G D
Is bound to be the death of me, Lord, Lord,
G D
Is bound to be the death of me.

John Henry said to his Captain,
"I ain't nothing but a man,
But before I'll let your steam drill beat me down,
I'll die with my hammer in my hand, Lord, Lord,
I'll die with my hammer in my hand."

John Henry said to his shaker,
"Shaker, why don't you sing?
I'm throwin' twelve pounds from my hips on down,
Jes' listen to the cold steel ring, Lawd, Lawd,
Jes' listen to the cold steel ring."

John Henry got a thirty pound hammer,
Beside the team drill he did stand.
He beat that steam drill three inches down,
And he died with his hammer in his hand, Lord, Lord,
He died with his hammer in his hand.

John Henry had a little woman,
Her name was Julie Ann,
She went down the track never lookin' back,
Says, "John Henry, you have always been a man, Lord, Lord,
John Henry, you have always been a man."

John Henry was hammerin' on the mountain,
An' his hammer was strikin' fire,
He drove so hard till he broke his pore heart,
An' he laid down his hammer and he died, Lawd, Lawd,
He laid down his hammer an' he died.

They took John Henry to the graveyard,
And they buried him in the sand,
And ev'ry time that train comes roaring by,
Says, "There lays a steel-drivin' man, Lord, Lord,
There lays a steel-drivin' man."

Gainer (1977:242)

John Henry is the obvious hero, but upon closer examination of the song the most powerful force in the scene is nature. It was no secret at the time that the completion of the C & O

Railroad would mark the end of the Appalachians as a barrier. Likewise it is no accident that the song characterizes a death which happened on the tunnels of that very railroad. John Henry, having beaten the strongest railroad construction machine was no match for the providence that served to keep Appalachian space in order.

CULTIVATING THE IMAGE

Even though railroads were built as the tool for resource exploitation, they provided the means for many upper and middle-class outlanders to experience the mountains. The springs of Appalachia were badly crippled by the Civil War, but they had a rebirth with easy rail access, and gave rise to an era where the mountains became a place to luxuriate in the cool air and hot springs of the region. There were the palatial Homesteads and Greenbriers, and there were literally hundreds of other smaller retreats, each boasting of the scenery and the picturesqueness of the environment. A recent work by Marshall Fishwick (1978) discusses the advertising techniques used by the springs emphasized the "recklessly, perhaps hopelessly" romantic settings of the places as a major selling point.

> *After all, these springs were right next to the primeval mountain forests; danger still lurked out there despite the Arcadian scene within the hotel grounds. The contrast was expressed constantly in 19th century travel literature: "The traveler is charmed by the sudden view of his resting place, surrounded on all sides by lofty mountains and the mysterious forests. . . . "*

Travelers did not understand the symbolism in the land, and they did not understand the depth of the relationship between mountain landscape and mountaineer. Similar to the case of the mine superintendents' homes, when American travelers first gained access to the region, they discovered a society that did not share their desire for profit. Discursive thinkers with technologized minds, the American mainstream had to find a category to fit these curious people. "Fatalistic" became the label to describe a society that praised "worthless" lands.

In her travel book, The Spirit of the Mountains, Emma Miles describes her experiences traveling in the mountains about 1910. Her insight is useful as an outsider's account of contact with the sublime experience of zionistic hero worship:

> *I once rode up the Side with a grandmother from Sawyer's Springs, who cried out, as the overhanging curve of the bluff, crowned with pines, came into view: "Now ain't that finer than any picter you ever seed in your life? - and they call us poor mountaineers! We git more out o' life than anybody."*
>
> *The charm and mystery of bygone days broods over the mountain country—the charm of pioneer hardihood, of primitive peace, of the fatalism of ancient peoples, of the rites and legends of the aborigines. To one who understands these high solitudes it is no marvel that the inhabitants should be about mystics, dreamers, given to fancies often absurd, but often wildly sweet.*
>
> *Nothing less than the charm of their motherland could hold them there. . . .*

Ms. Miles has all the heart of Jefferson in his description of the Potomac, but for Mrs. Miles, there can't be a hero . . . unless, of course, it is "one who understands these high solitudes." Ms. Miles goes on to explain:

> *Occasionally a whole starved-out family will emigrate westward, and, having settled, will spend years simply waiting for a chance to sell out and move back again. All alike cling to the ungracious acres they have so patiently and hardily won, because of the wild world that lies outside their puny fences, because of day-dream vistas, blue and violet, that lead their eyes afar among the hills. . . .*

Ungracious acres and day-dream vistas are not landscape-heroes. Neither are people who build puny fences heroes. The early Industrial Era in the Southern Highlands is important for it provides us the stereotype of the region and its people that exists to this day in most of mainstream America. The many people who traveled to springs on the railroad lines noticed a broken region with failing farms and industrial towns. This image is especially dominant in Hollywood. "The Beverly Hillbillies," "The Dukes of Hazzard," and "Gomer Pyle" are Hollywood's response to books like The Spirit of the Mountains. To Hollywood, the Appalachians are a land of hopelessly simple people who regard their landscape as profane, in contrast to the rest of America which has a cast of deep people who respect pristine landscapes. Real research into both may reveal that historically the reverse has been true.

AUTOCHTHONISM, TRACTORIDOLISM AND ROADS WITHOUT RAILS

During the early part of the Twentieth century, a new form of machine was introduced into the Appalachian garden. The tractor and the automobile made their debut in the mountains, forever changing the conception of time and space. They were rapidly assimilated into the culture because they offered renewed hope for survival in the region. To the farmer who was just eking out a living of marginal lands, mechanized equipment must have appeared as a godsend. It represented a chance to remain on the farm, the only alternatives being the dismal work of the industrial towns or sharecropping in the flatlands. Even though many farms' finances were too small and terrain was too steep for large machinery, the small-scale equipment that rumbled over the mountains in the early 1900's presented new hope for the farmer and earned a place of honor in his heart and fields.

In the early days of mechanization, farm machinery was treated symbolically as any other working entity on the farm. The equipment shed was built around the barnyard, and in the daytime the machine shared the same terrain of the husbandman on the slopes. A new Appalachian identity became wound-up into this rolling symbol of progress.

The mountaineers' relationship with nature changed with a shift in the use of his own resourcefulness. With the speed of the tractor, the view of the farmhouse in the valley became more obscure. The motion of equipment turns a picturesque scene into the blur of the technological sublime. The fixed image changes constantly, producing a moving picture. The foreground becomes non-existent, and the middle-landscape moves, voiding its symbolic permanence. Even though farm machinery occupied a modest position in the landscape, it served to captivate the focus of attention through its speed. The transformation of space and the condensation of time it caused have dubbed the tractor as a hero of the Appalachian landscape.

The automobile has not enjoyed the same reputation of the tractor in the Highlands, particularly because rather than a savior of the fields, automobiles on roads reached into the valleys and coves for the specific purpose of removal of something. Improvements in road building hit closer to home than the railroads, for they left no corner of the region untouched. In the Highlands, there are two types of roads, each held in equal contempt: tour roads and roads to cities.

Tour roads were planned especially to gain access into inaccessible areas, taking the tourists into the most isolated and preserved counties in the region. Without a doubt, the most famous scenic roads planned for the Southern Highlands were the Blue Ridge Parkway and the Skyline Drive. Beginning as early as 1909, the resort industry had schemes for a "Crest of the Blue Ridge Highway," which perched on the mountaintops would provide a balcony view of the borrowed scenery below.

What a contradiction this road must have been to the proponents of the zionistic outlook, for the Parkways would capture the mountaintop and hold their farms below on display for the tourist. The Blue Ridge Parkway was constructed beginning as a W.P.A. project in the 1930's. A favorite of President Franklin D. Roosevelt, it was met with the same success as the B & O Railroad's artists' journey, hosting a whopping 19 million visitors on the fiftieth anniversary of its beginning. A mountain is no longer a hero when it can be driven over at Parkway speed. As objects become obscure, their place in the frame of the landscape takes on less meaning. Speed turns the picturesque into a technological sublime. As the author of the 1859 Harper's article so clearly pointed out,

Fig. 3. 1930's borrowed landscape scene from the Skyline Drive.
(Norfolk/Southern Railway Archives)

the awe of the experience is absorbed in the accelerated passage of space. The sublimity of the entire Blue Ridge was sacrificed for the farmer for a chance to let the tourist get a commanding view of his picturesque land below.

While the parkways were built on the hilltops, the myriad interstate, state and local roads have been constructed reaching into the far heights of the valleys and coves. As progress in road construction continued, contempt for the city and its machines grew in the mind of the mountaineer. In a study of Appalachian literature, H. R. Stoneback (1986) discusses the emerging image of the highway in mountain literature:

> *It seems to me that . . . somewhat sentimental novels suggest the fundamental patterns of a century of mountain fiction: the roads come to the hills, bringing the machine to the garden, and the mountain autochthons either lose their Eden as they go down the deracinated road to the flatland cities or they experience a more fortunate fall and return to the mountains to reclaim the garden. Scores of works play variations on these themes.*

Whether on the railroad or highway, easy mobility has been one of the chief agents of change in the perception of Appalachian space. The roads and the railroads brought tourists to the mountains that separated the insular coves of the Southern Highlands. Contact with the outside nation, its evangelical and mainstream religions, its industrial capitalism and its wealthy visitors clearly had a role in changing the mountaineers' perception of the mountains.

Not only did the roads and railroads bring changes into the region, their physical presence changed the perception of the region's landscape. Located in some cases on the ridgeline of the mountains and spanning formerly impassible gorges, the technological advances between 1858 and 1940 changed the mountain sense of the sublime. Where formerly, the mountains had a substantial hold on travel and land use in the region, by the turn of the twentieth century they had been reduced to surmountable objects by engineers. Objects which had taken hours and days to pass by horseback took a few minutes by 1940. If the mundane land uses of travel and resources exploitation weren't enough, the mountains appeared topographically and metaphorically below the emerging popular travel along parkways with their celestial balconies. No matter what the outside influence had done to this point, Jefferson's family farm was still alive in Appalachian space. The modernization caused by a brush with the outside nation had provided plenty of economic and social changes, but in the isolated coves of the mountains, remnants of the man-land relationship of Appalachian space were still apparent in the landscape. On the eve of World War II, the house was typically located in the coves of the mountains and the fields still surrounded the farm.

III. WAR ON THE MOUNTAIN

Using landscape as an indicator, war is the event in human experience which creates the most heroes. The landscape always changes with war, and it always changes after war. Landscape is never the emergent hero of a war. The human race always is looking for scapegoats, and being witness to every death and atrocity that war creates, landscape is suspect of villany in every case in history. The landscape of the Southern Highlands, until World War II, had had a history of very little war. In comparison with the rest of the U. S., few Revolutionary or Civil War battles had happened in the mountains and due to the lack of organization among the Indian tribes of the region, barring local incidents, the region as a whole was settled without much hostility. The land use pattern that had evolved in the Southern Highlands was a landscape of peace. It was practically and metaphorically a landscape of peace.

The most significant changes in rural Appalachian land use patterns have occurred since World War II. The effects of World War II, the second major form of assault on the cultural land use patterns of Appalachia, finished off what the first had begun. The second attack on Appalachian Space murdered the spacial patterns altogether, for this blow, in contrast to the earlier one being exploitation of the mountain culture from the outside, was a change in the culture from within. The second blow to Appalachian Space came in the form of exposure of mountaineers to foreign cultures during World War II, the most foreign of which, especially in its technologies, was the American culture. The veterans of World War II returned home in the late 1940's with a different outlook on their place in the environment. This exposure to not only the horrors of war, but the victorious attitude that pervaded the allies' mentalities promoted a change in the structuring of the returning veterans' position in society. The change in position brought about a change in Appalachian space.

There have been regional trends, but these only account for some minor changes in the rich land-man pattern described earlier. For instance, land subdivision has been rampant in some parts of the Southern Highlands since the war, particularly in the North Carolina highlands. Within the entire region, subdivision has not been any more rampant in the Southern Highlands than in any other region in the country. Roadways have been improved since the war in the Highlands, but this is a national trend as well. The interstate highway system has been completed in the region, bringing in the usual nationally syndicated and clustered fast food and motel chains, but their effect on farming patterns has been to annihilate only those farms unfortunate enough to be near the highway or an interchange. Railroad use has declined steadily as highways have been added and improved.

The real change in the land use patterns of the region since World War II is seen at the detail of the family farm. Within the last forty years, the new houses constructed in the region have been built on the hilltops. Typically, the houses are mobile homes or modular. No longer is the log house constructed from the environment, but the house is rather brought into the environment in some form or another. The material change is inevitable, chestnut trees aren't to be found anywhere, and other materials, (including many "lincoln log kits") are available and cheap.

The locational issue was not inevitable. The locational criteria for rural housing have changed because the religious or organic ideal of man in the mountain environment has changed. The vernacular talent for locating houses within the wholeness of a farm has been lost. The newer constructions do not share the modest location at the cleft in a complete landscape composition, even though they may be owned by the family which has owned the property for generations. The significance of houses on hilltops is vast, for this pattern indicates the keystone of Appalachian space has been pulled out of the entire order. Houses on hilltops indicate that the family farm does not function as an organism with the home in the heart. They indicate that the mountains have been conquered even by that entity which previously had been placed reverently at its feet. Cemeteries lose their relative position, and mountains have been transformed from the status of "sublime wild nature" to "picturesque homesites."

The reasons for this change in land use reveal that there has been some upset that has occurred within the order. The structure of Appalachian space had withstood immense technological assault on the mountains from the outside. Even though technological advances and industrialization had penetrated the mountains, they hadn't wrecked the fundamental ordering of Appalachian space. The 1940's, however, was a decade when the individuals of Appalachian society experienced exposure to the outside American culture. The World War II effort drew essentially a generation of men overseas and women to cities.

Appalachian men went and fought in overseas lands. Those in Europe probably did not see agricultural land use patterns extremely different from the ones at home, for the ancestral roots of the region were German and Scotch-Irish. They did see, however, the incredible destruction and chaos of war. It is not insignificant that many of the major battles of World War II consisted of taking mountains and holding them. For example, in mid-August 1944, American troops hit the beach at St. Tropez and marched up the Rhone to defeat Hitler in the Vosges mountains. The psychology of war in general deals with the mastery of landscape position, and mountaintops are obviously the most defensible places.

HEROES DURING THE WAR

During World War I as well as World War II, the popular way to vent pressure of the war was to sing. In World War II, regional songs were coined. The heroines of the songs were generally a fantastical image of women. Along with the chart-topping "God Bless America" and "Deep in the Heart of Texas" was the song "She'll be Comin' Round the Mountain." Even though this song is obscure in origin, the contraction in the title indicates it may be from the Appalachian Region. If it is, the image would be somewhat unexpected from a peacetime Appalachia. It is of a woman, driving six white horses, coming to meet "us." If one can get over the fantasy of the image, the message is clear. The woman is the new heroine of the Highland Landscape, not the landscape itself or even technology. A second hero of the war was the weaponry of war. The bulldozer, for example, America's secret weapon of the wars, received top billing from the engineering authors. The construction machine, in contrast to all the war destruction machines, emerged after the war with hero status.

When Rome expanded its empire two thousand years ago, the houses were likewise expanded to proclaim the riches of victory. Similarly, when the Allies emerged victoriously from World War II, the styles of the U. S. changed to reflect this. At first women's styles were reminiscent of soldiers' and sailors' uniforms, only quickly to sway back to effeminate dress (Jenkins, 1977). American cars expanded, grew fins similar to rockets, and hugged the ground. Suburbia sprawled, for the middle class was ready to announce each winner's spoils, and the single-family house was the

Fig. 4. Traditional post-World War II siting: The farmhouse has crept out of the valley. Note the former family Homestead in the Valley beyond.

accepted way to do it.

In the Southern Highlands, the expansionist mentality caused the deterioration of the zionistic consciousness of Appalachian space, and the subsequent decay of that land use ideal. Since the first settlers in the region in the 1730's had never feared attack, there never had been the need to locate on the hilltop. The expansionists from World War II located houses on hilltops. Houses are not only used to indicate relative social position, but they are placed in high places as a response to fear. The mine superintendents' houses come to mind, as well as this new generation of houses across the Highlands. It is possible that the society, taken from what they thought was Eden, returned after World War II to find it a foreboding place; however, it is more likely that the new culture is afraid of something creeping into the garden.

In Appalachia there is frequently a practical reason for action which is backed by mythical explanations. In the case of the houses on the hilltops, there is a simple technological answer. The technologies of the bulldozer make it possible to excavate hilltop land and create roadways to it. Well insulated houses can perform under the adverse conditions, and now wells can be drilled and pumped cheaply. These practical excuses in no way justify houses on hilltops against the earlier scriptural code. The broadened horizons brought to Appalachia as a result of World War II have set a new code for Appalachia's horizon.

NEW HEROES OF APPALACHIAN SPACE

The husbandman returned from World War II with a lost concept of the land as a source of expression and protection. The thrill of capture has progressed into the family farm; there is an experience of the technological sublime when capturing a mountain with a bulldozer. The emerging hero of Appalachian space is the person who can afford the hilltop house. The Southern Highlands are rapidly becoming an ordinary place. After a century of aesthetic siege, the holistic farm land use pattern is beginning to deteriorate. The new heroes of Appalachian space are the victors of World War II. Their presence is established by capturing the high point of the land. Their presence may be the result of fear or pride, but one fact remains: Appalachia is no longer the form statement of a culture at peace.

In the Southern Highlands, the traditional cultural landscape was intrinsically ordered to emphasize a man-land experience that transcended society, religion and myth. By noticing the relative elevation of elements in the Highland landscape, it becomes apparent that the hero of Appalachian space has changed twice in the last one-hundred and thirty years. Through the metaphor of heroes, this paper has dealt with prominent changes in the ordering of the Appalachian space. Spacial perceptions have changed as the travel industry has changed form 1859 to the present, and spacial transformations have occurred in the post-war era from 1945 to 1986. These "improvements" have shifted the primary determinant of land use patterns in the region. Modernization of the Southern Highlands has changed the way people have regarded the mountains. With every technological advance, the mountains become a little less heroic, a little less sacred, and the natural environment becomes less meaningful.

The newest development in the Southern Highlands region is the predominance of satellite television reception dishes placed on and around the old houses and the new. Given their location in the coves, many of the old houses were never able to receive television waves, even if they were wanted. Now there is a grand effort to end isolation of the last remnants of the culture. The isolated culture of the Southern Highlands regions is finally obliterated, the last victim of World War II.

BIBLIOGRAPHY

"Artists' Excursion Over the Baltimore and Ohio Railroad," in Harper's New Monthly Magazine, (n.a.), vol. 19, no. 109 (6/1859). New York: Harper and Brothers, 1859.

Bowman, Waldo G., H.W. Richardson, Nathan Bowers, Edward Cleary, and A.N. Carter. Bulldozers Come First. New York: McGraw-Hill, 1944.

Drake, Richard. Mountaineers and Americans. Richard B. Drake, 1976.

Eller, Ronald D. "Industrialism and Social Change in Appalachia, 1880 - 1930: A Look at the Static Image," in Colonialism in Modern America: The Appalachian Case, Ed. Helen Lewis et al. Boone: Appalachian Consortium, 1978.

Eller, Ronald D. Miners, Millhands and Mountaineers. Knoxville: Univ. of Tennessee, 1982.

Fishwick, Marshall. Springlore in Virginia. Bowling Green State University: Popular Press, 1978.

Gainer, Patrick. "Folksongs," in Mountain Heritage. Ed. B.B. Maurer. Parsons, W. Va.: McClain Press, 1977.

Humphrey, Richard. "Religion and Place in Southern Appalachia," in Cultural Adaptation to Mountain Environments, Ed. Patricia D. Beaver and Burton Purrington. Athens: Univ. of Georgia, 1984.

Jackson, J.B. Discovering the Vernacular Landscape. New Haven: Yale, 1984.

Jackson, J.B. The Necessity for Ruins. Amherst: Univ. of Mass. Press, 1970.

Jefferson, Thomas. Notes on the State of Virginia. Ed. William Penden. Chapel Hill: U.N.C. Press, 1954.

Jenkins, Alan. The Forties. London: Heinemann, Ltd., 1977.

Jolley, Harley. The Blue Ridge Parkway. Knoxville: Univ. of Tenn. Press, 1969.

Kattwinkel, Kevin J. "Barns of Southwest Virginia." Blacksburg Va.: Virginia Polytechnic Institute, n.d.

Martin, Charles E. Hollybush: Folk Building and Social Change in an Appalachian Community. Knoxville, Univ. of Tenn. Press, 1984.

Maurer, B.B. (Ed.) Mountain Heritage. Parsons, W. Va.: McClain Press, 1977.

Miles, Emma. The Spirit of the Mountains, Ed. David Whisnant. Knoxville: Univ. Of Tennessee, 1975.

Novak, Barbara. Nature and Culture: American Landscape Painting 1825 - 1875. New York: Oxford Univ. Press, 1960.

Opie, John. "A Sense of Place: A World We Have Lost," in An Appalachian Symposium, Ed. J.W. Williamson. Boone: Appalachian Consortium, 1977.

Opie, John. "Where American History Began: Appalachia and the Small Independent Family Farm," in Appalachia/America, Ed. Wilson Somerville. East Tennessee State Univ., 1981.

Raitz, Karl and Richard Ulack. Appalachia, A Regional Geography. Boulder, Colo.: Westview Press, 1984.

Smith, Lawerence J. The High Alleghenies. Tornado WV: Allegheny Vistas, Inc., 1982.

Stilgoe, John. Personal discussions. Harvard University, Graduate School of Design, Spring, 1987.

Stoneback, H.R. "The Road in Appalachian Lore and Literature," in Blue Ridge Parkway: Agent of Transition, Ed. Barry Buxton. Boone: Appalachian Consortium, 1986.

Vale, Thomas R. and Geraldine R. Vale. U.S. 40 Today. Madison: Univ. of Wisconsin Press, 1983.

Wagner, Melinda. "America's Alter-Ego." Radford University Magazine, 3, no. 1. 1981. pp. 6-9.

Whisnant, David. "Introduction," in The Spirit of the Mountains. Knoxville: Univ. of Tennessee, 1975.

Zelinsky, Wilbur. "The Log House in Georgia," in Geographical Review (Jan., 1953). New York: American Geographical Society, 1953.

The Impact of Parkways on Development in Westchester County, New York City, and the Metropolitan New York Region

Domenico Annese, FASLA, Vice President, Clarke + Rapuano Inc.

Apart from their physical appearances, what is it that actually distinguishes parkways from highways and expressways, since they are all roads for transportation? I must say, recreation, recreation in the form of driving for pleasure and recreation in the use of a parkway's landscape and the parks it serves. The concept of the parkway in the New York metropolitan area has from the start been grounded in social concerns for light, air, recreation and esthetics rather than in the utilitarian purposes of transportation. Beginning with Olmsted's plan for Eastern and Ocean Parkways in Brooklyn, which he envisioned as broad boulevards with tree-lined malls for strolling, parkways in New York City were conceived as pleasure drives, serving as gateways to large parks.

America's romance with the automobile really grew out of its old love for the horse and buggy. The Sunday afternoon drive in a horse and buggy was a favorite pastime. What the automobile did was to bring that pastime to the masses. Indeed, during the fifties, the Bureau of Public Roads, the Federal Highway Administration's predecessor, liked to claim that pleasure driving was the most popular form of recreation in the nation. Remembering my youth, driving from Bronx Park to Kensico Dam on the Bronx River Parkway was a favorite pastime of our family on Sundays.

In their influence upon urban development, the parkways can be compared to the park squares where the frontage blocks and surrounding neighborhood became prime locations for residences because of the light and air and recreation afforded by the square. The great example, of course, is Central Park, the super park square of all! Along Mosholu and Pelham

Parkways in The Bronx, which were established in 1888 as connecting links between Van Cortlandt, Bronx and Pelham Parks, there developed fine residential communities - single and two family residences, deluxe apartment buildings with elevators, walk-up apartment buildings, a variety of housing serving all social levels. Today, a century later, the neighborhoods along Mosholu and Pelhám Parkways are the most stable in The Bronx.

In Brooklyn, Olmsted's Eastern and Ocean Parkways became fashionable residential boulevards and continue to be so today. In 1987, the New York City Landmarks Preservation Commission designated Eastern Parkway as a scenic landmark having "a special character, special historical and aesthetic interest and value as part of the development, heritage and cultural characteristics of New York City." It is included in the National Register of Historic Places and is therefore protected from "improvements for traffic operations."

The parkways of New York created in the 19th century for horse and carriage were the products of purposeful design, but not so with the 20th century automobile parkway. By the beginning of this century, New York City was already beset with traffic congestion and the age of the automobile and truck was being foreseen. Plans for grand highways and bridges, and even tunnels, were conceived but not a parkway just for automobiles, that is not until the Bronx River Parkway was built. One can very well ask, would there ever have been any modern parkway if the Bronx River Parkway had never been built? But that question begs another: would the idea for the Bronx River Parkway have ever risen had not the water fowl in the New York Zoological Park, popularly known as The Bronx Zoo, died in the summer of 1904 from diseases caused by the polluted Bronx River? The State Legislature had for twenty years debated plans for a trunk sewer to clean up the Bronx River valley. William N. Niles, a member of the Board of Governors of The Bronx Zoo, decided to take action and, in 1906, he succeeded in getting the Legislature to set up a commission to study the river. The commission issued a report recommending that a park be combined in the plan for the sewer. And so, in 1907, the Bronx Parkway Commission was created.

The construction of a roadway in the combined linear park and sewer project was included in the mandate of the Commission although whose idea it was has never been established. A road in the park would provide city residents with access to New York City's Kensico Dam and Reservoir, then under construction, and also would be a handsome entrance to the City from the north. Since New York City was paying 75% of the project's cost and Westchester County only 25%, one may assume that City officials had a strong interest in the road. Besides, the fact that the road would provide access to Bronxville, Scarsdale, Hartsdale and other new subdivisions along the Bronx River was evident to the three-man commission, two of whom were associated in real-estate development.

By 1916, the grading on some sections had been completed but no paving or landscaping had been done. World War I interrupted the project; the parkway was completed in 1924, extending 16 miles from Kensico Dam in Valhalla to Bronx Park in New York City. The Bronx River Parkway was a popular success, so much so that the Westchester County Parks Commission was created in 1922 and the Bronx River Parkway was transferred to the new commission in 1925 when the Bronx Parkway Commission was terminated. The new commission quickly developed a scheme of parks, parkways and outdoor recreation for Westchester County. Dictated by the north-south valley geography of the county, routes were planned in 1923 along Saw Mill, Grassy Sprain, and Hutchinson Rivers with east-west connecting routes. In the decade from 1922 to 1933 Westchester County developed a remarkable system of parkways that was built just for the automobile. As the railroads had in the mid-nineteenth century, the parkways brought another period of rapid suburbanization to Westchester County .

The success of the park and parkway systems in Westchester County was not lost upon the business and political leaders of New York

City but it took one man to galvanize plans and dreams. I am referring to Robert Moses, of course. It was in 1922-23 that Robert Moses' dream of beaches and parks for Long Island began to take form as he tramped the woods, marshes and beaches and searched out records. He imagined for Long Island a network of parks and beaches connected by parkways similar to the system evolving in Westchester County. A loyal supporter of Governor Alfred E. Smith and an assistant in his administration, the only reward Moses asked of Gov. Smith was the state job of running parks - without salary. So, in 1924, he got the Legislature to establish the Long Island State Park Commission, with himself appointed as head. By 1936, the system of parkways in Long Island was built and after World War II extended further eastward.

The demand for housing after World War II brought phenomenal suburbanization to Long Island as potato field after potato field became one Levittown after another, interspersed with shopping centers. Subdivisions crept eastward along the routes of the Northern and Southern State Parkways. Along the Northern State Parkway, large estates were subdivided, a process that began when the parkway's right-of-way was carved out and appropriated. The utilitarian function of the parkways for transportation accelerated as suburbanization increased so that peak hour traffic was no longer confined just to weekends when city visitors to the parks and beaches jammed the parkways. Lewis Mumford was always critical of the undisciplined and linear development in Long Island which, he claimed, was spawned by the parkways. However, consider the climate of the post World War II times: millions of returning veterans, lack of housing, GI insured mortgages, new technology in producing mass, affordable housing, and easily developable land. The Levittowns were inevitable. If the parkways had not been there, other highways would have been built - ordinary highways, not limited access expressways, for that era was still to come a decade later.

In 1934, Robert Moses became New York City's Commissioner of Parks under Mayor Fiorello La Guardia. He was now able to put into effect the proposals he had set forth for New York in 1930 as chairman of the New York Park Association's Metropolitan Conference on Parks. Wearing his two hats as head for New York City's parks and the Long Island State Park Commission, he coordinated the construction of parkways in Brooklyn and Queens with those of Long Island, using the same team of landscape architects and engineers. Geographically, Brooklyn and Queens are part of Long Island. The parkways connected with existing and proposed new parks, some of which were still then only dumps and landfills. Notably, the Belt Parkway which circles along the shores of Brooklyn and Queens, has preserved the waterfronts in a continuous park and provides access to the many beaches on the Atlantic. I leave to your imagination the high-rise complexes that would today occupy much of those shores if the Belt Parkway had not been built. In Manhattan and The Bronx, the focus was northward to connections with the parkways in Westchester County. Here the emphasis was on the West Side Improvement along Manhattan's Hudson River shore and Olmsted's Riverside Park, a project which had languished since 1891 when a special commission had made its report for a general purpose road and "grand equestrian promenade, corresponding in character to Rotten Row in London, but in every attraction far superior." That plan was translated into the modern Henry Hudson Parkway. How Robert Moses sought and found funds for its construction is a story of its own.

What did the Henry Hudson Parkway achieve? It captured the Hudson River waterfront from coalyards, boatyards and other commercial uses and covered the New York Central Railroad which barred access to the river. It doubled the acreage of Riverside Park. It provided New York City with gateways from the north and from the west via the George Washington Bridge. It made a grander "front yard" for the apartment buildings along Riverside that look out upon the Hudson River. It provided play and sports facilities for the adjacent neighborhoods.

Across the Hudson River, on the west side in New Jersey, the stage was set for a new parkway that would extend from Palisades Interstate Park, at George Washington Bridge, 35 miles north to Bear Mountain State Park, connecting via Bear Mountain Bridge to the parkways in Westchester County on the east side of the Hudson River. At the beginning of this century, the governors of New York and New Jersey established the Palisades Interstate Park Commission to preserve the palisades - those spectacular cliffs of igneous rock intrusions that form the New Jersey shore of the Hudson River - and to save them from the quarry operators. With the success of the Woolworth Building and dawn of the skyscrapers, there also came the demand for stone aggregate for concrete. New Yorkers, who looked across the Hudson River, were shocked by the despoilation the quarriers were wracking upon the Palisades. Theodore Roosevelt, then governor of New York, authorized the initial funds for purchase of land along the New Jersey shore and the face of the Palisades, an illegal action because he expended funds out-of-state, in New Jersey, without the authority of the New York State Legislature.

Two decades later, John D. Rockefeller, Jr. bought the estates at the top of the Palisades to keep them from being developed with subdivisions and apartment buildings. He donated the land to Palisades Interstate Park, thereby making the Palisades Interstate Parkway a reality. The parkway was planned and designed during World War II and built during the post-war decade.

The Palisades Interstate Parkway is again another instrument for transportation that was planned and designed primarily for recreation. It was designed, however, to higher traffic and operating standards than the parkways of the twenties and thirties, namely 70 miles per hour design speed. The parkway was routed through open land in Rockland County and brought to that county in the sixties and seventies the same sort of suburbanization that the Northern and Southern State Parkways had brought to Nassau County on Long Island, but with less density because of the more rugged topography. Although the Palisades Interstate Parkway was graded for a future third lane, the Interstate Park Commission has consistently refused to widen the roadways to three lanes for reasons of esthetics and pleasurable driving. It considers 3-lane roadways esthetically unsuitable to the parkway's character and purpose.

With the passage of its Parkway and Freeway Act in 1946, New Jersey also embarked on a parkway program. In less than ten years, it planned, designed and built the Garden State Parkway, extending 162 miles from Paramus in Bergen County - across the Hudson River from New York City - to Cape May at the southernmost tip of New Jersey. The Garden State Parkway was designed to serve the beaches and resorts along New Jersey's Atlantic seashore. Recreational areas along its route were carefully considered, primarily picnic areas at about 25-mile intervals and a 225-acre park. A toll road, limited to automobiles and buses, its construction and operation are financed by bonds issued by the Garden State Parkway Authority. Unlike New York's parkways, the Garden State Parkway was not conceived as an integral part of a park system. Nevertheless, its primary purpose was recreational, to serve beach traffic and relieve the incredible congestion it caused.

The Garden State Parkway accelerated suburban growth, although Bergen and Union Counties at its northern end were already heavily developed when the parkway was built. Daily, it serves commuter automobile traffic, including buses, unlike the parkways in New York which prohibit buses.

The parkways have been beneficial in numerous ways to urban development in the metropolitan New York region. Most importantly, they have preserved corridors of natural features, such as the stream valleys of Westchester County, the Hudson River shoreline of Manhattan, the seashores of Brooklyn, Queens and Long Island, and the Palisades of New Jersey. Secondly, they provide recreation to their adjacent neighborhoods as well as being the means for getting to parks and beaches. And thirdly, they have helped control the quality of development and restrained blight. That the parkways have been so beneficial can be attributed to the social concerns from which they sprang: concerns for light, air, recreation and esthetics and only lastly, in my opinion, for transportation.

This thesis is readily summed up in the definitions, Gilmore D. Clarke, landscape architect and leading parkway designer, gave to parkways and freeways: The parkway is a "strip of public land dedicated to recreation, over which abutting owners have no right of light, air, or access" whereas the freeway is a "strip of public land dedicated to movement, over which the abutting owners have no right of light, air, or access."

The Parkway in New York City

Ethan Carr

NINETEENTH CENTURY ORIGINS

By the mid-19th century New York City had become the great commercial metropolis of North America. The sustained growth of New York had been complemented by ambitious city and state public works which, like the Erie Canal (1825) and the Croton Aqueduct (1842), dynamically affected the character and potential of the metropolitan area. In at least one respect, though, public planning had proved totally insufficient. The streets of Manhattan were laid out according to a strict rectilinear grid that had been published in 1811.[1] The hundreds of identical rectangular blocks which resulted were eminently practical for development, but left inadequate provision for open space. By 1850, these blocks had been developed as far north as 42nd Street and the city's population surpassed 500,000; yet the total area of parks and public squares was less than 70 acres.[2] The absence of an adequate city plan threatened to make the city uninhabitable.

Drastic solutions were called for, and in 1856 the city acquired about 770 acres (later expanded to 840) out of the heart of Manhattan's grid plan for the creation of Central Park. The park was an enormous popular success, and because of increased tax assessments, a successful investment for the City as well.[3] The success of Central Park changed the future of American cities by demonstrating the financial as well as aesthetic desirability of innovative city plans. During the 1860s, as city administrators anticipated accelerated growth in new, suburban wards of New York in northern Manhattan, the Bronx and Brooklyn, they called on landscape architects and civil engineers to devise new strategies for urban expansion.

Among the most influential city planning features subsequently invented for the New York metropolitan area was the "parkway." Frederick Law Olmsted and Calvert Vaux, the designers of Central Park (1858) and Prospect Park (1865), first coined the term "parkway" in a report to the Board of Commissioners of Prospect Park, Brooklyn in 1868.[4] It was in the City of Brooklyn, New York's most important suburb, that the concept was first realized. The "Parkway plan" presented by Olmsted and Vaux attempted to redress the inadequacies of existing street arrangements, which lacked any kind of express throughway for surface transportation. The parkways they proposed were noncommercial through roads, designed for "pleasure-riding and driving...[with] ample public walks, with room for seats, and with borders of turf in which trees may grow of the most stately character."[5] These linear parks were intended to provide relaxed and scenic access to the amenities of regional parks (in this case Prospect Park), and to engender continuous "parkway neighborhoods" —neighborhoods more open, healthy and attractive than any yet known in large American cities.

The two landscape architects made clear that this was no utopian scheme; they stressed that city government could expect a profitable return on their parkway investment through increased tax assessments along the new roads. Eastern Parkway (1870-74), from Prospect Park to Ralph Avenue, and Ocean Parkway (1874-76), from Church Avenue to Seabreeze Avenue in Brooklyn are recognized as the first parkways ever built. They are both designated New York City Scenic Landmarks. The entire parkway plan for Brooklyn, however, was never accomplished. Such progressive and comprehensive schemes for residential development (including the plans for the 23rd and 24th wards of the Bronx presented by Olmsted and J. James R. Croes in 1876) were considered impractical, and never fully implemented in New York or Brooklyn. The benefits of regional parks and connecting parkways, however, had been established. In 1888, the City of New York acquired 4,000 acres of the Bronx for a system of regional parks.[6] The parks were connected by park access roads called the Mosholu, Pelham, Bronx and Crotona Parkways. These parkways, like Eastern and Ocean Parkways in Brooklyn, were essentially treelined boulevards. Their inspiration lay in the wide avenues of Berlin and Paris, although they were—like the word "parkway" itself—uniquely American adaptations.

THE MODERN PARKWAY

The first modern automotive parkway with restricted frontage, limited access, and grade separations was built along the Bronx River in New York City and Westchester County early in the 20th century. The Bronx River Parkway was initiated in 1906 as a river conservation effort, similar in many ways to the Muddy River Improvement Proposal (1881) devised by Frederick Law Olmsted for the Muddy River in Boston.[7] The Muddy River, like the Bronx River, had become sluggish and polluted, and resulted in a serious health hazard. Olmsted's improvement called for creating a landscaped ribbon-park along the river's banks, which eliminated the residences and businesses which were the sources of pollution. The Muddy River Improvement also featured a continuous carriage driveway, which took advantage of the natural right-of-way of the riverbed.

In the Bronx, similar improvements on the Bronx River lagged until after World War I. It was not until 1923 that the linear park and winding roadway designed by Hermann W. Merkel and Gilmore D. Clarke was complete between Bronx Park in New York and White Plains in Westchester.[8] The automobile, of course, had proliferated in the meantime, and the beautifully landscaped, curvilinear Bronx River Parkway was greatly appreciated by car owners. As they drove along it at 35 miles per hour, they experienced constantly changing, picturesque views of the restored river and the surrounding park. The convenience and beauty of the many rusticated stone bridges that carried intersecting traffic over the parkway were equally unprecedented. The parkway was a great success, and was followed by a remarkable series of automotive parkways built by the Westchester County Parkway Commission in the 1920s. Designed by Gilmore Clarke and the Westchester County Parkway Commission, 88 miles of suburban parkways were built by 1933, including the Saw Mill and Hutchinson River Parkways.[9]

These roads had parallels in another developing suburb of New York, Nassau County on Long Island, where Long Island State Park Commissioner Robert Moses was also building a system of suburban parkways. Roads like the Northern and Southern State Parkways, designed by Clarence C. Combs, made the beaches and countryside of Long Island finally accessible to New Yorkers, who for years had been barred from this recreation by poor roads, traffic jams, and the lack of any kind of public access to the beach. By 1929 Moses had acquired 9,500 acres of parkland on Long Island and completed the Southern State Parkway through Nassau County. His greatest success came that August, when Jones Beach State Park and the Wantagh causeway opened. Jones Beach, with its sumptuous bathhouses, campanile water tower and parking for thousands of cars, was an unprecedented public park development. The popularity of Jones Beach was comparable to the success of Central Park 71 years earlier, and was to have just as far-reaching consequences. 350,000 people crowded on to the beaches during the park's first month of operation alone.[10] Most of those people drove on the Southern State and Wantagh Parkways to get there. In the 1930s Jones Beach became a model for large-scale park development, and modern arterial parkways became an integral part of planning for recreational land use.

THE URBAN PARKWAY IN NEW YORK CITY

Robert Moses and his design and engineering staff at the Long Island State Park Commission were already planning for the park and parkway needs of New York City while developing Long Island in the 1920s. The New York Park Association's Metropolitan Conference on Parks, which Moses chaired, presented an ambitious set of proposals for the city in 1930.[11] The conference's report recommended the immediate acquisition of thousands of acres of undeveloped land for parks, and the construction of a system of parkways and river crossings around and through the city to connect with the suburban parkways in Long Island and Westchester. The Henry Hudson Parkway, the Belt system of parkways, the Bronx-Whitestone and Verazzano Bridges—all of which were subsequently built—were initially set forth in this pioneering planning report.

When Mayor Fiorello La Guardia created a unified Department of Parks for the five boroughs of New York City in 1934, Moses, as sole Park Commissioner, was given the means to implement his urban parkway plan. The major appeal of the city Park Commissionership for Moses was the chance to bring his regional parkway program to "a logical conclusion." "You cannot work out a logical [parkway] development for the suburbs," he pointed out, "unless you know what the city is going to do."[12] After 1934 the city carried out precisely the Park Commissioner's plans. Between 1934 and 1940, Moses oversaw the building of over 70 miles of parkways within city limits.

The first arterial parkways within New York City had been started in 1929 under Mayor James J. Walker. The eastern portion Grand Central Parkway had been mapped with an overly narrow easement, and a similar problem existed with the Interborough Parkway, which had been laid out from the Grand Central through Forest Park to Eastern Parkway in Brooklyn. Although dissatisfied with the narrow, twisting right-of-ways inherited in 1934, Moses quickly pushed the parkways to completion. An innovative, "cloverleaf" interchange of the Interborough and Grand Central Parkways soon appeared at the southern end of the newly-acquired Flushing Meadows Park. The interchange, known as the "Pretzel," became a familiar symbol of arterial road progress, and an early monument of Moses's emerging system of urban parkways. Looking back on these first projects, he later said, "We learned not to waste time on explanations and post-mortems, and to go on to the next thing, always hoping that it would be a fresh, new project without unfortunate inheritances."[13]

The next project was never long in coming. The city Park Commissionership was only one of the means by which Moses funded parkway projects. In 1934 two public authorities were created to issue bonds: the Henry Hudson Parkway Authority and the Marine Parkway Authority. Moses was named sole commissioner of both. In 1934 La Guardia also appointed him to the Triborough Bridge Authority, which since 1929 had floundered in the attempt to create a bridge and highway complex between Manhattan, the Bronx and Queens to serve as the heart of an arterial road system for the city. New Deal public works programs such as the Civil Works Administration and, after 1935, the Works Progress Administration were also funding park, parkway and river crossing projects, all of which were now being carried out hand in hand under Moses' unified authority. Because of the Park Commissioner's unique administrative situation, the Parks Department design and engineering staff supervised a wide variety of park, road, bridge and other construction projects.

Much has been written about Moses' personal motivations for acquiring so much control over public works projects in the New York metropolitan region; ultimately the effect of his monopoly over important public planning decisions may have been negative. But in the crisis atmosphere of the Great Depression, Moses embodied a kind of public works martial law which seemed justified in the economic emergency. New York received more than any other city in federal work relief funds, and no other individual in the country exploited the New Deal as effectively as Robert Moses.[14] Moses revealed what he often called the "silver lining" of the Great Depression: by 1940 he had completely rebuilt New York's park system. In his first six years as Commissioner he added 6,000 acres of parkland and built New York's parks into the premier system of recreation facilities in the country.[15] At the same time, he was creating an urban parkway system which was—and remains—unmatched anywhere.

THE WEST SIDE IMPROVEMENT

The Henry Hudson Parkway and Riverside Park were the first, and in some ways the best, examples of how Moses worked in New York City, where planning public works was more complex and more expensive than it had been on Long Island.[16] The development of the West Side of Manhattan was one of the oldest and most difficult public development problems in the city. Since the middle of the 19th century, the Hudson River Railroad (later part of the New York Central) had occupied the right-of-way along the shore of the Hudson. The land for Riverside Park was acquired in 1872, but the plans for the park by Olmsted and Vaux concentrated on Riverside Drive which wound its way along the upper portion of the narrow ribbon of parkland, and left the waterfront unimproved and inaccessible. As early as 1891 proposals were made for the expansion of Riverside Park, the covering of New York Central's tracks, and the construction of a much needed highway out of the city to the north. In 1904 property was even acquired for the construction of a bridge over the Harlem River Shipping Canal at the northern tip of Manhattan. Plan after plan, however, was abandoned because no one could finance the combined costs of such a development.

In 1934, Moses implemented his plans for the West Side Improvement, which called for doubling the area of Riverside Park by covering the railroad tracks with a promenade, and extending the shoreline with landfill. The Henry Hudson Parkway was proposed to run the length of the park from 72nd Street, where it met the elevated highway begun by Borough President Julius Miller in 1927, north to the Saw Mill River Parkway in Westchester. The new park and parkway were designed by Gilmore Clarke, and financing for the job was assembled from a wide variety of sources including a New York State loan to the Grand Central Railroad for railroad grade crossing eliminations, federal, state and city grade crossing elimination funds, and Federal highway and work relief funds. The Henry Hudson Bridge over the Harlem River Shipping Canal was financed by the sale of Henry Hudson Parkway Authority bonds.

The Henry Hudson Bridge and the northern part of the Henry Hudson Parkway opened on December 12, 1936.[17] The rest of the West Side Improvement, including the new Riverside Park, was dedicated on October 12, 1937.[18] To complete the West Side Improvement, Moses had overcome monstrous financial and administrative difficulties that had frustrated generations of city planners. Typically, the parkway construction was coordinated with surrounding park expansion and development. The Henry Hudson Parkway itself, surrounded by hundreds of acres of parkland and offering magnificent views of the Hudson River and New Jersey Palisades, today remains one of the most dramatic automotive entrances to an American city.

THE MARINE PARKWAY

The Marine Parkway Authority was also created in 1934, and financed the construction of the Marine Parkway (through Marine Park in Brooklyn) and the Marine Parkway Bridge. The bridge, which carried traffic across the Jamaica Inlet to the Rockaway Peninsula and Jacob Riis Park, was the longest liftspan bridge in the world when it opened on July 3, 1937.[19] More importantly, the parkway and bridge connected Jacob Riis Park on the Rockaway Peninsula to Brooklyn's Shore Parkway and the rest of the Belt system of parkways, which was intended to girdle the boroughs of Brooklyn and Queens.

Jacob Riis Park was improved and enlarged in time for the opening of the Marine Parkway and Bridge. In general, major park expansion was part of Moses' parkway program, and Jacob Riis Park was developed into "another Jones Beach" according to Mayor La Guardia.[20] Marshland was filled, the beach was increased in width by 700 feet, and a new boardwalk was built. The existing bath house was remodeled and expanded. The parking field at Riis park was 70 acres, the largest paved parking space in the country at the time. Marine Park, however, which was also scheduled for extensive recreational development, has remained mostly an undeveloped wetland. In 1974 over half of it was ceded to the Gateway National Recreation Area.

THE GRAND CENTRAL PARKWAY AND FLUSHING MEADOWS PARK

The most significant example of combined park and parkway development took place in Flushing Meadows, Queens, where the Grand Central Parkway Extension was under construction. While the Triborough Bridge was still unfinished, it was clear that the Grand Central Parkway would have to be extended if the bridge were to have an adequate approach from the east. The obvious route was through the swamps and ash heaps of Flushing Meadows where inexpensive land would be available. In fact, if the entire area were to be acquired, it could provide a sizable park to the east of the parkway route. Most of the land was acquired in 1934; the Grand Central Parkway Extension was begun north through Flushing Meadows and along Flushing Bay, connecting the Triborough with the Long Island state parkways.

Over the next four years massive improvements were made to the Flushing Meadows property along the Grand Central Parkway Extension to prepare it as the site for the World's Fair of 1939.[21] The ash heaps were leveled, the swamps drained and filled, and two lakes were excavated. The Flushing Meadows Improvement was designed and supervised by Moses' Parks Department, and after the Fair closed, the site was converted into a completely new, 1,200-acre city park: Flushing Meadows-Corona Park.

THE BELT PARKWAY

The greatest parkway to be built in New York City was actually a circumferential system of parkways around Brooklyn and Queens that came to be known as the Belt Parkway. Work on the seawall and landfill that would eventually support Brooklyn's Shore Parkway, the first section of the Belt, was begun in 1930 as an early work relief project. Moses's Park Department built on these foundations when they finished the two-mile long section of the Shore Parkway which opened near Fort Hamilton in 1934. The Shore Parkway Extension through Dyker Beach Park to Besonhurst Park opened on December 12, 1936, the same day as the Henry Hudson Bridge dedication.[22] With the improvements made by Brooklyn Borough President Raymond V. Ingersoll to Guider and Emmons Avenues along the shore near Coney Island, the route of the Belt Parkway had taken shape on the Brooklyn waterfront by 1937.

In December, 1937 the Parks Department published a list of new parkway proposals.[23] In the Bronx, the extensions of the Bronx River and Hutchinson Parkways were proposed. For Brooklyn and Queens the completion of the Circumferential Parkway (later shortened to the Belt Parkway) was described. Although in Brooklyn the Shore Parkway was already well underway, in Queens entire new parkways were required to complete the Belt. The Cross Island Parkway was planned to extend from the Bronx-Whitestone Bridge along Little Neck Bay, through Alley Pond Park and down the eastern border of Queens to the Laurelton Parkway, which extended to Brookville Park. The Southern Parkway stretched the remaining distance through southern Queens to the Shore Parkway near Marine Park.

In all, the proposal for the completion of the Belt Parkway described a system of parkways totalling almost 35 miles. "Landscaped parkways, restricted to pleasure vehicles," wrote Robert Moses in an accompanying justification for the request, "have proven not only to be the most efficient way of providing for a smooth flow of traffic, but also to be great neighborhood assets...especially if provision is made for neighborhood playgrounds and walks along these parkways so that they can be enjoyed by local residents and pedestrians as well as motorists."[24]

Moses's optimism was shared by the Board of Estimate which appropriated $16,000,000 for construction. On October 12, 1938 the Federal government granted $12,000,000 in emergency public works funds to supplement the city funds, and on November 16 work began. Sixty-five bridges and overpasses were built and millions of cubic yards of fill were moved. The Belt Parkway more than doubled the total length of parkways in the city when it opened on March 20, 1940.[25] It skirted or traversed 26 park areas totalling 3,550 acres, and most of these park areas were improved in conjunction with the parkway construction. In large, regional parks like Alley Pond, facilities of all types were built and large parking areas were provided for motorists. Other parkway amenities included waterfront pedestrian promenades, ballfields, playgrounds and bike paths which still line much of the route of the Belt Parkway.

THE END OF THE PARKWAY ERA IN NEW YORK

The opening of the Belt Parkway in 1940 effectively ended the parkway phase of arterial highway construction in New York City. The routes for parkways had been chosen mostly along waterfronts, through parks, and around the edges of the city. After World War II, few new parkways were planned. Instead commercial highways, called expressways, were built directly through the city, often cutting into dense, heavily populated neighborhoods. The expressways, many of which were part of the new Interstate Highway system, were pragmatically engineered, without landscaped right-of-ways or recreational uses in mind. A golden age of parkway construction in New York City had come to an end.

Many of the parkways depicted in "The Parkway in New York City: 1934-1940" (an exhibition of photographs from the New York City Parks Department Photo Archive also submitted to this conference) no longer resemble their original condition. As residential development increased in surrounding suburbs, lanes were added to the parkways to accommodate increased commuter traffic. This only led to more commuter driving and increased congestion—a now familiar phenomenon—necessitating further widening of the roadbeds. In 1978 maintenance responsibilities for parkways were transferred from the Parks Department to the Departments of Transportation and Sanitation, an indication that officials at that time felt the roads were little different from the commercial expressways and interstates built after World War II by other agencies.

But parkways are much more than commuter traffic arterials. Still officially mapped as New York City parkland, their wide, landscaped routes survive (or may be restored) in many areas. Parkways were planned and built in conjunction with the acquisition and development of thousands of acres of parks, especially in Brooklyn and Queens. They constitute a system of environmental corridors running through the city, connecting larger parks and waterfronts to one another, and to more crowded urban areas. Together, the parkways and parks planned and developed in New York in the 1930s recast the city's topography, and forever changed the patterns of urban life.

During the parkway era of road construction in New York, the original concept of parkways as landscaped, recreational facilities survived. If the historic importance and environmental significance of New York's parkways are realized, the viability of the roads may be resuscitated. The importance of urban parkways as parkland, all but forgotten, should be a key to their future management and restoration.

NOTES

1. The Commissioners' Plan or Randel's survey was the work of three commissioners, Gouverneur Morris, Simeon DeWitt, and John Rutherford, who were appointed in 1807. The plan was surveyed and drawn

by John Randel, Jr. (Stokes, Vol. V, 1926, p.1531)

2. In an annual address to the Common Council in 1850, Mayor Caleb S. Woodhull pointed out the lack of parks in New York: "All the public squares below 42nd Street comprise only, in the aggregate, about 63 acres, being less (all together) than one-fourth the size of one of the large parks in the city of London." (Stokes, Vol. V, 1926, p.1826)
3. The Board of Commissioners of the Department of Public Parks (a city agency created in 1870 to replace the Board of Commissioners of Central Park) published tables comparing the costs of acquiring and building Central Park against the increased revenues from higher tax assessments on surrounding properties. (Second Annual Report of the Board of Commissioners of the Department of Public Parks, New York, 1872) It was the careful analysis of the Park Commissioners (specifically Frederick Law Olmsted in this case) that first demonstrated the financial benefits a municipal government could expect from developing large parks.
4. Fein, 1967, pp.129 ff.
5. ibid., p.159
6. The citizens' commission created to select the Bronx parkland made a full report in 1884. Report of the Commission...23rd and 24th Wards of the City of New York (New York, 1884)
7. Zaitevsky, 1982, pp.81 ff.
8. Downer, et al., 1925
9. Wilson, et al., 1986, p.97
10. The Architectural Forum, Dec., 1936 ("Pattern for Parks"), p.497
11. Program for Extension of Parks..., Metropolitan Conference on Parks (New York, 1930)
12. The New York Times, Jan. 19, 1934, p.2;6
13. Moses, "The Changing City," 1940
14. Millet, 1938, pp.38-41
15. Six Years of Progress, N.Y.C. Parks Dept., 1940, pp.38 ff.
16. Caro, 1975, pp.525 ff.
17. Opening of the Henry Hudson Parkway, N.Y.C. Parks Dept., 1936
18. West Side Improvement, N.Y.C. Parks Dept., 1937
19. Marine Parkway, N.Y.C. Parks Dept., 1937
20. Shore Parkway Extension . . ., N.Y.C. Parks Dept., 1936, p.8
21. The Flushing Meadows Improvement, N.Y.C. Parks Dept., 1939
22. Shore Parkway Extension . . ., N.Y.C. Parks Dept., 1936, p.8
23. New Parkways in New York City, N.Y.C. Parks Dept., 1937
24. ibid., p.4
25. The Belt Parkway, 4 N.Y.C. Parks Dept., 1940

BIBLIOGRAPHY

Report of the Commission to Select and Locate Lands for Public Parks in the 23rd and 24th Wards of the City of New York, Luther R. Marsh, Pres.; John Mulally, sec. (New York, 1884)

I.N. Phelps Stokes, The Iconography of Manhattan Island (New York, 1915-1928)

Jay Downer and James Owen, Public Parks in Westchester County (New York, 1925), Reprinted from History of Westchester County, Alvah P. French, ed. (New York, 1925)

Program for Extension of Parks and Parkways in the Metropolitan Region, Submitted by the Metropolitan Conference on Parks, Arsenal, Central Park, New York City, February 25, 1930 (New York, 1930)

"Pattern for Parks," The Architectural Forum, Dec., 1936

New York Advancing 1934-1935, Rebecca B. Rankin, ed. (New York, 1936)

"Robert (or I'll Resign) Moses," Fortune, June, 1938

John D. Millet, The W.P.A. in New York City (Chicago, 1938)

Robert Moses, "The Changing City," The Architectural Forum, March, 1940

Albert Fein, Landscape into Cityscape (New York, 1967)

Robert Moses, Public Works: A Dangerous Trade (New York, 1970)

Robert Caro, The Power Broker (New York, 1975)

Cynthia Zaitevsky, Frederick Law Olmsted and the Boston Parks System (Cambridge, 1982)

New York City Parks Department Publications: These brochures and unpublished papers are part of the New York City Parks Department Archives (Northwest Turret, The Arsenal, Central Park, New York, N.Y. 10021)

Opening of the Henry Hudson Parkway, Dec. 12, 1936, Robert Moses et al.

Shore Parkway Extension and Marine Parkway, Dec. 12, 1936, Robert Moses et al.

New Parkways in New York City, December 7, 1937, Robert Moses et al.

West Side Improvement, October 12, 1937, Harry Sweeny, Jr., ed.

Marine Parkway, July 3, 1937, Robert Moses et al.

Completion of the Henry Hudson Bridge and Approaches, May 7, 1938, Robert Moses

The Flushing Meadows Improvement, vol.3, no.8, May 15, 1939. Final publication with complete resume of all improvements to date... Harry Sweeny, Jr., ed.

The Comprehensive Parkway System of the Metropolitan Region, Paper presented to the American Society of Civil Engineers by Robert Moses on January 19, 1939 (unpublished transcript)

The Belt Parkway, 1940, Clinton F. Loyd et al.

Six Years of Park Progress, New York City Department of Parks Annual Report, 1940

Thirty Years of Progress, New York City Department of Parks Annual Report, 1964

From Carriageway to Parkway: Evolution of the George Washington Memorial Parkway

Bacil B. Warren

The idea of a monumental highway from Washington, D.C., to the home of George Washington at Mount Vernon came into being over a hundred years ago[1]. But an important element of the story had roots going back much farther.

To learn the full story of the George Washington Memorial Parkway and how it came to be built, we have to go back to the time of the Constitutional Convention.[2] Both before and after that great event, from 1783 to 1790, when the states were newly united or about to be, they wrangled furiously over the location of their new capital.

It is well known that the Potomac area won a narrow victory only after Virginia and Maryland each offered to cede ten square miles to the national government. Somewhat less well known is that they also promised to provide substantial funds to help erect government buildings.[3]

AN ADVANCE FROM RICHMOND

In the Virginia Legislature spirited debate continued, even after the delegates agreed to supply $120,000 for buildings. The main question was very simple. Was this sum to be a gift or a loan? The fledgling government clearly could not repay the money, not now. Yet why not try to get it back sometime?[4]

A young man among the Virginia legislators rose to his feet. His name was John Marshall, and he was later to become Chief Justice of the United States. He suggested a compromise:

use the word "advance."[5] Do not lend the money; do not give the money; advance the money.

The advance of funds was promptly approved, but the tantalizing question still remained, and people would be arguing about the meaning of the word "advance" long after John Marshall and all the other members of that legislature were dead.[6]

Although the advance was legally authorized, the national government found it exceedingly difficult to extract the money from the state of Virginia. President Washington found it necessary to make a personal call on Virginia Governor Beverley Randolph in Richmond to secure the first installment.

In a letter to the Commissioners of the District of Columbia on April 13, 1791, the President wrote that the Virginia treasury was empty. Then he added:

> *P.S. Since writing the foregoing I have again conversed with Governor Randolph, and have drawn upon him, payable to your order, for forty thousand dollars, being the first installment; one thousand of which he hopes to have ready within a few days. . . .*[7]

Those funds not only helped to begin construction of, specifically, the capitol building, but they did something else. In the final analysis they also paid for the first leg of the George Washington Memorial Parkway.[8]

But that was far in the future. For fifty years Virginia forgot about the doubtful debt owed or not owed by the central government. When, after half a century, the U.S. showed a fiscal surplus for the first time, Virginia began a sporadic and entirely unsuccessful effort to convince Congress that the "advance" was indeed a loan.[9]

After trying to collect the money off and on for nearly 20 additional years, the Commonwealth of Virginia seemingly gave up the fight, but only on the surface. Some 70 years after the "advance," Virginia adopted a curious method of seeking payment.[10]

SURROGATE COLLECTORS

At that time efforts were being made by a group of Virginians to launch a railroad to be called the Orange and Alexandria line. Asked to support this effort, the legislature assigned its claim of $120,000 against the federal government to the developers of the railroad.[11] They said, in effect, "If you can collect this money, it's yours."

Naturally enough, the railroad could never collect, but that did not end the story. Events were already in motion that would give that Virginia claim another life.

These events began in 1838 with the movement to build a suitable memorial to George Washington.[12] Fund raising proceeded for ten years, and construction of the familiar Washington Monument began in 1848.[13]

FAULTY TOWER

Even before the 555-foot obelisk was started some were saying it was all wrong,[14] that while thousands of dollars were being raised to erect an inappropriate stone monument, Washington's home at Mount Vernon, close by his tomb, was falling into ruin. The home and tomb, they felt, should be the most important national shrine for the great Commander in Chief.[15]

The mansion at Mount Vernon had been offered for sale to both the national government and the Commonwealth of Virginia, but both had refused. The Mount Vernon Ladies Association of the Union raised two hundred thousand dollars by popular subscription and purchased Mount Vernon in 1858.[16]

Immediately following the civil war, public contributions grew rapidly, the house was completely restored and refurbished — also refurnished in the style of Washington's day — and soon the Washington estate was one of the leading attractions for visitors in the D.C. area.[17] It might have attracted even more people, except for the difficulty of access. The establishment of boat service helped some, but land routes to the mansion were long and arduous.[18]

NOBLE CONCEPT

It was in 1886, one year after the dedication of the Washington monument in the District[19] when a leading citizen of Alexandria,

Virginia, Washington's "hometown," had his grand idea.[20]

H. B. Harlow, then city treasurer, envisioned a great carriageway, leading from the capital, which the first President helped to plan, to the mansion where he had lived most of his life, and on the grounds of which his tomb was situated.

This avenue would not only serve as a suitable tribute to our first President, it would make travel to Mount Vernon an uplifting experience, would serve as a spiritual preparation for entrance into the General's home, and it would link the two existing monuments into one truly fine memorial.[21]

It happened that Harlow's friend, C. C. Carlin, was the Alexandria correspondent of The National Republican, a leading Washington newspaper. Carlin not only wrote a story about Harlow's inspiration, he submitted it personally, and Harlow went with him. They laid it before the editor, Col. E. W. Fox.

Col. Fox liked the story, liked the idea, and became a strong advocate. What was ultimately to become the George Washington Memorial Parkway was officially launched.[22] But more than 40 years of political maneuvering lay ahead.

Col. Fox wrote a number of favorable editorials about the plan, and after the printing of one of these, on September 18, 1887, a group of business and political leaders from both Washington and Northern Virginia met to form the Mount Vernon Avenue Association.[23]

By this time, the idea had become quite grandiose. This was the stated purpose of the association when it was formally convened in 1888:

> *The general object is to build a roadway of noble proportions from Washington to Mount Vernon.*[24]

And noble was no overstatement. They described their avenue as a great highway combining the idea of the Appian Way at Rome and of London's Westminster Abbey. It was to be a roadway, a park, a cemetery, an outdoor hall of statues, and a mausoleum, all wrapped in one.

ECLECTIC PLANNING

The thoroughfare was to be 17 miles in length, with a proposed width of 250 feet. The entire project would be divided into sections, giving one to each state.

It was suggested by the association that each state on its section should erect statues or monuments to its outstanding citizens, and should plant trees and flowers indigenous to its locality.[25] It does not require much imagination to see what the heterogeneous result would be.

It was further proposed that each state be requested to build upon its reservation a permanent home, an exposition building for the purpose of advertising its educational, industrial, and agricultural advantages, and to place in the building a topographical map.

These buildings could also be used for meetings of visitors from the state to the capital. (And today, could provide offices for state lobbyists.) The Commonwealth of Virginia evidently approved all of this, since the legislature gave the Mount Vernon Avenue Association a state charter.[26]

FUNDING SOLVED

What is more, someone remembered that old debt, owed or not owed to the state by the federal government. Since the Orange and Alexandria Railroad had never been able to collect, the legislature in Richmond endowed the association very handsomely by reassigning the debt to it.[27]

They said, in effect, "We give you the authority to build your grand avenue, and here is a claim for $120,000 with which to fund it. All you have to do is collect the actual cash from Uncle Sam."

There must have been chortles and knee slapping in the legislative halls at Richmond, seeing that Virginia had been unsuccessful in collecting that debt for over 90 years. But the strange thing is, the Mount Vernon Avenue group very nearly succeeded before the number of years stretched to 100.[28] And, symbolically at least, they did collect the debt in the end. But virtually all original members of the association had died before it happened.[29]

Members of the association got to work on Congress with almost immediate success. On February 28, 1889, Congress directed the Secretary of the Army to survey and make cost estimates for a national road to Mount Vernon.[30]

THE HAINS REPORT

Lieutenant Colonel Peter C. Hains, of the Corps of Engineers, was selected for the job, a most fortunate choice. By January 4, 1890, he had given Congress a report laying out three major routes with multiple variations, and he had described the entire project in lyrical terms that clearly caught its spirit.[31]

Furthermore, while still thinking in terms of horse drawn vehicles, he began to forecast some aspects of a modern parkway when he wrote:

> *It should be wide enough to give it character, and still have room for future adornment and expansion. The grades should be light, the alignment in graceful curves.*[32]

It is worthy of note that Col. Hains' report made no reference to the association's flamboyant plans to make the avenue a cemetery, a garden of statuary, and a permanent exhibit for all the states. He envisioned a noble road, to be sure, but only a road.

From time to time, members of the association still spoke of the original plan, but it was never actually seriously considered again. Meanwhile, the association was highly optimistic. Its charter had been amended to allow the United States to build the road on Virginia soil. Col. Hains had devised an engineering plan that Congress seemed to favor. The U.S. was indebted to the association for a considerable amount. Everyone seemed to expect quick action. What happened next was indeed quick, but the action was totally unexpected.

PRE-EMPTIVE STRIKE

Early in 1892, with little or no advance notice, the Washington, Alexandria, and Mount Vernon Railroad commenced construction of an electric rail line over part of the most scenic route to Mount Vernon. By the end of September, trains were running regularly from the capital to Washington's home.[33]

It was in fact a railroad, but not in local terminology. Those who used it called it the Mount Vernon trolley. The trolley line took away all the momentum that had built up behind the Mount Vernon Avenue. Now it was easy to get to Washington's home, and it was a beautiful ride.[34] Though the Mount Vernon Avenue Association redoubled its efforts, the actual construction of its boulevard was now to be postponed for nearly forty years.

To the backers, it was a tragedy. But from our privileged viewpoint it is clear the delay actually worked to improve the parkway that finally emerged.

Washington himself always used an inland route when he traveled from his home to Alexandria. It was shorter and made the crossing of Hunting Creek, just south of Alexandria, much easier.[35] Col. Hains, in his study, seemed to favor this same alignment for the Mount Vernon Avenue, except that the avenue would follow the high ridges as much as possible.[36] The trolley line opened up a different way, and carried a great many people along the banks of the Potomac, showing them sweeping views of the majestic river.

THE GREENING OF WASHINGTON

More Americans were beginning to appreciate the superb natural setting of their capital. The city was now a century old, and people were beginning to compare it with other great national capitals. The U.S. Senate established an Arts Commission to "enhance the beauty" of the city and its surroundings, and by great good fortune, one of the Commissioners was Frederick Law Olmsted.[37]

In 1901 Mr. Olmsted made a personal survey of the various suggested routes to Mount Vernon,[38] walking along the ridges and the river banks, and probably also riding the trolley. He and the commission approved a route that started with the Memorial Bridge, then also under consideration, proceeded through Alexandria on the street Washington originally surveyed, and then followed the river all the way to Mount Vernon.[39]

IMPROVED BY SETBACKS

This even improved on the rail route, because the trolley left the river to cut across the great curve of the Potomac just before reaching Mount Vernon. Instead, the highway follows that curve. As it does so, it plunges from a high bluff to the river's edge, and the trees seem to part like a curtain to reveal a stunning view of Fort Washington across the Potomac.

So the long delay led to a simplified plan and a better route. Meanwhile, just two years after Mr. Olmsted made his survey, a group of people in New York City were looking at their own natural resources. In 1903 they proposed that the valley of the Bronx River be preserved as a park. Twenty-two years later, in about 1925, the Bronx River Parkway was completed.[40]

It was important that the Bronx be built first. Its designers developed techniques and solutions that helped immeasurably when the time came to build the road to Mount Vernon. For when its time finally came, this boulevard had to be built very fast indeed.[41]

And there was one final gain from the delay. By the time the great avenue was built, horses and carriages were no longer in the picture. We were building now for automobiles.[42]

Members of the Mount Vernon Avenue Association had not dropped their claim against the federal government, and strangely enough, Congress was taking them seriously. At every session since the debt was transferred to the association, a bill had been introduced, and it had been reported favorably by a number of congressional committees.

The Hon. Charles C. Carlin, Representative from Virginia, testified as follows before the House Committee on Claims, December 16, 1908:

> *Virginia's claim has been considered a dozen times by various committees of the House and of the Senate and has been reported upon 9 or 10 times favorably... It so happens that the committees have never managed to report at the same session of Congress; when the House would report favorably, the Senate did not report at all, and when the Senate reported the House did not, and the result has been that no action has been had on the claim.*[43]

The idea of the memorial highway, now linked with construction of the Memorial Bridge, also received increasing support. There were strong endorsements from many leading organizations and individuals, and from several presidents.[44]

MORE DELAY

Congress provided money to begin construction of the Memorial Bridge in 1913,[45] and it looked as though the highway would not be far behind; but then came the first World War, and the grand idea of Mount Vernon Avenue was dead once more, or at best, postponed.

The war that stopped the highway also brought about the decline of the trolley. Passenger and freight revenues both declined, and the line went into receivership in 1920,[46] but continued to run for several years.

In 1924 and 1926 Congress passed legislation creating the National Capital Park and Planning Commission, charged with planning the park system, both in the District of Columbia and its environs in Maryland and Virginia. A truly distinguished committee was chosen, and again Frederick Law Olmsted was among the members.[47]

The event that finally galvanized the Congress into building the Mount Vernon Avenue was nothing new. It had occurred almost two centuries earlier. It was the birth of George Washington. When lawmakers generally realized that the bicentennial of the first President's birth was approaching, rapid action took place.[48]

ANNIVERSARY POWER

On December 2, 1924, Congress created a high level United States Commission for the Celebration of the Two Hundredth Anniversary of the Birth of George Washington.[49] Being high level, the commission was also ponderous, and while it was still pondering Congress acted again.

On May 23, 1928, Congress authorized the Commission, acting through the Agriculture Department and its Bureau of Public Roads, to construct a memorial highway from the Arlington Memorial Bridge to Mount Vernon.[50]

Here at last was the goal the Mount Vernon Avenue Association had fought to achieve, but the association was not around to enjoy the occasion. So far as I have been able to learn, the organization disbanded during World War I. The federal government was now proposing to build its grand avenue at national expense. Nothing further was heard about Virginia's claim for $120,000, and I believe it is safe to say that the debt, if it was a debt, was fully if indirectly paid, 137 years after it was incurred.[51]

The Bicentennial Commission did act expeditiously on one matter. They purchased the disused right-of-way of the Mount Vernon trolley, and three miles of the most scenic portion was made part of the boulevard.[52]

The Bureau of Public Roads was now gearing itself for a maximum effort. Grading of embankments and construction of 12 stone-faced, reinforced concrete bridges was accomplished in 1930 and 1931. Paving was done in 1931. The Bureau deadline for completion of the Mount Vernon Boulevard was February 22, 1932, and they not only met it, but the highway was actually completed and opened to traffic on January 16 of that year.[53] The Bureau is proud of the job it did within restrictive time limits, and well it might be.

TALENT AT WORK

The bureau was also most fortunate in the help it sought. From Westchester County, New York, the bureau hired Jay Downer, Gilmore D. Clarke, and Henry Nye as consultants. All three had worked on the Bronx River and other parkways built by the Westchester County Park Commission.[54]

But the two men who rolled up their sleeves in the old World War I torpedo factory in Alexandria and actually designed the boulevard were Wilbur Simonson and R. E. Toms. Simonson, landscape architect, also from Westchester County, and Toms, the engineer, drew twenty-foot-long plans detailing the entire project.[55]

All of these outstanding consultants, engineers, and designers did not, of course, design a copy of the Bronx River Parkway. But they had solved some of the problems there, and they brought some of their concepts with them — as you can see by looking at the bridges in both thoroughfares.

AT LAST—A PARKWAY

Before construction was well under way, the Congress made an addition.[56] Up to now it had dealt with the Mount Vernon Boulevard; now it was talking parkway. The George Washington Memorial Parkway would incorporate all of the Mount Vernon Boulevard, and in addition it would extend up the Potomac, on both sides, to above Great Falls. Here, a bridge would cross the river, providing fine views of the Potomac River Chasm and the falls. On the Maryland side, the parkway would continue down river to Fort Washington.[57]

Part of this project has never been built. But the portion on the Virginia side, from Memorial Bridge to the beltway, is interesting because it had the advantage of later design.

The Mount Vernon portion has only sections of divided highway. The northern part is all divided. The lower part is partly limited access, a serious mistake. The upper section is entirely limited access.[58]

So far as costs are concerned, Virginia paid nothing for the first section, unless you count that $120,000. For all the rest, both Maryland and Virginia shared the costs of land acquisition with the federal government.[59]

What started as a grandiose carriageway became a pioneering parkway. The original idea was long delayed in becoming reality, and it profited from the delay. The basic plan was simplified and extended; and it was integrated into the total Washington park system.

Circumstances provided the parkway, in its development, design, and construction, with some of the best talent in the world.

ENTER NATIONAL PARK SERVICE

Since its completion, the parkway has been under the care and protection of the National Park Service, which has done a remarkable job of retaining the original concepts under the stress of increasing traffic.

In 1984 NPS began an extensive renovation of the Mount Vernon section, designed to "up-grade the parkway to 1932 standards."[60] The problem now is to determine what can be done to prepare the parkway for the 21st century without losing the attributes we all want to keep.[61]

What the original planners could never have anticipated was that in over 50 years of hard use, the parkway would change from a ceremonial drive to a major commuting thoroughfare.[62] That is what it is today, and yet it still retains much of its beauty, its charm, its aesthetic appeal — for some, even a certain spiritual quality.

Professor Frederick Gutheim, who wrote the definitive book on the Potomac River, calls the parkway an American art form.[63] Some see it as a living sculpture. It is clearly a work of art, and a national treasure.

I lived for a dozen years between the parkway and the river, in Wellington Villa south of Alexandria, and I made that beautiful drive along the Potomac twice a day at all seasons. One of my car pool members gazed at a view of the river framed by the trees, his face almost saint-like. He remarked, "That is truly uplifting. That's all the church I need."

I can't go quite that far, but that inspiring drive keeps my spiritual batteries fully charged from Monday through Friday.

NOTES

1. John R. Reavis, Mount Vernon Avenue (Washington, Mount Vernon Avenue Association, 1888), p. 3.
2. John Addison Porter, The City of Washington, Its Origin and Administration (Baltimore, Johns Hopkins University Press, 1888), p. 6.
3. Porter, p. 7.
4. Committee on Claims, U.S. House of Representatives, Hearings on Senate Bill 5252 to provide for the payment of certain moneys advanced by the States of Virginia and Maryland ... December 16, 1908 (Washington, U.S. Government Printing Office, 1909), p. 4.
5. Committee on Claims, pp. 5-9.
6. Committee on Claims, pp. 5-19.
7. John C. Fitzpatrick, ed., The Writings of George Washington from Original Manuscript Sources, Vol. 31 (Washington, U.S. Government Printing Office, 1939), pp. 280-281. Another letter from President Washington to the District Commissioners, dated August 29, 1793 [Vol. 33, p. 75] establishes that the promised funds had been received, but that not all had been expended for the designated purposes. Portions of the funds had presumably gone for streets, sewers, etc. Also see Donald Jackson and Dorothy Twohig, eds., The Diaries of George Washington, Vol. VI [Jan. 1790-Dec. 1799] (Charlotte, University Press of Virginia, 1978). George Washington's diary for April 12 and 13, 1791, confirms that he was in Richmond on those days and conferred with the governor, but makes no mention of the $120,000.
8. Committee on the District of Columbia, U.S. House of Representatives, Hearings on HR 26, an act for the acquisition, establishment and development of the George Washington Memorial Parkway, March 13 and 21, 1930 (Washington, U.S. Government Printing Office, 1930), p. 17.
9. Committee on Claims, p. 6.
10. Reavis, pp. 6 and 7.
11. Virginia General Assembly, joint resolution adopted March 15, 1850.
12. Eleanor Early, Washington Holiday (New York, Prentice-Hall, 1955), p. 47.
13. David L. Lewis, District of Columbia, a Bicentennial History (New York, W.W. Norton, 1976), pp. 20 and 21.
14. Alex J. Wedderburn, Mount Vernon Ave-

nue (Washington, Art Publishing Co., 1913), under heading "Mount Vernon Has Become a National Shrine" (pages not numbered).

15. Mount Vernon Ladies Association of the Union, Mount Vernon (Mount Vernon, Va., published by the association, 1974), p. 2; and David Murphy, manuscript Mount Vernon Avenue: Forty Years in Design, p. 2. (Mr. Murphy, now Branch Chief for Rights of Way Acquisition, Land Management Division, National Capital Region, National Park Service, prepared this material in 1979 for a program of graduate study in Urban Planning at The George Washington University, Washington, D.C. Much of the text was used in support of a nomination of the parkway for inclusion in the National Register of Historic Places.)
16. Mount Vernon Ladies Association, p. 19.
17. Wedderburn, under heading "Mount Vernon Ladies Association of the Union."
18. Murphy manuscript, p. 2.
19. Early, p. 47.
20. Wedderburn, under heading "Section for Each State."
21. Reavis, p. 3.
22. Wedderburn, under heading "Origin of the Idea."
23. Reavis, p. 3.
24. Reavis, p. 4.
25. Wedderburn, under heading "Section for Each State."
26. Virginia General Assembly, Joint Resolution adopted February 18, 1888.
27. Virginia General Assembly, Joint Resolution adopted March 5, 1888.
28. Murphy manuscript, p. 7.
29. Committee on District of Columbia, p. 17.
30. Lieut. Col. Peter C. Hains, U.S. Corps of Engineers, Report on a Survey of a National Road from Aqueduct Bridge to Mount Vernon, Virginia, contained in letter from the Secretary of War to the Speaker of the House of Representatives, U.S. Congress, January 9, 1890; printed for the House Committee on Appropriations (Washington, U.S. Government Printing Office, 1890), p. 1.
31. Hains report, pp. 2-8.
32. Hains report, pp. 3 and 4.
33. Murphy manuscript, p. 8.
34. Alexandria Gazette, Nov. 10, 1909, states the Washington, Alexandria and Mount Vernon Railway "now has a 5 cent fare."
35. Reavis, pp. 24 and 25.
36. Hains report, pp. 10-13.
37. Committee on the District of Columbia, pp. 4 and 5.
38. National Commission of Fine Arts, Annual Report for 1929 (Washington, U.S. Government Printing Office, 1930), p. 115.
39. Bureau of Public Roads, Department of Agriculture, The Mount Vernon Memorial Highway: History, Design, and Progress in Construction (Washington, U.S. Government Printing Office, 1930), p. 3; and National Commission of Fine Arts, pp. 115 and 118.
40. Committee on the District of Columbia, p. 34.
41. Bureau of Public Roads, pp. 3 and 5.
42. Washington Post, Dec. 13, 1931, article on "Designing 100-Mile-an-Hour Roads," p. 9.
43. Committee on Claims, pp. 5 and 9. The Hon. Charles C. Carlin is the same man who, 22 years earlier, had served as the Alexandria correspondent of the National Republican. It was he who took H. B. Harlow's great idea, the Mount Vernon Avenue, to his editor, Col. E. W. Fox.
44. Wedderburn, under heading "Endorsements by Eminent Men, Organizations, and Commissions."
45. National Commission of Fine Arts, p. 115.
46. Edith M. Spouse, "The Troublesome Road to Mount Vernon," in Fairfax Chronicles

(Fairfax County, Va., Office of Comprehensive Planning), May-July, 1981, p. 2.

47. Committee on the District of Columbia, p. 4.

48. Bureau of Public Roads, p. 3.

49. National Commission of Fine Arts, p. 115.

50. Committee on Roads, U.S. House of Representatives, Committee Meeting February 18, 1930 (Washington, U.S. Government Printing Office, 1930), pp. 1 and 2.

51. Committee on the District of Columbia, p. 17. Commenting on this matter, D. Allen Williams, Associate Professor of History, Corcoran Department of History, University of Virginia, Charlottesville, wrote in a personal letter to the author, April 1, 1983: "[The Virginia claim was] an interesting piece of Virginia legislative sophistry. The General Assembly was transferring money that did not exist, an uncollectible loan, to try to pay its share for a road it did not desire to build.... The good news is that the Federal government did build the Mount Vernon Memorial Highway ... paid for by federal funds."

52. Murphy manuscript, p. 12.

53. Donald M. Sweig, Ph.D., "A Historic New Road to Mount Vernon," in Fairfax Chronicles, Nov. 1982-Jan. 1983, Vol. 61, No. 4, p. 4.

54. Murphy manuscript, p. 15.

55. Alexandria Gazette (Alexandria, Va., George Mair, Editor and Publisher), May 21, 1984, "Parkway Designer Proud of Project," pp. 1 and 5.

56. Committee on District of Columbia, pp. 6 and 7; and National Commission of Fine Arts, p. 115.

57. President's Council on Recreation and Natural Beauty, A Program for Scenic Roads and Parkways (Washington, U.S. Department of Commerce, 1966), p. 1.

58. President's Council, p. 2.

59. Committee on District of Columbia, p. 15.

60. Alexandria Gazette, May 21, 1984, pp. 1 and 5.

61. Concrete Construction (Addison, IL, Concrete Construction Publications), "Mount Vernon Memorial Parkway," Vol. 29, No. 2, February 1984, p. 142.

62. Concrete Construction, p. 137.

63. Frederick Gutheim, Some Thoughts on the 50th Anniversary of the Completion of the George Washington Memorial Parkway, manuscript notes, not dated, copy provided to author by Prof. Gutheim; p. 1.

BIBLIOGRAPHY

Alexandria Gazette, Alexandria, VA: George Mair, Publisher. Nov. 10, 1909, "Letters Column," p. 3.

___, May 21, 1984, "Parkway Designer Proud of Project," pp. 1 and 5.

Bureau of Public Roads, U.S. Department of Agriculture, The Mount Vernon Memorial Highway, History, Design, and Progress in Construction. Washington: U.S. Government Printing Office, 1930.

Concrete Construction, "Mount Vernon Memorial Parkway," Vol. 29, No. 2, February, 1984. Addison, IL: Concrete Construction Publications.

Early, Eleanor, Washington Holiday. New York: Prentice-Hall, 1955.

Fitzpatrick, John C., ed. The Writings of George Washington from Original Manuscript Sources, Vol. 31. Washington: U.S. Government Printing Office, 1939.

Gutheim, Frederick, Some Thoughts on the 50th Anniversary of the Completion of George Washington Memorial Parkway. Manuscript notes, undated, copy provided to author by Prof. Gutheim.

Hains, Peter C., Lieut. Col., U.S. Corps of Engineers, Report on a Survey of a National Road from the Aqueduct Bridge to Mount Vernon, Virginia, contained in letter from the Secretary of War to the Speaker of the House of Representatives, U.S. Congress, Jan. 9, 1890. Printed for the

Committee on Appropriations. Washington: U.S. Government Printing Office, 1890.

Jackson, Donald and Twohig, Dorothy, eds., The Diaries of George Washington, Vol. VI (Jan. 1790-Dec. 1799). Charlottesville: University Press of Virginia, 1978.

Lewis, David L., District of Columbia, a Bicentennial History. New York: W.W. Norton, 1976.

Mount Vernon Ladies Association of the Union, Mount Vernon. Mount Vernon, VA: published by the association, 1974.

Murphy, David, Mount Vernon Highway, 40 Years in Design. Unpublished manuscript written May 1, 1979, as part of a program of graduate study in Urban Planning, The George Washington University, Washington, D.C.

Porter, John Addison, The City of Washington, its Origin and Administration. Baltimore: Johns Hopkins University Press, 1885.

President's Council on Recreation and Natural Beauty, A Proposed Program for Scenic Roads and Parkways. Washington: U.S. Department of Commerce, 1966.

Reavis, John R. Mount Vernon Avenue. Washington: Mount Vernon Avenue Association, 1888.

Spouse, Edith M. "The Troublesome Road to Mount Vernon," in Fairfax Chronicles, May-July 1981. Fairfax, Va.: Office of Comprehensive Planning, 1981.

State of Virginia, General Assembly, Joint Resolution adopted March 15, 1850.

------------- adopted February 18, 1888.

------------- adopted March 5, 1888.

Sweig, Donald M., Ph.D. "A Historic New Road to Mount Vernon," in Fairfax Chronicles, Nov. 1982-Jan. 1983, Vol. VI, No. 4. Fairfax, Va.: Office of Comprehensive Planning, 1983.

U.S. House of Representatives, Committee on Claims, Hearing on Senate Bill 5252 . . . to provide for the payment of certain moneys advanced by the States of Virginia and Maryland . . . Dec. 16, 1908. Washington: U. S. Government Printing Office, 1909.

-------------, Committee on the District of Columbia, Hearings on HR 26, an act for the acquisition, establishment, and development of the George Washington Memorial Parkway, March 13 and 21, 1930. Washington: U.S. Government Printing Office, 1930.

-------------, Committee on Roads, Committee Meeting, Feb. 18, 1930. Washington: U.S. Government Printing Office, 1930.

Washington Post, Donald E. Graham, publisher, issue of Dec. 13, 1931, p. 9, "Designing 100-Mile-an-Hour Roads."

Wedderburn, Alex. J. Mount Vernon Avenue. Washington: Art Publishing Co., 1913.

Urban Parkways in Madison and Dane County, Wisconsin, 1893-1987: A Midwestern Case Study

Paul Skidmore and Arnold R. Alanen, Department of Landscape Architecture, University of Wisconsin, Madison

The origins of parkway development in America are usually traced to situations that occurred in the eastern United States during the nineteenth and early twentieth centuries. Through the efforts of landscape architects such as Frederick Law Olmsted, Sr., Charles Eliot, H.W.S. Cleveland, John Nolen, and several other individuals, a number of notable parks and parkways were developed for public use and enjoyment. Olmsted's Central Park in New York City and Prospect Park in Brooklyn are excellent examples of the former, while the features incorporated into Olmsted's and Eliot's proposals for Boston's park system (the "Emerald Neck-

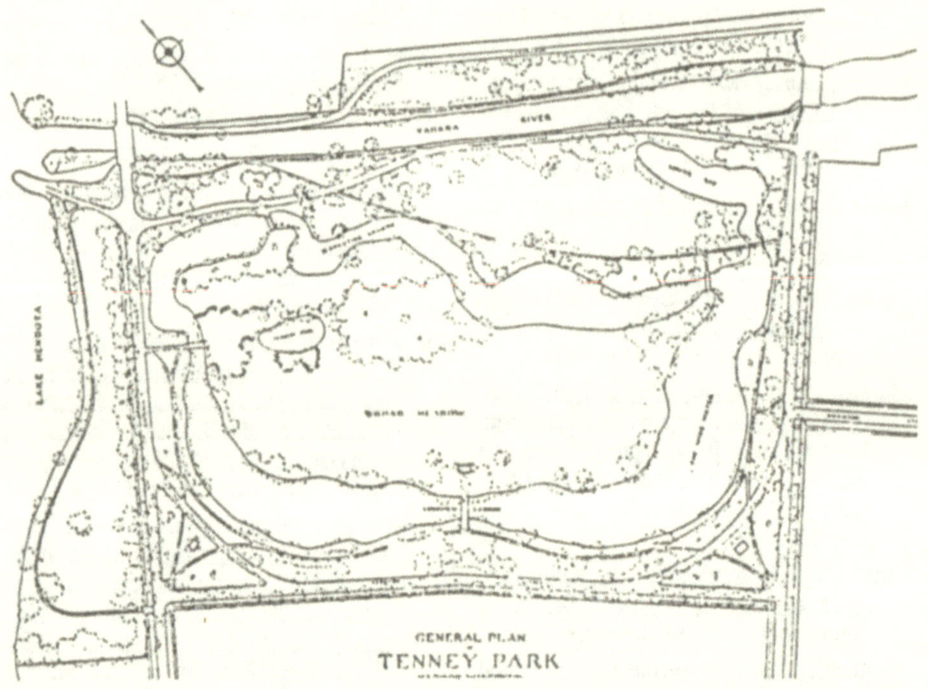

Fig. 1. Tenney Park in Madison, designed by landscape architect O. C. Simonds in the early twentieth century, is still noted for its free-form lagoons, island, and pedestrian bridges. (Source: John Nolen, *Madison: A Model City*, 1911)

lace") typify the best of the latter.[1]

When considering urban parkways, it is obvious that most scholarly attention has been given to developments in the eastern United States. This is only logical since most early parkways, and landscape architects, were situated in this region—the area of highest population density in the nation. Parkway developments that took place elsewhere. and often the landscape architects who designed them, have been ignored in most accounts—especially if the projects occurred in smaller cities and places. (Activities in large metropolises outside the eastern corridor such as Chicago, Kansas City and Minneapolis have been well documented.)

The parkways that emerged in several smaller cities are especially interesting since they often reflected, at least partially and at a reduced scale, the design and planning features utilized in the larger, better known facilities. In many cases the smaller centers have not been threatened by the same development pressures that the larger cities have encountered; thus, the physical evidence is more likely to be discernible. Finally, some of the smaller urban areas with a history of progressive planning traditions display a long and continuous history of parkway development that includes examples of various open space design and planning eras. Madison, Wisconsin, and its surrounding Dane County area, is one place where the history of a constantly evolving open space system can be traced over the span of almost one hundred years.

THE INITIAL DEVELOPMENT OF A SYSTEM

The development of urban parks and parkways was and is an integral part of the overall urban development fabric of Madison and Dane County. Early planners recognized the benefits of scenic and recreational parks, and included proposals for their development in city plans.

The first organized efforts at recreational-parkway planning in Dane County were carried out by the Madison Improvement Association (MIA). This private, non-profit organization was formed in 1893 by a number of prominent, civic-minded Madison leaders for the purpose of securing and developing recreational resources for city residents. The MIA initially raised $15,000 through donations, and hired the renowned architect Frank Lloyd Wright, from nearby Spring Green, Wisconsin, to design public boathouses for two of Madison's lakes. Shortly after these efforts were undertaken, the Association disbanded because of an inability to raise further funds.[2]

Shortly after the Association terminated its activities, a similar nonprofit group, with many of the same directors, was founded. This organization, the Madison Park and Pleasure Drive Association (MPPDA), was created in 1896 and raised money to buy land and develop it into recreational parks and scenic parkways.[3] Unlike its predecessor, the MPPDA was generally successful in achieving the goals of park and parkway development.

Initially, the Association used local volunteer help to develop its facilities. Unsatisfied with no more than sporadic success when pursuing this approach, the Association then made the decision to hire a design consultant in 1899. The directors hired the noted Midwestern landscape architect, Ossian Cole Simonds, to prepare detailed plans for proposed park projects. The most notable products resulting from his efforts were Tenney and Vilas Parks, both located in Madison.

Tenney Park and Vilas Park were significant additions to the MPPDA parkway system. Tenney Park, located on Madison's near east side, is known for its large free form lagoons, island, and pedestrian bridges (Figure 1). Vilas Park, situated on Madison's near southwest side by Lake Wingra, is also known for its lagoons, island, and pedestrian bridges, and has zoological gardens. Both parks have been modified and updated through the years, but they still show much of the form originally designed by Simonds.

In 1906 the Association decided to replace Simonds with a more "aggressive" designer. After a short stint with a local landscape architect, Emil Mische, the directors hired John Nolen, a prominent, Harvard educated landscape architect from Cambridge, Massachusetts to serve as a design consultant. Hired in 1909, Nolen was commissioned to continue the design development of the MPPDA's growing park and parkway system. Later that year he also was authorized to develop a comprehensive plan to guide the long-range future of the city of Madison.

The plan he prepared. entitled, Madison: A Model City, was presented to the Association in 1911. The "Nolen Plan," as it was referred to locally, was based on the City Beautiful concept of long vistas, wide boulevards, and centralized public facilities.[4] Furthermore, the plan called for Madison to be developed as a residential, University, and capital city. To achieve the goal of "a beautiful, well-ordered, free, organic city," Nolen proposed grand boulevards to connect the State Capitol to a proposed civic center on Lake Monona, along with another link between the Capitol and the University of Wisconsin (Figures 2 and 3).[5] Among other features, Nolen's City Beautiful proposal called for or featured:

1. The development of a city wide park system for Madison;
2. The development of automobile parkways that took advantage of Dane County's scenic beauty;
3. Recommendations to improve the scenic beauty of the city in general;
4. The development of an arboretum for the University of Wisconsin;
5. Guidelines for regulating development in Madison (a model zoning code); and
6. A prototypical suburban subdivision design.[6]

Nolen's services to the MPPDA also included the preparation of plans for some of the individual parks he identified in the general plans.[7] Although his proposals for Madison

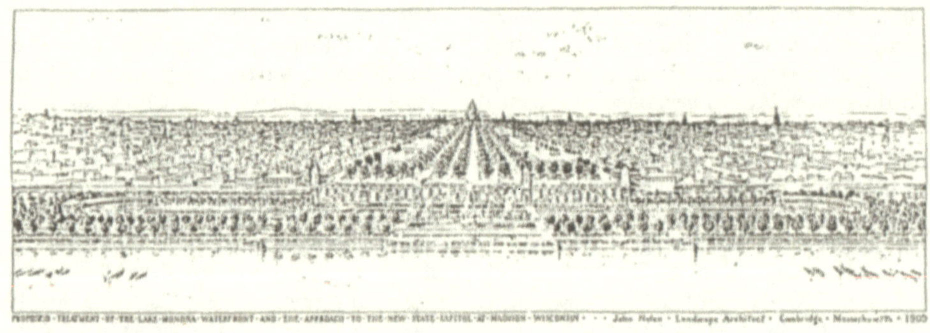

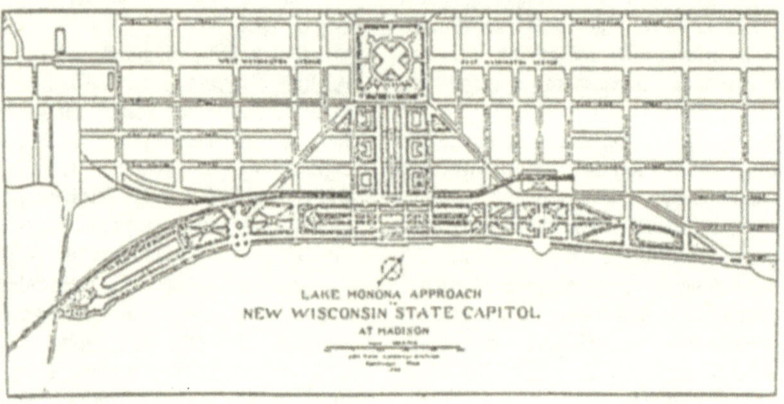

Top: ***Fig. 2. John Nolen, hired by the City of Madison to prepare a long-range plan in 1909, proposed a formal linkage between the State Capitol and Lake Monona.*** (Source: John Nolen, *Madison: A Model City*, 1911.)

Bottom: ***Fig. 3. Based upon City Beautiful planning concepts, Nolen's proposal called for long vistas and wide boulevards.*** (Source: John Nolen Papers, Cornell University Library, Ithaca, N.Y.)

were never fully realized, many elements were carried out and are still discernible today. The most notable accomplishments include the public purchase of waterfront areas, improved main thoroughfares, zoning regulations, and the development of an excellent park system.

The Park and Pleasure Drive Association continued to develop open space facilities after Nolen fulfilled his contract, even though other landscape architects were not hired. The Association continued with its activities in the Dane County Metropolitan Area until 1934, at which time it turned over all land and other assets to the newly formed City of Madison Parks Commission.[8] The Parks Commission has endured through the years, and still exists as the official agency responsible for developing and managing Madison's open space facilities.

Along with the efforts of the MPPDA, several notable landscape architects were designing subdivisions that expanded the Dane County urban parkway system. Besides consulting with the MPPDA, both John Nolen and O.C. Simonds designed "progressive subdivisions" in what was then rural Dane County. Nolen was responsible for Lakewood (later termed Maple Bluff), while Simonds designed Nakoma, a subdivision modeled after the Country Club District of Kansas City, Missouri.

Lakewood embodied Nolen's prototypical subdivision design, and contained many of his planning and development principles (Figure 4).[9] Originally the site was a low grassy beach that sloped toward the marshy waters of Lake Mendota. The area was dredged and filled, which accommodated a small tier of lots that were strung along a curvilinear plat. The central road, Lakewood Boulevard, was divided and typical of other pleasure drives in Dane County.

Nakoma was considered a very progressive subdivision when development began in 1915.[10] Based on an overall plan by O.C. Simonds, much of the detailed design was handled by local professionals (Figure 5). Streets were designed to curve gently along the base of the rolling topography, wide tree-lined boulevards were developed, and several community parks were included in the plan. Also dedicated were a 40 acre golf course and a community grade school. In addition, the subdivision was one of the first in the Dane County area to offer public water, electricity, and street improvements prior to development. Finally, Nakoma homeowners were required to sign an agreement that regulated the type of construction, the kind of use, and other subdivision features.[11]

The subdivisions were typical of a new generation of housing developments in the Dane County area. They included curvilinear streets that followed the natural topography, parks and open space for public recreational use, landscaped boulevards and street terraces to beautify the neighborhood, and building and deed restrictions (early zoning and building codes) to insure orderly and compatible growth.

The new housing developments also added significantly to the number of public parks and parkways in Dane County. Most of the new subdivisions were constructed outside the city limits but were eventually annexed to the City of Madison.

AN ERA OF EXPANSION

Dane County, and Madison in particular, experienced steady growth during the 1920's and 1930's. Subdivisions originally developed outside the city limits of Madison continued to be annexed, and the County's infrastructure was steadily improved to accommodate these developments (Figure 6). The University of Wisconsin was also growing steadily and emerging as one of the more prestigious land grant educational institutions in the nation. These factors, along with the continued growth and evolution of the MPPDA, contributed to the steady development of the County's urban parkway system.

In 1934, the Madison Parks Commission was created to develop and manage parkland areas with the city limits of Madison. The Commission, an agency of city government, essentially took over the assets and management of all parks and parkways that had been established by the Association.[12] Once the voluntary transfer was completed the Association disbanded and all of its functions were handled by the City of Madison. Since that time, park development has been managed by city personnel and funded primarily through tax levies.

Already during the 1920's, the progressive subdivisions developed early in the twentieth century were methodically being worked into the metropolitan service area of Madison. Nakoma was annexed to the City of Madison, and its parks, open spaces, and boulevards were transferred to the Parks Commission. Lakewood was incorporated into the Village of Maple Bluff, and provided its own government and parks commission. Several other subdivisions were created and absorbed into the urban fabric, with many having small community parks and parkways of their own. These subdivisions helped to create a pattern of parks and parkways that emanated outward from the city's center to the fringe areas of new growth.

The University of Wisconsin also contributed to and benefited from the early park developments of Dane County. Prior to 1915 the University did not offer formal courses in landscape architecture. A few planting design courses were taught in the horticultural department, but only on an occasional basis. This changed in 1915, however, when Professor Franz Aust was

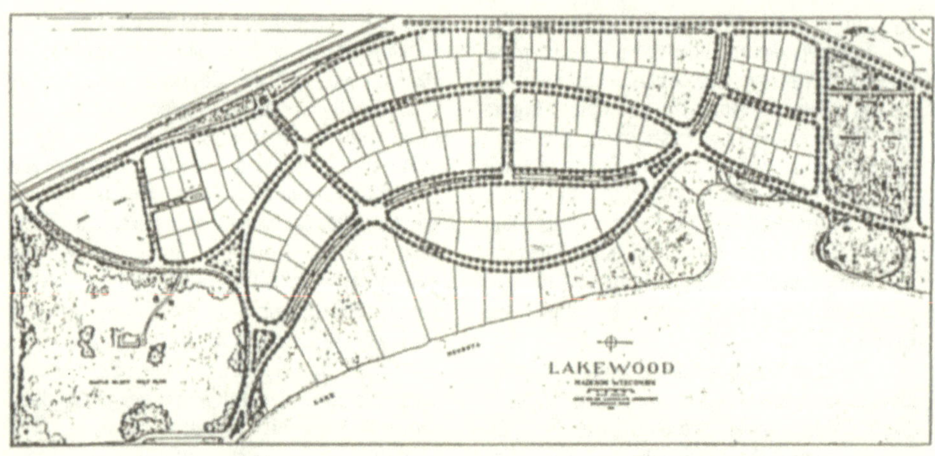

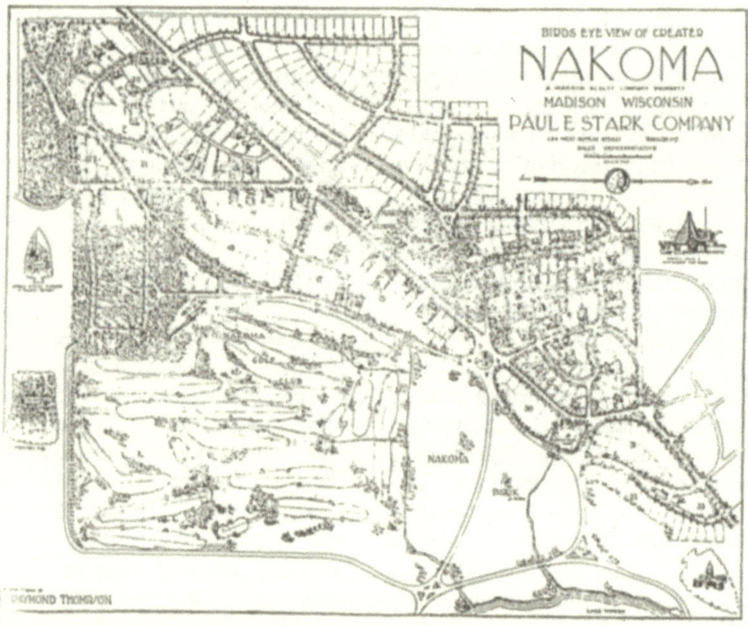

Top: ***Fig. 4. While employed in Madison during the early 1900's, John Nolen also prepared a subdivision plan for Lakewood.*** (Source: John Nolen Papers, Cornell University Library, Ithaca, N.Y.)

Bottom: ***Fig. 5. O. C. Simonds' overall plan for the subdivision of Nakoma began to be developed in 1915. Included in the plan were wide, tree-lined boulevards, several small parks, and a golf course.*** (Source: Paul Stark Company Archives, Madison.)

Following Page: ***Fig. 6. By 1925, several subdivisions—along with their parks and parkways—had been annexed by the City of Madison.*** (Source: Paul Stark Company Archives, Madison.)

hired to teach landscape architecture as a course of study in horticulture. Aust taught landscape architectural design and construction courses and relied upon other departments to complete the program with drafting and other offerings. Aust, who was educated at the University of Michigan under O.C. Simonds, later worked with Wilhelm Miller at the University of Illinois.[13] He was greatly influenced by the philosophy of using native plant materials in landscape design, and promoted these concepts through his teaching and practice.[14]

Several university officials, including Aust, participated in the planning and park development of Dane County during the 1920's and 1930's. Aust, for example, worked for the Madison Realty Company in designing and developing the Nakoma and University Heights subdivisions for the city. He provided detailed designs for parks, boulevards, and other recreational facilities, supervised the street tree program in Nakoma, and designed numerous individual residences in the area. Professor Dickson, a plant pathologist, and Professor Moore, a horticulturist, also helped Aust in the selection of plant materials for the parks. In addition to University officials who participated in this park endeavor, numerous students of Aust had the opportunity to assist in the drafting and field work for the projects.[15]

THE MATURATION OF A SYSTEM

One of the most radical developments in Dane County's parkway development occurred in the late 1950's and early 1960's when Professor Philip Lewis, Jr., of the University of Wisconsin developed his environmental corridor concept. While working for the Wisconsin State Planning Office in the early 1960's, Lewis determined that about 90 per cent of all significant natural resources in the state—such as fish and wildlife habitat—were located in "corridors" that flanked the streams, wetlands, and edges of other natural communities. Preserving these sensitive corridors, Lewis stated, was a vital priority for public officials. According to the landscape architect, designating these environmental corridors as park lands and developing them for recreational use would be beneficial to the public. Lewis also developed numerous plans during the 1960's to incorporate these environmental corridors into the park systems of the state. The "Madison E-Way System" plan, developed in 1971, was the first parkway proposal to utilize specifically designated environmental corridors.[16] Lewis proposed that Madison acquire and develop these corridors, and connect them to other city parks and historic/cultural centers. The "E-Way System" plan, in fact, served as the model for other parkway proposals in the area.

Lewis and others have subsequently developed parkway plans based on the environmental corridor concept. Most notably, Lewis proposed a parkway plan for Dane County that expanded the "Madison E-Way System," and he also designated a regional "E-Way System" that would connect regional environmental and cultural centers via Wisconsin's railways. Until now, however, the state plan has been basically unrealized.

Another important change in Dane County's parkway development has involved the rules that govern subdivision developments in rural areas. Ordinances regulating the platting of undeveloped land into subdivisions were strengthened during the 1960's and 1970's. As is currently true of many areas of the nation, most of Dane County's subdivision ordinances require that a developer dedicate a certain percentage of land in new plats to park and open space for the public use. Whereas such rules ensure that a certain amount of land will be dedicated within a given area, most developers usually designate the least buildable land within the plat for open space use. These areas, however, often have the highest concentrations of sensitive natural resources. Hence, designating them for public open space use has dual benefits: the natural resources are preserved and protected, and the open space areas are owned by the body public.

The Madison Parks Commission, and the Madison Parks Department and its staff, continued to grow throughout the 1960's. The Commission had a healthy budget by this time, and continued to acquire, develop, and main-

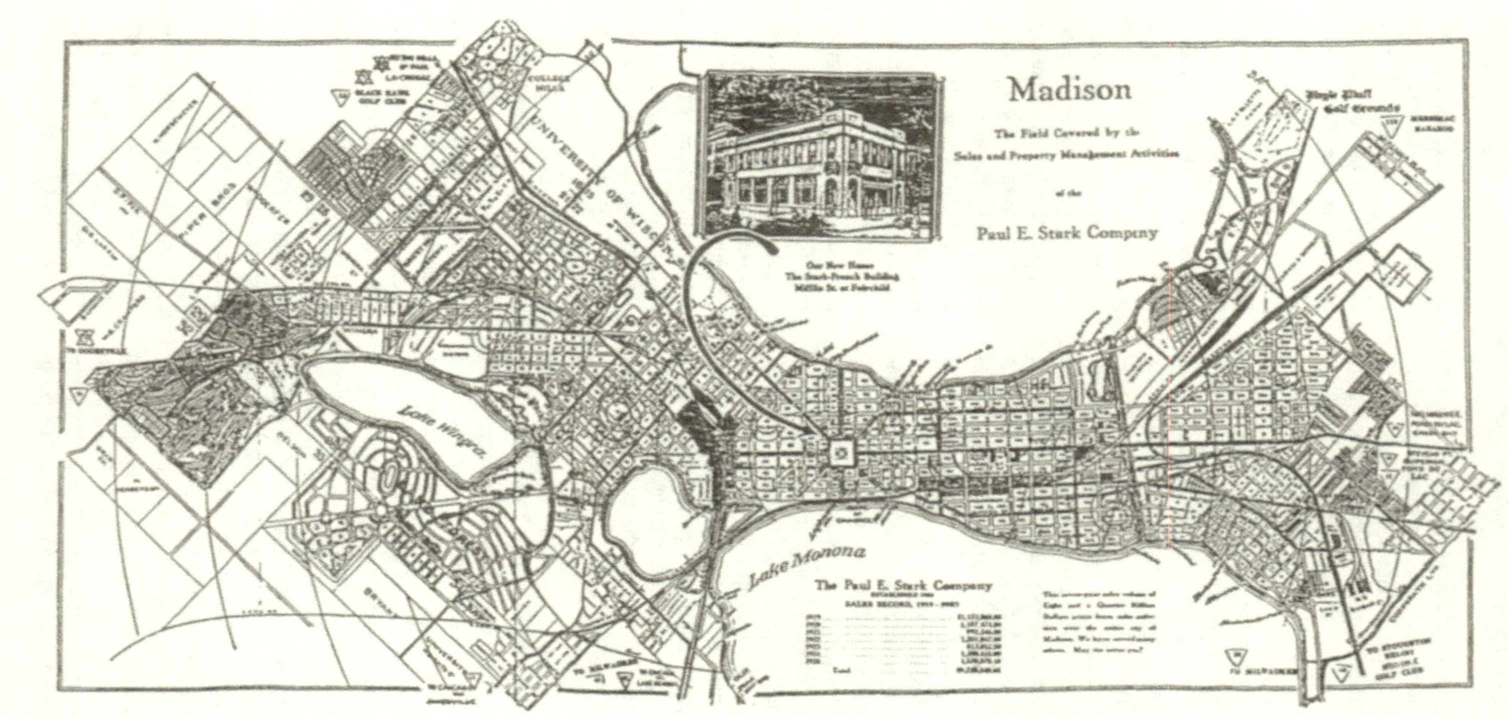
Madison
The Field Covered by the
Sales and Property Management Activities
of the
Paul E. Stark Company
UNIVERSITY OF WISCONSIN
Lake Wingra
Lake Monona
The Paul E. Stark Company

tain parks throughout the city. Also, many small outlying communities had developed their own park commissions and were in the process of implementing individual municipal park systems.

At the same time, Dane County, which had begun to implement its own facilities in 1935, was in the process of developing an extensive county-wide park system. This organization, the Dane County Parks Commission, originated in a manner similar to the Madison Parks Commission. It was created when a private parks organization similar to the MPPDA decided to disband. The group, based in rural Dane County, had developed only one park: Stewart Park in Mt. Horeb, which had been purchased in 1935 shortly after the formation of the parks department.[17] As was true of similar systems elsewhere, Dane County's parks have been selected because of their unique environmental or aesthetic qualities. Interestingly, most of Dane County's parks fall into the environmental corridors that originally had been identified by Lewis.

CONTINUED DEVELOPMENT

The parks and parkways of Madison and Dane County, Wisconsin continue to be developed in a number of ways. The acquisition, construction, and maintenance of scenic and recreational facilities have become an established part of urban and rural planning in the county.

The Dane County Parks Commission, now a well established organization, continues to develop county-wide park and recreational facilities. Since the time of its organization, it has purchased and developed a number of other parks throughout the county. In the 1970's the "E-Way System" concept proposed by Lewis began to be incorporated into planning efforts. Just recently the county conducted a groundbreaking ceremony to initiate a major effort to acquire and preserve numerous environmental corridors within its boundaries.[18] This effort was funded both by tax levies and private donations. The eventual goal is to create a county network of parks that are connected by environmental corridor "parkways." The parkways will have foot and bicycle trails, and also will serve to protect sensitive natural resources.

At the local level, several rural communities in Dane County have developed parks and parkways on a smaller but equally significant scale. Communities such as Fitchburg, Verona, and Sun Prairie have parks departments that acquire, construct, and manage recreational facilities within their jurisdictions. Many of these communities are developing pedestrian and bicycle parkways along environmental corridors that are similar to the approach of Dane County, and also are based on the environmental corridor concept.

Meanwhile, the Madison Parks Commission continues to develop and maintain urban park land on a large scale. According to local park officials, Madison's park system has become one of the largest, most diverse systems for any city of this size in the nation, and includes a zoo, botanical gardens, and numerous athletic and recreational facilities. Finally, throughout Dane County, local subdivision platting ordinances require that developers still must dedicate a percentage of their land for park and recreational purposes. This means that such facilities will continue to be preserved, even as urban development increases. As noted previously, most of the lands dedicated under these ordinances are considered marginal for building purposes, but they are, in fact, generally environmentally sensitive and usually found in corridors. Thus, the merger of historical and contemporary parkways continues in a unified and logical manner.

NOTES

1. See, for example, Norman T. Newton, Design on the Land: The Development of Landscape Architecture (Cambridge, Mass.: Harvard Univ. Press, 1971), pp. 267-317.
2. The Frank Lloyd Wright boathouses were never constructed, but in the early 1900's John Nolen was responsible for siting a similar structure. Constructed in or about 1908, the boathouse is considered the oldest public building in Madison. It still stands

in its original location in Brittingham Park and was placed on the National Register of Historical Places in 1973.

3. James Marshall (former MPPDA employee, and first Director of Parks for Madison), interview with Paul Skidmore, August 5, 1986.
4. "Special City Planning Section," Wisconsin State Journal (Madison), March 4, 1927.
5. John Nolen, Madison: A Model City (Madison: Cantwell Printing Co., 1911), p. 19.
6. Ibid.
7. Barbara Jo Long, "John Nolen: The Wisconsin Activities of an American Landscape Architectural and Planning Pioneer, 1908-1937," unpublished Master's Thesis, University of Wisconsin, Madison, 1978, pp. 28-29.
8. Marshall, interview.
9. Lance M. Neckar, "Progressives, Suburbs, and the Prairie Spirit: Suburban Development in Madison, Wisconsin, 1890-1920," unpublished Master's Thesis, University of Wisconsin, Madison, 1980, pp. 92-94.
10. Ibid., pp. 106-107.
11. The benefits and amenities of Nakoma were promoted in a monthly community newsletter published by the Madison Realty Company from 1915 to approximately 1923. Nakoma's land owners were required to sign an agreement prior to receiving title to their property. This contractual agreement, "for the development and protection of an ideal residential community," served as the legal means for regulating development and land use on individual lots.
12. James Mueller (Dane County Parks Planner), interview by Paul Skidmore, August 13, 1987.
13. Franz Aust's educational and employment history was traced primarily through an unpublished 1942 resume. Additional information was obtained from the University of Michigan's "Calendar" for 1911-1912, and from an interview with Aust's son, Alden, conducted by Paul Skidmore on January 29, 1987.
14. Paul Skidmore, "Franz Albert Aust—Pioneer Landscape Architect," unpublished paper, Department of Landscape Architecture, University of Wisconsin, Madison, 1985, pp. 12-14.
15. Ibid., pp. 8-10.
16. Philip H. Lewis, Jr., Madison E-Way System (Concept Chapter), unpublished report, University of Wisconsin, Madison, 1971, unpaginated.
17. Mueller, interview.
18. "First E-Way Section to Open June 6," Wisconsin State Journal, (Madison). May 4, 1987.

BIBLIOGRAPHY

Gerhauser, Frank E. "Success and Failure in Madison Urban Land Developments." Unpublished Master's Thesis. Madison: University of Wisconsin, 1923.

Lewis, Philip H., Jr. Madison E-Way System (unpublished report). Madison: University of Wisconsin, 1971.

Long, Barbara Jo. "John Nolen: The Wisconsin Activities of an American Landscape Architectural and Planning Pioneer, 1908-1937." Unpublished Master's Thesis. Madison: University of Wisconsin, 1978.

Nakoma Tomahawk. Newsletter published irregularly by the Madison Realty Company, Madison, c. 1915-1923.

Neckar, Lance M. "Progressives, Suburbs, and the Prairie Spirit: Suburban Development in Madison, Wisconsin." Unpublished Master's Thesis. Madison: University of Wisconsin, 1980.

Newton, Norman T. Design on the Land: The Development of Landscape Architecture. Cambridge, Mass.: Harvard University Press, 1971.

Nolen, John. Madison: A Model City. Madison, Wisconsin: Cantwell Publishing Co., 1911.

Skidmore, Paul E. "Franz Albert Aust— Pioneer Landscape Architect." Unpublished paper, Department of Landscape Architecture, University of Wisconsin, Madison, 1985.

Origins of the Baltimore–Washington Parkway: "Connecting the Great City of Baltimore with the Federal Capital"

Jere L. Krakow, Historian, National Park Service, Denver Service Center

One of the fascinating aspects of historical research is the developing of context and connections among phenomena. In the case of the parkways in the vicinity of Washington, D.C., linkages exist between them and the first parkway in Westchester County, New York. When the Bronx River Parkway opened in 1923, it embodied many concepts that had occurred before but that had not been unified until then. Specific elements combined in the 15-mile stretch to Kensico Dam included limited access, gentle curves, and a parklike setting that invited pleasure driving.

An in-depth look at the origins and development of a parkway constructed after several others had already been completed can provide insight into the history of parkways in the United States. For this purpose the Baltimore-Washington Parkway may serve as an example. It is not a classic recreational experience, such as the Blue Ridge Parkway, nor is it just another route to somewhere, such as the interstate highway system. Rather, it is a transitional project which represents a point on a continuum from the parkway to the freeway; it combines elements of both and as such can provide comparative data on road design and development in the United States. To assess origins and development it is necessary to examine some of the milieu spawning the parkway between Baltimore and Washington.

Gilmore Clarke, principal designer for Westchester County and later chairman of the Fine Arts Commission and consultant on the Mount Vernon Memorial Parkway, in charge of land use studies for the Baltimore-Washington Parkway, recalled the role of William W. Miles in the Bronx River Parkway effort. It seems that Miles, member of the zoological board for New York City, became concerned about the Bronx River as it flowed south into New York City, causing a filthy eyesore and sought the help of Governor Charles Evans Hughes in arresting resource deterioration. For Miles, a trip to visit Andrew Carnegie in Scotland stimulated his vision for the Bronx Valley. Miles observed a small stream running through the village at Inverness while visiting in Scotland. It was "in sharp contrast to the filthy, smelly waters of the Bronx River in New York."[1] Upon his return he lobbied the New York State Legislature for a bill to study the problem. At first unsuccessful, Miles persevered and in 1906 the legislature passed "a bill authorizing a commission of three, to be appointed by the Governor, to inquire into the advisability of preserving the waters of the Bronx River from pollution and creating a park reservation of the lands on both sides of the river."[2] The newly formed Bronx River Parkway Commission included Miles as Secretary and Counsel, and through its efforts secured passage of a bill to acquire land for a park, clean up the river, and, later, to provide a road through the parkland as a pleasant entryway to New York City from Westchester County.

A concern for the urban scene and the contiguous rural landscape coincided with the focus of reformers in American society at the time. The Age of Industrialism after the Civil War had brought about fundamental changes in American society. On the one hand, backward-looking Americans sought a return to the older, agrarian America when life seemed uncomplicated and conventional. On the other, industrialists recognized the changes wrought by exploitation of basic natural resources such as iron and coal, the changing transportation network, especially railroads, and the industrial sector which used combinations of the above and lured more and more workers to America's cities.

The reform movement affected all levels of government and dealt with such issues as crime in the cites, minority rights, and pure food and drug laws, to name a few. Most reformers were firmly entrenched in the middle class and therefore viewed the world from that perspective. Harvard historian Frank Friedel notes that they "believed in Social Darwinism—the idea of the survival of the fittest applied to human society" and possessed faith in the concept.[3] One element in that belief system was a faith in science and technology which translated into the notion that societal ills could be corrected through study and investigation. A favorite device used by the reformers, evidenced in the Bronx River Parkway project, was the investigative commission. Former New York governors Theodore Roosevelt and Charles Evans Hughes used them effectively to address problems called to their attention.

Cleaning up the Bronx River Valley by means of a commission investigating the issue of preservation fit well with a world view of solving problems through scientific means. The effort brought together those imbued with nature and those who viewed the future with optimism. A cleaned-up valley portended the urban populace communing with nature away from the teeming city to the south, yet suited the world view of the reformers who could claim it for a victory. Incidentally by 1923 they used their automobiles for a pleasuring experience, one that the masses ordinarily did not have available to them.

A concomitant development bespoke the importance of preserving and interacting with nature. In his well known work, Wilderness and the American Mind, Roderick Nash underscores the fact that wilderness of the early twentieth century "had attained the dimensions of a national cult."[4] Such defects in society as crime, slums, and corruption could be corrected by opportunities to touch nature through restored or natural landscapes like that along the Bronx River. Writing in the Chicago Plan of 1907, Daniel Burnham, active in the McMillan Plan for Washington, D.C., also expressed the need for nature when he said, "He who habitually comes in close contact with nature develops saner methods of thought than can be the case when one is habitually shut up within the walls of a city."[5] One might also identify elements of cleaning out less desirable residents (especially new immigrants), such as occurred in Westchester County, all in the name of progress.

One particular irony happened to be the desire to present a favorable entryway to New York City from Connecticut. If the city represented much that was wrong in the nation, should a pleasant entryway be used to embellish the image? Of course duality of thinking has no chronological or generational bounds, as we, too, elevate both wilderness and the city in the late twentieth century.

If entryway into New York City assumed importance, it likewise became very important to the nation's capital. A number of individuals lamented the negative impression gained in entering Washington, D.C., from either Maryland or Virginia. Gilmore Clarke raised the issue in a succinct way by calling existing highways in 1938 "ugly and sordid traffic arteries entering the city. There is hardly a more indecent approach to a great capital in all the world than the approach to Washington from Baltimore over United States Route 1."[6] His observation served as part of a rationale for parkway construction between the two cities.

Origins of the planning in the Federal City of Washington, D.C., preceded Clarke's concern by many years, beginning with the selection of Pierre Charles L'Enfant to design the city. George Washington chose the site on the banks of the Potomac "and set its boundaries four-square to the compass points . . . ."[7] During July of 1790 Congress established the location of the nation's capital on the banks of the Potomac, while Philadelphia remained the temporary capital for ten years. This allowed time to adequately plan the site and start the process which continues today.

L'Enfant, chosen by President Washington, had no particular background or experience in planning, and embodied "the artist of the army" concept.[8] He had designed Federal Hall in New York City and, besides being French (Americans loved the French), possessed a fine reputation.

Remarkably, between March and June of 1791, L'Enfant studied the natural setting and conceptualized a plan in first draft. It reflected the topography, tied grid streets together with major radial avenues and provided for "nodes of urban development" with other radial streets.[9] Sited in the plan were the president's residence, the Capitol, and the ceremonial route, Pennsylvania Avenue. The ten mile square area had a unity which transcended time; from key points the entire setting could be observed spreading from the confluence of the Anacostia and Potomac Rivers, including the coastal plain to the surrounding hills. "L'Enfant consistently stressed his aim to generate development of the city throughout its entire area, and the simultaneous development of its several major districts."[10]

Tributes to the physical setting and L'Enfant's plan came from a variety of travelers approaching Washington from the vicinity of the present Baltimore Washington Parkway. Frederick Gutheim underscores that from the north "travelers had a synoptic view of the town and its natural setting from the hills above the Bladensburg road."[11] It was a panorama which needed a grand entryway to the Federal City, an absence which was often lamented by Clarke and others.

The nineteenth century saw the populating of the Washington area at an ever increasing pace. L'Enfant's imprimatur remained and was accented as public and private buildings went up and development spread through and beyond the district. As in other cities, public transportation systems aided municipal growth. Urban areas like the capital city became targets of reform as concern mounted for improving the environment of more and more Americans. Planned urban design came of age, a panacea for the urban setting.

For twentieth century development of Washington, the McMillan Plan, named for Senator James McMillan of Michigan, guided the effort. A new wave of municipal revitalization had broken over the land. Initiatives from the aforementioned faith in science and technology were illustrated to the maximum at the World's Columbian Exposition held in Chicago in 1893. For the Federal City, the McMillan Plan of 1902 embedded in L'Enfant's original plan, served as a blueprint for revamping the mall, building a park system and grouping major buildings.

Specific elements of the plan concerned the matter of Washington area parkways. The routes identified in a conceptual fashion became in due course the George Washington Memorial Parkway on both sides of the Potomac River, and the Rock Creek Parkway from the creek mouth to the National Zoo. Another linkage of parks envisaged in the plan used the natural topography of heights to tie Civil War sites into a proposed Fort Drive. Later additions included the Baltimore-Washington and Suitland Parkways. Centered around the Chicago World's Fair design concepts, the individual expression of Washington, D.C., became the "City Beautiful" movement. This urban reform effort closely paralleled the ascendant progressivism of the age; social ills evidenced in American cities could be "fixed up" by applying scientific approaches to problems.

During the years before construction of parkways in the Washington area began, several agencies were responsible for planning. Beginning in 1910 the Fine Arts Commission directed implementation of the McMillan Plan recommendations. Duties of the Commission were to "advise on the location of statues, fountains, and monuments in the public squares, streets, and parks in the District of Columbia," plus make recommendations concerning public buildings.[12] In 1924 the newly designated National Capital Park Commission assumed some of the responsibilities and itself was replaced in 1926 by the National Capital Park and Planning Commission (NCP & PC). This commission originated in response to efforts to implement the City Beautiful movement and lead the nation to the promised land of planning verities. Both bodies consulted with the Commission on Fine Arts on planning matters in the District and adjacent areas of Maryland and Virginia. Parkways would be the principal "work program" of the NCP & PC, and were "basic elements in City Beautiful planning."[13] As automobile traffic proliferated throughout the 1920's, apprehension over its impact in metropolitan Washington mounted. One recommendation of the McMillan Commission regarded establishment of a parkway running between Mount Vernon and the capital city. Many people complained of the visually poor approaches to Washington's home and to the District from the Virginia side. The approach served as a reminder of the desire to improve all routes leading to the city. To that end the Capper-Crampton Act of 1930 became a means. Sponsored by Louis C. Crampton of Michigan, and Arthur Capper of Kansas, House and Senate District Committee Chairmen respectively, the legislation made $16,000,000 available for acquiring parkland in the District of Columbia. An early beneficiary from the act was the George Washington Memorial Parkway for which land was purchased along the Potomac. This proposed parkway along both sides of the Potomac linking together the Mount Vernon Memorial Highway and the Potomac Palisades area came from ideas presented by Milton Medary and Charles Eliot. It would serve to underscore the need for a suitable entryway into the nation's capital.

Likewise, another recipient was the future Baltimore-Washington Parkway. Drawing on popular thought about advantages of parkways throughout the United States, proponents of that route went into action. Arguments favoring the roadway during the 1920s revolved around the notion of traffic volume and a scenic entrance into both cities, and especially the capital, in addition to general bandwagon propensity for building parkways at the time. Writing to Charles Moore in 1925, Fine Arts Commission Chairman James Greenleaf urged that the route of such a parkway be

> *cut straight through vergin* [sic.] *territory from the north portal to the City at the end of 16th Street, instead of following the old line of roads out of Maryland Ave. through the narrow streets of Bladensburg and other villages.*[14]

Greenleaf based much of his opinion on remarks delivered by Jay Downer of the Westchester County Park and Parkway Commission, at a conference held at "Skyland in the Shenandoah Range."[15] Downer had argued for new road alignments as being least disruptive to local residents, commercial establishments, and control of access. Notably Downer viewed

> *a parkway, not necessarily as a boulevard of uniform width lined with double rows of trees but a narrow park of varying width through which single or double lines of traffic way wended, all as best suited local topography and conditions.*[16]

Frederick Delano, Chairman of the NCP & PC, strongly supported the new parkway proposal as a means of "connecting the great city of Baltimore with the Federal Capital."[17] In the same communique, Delano expressed support for the parkway to Col. C.O. Sherrill, Chairman of the National Capital Park Commission, countering opposition Sherrill had received from a "Baltimorian" complaining of costs. Delano also made his opinion clear about design matters, saying that a parkway should be a "strip of varying width with roadways on the outer edge and park between, which should be liberally planted with trees wherever possible or retained as forested land."[18] Delano added that a parkway should vary "in width from 100 to 1000 feet," with an average of about 300 feet.

The "Manufacturers Record," a periodical published in Baltimore, took a keen interest in the highway in the mid 1920s and exchanged correspondence with Colonel Sherrill about a speech he had made in Baltimore during the fall of 1925 favoring a boulevard between the cities. Writing to Sherrill later that fall, Baltimore writer Victor Power sought material for an article in the publication supporting the road and raised the initial tie between the route and various nearby military installations. Power stated that

> *the road would have certain military importance and significance. Within call of the roadway would be Fort Myer, Camp Meade, Fort Howard, Baltimore, the Naval Academy, Annapolis, not counting the military adjuncts and establishments in Washington.*[19]

A final point in the letter cut to the heart of funding the effort: linking the military installations with the roadway would "move the administration to help finance it as a war insurance measure."[20]

Advocacy for a parkway gathered momentum during the late 1920s when groups like the NCP & PC took up the effort. Ulysses S. Grant III, Executive Officer, expressed to William

Ellicott the desire of the Commission for the parkway, calling attention to its recommendation in annual reports from 1927-1929. He also pointed out that the pending Capper-Crampton bill included monies for parkway construction as far as Camp Meade.[21] In the same letter Grant raised the matter of a regional planning commission in the Baltimore area advocating the parkway. Near the District, the Maryland National Capital Park and Planning Commission (founded in 1927) would be active in directing and coordinating planning related to projects of mutual interest such as that proposed in the parkway concept.

By 1930 it became apparent that the major impetus for establishment of a parkway came from the Washington end of the route. Maryland would have to develop a lobbying effort and build a portion of the route on land between Baltimore and Camp Meade acquired from private interests. Members of various Washington area planning agencies often used arguments specifying the economic advantage that accrued to Westchester County, New York, after the parkway opened there in 1924.

A major portion of the rationale for building the Baltimore-Washington road can be found in a report by T.C. Jeffers, NCP & PC Landscape Architect.[22] The purpose, according to Jeffers, was "to attract as much of the passenger vehicle traffic from the present Baltimore Boulevard as possible," leaving this already congested highway to bus and freight traffic.[23] In order to do this, Jeffers advocated the creation of "a high speed driveway in as direct a line as possible with large radius curves and a minimum number of highway crossings."[24] He added that "border roads" should divert local traffic to major crossings of the parkway. Jeffers also drew up a proposed route for the parkway by September of 1932, all the way to Camp Meade which reflected widths advocated earlier by Delano.

Preliminary plans for routes included one that ran from Anacostia River Valley to Indian Creek then to Laurel before crossing to the Patuxent and Patapsco Rivers. A portion of the route crossed the ongoing Beltsville development of the United States Department of Agriculture (USDA). Workers cleared deadfall from some portion of these lands. All live trees and shrubs were to be protected, and especially was this true in the case of small dogwood trees.[25] Studies of land use near the routes increased by the mid 1930s when Gilmore Clarke assumed charge of those studies.[26] Clarke was nationally known in the field of land planning and parkway design.

Designers such as Jeffers sought to include diversity in the route by considering topography which would permit "various kinds of recreation," such as informational waysides, and lakes near Branchville.[27] Said Jeffers, "picnic areas are to be provided at suitable locations" for both residents and through travelers that they may have "pleasant resting and lunching places."[28] Of note, he added the opinion that "It might be desirable to establish a model wayside camping ground for tourists," on the Beltsville property.[29] This suited other design concepts being considered; as Nolen expressed to Delano, a parkway should be a "limited way but the dual highway is the coming thing for intercity and regional routes."[30]

Advocates addressed many regional issues including roadways, in a Maryland planning document prepared in 1937.[31] Of the new roads being endorsed in the report, one was a divided four-lane route running between Washington and Baltimore. Discussion of the parkway to Baltimore included traffic survey information gathered by the United States Bureau of Public Roads in 1932. This indicated some "18-1/2 percent of the travelers had as their origin or destination locations other than Maryland, Virginia, or the District of Columbia."[32] In short, intercity needs dominated design considerations.

Design concepts employed in the report buttressed those noted above and pointed up how many road engineers looked to railroads for the success of such concepts as "limited access separated as to direction, and scheduled for fast express and slow-moving freight."[33] Applied to highway design, the parkway concepts in due course evolved to the design of freeways on the American scene. The Maryland report was circulated for comment and a point made by the NCP & PC, prepared at the request of the National Park Service, expressed disagreement over the definition of "parkway." Reviewers wrote that

> *the term parkway has been pretty definitely tied down by legal definition as "an attenuated park with a road through it." Three characteristics determine a parkway: (1) linear form, (2) a road through it, (3) no right of light or air or access to abutting property.*[34]

Delano also circulated the report to members of Congress to make them aware of coordinated planning efforts and of the need for interstate cooperation as rapid growth continued.

Other avenues taken to muster public support consisted of press releases and feature articles in local newspapers by such advocates as Gilmore Clarke. Not only did Clarke explain why a parkway was needed between the two cities of Washington, D.C., and Baltimore, but he laid out many elements of design to enhance public knowledge.[35] The more important elements called attention to such concepts as limited access, controlled right-of-way, absence of at-grade crossings, entrances and exits on the right-hand side, and divided roadways.[36] Clarke urged that beauty and efficiency should be uppermost as highway engineer and landscape architect closely collaborate, that roadsides and structures should harmonize with the environment and topography, and parking spaces should be away from traffic but provide for those desiring to stop.[37]

During the summer of 1939 a sizeable addition in acreage to Camp Meade carried implications for the parkway route. The War Department obtained money to add nearly 10,000 acres to the reservation. At a conference late in July, the Camp Meade Commander agreed with the planning commissions present to permit the parkway to follow along the edge of the new addition.[38] The land purchase closed most of the gap between Camp Meade and the Agriculture Research Center. Secretary of War Harry H. Woodring advised Delano during the summer of 1940 that as soon as funds became available, land would be acquired,

> *including the route for this highway, and the War Department will favorably entertain a further request from the proper agencies to use and occupy so much of War Department lands as are necessary to construct the highway in the location herein approved.*[39]

Just before Pearl Harbor and American entry into World War II, cost estimates began to appear in the range of $12,000,000 to $15,000,000.[40] Wilson Ballard, Chief Engineer of the Maryland State Roads Commission, expressed concern about funding the parkway, though Director of Planning for the NCP & PC, John Nolen, tempered that view. Nolen and Chairman Delano believed that, although the project seemed costly, monies in an amount greater than "50 percent Federal funds might be available under the Federal Aid Road program," since several federal installations lay along the proposed route.[41] During 1942 the Franklin D. Roosevelt Administration released $2,000,000 of National Industrial Recovery Act (NIRA) funds for the Baltimore-Washington Parkway.[42] It provided land acquisition from the Peace Monument at Bladensburg to Greenbelt and from Laurel Road to the Jessup entrance of Fort Meade. Survey work secured funding from both the NCP & PC and the Maryland NCP & PC whose sources included appropriations made under the Capper-Crampton Act of 1930.

It became more apparent during the war years that federal largesse would be tapped for the parkway and for the management of some portion of it. Originally, the State of Maryland planned to construct it; however, by 1943 the NCP & PC believed that "at least the section from Washington through Fort Meade should be a Federal project, maintained and controlled by the National Park Service."[43] Commission minutes went on to add that the parkway simply extended from the Anacostia River Parkway, a portion of the District of Columbia park system, thereby "making it eligible for construction by the National Park Service."[44] Sections of the road not funded by the NIRA could be funded by the NPS, but only "as a post-war project."[45] For Maryland, it likely meant funding the portion from Fort Meade to Baltimore, though the NCP & PC specifically sought funding it all the way to Baltimore.[46]

A sticky issue constantly raised in the documents pertained to the route to be followed. Various federal agencies had differing points of view, and so did the different planning commissions. The major problem related to the portion of the route running from New York Avenue to Greenbelt. The NCP & PC preferred the Anacostia route, while the Public Roads Administration favored a route on the higher land to the east. Though the route would enter the District at New York Avenue (same as at present), Delano desired a feed into the "Anacostia River Parkway southwest to Constitution Avenue, underpassing all bridges, and finally continuing to the proposed river crossing at Alexandria and over the George Washington Memorial Parkway to Fort Washington."[47]

Capper-Crampton funds could be used along the Anacostia River for extension of the park system, but not in "construction of roads. . . except if and as Federal aid highways."[48] As typically happens, the opposing interests each compromised to some extent, due to the persuasiveness of impending loss of funds due to the deadline, and to the endorsement of the easterly route by NPS Architect, Thomas Vint.

In the Beltsville area the USDA granted a right-of-way across its property that ranged from 400 to 800 feet wide and encompassed 153.868 acres. Right-of-way acquired at Fort Meade comprised 94 acres and some "206 acres from the Federal Public Housing Authority through the Greenbelt area."[49] It remained, however, for umbrella legislation to be enacted by Congress in order to lay out the provisions of the new parkway between Washington and Baltimore. The drafting of legislation coincided with construction on small sections of the road using FIRA funds, with deliberations about underground utility conduits, and with discussions over whether to allow buses on the parkway. Late in 1946 Park Service Associate Director Arthur E. Demaray sent a draft of a proposed bill to Commissioner Thomas MacDonald of the Public Roads Administration.[50] The draft attempted to grapple with the matter of administering and funding the parkway. After many exchanges of comments on the various sections, the bill was introduced in the House of Representatives April 8, 1948, and referred to the Committee on Public Works.[51] While subjected to rigorous examination and review, it remained basically intact, though not passed and signed into law until President Harry S Truman did so in August, 1950.

The law provided that the parkways be administered by the Secretary of the Interior through the NPS; monies for parkways would be appropriated yearly to the NPS and be used for "continuing the construction, development, maintenance and policing of the Baltimore-Washington...Parkways."[52] Land for the parkway to Baltimore would be acquired by the United States and considered as an extension "of the park system of the District of Columbia and its environs."[53] Camp Meade remained the northernmost point of federal control while Anacostia Park served as the southern limit. Specific design considerations called for the parkway to be

> *administered as a limited access road primarily to provide a dignified, protected, safe, and suitable approach for passenger vehicle traffic to the National Capital and for an uninterrupted means of access between the several Federal establishments adjacent thereto and the seat of government in the District of Columbia.*[54]

Determining types and classes of vehicles using the parkway, plus the location of access points, was to be controlled by the Secretary of the Interior with concurrence of the Federal Works Agency. Cost estimates of the federal portion of the parkway fell in the $15,000,000 range, while Maryland estimated the same amount for the twelve miles from Jessup to the Baltimore city line.[55]

Portions of the route between the two metropolitan areas were in the early stages of construction by 1943, and subsequent sections were completed before passage of the legislation of 1950. Federal appropriations increased after 1950 and resulted in completion of the entire parkway in October, 1954. Reporter Wes

Barthelmes, of the *Washington Post and Times Herald*, wrote a lengthy article extolling the importance of the new road. It would, he said, supplant Route 1 (Washington-Baltimore Boulevard) and rectify "the delays and seedy and cluttered appearance along. . . Suicide Lane, alias Bloody Mary. . . , where since 1942 there have been 347 persons killed and 4688 injured in 9428 accidents."[56] Senator Millard Tydings, Maryland, also spoke glowingly of the new parkway and the contributions it made to Maryland and the nation as an important military defense highway and route of escape in the event of a nuclear war.

Illustrative of the joint effort by the Federal Government and the State of Maryland, the portion to Jessup from the District was known as a parkway while the state portion was labeled a freeway. By whatever name, traffic counts the first week showed a daily average of 21,000 vehicles using it, some 6000 more than expected.[57]

With completion of the Baltimore-Washington Parkway, a major alternative route between the two cities became operational. The original idea for such a roadway, and the shaping of it into reality constitute a significant contribution to the history of modern highways in the United States. In this case study can be seen important design concepts leading from parkway to freeway. The application of principles derived from such sources as railroad design and other parkway experiences enabled the development of the Baltimore-Washington and advanced road design further along the continuum of parkway to freeway. Limiting access, eliminating at-grade crossings, and developing acceleration and deceleration lanes became commonplace concepts in public road design due to their application on such as the Baltimore-Washington Parkway.

A final important lesson from that experience relates to the interaction of various planning commissions, federal agencies, and state agencies. Though all had turf to protect and constituencies to consider, communication and compromise permitted the public to benefit from the collective effort.

The parkway met most of the goals expressed early on in the project, except for the provision of a quality entryway into the Federal City. This effort continues and, like planners and designers earlier in this century, a vision guides those who continue to seek an improved entryway into the nation's capital.

NOTES

1. Washington Star, June 5, 1938, National Archives, Record Group 328, Box 126.
2. Norman T. Newton. Design on the Land: The Development of Landscape Architecture (Cambridge: The Belknap Press of Harvard University Press, 1974), pp. 598-599.
3. Frank Friedel. America in the Twentieth Century, fourth edition (New York: Alfred A. Knopf, 1976), p. 4.
4. Roderick Nash. Wilderness and the American Mind, revised edition (New Haven: Yale University Press, 1975), p. 140.
5. Charles N. Glaab and A. Theodore Brown. A History of Urban America (London: The Macmillan Company, 1972), p. 262.
6. Washington Star, June 5, 1938, National Archives, Record Group 328, Box 126.
7. Frederick Gutheim. Worthy of the Nation: The History of Planning for the National Capital (Washington, D.C.: Smithsonian Institution, 1977), p. 2.
8. Ibid., p. 16.
9. Ibid., p. 25.
10. Ibid., p. 26.
11. Ibid., p. 20.
12. Ibid., p. 152.
13. Ibid., p. 171.
14. Greenleaf to Moore, letter dated June 9, 1925, National Archives, Record Group 328, Box 126.
15. Ibid.
16. Ibid.
17. Delano to Sherrill, letter dated September 30, 1925, National Archives, Record Group 328, Box 126.

18. Ibid.
19. Power to Sherrill, letter dated October 21, 1925, National Archives, Record Group 328, Box 126.
20. Ibid.
21. Grant to Ellicott, letter dated March 10, 1930, National Archives, Record Group 328, Box 126.
22. "The Baltimore Parkway," unpublished report dated September 16, 1932, National Archives, Record Group 328, Box 126.
23. Ibid.
24. Ibid.
25. Demaray to Symons, letter dated July 30, 1934, National Archives, Record Group 328, Box 126.
26. Nolen to Wirth, memorandum dated May 17, 1935, National Archives, Record Group 328, Box 126.
27. Jeffers, unpublished briefing sheet dated June 4, 1935, National Archives, Record Group 328, Box 126.
28. Ibid.
29. Ibid.
30. Nolen to Delano, memorandum dated March 16, 1936, National Archives, record Group 328, Box 126.
31. Maryland State Planning Commission, "Regional Planning, Paret IV- Baltimore-Washington-Annapolis Area," November 1937, National Archives, Record Group 328, Box 126.
32. Ibid.
33. Ibid.
34. National Capital Park and Planning Commission, "Comments on Report of Maryland State Planning Commission on State Recreational Areas," unpublished 1938?, National Archives, Record Group 328, Box 126.
35. Washington Star, June 5, 1938, National Archives, Record Group 328, Box 126.
36. Ibid.
37. Ibid.
38. Delano to MacDonald, letter dated July 31, 1939, National Archives, Record Group 328, Box 126.
39. Woodring to Delano, letter dated June 8, 1940, National Archives, Record Group 328, Box 126.
40. Minutes of National Capital Park and Planning Commission, September 1941, National Archives, Record Group 328, Box 126.
41. Ibid.
42. Demaray to Fleming, letter dated September 28, 1942, National Archives, Record Group 328, Box 126.
43. National Capital Park and Planning Commission Minutes, November 4, 1942, National Archives, Record Group 328, Box 126.
44. Ibid.
45. Ibid.
46. Ibid.
47. Delano to Ballard, letter dated September 19, 1941, National Archives, Record Group 328, Box 126.
48. Director to Associate Director, National Park Service, memorandum dated September 7, 1944, National Archives, Record Group 79, Box 2835.
49. Ibid.
50. Demaray to MacDonald, letter dated December 30, 1946, National Archives, Record Group 79, Box 2835.
51. HR 6177, National Archives, Record Group 328, Box 127.
52. Draft of Bill, National Archives, Record Group 328, Box 129.
53. Ibid.
54. Ibid.
55. Washington Star, August 4, 14, 1950, National Archives, Record Group 328, Box 129.
56. Washington Post and Times Herald, October 4, 1954, National Archives, Record Group 328, Box 129.

57. Washington Star, October 30, 1954, National Archives, Record Group 328, Box 129.

BIBLIOGRAPHY

Primary Sources

National Archives: Record Group 79, National Park Service.

Record Group 328, National Capital Park and Planning Commission.

Secondary Sources

Friedel, Frank. America in the Twentieth Century, fourth edition. New York: Alfred A. Knopf, 1976.

Glaab, Charles N. and A. Theodore Brown. A History of Urban America. London: The Macmillan Company, 1972.

Gutheim, Frederick. Worthy of the Nation: The History of Planning for the National Capital. Washington, D.C.: Smithsonian Institution, 1977.

Nash, Roderick. Wilderness and the American Mind, revised edition. New Haven: Yale University Press, 1975.

Newton, Norman T. Design on the Land: The Development of Landscape Architecture. Cambridge: The Belknap Press of Harvard University Press, 1974.

Congress and the Development of the Natchez Trace Parkway, 1834 - 1946

Philip A. Grant

On February 20, 1934 Senator Hubert D. Stephens of Mississippi introduced a bill calling for a $50,000 appropriation in order to initiate a survey of the Natchez Trace, which during the seventeenth and eighteenth centuries had been a major Indian trail extending through the states of Mississippi, Alabama, and Tennessee. The Stephens Bill, having the avowed objective of constructing a federal road bearing the name Natchez Trace Parkway, read as follows:

> ***Be it enacted by the Senate and House of Representatives of the United States of America in Congress assembled,*** *That there is appropriated out of the Treasury of the United States a sum not exceeding $50,000 to be used by the Department of the Interior through the National Park Service with which to make a survey of the Old Natchez Trace throughout its entire length from the section of Tennessee about Nashville to Natchez, Mississippi, the same to be known as the "Natchez Trace Parkway." The said survey shall locate the Natchez Trace as near as practicable in its original route. An estimate of cost of construction of an appropriate national parkway over this route, and such other data as will be valuable shall be obtained by said survey with the objective of determining matters concerning the construction of the Natchez Trace Parkway.*[1]

The Natchez Trace Parkway Survey Bill was immediately referred to the Senate Committee on Post Offices and Post Roads. After scrutinizing the measure for approximately eight weeks, the Post Offices and Post Roads Committee issued a favorable report on the bill.[2] On April 30, 1934 the Senate, allotting only a few minutes for floor debate, passed the Natchez Trace Parkway Survey Bill by voice vote.[3]

The Natchez Trace Parkway Survey Bill was dispatched to the House of Representatives and promptly submitted to the Committee on Roads. The Roads Committee two days later unanimously recommended its passage to the

House.[4] On May 7 Representative T. Jeff Busby of Mississippi persuaded his colleagues to pass the bill without the formality of a roll call. The Natchez Trace Parkway Survey Bill was thereupon signed into law by President Franklin D. Roosevelt on May 21, 1934.[5]

The Natchez Trace Parkway Survey Act was only one of the four hundred and eighty-six laws approved by the Seventy-Third Congress in 1933 and 1934. The appropriation of $50,000 was certainly a modest one for a Congress which authorized an overall total of $13,141,600,000 in federal spending. It would, of course, be the responsibility of future Congresses to review the findings of the survey and determine the feasibility of the Natchez Trace Parkway.[6]

Of distinct importance to the future of the proposed Natchez Trace Parkway was the Federal Highway (Hayden-Cartwright) Act of 1936. The Federal Highway Act, authorizing one-half billion dollars for the construction and improvement of roads throughout the nation, was the most comprehensive such measure ever approved by Congress. Section 5 of the statute was especially relevant to the Natchez Trace Parkway. It read:

> *For the construction and maintenance of parkways, to give access to national parks and national monuments, or to become connecting sections of a national parkway plan, over lands to which title has been transferred to the United States by the States or by private individuals, there is hereby authorized to be appropriated the sum of $10,000,000 for the fiscal year ending June 30, 1938, and $10,000,000 for the fiscal year ending June 30, 1939: Provided: That the location of such parkways upon public lands, national forests, or other federal reservations shall be determined by agreement between the department having jurisdiction over such lands and the National Park Service.*[7]

While the House and Senate passed their respective versions of the Federal Highway Bill by voice votes, the House adopted the conference report on the measure by a roll call. The House approved the conference report by a 238-87 majority. The most pronounced support for the bill emanated from congressmen representing districts in Mississippi, Tennessee and Alabama, states in which the Natchez Trace Parkway would be located. Congressmen from these states voted 20-1 in favor of the conference report.[8]

Shortly after the Seventy-Fifth Congress was called to order in 1937 Representative Aaron L. Ford of Mississippi offered legislation to finalize the status of the Natchez Trace Parkway. The text of the Ford Bill, designed to remove any doubt as to the national government's jurisdiction over the parkway, was worded as follows:

> *. . . That all lands and easements heretofore and hereafter conveyed to the United States by the States of Mississippi, Alabama, and Tennessee for the right-of-way for the projected parkway between Natchez, Mississippi and Nashville, Tennessee, together with sites acquired or to be acquired for recreational areas in connection therewith, and a right-of-way for said parkway of a width sufficient to include the highway and all bridges, ditches, cuts, and fills appurtenant thereto, but not exceeding a maximum of two hundred feet through Government-owned lands (except that where small parcels of Government-owned lands would otherwise be isolated, or where topographic conditions or scenic requirements are such that bridges, ditches, cuts, fills, parking overlooks, and landscape development could not reasonably be confined to a width of two hundred feet, the said maximum may be increased to such width as may be necessary, with the written approval of department or agency having jurisdiction over such lands) as designed on maps heretofore or hereafter approved by the Secretary of the Interior, shall be known as the Natchez Trace Parkway and shall be administered and maintained by the Secretary of the Interior through the National Park Service, subject to the provisions of the Act of Congress approved*

August 25, 1916 (39 Stat 535), entitled "An Act to establish a National Park Service, and for other purposes," the provisions of which Act, as amended and supplemented, are hereby extended over and made applicable to said parkway: Provided, That the Secretary of Agriculture is hereby authorized, with the concurrence of the Secretary of the Interior, to connect with said parkway such roads and trails as may be necessary for the protection, administration, or utilization of adjacent and nearby national forests, and the resources thereof: And provided further, That the Forest Service and the National Park Service shall insofar as practicable, coordinate and correlate such recreational developments as each may plan, construct, or permit to be constructed, on lands within their respective jurisdictions, which, by mutual agreement, should be given special treatment for recreational purposes.[9]

While the House Committee on Public Lands urged passage of the Ford Bill in July 1937,[10] the measure did not reach the House floor until February 1938. After a short, but somewhat spirited discussion, the House passed the Ford Bill by a margin of 200-118. As had been evident with the Federal Highway Bill of 1936, congressmen from Mississippi, Alabama, and Tennessee mobilized in behalf of the bill. Indeed House members from the three states voted 18-0 for the bill.[11]

On April 29, 1938 the Senate Committee on Public Lands and Surveys endorsed the Ford Bill. With a minimum of debate the bill was approved by the Senate on May 3, and thirteen days later President Roosevelt affixed his signature to the measure. Thus, on May 18, 1938 the Natchez Trace Parkway officially came into being.[12]

Funding for the planning and development of the Natchez Trace Parkway was included in the annual appropriation bills for the Department of the Interior. For the 1938 and 1939 fiscal years Congress approved identical sums of $1,500,000. In 1940 and 1941 the appropriations were $1,350,000 and $1,600,000 respectively. In 1942 the House and Senate agreed upon a substantially reduced figure of $700,000. Because of the extraordinary and unprecedented demands placed upon the government by the nation's involvement in World War II, the 1943 appropriation was a mere $80,740.[13]

While the annual amounts reserved for the Natchez Trace Parkway were quite modest, congressmen from the Northeast and Midwest frequently alleged that the states of Mississippi, Alabama, and Tennessee were receiving preferential treatment. These congressmen argued that the Natchez Trace Parkway was not connected with any functioning interstate highway system and that the annual federal expenditures for its construction were unnecessary and unjustified. The critics of the parkway maintained that only a small minority of the nations's population would benefit from its completion.[14]

One of the most outspoken leaders of the economy block on Capitol Hill was Representative Edward H. Rees of Kanasas. Rees, a conservative Republican serving a rural constituency in the Great Plains, was destined to spend twenty-four years in the House. In 1939 and 1941 Rees offered amendments to delete all funds proposed for national parkways, the effect of which would have been to suspend construction of the Natchez Trace Parkway. The 1939 and 1941 Rees Amendments were rejected by respective tabulations of 118-7 and 67-39.[15]

Two of Rees' Republican colleagues were Representatives John Taber of New York and Robert F. Rich of Pennsylvania. Taber and Rich, who were to serve a combined total of sixty years in the House, were determined to eliminate the Natchez Trace Parkway clauses of the appropriation bills for the Department of the Interior. The House, however, rebuffed their attempts to frustrate adoption of the 1938 and 1940 conference reports for Interior Department Appropriations. The 1938 conference report was approved by a 204-127 majority, while the 1940 conference report passed by a 197-156 margin. The unanimous votes of 21-0 cast by congressmen from Mississippi, Alabama, and Tennessee provided substantial proportions of the margins of victory for the 1938 and 1940 conference reports.[16]

An analysis of the various roll calls in the House of Representatives indicated that many congressmen from the Midwest and Northeast were clearly hostile to the Natchez Trace Parkway. Of the one hundred and eighteen votes recorded against the Ford Bill in 1938, sixty were cast by congressmen from the Midwest and forty-seven by members from the Northeast. On adoption on the 1938 Interior Department Appropriation conference report, midwesterners accounted for sixty-four and northeasterners for fifty-two of the one hundred and twenty-seven negative votes. On the 1940 Interior Department Appropriation conference report congressmen from the Midwest provided eighty-two and their colleagues from the Northeast sixty of the one hundred and fifty-six dissenting votes.

The proponents of the Natchez Trace Parkway were quite fortunate, however, in having several illustrious Southern Democrats on their side. Especially prominent were Representatives Joseph W. Byrns of Tennessee, Speaker of the House between 1934 and 1936, and William B. Bankhead, who occupied the speakership from 1936 to 1940. Also influential were Senators Pat Harrison of Mississippi, Chairman of the Finance Committee, 1933-1941, and Kenneth D. McKellar of Tennessee, who presided over the Post Offices and Post Roads Committee from 1933 to 1946 and was a senior member of the Appropriations Committee during the same period.[17]

Other Southern Democrats who became energetic spokesmen for the Natchez Trace Parkway were Senators John H. Bankhead of Alabama and Representatives John E. Rankin, William H. Whittington, and Ross A. Collins of Mississippi, Joe Starnes of Alabama, and Albert A. Gore of Tennessee. Bankhead, the brother of Speaker William B. Bankhead, was a veteran member of the Senate Appropriations Committee. Rankin and Whittington chaired the House World War Veterans' Legislation Committee and the House Flood Control Committee respectively. Collins, Starnes, and Gore served on the powerful House Appropriations Committee, the panel having the exclusive responsibility of initiating spending bills. These six gentlemen, who spent an aggregate total of one hundred and thirty-five years on Capitol Hill, represented states or districts which would be enhanced by the completion of the Natchez Trace Parkway.[18]

The annual appropriations furnished by Congress enabled the National Park Service to acquire considerable land and undertake actual construction of the Natchez Trace Parkway during the late nineteen thirties. By 1940, 9,814 acres had been secured and 86 miles of the parkway were either completed or under construction. Two years later the acreage had grown to 12,834 and mileage had increased to 105. By the final year of the Third Roosevelt Administration in 1944, the Park Service was exercising control over 13,649 acres and the number of miles was 117.[19]

Beginning in the latter half of 1943 all federal road construction was suspended for the duration of the war. While there was considerable doubt over the projected length of World War II, it was anticipated that construction of the Natchez Trace Parkway would resume within a reasonable time after the attainment of an international peace settlement. Indeed the needs of the future were apparent in the Federal Highway Act of 1944, a measure which authorized $10,000,000 for national parkways during each of the first three years of the postwar period.[20]

Among the congressmen whose long and distinguished careers have largely paralleled the development of the Natchez Trace Parkway over the past half century is Representative Jamie L. Whitten of the First District of Mississippi. A member of the House since 1941 and Chairman of the Committee on Appropriations since 1979, Whitten in late 1984 recalled the circumstances surrounding the early years of the Parkway. Whitten at that time explained that "the problems of funding, of securing rights of way, of starting work at various places along the route, were not always easy nor were the reasons always apparent." While attending the dedication of a parkway bridge in his honor in Dennis, Mississippi, Whitten declared:

> *As modern as hard surfaced roads and great bridges can make it, the Trace is as*

close to the natural beauty of years ago with forests and trails, valleys and hills, much as they were in the beginning. When finished it will connect New York and Washington with New Orleans by way of Nashville and Natchez, a great tourist attraction.

The Natchez Trace Parkway will eventually extend a length of four hundred and fifty-four miles. The bulk of the mileage of the Parkway was constructed over the period from 1947 to 1966. During these two decades an additional total of one hundred and ninety-four miles was completed. Notwithstanding the impressive progress made between the years shortly after World War II and the latter half of the nineteen sixties, it must be remembered that the origin and planning of the Natchez Trace Parkway took place during the presidency of Franklin D. Roosevelt.

NOTES

[1]United States Senate, S. 2825-A bill to provide for an appropriation of $50.00 with which to make a survey of the Old Indian Trail known as the "Natchez Trace," with a view of constructing a national road on this route to be known as the "Natchez Trace Parkway," February 20, 1934; Jonathan Daniels, The Devil's Backbone: The Story of the Natchez Trace (New York: McGraw-Hill Book Company, 1962); Clement Eaton, The Growth of Southern Civilization, 1790-1860 (New York: Harper and Brothers Publishers, 1961), pp.31-32; Harnett T. Kane, Natchez on the Mississippi (New York: William Morrow and Company, 1947), pp. 61-78; "Natchez Trace," The Encyclopedia of Southern History (Baton Rouge: Louisiana State University Press, 1979), pp. 879-880.

[2]A key paragraph in the Post Offices and Post Roads Committee report asserted: "The Natchez Trace is located throughout almost its entire length on highlands between watersheds on the most suitable route over which to establish the national parkway through a section of the country greatly in need of such road facilities from a national standpoint to connect the North and East with the Natchez, New Orleans, and the southwest section of the country." United States Senate, Report Number 740, April 17, 1934.

[3]United States Congress, Congressional Record (Washington: United States Government Printing Office, 1934), LXXVIII, 7290-7281.

[4]The Roads Committee concluded: "A great necessity is shown for the construction of a road over this route because road facilities are woefully lacking in that section from a national standpoint need. Most of the people who travel long distances live in cities, own no land, and pay no part in the construction of roads unless the National Government renders assistance....We feel that the survey of this route is an important first step in the right direction, and recommend the passage of the bill." House of Representatives, Report Number 1442, May 2, 1934.

[5]Congressional Record, LXXVIII, 8266-8267; The Statutes at Large of the United States of America, 1933-1934 (Washington: United States Government Printing Office, 1934), XLVIII, 791-792.

[6]Department of Commerce, Historical Statistics of the United States, Colonial Times to 1970 (2 vols.; Washington: United States Government Printing Office, 1976), II, 1081, 1104, 1114.

[7]House of Representatives, H.R. 11687-A bill to emend the Federal Aid Highway Act, approved July 11, 1916, as amended and supplemented, and for other purposes, March 9, 1936; Fredrick L. Paxson, "The Highway Movement, 1916-1935," American Historical Review, January 1946, pp. 236-253.

[8]Congressional Record, LXXX, 8704-8705; Times, New York, N.Y., April 17, 1936, p.2; June 22, 1936, p.14.

[9]H.R. 6652-A bill to provide for the administra-

tion and maintenance of the Natchez Trace Parkway in the States of Mississippi, Alabama, and Tennessee, and for other purposes, April 26, 1937.

[10]The Public Lands Committee report contained a July 3, 1947 letter from the Acting Secretary of the Interior. The Acting Secretary stated: "The area through which the proposed parkway passes best represents the antebellum South, for it suffered less than did other sections during the War between the States. Many historical features, including the old Indian trails, romantic Natchez on the Mississippi, and the opening of the Old Southwest, make the proposed parkway of national interest." House Report 1277, July 21, 1937.

[11]Congressional Record, LXXXIII, 1422-1436.

[12]Senate Report 1627, April 29, 1938; Congressional Record, LXXXIII, 6286; Statutes at Large, LII, 407-408.

[13]House of Representatives, Hearings on the Interior Department Appropriation Bills, 1938-1943 (Washington: United States Government Printing Office, 1938-1943); Statutes at Large, L, 546-616; LII, 251-342; LIII, 685-738; LIV, 406-462; LV, 303-361; LVI, 506-561.

[14]Between 1938 and 1943 expenditures for the Department of the Interior amounted to $1,207,907,000. During the same period total federal expenditures were $151,320,644,000.

[15]Congressional Record, LXXXIV, 2992-3000; LXXXVII, 4061-4064.

[16]House Report 1178, July 1, 1937; House Report 2173, May 10, 1940; Congressional Record, LXXXI, 4796-4797; LXXXVI, 7126-7129; James Giglio, "John Taber," Dictionary of American Biography, Supplement Seven (New York: Charles Scribner's Sons, 1981), pp. 733-734.

[17]Stanley J. Folmsbee, "Joseph Wellington Byrns," Dictionary of American Biography, Supplement Two (New York: Charles Scribner's Sons, 1958), pp. 82-83; J.M.Galloway, "Speaker Joseph W. Byrns: Party Leader of the New Deal," Tennessee Historical Quarterly, Spring 1966, pp. 63-76; Walter Heacock, "William B. Bankhead and the New Deal," Journal of Southern History, August 1955, pp. 344-355; Albert D. Kirwan, "Byron Patton Harrison," Dictionary of American Biography, Supplement Three (New York: Charles Scribner's Sons, 1975), pp. 344-345; Thomas K. McCraw, "Kenneth Douglas McKellar," Dictionary of American Biography, Supplement Six (New York: Charles Scribner's Sons, 1980), pp. 418-420; Dean Pope, "The Senator from Tennessee," West Tennessee Historical Society Papers, 1966, pp. 102-122; Martha H. Swain, Pat Harrison: The New Deal Years (Jackson: University of Mississippi Press, 1978).

[18]Walter Goodman, "John Elliott Rankin," Dictionary of American Biography, Supplement Six, pp. 525-526; J.B. Key, "John Hollis Bankhead," Dictionary of American Biography, Supplement Four (New York: Charles Scribner's Sons, 1974), pp. 49-51; Lawrence F. Kennedy (comp.), Biographical Directory of the American Congress, 1774-1971 (Washington: United States Government Printing Office, 1971), pp. 768-769, 1018, 1744-1745, 1917.

[19]Department of Commerce, Statistical Abstract of the United States, 1942 (Washington: United States Government Printing Office, 1943), p.1029; Department of the Interior, Information Relating to the National Park Service, 1944 (Washington: United States Government Printing Office, 1944), p. 33.

[20]Statutes at Large, LVIII, 838-843.

BIBLIOGRAPHY

Daniels, Jonathan: The Devil's Backbone: The Story of the Natchez Trace (New York: McGraw-Hill Book Company, 1962).

Department of Commerce: Historical Statistics of the United States, Colonial Times to 1970 (2 vols; Washington: United States Government Printing Office, 1976).

Department of Commerce: Historical Abstract of the United States, 1942 (Washington: United States Government Printing Office, 1943).

Department of the Interior: Information Relating to the National Park Service, 1944 (Washington: United States Government Printing Office, 1944).

Dictionary of American Biography (New York: Charles Scribner's Sons, 1958-1981).

Eaton, Clement: The Growth of Southern Civilization, 1790-1860 (New York: Harper and Brothers Publishers, 1961).

Encyclopedia of Southern History (Baton Rouge: Louisiana State University Press, 1979).

House of Representatives: Hearings on the Interior Department Appropriation Bills, 1938-1943 (Washington: United States Government Printing Office, 1938-1943).

House of Representatives: Reports on Public Bills and Resolutions, 1933-1944 (Washington: United States Government Printing Office, 1934-1944).

The Statutes at Large of the United States of America, 1934-1944 (Washington: United States Government Printing Office, 1934-1944).

United States Congress: Congressional Record (Washington: United States Government Printing Office, 1934-1944).

United States Senate: Reports on Public Bills and Resolutions, 1934-1944 (Washington: United States Government Printing Office, 1934-1944).

UNTITLED SAM WANG

IV. Environmental and Economic Perspectives

"In my recent work," says Sam Wang, "I play with an intimacy with the subject . . . in terms of the viewer's heightened sense of participation in the scene. The content is very much influenced by the tools I use: a camera I built that captures the whole image-circle projected by a wide-angle lens. Coincidentally, the circular format also conveys a sense of perfection, serenity, and dignity, or perhaps our longing for such."

An Economic Framework of the Blue Ridge Parkway Area

Paul E. Lovingood, Jr. and Lisle S. Mitchell, Department of Geography, University of South Carolina, Columbia, South Carolina

The Blue Ridge Parkway Area, as defined here, consists of the twenty-nine counties in North Carolina and Virginia through which the Parkway traverses for a distance of almost 500 miles (Figure 1). This linear grouping of counties is often thought of as homogeneous in terms of terrain and cultural characteristics. It is true that the counties that make up this region are classified as low mountains and thus share similar characteristics of local relief, slope, morphology, natural resources, flora and fauna. On the other hand, the nature of the cultural traits of these twenty-nine counties is much more heterogeneous. It is the variance in the cultural aspects of the region that is of concern, especially the variety of economic phenomena. The purpose of this presentation is to investigate, from a geographic perspective, the economic framework of the Blue Ridge Parkway Area.

There is no one right way to analyze the economic landscape of a region. Every discipline and every researcher within a given discipline will formulate a unique method of study. Within the context of the social sciences, all academic disciplines examine the same regions and use the same data sources; however, the results of their separate investigations will be different because of their distinctive approach.

Economic geographers are concerned with the physical manifestation of business activities and facilities on the landscape and tend to display these impacts on maps. Such information on two-dimensional representations may be viewed from four perspectives (Pattison, 1964). First, economic landscapes may be studied in terms of the natural resources required to operate an industrial enterprise. Second, the economic scene may be analyzed on the basis of how the resident population relates to and utilizes the resources of the natural environment. Third, the spatial arrangement, interrelationships, and dynamics of economic activities in an area may be examined. Fourth, a description of the industrial features that give character and uniqueness to a region may be presented. The perspective emphasized in this presentation is the distribution of business establishments by counties in the Blue Ridge Parkway Area, but the human-environment relationships and the description of regional character will be considered in the explanation of areal patterns.

RESEARCH DESIGN

Data. Standard Industrial Classification data of the County Business Patterns (U. S. Department of Commerce, 1986) was the primary data utilized. The total number of establishments in each of the twenty-nine counties, for ten different business types, was analyzed using standard statistical techniques and presented in the form of computer produced maps and diagrams. The data for the Virginia counties excluded information for "independent cities" and thus it was necessary to gather statistics for each of the eight legal entities within the study area and add them to the appropriate counties. This procedure standardized the data for all counties and made them comparable.

Methodology. The approach followed here was to identify the study area by mapping the twenty-nine counties adjacent to the Parkway (Figure 1). A map of the resident population of the counties was prepared to illustrate the configuration of the primary human resource of the region. After the area was defined and the population distribution mapped it was necessary to array the data for each of the Standard Industrial Classes (SIC) by the number of business establishments in each county. The data were then classified into discrete classes based on the "natural" breaks in the data. This procedure resulted in four or five homogeneous classes for each of the ten types of establishments. The total number of establishments in each county were treated in the same manner. The ten maps produced following this technique were then

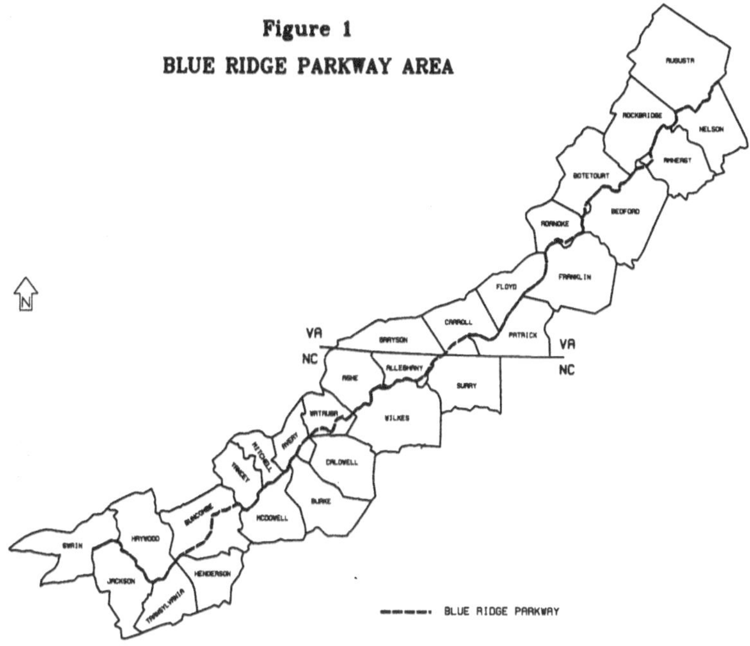

Figure 1
BLUE RIDGE PARKWAY AREA

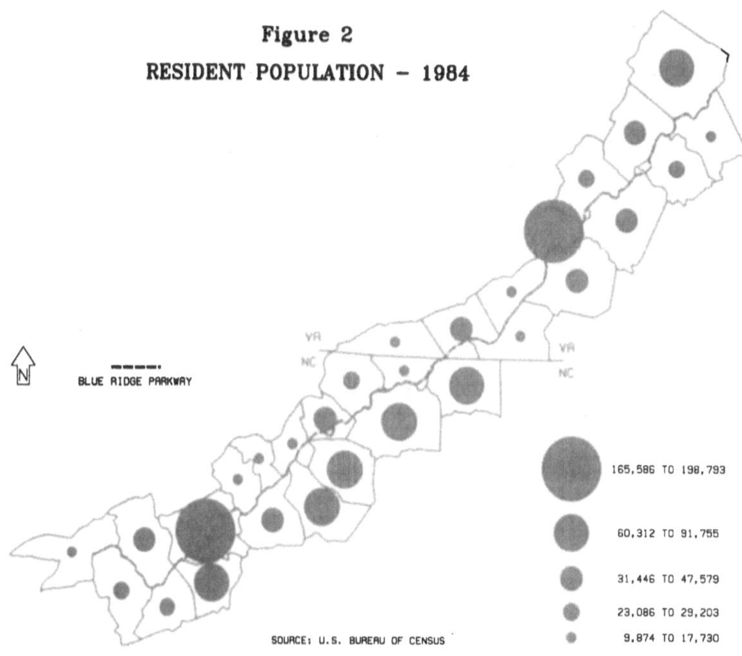

Figure 2
RESIDENT POPULATION – 1984

analyzed from a geographic point-of-view.

To achieve a holistic perspective of the economic landscape of the study area a hierarchical grouping procedure was used to develop multifactor regions. This technique analyzes all ten types of enterprises and then places counties into homogeneous groups or regions. The regions vary statistically between groups but the variance within groups is minimized. This procedure provides useful insights into the economic similarities and differences between counties because it makes possible the mapping of the regions or groups. A summary of the findings is restated and the study concluded by noting some implications for the Blue Ridge Parkway and its bordering counties.

POPULATION DISTRIBUTION

It was assumed that the reader would be familiar with the Parkway and the twenty-nine counties included in the study area (Figure 1), and that a detailed description of the route and the physical geography of the area was unnecessary. The distribution of population, however, is less likely to be known and is portrayed on Figure 2. Roanoke and Buncombe Counties are by far the largest population centers with about 199,000 and 166,000 individuals respectively. These two metropolitan counties dominate the study area in terms of human resources as well as in all ten types of business establishments.

Six counties are included in the second population class with between sixty and ninety-two thousand individuals each. Only one of these counties, Augusta, is located in Virginia. The remaining five counties are found in North Carolina to the south and east of the Parkway. These population concentrations probably exist because of superior natural resources, excellent access afforded by interstate highways, and proximity to the manufacturing region of North Carolina, South Carolina, and Georgia known as the "fertile crescent." There are seven third-order counties which have populations from thirty-one to forty-eight thousand individuals. Four of the counties are adjacent to the two largest urban counties and the remaining three are in proximity to the counties in the second class. Populations in the smallest two classes have no discernible spatial pattern except that seven of the nine least populated counties are found to the north and west of the Parkway.

BUSINESS ESTABLISHMENTS

Total Business Establishments. The spatial distribution of total business establishments is demonstrated on Figure 3. Roanoke and Buncombe are by far the most important counties in this regard. Buncombe County has more than twice the establishments of the highest-ranking county in the second class (4,258 to 2,058) and Roanoke has more than five times as many establishments as the lowest-ranking county in this class (5,414 to 1,056). The counties in the second class are predominately found in North Carolina (six of seven) on the south and east side of the Parkway. There are eight counties in the third class, four in each of the two states. They tend to be located near the larger business centers. The two smallest classes of counties are evenly divided between the two states and are counties with the smallest populations.

A look at total business establishments for the area as a whole is presented in Figure 4. This graph illustrates the relative importance of each type of business as a percentage of the total. Services and retail trade establishments stand out as the dominant type of business in the study area with 28.7 and 28.2 percent respectively. Providing personal services and material objects to the population are primary roles of business centers in a modern economy, and thus these statistics are expected. Contract Construction is the third ranked business with 10.2 percent. There is a constant need to repair and replace aging structures and transportation links as well as to meet the construction needs of ever expanding public and private enterprises.

The most surprising factor found in Figure 4 is the relatively large percentage of businesses that are unclassified (8.3 percent). This figure is well above the 2.3 percent of unclassified business for the entire Southern Highlands (Lovingood and Reiman, 1986). Manufacturing and Finance, Insurance and Real Estate are

Figure 3

TOTAL BUSINESS ESTABLISHMENTS

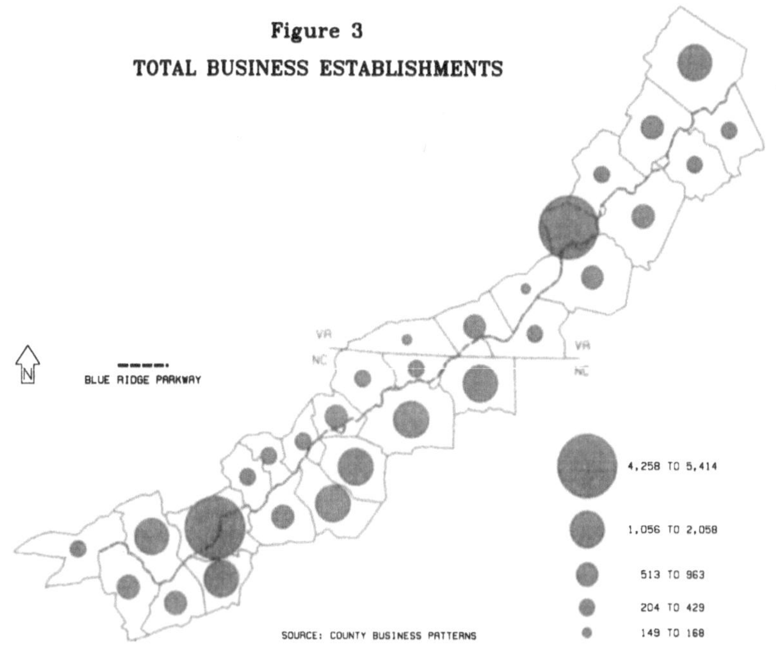

Figure 4

SPECIFIC ESTABLISHMENTS AS A PERCENT OF TOTAL ESTABLISHMENTS

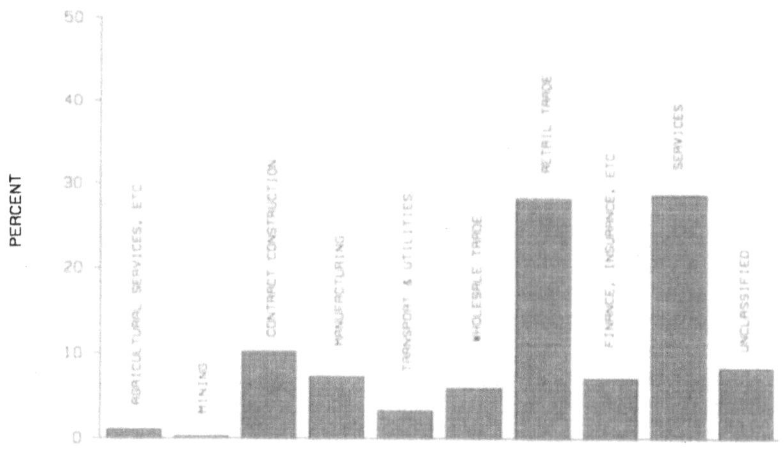

SOURCE: COUNTY BUSINESS PATTERNS

the fifth and sixth most important business types in the Parkway Area with 7.2 and 7.0 percent respectively. Manufacturing is one of the most basic forms of economic income and the activities of financial institutions are fundamental to the continued growth and development of a region. Wholesale Trade with 5.9 percent and Transport and Utilities with 3.3 percent are the seventh and eighth ranking business types. Wholesaling, of course, plays an important role in the distribution of material goods to retail outlets, and although transport and utilities enterprises are small in relative terms they are extremely important to the functioning of a modern society. Agricultural, forestry, fishing, and mining establishments make up the two smallest classes of business enterprises. Environmental and resource limitations probably account for these small values.

Agricultural, Forestry, and Fishing Establishments. These types of establishments are relatively unimportant in the economic landscape of the Blue Ridge Parkway Area as there are only 281 such establishments. Agriculture, forestry, and fishing are insignificant economic activities along the crest of the Blue Ridge Mountains due to a lack of resources and government contract of land. Therefore, the enterprises that provide goods and services to such concerns are limited in number. About thirty-one percent of all such establishments are located in the urban counties of Roanoke and Buncombe (Figure 5). These counties, on the average, have more than twice as many establishments as the seven counties included in the second class. Six of the counties in class two are found in North Carolina which indicates a better resource base. The numerical differences between the three smallest classes are minute and there is no discernible spatial pattern.

Mining Establishments. Mining is of little economic significance in the study area and the provision of goods and services to this industry is also unimportant. The total number of establishments serving the mining industry is only sixty-nine for an average of 2.4 businesses per county. Roanoke with twelve such establishments is the only county in the highest classification. Rockbridge and Buncombe Counties make up the second class and they only contain nine and six establishments respectively. The seven counties included in the third class are all above the regional average with either three or four establishments each. A majority of the counties (19) have less than the regional mean, and almost one-third have no businesses providing goods or services to mining companies.

Four of the ten counties in the top three classes are found in Virginia (Figure 6). Roanoke is the primary county and the other three, Rockbridge, Augusta and Amherst, are clustered at the northern end of the Parkway Area. Two linear groupings of three counties each are found in North Carolina. One group is located on the north side of the Parkway and consists of Buncombe County to the south and Yancey and Mitchell Counties to the northeast. The other agglomeration includes Caldwell, Wilkes and Surry Counties and lies on the south side of the Parkway.

Contract Construction Establishments. Three counties are included in the highest class of construction businesses (Figure 7). Augusta County is included with the usual leaders. A concentration of construction activity in Roanoke and Buncombe Counties is obviously related to their large populations and continuing growth and development. Augusta County, although it does not contain a dominant primary urban center, does incorporate two fairly large concentrations of population in Staunton and Waynesboro. It also embodies a significant number of small urban places, because it is a large county in physical size. The county, furthermore, is served by Interstate Highways 81 and 64 and these super thoroughfares provide easy access to Charlottesville and Harrisonburg.

Six of the seven counties comprising the second-ranked class are found in North Carolina, the only exception being Bedford. These counties, with two exclusions, are associated with second-level population centers and are located to the south of the Parkway. Haywood and Watauga Counties, the exclusions, have relatively small resident populations but they possess considerable tourist appeal and educational opportunities. Thus, construction activities related to these enterprises probably ex-

Figure 5

NUMBER OF AGRICULTURAL, FORESTRY AND FISHERIES ESTABLISHMENTS

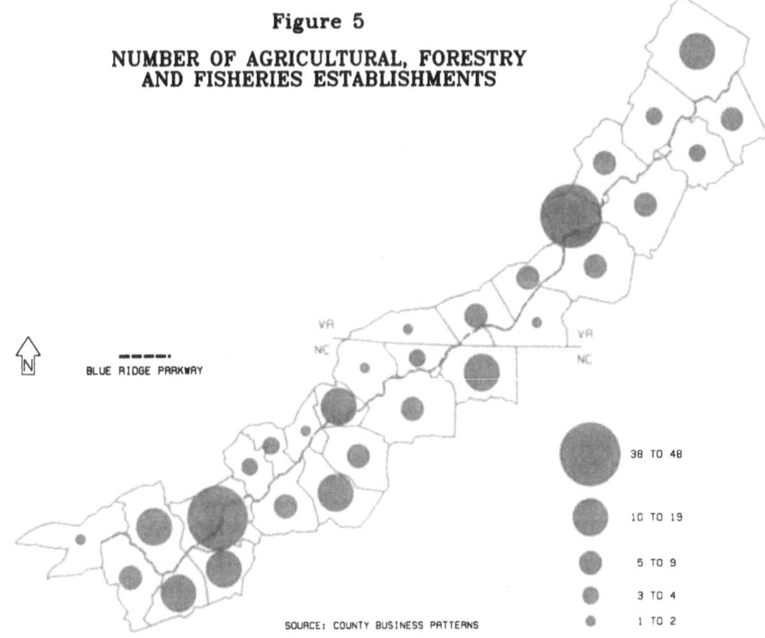

Figure 6

NUMBER OF MINING ESTABLISHMENTS

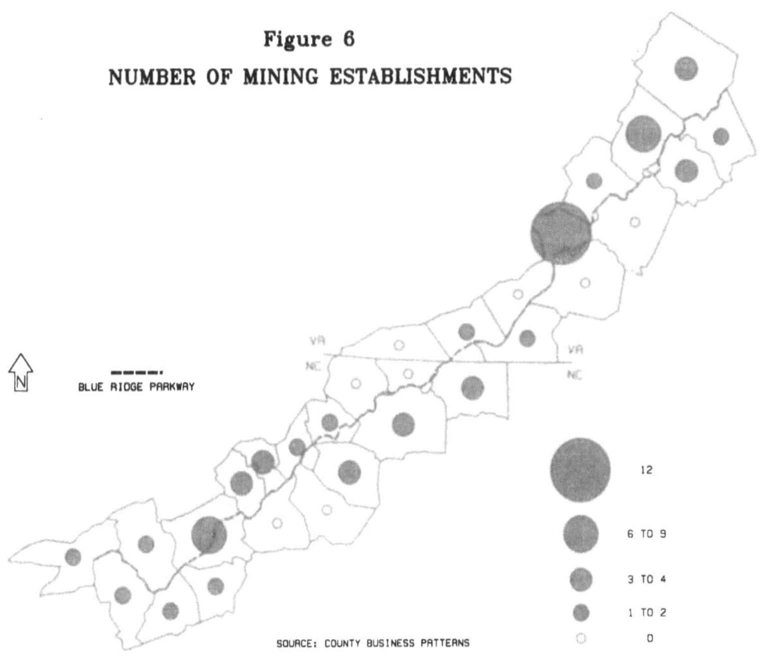

plain why these two counties are anomalies. None of the remaining counties contain more than ninety construction enterprises and none of the three lower classes of these establishments have recognizable spatial patterns.

Manufacturing Establishments. Manufacturing is the fifth most important business type in the study area based on comparative statistics. A total of 2,026 establishments are in operation for an average of almost seventy per county. Only ten counties have more than the average number of businesses and they comprise the first two classes (Figure 8). Roanoke and Buncombe Counties are included in the top class. These counties contain more that one-quarter of all the manufacturing establishments and have more than twice as many as the second-class counties. The six counties in the second class are perfectly correlated with the secondary population centers. Five of the counties are located in North Carolina on the southeast side of the Parkway. Augusta County, the sole Virginia representative, is situated at the northern end and on the northwest side of the Parkway.

Four of the six counties that make up the third class are found in Virginia. All of these counties are adjacent to at least one county in the first two classes. This finding points to the tendency for manufacturing firms to agglomerate. Fifteen counties make up the two smallest classes and their locations reflect limited population bases, a lack of natural resources and limited transportation linkages to major areas of consumption.

Transportation and Other Public Utility Establishments. There are only 927 establishments that provide transport and utility services in the study area, the third smallest business category. Although these functions may be the most important for society at large, they do not make much of an impact on the visible economic landscape. Buncombe and Roanoke Counties have almost 31 percent of the total establishments (Figure 9). The 152 and 131 businesses in the two counties are much larger than the totals in the second class. Six counties are included in the second class. All of them are counties with relatively large resident populations and five of the six are located in North Carolina. The three smallest classes contain twenty-one of the twenty-nine counties in the study area, but only account for 345 establishments or about 37 percent of the total. Spatially, these counties tend to cluster around the more highly populated counties.

Wholesale Trade Establishments. Location is probably more important to wholesaling than any other type of business activity considered in this paper. The need to be central to a large productive and consumptive service area is paramount and this principle explains the importance of Roanoke and Buncombe Counties (Figure 10). Even within the highest class there is great disparity as Roanoke has 219 more wholesale businesses than Buncombe. Roanoke's location at the southeastern end of the highly productive Shenandoah Valley explains its numerical superiority. Buncombe County has better access than Roanoke because of the intersection of Interstate Highways 40 and 26, but its mountain environment and limited service area reduce its locational significance as a wholesale center. The two largest centers account for more than 48 percent of all wholesale establishments in the Blue Ridge Parkway Area.

Only four counties are included in the second class and three of these are located in North Carolina. Henderson County is adjacent to Buncombe, and Wilkes and Surry Counties are spatially connected just south of theNorth Carolina-Virginia border. Augusta County is the sole Virginia representative and it is located at the northern tip of the Parkway. Nine counties are included in the third class, four in Virginia and five in North Carolina. These counties tend to cluster and to be in proximity to counties with large resident populations. The remaining counties are of limited importance as wholesaling centers.

Retail Trade Establishments. Direct provision of goods to the general public is the second most important economic activity in the study area in terms of total establishments. Retail activity is highly correlated with population and thus the primary position of Roanoke and Buncombe Counties is as expected (Figure 11).

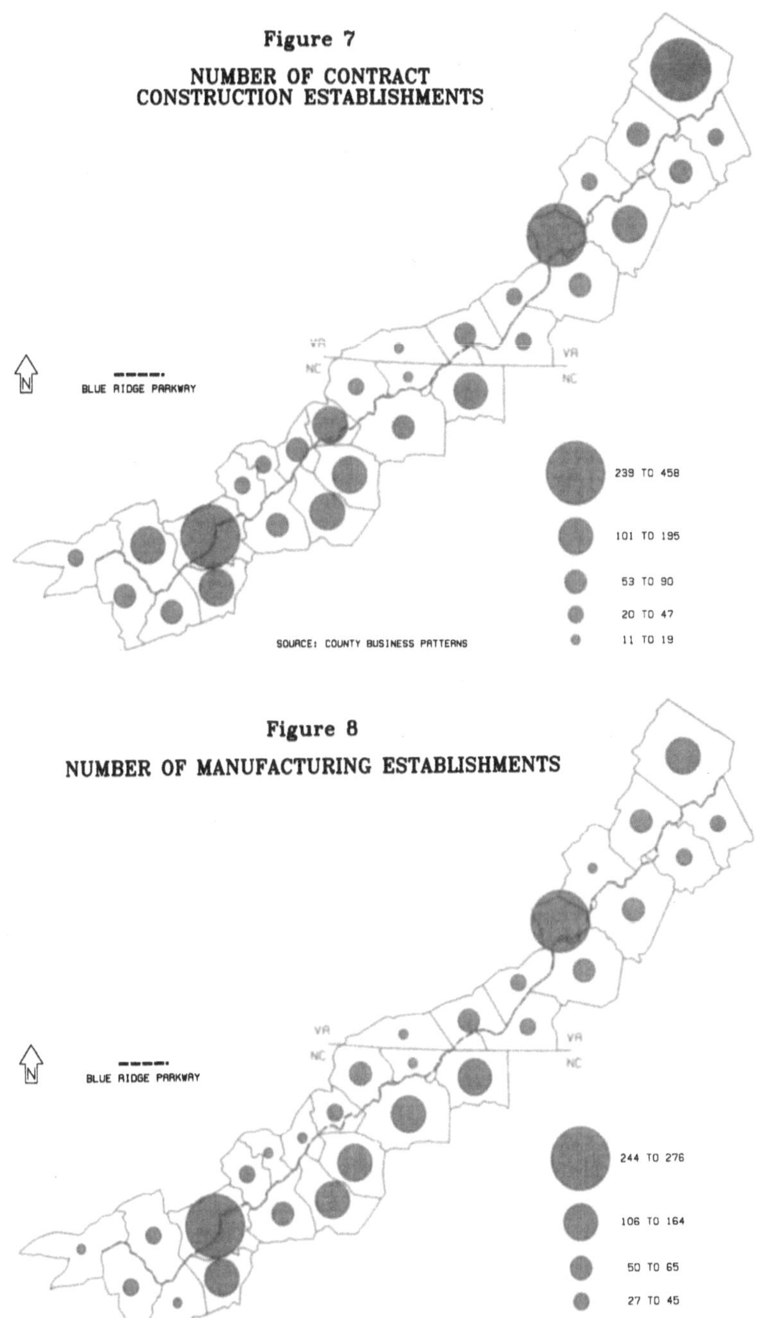

Figure 7

NUMBER OF CONTRACT CONSTRUCTION ESTABLISHMENTS

Figure 8

NUMBER OF MANUFACTURING ESTABLISHMENTS

These counties have more than twice as many establishments as the second class of retail centers. Seven of the eight counties included in the second class are found in North Carolina. Six of the eight secondary retail centers have significant residential populations. The two exceptions, Haywood and Watauga Counties in North Carolina, are explained by a concentration of tourism and educational facilities and activities. Resident populations in these counties would not support such a large number of retail establishments, but tourists and students provide the necessary monetary base. The third class of retail counties, of which there are five, are located in proximity to counties with larger populations. Fourteen counties are included in the two smallest classes and are evenly distributed in the two-state area. They tend to be positioned in physical environments that are extremely rugged and as a result have poor access.

Finance, Insurance and Real Estate Establishments. Services provided by various finance, insurance and realty firms are concentrated in the three counties of Roanoke, Buncombe and Augusta (Figure 12). Although these counties are much larger in terms of total establishments than all other counties there is also great variation within this class. Roanoke has 205 more businesses than Buncombe, and Buncombe has 153 more than Augusta. This variance, for the most part, reflects the differences in the economic base and resident populations of these counties. All seven counties in the second class are located in North Carolina. This location clearly reflects the importance of population size, tourist attractions and educational facilities to these counties. The three lowest classes include nineteen counties none of which has one-tenth the number of establishments as Roanoke. In fact, all of these counties added together do not have the number of financial businesses of that county. These counties do not possess a productive environment or the linkages necessary to be financial, insurance or real estate centers.

Services Establishments. Services establishments are absolutely and relatively the most significant type of business activity in the Blue Ridge Parkway Area. The Metropolitan Counties of Roanoke and Buncombe make up the first class (Figure 13). Both counties have more than twice as many services businesses as the next highest county. Nine counties, two in Virginia and seven in North Carolina, are included in the second class of services establishments. The Virginia counties are Augusta and Rockbridge located on the north and west side of the Parkway, and at its northern extremity. Five of the North Carolina counties are on the south and east side of the Parkway and have relatively large populations. Haywood and Watauga Counties on the northwest side of the Parkway have limited permanent populations but possess several tourist and educational centers that provide an extensive range of personal and public services. None of the remaining eighteen counties are out of the ordinary in terms of the number of services establishments.

Unclassified Establishments. Establishments that are unclassified cannot play a significant role in characterizing the economic nature of the study area. These businesses are either difficult to classify or for some reason do not fit into the specific definitions used by the Department of Commerce. Nevertheless, the distribution of such firms is illustrated in Figure 14. Almost 30 percent of the total are found in the first class which includes Roanoke and Buncombe Counties. Only four counties are included in the second class and they account for more than 21 percent of the total. Thus, six counties account for slightly more than 50 percent of all unclassified establishments. This finding is to be expected because the most unusual types of establishments tend to be found in major population centers. The remaining twenty-three counties are relatively unimportant because on the average they account for little more than two percent of the unclassified establishments.

As a result of the above analysis a number of findings about the distribution of business enterprises in the Blue Ridge Parkway Area are fairly obvious. First, Roanoke and Buncombe Counties dominate the economic landscape of the study area. Second, there is a fairly high correlation between the location of business

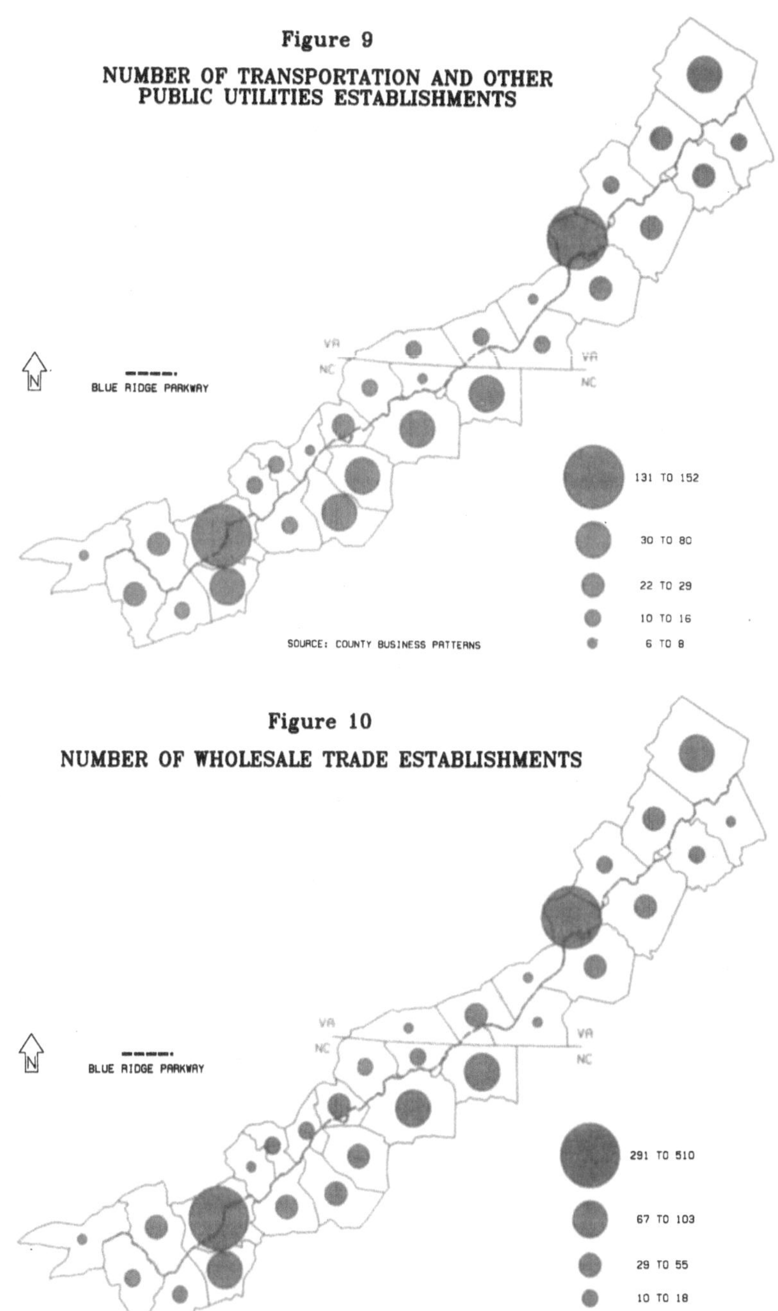
Figure 9
NUMBER OF TRANSPORTATION AND OTHER PUBLIC UTILITIES ESTABLISHMENTS
N
BLUE RIDGE PARKWAY
VA
NC
VA
NC
131 TO 152
30 TO 80
22 TO 29
10 TO 16
6 TO 8
SOURCE: COUNTY BUSINESS PATTERNS
Figure 10
NUMBER OF WHOLESALE TRADE ESTABLISHMENTS
N
BLUE RIDGE PARKWAY
VA
NC
VA
NC
291 TO 510
67 TO 103
29 TO 55
10 TO 18
4 TO 9
SOURCE: COUNTY BUSINESS PATTERNS

types and population. Counties with the largest populations tend to have the highest number of establishments of all types. Thus, eight counties, six in North Carolina and two in Virginia, stand out as concentrations of business establishments. Third, in most business categories, counties in Virginia are not as significant as those in North Carolina. Fourth, several counties contain more businesses than would be expected. Augusta in Virginia is outstanding because of its physical size and situation with regard to transportation routes and urban centers. Haywood and Watauga in North Carolina are above average because of their concentration of tourist and educational facilities and activities. Fifth, those counties that usually appear in the three lower classes of business types are lacking in some natural and/or human resources.

REGIONS OFTHE BLUE RIDGE PARKWAY

Six formal regions were developed using the hierarchical grouping procedure as discussed in the section on methodology (Figure 15). Each region is homogeneous in terms of the ten types of enterprises used in this study. This means the difference in the data varies more between the regions than it does within a given region (Figure 16).

There are three single-county regions: Region 2 - Buncombe, Region 5 - Augusta and Region 6 - Roanoke (Figures 15 and 16). As noted in the previous discussions of the ten individual enterprise types these three counties dominate the statistics. All of these counties have large, productive service areas and excellent transportation and communication networks. Roanoke and Buncombe by their very size are important business centers and this concentration of business enterprises acts as a magnet in attracting and maintaining a high level of economic activity. Augusta County, with the independent cities of Staunton and Waynesboro, is not as dominant as Roanoke and Buncombe but because of its large physical size, numerous small urban-like places, significant population and excellent accessibility is classified as a single-county region.

Region 3 consists of seven counties all in North Carolina. The average number of specific establishments in these counties is lower than in the three single-county regions but above those found in other multi-county regions (Figure 16). Five counties in this region (Henderson, Burke, Caldwell, Wilkes, Surry) have populations varying between 60,000 and 90,000, are located on the southeast side of the Parkway with relatively productive hinterlands and have good access because of interstate highways. The other two counties (Haywood and Watauga) are located on the northwest side of the Parkway in the mountains proper, contain tourism and educational complexes, and have better than adequate access routes due to their location in relation to the Parkway. These counties are not in the same economic class as the three single county regions; nevertheless, they contain large numbers of establishments of most types and are important generators of economic activity.

Region 4 is made up of six counties, three in each state. These counties have no discernible spatial pattern except that four of them share a common boundary with one of the three single-county regions. One of the other two counties (Jackson) is relatively close to Buncombe County, but Carroll County, Virginia is relatively isolated from the most significant regions. Region 4 is not poverty stricken in terms of businesses but it is some 30 to 40 percent below that of Region 3. Region 1 is the largest with 13 counties, seven in Virginia and six in North Carolina. These counties have limited numbers of business establishments (Figure 16). In a real economic sense this region is poverty stricken because it is lacking in the facilities and attendant activities that constitute a viable economy. In spatial terms the seven counties in Virginia have no recognizable pattern; if anything, the distribution resembles a hop-scotch because the counties tend to skip back and forth across and along the Parkway. All of the Region 1 counties in North Carolina are located on the northwest or mountain side of the Parkway, and this reflects the ruggedness of the physical geography and its limited resource base.

Figure 11

NUMBER OF RETAIL TRADE ESTABLISHMENTS

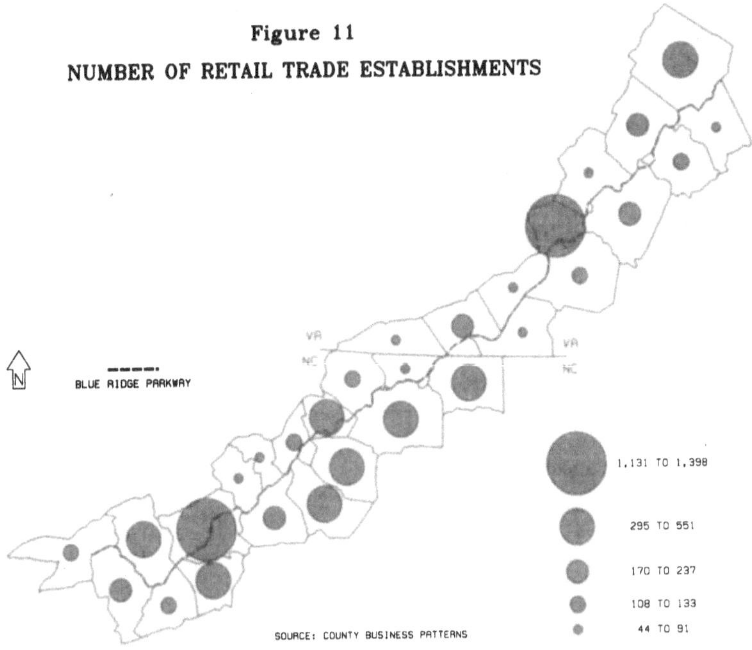

Figure 12

NUMBER OF FINANCE, INSURANCE AND REAL ESTATE ESTABLISHMENTS

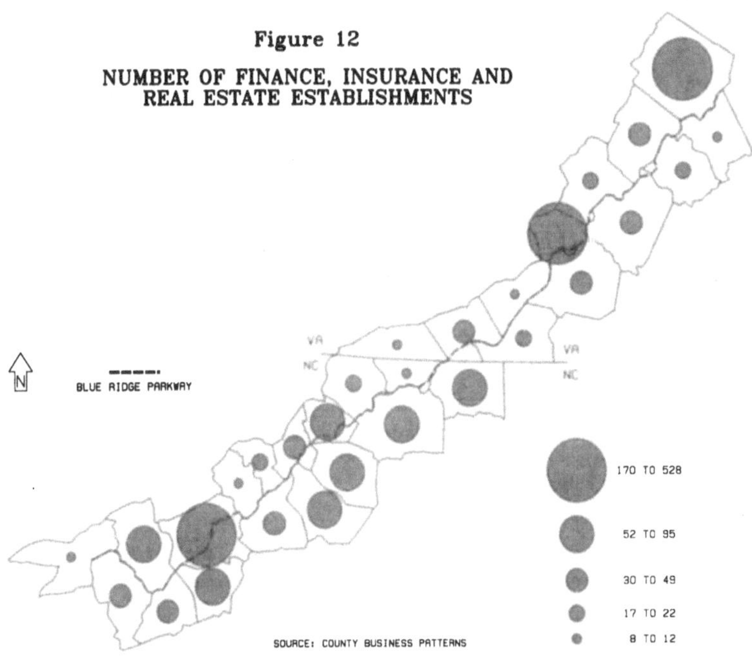

The regionalization scheme formulated here has identified six regions, each homogeneous in terms of the number of and type of business establishments. Three of the regions consist of a single county. These counties, Roanoke, Buncombe and Augusta, have large numbers of establishments and thus dominate the economic landscape. The economic superiority of these three regions is explained by their location in productive service areas and nearness to major transport arteries. One additional region, Region 3, consists of seven economically viable counties. None of these counties can compete with the three dominant regions but they do have the mix of business types and number of establishments that constitute above average economic conditions. The site and situational characteristics of these seven counties are not as strong as the leaders but they differ more in degree than in kind. Regions 1 and 4 consisting of nineteen counties are economically disadvantaged compared to the other regions. Their locations with regard to the physical and cultural resource requirements of a post-industrial economy are poor.

A comparison of the Virginia and North Carolina counties that make up the Blue Ridge Parkway Area reveals that the Virginia counties, as a whole, are considerably worse off in terms of economic indicators. With the exception of Roanoke and Augusta Counties, all of the other Virginia counties are found in Regions 1 and 4, the two poorest regions (Figure 16). Only Roanoke and Augusta Counties on the northern side of the Parkway are in a position to take advantage of the productivity of the Shenandoah Valley, and the southern counties are adjacent to the relatively sterile upper Virginia Piedmont. North Carolina, on the other hand, only has one of the three major economic centers, but it also contains all of the counties that make up Region 3. These counties are all economically viable because of their location in proximity to the manufacturing centers of the "fertile crescent," excellent access routes, or to the existence of tourism and educational complexes in scenic mountain areas. While the counties in North Carolina are generally better off than those in Virginia, nine of the seventeen counties, more than one-half, are classified in the two establishment poor regions (Figures 15 and 16).

CONCLUSIONS

The counties of the Blue Ridge Parkway Area are not homogeneous in terms of the number of and/or type of business establishments. Rather, the study area is heterogeneous and has been analyzed in terms of ten specific establishment types and one regionalization scheme. Each of the ten establishment types has different spatial distributions as illustrated in Figures 5 through 14. Although these patterns are fundamentally different there are a large number of similarities as noted above. A holistic view of the entire study area was presented spatially in Figure 15 and aspatially in Figure 16. These illustrations show that the study area can be logically divided into six homogeneous, formal regions. Three of these are single-county regions which are the principal economic growth poles along the Parkway. The three multi-county regions are at three different economic levels: prosperous, poor, and poverty-stricken.

The Blue Ridge Parkway with its twenty-nine counties has been analyzed from an economic geography perspective. Similarities and differences between the physical and cultural environments have been noted and the regions of economic viability have been identified. There are six implications of these findings for the Parkway. First, prosperous counties continue to attract business establishments and thus the Parkway traveler is well served when he or she stops in one of these counties. Second, increased economic growth adjacent to the Parkway may alter the natural, park-like vistas that are an important part of the Parkway experience. Third, the recently completed routeway may serve as a magnet to attract even more travelers to the area and thus further enhance the economic growth of surrounding counties. Fourth, continued growth and development may cause serious congestion along the Parkway, especially at entrance and exit points. Fifth, increased travel along the Parkway may increase the rate of deterioration of the pathway

Figure 13
NUMBER OF SERVICES ESTABLISHMENTS

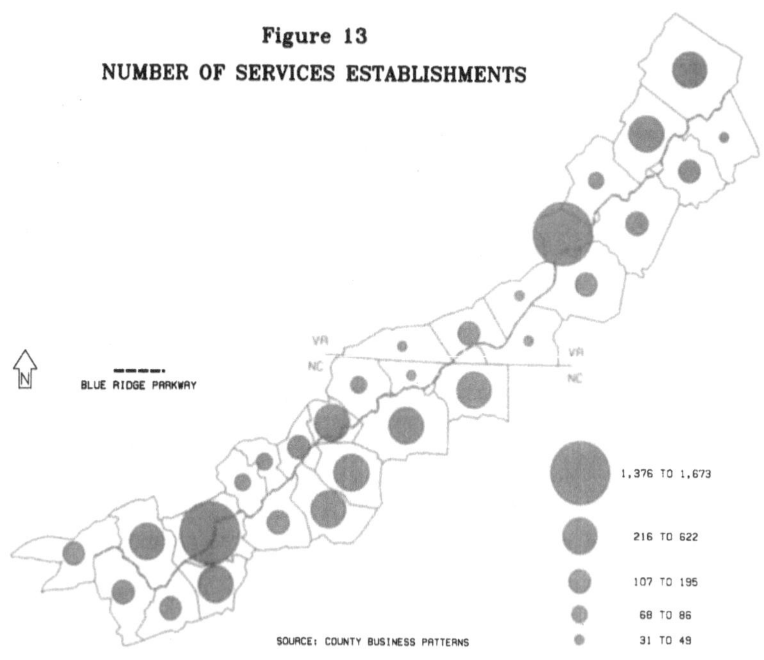

Figure 14
NUMBER OF UNCLASSIFIED ESTABLISHMENTS

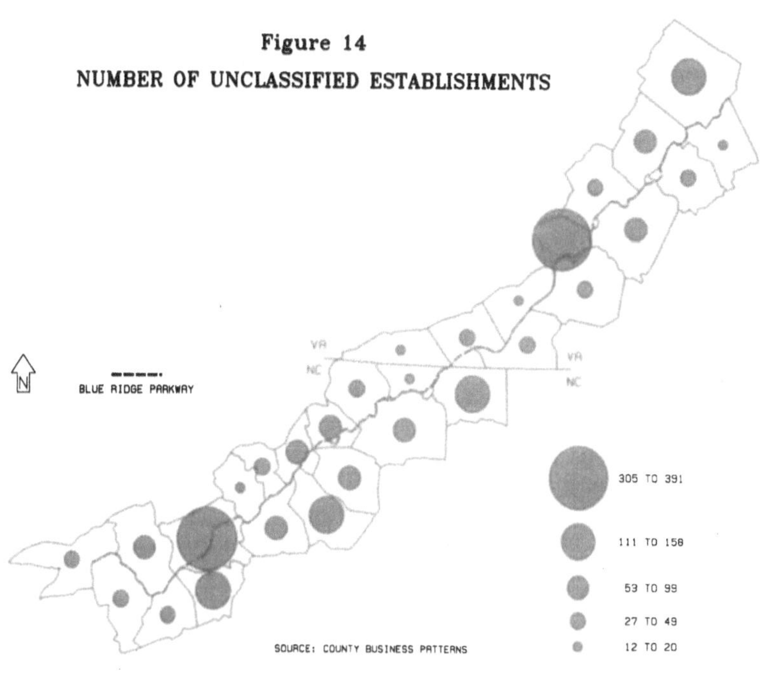

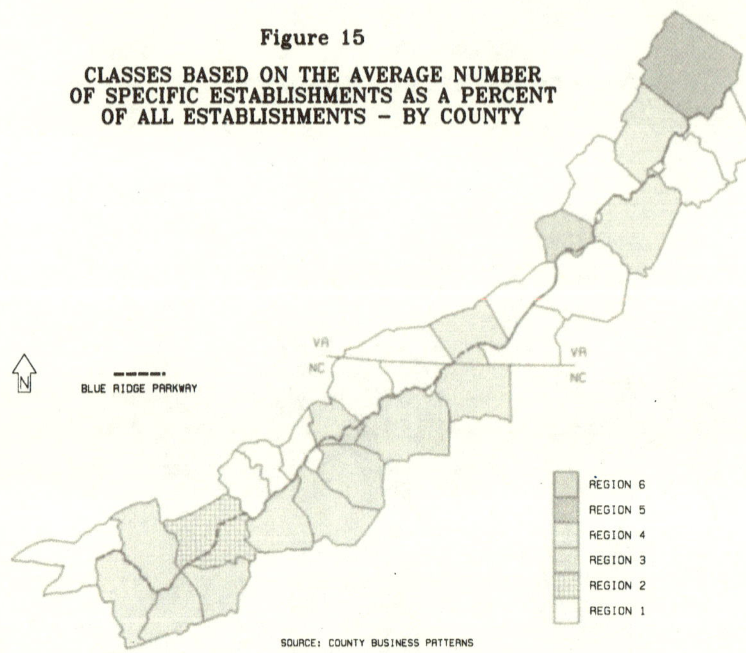

FIGURE 16

CLASSES BASED ON AVERAGE NUMBER OF SPECIFIC ESTABLISHMENTS AS A PERCENT OF ALL ESTABLISHMENTS

	REGIONS					
ESTABLISHMENTS	1	2	3	4	5	6
Agricultural Services, Forestry & Fisheries	3	38	12	8	19	48
Mining	1	6	2	2	4	12
Contract Construction	34	381	124	78	239	458
Manufacturing	28	276	106	48	112	244
Transportation & Other Public Utilities	13	131	37	20	80	152
Wholesale Trade	12	291	60	29	103	510
Retail Trade	88	1,131	386	186	551	1,398
Finance, Insurance, & Real Estate	17	323	69	41	170	528
Services	76	1,376	330	177	622	1,673
Unclassified	31	305	104	56	158	391
Region Size (Counties)	13	1	7	6	1	1

and to related facilities. Sixth and last, the Parkway and the twenty-nine adjacent counties exist in a symbiotic relationship and any alterations of the surrounding environment or the Parkway itself will result in either advantageous or deleterious transformations. In general, the economic framework of the Blue Ridge Parkway Area is normal and change is most likely to occur in those counties with the largest populations and the greatest number of business establishments.

BIBLIOGRAPHY

Lovingood, Paul E., Jr. and Robert. E. Reiman, "A Regionalization of County Business Patterns in the Southern Appalachians". Paper presented at the annual meeting of the Southern Regional Science Association. March 1986.

Pattison, William D., "The Four Traditions of Geography". The Journal of Geography, Vol. 63 (1964), pp. 211-216.

SAS Institute Inc. SAS User's Guide: Statistics. Cary, North Carolina: SAS Institute Inc., 1982.

U. S. Department of Commerce, Bureau of the Census. County Business Patterns, 1984, North Carolina. Washington, D. C.: U. S. Government Printing Office, 1986.

U. S. Department of Commerce, Bureau of the Census. County Business Patterns, 1984, Virginia. Washington, D.C.: U.S. Government Printing Office, 1986.

Ward, J. H., "Hierarchical Grouping to Optimize an Objective Function". Journal American Statistical Association, Vol. 58 (1963), pp. 236-244.

Waugh, T. C. and J. McCalden. Gimms Reference Manual. Edinburgh, Scotland: Gimms, Ltd., 1983.

Enhancing the Parkway Experience Through Side Trips to North Carolina State Parks

William W. Davis and Margaret F. Plemmons

FOREWORD

The Blue Ridge Parkway in North Carolina is no less than a scenic wonderland, each season as glorious as the one preceding it. The vastness of the mountaintop panorama, with the fresh air and the quiet wonder, provides a healing calm for a nation moving far too quickly to appreciate its remaining heritage.

As the Blue Ridge Parkway opens a door to the beauty of the once-inaccessible mountain treasures, the nearby state parks in North Carolina provide just the right opportunity for an interactive experience with our natural heritage itself.

The following narrative describes the protected areas of the western region of North Carolina which have been preserved as state parks. The historical significance, the geological, biological, and scenic attractions, and the recreational opportunities are outlined for each park. It is the hope of the North Carolina Department of Natural Resources and Community Development's Division of Parks and Recreation, that Blue Ridge Parkway travelers will enhance their experience on the Parkway through side trips to North Carolina state parks, the wonders of which belong to all of us.

MOUNT MITCHELL STATE PARK

The year 1914 was a turning point in the mountain region of North Carolina. Fraser fir and red spruce, previously plentiful on the mountaintops, were being destroyed by logging companies. Early conservationists were alarmed. So was Governor Locke Craig.

Governor Craig took action, and the 1915 General Assembly authorized the purchase of 1,224 acres of land to ensure that Mount Mitchell,

Mount Mitchell

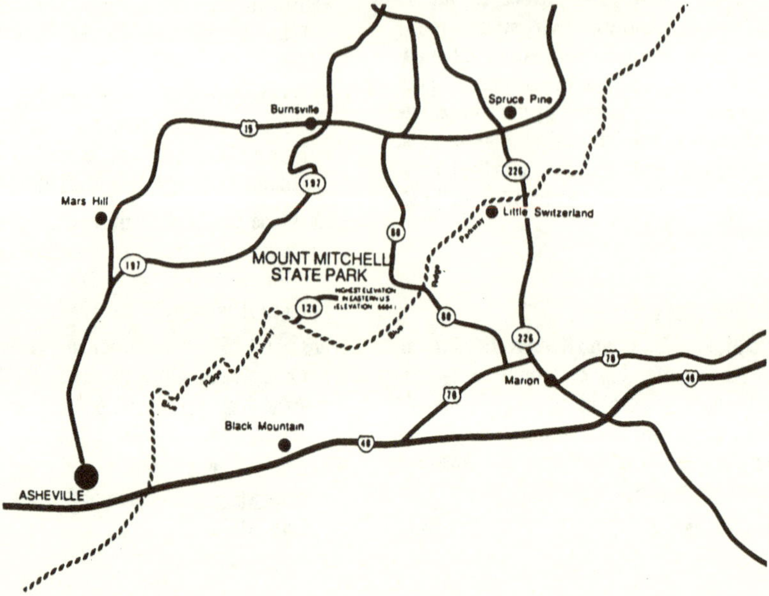

"the most noted mountain in the eastern portion of the United States, was preserved in its original beauty and grandeur, for ourselves and our posterity" as North Carolina's first state park.

The highest peak in eastern America, Mount Mitchell, stands 6,684 feet high in the Black Mountain range. Many other peaks within the park and surrounding National Forests soar to over 6000 feet. These mountains were the battleground of the Cherokee, Catawba, and Iroquois Indian tribes in the 1600's.

Mount Mitchell was named for Dr. Elisha Mitchell, who fell to his death in 1857 while verifying his earlier (1835) measurement of the height of the mountain, previously called "Black Dome." He is buried at the summit of his mountain.

When Mount Mitchell first became a state park, there were few visitors because of the inaccessibility of the region. Those who did visit generally drove on privately-owned toll roads to the old logging camp, Camp Alice, and hiked the remaining mile to the summit of the mountain.

The Roosevelt Administration's federally funded work program for the unemployed, initiated in the 1930's, gave a new thrust to the development of national parks. Mount Mitchell benefited from the federal program as the Civilian Conservation Corps provided manpower for the concession stand construction, water system installation, trail blazing, and general park landscaping.

But it wasn't until 1946 that State Road 128 was built from milepost 355 on the Parkway to the summit, allowing Mount Mitchell's visitation to soar. Today's visitors can enjoy a meal at the restaurant from May through October. There are nine tent campsites, available on a first come first serve basis. Other camping facilities are located in the surrounding Pisgah National Forest. Near the summit are picnic areas with grills, and a snack bar. A museum is located along the short walk to the summit where an observation tower provides a 360-degree view of the Black Mountains. Eighteen miles of trails enable those who wish to hike to the famous summit and at least four other peaks of over 6500 feet elevation to do so. These trails connect to many trails in the Pisgah National Forest, providing opportunities for hikes of any length.

Much of Mount Mitchell is mica gneisses and schists. The alpine-type flora near the summit is similar to Canadian alpine communities. In the summer, the slopes are covered with bearberry, rhododendron, white hellebore, blue bearded Clinton's lily, and other flowering plants. The interpretive rangers offer guided nature hikes and educational programs.

MOUNT JEFFERSON/ NEW RIVER STATE PARKS

Mount Jefferson and New River State Parks lie only ten miles from each other in the northwestern corner of North Carolina. Both are accessible from milepost 261 on the Parkway by way of Highway 16 North. Mount Jefferson can be clearly seen from the overlook at mile marker 266.

An enjoyable 30 mile loop allows one to visit both parks. Take 16 north 0.5 miles to 163 west. After passing several views of the South Fork of the New River, at 9 miles from the Blue Ridge Parkway, a sign directs you to the entrance of Mount Jefferson State Park. After visiting Mount Jefferson, turn right on 16 and follow the signs to New River State Park 6.6 miles to the bridge over the New River at NC 88. Turn under the bridge and drive 3 miles downstream along the river on a gravel road to the Wagoner Road Access. After returning to 16 south follow along the South Fork of the New River 7.3 more miles to the Blue Ridge Parkway.

Prior to Mount Jefferson's acceptance into the state park system, it was called Panther Mountain. It has since been re-named after President Thomas Jefferson's family.

Mount Jefferson is noted for its 541 acres of beauty between the North Fork and the South Fork of the New River.

A panoramic scene including three states may be viewed from the 4,683-foot summit of Mount Jefferson. Whitetop Mountain in Virginia, Grandfather Mountain in North Carolina and mountains in Tennessee can be seen on clear days. Millions of years ago, the mountain itself was part of a large plateau. Most of this plateau has eroded leaving Mount Jefferson more than 1600 feet above the surrounding terrain.

One of the most outstanding chestnut-oak forests in the nation is located on the summit. A heavy undergrowth of purple Rhododendron, mountain laurel and flame azalea completes the vegetational community. Dead chestnut trees still stand in the upper elevations. Chestnut saplings reaching as high as 12 feet sprout from the roots of the old chestnut trees. Wild flowers which grow profusely include iris, jack in the pulpit, galax, solomon seal, dutchman's breeches, as well as dutchman's pipes.

The Rhododendron Trail, a self guided one hour walk, provides information on natural history, human history, and legends of the mountain. The cave near the top of the mountain is said to have been part of the Underground Railroad. The Summit Trail leads to a firetower with excellent views of the pastoral valley as well as surrounding mountains.

Picnickers can enjoy themselves surrounded by rhododendron, usually in bloom in June.

Only a few miles from Mount Jefferson, New River State Park offers the Parkway traveler 498 acres at three sites on a 26-mile stretch of the New River.

Famous for canoe outings, the Wagoner Road access in the park is the state's most popular "put-in" point for canoe outings. Two canoe campgrounds and canoe rentals are available through nearby commercial outfitters.

The New River park currently consists of three access sites along the river. The first site is the Wagoner Road Access which is 3 miles downstream along a gravel road (NC secondary road 1588) off of N. C. Highway 16 N at Index, N. C. approximately eight miles SE of Jefferson, N.C. The second site, the U. S. 221 Access which can only be reached by canoe, is approximately 1 mile upstream, south, of the bridge

Mount Jefferson

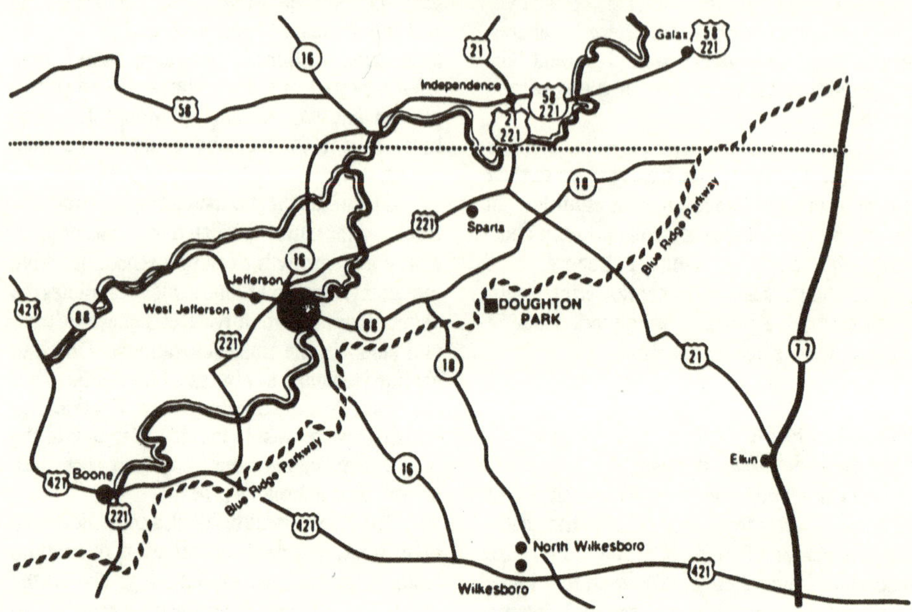

New River

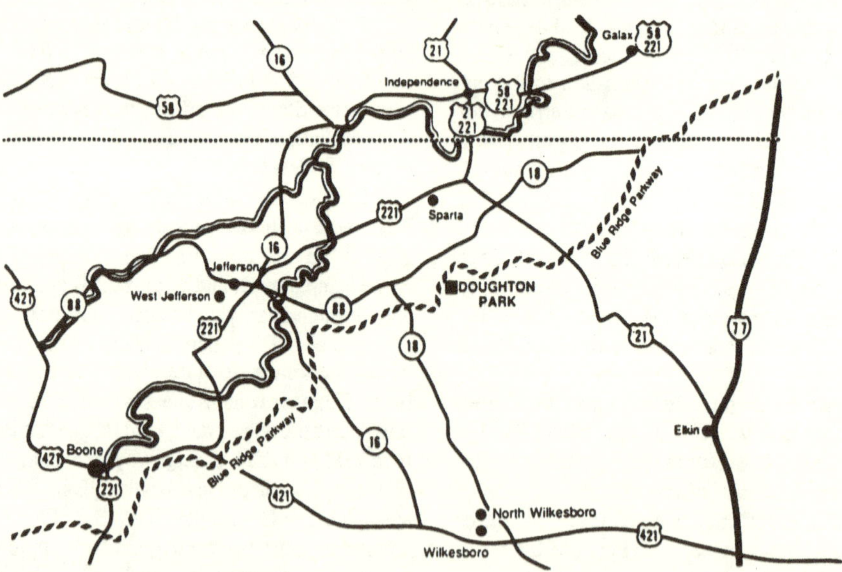

crossing the river at Scottville, N.C. A primitive campground with water and pit toilets is located at this site. The third access, the Alleghany County access, is located approximately 1 mile upstream, south, of the state line. This site is also accessible only from the river and provides primitive camping with water and pit toilets as well as a rough shelter-office building. Development plans for this site propose a full facility drive in tent and trailer camping area as well as extensive hiking and bridal trails.

On June 30, 1987, Governor Jim Martin announced that the State had approved financial assistance to Ashe County to build a canoe access facility at the NC 88/16 bridge near Index. Ashe County will match this grant with local funds as well as operate and maintain this site. The development of this access site will greatly facilitate public use of the river.

Despite its name, the New is the World's second oldest river. Hundreds of millions of years ago it formed the headwaters of the Teays River. The Teays, which pre-dated the Appalachian Mountains, was a huge river that contained the Mississippi and Ohio Rivers as tributaries. Glacial activity in the last million years changed the river channels of the Teays, but did not directly affect the New River. Today the river channel exists essentially the same as it did in prehistoric times. Three species of endangered plants are found along the river: the Virginia spiraea, waterstar mudplantain, and Carolina saxifrage. In addition, six aquatic species which are threatened or of special concern live in the river's waters. These species include a snail, a crayfish and four fish.

In the 1960's, the Appalachian Power Company was granted a permit to construct a hydro-electric facility on the river. The series of dams required for this facility would have flooded the valley and destroyed the unique natural habitats. After a long fight by local citizens and supporters across the country, the New River was protected from dam construction by inclusion in the Scenic River System.

The best way to appreciate the beauty and history of the region is by canoeing the 26.5 mile "Scenic River" stretch of the New River as it flows north from Dog Creek to the N.C.-Va. line. Beginning and intermediate canoers will be challenged by the few rapids.

STONE MOUNTAIN STATE PARK

Stone Mountain State Park lies between New River and Pilot Mountain State Parks. Stone Mountain is actually a 350 million year old dome-shaped granite mass with a circumference of over three miles. This awesome feature has been a state park since 1969 and is listed on the National Registry of Natural Areas.

A dramatic view of Stone Mountain can be seen from the overlook located at milepost 232 on the Blue Ridge Parkway. To reach the park at milepost 229 take US 21 South for 10 miles, then turn right on state road 1002. Park signs lead the way to the entrance, which is deep in the mountain woods.

Originally the hunting grounds of the Catawba Indians, Stone Mountain's wilderness environment is habitat for bear, cougars, and a herd of feral goats. Fishermen enjoy both stocked and native trout streams. The 200-foot Beauty Falls is an unequalled attraction.

The park includes both mountain and piedmont vegetation. Along streams and in moist coves are found a variety of trees such as hemlock, beech, tulip poplar, basswood, northern red oak, sweet birch, fraser magnolia, silverbell, and hickory. Rosebay rhododendron often dominate the understory along creeks. Away from the creeks flowering herbs dominate the forest floor in spring and summer.

A transition of species occurs with changes in elevation. Oak forests, with subcanopies of dogwood and sourwood, dominate the open, drier slopes. A shrub community of bearberry, blueberry, and mountain laurel is common. An abrupt change from the oak forest to pine forest often occurs along the driest ridges, with the pine forest dominating the drier ridges. Catawba rhododendron are also found on the upper slopes and ridges of Stone Mountain.

The 11,285 acre Stone Mountain State Park is relatively undeveloped. Both tent and backcountry camping are available. Trails, including continuous loop trails, rate from easy to strenuous. One of the most popular trails crosses

Stone Mountain

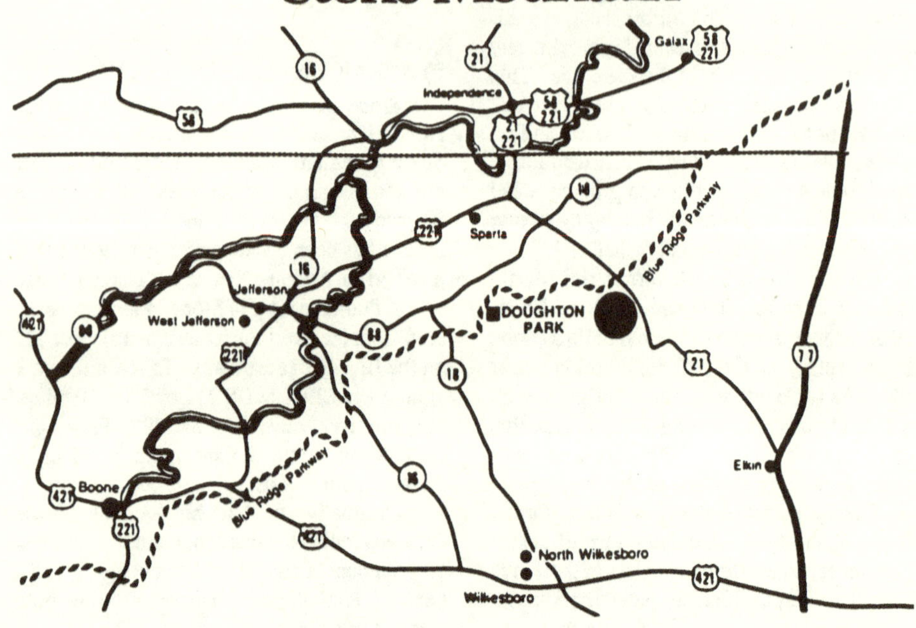

Pilot Mountain

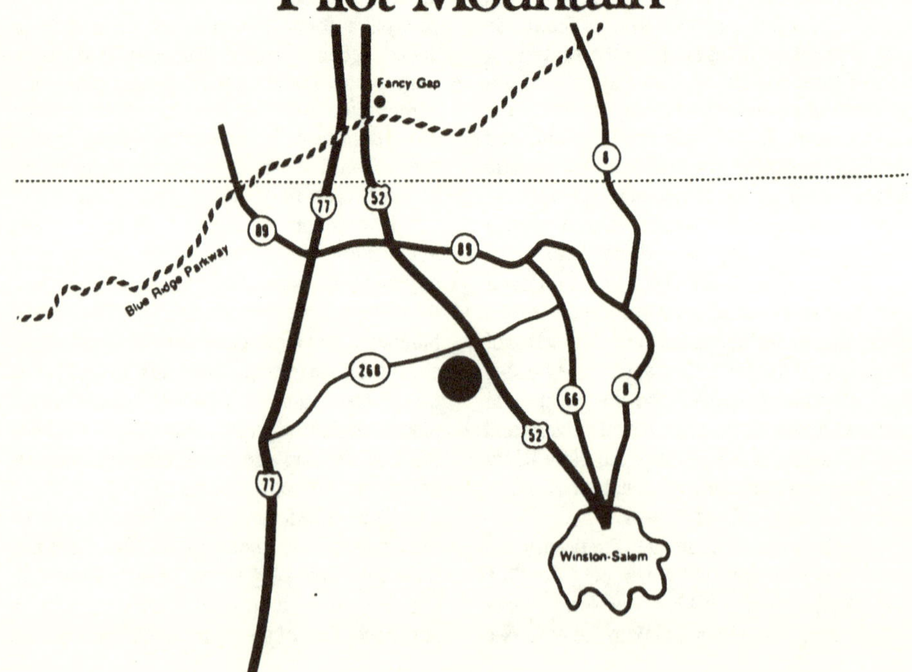

the top of Stone Mountain providing tremendous views of the Blue Ridge Escarpment and the park interior. The trail descends near 200 foot tall Beauty Falls and returns through the forests along Big Sandy Creek. Young visitors often slide down slick stream rocks into deep, cool pools of pure mountain water. Birdwatchers hold hikes several times each season. Many resident and migratory species, including the ruffed grouse, the pileated woodpecker, and the scarlet tanager have been identified.

Rapelling is a popular sport for hardy climbers who enjoy the challenge of the bare mountain face. Professional rapellers hold informative seminars which are of wide appeal to curious visitors. As in the other state parks, interpretive rangers lead nature hikes and host school groups for environmental education outings. There is also a guided nature trail designed for visitors to learn about the wilderness habitat at their own pace.

PILOT MOUNTAIN

Pilot Mountain State Park covers 3,748 acres on the western end of the Sauratown range. For Parkway visitors, it is very simple to locate from milepost 199 in Fancy Gap, Virginia. From there, Highway 52 South leads directly to the park entrance, 30 miles away.

Pilot Mountain was dedicated as a National Natural Landmark in 1970, due to its visually stimulating appearance. Pilot Mountain commands the landscape for miles around with its unique shape. The Indians called it "Jomeokee" meaning "Great Guide" or "Pilot". 3,000 square miles are visible from Big Pinnacle, a 200-foot tall quartzite marvel which begins 1400 feet above the valley floor.

A paved road leads to the Little Pinnacle where picnic facilities are located. A short walk to the Little Pinnacle overlook provides a view of the Big Pinnacle and Dan and Yadkin River Valleys. Trails of varying length and difficulty begin here. Rapelling is permitted on the Little Pinnacle but not the Big Pinnacle.

The chestnut-oak forests provide habitat for many species of wildlife. Ravens populate the knob, one of their few remaining habitats. Over 70 families of vascular plants can be easily identified in the park, and in the spring the summit area is covered with rhododendron and mountain laurel. Both resident and migratory songbirds make the atmosphere of Pilot Mountain restful and appealing.

The Yadkin River Section of the park, which is connected with the pinnacle section by a corridor, consists of 1300 acres on the Surry and Yadkin County sides of the Yadkin River as well as two large islands in the river. To reach this section by roads, exit the main section of the park on US 52 South, turn right at the Pinnacle exit and follow signs to the park. The last mile is currently a gravel road. A group camping area as well as picnic areas are located in this section of the park. Gravel roads lead to the river, where fishing is permitted. Sunfish and catfish are the most common fish.

A canoe access site is located on the Yadkin County side of the river near East Bend. There is also a primitive canoe-access campground available on the larger island. This is part of the 165 mile long Yadkin River Trail.

A six mile long Corridor trail descends from the pinnacle to the Yadkin River. This trail is used by hikers and horseback riders. The Sauratown Trail, which connects Pilot Mountain with Hanging Rock, is also used by both hikers and horseback riders.

Other activities visitors enjoy include family camping, picnicking, fishing, and interpretive programs. Pilot Mountain's location is ideal for stargazing. Astronomy programs are often conducted at Pilot Mountain State Park during the clear nights of the summer and fall.

HANGING ROCK STATE PARK

Citizen involvement and volunteer assistance are vital factors in the development of state parks. Often, parks are created on land obtained through a combination of purchased and donated tracts. One such park is Hanging Rock State Park, which was developed in 1935 on 3000 acres in the Sauratown Mountains donated by citizens of Stokes County and Winston-Salem.

Hanging Rock is conveniently located in

Hanging Rock

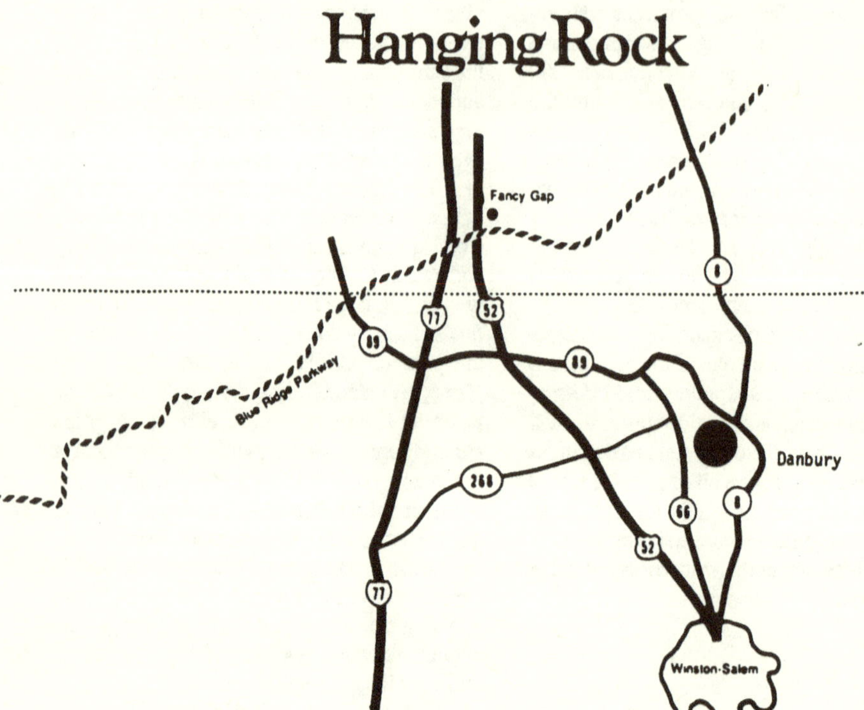

Sauratown Trail

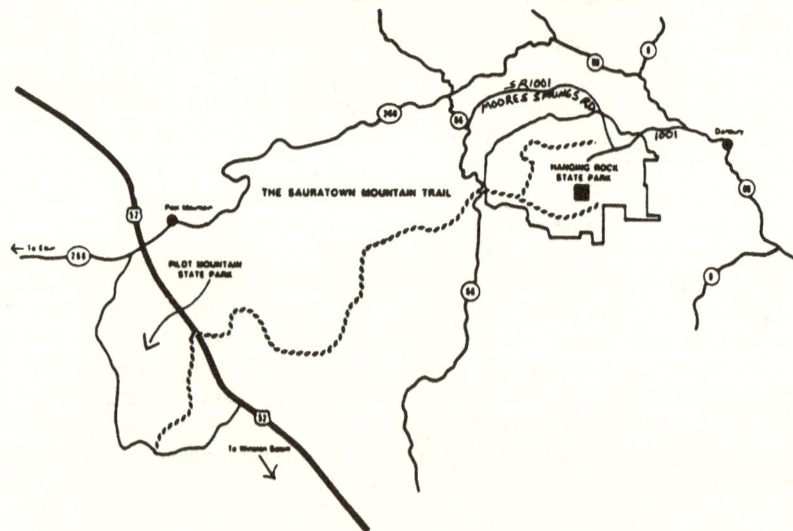

the north central part of the state, and only a 40-minute ride from the Blue Ridge Parkway at its closest point. From milepost 165 in Virginia, Highway 89 (connecting with Highway 8 in North Carolina) leads into Danbury, North Carolina, where there are signs for the park.

The easternmost mountain in North Carolina, Hanging Rock is a mountain away from the mountains. Its mountainous topography and piedmont location allow piedmont and mountain ecosystems to co-exist. Here geology and vegetation similar to the Blue Ridge are found amid the Piedmont, providing a comprehensive view of both regions in just one state park visit!

The major features of the park are the quartzite-capped rock outcrops, especially Hanging Rock, Moore's Knob, and Cook's Wall. Notable structures in the park include an observation tower on Moore's Knob.

Visitors to Hanging Rock may participate in active recreation, such as swimming, canoeing, hiking, and climbing. Rock climbing is allowed on Moore's Knob and Cook's Wall but not on Hanging Rock itself. The lake created by the CCC is popular for swimming and boating. Educational programs are offered several times each month by trained staff members.

Hanging Rock provides a varied habitat for over 300 species of identifiable mountain and piedmont flora. The elevation climbs from 1000 feet at the gate to 2579 feet at Moore's Knob. This is one of the few regions in which Carolina and Canadian hemlock grow together. Table Mountain Pine and chestnut oak are the major trees. Mountain camelia, catawba and rosebay rhododendron, mountain laurel, the deciduous pinxter flower, azalea, trailing arbutus, and galax, flowers normally found in the mountains, provide an extended blooming season. Sundew is also found here, 100 miles out of its normal range.

There are currently over 18 miles of trails to guide visitors along scenic heights, waterfalls, and rocky ridges. A new trail under construction will lead to the Dan River. A canoe access site and primitive campground which will be part of the Dan River Trail are under development at the Dan River where it runs through the park. The transition of habitat from the Dan River to the rock peaks provides food and habitat for varied wildlife. Raccoon are plentiful and there are populations of deer, gray fox, bobcat and numerous reptiles, and amphibians. Birds, particularly those suited to upper canopy forests, are common.

All of this combines to make camping in the park appealing to vacationers. Hanging Rock also offers cabin rentals, which must be reserved months in advance.

An added appeal of Hanging Rock State Park is that horsemen and hikers can travel directly from one state park to another, Pilot Mountain, using the Sauratown Trail. (See map below.) Twenty miles in length, this trail traverses public roadsides and private land, made possible through cooperative agreements with landowners. This is a magnificent example of citizen cooperation and a sharing of our fine resources so that we may all appreciate them.

A special feeling is created by the facilities constructed by the Civilian Conservation Corps in the 1930's and 1940's. The large stone and notched exposed beam-covered picnic shelters, a stone bathhouse overlooking the lake, and rock walls are all reminiscent of the Blue Ridge Parkway.

SUMMARY

More than half the population of the United States is within easy access of the Blue Ridge Parkway. With the recognition of the importance of natural heritage preservation by the state and many citizens organizations, the western region of North Carolina boasts many state parks not to be missed on a trip down the Blue Ridge Parkway. The design and splendor of the Parkway itself force us to slow down and open our eyes to the natural beauty which has existed through the ages. North Carolina's state parks provide the opportunity to explore and appreciate it.

Across North Carolina, more than 45 additional state parks and recreation areas are within easy access of major population areas, just waiting for visitors to discover the habitats and natural features so vital to our past, and preserved for our future generations.

A Deeper Understanding of the Landscape Awaits Interpretation by the Traveling Parkway Visitor

J. Dan Pittillo

INTRODUCTION

Parkways are generally considered to be resources and sites for leisure uses such as driving for pleasure, biking, hiking, viewing, and photographing. But are the managers really providing the visitor with the greatest value that a parkway might offer, namely its relationship with the natural landscape setting? Is there an effort to provide parkway visitors valuable understandings of the natural landscape that modern science has discovered? The example of the Blue Ridge Parkway will illustrate where we have the opportunity to go if a program of active interpretation is developed.

In this brief essay the objective is to describe some examples of research and field observations that are available for interpretation for the Parkway visitor. First we will look at some good examples of interpretation that should be developed. Among them are newly developed theories of how the Blue Ridge relates to the mountain building processes of plate tectonics. Paleoecologists have been able to piece together some ideas of what happened in the more recent past. Botanists have found that many of the rare relict plants of the higher elevations along the Blue Ridge Parkway are related to past climatic influences and distributions. Endangered or threatened plánt populations are a valuable resource that find their habitats continually impacted; these need protection and understanding by managers and visitors of the Parkway. Lastly we will suggest some ways that might be considered in development of the interpretative program.

How the earth, plants, and animals interact and how they can be viewed are valuable lessons to the astute Parkway visitor. The Parkway visitor can, in his leisure, enjoy the more rewarding depth of understanding of the beauties of Earth and not feel the Parkways are simply a place to speed from point to point. The mystery of the unknown and the path toward understanding are among the most rewarding experiences of the human mind. Parkway visitors can be provided this deeper understanding at their leisure.

THE RISE OF THE APPALACHIANS

As travellers approach the 2000-4000 feet of relief of the Blue Ridge Mountains, how often have they pondered, "How did these mountains come to be and how long have they been here?" These questions have been answered in part many times before and usually differently as scientists have added new facts. In the first half of this century, scientists dated the Blue Ridge of the Appalachian Mountains as one of the older ranges in the world, with the rocks of such places as Whiteside Mountain initially estimated about 250 million years old (Keith 1907, p. 4), but rocks of the Whiteside area are now considered much older, about 400 million years as the minimum (McNiff 1967). It was only after the International Geophysical Year, which began in 1957, that the general concept of Wegener on Continental Drift became more accepted in the expanded concept of Plate Tectonics (cf. Wilson 1963 and Scientific American 1970).

Following the acceptance of the general concept of Plate Tectonics, the Appalachians are now theorized to have involved many episodes that culminated around 300-275 million years ago (Oliver 1980). To the east, a vast sea, know as the Proto-Atlantic, was spreading 800-700 million years ago. Some microcontinents (or islands and peninsulas) formed to the east. Then 600-500 million years ago the Proto-Atlantic began to close and the microcontinents were thrust upon the North American continent. Around 400-350 million years ago an island arc formed to the east and this was subsequently thrust upon the North American continent as Africa collided with North America. Geologists now theorize that the North American crust was coming from remnants of the smaller microcontinents and volcanic islands that became fused to form our present Blue Ridge and Piedmont (Hatcher 1978; Oliver 1980). Recent seismic techniques for underground exploration indicate that the existing Blue Ridge is an overthrust sheet of metamorphic rocks covering sedimentary rocks similar to those presently found in eastern Tennessee. This has led to speculation about the possibility of gas being trapped beneath the Blue Ridge (Oliver 1980).

It is this ancient landscape that the Parkway visitor sees. The visitor is mainly impressed by the dense and extensive green mantle of forests that cloak the mountains to their peaks, sustained by the deep layer of moist soil that was produced by the decay of the rocks during thousands of years. Only occasionally is the forest cover broken by a rock outcropping. More frequently the break in this tree mantle is a product of human activities, with pastures, crops, developed areas, etc., most common in the valleys below the Parkway. It might be enlightening to muse what it might have been like to stand in the southern Appalachians on a mountain at 10,000 feet elevation during the age of dinosaurs. It certainly would reveal a different vision than the present scenery.

THE UNEARTHING OF THE PAST HISTORY

We are now able to learn many details of more recent history by probing the sediments of recent deposits. This is because of advances in aging sediments by a process called thermolumenescence. Combined with study of the prefossil deposits of plant pieces and pollen, this allows our reconstruction of some interesting past events. One site that has proved especially valuable is at Flat Laurel Gap near Mount Pisgah. Paleoecologists have recently produced the following story for the site (Shafer 1985).

About 12,000 years ago when the permafrost melted, a fine, mustard-colored silt washed from melted permafrost slopes and was deposited in the basin at Flat Laurel Gap. Around 9,000 years ago there were deluges of rainfall, resulting in debris avalanches, some of which also moved down into the basin. The botanical record stretches back to 3,000 years ago and has a dominance of heath species that continues to the present, the longest known southern Appalachian record. These heath species consist of rhododendrons, mountain laurel, blueberries, and other heaths, but include some species now extirpated from the site, such as leatherleaf (Chamaedaphne calyculata) and bog rosemary (Andromedia glaucophylla). Some other events of note include the extirpation of Fraser fir (Abies fraseri) in the late 1800's and American chestnut in the 1930's.

It is noteworthy that within the glade of Flat Laurel Gap there remains an open stony flat with an active patterned ground, a geologic term for sorting of coarse to fine materials by alternative freezing and thawing. Apparently the freeze-thaw action on the small boulders and gravel that now occurs within the stony flat during the relatively milder winters of this interglacial time is strong enough to produce small polygons of sorted stones that are about 15-20 cm across.

Besides the ancient heath community of Flat Laurel Gap, another species of note here is the bog asphodel (Tofieldia racemosa var. glutinosa). This small lily blooms in the early summer with a spike of white flowers covered with sparkling red glands, like small ruby gems throughout the inflorescence. This "botanical gem" is found scattered along the Appalachians and into Canada.

THE NECKLACE OF BOTANICAL GEMS

Throughout the growing season, colorful plants are draped from the banks and along the shoulders of the Parkway much as the necklace of sparkling gems of a princess. These showy plants, as well as the rare and endangered plants of the states of North Carolina (Pittillo and Govus 1978) and more recently of Virginia (Coleman and Pittillo 1987), have been mapped and described in the "manual" of important plant habitats for the National Park Service. In Virginia, many of these have been transplanted during and following the construction of the

Parkway, producing displays such as the red spruces at Bluff Mountain (mile 51.2) and purple rhododendrons at Laurel Springs (mile 9.3). In many places the Parkway crosses or encompasses beautiful examples of old growth plant communities, also included in the "manual."

The public considers Craggy Gardens as one of the outstanding "botanical gems" of the Blue Ridge Parkway. This area has long been sought out for its colorful June displays of purple rhododendron (Rhododendron catawbiense). Over the years, additional botanical finds have made this one of the most significant sites in the southern Appalachians. Many of the Craggy Garden species have affinities to the tundra of the northern Appalachians or farther north in the Arctic tundra. Among the alpine types are spreading avens (Geum radiatum), deerhair bulrush (Scirpus cespitosus var. callosus), and single-flowered rush (Juncus caroliniamus). Not only are these plants listed by the state of North Carolina for protection, but their connection with ancestral stock during the glacial periods is significant. Their rareness, then, like a diamond, makes them a valuable part of this "botanical necklace."

The dwarfed beeches and yellow birches of the Craggies point to another curiosity in this string of botanical gems. About five miles to the north the Craggies abut the Black Mountains. The Black Mountains extend up to 6,684 feet in elevation atop Mt. Mitchell and the spruce-fir forests extend down to 4,500 feet generally. Looking toward the Black Mountains from Craggy Pinnacle, the dark line of the spuce-fir forest extends downward considerably below the tops of the Craggies. The Craggies rise to slightly over 6000 feet at Craggy Dome and yet, except for a few scattered clumps of Fraser fir and red spruce, are covered primarily with deciduous birches and beeches. This curiosity is yet to be explained but suggestions include the devastation of the spruce-fir forest by the weather changes during the past. Past weather would have played a role in this elimination of the spruce-fir forest in this ecotonal hypothesis that W. H. Whittaker (1956) and A. F. Mark (1958) proposed in the 1950's. In this hypothesis the spruce-fir forest moved up during the warm interglacial period about 5000 years ago and on intermediate peaks the spruce-fir was eliminated. When cooling followed and the spruce-fir generally moved down the slopes, those intermediated peaks not having spruce-fir became grass balds or became dominated by other species such as heaths. In the Craggies, the heaths presumably were replaced by beeches and yellow birches which became dwarfed by the stressful and severe weather. Another hypothesis that should not be overlooked is the possibility that the spruce-fir forest was lost by fire or a combination of fire and weather damage and has not yet been replenished. The small clumps of trees near the outcrops on the south and east sides of Craggy Dome are somewhat similar to clumps that remain in some areas devastated by fire in the Graveyards area of the Balsam Mountains.

In the Balsam Mountains to the south are a few more botanical gems that possibly date to glacial times. While working on another project in early summer of 1978, I noticed a grape fern which seemed out of season (our common grape ferns come up in late summer or fall). It turned out to be the little-leaf grapefern (Botrychium simplex), known generally for Pennsylvania northward to the tundra. There was a good colony on Richland Balsam and later another colony was found farther east at Beech Gap. These have been observed for the past decade or so and generally are decreasing in numbers. A more diligent search in May of 1987 resulted in an additional site with only two plants noted. The interesting thing is that all of these plants are located at high elevations (above 5700 feet) and only on scraped shoulders and banks of the Parkway. I understand that it takes a long period for the gametophytes (the tiny plants scarcely larger than a fingernail that bear the gametes, sperms and eggs) to grow enough to produce sporophytes (the larger ferns we see with the spore-bearing brown dots on the leaf or in this case tiny bead-like clusters that look like miniature green grapes before they ripen) and it had been about 20 years since the construction of the Parkway has been completed. I also learned that a mycologist had discovered that fungus spores can grow from ancient mud deposits. This led me to speculate that it might be possible that these little-leaf grapefern plants developed from ancient spores in soils recently exposed by the Parkway construction. Now comes the more difficult task of getting more substantial evidence for this speculation.

Many of the botanical gems of the Parkway are more familiar than these. In spring throughout the 470-mile length of the Parkway a showy display of such plants as flame azalea, mountain laurel, and three species of rhododendrons are delightful to the Parkway travellers. But there is an abundance of wildflowers growing throughout the Parkway to make any part of the summer worth the trip. Trilliums are found in the open forests before the leaves shade them out. Irises, buttercups, fire pinks, bluets, daises, black-eyed susans, phloxes, sundrops, oswego tea, coneflowers, blue bells, monkshoods, goldenrods, asters, gentians, and turtleheads, will give you an indication of the progression of the botanical gems through the growing season. Would anything less than a "necklace of gems" be a suitable metaphor for these beauties of the botanical world?

EVENTS IN THE LIVES OF PLANTS

What happens when we pay close attention over a period of time to the activities of a plant instead of simply enjoying its beauty for the moment? Have you ever watched the bees scrambling over the flowers of wild celery (Angelica triquinata)? Sometimes the bees tumble off in a drunken stupor. Alas, bees have their own form of pot plants! On a more serious note, the bees are serving the important function of cross pollination. But to my knowledge, the cause of the observation of drunkenness has yet to be explained.

Two common early blooming plants of the woodlands are squirrel corn (Dicentra canadensis) and Dutchman's breeches (D. cucullaria). These close relatives may be recently derived from a common ancestor if the observations and suggestions by Leslie Bishop (1980) are correct. In her study of these two species at Red Bank Cove (a beautiful natural area near milepost 441 and Balsam Gap in the Balsam Mountains of North Carolina), she found that Dutchman's breeches tend to bloom earlier than squirrel corn and thereby have less competition for the bee pollinators. So perhaps these two species recently evolved and are continuing their divergence from each other by timing their blooming further apart.

Have you ever noticed how the coloration progresses in witch-hobble (Viburnum alnifolium)? Rather than the green leaves turning red at once, red blocks appear irregularly on a given leaf and in different parts of a given plant. What is the basis of this? To my knowledge, no one has investigated this phenomenon. So here is another example of one of the mysteries that the careful observer can find and attempt to solve in his visits to the Parkway.

INTERPRETIVE CENTERS AND INTERPRETERS

There is much scientific knowledge accumulating about the natural world. This knowledge diminishes the margin of the unknown as our society matures. When the Parkway visitor travels from the lowlands to the Parkway for the first time, the mystery of the mountains diminishes to some degree. But here he may see new mysteries or perhaps, with a little suggestion from a talented interpreter, can have a different way of looking at familiar things and begin to gain a deeper understanding of the phenomena that surround him. If the Parkway is going to help visitors deepen their appreciation for our National Parks, it is very important that a good program of interpretation be maintained. Unfortunately, too much of the Parkway's financial resources get channelled into the day-to-day maintenance activities such as replacing pavement, repairing buildings, paying rangers, etc., and interpretation always seems the last thing to be funded. This must change if the natural resources are to be properly appreciated and not destroyed in the push to widen the road, build another trail, clear away the brush, or manicure the grass.

One of the most valuable physical assets of any park is the interpretive center. The Parkway is such an elongated park that one center is not, for practical purposes, the best solution. Thus it may be more reasonable to place several interpretive centers at appropriate places. In the southern end, the only interpretive center is at Craggy Gardens. While this is a good location for such a center, it is not open over a considerable portion of the year due to weather conditions. It is not used effectively for interpretation at the present time. It is primarily a book store and information point. This is unfortunate and badly needs changing.

A second means of interpretation is by providing personal interpreters. This may be the most effective one, just as a teacher is better than a television program for teaching children how to write. The interpretive staff needs to be expanded considerably and programs offering interpretation for different groups should be a primary objective of the Parkway. There are usually interpretive programs associated with campgrounds and this is as it should be. There should be interpreters associated with each interpretation center. The interpreter should be well versed in the features of the location. It certainly should be possible to hire local people to either develop or carry out the interpretive program for the busy season.

The entire interpretive program of the Parkway needs review. It may be found that there is a direct relationship between the quality of interpretation and the quality of the experience of the visitor. If a visitor has a quality experience and learns more about his world, he may be more respectful of the Parkway, national parks, and nature in general. This can be translated to producing less stress on the biosphere and more care in conserving diminishing natural resources. In this way our society may improve, providing a higher quality of life for all of us.

BIBLIOGRAPHY

Bishop, Leslie. 1980. Competition for pollinators: Interactions between Dicentra cucularia and Dicentra canadensis. Masters Thesis, Western Carolina University, Cullowhee, NC. 30 p.

Coleman, D. A. and J. D. Pittillo. 1987. Important plant habitats of the Blue Ridge Parkway, Roanoke to Rock Fish Gap, Virginia. Blue Ridge Parkway, National Park Service, Asheville, NC. 110 p.

Hatcher, R. D. Jr. 1978. Tectonics of the western Piedmont and Blue Ridge, southern Appalachians: Review and speculation. Am. J. Sci. 278: 276-304.

Keith, Arthur. 1970. Geologic atlas of the U. S. — Pisgah folio. No. 147. U. S. Geological Survey, Washington.

Mark, A. F. 1958. The ecology of the southern Appalachian grass balds. Ecol. Monog. 28:293-336.

McNiff, J. M. 1967. Geology of the Highlands-Cashiers area. Dissertation, Rice University, Houston. 100 p.

Oliver, J. 1980. Exploring the basement of the North American Continent. Am. Sci. 68: 676-683.

Pittillo, J. D. and T. E. Govus. 1978. A manual of important plant habitats of the Blue Ridge Parkway from the Great Smoky Mountains National Park to Roanoke, Virginia. Blue Ridge Parkway, National Park Service, Asheville, NC. 446 p.

Shafer, D. S. 1986. Flat Laurel Gap bog, Pisgah Ridge, North Carolina: Lake Holocene development of a high elevation heath bald. Castanea 51:1-9.

Scientific American. 1970. Continents adrift. W. H. Freeman Co., San Francisco. 172 p.

Wilson, J. T. 1963. Continental drift. Sci. Am. 208 (4): 86-100.

Whittaker, R. H. 1956. Vegetation of the Great Smoky Mountains. Ecol. Monog. 26:1-80.

Preserving and Protecting the Parkways of Washington, D.C.

Steven Elkinton and Lou A. DeLorme, IV

ABSTRACT

Built as an outgrowth of the City Beautiful Movement and the U.S. Senate's McMillan Plan in 1902, the five parkways of Washington, D.C., today face a variety of problems and opportunities.

Changing safety standards, tighter environmental controls, and decreasing maintenance budgets have all affected the parkways. The growing metropolitan area threatens scenic buffers and rural vistas, as well as causing heavy commuter use at rush-hour, overshadowing their intended use as scenic city entrances. Most of the parkways have become radial arms of the area's arterial highway system, connecting the beltway to the city center. Increased volumes and faster cars create pressure for more lanes; while the clearing of adjoining land destroys the slender woodlands along the Parkways' edges.

How are the parkways of Washington adapting to increasing urban growth and change? National Capital Region is experimenting with a variety of answers. The fundamental policies governing parkway design, use, and management remain intact—but new efforts include wider turf shoulders, timber guardrail, stone walls, skid-resistant bridge decks, bicycle trails, landscaped drainage and retention systems, restoration of meadows and woodland communities, and selection of available native species for specimen and buffer plantings.

Such adaptations preserve the original intended appearance of these special roads, while allowing them to meet new safety standards and the changing conditions of the Nation's Capital.

INTRODUCTION

The concept of Parkways first appeared in the Washington, D.C., area late in the 19th century. A set of alternatives was considered by the Army Corps of Engineers for the Mount Vernon Highway in the 1890s. The Senate District Committee's The Improvement of the Park System of the District of Columbia (known as the McMillan Plan in honor of the Committee's chairman) recommended eight separate parkways as part of a comprehensive park plan for greater Washington. Two of those roads were eventually built: the Mount Vernon Highway and the Rock Creek and Potomac Parkway.

Plans by the National Capital Parks and Planning Commission (NCPPC) in the late 1920s called for a series of radial streamside of riverside parkways providing scenic entrances to the capital city. The short Dalecarlia Parkway (now under the jurisdiction of the District of Columbia) was built as a result of these plans. In 1930, the Capper-Cramton Act financed the acquisition and development of the NCPPC's Park and parkway plans, specifically establishing a commission to purchase land for and build the George Washington Memorial Parkway on both sides of the Potomac River.

During World War II the remaining two parkways were built to connect the city to important suburban military bases: the Suitland Parkway to Andrews Air Force Base and the Baltimore-Washington Parkway to Fort Meade (now the National Security Agency). In fact the "B-W" Parkway immediately became a major inter-city route, soon connecting the Baltimore and Washington beltways to each other. [For a more complete history of these parkways, see the paper by Dr. Jere Krakow, "Parkways of the Nation's Capital" in this volume.]

Figure 1-2 shows the four parkways regionally and in the District of Columbia. Today they are administered by the National Capital Region of the National Park Service.

Since these Parkways were completed in the 1950s, the Washington metropolitan area's population has tripled (Figure 3), and the public has come to accept inter-state highways as the norm in high-speed travel. Yet when parkways

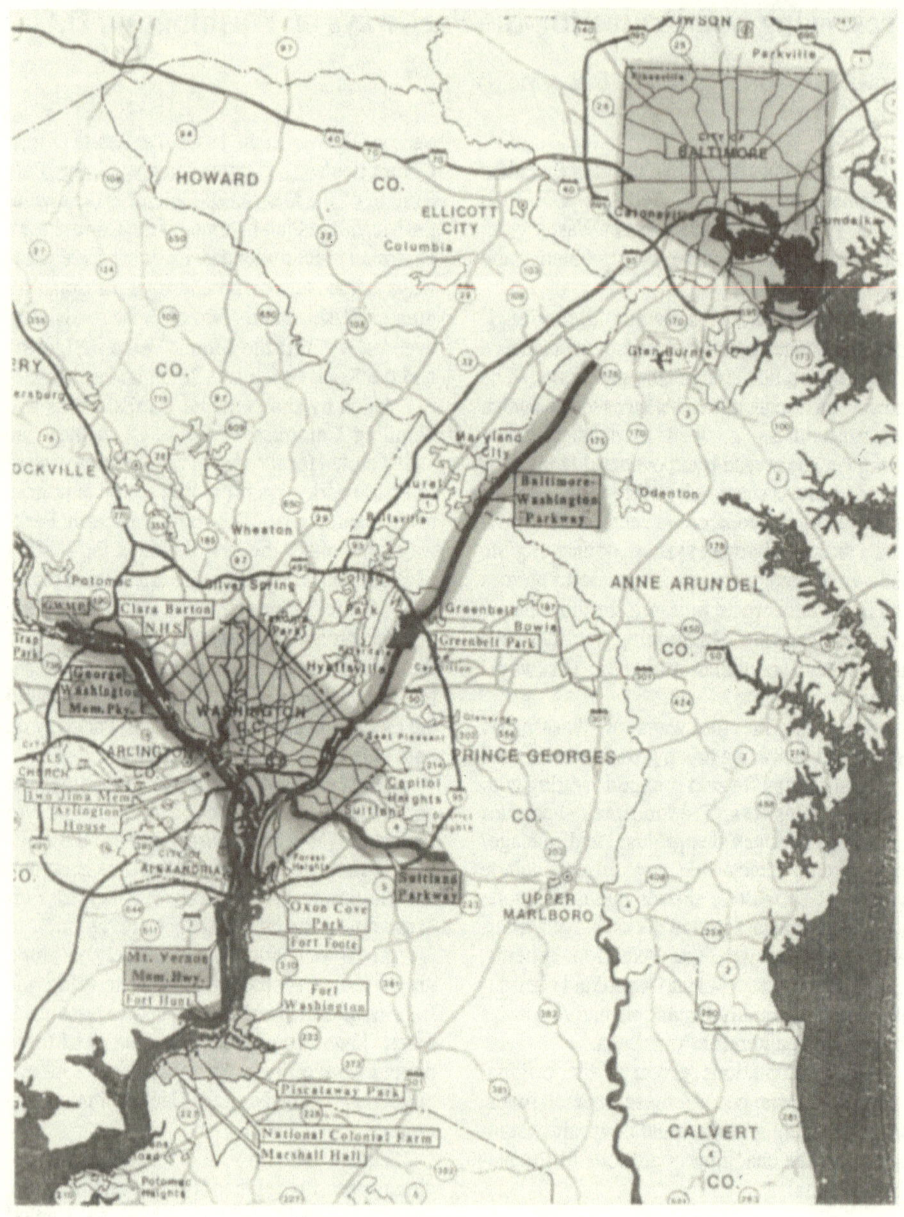

Fig. 1-2. Washington and Baltimore metropolitan areas showing the parkways in and around Washington, D.C.

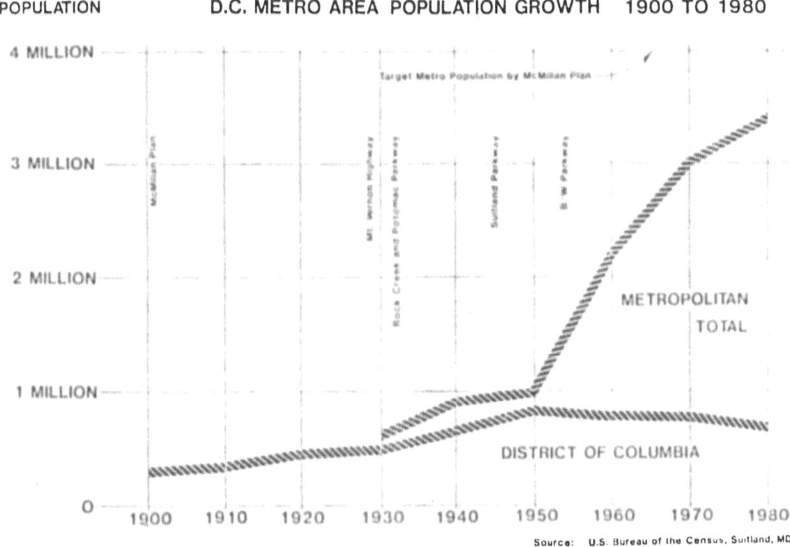

Top: *Fig. 3. Population growth in the Washington Metropolitan Area since 1900. Note the total has more than tripled since 1950, even though the District's population has stayed about even.* Bottom: *Fig. 4. Typical parkway scene along the Suitland Parkway, with gentle horizontal and vertical curvature and two lanes in each direction.*

have been threatened with conversion to interstate standards, as in 1970 when the "B-W" parkway was offered to the state of Maryland for conversion to a state expressway, the public has strongly indicated its support to keep them as scenic alternatives to such highways. Surrounded by increasing urbanization, the parkways face a full array of problems.

This paper is a brief overview of some of the measures which are currently being used to preserve and protect these four parkways' scenic character. Many of the illustrations were filmed on video, so they are not reproduced here. Reproductions of those slides and charts that relate to the text are included at the end.

PARKWAY CHARACTERISTICS

Although each Parkway was built under different circumstances at different times, they have many characteristics in common, including:

- broad, gentle horizontal and vertical curvature [Fig. 4]
- paved roadway limited to two lanes each way [Fig. 4]
- views to scenic features nearby
- where possible, landscaped medians
- accents on landmarks, such as the Washington Monument.
- wide, grassy shoulders (when topography allows) [Fig. 5]
- wide rights-of-way, preserving woodland buffers [Fig. 5]
- extensive landscaping, including overhanging trees creating alternating bands of sun and shade
- stone-faced bridge and drainage structures

(Characteristics which are unique to each parkway are not discussed in this paper.)

PROBLEMS

Today these parkways face a range of problems caused by their location in an increasingly urbanizing metropolitan area, their age, changed highway safety standards, and changing environmental protection standards. Most critical is the increased volume of traffic, much of it occurring at morning and evening rush hour [Fig. 6]. None of these roads was designed for commuter traffic, yet the majority of their use is commutation.

Increasing population and urbanization also causes changes in adjacent land use, so that woodlands and fields give way to shopping centers, housing, industrial parks, and in some areas, clusters of high-rises [Fig. 7]. Streams deteriorate hydrologically as adjacent watersheds are cleared and developed. In many areas, dumping is common along the parkways.

As the urban area grows and additional highways and utility corridors are built, new bridge crossings, powerlines, and underground cables approach and cross the parkway corridors from all sides, disrupting their scenic continuity. Such land use changes damage the drainage and the visual setting of the parkway, often destroying its intended scenic quality.

Many parkway problems are due to age and heavy use: deteriorated pavement, eroded drainage ways, weathered curbs, rutted shoulders, corroded bridge decks and railings. Others stem from inadequate initial design or incomplete installation: at-grade intersections, unpaved ramps, low bridge clearance, tight curves, and poor stopping sight distances. Since their original construction, the parkways' adjoining vegetation has often flourished, obscuring views and creating tangled thickets.

Additional problems are related to changed safety standards, and have led to the interim installation of unsightly guardrails and a proliferation of signs. Since the 1950s, annual accident totals have roughly paralleled population growth, increasing three times in 30 years (1,100 in 1951; 3,700 in 1986). Of these, only 1% or less are fatal. Since 1970, numbers of accidents per year have remained about the same from year to year.

MEETING THE CHALLENGE

Between the late 1950s and the late 1970s, all four of these parkways enjoyed heavy use.

Each was occasionally repaved as needed, but no major capital improvements were made, other than the introduction of off-road bicycle trails along the Mount Vernon Highway and the Rock Creek and Potomac Parkway [Fig. 6]. By 1980 it was clear that all of them needed major rehabilitation work. In the case of the Mount Vernon Highway, this work was considered historic rehabilitation since the road was considered eligible for the National Register of Historic places. In 1983, a 5-cent per gallon gasoline tax was passed by Congress, with the provision that a significant proportion of that revenue be used on federal roads, including Park roads. As a result all four parkways are in the midst of being rehabilitated, starting with Mount Vernon Highway (almost complete), Suitland Parkway (construction about to commence}, and proceeding to the B-W and Rock Creek and Potomac Parkways (feasibility and engineering studies still being completed).

Funding for this work is available from four separate sources: special Congressional authorizations drawing on the General Highway Trust Fund, the Federal Lands Highways program, National Park Service bridge and cyclic maintenance funds, and the NPS line-item construction budget. Project funded under the last three sources must compete against similar projects on a national basis. In certain cases this funding covers bicycle trail and landscaping rehabilitation, in other cases not.

CONSISTENT POLICIES

These recent rehabilitation projects occur under the umbrella of parkway policies which have changed little since the 1930s. These roads are seen as neither parks nor highways, but as scenic experiences in themselves. Since each is unique, no specific parkway standards have been written. Traffic speed limits have not been reduced. Parkway shoulders are to remain grass. Access to private property owners is consistently denied. And despite increased traffic demands, the parkways have not been widened in the belief that more than two lanes of pavement in either direction destroys scenic parkway character.

ENGINEERING CHANGES

Since these roads were first built, highway standards have changed—especially the requirements for clearance between the travel way and permanent obstructions (trees, guardwalls, bridge abutments, etc.). In addition, faster speeds and extensive testing have meant that stopping sight distances are longer than in the 1950s.

As each of these parkways has been prepared for rehabilitation, all of these factors have been taken into account. Where feasible, acceleration and deceleration lanes have been lengthened Vertical curves creating blind spots near intersections have been lowered [Fig. 8]. Bridge decks have been widened to allow for emergency stopping, and the bridge abutments and parapets protected with guardwalls [Fig. 9]. Grassed shoulders have been widened and hardened by the addition of aggregate into the soil mix to promote stability. Drainage structures have been extended and repaired, retaining their distinctive stone-faced headwalls or paved flowlines [Fig. 10]. Stream flowlines have been stabilized with rip-rap to prevent scour and erosion. Re-establishing mountable curb-and-gutters along the roadways has sometimes meant re-building or replacing earlier storm drain systems. This also adds a foot or two to the travel way for greater safety and edge definition.

The largest cost item in each project is replacement of the pavement. In some cases, such as the Mount Vernon Highway, this only involved replacing weathered concrete slabs. In others, the original concrete was kept, but the joints were replaced and an overlay of asphalt was installed. In certain cases, new technology has allowed joints to be carried up through the asphalt covering to minimize annoying rhythmic bumping.

Two innovations deserve special attention, since they were designed to balance the higher safety needs with the parkways' scenic appearance. Both are guidance structures to help prevent cars from hitting trees, ravines, or on-coming traffic. Both were crash tested by the Federal Highway Administration and proved equal in strength and durability to standard

Top: *Fig. 5. Grassed shoulders, landscaped margins, and wide wooded buffers all help create the scenic charm of the George Washington Memorial Parkway.*

Center: *Fig. 6. Heavy rush-hour traffic on the Rock Creek and Potomac Parkway.*

Bottom: *Fig. 7. Aerial view of the George Washington Memorial Parkway passing around Rosslyn, Arlington County, Virginia.*

Top: *Fig. 8. Cutting down a vertical curve along the Mount Vernon Highway.*

Center: *Fig. 9. Supplemental concrete guidance structures protecting the railings of a bridge along the George Washington Memorial Parkway.*

Bottom: *Fig. 10. A concrete drainage chute with cobbled apron along the Mount Vernon Highway.*

metal highway guardrails. One is a timber guardrail, reinforced with steel backing and angle irons. The other is a smooth-surfaced stone-faced guidewall. Both are more expensive than standard interstate "W-Beam" guardrail, yet both harmonize well with the scenic character of the parkways. In addition, an alternative type of post-and-cable barrier has successfully prevented accidents on the outsides of high-speed curves.

STILL TO COME

Certain protection and enhancement measures have not been covered by this set of rehabilitation efforts so far. These include pro-active outreach to have local jurisdictions establish protective buffers along the edges of the parkway rights-of-way. This is especially important where high-rise buildings can break above the tree line and ruin the parkway's scenic edge. A related issue is controlling garish signs which easily ruin scenic quality. Legally such issues are addressed as "public nuisances." Also, naturalized landscaping has yet to be successfully applied along these roads to lessen the amount of mown turfgrass while creating more scenic diversity. Currently a 5-acre wildflower project is underway along the George Washington Memorial Parkway in honor of Lady Bird Johnson, and various key entry sites are being considered for colorful annual flower displays.

CONCLUSION

Not since they were built, have the four Washington D.C.-area parkways managed by the National Park Service undergone such significant repair and rebuilding as is now underway. Increasing conflicts between the desired parkway appearance and highway engineering standards make these projects especially difficult to design. Although their urban setting and role has changed significantly, consistent policy seeking a balance between safety and scenery has set the stage for innovative engineering and landscape design which will perpetuate their unique character into the 21st Century.

Each rehabilitation project is a cooperative effort among the Federal Highway Administration, the Park Service's Denver Service Center, the individual parkway's staff, and the NPS's National Capital Region office.

As the Washington metropolitan area has grown and the public has come to accept interstate highways as the norm for high speed travel, one could ask, "Is the concept of a scenic parkway in the city obsolete?" The definite answer is "No." These roads have become a beloved part of Washington's park and road systems, providing visitor and commuter alike a scenic alternative to other urban roads.

ACKNOWLEDGMENTS

The following people provided materials and helped with the preparation of this presentation:

John Byrne, Superintendent, George Washington Memorial Parkway

William Clark, Photographer, National Capital Region, NPS

Georgia Ellard, Superintendent, Rock Creek Park

Manus J. Fish, Regional Director, National Capital Region

Peggy Fleming, Naturalist, Rock Creek Park

Lt. Fogerty, Information Services, U.S. Park Police

Bob Ford, Resource Manager, Rock Creek Park

Patrick Gregerson, Planner, National Capital Region

Bob Hickman, Site Manger, Greenbelt Park and Baltimore-Washington Parkway

John Parsons, Associate Regional Director for Land Use Coordination, National Capital Region

Al Teikari, Engineer, Federal Highway Administration.

New Roles for Urban Parkways

George C. Hemmens, School of Urban Planning and Policy, University of Illinois at Chicago

Chicago has an extensive urban parkway system that was once the pride of the city and served as a framework for the physical plan of the city. The parkway system is a series of boulevards that connect major parks and link up with other boulevards to form a ring through what were once the prime residential areas of the city. Today both the boulevards and the parks are in a sad state, having been neglected for a long time. Within the past few years official attention has once again been given to the boulevards. In addition to some refurbishing efforts, the city's planners are examining the potential of the boulevards to again play a major role in the structuring and functioning of the city. This report discusses possibilities for renewal of the boulevards, using Chicago as context.

HISTORY OF CHICAGO'S BOULEVARD SYSTEM

The history of Chicago's boulevards begins with State legislation in 1869 that authorized three park districts (South, West and Lincoln) to develop parks, boulevards and pleasure drives in their parts of the city. Olmsted and his associates were retained to lay out the South parks and boulevards and by 1871 the basic plan for what are now Washington and Jackson parks, the Midway Plaisance which connects them and other boulevards was completed and some construction was underway. William LeBaron Jenney and his associates were retained to lay out the West parks and connecting boulevards. Between 1870 and 1872 they developed the plans for Humboldt, Garfield and Douglas parks and connecting boulevards and construction was begun. Development of the North parks was much delayed by legal challenges and organizational problems. No large inland parks were developed but some boulevards were laid out and partially developed. The west boulevards connected with the south boulevards and parks at Gage Park, and with the north boulevards at Logan Square forming three sides of a rectangle with the lake and a proposed lake shore boulevard as the fourth side. This rectangle provided the basic structure of the system, roughly 27 miles, and other boulevards and parks were connected to it.

The boulevard and park system was largely in place by 1880. At that time Chicago was claimed to be second only to Philadelphia in park space and its park and boulevard system was considered a model for the nation.[1] The boulevards had a variety of designs to serve different uses.[2] Two Olmsted designed boulevards illustrate the differences. Drexel Boulevard had a one-hundred-foot-wide central park strip designed to "invite rest and contemplation" with one-way streets on either side of the park strip. This park strip was heavily developed with plantings, curving walkways, seating areas and fountains. Grand Boulevard, now Martin Luther King Drive, had a wide central drive suitable for through traffic flow, narrow park strips on either side of the central trafficway and then local service streets on the other side of the park strips. Major pieces of the system were not completed until later. Jackson Park, along with the Midway Plaisance, the site of the Columbian Exposition of 1893, was not developed as a park until after the fair and then not according to Olmsted's plan.

Daniel Burnham, with his colleague, Edward Bennett, planned major additions to the park and boulevard system in the 1909 Plan of Chicago. One of their aims was to create a much larger park system in Chicago and restore Chicago to a national leadership position in parks and recreation. Tree lined boulevards connecting the parks were a feature of the plan. Burnham proposed an arc shaped boulevard with three major new parks along it extending outward from the existing boulevard rectangle. This major boulevard was designed like Grand Boulevard as a wide linear park with trafficways on either side. It was designed to serve both as a pleasure drive and as a major circumferential road. The other major boulevard proposal in the 1909 plan was for the boulevard along the lake shore. Following the 1893 fair he proposed developing the south lake shore of the city as a series of parks, partly on islands, accompanied by a parkway that would connect the center of the city with Jackson Park and the south shore.

Burnham's views on boulevards are shown in his discussion of the proper location of recreation facilities and in his proposed stratification of the street system. First, he noted with satisfaction that in locating the new, small, recreation parks developed in the first years of the twentieth century that "the principle has been followed as far as possible of locating them on the proposed circuit boulevards."[3] He further suggested that even the larger playgrounds should be located on or adjacent to boulevards "in order that they may be reached from one another by passing through a continuous line of planting."[4] Second, he proposed a three part classification of streets: the street; the avenue; and the boulevard. The street provided local access. The avenue was to be the major traffic carrying street. He proposed a number of diagonals superimposed on Chicago's existing grid system to supplement major gridiron "avenues." The boulevard he thought should be "designed primarily as a combination of park and driveway."[5] He described the boulevard as "the streets where all heavier traffic is excluded; the streets lined with commodious and even fine dwellings; the streets where grass and trees and shrubs assert themselves, and where there may well be continuous playgrounds for the children of the neighborhood, such as many Chicago boulevards now provide."[6] Burnham also approved the location of light industry along boulevards where they were near railroads because "the working people will then enjoy a maximum of fresh air and light; and so will work with greater effectiveness."[7]

Clearly Burnham viewed the boulevards as part of the park system serving adjacent communities and serving as pleasure drives connecting the major parks and as walkways connecting minor recreation facilities. The carriage drive and promenade aspects of the system, since they would obviously serve the wealthy, and the proposal that boulevards be lined with "commodious and even fine dwellings" that would be occupied by the wealthy are some of the features of Burnham's plan that later led to criticisms of elitism and grandiosity. The image of children of the poor playing in the median parkstrip, having come from the interior of neighborhoods whose facilities or housing Burnham did not include in his plan, and providing part of the romantic scenery for the wealthy on a Sunday afternoon tour, easily generates criticism and dismissal of Burnham's ideas. But such criticisms are unfair in focusing only on part of Burnham's thinking.

It is true that Burnham thought of the city largely from the perspective of his own social class and he thought grandly. For example, the median park strip in his proposed giant arc boulevard was a city block wide. At the same time, however, he had more imagination and more insight into changing urban structure than most of his colleagues. He foresaw that the existing railroad freight yards in the city would eventually be abandoned and proposed turning them into recreation areas connected to his proposed inner loops of avenues and boulevards. He used the existing and proposed boulevards both to provide the traveler with a sense of the structure of the city and to improve the flow of traffic through it.

The history of urban parkways in Chicago is a story of faded glory. First, there were the beautiful early boulevards and parks that were important in forming the built structure of the developing city. Then there were Burnham's plans for extension of the boulevards and a larger role for them in shaping and serving the city. But since then there has been only neglect and decline with the end result that an important part of Chicago's heritage has been essentially lost.

The grand arc boulevard and the associated parks were never developed. The lakefront drive was developed but without the accompanying parks. So the boulevard and park system in Chicago is largely what existed at the turn of the century. Since then the major changes have been administrative. A single park district was formed in 1933 to manage the Chicago parks and boulevards. In 1959 the park district turned over the maintenance of the boulevards to the City of Chicago, but retained control of the parks. The last major improvements to the boulevards were made in the 1930s by the Works Progress Administration.

Subsequent Chicago plans have generally ignored the boulevard system. The 1966 comprehensive plan for the city shows a schematic and incorrect map of the boulevard system as part of the recreation section of the plan but does not propose improvements in the system or propose using it as a framework for the recreation proposals that are in the plan.[8] Instead a park mall consisting of small parks and playlots connected by specially landscaped sidewalks is proposed. The 1982 comprehensive plan ignores the boulevards.

INHERITORS OF THE BOULEVARDS

There are many reasons for the decline of interest in the boulevards. Primary among the usual reasons given are changes in transportation technology. The rise of automobile ownership and commuting use, the increase of truck traffic, and the development of urban expressways to accommodate daily commuting are said to have rendered the exclusively automobile boulevard less valuable. At the same time the change in life style and the resulting changes from nineteenth and early twentieth century development patterns to low density urban and suburban development are said to have rendered the inner city parks and connecting boulevards obsolete.

There is much factual truth to these explanations. In Chicago, however, and perhaps in other cities the change in occupancy of the adjacent neighborhoods has been a major factor in the decline of the parks and boulevards. The in-migration to these neighborhoods of minority populations, the subsequent complete racial changes of the area, the increasing poverty, the decrease in property maintenance, and finally property abandonment is a sad, familiar story of the fate of Chicago's inner neighborhoods. The blame for the decline of these neighborhoods is usually placed on block-busting tactics of realtors, the actions of absentee landlords, the condition of poverty, and the in-migrants themselves. Less attention is given to the effects of public action and inaction in the decline of these areas. In Chicago the inner city parks and connecting boulevards, especially those in minority residential areas, have been allowed to deteriorate for at least 30 years. Recent lawsuits against the Park District have resulted in a finding that the parks in minority areas, including the historic parks connected by the boulevards, have not been equitably cared for, and the court has required major reinvestment in facilities and maintenance. In 1959 responsibility for the boulevards was assigned to Chicago's Department of Forestry. Since then maintenance of the boulevards has steadily declined. The independent forestry department was changed to a Bureau within Public Works and its budget allocation for new planting and maintenance throughout the city has been reduced. In 1980 the Bureau's budget was halved, and this cut has not been restored. There has been little or no new or replacement planting and little maintenance of planting or other features such as fountains and statues. In 1985 the city was providing minimal maintenance, essentially cutting the grass, on 300 acres of greenway on the boulevards. Another 155 acres were not routinely maintained. The net result is that the parks and boulevards are in very poor condition.

Today, development adjacent to the boulevards is of very mixed quality. In some areas the housing along the boulevards remains in relatively good condition. That housing was originally the best in the area. The original housing quality combined with the environmental quality and desirability of the boulevard location has helped preserve the housing while other nearby housing has deteriorated badly. In other areas there are many abandoned, boarded-up buildings along the boulevards and many gaps in development where deteriorated buildings have been pulled down. There has been considerable non-residential intrusion on the formerly residential boulevards, especially at major intersections. Often this involves replacing existing mixed use commercial and residential buildings which provided local retail services with national chain fast food restaurants and gas stations. These changes significantly damage the character, scale and continuity of the boulevards. Restriction of the boulevards to automobile traffic continues, but few of the boulevards retain their original pleasure drive character. Those boulevards located so that they are convenient for rush hour traffic have become major commuting routes.

RENEWAL OF THE BOULEVARDS

The boulevards are still a major asset to Chicago. Their appearance and condition are poor, but they still provide special character to the areas they pass through and they still provide connection to the major inland parks in the city. Further, the boulevard system gives a special sense of identity to the neighborhoods they pass through. The landscaped park strips tell the traveler she is in a special place and helps her locate herself in the largely undifferentiated gridiron structure of Chicago. Even today, regardless of their condition, when you cross a boulevard or drive on one in traveling through the city, you experience an aesthetic response to the change in the city pattern and to the special design of the boulevard.

One-half million people live within three blocks of a boulevard in Chicago according to current estimates. That is one of every six residents of Chicago. The boulevard system goes through 20 of the 77 official community areas in Chicago. So the boulevards affect many and may serve as a rallying point for renewal of the neighborhoods.

The City of Chicago has recently begun to examine the boulevard system and consider ways to improve it. This interest seems to have been promoted in part by residents adjacent to the boulevards in neighborhoods that are experiencing stabilization and redevelopment, and in part this interest reflects the commitment of the current city administration to making improvements in the living conditions of inner city neighborhoods. In this section I will review the recent and current efforts to improve the boulevards in Chicago and then identify and discuss issues about adapting boulevards to fit into the changing city.

The first boulevard improvement project, in 1986, was to restore segments of King Drive and Garfield Boulevard on the city's south side. Both boulevards connect to Washington Park, an Olmsted designed major park which is further connected to Jackson Park and the lakefront by the Midway Plaisance. The two boulevards were originally very different. King Drive featured a central roadway flanked by 3-foot medians and one-way local service streets and finally 16-foot parkway strips. The original planting was a formal pattern of trees six in a row (two on each median, one on each parkway strip) and about 16 rows per block.

Garfield Boulevard was designed with a central 80 foot median flanked by two-way 40 foot streets and a 20 foot parkway strip. The original planting featured trees, bushes, hedges and flower beds laid out in an informal pattern with curving paths and seating areas in the central median. Little of the original planting remains on Garfield, but the original tree planting design on King Drive is still evident. Development along King Drive, once one of the most elegant boulevards in the city, is mixed. Many stately homes remain and some have recently been repaired, but there are gaps in development and some dilapidated structures. Development along this stretch of Garfield Boulevard is in worse condition and there are more gaps in development. King Drive has become a major traffic facility carrying south side residents to and from Chicago's Loop. Regular local buses also use King Drive.

After a lengthy process of joint planning with local community groups, the local alderman's office and other city departments, the planning department prepared a renewal plan for eight blocks of King Drive and 16 blocks of Garfield Boulevard. The plan calls for restoration of the formal tree planting scheme on King Drive and adding trees in an informal pattern to Garfield Boulevard. Extensive restoration of grass areas will be undertaken along with curb and sidewalk improvements. Community Development Block Grant funds will be used for the boulevard planting program, but other regular city funds will be used for the remainder of the project. These other funds include the street tree program of the forestry department, public works funds for street improvements and the alderman's earmarked funds from an issue of general obligation bonds.

This pilot project has become a model for boulevard improvement in Chicago. The model features extensive community involvement, cooperative efforts of city departments using regular funds, cooperative funding and participation from the alderman's office, and limited use of special funds. The local residents are encouraged to participate and given major influence in the planning process. In turn the city expects the community to participate in implementation. Use of the alderman's discretionary funds is one form of participation in implementation. The community is expected to water the grass and trees, pick up debris and litter, get involved in "adopt a block" programs involving garden planting and spot mowing, and get involved in "adopt a tree" programs. The reliance on the community for a significant part of the boulevards' maintenance reflects the reality of very limited current maintenance funds and no new maintenance funds tied to the improvements. The city expects the community to undertake this maintenance out of self interest. The assumption is that boulevard improvements will increase land values adjacent to the boulevard and promote reinvestment as well as improve the quality of life in the neighborhood.

Since this first project the city has begun four additional boulevard improvement projects using this approach. The most advanced of these focuses on Palmer Square in the northwest part of the city, and includes Kedzie and Humboldt Boulevards which connect at Palmer Square, and Logan Boulevard which completes the northwest boulevards.

The neighborhoods in this area have experienced considerable population change in the past, including a large inflow of Hispanic households, and have recently undergone considerable renovation and gentrification with an accompanying inflow of young, white professionals. Given the rapid rise in housing costs in the gentrified north side neighborhoods closer to Lake Michigan, areas such as Logan Boulevard and Palmer Square have become attractive investments for developers and the so called "urban pioneers." These neighborhoods are generally in good condition and contain good quality housing stock. Along with the push for better public services has come a push for improvement and better maintenance of the boulevards. All of the development along these boulevards has been designated an historic area and the areas have had recent zoning changes to reduce the permissible density of development, all with the support of local residents.

The residents along the northwest boulevards and squares are well organized. Both squares and the three boulevards have their own homeowner's association and an overall area homeowner's association unites and coordinates them. For several years these groups have operated tree planting and maintenance programs on the boulevards to supplement the limited efforts of the City. The residents have participated enthusiastically in the planning for renewal of this area. The renewal will focus on Palmer Square. The square contains a large central median, 240 feet wide and 1280 feet long, that was originally designed as an informal landscaped garden for strolling and sitting. It was surrounded by wrought iron fence and was heavily landscaped with flower beds, shrubs and trees. At one time a full-time gardener was assigned to the Square.

Little of the original vegetation remains, and the character of the square today is an active recreation area. The square is used by a nearby Boy's Club for baseball and other organized recreation. Parochial schools adjacent to the square use it for recreation. Neighborhood children play in the square. Adults jog around its perimeter and use it for active recreation and sitting.

The planning process in the Palmer Square project followed the original model closely and successfully. Similar participation, funding and maintenance plans have been established. In the planning process a number of issues emerged that suggest some possible difficulties. The boulevard residents, particularly on Logan Boulevard, want traffic slowed and discouraged through addition of stop signs. The city's practice is to give the boulevard through street treatment to enhance its contribution to traffic flow. Residents around the square proposed a planting design that would greatly restrict the use of the square for active recreation and organized sports. The cost of such development and the maintenance problems both seem prohibitive to the city. In addition, there is considerable disagreement on the best use of the medians. All along these boulevards, medians are used for active play by neighborhood residents, by others, and by local schools and churches. The current plan will give the square a perimeter jogging path, two large grassed open areas, new benches and repaired baths, and many new trees massed in clusters. The plan is a compromise among the different interests and depends heavily on the community for implementation and maintenance.

There have been different responses in the three other areas where planning for boulevard renewal projects has begun. In the poorest area the community has not participated actively and has raised questions about the desirability of the project. There appears to be some fear that improvement of the boulevard will lead to gentrification. In poor and less organized communities there also appears to be some questioning of the assumption that the community should contribute its time and labor to the provision of public services.

Two major projects, a citizen task force study and the initiation of a comprehensive plan for the boulevards show the city's increased interest in the boulevards, and the emergence of a strategy of using boulevard restoration as a catalyst for inner city neighborhood renewal. In January 1986 Mayor Harold Washington established a citizen Task Force on Neighborhood Land Use and assigned it five tasks. An examination of the boulevards and recommendations for their renewal was one of these. After a thorough review, the Task Force recommended: 1) that the City make a major commitment to restoration and maintenance of the boulevards; 2) develop a comprehensive plan and program for the boulevard system; 3) develop a coordinated public and private program for financing and maintaining boulevard improvements; and 4) centralize responsibilities for the boulevard system that are now divided among many public agencies. The Task Force report has not been officially adopted, but has been credited by city officials with stimulating action on boulevard improvement. The Task Force generally accepted the assumption that boulevard restoration would generate reinvestment along the boulevards, but raised questions about the appropriate character of the boulevards and their role in the overall city structure. Specifically, they questioned "how active a role should the boulevards have as traffic routes or as a recreational space?"[9] On the traffic issue, the report noted how historically the boulevards had been turned into major traffic routes in the early twentieth century by removal of streetcars, placement of stop signs on cross streets, and establishment of higher speed limits. The task force had a clear recommendation on this issue: "limitation of traffic volume and speed on the boulevards in order to retain their residential and park character."[10] Their other recommendations have a similar character. They tend to support restoration of the boulevard system to its original character and role to the extent feasible. To some extent they suggest a difficult, dual role and identity for the boulevards. On one hand they argue the importance of the boulevard as a city-wide system that has symbolic importance and land development effects at the city scale. On the other hand they argue for their importance at the local, city block scale and support local involvement and influence.

The city is now finalizing specifications for a comprehensive plan of the boulevards to be prepared with the support of grants from the National Endowment for the Arts and the National Park Service. It is too early to tell how that plan will develop, but early indications are that it will focus mainly on the boulevards and give relatively little direct attention to the question of neighborhood development. An analysis of existing conditions of vegetation and recreation use, prototype design proposals for boulevard segments and standards for planting, signage and furnishings will probably be included.

ISSUES IN BOULEVARD RENEWAL

The planning of improvements to Chicago's boulevards raises a number of questions about the appropriate role and function of urban parkways in American cities at the end of the twentieth century. The plans and improvements that are made now will set the framework for urban parkways in the twenty-first century. Chicago's boulevards, designed and implemented at the end of the nineteenth century, have not survived as important sources of strength in the urban fabric in this century. Although much of their decline may be due to technological change and to economic and racial shifts in the city, it is appropriate to ask whether restoring the boulevards to an approximation of their former condition is the right course of action. I will briefly review the issues I have identified in connection with the restoration of Chicago's boulevards. These are traffic capacity, character, adjacent land use, contribution to urban structure, and control. The traffic issue is, I think, the critical one.

TRAFFIC

Travel on Chicago's boulevards is restricted to automobiles, but there is little resemblance between the present traffic pattern and a leisurely pleasure drive. The boulevards, which are located so that they readily serve commuter traffic, function as arterial streets during rush hours. They carry a large amount of traffic, up to 25,000 vehicles per day currently, and yet retain their special character. In Chicago, as in most other major American cities, it is unlikely that any more expressways will be built. Their high cost and the considerable disruption and destruction of neighborhoods that their construction causes suggest that new expressways are financially and politically infeasible. Existing expressways are seriously overcrowded and the very expensive minor modifications that can be made to increase their capacity will not solve existing problems. Most of the commuting traffic that clogs the expressways is automobiles.

A sizeable portion of that traffic could be served by existing and new parkways and boulevards. The legal speed on boulevards would be considerably less than expressways, say 35 rather than 55 miles per hour, but the actual travel speed would likely not be much different during rush hours. From a financial and political perspective, the possibility of improving traffic carrying capacity of existing boulevards and creating new ones seems more feasible than building or rebuilding expressways and existing arterial streets.

Current thinking, however, is strongly opposed to using the boulevards as major traffic carrying facilities as shown by the Mayor's Task Force's report on boulevards. Some of the objection is based on practical experience with poorly designed changes to accommodate traffic on the boulevards. In Chicago most of the actual investments in the boulevards in the last forty years or more have been for traffic carrying improvements. These have involved cutting cross streets through medians and historic squares. Some street widening projects to extend the boulevards have been done clumsily, resulting in unattractive rear yards and garages facing the boulevard. These are serious problems; however, they can readily be avoided by sensitive design.

Most of the objection to using the boulevards as major traffic moving facilities comes from an interest in preserving and restoring a style and quality of urban life that we associate with an earlier time. The urban parkway, part park, part pleasure drive, lined with pleasant homes generates feelings of stability, serenity and security. The association of these feelings with this street design have been reinforced over the years by the design of high cost and quality residential areas with parkway like streets with decoratively planted central medians. I suspect that the impetus to restore Chicago's boulevards to their historic role is influenced strongly by this suburban idyll, the romantic subdivision. The reality of Chicago's boulevards is that many of them have been major trafficways for 50 years and longer. They are integrated with the arterial system, although not in the way proposed by Burnham.

I think traffic capacity is the critical issue in developing a renewed role for boulevards in Chicago and for urban parkways in general. Once this issue is resolved, the other issues of character, adjacent land use, etc. will be readily resolved. In Chicago the present situation of the boulevards and the general context of highway and public works improvements argue that the boulevards should assume a significant role in traffic movement. Consider the highway investment situation. Chicago's last planned inner-city expressway, the crosstown, was cancelled several years ago due in part to public opposition. The expense, social and economic disruption, and traffic inducement characteristics of expressways provide strong reasons to believe that no more will be built. The expressways are seriously overcrowded. So are the arterial streets. Arterial streets are very expensive to improve. And in my experience, arterial street widening and traffic improvement projects often result in a serious decline in amenity and physical appearance of the streets. Further, existing curb cuts and cross streets limit traffic carrying capacity.

Existing boulevards, especially those common in Chicago, designed with a center traffic way, side medians and side streets can carry substantial traffic volumes. Historically, there were limited cross street cut throughs on the boulevards in Chicago enhancing traffic flow. For relatively small investments those boulevard segments located to serve major traffic flows can be upgraded to carry more automobile only traffic without serious negative effects on adjacent development. Interestingly, recent new developments along the boulevards have chosen to locate their auto and pedestrian entrances on the side street rather than the boulevard, reducing traffic conflicts yet retaining the development character of the boulevards.

Extension of the boulevard system to create a more complete system and to better connect it to the arterial streets and expressways would be the most sensible way to improve service to the ever increasing automobile traffic in Chicago, I believe. In addition, development of new boulevard/parkways in deteriorated areas may provide an important stimulus to development. An example of how relatively low cost boulevard construction could serve these multiple purposes is provided by a recent planning project in Chicago. Architecture and planning students at the University of Illinois at Chicago undertook a year long review and design study of development plans for the city's near south side. Contrary to the city's plans, the students proposed a redevelopment scheme that focused on a new north-south boulevard through the area that would serve as a spine for redevelopment and connect the downtown Loop with King Drive and the boulevard system on the south side. In addition this new boulevard would create direct, classy connections between the Loop and McCormick Place, the city's convention center, and the Loop and Chinatown. Neither is now well connected to downtown in the city street system. The new boulevard would also connect to major arterial streets serving the southwest side, improving those connections to the Loop.

The students' design shows how a boulevard can be built into existing urban structure relatively easily. It also shows how different segments of a boulevard can be designed to fit the adjacent development context while still creating the sense of special boulevard identity along the entire route and providing substantial through traffic carrying capacity. There is even successful experience in Chicago with direct connection of restricted, automobile only parkways with unrestricted arterial streets, for example, Fullerton Parkway.

CHARACTER OF THE BOULEVARDS

The original purposes of the boulevard as pleasure drive and park strip led to designs for passive and active recreation. As on Garfield Boulevard these designs often featured pedestrian strolling and sitting in garden like settings. It does not seem reasonable to restore these designs. Significant conflicts are emerging in the city's boulevard restoration projects. Today, even on those boulevards that carry relatively light traffic, people must contend with relatively fast traffic and auto fumes. Nevertheless adjacent residents and institutions want to continue to rely on these medians for youth and adult recreation.

For security reasons, neighborhood residents are also unlikely to want dense, decorative planting. However, in Palmer Square the residents sought restoration of at least some of the original design in the style of an English garden. Recognizing that while one-time funds for restoration may be made available, and additional maintenance funds will be very difficult to obtain, the city is arguing that low maintenance designs and hardy plantings will be necessary.

These emerging conflicts over the use of the boulevard park strips go directly to the issue of the character of the boulevards. In those communities where residents have been active in maintaining the boulevards there is a natural tendency to regard the park strips as local facilities that primarily serve local activities. Active youth recreation is probably the most common activity. The park strips are valued as recreation spaces because they are close to home, there aren't good alternatives close by, and, in some cases, concern about youth gangs in the larger active sports oriented parks and playgrounds off the boulevards. None of these seem compelling reasons to turn the boulevards into local parks and playgrounds. In most neighborhoods adjacent to the boulevards there is vacant land available for playground development. Much of this vacant land is city owned, acquired through urban renewal. It would be more appropriate to develop local parks and playgrounds in these areas. With the existing gaps in boulevard development, it would be possible to locate such playgrounds within a block or two of the boulevards and connect them to the boulevards with greenways as part of a coordinated strategy of neighborhood renewal accompanying boulevard restoration.

Limited, passive recreation with the boulevard serving primarily as a drive and walkway and less as a park seems the most appropriate character for the restored boulevards given the inevitable conflicts with traffic. Enhancing the boulevards for traffic use will further reduce their suitability for active recreation. Since active recreation facilities can economically be developed off the boulevards and the economic benefits of boulevard traffic enhancement are likely to be large, this seems a reasonable tradeoff. The benefits to neighborhood redevelopment of interior park development further support this approach.

ADJACENT LAND USE

The boulevards created prestige locations and the resulting adjacent development was often more substantial and more expensive than the development a few blocks away. Today the redevelopment potential of boulevards is reflected in the generally better maintenance and value retention of housing along the boulevards and the efforts of boulevard residents to maintain and improve the boulevards. Two land use questions must be answered to develop sound plans for the boulevards. First, what are appropriate adjacent land uses for the future; and second, will restored boulevards have significant attractive power for new development? Chicago, in its first boulevard projects, is taking a cautious attitude toward the development drawing power of boulevards. They have adopted two strategies: following reinvestment on boulevards; or selecting stable areas that have withstood neighborhood change and are judged to have some potential for reinvestment. This passive attitude leaves the issue of the kind of adjacent development up to land developers. There are no special zoning restrictions, design guidelines or other development controls for the boulevards. Over the years the major changes on the boulevards have been loss of housing in the most distressed areas and the replacement of combined residential/local commercial buildings by auto oriented regional commercial development at major boulevard intersections. In the distressed areas, the most likely possibilities for new development along the boulevards are further auto oriented commercial developments and multi-family housing. Both would create a very different scale and visual sense from the original concept of a residential drive.

There are two aspects of the adjacent land use issue: the kind of activity and the physical design of it. Visually, we expect an urban parkway to be fronted by a wall of low scale buildings. The historical pattern in Chicago is residential development of two to six stories. The wall of development helps define the parkway as a path in the city and is a desirable characteristic that should be continued. Adjacent development also gives some sense of the neighborhood being transversed. Occasional open space breaks in the wall provide visual variety and a further sense of the community. These can be created by greenways, leading to adjacent parks, by landscaped cross streets and by institutional land uses in landscaped settings. The kinds of land uses that best suit the desired visual characteristics of the boulevard are residential, mixed use residential/commercial and institutional. Those least suited are auto oriented commercial and industrial. However, the actual design of development is more critical than the use. Dispersed high rise residential structures surrounded by parking lots would be as inappropriate as a used car lot.

Special development controls for the boulevards with compensatory incentives for quality development are essential if the special character of the boulevards are to be restored and maintained. This has been recognized by the residents of the northwest boulevards who initiated the downzoning of those areas. However, simple downzoning is not a solution to the problem. To the extent that renewed boulevards are attractive to development and return the public's investment through neighborhood revitalization, some increase in adjacent land values and pressure for more dense development is inevitable. Again, this can be turned to advantage by linking boulevard and neighborhood revitalization by, for example, giving density increases and other incentives off the boulevard in exchange for appropriate scale development on the boulevard.

URBAN STRUCTURE

When you drive across, onto or along a Chicago boulevard you experience being in a special place and you have a sense of where you are in the city. The boulevards historically served as a major structuring element in the city's fabric. They give a particular kind of legibility to the city because of their design, travel speed and historic role of connecting major parks and creating major nodes. Expressways generate only the image of the central city connected to the suburbs and a large, undifferentiated landscape between the two. Boulevards generate images of neighborhoods and major public spaces. Further they give a sense of the connection between places within the city and of the institutions, such as churches, which serve the city. In short, the boulevards structure and reveal the city in a way that expressways cannot and commercial arterial streets generally do not.

The Mayor's Task Force acknowledged the special role of boulevards and called for unique street signage, ornamental lighting fixtures and other features to improve the legibility and identity of the boulevard system. These are useful actions, but to the extent that they are only an attempt to restore the past they are sentimental and fail to develop an appropriate image and role for boulevards in the twenty-first century. The possibility of adding to the boulevard system to develop a major, specialized traffic system serving automobiles only presents the opportunity to recreate the urban parkway as a major structuring element in the city's redevelopment in the future.

CONTROL

Finally, there is the issue of who is to control development along the boulevards; who is to decide on the character of the boulevards themselves? I have already discussed some potential conflicts between local residents and city-wide interests in deciding the future of the boulevards. Local residents are particularly concerned with traffic reduction, local use of the park strips, appearance and property value enhancement, especially in the areas experiencing reinvestment. City-wide interests are necessarily concerned with improving traffic flow, the system level functioning and urban structural effects of the boulevard. Currently, the city is committed to active involvement of local citizens in planning the redevelopment of boulevard segments. Partly this reflects the political philosophy of the present city administration. But it also reflects the practical necessity of depending on local residents for at least some of the maintenance of new plantings, and of depending on funds under the control of the local alderman for a significant part of the projects' cost.

An appropriate balance between local control and city wide control over boulevard renewal will be very difficult to establish. It is complicated by the very different attitudes in the adjacent neighborhoods. It is already apparent that in some of the poorest neighborhoods most in need of the reinvestment that boulevard improvement might bring, local residents fear gentrification and displacement as a result. In other neighborhoods private reinvestment is being promoted and boulevard improvement is recognized as an asset toward that end. On balance, I think this is an issue where city wide interests must prevail, but to avoid and learn from the mistakes of urban expressway planning a cooperative, negotiating relationship with neighborhoods will have to be established, and the legitimacy of neighborhood interests will have to be recognized and respected. The task will be easier if the planning is expanded from the boulevard itself to include adjacent development, creating the possibility of trading-off boulevard and interior investments.

CONCLUSION

In developing a comprehensive plan for the boulevards, Chicago has the opportunity to design boulevards for new and renewed functions in the city. The issues discussed above make clear that there will be strong pressures to adopt a romantic attitude toward boulevards attempting to restore and conserve their former functions. There will also be strong pressures to treat the boulevards as a local problem focusing on the interests of adjacent landowners and to limit the plan to the right-of-way, viewing the boulevard as a thing in itself. There is, however, a need to imagine new roles for boulevards and correspondingly new forms and to plan concurrently for adjacent land development and neighborhood revitalization.

Proposing boulevards to be major traffic facilities seems incongruous, but a well designed boulevard with a central trafficway flanked by park strips and then by local streets may be the desirable and feasible method of providing needed capacity for predicted increases in auto travel. At the same time, adjacent land uses are protected from direct contact with heavy traffic and benefit from the added plantings and open space. Further, a system of such boulevards would do much to restore legibility and an understandable scale of the city to people traveling in it.

Some existing boulevards may appropriately be separated from this system if they are not essential to traffic flow. Such segments could function as small linear parks and neighborhood control could be granted in exchange for neighborhood maintenance. Those boulevards that are essential to the system of boulevards and to traffic flow would be integrated with the arterial street system similar to the proposals of Daniel Burnham and Edward Bennett in the 1909 Plan of Chicago. As part of a system that serves the entire city, boulevards would once again be a major structuring influence in the city fabric. They could create substantial potential for adjacent development and redevelopment. In conclusion, urban parkways have a future in a city like Chicago, but to realize that future they may need to be different from the pleasure drive and park strip of the past.

ACKNOWLEDGMENT

Maria Choca and Art Traczyk of the Chicago Department of Planning graciously provided information on Chicago's boulevard restoration projects.

NOTES

1. Burnham (1909), p. 42
2. Ranney (1972), p. 5
3. Burnham (1909), p. 44
4. Burnham (1909), p. 44
5. Burnham (1909), p. 82
6. Burnham (1909), p. 84
7. Burnham (1909), p. 85
8. Chicago Department of Development and Planning (1966), p. 40
9. Mayor's Task Force (1987), p. 8
10. Mayor's Task Force (1987), p. 12

BIBLIOGRAPHY

Daniel H. Burnham and Edward H. Bennett, Plan of Chicago. Chicago: The Commercial Club, 1909.

Chicago Department of Development and Planning, The Comprehensive Plan of Chicago. City of Chicago: December 1966.

Chicago Department of Planning, Boulevard Restoration: A Catalyst for Neighborhood Revitalization. City of Chicago: September 1986.

CITY LAB, A Boulevard Plan for Chicago's Near South Side. College of Architecture, Art and Urban Planning, University of Illinois at Chicago, September 1986.

Mayor's Task Force on Neighborhood Land Use, Boulevards. City of Chicago: May1987.

Victoria Post Ranney, Olmsted in Chicago. Chicago: The Open Lands Project, 1972.

"Hillbilly Sold Here": Appalachian Folk Culture and Parkway Tourism

Jean Haskell Speer, Ph.D., Director, Appalachian Studies Program, Virginia Polytechnic Institute and State University, Blacksburg

Traveling the Blue Ridge Parkway to most any tourist destination in Appalachia demonstrates the extent to which folk culture of the region has become a commodity to be bought and sold. Postcards, calendars, articles of clothing, foods, and artifacts present to the tourist myriad perceptions of the region's traditional culture and become an unwitting and skewed biography of the region for those who do not know its life story.

In this paper, I examine the role of folk culture in the economy of Parkway tourism in Appalachia. The study begins with an analysis of the mythology of Appalachia and two of its dominant mythic images, mountaineer as romantic hero and hillbilly as trickster or buffoon. I then consider the ways in which these images have been exploited in the development of tourism in the region, from the early days of mountain travel to the present. Historic sites, commercial attractions, craft and souvenir shops, and tourist resorts have always molded and marketed these mythic images for the most avid consumer—the tourist.

To discover the rhetorical and ultimately the economic impact of using folk culture in tourism, I analyze some of the strategies behind particular instances of "hillbilly" marketing, and the perceived effect on the tourist and tourist dollars in Appalachian states. For example, historic sites and tourist concessions along the Blue Ridge Parkway offer an interesting case study. Finally, I consider the political and moral implications of making folk culture a commodity for promoting parkway tourism in Appalachia or in any region.

THE MYTHOLOGY OF APPALACHIA

A few years ago when I was in Europe, I found myself on a train to Zurich in an interesting conversation with a man from Switzerland. After exchanging pleasantries, he asked me about my work in the United States. He had no problem understanding my teaching and research in communication, but my work in "Appalachian Studies" left him perplexed. I explained that I taught and wrote about all aspects of life and culture in the Appalachian mountain region of America. He frowned. "You know," I said, "quilts, dulcimers, coal mining, moonshine" —picking some of the most widely known, romantic symbols of the region. he brightened. "Ah," he smiled, "hilleebeellies." Reluctantly, I agreed, "something like that."

I was amazed (and a little chagrined) that the mythology of Appalachia was so widespread and its most potent symbols so firmly entrenched even outside America. I asked myself how this mythology had gotten communicated so widely and with such effectiveness. The answer to that question is complex, involving worldwide perceptions of mountain cultures, the media, and, to no small extent, tourism.

What is the mythology of Appalachia? Whether you've realized it consciously or not, you probably know it or parts of it just as my train companion in Switzerland did. From the time Appalachia first became clearly identifiable as an American region (near the beginning of the twentieth century), its mythology was taking shape. And it took its shape in the rapidly developing new media for public consumption at the beginning of the twentieth century — mass-produced newspapers, magazines, cheap novels, photographs, traveling exhibitions, silent films, fund-raising speeches (for work in the new discipline of social welfare), and promotional campaigns to attract tourists to the mountains.

In fact, the word "hillbilly" first appeared in print in 1900 in a newspaper, the New York Journal. The reporter defined a "Hill-Billie" as a "free, untrammeled white citizen who lives in the hills...has no means to speak of, dresses as he can, talks as he pleases, drinks whiskey when he gets it, and fires off his revolver as fancy takes him."[1] By the 1920s, the fundamental elements of the mythology were well-established, but touched by the romanticism so characteristic of conceptions of "native" or "primitive" peoples of the period. (Remember that anthropology and folklore were new academic disciplines of the time.) For example, American playwright Percy MacKaye, after a trip to the Kentucky mountains in 1924, declared in an article in one of the new "serious, scientific" magazines of the period that he had encountered "untamed mountaineers, a rare, unclassified species of the *genus homo*—strange wildflowers of the human spirit, hardy, wayward, shy, fantastic, beautiful, and doomed to extinction." Going on to contrast mountaineers with the "standardization" he perceived in "civilized life," MacKaye wrote:

> *Over there in the mountains are men who do not live in cages: a million Americans who do not chase the dollar; who do not serve time-machines; who do not learn their manners from the movies, or their culture from the beauty parlors: illiterates, who do not think what they are told to in type; "lazy" people, who have leisure to lean on their hoes and discourse religion and poetry with the dawns and sunsets; old-fashioned "Independence" folk, who take "liberty and the pursuit of happiness" for granted; untamed Americans, who do not ask for "licenses" to live.*[2]

MacKaye added to his story of the mountaineers his personal "vacation" photos made on the trip. This is the image of the mountaineer as romantic hero—the last vestige of the American pioneer.

Another version of the mythology is the hillbilly as buffoon, developed as early as the nineteenth century but solidified in "L'il Abner," the cartoon strip created by Al Capp from the 1940s to the 1960s. In this set of images, the hillbilly dashes around in jalopies or broken-down trucks on bad roads, wearing battered clothing, slouch hats and overalls, trafficking in moonshine, eating great quantities of ham (and less familiar foods), and being hopelessly ignorant of the ways of civilization." This is the image of the mountaineer as buffoon.[3] (Interestingly this image of hillbilly life served as the basis for what is probably the most popular tourist attraction in the Ozarks—"Dogpatch, U.S.A.")

Stories of the region were so widespread in newspapers, magazines, on the stage, in cheap novels, in nickelodeon silent films, in photographs, and in tourism promotions, and the elements of the stories so coherent, that as early as the 1930s one outraged mountain sympathizer was able to write: "People from other sections of the country almost without exception, believe that our mountain people are poor, uneducated, benighted folks, without culture in any degree, living in cabins, and existing wholly upon corn pone, fat bacon, and blocade {sic} liquor."[4]

Mountaineers have been called "pure, Anglo-Saxon stock," "our contemporary ancestors," portrayed as living a pioneer lifestyle isolated from the rest of forward-moving, industrialized, contemporary America. Mountaineers are, according to the mythology, resistant to progress because they are ignorant, tradition-bound, stubbornly proud people, with a zeal for individual liberty bordering on anarchy and certainly leading to violence. And in the consistent inconsistency of mythology, not only are they *actively* resistant to change, but *passive* in the face of any change forced upon them—a passivity born of ignorance, indolence, and bizarre religious beliefs based on superstition and fatalism.

Today, the mythology is, if anything, more firmly entrenched and more fully articulated. One current analyst writes (and it's worth quoting in full since it explicates the mythology so well):

> *The stereotype of the mountaineer is an image of the man as tall, gaunt, perhaps stooped, with a deeply lined face and drawn features, hollow eyes and a thin set mouth. He wears overalls that are dusty and patched. His hair is an undefined color between brown and gray. His wife has stringy hair, unhealthy looking skin, and is old for her age, having gained weight as a result of poor dietary habits and having too many children. Around this couple, a small herd of children run wild about a homestead which consists of a broken-down, wooden house, with a leaning porch. The image is American Gothic gone stale. The family receives a welfare check in the mail each month. The man goes off in the afternoon to sit in the shade with his buddies. They pass the jug of corn licker round and round. They don't do much but watch the road: "I could see the car going by on the highway if I bothered to turn my head." Hillbillies are presumed by outsiders to be ignorant and illiterate, incestuous and therefore genetically flawed, poverty stricken, violent, and generally savage. . . .*[5]

No matter what the realities of Appalachian life may be, the mythology is far more pervasive in American life and, I fear, throughout the world. As cultural analyst David Whisnant has commented, "to this day there are a thousand people who 'know' that mountaineers weave coverlets and sing ballads for everyone who knows that millions of them have been industrial workers for a hundred years, have organized unions and picketed state and national capitals in pursuit of their constitutional rights, and have laid their bodies in front of stripmine bulldozers and overloaded coal trucks. Or that, today, they shop at K-Mart and Radio Shack, drive Camaros, and watch as much television as people anywhere."[6]

THE MYTHOLOGY AND TOURISM

Mountains became a fashionable, even cultish, tourist destination in Europe and America beginning in the late eighteenth century and lasting well into the early twentieth century.[7] Enthusiasm for mountain travel reached its zenith during the Romantic period of the nineteenth century, coinciding with the coming of railroads to take the tourists into mountain areas. Orally circulated stories and published accounts by travellers into the southern Appalachian mountains contributed significantly to the creation and dissemination of the mythology of Appalachia.

By the late 1700s, stories of mythic proportions were already circulating among travellers about the exploits of such intrepid mountain men as Daniel Boone and Davy Crockett (mountaineer as hero). A typical written account of early travel in the mountains is journalist Anne Newport Royall's description of the people she encountered in the southwest Virginia territory. In her account, you can already hear the mythic images taking shape: "These counties, remote from commerce and civilized life, confined to their everlasting hills of freezing cold, all pursuing the same employments, which consist in farming, raising cattle, making whiskey (and drinking it), hunting and digging *sang* (ginseng), as they say, present a distinct republic of their own, every way different from any people."[8]

By 1867, the first "hillbilly as buffoon" character appears as Sut Lovingood in a cycle of stories by George Washington Harris, popular with travellers to the mountain region. Sut, who speaks in a heavy mountain dialect and drinks moonshine, is a mountaineer, as Harris describes him, "among a crowd of mountaineers full of fun, foolery, and mean whiskey."[9]

Shortly after the American Civil War, improved transportation brought a flood of people to the mountains of Appalachia. Some came as tourists to see the beauty of the mountains and spend summers in the cool, disease-free environment. Some came to mine the region's abundant natural resources (timber, coal, etc.); some came representing churches or charitable organizations to mine what were thought to be the region's lost souls (the mythology already at work). Some came to find and sell—literally sell—to the American people the commodities of what one early writer called, "a strange land and peculiar people."

These early taproots of the mythology of Appalachia took hold and in a fertile period from 1875-1935 grew as dense and complex and tenacious as a thicket of mountain laurel. The outpouring of rhetoric about theAppalachian region in this period is nothing short of phenomenal. In just the first two decades (1875-1895) more than two hundred novels and stories were published which described mountain people as "quaint and isolated, living peculiar lives in the shadow of awe-inspiring peaks."[10] Countless non-fiction books and magazine articles, particularly travel accounts, frequently illustrated with engravings or later, photographs, sold vigorously, as did untold newspaper stories of mountain life.

In more recent years, the mythic icons of hillfolk have come into the consciousness of most people through the visual media—television and film, photography, cartoons, and marketing campaigns to sell land in the mountains and to promote tourism. In the early development of the mythology, photographs helped sell the stories of the hillbilly to the public outside the region; in the 1940s, 1950s, and 1960s (with the first automobile tourism boom in Appalachia) cartoonist Al Capp's L'il Abner series and Billy DeBeck's Snuffy Smith forever inscribed the mythic icons of "hillbilliness" in the public mind; in the 1960s, news photographers and documentary filmmakers animated the cartoon icons with real mountain people, as they saw them, in reporting Johnson's War on Poverty. The 1970s reproduced images of the mountaineer as pioneer hero in the back-to-the-land nostalgia craze. The icons of Appalachia have by now become so widely known that they are used to sell calendars, kitsch, real estate, food, and tourism. The Appalachian story has become a commodity which sells well.

Take a trip anywhere in the mountains today and you can buy souvenirs of mountain life ranging from the ridiculous to the sublime, from a hillbilly calculator (a cardboard cut-out of a hand with the digits numbered) to a stunningly crafted cathedral window quilt. You can visit John Rice Irwin's attractive Museum of Appalachia (i.e., rural, traditional Appalachia) in Norris, Tennessee, or the garishness of Gatlinburg, Tennessee with its Ripley's Believe It or Not museum, giant waterslides, and the worst hillbilly kitsch imaginable.

One of the most popular destinations in southern Appalachia is the Blue Ridge Parkway which attracts twenty million visitors a year. The Blue Ridge Parkway's interpretation of Appalachia and the role of its concessioners in marketing the mythology of Appalachia offer an interesting case study in the interplay between culture and commerce.

THE BLUE RIDGE PARKWAY AND APPALACHIA

Designers and administrators of the Blue Ridge Parkway early on made a decision to protect and interpret the cultural history of the area through which the Parkway passed. In the 1930s when landscape architect Stanley Abbott began designing the Parkway, he said: "Through much of its length the parkway goes through a 'managed landscape' and I think it has been pretty clear and relatively unquestioned with the (Park) Service that the problem was to marry ourselves to that managed landscape. This has required a feeling for the rail fence, the old barn, and the farm field" to which he later added, "The picture of . . . simple homestead culture . . . (is) as interesting a part of the Blue Ridge as the natural scene around (it)."[11] Abbott, always a strong image-maker, chose an apt metaphor when he described the Blue Ridge Parkway's relationship to the surrounding cultural area as a marriage—sometimes it has been a blissful relationship, sometimes stormy, but nonetheless a permanent and enduring relationship.

What Abbott called a "simple homestead culture," much of it the vestiges of a pioneer culture still visible in the 1930s in parts of the mountains, became the focus for the Parkway's interpretation of Appalachia—the mountaineer as romantic hero. In this approach the Blue Ridge Parkway has been remarkably and admirably consistent. A Parkway visitor encounters miles of split rail fences, preserved log cabins, an entire farmstead (the Johnson Farm) at Peaks of Otter, a working gristmill at Mabry Mill, and numerous craft exhibits. The parkway has been sensitive (perhaps even a little defensive) in portraying mountain life with dignity and trying to avoid negative stereotypes about the region. Nowhere is this more apparent than in the parkway Guidebooks (1976), when a fictional character, Uncle Newt, who speaks in mountain dialect, is introduced to add "local color" to the Guide. Immediately the author of the Guide hastens to add: "To avoid any misunderstanding: Many of our local contacts had college degrees, spoke perfect English, and, like Uncle Newt, were gracious and helpful. Uncle Newt was born out of love and admiration for the mountainesque local color he represents."[12]

Recently the Blue Ridge Parkway administration has come to realize the unique role that parkways can play in cultural interpretation of any area. More than any single destination park or tourist attraction, parkways move visitors through actual as well symbolic time and through real cultural space. Visitors can see the dynamics of culture, both continuity and change. Rather than simply showing visitors the preserved, hermetically sealed, pioneer past of the mountains, the Parkway can help visitors understand the region's past, the ways in which mountain life has changed (and how it has stayed the same), and some potentials and problems for the future of the mountains. There are encouraging signs (too numerous to discuss here) that the Parkway is moving toward this approach.[13]

For most tourists, the real buying and selling of the commodities of mountain life takes place at the gift shops operated by concessioners at numerous Parkway locales (e.g., Doughton Park, Cherry Hill, Northwest Trading Post, etc.). Just last week I took a trip down the Parkway from near Blacksburg, Virginia, deep into North Carolina stopping at nearly every concession area to see the current state of "marketing the mountains." First, let me say that what I found was mostly pleasing. Many of the concessions had for sale largely locally made products of generally good quality representing mountain cultural traditions still vital today (i.e., basketmaking, quilting, beekeeping, woodcarving, etc.). The concessions do a particularly good job with regional foodways both in their restaurants and in the foods (apple butter, jams, preserves, relishes, etc.) they sell as souvenirs. (The buckwheat cakes are deservedly famous; the mountain trout, country ham biscuits, grits, and tomatoes are excellent; and at the Northwest Trading Post in North Carolina you can sample a true mountain delicacy—molasses stack cake). Perhaps the food tastes so true because local people staff the kitchens.

The false notes that I found were few but shrill and inevitably the product of nonlocal companies. At the Northwest Trading Post, so fine in most ways, I found a T-shirt, made in Texas, with a drawing of a hillbilly stereotype (slouch hat, slouched position, log shack in the background) with a buxom, young woman standing over the hillbilly, posterior protruding from short shorts (patched, of course!) toward the viewer. Across the top of the T-shirt written in rustic letters were the words: "Thrills in the Hills." Here was a shirt that combined negative cultural stereotyping and sexism all in one. The mountaineer as buffoon.

Another T-shirt, discovered in the gas station at Crabtree Meadows, portrayed the stereotypical hillbilly with all his cultural baggage—sleeping against a tree in slouch hat and tattered clothes, hound dog sleeping by his side, a moonshine jug "right handy" (clearly identifiable by the XXX's on it) and flies circling the whole lot. The shirt read, "Laid Back in North Carolina" or "Kicked Back in North Carolina" in another version.

Finally, in the coffee shop/gift shop at Doughton Park, prominently displayed beside the cash register, I bought the "Hillbilly Joke Book," published in Texas, mostly about the Ozarks (but aren't hillbillies the same everywhere?), which must contain every hillbilly stereotype ever known.

These may seem like minor concerns but it is jarring to see the people of the mountains presented as "independent pioneer and mountain tackey"[14] all at the same time, and in the same place (though it does pointedly reveal much of the ambivalence mainstream American culture has always felt about Appalachia). Similar items depicting negative stereotypes of Black people or Native Americans would bring howls of protest to the Park Service from the tourist public.

Does it really matter that a few pieces of hillbilly kitsch are sold along the Blue Ridge Parkway, especially when some of these items sell well? (A Blue Ridge Parkway official once told me that it was unfortunate but true that a lot of the nonlocal, poorer quality items sold much better than the locally made goods, a strong argument made by the concessioners, proving that the economics of culture frequently dominate sensitivity to culture.) I think it does matter, particularly because it puts the Park Service, a federal agency that in recent years especially has tried to be sensitive to the politics of culture, in the awkward position of seeming to hawk ethnocentrism and sexism. The very culture the Parkway celebrates mile after mile gets denigrated quickly when a kid buys the hillbilly joke book as her souvenir to take back home from the mountains.

Do hillbilly stereotypes really hurt anyone? Do they really have any significant effect on anyone or anything or are they only harmless fun? The answer to these questions is complicated but a few examples may demonstrate that perceptions of cultural difference always have effects.

Many of my students at the university who come from southwest Virginia or other parts of Appalachia tell me that they struggle with their cultural identity because for so long they have been made to feel ashamed of their mountain "hillbilly" heritage. These are exceptionally bright students from mostly middle class or upper middle class homes. Think of the effects on mountain young people who have fewer inner strengths and less moral support.

More pertinent to the subject of parkways, the controversial story of the building of the Skyline Drive (and the Shenandoah National Park) centers on cultural perceptions of mountain residents. A decision was made to resettle all mountain residents out of the area when the park and parkway were to be built, "for their own good." The motives of some of those involved in the resettlement were high-minded, believing that the mountain people would benefit from access to jobs, better housing, education, and health-care. But many found it easy to justify displacement of the residents because they believed the mountaineer's way of life simply wasn't "worth saving," according to one of the project engineers.[15] A Park Service historian of the period (1935) wrote, "the area . . . is almost destitute of the remains of a mountain culture"[16] and a caption under a photograph in the plan book for the project stated: "The picture . . . tells the story of moronic but contented mountain folk of the average type."[17] And finally, another engineer from the road building project resisted putting mountain residents to work on the road, calling them "a bunch of hillbillies" and adding, "Oh these hillbillies, they won't work. They don't know anything. They're lazy. They won't work."[18] But the mountaineers did work on the road and research in recent years has shown that the widespread perceptions of "no culture" among the inhabitants of the Shenandoah area simply were not based on evidence which has proven contradictory (i.e., that there was a rich culture operating but not visible to those who saw only what they wanted to see).[19]

CONCLUSION

What can we learn from the experience of Appalachia useful to those interested in parkways? Parkways by their nature attract people—usually great numbers of people—to places where other people live and enact their culture. Parkway planners have to make a decision, either consciously or subconsciously, about their stance toward the local culture and its interpretation. Fredric Jameson argues that efforts at interpretation are plagued by a binary opposition between Identity and Difference; that is, we are faced with the dilemma of either affirming the Identity of the culturally Other with ourselves, or affirming the radical difference from ourselves.[20]

If we take the first stance, we say " 'they' are just like us" and we fail to "touch the strangeness and the resistance of a reality genuinely different from our own."[21] If we take the second stance, we say "'they' are so different from us we can never understand," which casts us in the role of gaping tourists. Both positions have moral consequences which are made clear in Tzvetan Todorov's The Conquest of America: The Question of the Other, an historical case study of the white European encounter with the American Indian.

Todorov points out that the Christian missionaries too easily identified with the indigenous peoples and he asks: "Can we really love someone if we know little or nothing of his identity; if we see in place of that identity a projection of ourselves or our ideals?...Doesn't one culture risk trying to transform the other in its own name, and therefore risk subjugating it as well? How much is such love worth?"[22] On the other hand, Todorov views Columbus as guilty of affirming the radical Different of the native peoples, "the failure to recognize the Indians, and the refusal to admit them as a subject having the same rights as oneself, but different. Columbus discovered America but not the Americans."[23]

The people of Appalachia have been victims of both stances. Like the missionaries and the Indians, Appalachia has been "loved" too much by reformers of one kind or another who have believed mountain people are just like them if only they had the opportunities; who have wanted to make mountain life just like mainstream American culture; who have wanted to help those "poor, culturally isolated mountain folk" get some real culture. One mountain poet has described "How America Came to the Mountains" as "an awful storm."[24]

On the other hand, mountain people are often seen as so different that they can't be like mainstream Americans, and in fact, we don't want them to be. We prefer them to be what we imagine them to be.

How do those faced with this dilemma—Identity and Difference—resolve it? There is no easy answer but I offer three words of advice: Listen, See, and Question. First, listen with empathy to the people whose culture is to be interpreted and, usually, marketed. The Blue Ridge Parkway has been doing this well in recent years with public forums and community involvement. The Roanoke EXPLORE project has discovered that local people need to be and will be heard on the plans for this park and parkway. Second, try to see with new eyes, to look at things, as anthropologist Clifford Geertz says, "from the native's point of view."[25] And, finally, we must ask ourselves, as cultural interpreters, some hard questions about our own motives; we must try to see around our own blinders to the political and moral implications of our visions and plans; we must be constantly alert to our own cultural hegemony.

Using folk culture as a basis for interpretation or marketing along a parkway is a serious and sensitive issue. But Appalachian poet Jim Wayne Miller summarizes with acerbic wit the difficulties of combining folk culture and tourism is his poem, "The Brier Losing Touch with His Traditions"[26]:

THE BRIER LOSING TOUCH WITH HIS TRADITIONS

Once he was a chairmaker.
People up north discovered him.
They said he was "an authentic mountain craftsman."
People came and made pictures of him working,
wrote him up in the newspapers.

He got famous
Got a lot of orders for his chairs.

When he moved up to Cincinnati
so he could be closer to his market
(besides, a lot of his people lived there now)
he found out he was a Brier.

And when his customers found out
he was using an electric lathe and power drill
just to keep up with all the orders,
they said he was losing touch with his traditions.
His orders fell off something awful.
He figured it had been a bad mistake
to let the magazine people take those pictures
of him with his power tools, clean-shaven,
wearing a flowered sport shirt and drip-dry pants.

So he moved back down to east Kentucky.
Had himself a brochure printed up
with a picture of him using his hand lathe
bearded, barefoot, in faded overalls.
Then when folks would come from the magazines,
he'd get rid of them before suppertime
so he could put on his shoes, his flowered sport shirt
and double-knit pants, and open a can of beer
and watch the six-thirty news on tv
out of New York and Washington.

He had to have some time to be himself.

NOTES

[1]Quoted in Archie Green, "Hillbilly Music: Source and Symbol," Journal of American Folklore, 78 (July 1965), 204.

[2]Percy MacKaye, "Untamed America: A Comment on a Sojourn in the Kentucky Mountains," The Survey 51 (January 1, 1924), 327.

[3]For a discussion, see Stephen W. Fisher, Identity as Symbolic Production: The Politics of Culture and Meaning in Appalachia. Ann Arbor: University Microfilms, 1977. Ph.D. Dissertation, Princeton University, 1977, p. 30.

[4]Julia Montgomery Street, as quoted in Charles Alan Watkins, "Merchandising the Mountaineer: Photography, the Great Depression, and Cabins in the Laurel," Appalachian Journal, 12 (Spring 1985), 220.

[5]Fisher, p. 29.

[6]David Whisnant, All That Is Native and Fine: The Politics of Culture in an American Region (Chapel Hill: University of North Carolina Press, 1983), p. 13.

[7]See, for example, Paul P. Bernard, Rush to the Alps: The Evolution of Vacationing in Switzerland (New York: East European Quarterly, 1978); and, Maxine Feifer, Tourism in History (New York: Stein and Day, 1985).

[8]Anne Newport Royall, as quoted in Voices from the Hills: Selected Readings of Southern Appalachia, ed. by Robert H. Higgs and Ambrose N. Manning (New York: Ungar, 1975), p. 73.

[9]George Washington Harris, Sut Lovingood, Yarns Sun by a "Nat'ral born durn'd fool." Warped and Wove for Public Wear. (New York: Dick & Fitzgerald, 1967), p. 19.

[10]Carvel Collins, "Nineteenth Century Fiction of the Southern Appalachians," Bulletin of Bibliography, xviii (1942), p. 186.

[11]Quoted in Douglas Swaim, "Stanley Abbott and the Design of The Blue Ridge Parkway," Blue Ridge Parkway: Agent of Transition, ed. by Barry M. Buxton and

Steven M. Beatty (Boone: Appalachian Consortium Press, 1986.)

[12]William Lord, Blue Ridge Parkway Guide (Asheville: Hexagon, 1976), p. 5.

[13]Parks Lanier in "Mabry Mill as Metaphor," in Blue Ridge Parkway: Agent of Transition, p. 164, makes the interesting suggestion to replace utilitarian placards explaining the artifacts at Mabry Mill with the words of contemporary Appalachian poets.

[14]Charles L. Perdue, Jr. and Nancy J. Martin-Perdue, "From Independent Pioneer to Mountain Tackey: Socioeconomic Determinants of Cultural Paradox," paper presented for the American Folklore Society, 1977, p. 3.

[15]Perdue, p. 2.

[16]Perdue, p. 2.

[17]Perdue, p. 3.

[18]Gwen Russell Harvey and Alice Hoffman, "A New Deal for the Mountain Folk: Recollections of the Resettlement Administration," Blue Ridge Parkway: Agent of Transition, p. 94 and p. 96.

[19]See Charles and Nancy Perdue, "Appalachian Fables and Facts: A Case Study of the Shenandoah National Park Removals" Appalachian Journal, 7 (1980).

[20]Fredric Jameson, "Marxism and Historicism," New Literary History 11 (Autumn 1979), 43. I am grateful to my colleague Dwight Conquergood of Northwestern University for this and the Todorov reference that follows.

[21]Jameson, p. 43.

[22]Tzvetan Todorov, The Conquest of America: The Question of the Other, trans. Richard Howard (New York: Harper & Row, 1984), p. 168.

[23]Todorov, p. 40.

[24]Jim Wayne Miller, "How America Came to the Mountains," The Mountains Have Come Closer (Boone: Appalachian Consortium Press, 1980), p. 47.

[25]Clifford Geertz, The Interpretation of Cultures (New York: Basic Books, 1972).

[26]Jim Wayne Miller, "The Brier Losing Touch with His Traditions," The Mountains Have Come Closer, p. 44.

Area Development Effects on the Colonial Parkway, Colonial National Historical Park, Virginia

Peter Baril

Colonial National Historical Park was established by presidential proclamation as Colonial National Monument on December 30, 1930, to commemorate the beginning and end of the English-American colonial experience. Congressional authorization earlier that year had specified that the park would be created "... to preserve the historic structures and remains ... for the benefit and enjoyment of the people."[1]

President Herbert Hoover reiterated the purpose of the park as established by the Congressional authorization, and further stated that the park would be comprised of Jamestown Island, passage through the city of Williamsburg, the Yorktown battlefield, and ". . . areas for highways to connect said island, city and battlefield."[2]

Spurred by the Great Depression, construction on the Colonial Parkway began in 1931, after suitable land cessions and purchases had been made. Work was interrupted by World War II, and it was not until 1956 that the Colonial Parkway was completed.

Three lanes wide, the Parkway fronts the James and York Rivers for approximately half its twenty-three mile length. Away from the Rivers, the roadway traverses low hills which are maintained in forest. The right-of-way includes several Confederate forts, the ruins of two seventeenth century plantation houses, and the site of at least one Indian village. The soil very likely holds undiscovered archeological remains. Interpretive signs located along its length allude to events as diverse as a sixteenth century Jesuit mission in the area, the brief presence of young George Custer, and colonial real estate.

The forested boundaries of the Parkway today are home to a variety of animals. White-tailed deer often are seen along the roadside or scampering across the paved surface, even within the Williamsburg city limits. Opossums and raccoons are seen frequently. Great blue herons fish in the shallow water of the James and the marshy tributaries feeding it. Especially lucky visitors are able to observe pileated woodpeckers, ospreys and bald eagles. Selective planting of redbud, dogwood, and locust trees provide a continual show of flowers through much of the spring.

From the beginning, the Parkway was planned as a motor road, and the primary management consideration was scenery, a visually pleasant conduit between two places in which strikingly important historical events took place. Turnouts have been placed strategically so as to afford the best view of the two rivers and the water traffic on them. Where the road is out of sight of water, the pullovers are fewer and keyed to some other scenic feature, most notably a large oak tree thought to date to the colonial era. In only one case does the Parkway provide paved access to an area whose primary interest is historic. One of the smallest and least used turnouts, it calls attention to the presence there of a seventeenth century paper mill.

The size of the pullovers argues that most of them were intended by their designers for short term use. Only three will hold more than a dozen cars. Lack of any access from the bluff areas to the riverfronts below them also indicates that the planners did not envision recreational use of those beach areas. Visitors were meant to use the turnouts to read the interpretive signs, take in the view for a few minutes, and be on their way. Two picnic areas adjacent to the road were intended for recreational purposes, it is true, but their largely wooded character and locations show they were not meant for anything more vigorous than a cookout. Certainly there are none of the amenities associated with more active recreation, no horseshoe pits, softball diamonds or bath houses.

The construction dates of the two picnic areas located along the Parkway also indicate that they were not considered a critical need by the first park planners. Ringfield Picnic Area was cleared and set up in 1956, and Great Neck Picnic Area did not follow until 1963.[3]

The lack of consideration given to recreational uses of the Parkway is also shown in the adoption of a special federal regulation which prohibits landing or launching boats in the park.[4]

It should come as no surprise that the National Park Service has trouble restricting or channeling visitation to fit the strictures of Congress, President or park planners. In some cases their intentions have been merely exceeded. In others they have been contradicted entirely.

Citizen requests for greater recreational access to the park and for a widened spectrum of permitted activities have been heard practically from the moment the park was established. Representative of this type of public reaction to the park is a letter received in July, 1951, which complained of a lack of parking on the Parkway and a ban on parking on the grass. The park superintendent stoically replied that the purpose of the Parkway is not to provide local recreational facilities, and random parking would destroy the beauty of the roadway.[5] Often, however, Park Service reaction to rising recreational pressure has been much more equivocal.

In response to a perceived public demand for swimming, the National Park Service created a paved parking area parallel to the Parkway between College Creek and the existing turnout west of the creek. Since the park did not provide lifeguard protection, when drownings occurred there were claims for damages. The parallel parking area was removed in 1971 to prevent continuation of government liability and the James River shoreline has been effectively closed to swimming since that time.[6]

Rising area population has resulted in a much higher use of the Colonial Parkway as a commuter route. Development of York and Gloucester Counties as suburban areas for people who work in Williamsburg or at the military installations next to the parkway has accentuated this tendency. Though there are seldom traffic jams such as occur in cities, there is little doubt this sort of use is increasing and will continue to rise in the future.

This commuter traffic is concentrated on the portion of the Parkway between Yorktown and Williamsburg. The western suburbs of Williamsburg do not rely on the Parkway as a transportation artery and it is unlikely they will come to do so.

The growth of the Yorktown-Williamsburg-Jamestown triangle will bring about a greater insularity for many of the animals living in the park. Disappearance of game animals from private land near the park probably will result in more poaching of animals along the Parkway, where access is easy, deer browse near the roadside in winter, and the long sight lines make it difficult for the rangers to conduct surveillance.

Military spending affects the Parkway because of its proximity to the Yorktown Naval Weapons Station. Any buildup of the armed forces translates into more employees at this installation. Many of them travel on the Parkway, concentrating at the shift changes when traffic is very heavy.

People driving to and from work normally would not be said to be recreating, but there is reason to believe many of them use the Parkway because of its scenic values as well as for convenience. An alternative commuter route from Yorktown to Williamsburg exists. In length it is little more than a mile longer than the Parkway route, and if speed limits are not exceeded and one has reasonable luck with traffic lights, is not substantially more time consuming. No scientific work has been done to date to determine the extent of its use between Yorktown and Williamsburg, but judging from observation, this use appears to be light.

It is necessary for the National Park Service to evaluate types of recreational use and act as arbiter to determine what is appropriate and to prohibit what is considered inappropriate. Often this is not easy. A body of literature has grown up within the agency to guide the staff within any individual park and to assure uniformity throughout the system. Chapter 36 of the Code of Federal Regulations, for example, prohibits hunting in all areas of the National Parks except as specifically allowed in the enabling legislation of an area.[7] Hunting and trapping are prohibited along Colonial Parkway, though both are sometimes done illegally.

Taking mammals, birds, reptiles, or amphibians is prohibited, but fishing is only regulated. Since the tidal waters of the York and James are considered salt water, no state license is required, there is practically no limitation on catches, and parking is easy and free. Fishing thus offers a source of inexpensive recreation that contains the added prospect of an economic advantage to those engaging in it.

Fishing attracts substantial numbers of persons to the Parkway, many of whom come equipped to make a day of it. At the height of the season they are numerous enough to fill some of the parking areas along the road, effectively barring access to others and making it difficult even to read the interpretive signs. In addition to this effect, some of the less conscientious fishermen and women leave litter behind and their use has resulted in the creation of a number of impromptu trails from the parking areas to the water. Shoreline vegetation has been trampled and the beach areas destabilized.

The beaches along the James and York Rivers are utilized for purposes other than fishing. Though it might seem odd for a peninsula, there are few public beaches available in the area, and because of this, shorelines in the park have been visited heavily for many years. This use is concentrated somewhat and probably is governed by the availability of parking. In fact, it does not seem coincidental that the three largest Parkway turnouts are located near the three best beach areas. Earlier we argued that recreational use was not catered to by the Parkway planners, but these three beach areas would seem to be exceptions. However, since they were established, they have come to be used extensively for sunbathing and picnicking.

As do the fishermen, people coming to the beaches in the park often stay for the day. Sunbathing in itself might be considered a non-consumptive use and basically compatible with the purposes of the park. It must be noted, however, that the numbers of these users sometimes is so great that a deterioration of the resource is inevitable. Foot traffic from the parking areas has created more of the eroding trails already mentioned, trails which, judging from visual rather than empirical evidence, are becoming more numerous and suffering greater soil loss as time passes. Many people bring their lunches or other refreshments, and some leave their refuse when they depart. The park must either pay to clean up this trash, or accept a littered landscape, or establish a continual law enforcement presence in these places.

Once again, areas that receive substantial visitation for recreational purposes experience trampling of the shoreline vegetation and destabilization of the shoreline itself. This is particularly significant in the vicinity of College Creek, where the shoreline is moving back due to natural processes, and where a Confederate fort is but a short distance from the beach. Preservation of the historic remains is the reason the park exists, and anything that endangers the old structures is *a priori* unacceptable.

Since so many people desire to use the beaches near the Colonial Parkway, and since the National Park Service Organic Act of 1916 mandates accessible resources for the benefit and enjoyment of the visitors, the park comes under intense pressure to provide recreational facilities. For example, persons who come to one of the small park beaches for the day will need to relieve themselves sometime during the course of their visit. No provision has been made for this understandable human need, so people must either leave the area or find momentary privacy in the nearby bushes. Because parking often is at a premium on weekends, there is a clear preference for the bushes.

Interestingly, there has been no clamor for bathrooms from the visitors. Nor has there been any such insistence from either federal or state public health officials. What there has been is pressure for more parking, primarily at Indian Field Creek. Visitors confronted with a full parking lot often park on the grass, an unacceptable practice for both legal and resource management reasons. In an attempt to cope with this heavy use, the park in 1982 set up an overflow lot next to the paved parking area. Even this additional space has been insufficient during peak visitation times, however, and the problem persists. In an addition to this, the bare soil and log barriers of the temporary parking area are ugly. By almost everyone's estimation, so is the long line of parked cars which are there on spring and summer weekends.

It can be argued that if this area is crowded with sunbathers, there must be significant numbers of people who do not object to crowding, and who wish to use the park for this type of passive recreation. Trying to cope with such a contention, the park managers at Colonial National Historical Park have worked to define what kind of use is appropriate. A Compilation of Regulations has been issued by the park superintendent for this reason. The compendium prohibits a number of recreational activities in the park, including boating in park waters, fishing in park impoundments, snowmobiling, and skateboarding. The Colonial Parkway is closed to horseback riding, kite flying, ball games, frisbee throwing and other activities not directly related to the historical theme of the park.[8] No determination has been made whether fishing or sunbathing are related to the historical theme of the park.

The American scene has changed considerably since President Hoover established Colonial National Monument in 1930. So have recreational activities. People do still sometimes drive for pleasure, but driving is seldom thought of as a recreational activity. Many people ride bicycles and jog for fun, however, a situation which the Parkway planners half a century ago cannot be blamed for failing to anticipate. Sunny weekends bring out groups of these enthusiasts, but individual cyclists and runners can be seen almost every day.

Neither bicyclists nor joggers have a significant physical effect on the road. It is sometimes contended that bicycle tires exert enormous stresses on a road surface, but there is no noticeable evidence that two-wheeled vehicles have caused any wear to the Colonial Parkway. There do not seem to be any worn pathways along the side of the Parkway caused by runners. The impact of bikers and joggers is rather on the traffic conflicts they sometimes have with automobiles. Drivers habitually swing into the middle lane of the Parkway to pass cyclists, as they should, but use of the middle lane can be dangerous. The motorist who is distracted sometimes does not see a runner or bicyclist. Runners who have the sun at their backs must be especially careful. There was one serious injury to a bicyclist during the summer of 1987, and as long as they share a comparatively narrow winding road with motor vehicles the potential for a serious accident must be considered high.

In the 1970's, proposals were made for a bicycle-jogging path alongside the Parkway. Some provision for this bikeway was made, but when it became obvious that funding would not be available in the near future the effort was shelved, and the likelihood of such a pathway is now remote. The idea has produced a rather odd bridge in the park, however, a bridge which includes a completely unused auxiliary crossing for bikes and foot traffic.

During the day, recreational use can be given at least an ephemeral connection with the original purpose of the park, but when the sun sets little justification for visitation can be made. In fact, much of the after dark visitation to the Colonial Parkway is for sexual relations and for drinking. The impact of this type of recreation is, once again, the quantities of litter produced, the pedestrian traffic on eroding bluff surfaces, and the drain this use puts on park personnel resources. There is no possibility, however, that the Parkway will be closed at night, and so the problems posed by nighttime visitation will persist.

There is scarcely a problem in the park that will not become worse in the future if the trends so evident today will continue, and all indications are that the area will see more of the same in coming years. There seems little reason, for example, to doubt the current population growth of two percent per year will continue. Although the parallel is inexact, again there is every cause to believe this population growth will bring about similar increases in numbers of users of the Parkway. In fact, the visitation increase might exceed area population growth because that growth is uneven.

Two nearby municipal parks, Newport News Park and Waller Mill Park, receive heavy summer use for recreational purposes, but neither has a beach and the Colonial Parkway therefore will remain the focal point for sunbathers who do not want to drive as far as Virginia Beach. Demographic changes might work to the advantage of the park in this case, as the vast majority of these visitors are young. If the William and Mary student population remains stable and the military installations do not increase their rosters, this type of use should not become more intense.

The rapid growth of the Williamsburg metropolitan area has also brought about other changes in the character of the Colonial Parkway. Because it crosses the peninsula, the Parkway must itself be crossed by any land traffic in the area. Numerous bridges now span the old road, including Interstate Highway 64, and though the National Park Service insisted that any bridge over the Parkway must be faced with brick to make it visually compatible, there is still an individual and cumulative effect of noise and visual intrusion.

This type of impact also has been caused by the clearing of adjacent land for suburban residences and businesses. During summer these structures are hardly visible from the roadway, but when the leaves fall the narrow corridor of vegetation owned by the park is inadequate to screen nearby buildings. As land has become more scarce there has been a greater propensity to build higher structures. A recent case involves plans for a five-story hotel very close to the Parkway.

Area development has caused siltation of the small streams which cross beneath the Parkway. It has brought about noise pollution, and the larger numbers of nearby residents have contributed to air pollution with their automobiles and wood fires. In trying to provide facilities for the local population, the Park Service has consented to several utility corridors above and below the road surface. Electric and telephone lines now cross the Parkway, as do several water lines, one natural gas line, and even a line for cable television. The entry road to one housing development empties on to a Parkway access road, and in 1983 the park superintendent turned down a request for a second similar access.[9]

As must be clear by now, it is time for a comprehensive analysis of the Colonial Parkway, its capacities and objectives, and what can be done to reconcile a public which desires more intensive recreation with a park which is mandated to preserve historic features. Just such a review is now being made as part of a general management planning process in the park. Public involvement in this process will be solicited, but the park must make management decisions based on the intent of Congress and the President rather than the desires of people in the neighborhood. It is in trying to please everyone that the National Park Service manages to please no one.

NOTES

1. 46 Stat. 855
2. 46 Stat. 3041
3. Superintendent's Monthly Report, September 1956, and October 1963, unpublished, Chief Park Historian's office, Colonial NHP.
4. Ibid, July, 1951.
5. 36 Code of Federal Regulations SS7.1
6. Interview with Trent R. Taylor, Park Ranger and lifetime resident of Newport News and Williamsburg, Virginia.
7. 36 Code of Federal Regulations SS2.2
8. Compilation of Superintendent's Orders, April 10, 1987, unpublished, available at the Superintendent's office, Colonial National Historical Park.
9. Recollection of the author.

The Need for a National System of Scenic Highways

Edward McMahon, Executive Director, Coalition for Scenic Beauty

I come today to present only one simple, but I believe compelling idea. We must establish a national system of scenic highways in the United States.

Let me invite you to take a short imaginary drive along one of our federal interstate highways. Let's take a trip down Interstate 45 from Houston to the Gulf city of Galveston. Or along Interstate 10 through Florida, Mississippi and Louisiana or on Interstate 40 across North Carolina, into the Appalachians and then westward across Tennessee, Arkansas, and Oklahoma. What would we see?

Thousands of billboards of every description, towering over the fields, riding the hills, dominating the landscape and the largest number of them advertising alcohol and tobacco, products channeled by federal law off our airwaves and on to our landscape.

Most of our journey we would have been outside developed urban areas, yet rarely would our vista have been free of billboards.

Any person aware of the existence of the Federal Highway Beautification Act would quickly assume that this disgraceful mess must have been created prior to 1965. Such an observer might complain that the beautification program has still not gotten around to cleaning up these roads.

Would an observer believe that the worst of this blight had been created since the passage of the Beautification Act? Believable or not, that is exactly what has happened - and continues to happen even as I speak.

Would the observer believe that almost $220 million has been spent to remove billboards on such roadways in America? Well, once convinced, any taxpaying observer should be outraged at this waste of public money.

Why does America need to preserve scenic highways? Several reasons: first, to meet the recreational needs of those millions of Americans who drive for recreation and pleasure; second, to provide for preservation of routes of historical significance in urban and rural areas; third, to provide for the recovery and conservation of natural beauty and cultural diversity along designated scenic routes; and fourth, to maximize the potential of little used and bypassed sections of highway and return economic vitality to distressed areas through promotion of tourism.

NEED

All American highways were scenic highways when settlers first carved them out of the wilderness. But scenery was the last thing early trailblazers and road builders had in mind. They merely wanted to get from here to there, the fastest way possible.

We now know how civilization has altered or in places demolished the pristine look of America—with highways bearing a large share of responsibility. Yet, even a generation ago, a drive in the country was still an American institution.

Families packed a picnic and a road map and set out to discover the wonders of rural America. But today much of our countryside looks depressingly familiar. City blends with suburb. Suburb blurs with rural areas. Every place is coming to look like every place else.

Today's drive in the country rewards us with endless vistas of mammoth billboards and flashing signs. Drink this! Smoke that! Eat here! Fly there! The proclamations combine to obliterate our scenery.

Our distinctive rural landscapes are rapidly disappearing. In some places—like East Tennessee and Western North Carolina—the clutter is so bad, you literally can't see the mountains for all the billboards. Likewise, in many country towns the tallest structures are no longer steeples or silos but towering signs—many ten stories high. The day is fast approaching when the unspoiled American landscape will endure—like an endangered species—only in national parks and preserves.

Government must act to protect a vital but rapidly vanishing part of our heritage—unspoiled roadside America.

Like it or not our perception of America is sharply influenced by where autos can go. We see relatively little of anyplace on foot. The vast majority of all Americans will never raft a wild river or hike through an unspoiled wilderness.

America the Beautiful for most people today is what they can see from our streets and highways. Moreover, numerous surveys indicate that driving for recreation is one of America's leading forms of outdoor recreation. Millions of tourists, day trippers, and recreational drivers want to get away from the boredom and blight all too common along our primary and interstate highways. Instead, they seek unspoiled scenery and unobliterated architecture. They want to visit historic sites, stop and relax at parks and picnic areas, and see farmland and forests not truckstops and billboards.

The need for scenic highways is easily documented. Nearly half (43%) of all Americans drive for pleasure according to the 1986 Market and Opinion Research (MOR) Survey conducted by the President's Commission on Americans Outdoors. Pleasure driving to view historic, natural or pastoral sites comprises some 15% of all vehicle miles driven. Indeed the President's Commission on Americans Outdoors found that "driving for pleasure" was the 2nd most popular form of outdoor recreation ranking behind only "walking for pleasure." "Sightseeing," another form of outdoor recreation which typically involves driving, ranked third.

Last year, the Blue Ridge Parkway was America's most visited national park. In 1986, over 19 million people drove on the parkway—a road for travelers who want unspoiled scenery and spectacular vistas—a road without billboards, truckstops, or commercial clutter.

The Natchez Trace Parkway (another scenic highway) ranked third among U.S. parks with over 13 million visitors. Likewise the annual pilgrimage of millions to Vermont's Route 100 or California's State Route 1 and the popularity of books like Blue Highways indicate that Americans yearn to explore unspoiled scenic highways.

By setting up a national system of scenic roads and highways, America can preserve an important but rapidly vanishing part of our heritage. Doing so will also fill a massive gap in natural resource protection policy while at the same time meeting one of the major unmet needs of Americans outdoors.

In her book Country Adventures, Elizabeth Mooney writes of "country roads, innocent of stop signs, billboards, 18 wheel trucks and the attention of road graders. We should be collecting them like diamonds, because they're not making any more of them. They're a last inheritance from the people who came before us and they lead to places that soothe the souls of city folks. They are our compensation for rush hour traffic."

IMPLEMENTATION

Setting up a national system of scenic roads and highways would be relatively simple. The Parkway system could be designated by using existing secondary (primarily two-lane) roads. Designated routes would take advantage of little used secondary roads and would travel through scenic, historic, geologic, and pastoral areas of the nation. Routes would be designated to offer alternative travel routes to high speed, heavily traveled, commercialized highways.

To ensure that all areas of the country are represented in the system, designated routes should be outlined as part of a nationwide scenic routes plan. Unlike traditional national parks which require massive outlays of funds and fee simple ownership of large tracts of land, the scenic highways would depend on low cost land protection measures such as scenic easements and prohibitions against outdoor advertising.

Whenever a road or highway is designated as part of the system, regulations would apply to protect the view from the road. Billboards, junkyards, strip mines, and other inappropriate uses would be prohibited or simply screened from view. Scenic easements and private land trusts could be used to protect important features of the built or natural environment. However, except for the occasional development of roadside parks and picnic areas, little land acquisition would be required.

To establish, maintain and enhance the system of scenic roads Congress could rely on existing highway funding sources. Alternatively, however, it could enact a highway user fee of $250 - $500 per year on each of the over 500,000 billboards which now line our federal interstate and primary highways. This money could be placed in a "beautification superfund" which would be used to maintain and enhance the scenic highways system. The money could pay for roadside landscaping, scenic easements, wayside parks, bike paths, historic sites, etc.

Currently billboards are the only "user" of the federal highways which pay no road user taxes, tolls, or fees. In this regard it is important to recognize that billboards derive no value from the private land they stand on but from the public roads they stand next to. To understand this principle simply imagine leaving every billboard in America standing exactly where it is but turn it around so that it cannot be viewed from the road. The structure immediately loses all value. Since the 1930's courts have recognized this as the "parasite principle." One court put it this way: "Billboards are parasitic use, living off a public investment, without rendering a public service."

Billboards are now flourishing along our federal interstate and primary system. There is no reason why they shouldn't be charged for their use of our highways. A road user tax on billboards can generate needed revenue while helping to enhance and restore the visual integrity of our landscape along the scenic highway system.

ADVANTAGES

A system of scenic roads and highways would have many advantages. It will preserve a rapidly vanishing part of America's heritage. It will meet the recreational needs of the vast majority of Americans who have little access to traditional national parks and wilderness areas and it will return economic vitality to distressed rural areas through promotion of tourism.

As tourists Americans collectively spend billions of dollars seeking unspoiled natural beauty and unblemished historic character. Indeed our scenic heritage is one of our greatest economic as well as physical assets. States like Maine, Vermont, Hawaii, Oregon and Washington have recognized that preserving scenic beauty pays. Establishing a national system of scenic highways will maximize the potential of little used and bypassed sections of highway and will bring tourists into depressed areas along the designated routes.

Perhaps most importantly there is a special need to protect rural communities and landscapes that have unique and complex ecological, cultural and historic qualities and a definable sense of place. Yet to date, roadside America has been ignored as a natural and economic resource worth preserving and enhancing.

Americans have always drawn strength and inspiration from the beauty of our country. America's greatest leaders—from Thomas Jefferson to Teddy Roosevelt to Lady Bird Johnson—have all recognized that when we degrade America's beauty we diminish the American spirit. For Americans today America the Beautiful is what they see out the window of a car. Unless we want our children and grandchildren to grow up in a blighted, homogenized world of endless clutter we must act now to protect what's left of our roadside heritage.

"LINVILLE AREA, BLUE RIDGE PARKWAY" JOHN SCARLATA

V. Management

John Scarlata is a professor of photography at Virginia Intermont College. He resides in North Carolina near the Parkway. John, who works with large-format cameras, helps us perceive the essence of what we look at. Here, his cameras have been turned toward the Parkway.
—Gilbert W. Leebrick

Accident Analysis as a Decision Tool in Rehabilitating Park Roads

Richard G. Wasill, P.E., Project Development Engineer

BACKGROUND

In 1986, the Western Direct Federal Division (WDFD) of FHWA was requested by the National Park Service (NPS) to design and construct an 18 mile resurfacing project in Mt. Rainier National Park from the Nisqually entrance to the Paradise visitors complex. This project was programmed for minor widening to attain a uniform 24 foot width, to make minor drainage corrections, and to make several spot safety improvements along the route under a RRR concept. Our design procedures require the identification of any exceptions to full standards which, in this case, consist of the NPS Park Road Standards adopted in 1984. The park road standards for this route warrant a 35 mph design speed with a 28 foot paved top width for the estimated 1,700 ADT. The maximum regulatory speed is posted at 35 mph. By way of comparison, AASHTO Recreational Road Standards would require a roadway width of 26 to 32 feet.

The original construction of the Nisqually Entrance Road was completed in the late 1920s and predated current engineering standards with regard to roadway design. The proposed resurfacing with minor widening precluded substantial alignment correction. A comparison of design exceptions for this resurfacing project (see Figure 1, Highway Design Standards Checklist) indicates approximately 90 curves on the 18 mile route which do not meet the horizontal criteria for 35 mph. In addition, approximately 20 percent of the curvature exceeds the maximum superelevation rates, and approximately 40 percent of all curves do not provide adequate superelevation runoff. The proposed RRR widening to 24 feet results in substandard shoulder width throughout the length of the project.

Due to the substantial numbers of exceptions and potential for associated risks, a comprehensive accident analysis was performed on an interagency basis to ensure that the proposed work properly addressed areas where safety enhancement should be incorporated into the project. This paper provides a brief summary of that comprehensive report dated August 1986.

INTRODUCTION

There have been occasional differences of opinion with regard to the interpretation of the National Park Service standards. A frequent NPS position is that the 1984 NPS standards are considered as guidelines only. FHWA's position and policy are that these provide both guidance and standards, particularly the latter where minimum numerical values are used. Notwithstanding this difference of opinion, there are provisions for discretionary action in the adoption of exceptions, provided those exceptions are made through conscientious and rational addressing of the local situation and circumstances. FHWA's responsibilities as design experts are to insure that those exceptions to standards are identified so that they can be properly considered in making the ultimate management decisions on the improvement.

In late July, an accident analysis was performed for this route by FHWA and NPS personnel. This analysis consisted of a review of accident reports collected from the files of the Mount Rainier National Park as well as a field review of the route to evaluate accident locations and/or potential design inconsistencies from an engineering viewpoint.

ACCIDENT HISTORY ANALYSIS

Since the park rangers are the enforcement authority, Mount Rainier National Park, like most parks, maintains a wealth of accident information. Unfortunately, some of the problems which plague other agencies are common to the NPS system; namely, ease of information retrieval and identification of specific highway

Federal Highway Administration Western Direct Federal Division

Highway Design Standards

Project Number: MORA 14-1(1)

Project Name: Nisqually-Paradise

Location: Mt. Rainier National Park

Type of Project: __ New Construction __ Reconstruction ✓ RRR

Description of Work: Minor grading, minor base, and bituminous pavement.

System:
- __ Federal-aid Primary
- __ Federal-aid Secondary
- __ Off System (Co. Road)
- __ Other:
- ✓ National Park Service
- __ Forest Service
- __ Bureau of Land Management

Functional Classification: Primary Park Road

Traffic	Year	ADT			Percent Trucks		D
		Average	Seasonal	DHV	DHV	ADT	
Current			1,700 seasonally adjusted				
Future			unknown, not projected				

Terrain: Mountainous Design Speed: 35 mph with exceptions

Posted or Regulatory Speed Limit: 35 mph with posted 20-25 mph areas

Geometric and Bridge Criteria	Standard	As Designed	Exception
Horizontal Curvature	15° maximum	80° maximum	90± curves
Superelevation	0.08	0.10	20%
Superelevation Runoff	AASHTO 1984	60%	40%
Crown	0.02	0.02	None
Gradient	13% maximum	7% maximum	None
Stopping Sight Distance	225'	Approx. 225'	Trees may limit sight distance
Travel Way Width	11-12'	11'	None
Shoulder Width	3	1±	All
Horizontal Clearance	N/A		
Vertical Clearance	N/A		
Bridge Width	N/A		
Bridge Loading	N/A		
Clear Zones/Guardrail/Br. Rail	12' minimum	1.0' minimum	Nearly full length

Reasons and descriptions of exceptions to standards including analysis of associated risks:

See attached sheets. Due to the significant number of exceptions, WDFD performed an Accident Analysis (See August 1986 report).

A meeting was held on 8/27/86 with FHWA and NPS personnel to review proposed work—see minutes.

Design considerations proposed to mitigate exceptions:

Redude excessive super elevation to 0.10 max. Add curve widening. Performed "speed" study using ball-bank indicator to ascertain appropriate warning signs. Final surface to be open graded friction course using AC-20R. Guardrail not warranted based on the accident analysis. Intersection improvement at Upper Ricksacker. Signt distance improvement at Kautz Creek area.

Fig. 1. Highway Design Standards Checklist

locations. (The NPS is currently developing a Service Wide Traffic Accident Reporting System, STARS, which is scheduled to be implemented in 1987 and is intended to correct these deficiencies.)

Mount Rainier National Park (MORA) provided the review team with a "spot" map showing general accident locations and type covering 1979 through 1985. Individual accident reports were available for the most recent 3 years of record. A detailed review of individual accident reports for 1985 and 1984 was made with the various factors summarized and subsequently grouped for statistical comparison. Figure 2 shows a summary for the most recent 2 years of record with the types of occurrences expressed as a percentage and compared to two published statistics: the National Safety Council, 1983, statistics for all Rural Roadway Accidents with Property Damage greater than $250; and US Route 12 in Idaho, a narrow two-lane road with similar topography also with property damage greater than $250.

Comparison of the data needs to be made with caution due to obvious differences in the routes and type of information collected. For instance, the NPS reports all accidents, regardless of how minor, so long as they are aware of them while each of the comparable statistics exclude property damage of less than $250. Also, the low speed of the road investigated is not necessarily comparable to the range of speeds included in both the NSC and US 12 data. Nevertheless, by comparing the "norms" one can begin to appreciate the types of safety deficiencies prevalent along the route.

Some of the more interesting observations are summarized as follows:

1. Thirty percent of the 1984-85 accidents were run-off-the-road type accidents resulting in collisions with embankments, backslopes, trees, walls, and signs. This is lower statistically, however, than the National Safety Council average rate of 43 percent for all rural roads. Of greater significance are the cumulative rates of 12.5 percent sideswipe meetings (vs. 5.8 percent NSC); head-ons 11.3 percent (vs. 5.2 percent*); rear-ends 8.8 percent (vs. 7.4 percent NSC); parked vehicle (in or near roadway) 7.5 percent (vs. 2.7 percent to 3.8 percent), which individually and cumulatively are indicative of a narrow roadway problem. (*164 miles Idaho Route 12, two-lane rural mountainous—12 percent trucks)
2. A figure of 42.5 percent of the 1984-85 accidents occurred on snow or ice with 13.8 percent on wet pavements and 43.8 percent on dry pavements. The winter rates are substantially higher than the NSC ice/snow rate of 14.5 percent; however, this is not necessarily inconsistent with other all-season mountainous roads at high altitudes. The high snow/ice rate appears related to excess superelevations and narrow roadway.
3. The majority of accidents (87.5 percent) were Property Damage Only (PDO) with statistically low injury rates primarily attributed to the low speed character of the roadway.
4. Speeding and alcohol were just slightly above the norm.
5. Extremely significant is the statistic that 87.5 percent of the 1984-85 accidents involved a downhill grade (contributor to excess speed) and/or a horizontal curve (excessive superelevation, snow, ice, sideswipes, and head-ons).
6. A figure of 6.3 percent of the total accidents and 17 percent of the run-off-the-road accidents involved tree hits.
7. In general, increasing traffic is synonymous with increasing accidents although exceptions have been noted (Ref. 3). The following table compares total accidents for 1983, 1984, and 1985 with typical monthly park visitation statistics and shows that accident rates were highest during low-volume periods.

MORA 14
Mt. Rainier National Park
Nisqually-Paradise Road
1984 - 1985

	Rate	Percent	NSC* US 12, Idaho**
Accident Type:			
Run-Off-Road (embk, tree, wall, sign)	24/80	30.0	43.0*
Sideswipe Meeting (0% passing)	10/80	12.5	5.8*
Overturn (includes some RDR)	10/80	12.5	12.6*
Head-On	9/80	11.3	5.2**
Rear-Ends	7/80	8.8	7.4**
Parked Vehicle (in or near roadway)	6/80	7.5	2.7-3.8*
Hit Tree	5/80	6.3	2 ±*
Avoid Deer	3/80	3.8	0.8*
Angle	2/80	2.5	2.2**
Turning	1/80	1.2	7.4**
Road Surface:			
Wet	11/80	13.8	19.8*
Dry	35/80	43.8	62.8**
Snow/Ice	34/80	42.5	14.5*
Light Conditions:			
Day	55/80	68.8	63.3**
Night	17/80	21.3	30.9*
Dawn/Dusk	7/80	8.8	5.3**
Injury Type:			
Fatal	0/80	0	2.4**
Injury	10/80	12.5	47.3**
Property Damage Only	70/80	87.5	
Other Contributing Factors:			
Single Vehicle	46/80	57.5	
Multiple Vehicles	34/80	42.5	
Speed	24/80	30.0	28.1*
Alcohol	13/80	16.3	11.0**
Down Hill/Horizontal Curve	70/80	87.5	

Accidents/Mile/Year = 80/18.5/2 = 2.1

*National Safety Council 1983 statistics—All accidents rural roadways: Property Damage Only>$250

**US 12, Idaho, rural two-lane, narrow road with 14 percent trucks on 164 miles: Property Damage Only>$250

Fig.2. MORA summary of accidents.

Month	Total Accidents 1983-1985	Typical Monthly Visitation(1985)
January	21	30,598
February	28	28,137
March	4	35,637
April	5	38,089
May	9	90,737
June	8	232,048
July	16	368,801
August	22	402,336
September	15	225,289
October	10	118,959
November	13	44,809
December	23	?

FIELD OPERATIONAL SAFETY REVIEW

Having developed a "feel" for the types of accidents and armed with the "spot" map, the second part of the accident analysis included a field review for the specific purpose of viewing the various accident locations and identifying roadway design inconsistencies and comparing them to the types of accidents just recorded.

Many of the accident locations involved extremely sharp curvature in areas of tight terrain, and corrective action would require substantial costs to improve alignment, which was clearly outside the scope of this RRR project. The majority of these accidents were attributed to excessive speed for the local situations due to the reduced curvature. Again, correction of some of these major areas was clearly beyond the intended scope of the program funding; however, correction of superelevation will be made and curve widening added where feasible. Monitoring of these locations will be performed with a view toward future spot safety improvements. During the field review, several areas were identified as having a high potential for corrective action at minimal cost. Corrections of these areas posed very little if any environmental impacts with regard to those covered in the Environmental Assessment.

KAUTZ CREEK EXHIBIT AREA

The Kautz Creek Exhibit Area is characterized by a set of reversing horizontal curves partially hidden by a combination of crest and sag vertical curves. Accidents in this general area showed a significant number of vehicles losing control even in good weather, and almost all involved the horizontal curvature in combination with this "hidden" alignment. A warning sign is indicative of a problem in this area and the site was proposed by FHWA for corrective action. A culvert currently at the crest of the vertical curve is slated for replacement and will entail regrading the roadway in this area. FHWA has proposed lowering the crest vertical curve by approximately 2 feet and raising the sag vertical curve approximately 3 feet, with virtually no change in the curvilinear alignment through this area and little or no impact on the environmental vegetation. The cost to correct this sight distance problem is clearly insignificant with regard to the planned expenditures, and agreement was reached to include correction in the project.

CHRISTINE FALLS ROCK OUTCROP

A rock outcrop at the Christine Falls area showed visual evidence of scarring. Of concern here was the fact that traffic in this tight area tends to shy away from the rock and cross the centerline as evidenced by the wear on the centerline stripe and as further evidenced by observation of traffic in the area. Analysis of accidents typify downhill-horizontal curve involvement and several run-off-the-road accidents hitting the ditch and rock backslope. While the accidents did not indicate hits of this particular rock, there was concern that the location of the uphill bridge parapet could inadvertently lead a motorist head-on into the rock, which encroaches approximately 2 feet beyond the rock wall. Obviously, removal of this rock has caused some concern to the park with regard to protection of the existing structure and effects on closure of the road. Agreement was reached to remove this rock outcrop with expansive chemicals under controlled conditions.

LOWER MILLER INTERSECTION

Analysis of the types of accidents occurring at the Lower Miller Intersection again indicated significant downhill horizontal involvement.

Of specific concern was a gap in the existing guide walls for a length of approximately 335 feet which originally was proposed by FHWA to be closed with guardrail and which the park has requested to be closed with matching guide wall. FHWA agreed to close this with matching guide wall, recognizing the serious consequences should a vehicle miss the curve and go off the road in this area. While this is not necessarily considered a crash worthy facility from the standpoint of normal highway safety appurtenances, it is recognized that speeds are low in this area and that the intent is to match the existing wall structure and provide continuity and park aesthetics through the area.

UPPER MILLER INTERSECTION

The Upper Miller Intersection had very poor geometrics. This resulted from the fact that the approach road used to be the main park road and had become an approach road with an extremely obtuse angle to the relocated main park road. At the time the relocated park road was constructed, a proper intersection was not provided. Reverse superelevation was also present on the mainline.

Curvature on the main park road immediately preceding the intersection placed traffic in a "blind spot" to the approaching intersection traffic. During our brief observation of this location, a near-accident occurred when a motorist inadvertently thought no traffic was coming and as he pulled out, there was a vehicle which had been in the blind spot causing evasive action to be taken by both vehicles. Although no accidents were indicated at this area for 1984-85 and only eight accidents had been identified since 1979, this was an obvious type engineering corrective action that could be corrected with minimal additional expenditure. The change in use of the two roadways should give major emphasis to the main park road and relegate the one-way approach to a minor status approach at a right angle. This involved a minor relocation and the removal of several very small trees which obstruct sight distance at this location.

ROADSIDE SAFETY

Much of the roadside along this 18 mile route is characterized by the close proximity of native fir and hemlock trees, many of which were never cleared during original construction. They serve to lend character and confinement to the corridor and in some instances restrict sight distance. Their awesome presence probably accounts for greater shy distance from the shoulder, contributing to a higher than normal on-road, head-on, and sideswipe type accidents. New construction standards for this class of road and this traffic volume would generally require a minimum of 12 foot clear roadside area to enable an errant motorist to safely recover control of a vehicle. This has been an area of concern throughout the project programming and development stage. This amount of clearing would be inappropriate for this project based on environmental concerns and to some degree verified by accident analysis.

A number of these trees exhibited "bumper disease," some of which were documented vehicle hits and others were suspected as being maintenance snowplow scuffings. The removal of these trees became an extremely sensitive environmental issue and although the preferred alternative in the Environmental Assessment clearly indicated removal of approximately 90 trees, the final FONSI issued by the National Park Service compromised by indicating a maximum of 20 trees to be removed. Numerous field reviews were made to individually prioritize those trees for removal.

GUARDRAIL

Guardrail, unlike other design areas, falls into the guideline category as opposed to standards. At present there is no guardrail on the entire 18 mile route with the exception of the few guide walls as previously discussed. Design procedures utilized by the Western Division to supplement NPS standards follow the AASHTO guidelines which permit cost effective analysis with regards to the installation of guardrail. The typical cost analysis curves, however, are based on high speed facilities which clearly were not appropriate in this instance. Predicted collision frequencies were ten times those actually encountered in this accident analysis.

Based on the accident analysis and severity, it was not cost effective to install guardrail throughout this project at this time. Guide wall will be installed at the Lower Miller intersection due to the potential hazard at that location. This analysis was unable to identify any specific "high accident" locations which would warrant guardrail at this time. MORA should continue to reevaluate the locations of run-off-the-road accidents to assess the need for guardrail.

ROADWAY WIDTH

The analysis of accidents from Exhibit 2 are indicative of narrow roadway conditions and inadequate shoulder widths. Improving roadway width from 22 feet to 24 feet is estimated to cost $160,000/mile and should reduce total accidents by 9 percent (Ref. 3). Improving the roadway width from 22 feet to full standard 30 feet is estimated to cost in excess of $1,000,000/mile and would be expected to reduce accidents by 21 percent. The proposed RRR project will preserve and extend the service life of the roadway structure and address a significant portion of the total accident reduction potential. The NPS program decision to treat this project as a RRR project rather than upgrade to full NPS standards is clearly defensible. Curve widening will be added whenever possible.

SPEED STUDY

Further analysis of the project also revealed many of the horizontal curves had superelevations well in excess of normal maximums, and in many cases, approaching 16 percent. The proposed project will correct these superelevations to a maximum of 10 percent. Under present design procedures the maximum superelevation would be limited to 8 percent. Correction of the superelevations to a maximum 10 percent presents concern from the standpoint that the flatter superelevation will necessitate lower driving speeds during dry weather. The flattening of these superelevations, however, should reduce the types of on-roadway accidents attributable to the excessive superelevations during ice and snow conditions. In order to fully evaluate the significance of the proposed changes in superelevations with little or no change in alignments, FHWA performed a speed survey using a ball bank indicator to document existing safe running speeds as well as existing advisory and posted speed limit criteria. A listing of recommended signs was included in the project. Upon completion of construction, we will again run a speed study to make final recommendations for posting those areas where restricted speeds are warranted.

RESURFACING

The surfacing selected for this project was an Open Graded Asphaltic Friction Course. This material was selected for a variety of reasons. Structural improvement was not generally required and, therefore, minimal thickness was indicated. OGAFC is designed to be placed in a 3/4 inch lift. This thin lift also permits a wider roadway section for a given subgrade (or existing surface) width. Since all materials must be obtained from outside the park, the reduced quantities minimize haul costs and damage. This type material is also noted for its improved "wet weather" skid characteristics and its resistance to reflective cracking. Enhancing the characteristics of OGAFC by using asphalt fortified with rubber was recommended to improve the toughness and tenacity of the wearing course in this elevated environment, and to hopefully improve some of the snow and ice "benefits" reported in past evaluations of OGAFC. OGAFC surfaces typically retain a "darker" color and promote faster surface thawing of snow and ice.

SUMMARY

An accident analysis was performed on a proposed RRR project to ensure that appropriate safety enhancements were incorporated into the project. The analysis consisted of a detailed review of accident records covering a 2 year period as well as a field review to identify potentially hazardous areas. The analysis when coupled with identified exceptions to NPS standards served to support various safety enhancements and mitigations for remaining exceptions.

Accident costs clearly demonstrated the appropriateness of a minimal widening RRR overlay project in lieu of total reconstruction to full NPS standards.

Analysis of accident injury rates and severity on this low speed facility confirmed that application of "cost effective" barrier warrants were inappropriate for this facility since the data used to develop the warrants had been based on "high speed" facilities.

Accident analysis indicated significant accident characteristics including snow and ice conditions, downhill, horizontal curvature, excessive speed, and excessive superelevation. Speed studies with a "ball bank indicator" were used to identify improper curve speed postings, and after proposed milling, leveling and overlaying of the pavement surface, will be used to ensure proper posting and sign locations.

Special surfacing material was selected for durability and improved frictional characteristics.

All agencies face limited funding with regard to rehabilitating and maintaining their facilities and not all facilities can be brought to full standards. Exceptions to these standards need to be fully addressed to ensure that appropriate consideration is given to highway safety. Accident analysis is one method to ensure appropriate attention is given.

BIBLIOGRAPHY

1. "Park Road Standards," National Park Service, 1984
2. "Highway Safety Engineering Studies—Procedural Guide," FHWA TS-81-220, November 1981
3. "Technical Note No. 2—Accident-Width Relations for Single-Carriageway Rural Highways," J. R. McLean, Australian Road Research Board
4. "Guide for Selecting, Locating, and Designing Traffic Barriers," AASHTO, 1977
5. "Environmental Assessment of Nisqually-Paradise and Stevens Canyon Roads," Mount Rainier National Park, February 1986
6. "Finding of No Significant Impact" (FONSI), Mount Rainier National Park, Package 344B, Approved 5/30/86

The Art and Craft of Managing a National Parkway

Granville Liles

The completion of the "missing link" at Grandfather Mountain is certainly one of the most significant events in the history of the Blue Ridge Parkway. However, it is not as if suddenly the gates were opened for the first visitors, since the Parkway has been enjoyed by millions of visitors for the past fifty years.

The purpose of this paper is to discuss some of the highlights of the Parkway's history, and generally explain the development of policies and techniques that originated on the Blue Ridge. This statement also deals briefly with the six superintendents who have been responsible for its management. The Parkway could very well serve as a mirror of our society, reflecting the Great Depression, war, peace, recovery, the influence of politics, and the phenomenal increase of leisure in America.

When we consider the beginning years, it is also significant that the Blue Ridge was the first rural parkway in the world. At the time the parkway was proposed, it was so politically motivated that it was under construction before Congress finally got around to passing legislation in 1936 that officially designated it as the Blue Ridge Parkway.[1] The concept of a parkway connecting two existing national parks was approved by President Roosevelt in 1933. Most important is that the Secretary of the Interior assigned its management to the National Park Service.[2] Up to that time, that agency had been primarily responsible for the western parks, a steward of the frontier landscape.

A major departure from the traditional personnel policy of the National Park Service occurred in 1933 when the Director went outside the circle of career employees and appointed Stanley W. Abbott to be in charge of this new project. Abbott was a trained landscape architect with special experience on the Westchester County parks program of New York. Though still a young man, Abbott impressed someone that he had the talent and vision to do the job. He surrounded himself with other talented professionals, and in spite of the network of agencies involved, enabled construction to begin in September 1935 at the North Carolina state line.

Abbott and his staff did not have a handbook on policies, or written guidelines on standards, as are available today. Consequently, progress was often by trial and error. Since there was no precedent for a project of this type or scale, Abbott and his associates seized the opportunity to experiment with new concepts in location, design, architecture and cooperative land use. In the early years, these techniques and policies may have at times appeared experimental, but through the years many of them have survived the test of time and now serve as models worldwide.

When the idea of this parkway emerged in the thirties, the National Park Service had been established less than twenty years earlier in 1916. Nevertheless, this young land-managing agency was highly regarded and the career employees were considered among the best in the Government service. The esprit de corps and high morale had always been attributed to its first Director, Steve Mather.[3] When Mr. Mather stepped aside because of poor health in 1929, Horace Albright, his assistant, became the Director and served until 1933.

By the time the parkway concept was approved in 1933, the Service had its third Director, Arno B. Cammerer. He was a Matherman, and a trained landscape architect. Shortly after Cammerer became Director, the proposed parkway to connect the two national parks was approved.

The challenge that Abbott and his staff faced required flexibility of action, while on the other hand they had to work within the emerging framework of Park Service policy and legislated authorities. Recognizing the complexity of parkway management today we should not forget the unforeseen situations that faced the early planners and managers in designing and building a rural parkway of this magnitude. Foremost at the time was the issue of the right-of-way, comprising those lands which the States agreed to acquire on which the parkway was to be built. In the fall of 1934, the Bureau of Public Roads was designated as the agency to negotiate with the States for the required lands. The Bureau first proposed a uniform strip 100 feet on either side of the road center line The planners vigorously objected to such a limited right-of-way and convinced the Bureau engineers that it should contain at least 100 acres per mile, with an additional 50 acres per mile in scenic easement. The States wrongly assumed that the landowners would donate the lands for the parkway, and the local landowners were misled into thinking that they would have free access to this new "scenic" road, as they called it. After much negotiating, North Carolina did get legislation through the General Assembly in 1937 to acquire 125 acres per mile in fee simple. Virginia never officially accepted the 100 acres per mile requested, but did go along with acquiring a right-of-way between 400 and 800 feet in width. In North Carolina, before transferring the land to the Service, the State would include in the deeds reservations for private roads and other rights to the individual. In Virginia, the generosity of the State in giving private access rights prompted the Secretary of the Interior to issue an order in 1938 that there would be no more private roads connecting with or crossing the parkway motor road at grade.[4] There were so many private road crossings reserved, that years later the Parkway staff is still struggling with plans that will provide access to public roads via other locations and eliminate crossings at grade.

Parkway officials have always had as a goal a right-of-way that approximates 125 acres per mile, which is an average width of 1,000 feet. The width may vary so long as the average acreage is acquired. A parkway without an adequate right-of-way, or other land use control, will eventually lose its beauty and purpose and will be little more than an ordinary highway.

To give you a general idea of the acreage included in the right-of-way, Virginia has donated something like 15,000 acres and North Carolina has donated some 22,000 acres. These 37,000 acres comprise about 51 percent of the lands within the initial right-of-way. Approximately 29,000 acres have been transferred from the national forests in the two States, making a grand total of 66,000 acres. A little calculation and you can see that this exceeds the 125 acres per mile. What has really added greatly to the beauty and usefulness of the Parkway has been the private donations at Cone Park, Price Park and Linville Falls.

An important element in the 1936 Parkway Act was the provision that the Park Service and Forest Service were to coordinate their planning efforts for recreational facilities along the route where the parkway traversed lands of that agency, totaling some 180 miles. The location of the parkway through the National Forest has given it a wilderness character in many places. While competition between these two agencies dates back to Mather and Chief Forester Pinchot, the relationship on the Blue Ridge Parkway has been quite friendly through the years. Each agency appears to respect the policies of the other agency and the Parkway provides a setting for the public to see an excellent example of cooperation in land use planning and management.

Any account of the building of the Parkway would be grossly incomplete if it did not include the contribution of the Bureau of Public Roads (now the Federal Highway Administration). The participation of that agency goes back to the Twenties, when Director Mather entered into an agreement for its expert assistance in road design and construction in some of the western parks. In 1933, when the Secretary of the Interior designated the National Park Service as the Federal agency to be in charge of the Blue Ridge, he also requested that the Bureau of Public Roads assist in the design and construction. Ed Abbuehl, a key figure in the early planning and a right-hand man to Abbott, wrote an unpublished history of the Blue Ridge in 1948 and was very complementary of the assistance and cooperation of that agency. Abbuehl said, and I quote: "This project is the product of very close cooperation between the Public Roads Administration and the National Park Service. The two Roanoke offices were given great latitude and freedom in their work and were backed up 100 percent by their respective Washington offices."

Much of the land from Shenandoah National Park in Virginia to the Great Smokies in North Carolina had been subjected to such excruciating land use as subsistence farming and logging in a country of steep hillsides and thin acid soil. The land also reflected the damage from field and forest fires that swept across the mountains each spring. Abbott and his staff set about with plans to restore the land, preserve the local culture, and give the parkway some management directions that would survive for the next half century.

In 1937, Resident Landscape Architect Abbott devised a unique method of communicating with the neighbors. He issued a "News" letter, advising them that it would be published periodically and would be placed in the local stores, post offices, and other convenient places.[5] He promised to keep them informed about issues of interest, such as construction progress. For example, his first issue announced that 100 miles of the scenic Parkway could now be driven in the two States. He also informed the people that a major landscaping program would soon begin, and that he was considering leasing back the farm lands in the right-of-way to the former owners. The "News" turned out to be a marvelous public relations gesture. This message was needed to reassure the mountain people that the Government meant well, that the Parkway people were building something of beauty. To leaf through the 53 issues of the "News" published between November 1937 and April 1943 is to clearly see the evolution of policy and decisions, ranging from the prohibition of commercial vehicles, to a request to prevent forest fire, to a progress report of construction.

Fifty years ago this fall, Abbott announced that he wanted to "preserve the farm scene of grain, crops, orchards and pastures." The policy to lease back to them the agricultural lands, share responsibility in a lands improvement program, and restore the picturesque farm scene began then. This program has been faithfully continued by succeeding managers. By 1945, a more intensive program was inaugurated to make the parkway an example of good land stewardship. This included leasing back all lands suitable for farm purposes and the restoration of eroded fields. Lands not suitable for agriculture were allowed to return to forest. The result today is a mosaic of farms and forest, pasture and meadows of wild flowers. The Park Service rescued a perishable and shrinking resource, and to have seen the Southern Appalachians then, as I did, and to see it now is a dramatic experience.

My first assignment on the Blue Ridge began in early 1938, when appointed a landscape technician with the Bureau of Public Roads in North Carolina. A major landscaping program had been inaugurated that year in both states where the construction had been completed. Local workers were recruited from the unemployment rolls at 25 cents per hour. With some 200 men, we began the repair of the land from construction scars, planting trees and shrubs, and a general restoration of the landscape.

The first professional rangers were appointed in 1938 to provide protection for this new parkway. It was during my work as a landscape technician that I became intrigued with the duties of a ranger. I applied to Assistant Superintendent Weems for a ranger post, and subsequently got the job. My first assignment was the district from Grandfather Mountain to near Mt. Mitchell. The early rangers served as the eyes and ears of the Superintendent, and it was their duty to protect the resources, enforce the regulations, and educate the local people about this new parkway. Under the watchful eyes of Abbott and Weems, we learned some fundamental lessons in public relations, hard work, and resource management that served us well in long and useful careers.

Abbott announced in 1942 plans to preserve historic buildings such as Mabry Mill, the Trail Cabin, Puckett Home, and the Brinegar Cabin.[5] These were remnants of a fast disappearing Appalachian heritage in architecture. Because of that initiative, other buildings have been added to the list of structures on the preservation program such as the James River locks, the farmstead at Humpback Rocks, the Johnson Farm at the Peaks and others. These add greatly to the historic and cultural story of the region.

During the early years, a unique sign system was designed and perfected on the Blue Ridge that included the distinctive Parkway logo. This logo remains the dominant symbol of the area—a windswept white pine against a big blue sky and mountain peak with a road threading between, all in a circle of blue. The Parkway sign shop for years has manufactured informational and interpretive signs for park use nationwide, and for this alone the Parkway achieved considerable fame.

Mr. Abbott served as Acting Superintendent until 1944, when he elected to devote full time to the duties of Resident Landscape Architect. Sam Weems had been operations officer for several years with the title of Assistant Superintendent and was elevated to the Superintendent's position. This was a logical choice since Mr. Weems was thoroughly familiar with the parkway. He served with distinction from 1944 through 1966 as Superintendent. The Abbott-Weems era spanned more than thirty years and during this period more than 460 miles of the motor road was completed.

We have mentioned earlier the problems that have plagued all Blue Ridge managers because of the generosity of the states in reserving private roads that crossed the motor road at grade. Recognizing this threat to the safety of the visitors, as well as the visual impact, the Service sought Congressional authority to permit the purchase of such reserved rights. Congress passed legislation in 1961 authorizing the purchase of lands and rights, as well as the authority to exchange lands where the landowner and government would jointly benefit.[6] Many such crossings have been eliminated in the past twenty-five years by quitclaim deed where it was feasible to relocate access to a public road across Parkway lands. To better understand the severity of this situation, consider that at one time there were 350 public road easements on the 470 miles, plus some 475 private road easements. Since passage of the legislation in 1961 many of these have been extinguished to achieve a safer and more attractive parkway.[7] Present management is certainly aware of the handicap it suffers in controlling the situation.

In the mid-Forties, Weems realized that the regulation prohibiting hunting had created public relations problems among the local people, as well as the Forest Service and Fish and Game Commissions. Hunting was an old mountain custom, and the Parkway had completely disrupted this sport. After negotiations with these agencies, an arrangement was worked out to issue permits to hunters, allowing them to park in certain overlooks along the Parkway and walk to the hunting grounds on public lands open to hunting. This has greatly improved relations with all concerned, but is an example of policy development that accommodated an old mountain custom without compromising the law. Unfortunately, it was not possible to work out a suitable arrangement to allow the manufacture of illegal "moonshine."

Following the war years, the national parks faced severe problems of overuse, lack of maintenance and worn-out facilities. The Blue Ridge was no exception and the situation was compounded by the urgent need for construction funds. Conrad Wirth, who had become Director in 1951, proposed a massive improvement program for the parks to be achieved between 1956 and 1966, the Golden Anniversary of the National Park Service. Congress and the President supported the program which ultimately gave the parks more than one billion dollars to achieve the goal nationwide. The Blue Ridge Parkway became a principal beneficiary of this imaginative concept.

With funds available from Mission 66, the National Park Service and the Federal Highway Administration moved vigorously ahead to complete the Parkway motor road. By the end of 1967, thirty-two years after construction began, more than 460 miles were completed and opened to the public. Only the 7 1/2 miles around Grandfather Mountain remained unfinished.

I should mention here some special achievements during the Weems era. In 1948, the Moses Cone Memorial Hospital in Greensboro, North Carolina deeded an estate of some 3,500 acres to the Parkway, including the Flat Top Manor, the impressive summer home of the Cone family. In addition, the Cone Foundation contributes $10,000 annually towards its maintenance. In 1949, the Jefferson Standard Life Insurance Company of Greensboro also donated to the Park Service a 3,900 acre estate adjoining the Cone estate. In 1951, a donation from John D. Rockefeller, Jr. of $95,000 enabled the purchase of the Linville Falls area of 535 acres. These three properties, plus the majesty of Grandfather Mountain, give the Parkway a special quality of landscape components not found elsewhere.

The earliest record I can find of a public statement regarding the "tourist trade and the Parkway" appeared in Abbott's "News" in April 1940. He stated that "the capacity of the parkway to handle large numbers of people and the scenic quality of the Blue Ridge to attract them is unlimited." In addition, Abbott explained the plan to develop "day use" facilities—shops for the sale of gasoline, oil, food, and picnic supplies. He also announced plans for future overnight facilities at Rocky Knob in Virginia and Bluffs in North Carolina. He added: "We hope that those already engaged in tourist enterprises in the towns and cities nearby the Parkway will keep alive to the increasing needs of the tourist for new and well-rounded service. As we see it, there will be a new business opportunity for local people both on and off the Parkway, and this of course means the entire business community from the farmer who produces through to those who directly play host to the public."

In May of 1940, the Parkway advertised for bids on concessions to be located in Virginia (near Rocky Knob), and at the Bluffs in Aleghany County, for gasoline stations, food service, and handicrafts. No complete bids were received. Again in August of 1940, bids were asked for gasoline and food service. In December 1940, Abbott announced in the "News" that no bids were received. Ultimately, a nonprofit distributing corporation was organized, called National Park Concessions, Inc. and under negotiations provided visitor services at Cumberland Knob, Doughton Park, and later at Mabry Mill and Crabtree Meadows.

Other concession operations were authorized at the Peaks of Otter in Virginia and at Mt. Pisgah in North Carolina. The facilities were constructed with private capital and are operated by private corporations. Contracts are negotiated on a twenty-year basis with a portion of the profit going to the Government.

The operation of the Craft Center at the Cone Manor House is a special one because the merchandise is produced under contract with the Southern Highland Handicraft Guild. One of the most unusual concessions is the Folk Art Center on the Parkway near Asheville. The building was constructed with the help of private funds raised by the Guild. The original concept of this operation was to have been built at Price Park, but was approved for Asheville in early 1975. The Center offers regional crafts of the highest quality and provides demonstrations and exhibits of native crafts.

1946 was the first year that one million visitors came to the Parkway. It was not until 1951 that the first permanent interpreter was added to the staff.[7] Bill Lord had been a ranger and his talents for writing and interpretation earned him the first appointment as a naturalist. He is the author of the Blue Ridge Parkway Guide, published in 1961. This has been a standard reference for visitors for 25 Years. For a number of years, interpretation was achieved through signs, exhibits, literature and other innovative methods. Then came the physical improvements such as campgrounds, visitor centers, picnic areas and wayside stations where the interpreters could offer campground programs, illustrate talks, nature walks, tours and the like. The very nature of the Parkway, with its great length, poses a challenge for interpretation. Another excellent reference is Dr. Harley Jolley's The Blue Ridge Parkway.[8] Dr. Jolley served for many years as a seasonal interpreter and is probably the greatest authority on the history of the Parkway.

Is there some event in the past fifty years that reflects a major change in public attitude toward the parkway concept?

In 1961, Congress passed legislation authorizing the National Park Service and the Bureau of Public Roads to make a survey of a possible route of a parkway extension from the existing Blue Ridge south of Asheville to a point just west of Marietta, Georgia.[9] After preliminary studies, Secretary of the Interior Udall and Secretary of Commerce Hodges submitted a report to the President and Congress recommending that the extension of approximately 190 miles be constructed. About half of the mileage would be on lands under Forest Service ownership, and the two agencies were instructed to work together on the specific location in the National Forest. Between 1961 and 1968, the National Park Service, U.S. Forest Service and Bureau of Public Roads worked jointly on a more precise general location. Representatives of the Department of Transportation of North Carolina and Georgia were kept informed since they had expressed their willingness to acquire the right-of-way on private lands. All that remained was for Congress to pass legislation authorizing the extension.

In the fall of 1966, a major change occurred in the Parkway management when Superintendent Weems accepted an offer to go to Australia and assist that country in developing its national parks. The departure of Mr. Weems at the end of 1966 closed the Abbott-Weems era of watermark achievement.

Assistant Superintendent Jim Eden was selected as Weems' successor. Eden was a long-time career employee, experienced in the western parks, and a reliable understudy to Mr. Weems. Although Eden served only one year as Superintendent, he continued with the Abbott-Weems programs. He saw the completion and opening in 1967 of the section around Asheville and worked toward a solution of the Grandfather Mountain route. Before the end of 1967, a decision was made in the Washington Office that the administrative offices of the Parkway should be moved to Asheville. This was the first step that eventually led to the complete move of the headquarters from Roanoke to Asheville. Eden transferred to the Regional Office in Santa Fe at the end of the year, creating a vacancy in the Superintendent's Office.

It was my good fortune to be selected to fill the vacancy of Superintendent at the beginning of 1968, returning to the Parkway after an absence of 21 Years. During this time, I had served in three eastern parks and three western parks, and the Regional Office in Richmond, Virginia.

George B. Hartzog, Jr. became Director in 1964. Hartzog was one of the most dynamic and politically skilled Directors to serve in that post. During his nine-year tenure, he expanded the Service's role in urban recreation, environmental education, interpretation and historic preservation.

When I arrived on the Parkway in early 1968, the most urgent issue seemed to be the resolution of the 7 1/2 mile "missing link" around Grandfather Mountain that had been controversial for some 25 Years. In the spring of that year, planners and engineers seemed satisfied with their final location of the middle route. The only obstacles in the way of a settlement were refinements in the location, agreement on easements, and obtaining funds to begin construction. At this critical moment, we were fortunate to get Governor Dan Moore and Director Hartzog to meet in Blowing Rock on June 27, 1968 for a luncheon preceding the dedication of Jeffress Park. This meeting gave the Director and Governor a chance to discuss the urgency to complete the Parkway around Grandfather Mountain. Governor Moore promised the Director that he would deliver the deed for this final section in the fall if the Director would earmark funds to begin construction. They both held to the agreement, and on October 22, 1968 at a luncheon at Grandfather Mountain, the deed was handed over to the Director. The occasion ended with the traditional groundbreaking at nearby Beacon Heights. In keeping with the Director's promise, a contract had already been awarded for the two bridges that would link this section with those sections completed some thirty years earlier.

It is unfortunate that nearly twenty years have passed since that special event, but there are logical reasons for the delay. The National Environmental Policy Act of 1969 placed restraints on construction techniques, a lack of funds handicapped progress, and the decision to construct the complicated Linn Cove viaduct all contributed to the delay.

In the fall of 1968, the Parkway celebrated the occasion of the first ten millionth visitor in a year.

On October 9, 1968, Congress passed legislation authorizing the extension of the Parkway into Georgia.[10] It is perhaps ironic that the year that the last obstacle to completion of the original Parkway was overcome in North Carolina, Congress would authorize an additional 190 miles. As early as 1968, a tremendous amount of work had been devoted to this proposal. At that time there was considerable optimism that this project would move ahead. The states of North Carolina and Georgia were fully cooperative and by 1970 were ready to begin acquisition of private lands. The planners were working closely with the US. Forest Service since about half of the route would be on lands of that agency. The passage of the National Environmental Policy Act of 1969 opened the proposal to public involvement and inquiry. The location began to conflict with proposed commercial developments, particularly in the open gaps and choice areas; environmental groups voiced concern about the potential impacts. The Park Service had not yet prepared an environmental impact statement that might have satisfied the questioners. The Forest Service was probably opposed to the location and there was some indication that the Bureau of Outdoor Recreation was not fully supportive.

In 1974, it became apparent that alternate routes had to be studied in order to comply with the provisions of the National Environmental Policy Act. A few public hearings convinced the Park Service that the climate was not right to give the states the green light on land acquisition.

As late as 1976, after some pre-assessment hearings, there seemed to be considerable sentiment against the extension. By then, there were no funds available for construction, NEPA compliance was not met, and the attitude of the Service was to put the project on "hold." Now, after a lapse of more than ten years, it is reasonable to believe that this project cannot be revived. The estimated cost in 1970 was $87 million and today it would exceed that cost by many millions.

We mentioned earlier the historic significance of the deed received from the Governor of North Carolina in October 1968 that completed the last major land transfer in North Carolina. In Virginia, the Commonwealth transferred by deed in January 1975 several hundred acres at Mill Mountain near Roanoke. This land was acquired jointly by the City of Roanoke and the Commonwealth of Virginia.

Continuing consolidation of needed lands and interest in lands have occurred during the past twenty years and we hope that this program will continue. Legislation that really aided the Parkway was the Land and Water Conservation Act of 1964. This provided funds urgently needed to acquire parcels that were critical to the protection of the parkway. With money from this fund and the authority of the 1961 Act, the policy allows the purchase from willing sellers. What happens in the scenic corridor is critical to the future of the Blue Ridge. That includes not only the right-of-way acquired by the states, but the private lands in the outer zone such as the sweeping distant panorama. The government has no control over the outer zone, but what happens in that corridor helps the observer understand the nature, use and history of the surrounding lands. We have long known that the environment of the Blue Ridge country is indivisible and the preservation of the total resource depends upon the supportive behavior of the owners and managers of surrounding lands.

As mentioned earlier, the first Director of the National Parks, Steve Mather, established some high ideals and policies that have survived the test of time. The force and excellence of Mather has persisted, though modern-day managers may be less aware of Mather's legacy than earlier career employees. Nevertheless, some of the principles of management defined in 1918 seem to have prevailed, in spite of political changes and fallout that all agencies must face at times. Those searching for a better understanding of the ideals of the National Park Service would do well to read the story of Steve Mather by Robert Shankland.

During the sixties and seventies, Director George Hartzog exerted a tremendous influence on the parks. Some seventy new areas were added to the System while he was Director between 1964 and 1972. The Carl Sandburg Home in Flat Rock, North Carolina was acquired in 1969 and placed under the management of the Parkway for several years. In 1971, Hartzog made the decision to move the Parkway headquarters from Roanoke to Asheville. The reason given for the move was the additional work expected on the Parkway extension, although there may have been political reasons.

The location of the Blue Ridge in two states, traversing 29 counties, numerous planning districts, and eight Congressional districts has always required close coordination of management practices. To name a few of the complex problems would include the impact of developments along a 1,200 mile boundary, traffic circulation, problems of utility routes, control of billboards, and elimination of hazardous road crossings. Management has always been aware of the need to exert extraordinary efforts toward cooperation with states, counties and local groups. Fortunately, there have always been agencies, non-profit groups, and organizations that have had an exceptional interest in the Parkway and its purpose. One such organization has been the Appalachian

Consortium for which we are very proud.

I retired from the Superintendent's position at the end of June 1975. Selected to replace me was Joe Brown, an Assistant Director in the Washington Office. Joe had considerable field experience in a number of parks, as well as previous experience as an administrator of municipal parks. Some of his achievements include negotiating a contract for the Folk Art Center and initial progress on its construction. Brown was Superintendent for only two years, but progress continued on the Grandfather Mountain project. He continued to forge ahead on some of the other programs begun in the sixties, including land acquisition, grade crossing elimination, and exploration toward keeping the extension alive. The latter failed. With the retirement of the Regional Director in Atlanta in the late summer of 1977, Brown was selected to fill the Regional Director's position. This was an advancement.

Selected to fill the vacancy of Superintendent following Brown's departure was Gary Everhardt. Mr. Everhardt had served as Director for the past 2 1/2 years and was extremely qualified for the Parkway post. Gary had begun his career on the Parkway as an engineer and had served in the west as Superintendent before being selected for the top post of Director. While in that position, he administered a great increase in park development and interpretive programming for the American Revolution Bicentennial.

Mr. Everhardt has had an impressive ten years as Superintendent of the Blue Ridge. He managed the completion and dedication of the Folk Art Center. He planned and directed the 50th Anniversary of the Parkway that took place in September 1985. His skill and leadership in management certainly resulted in the completion of the Grandfather Mountain section and subsequent opening in September 1987. Everhardt has made progress on the proposal to construct a headquarters facility in Asheville by acquiring a choice piece of land. With his special talents at public relations, his dream of having a Parkway headquarters will surely come true. Superintendent Everhardt has followed the Mather tradition in stimulating a high degree of esprit de corps and is one of the most dynamic Superintendents in the Parkway's history.

We have said little about the economic impact of the Blue Ridge Parkway on this region, but it is impressive. A figure often quoted by Parkway officials is that the actual construction cost of the Blue Ridge is in the range of $130 to $140 million. We have no figure on the accumulated operating cost in the past 50 years, but it would be in the millions since the operating budget for this year alone is approximately $8 million. With 22 million visitors, that would be a cost to the government of 36 cents per visit. We are unable to accurately estimate the dollars spent by Parkway travelers in the two states annually, but 22 million visitors would conservatively spend a billion dollars a year along the Parkway. This makes a great impact and the neighboring communities have always shown a great interest in Parkway travel.

The completion of the motor road at Grandfather Mountain will close an era spanning 52 years of construction. However, it will usher in an opportunity to think and act in original and innovative terms of expanded visitor use, research, interpretation, transportation and land use control. The future opportunities are just as endless and challenging as they were fifty years ago. The Blue Ridge presents a particular ecological situation and management must consider its ecological health if it is to endure for the future. This parkway is not isolated on a mountain top, but is at the heart of regional considerations. It is not a self-contained area, carved out of the public domain, but a slice of rural America. It is an elongated park, fitted into a corridor that is harmoniously integrated into the natural landscape. We are proud of the Blue Ridge Parkway and the National Park Service.

BIBLIOGRAPHY

(1) Public Law No. 848, June 22, 1936, known as Blue Ridge Parkway Act

(2) Memo from Ickes to Cammerer, November 18, 1933, in National Archives

(3) Steve Mather of the National Parks, Robert Shankland, Alfred Knoph

(4) Unpublished History of the Blue Ridge Parkway, February 8, 1948, Edward H. Abbuehl

(5) Blue Ridge Parkway "News," November 1937 - April 1943 by Stanley Abbott

(6) Act of June 30, 1961 (75 Stat. 196)

(7) Unpublished History of the Blue Ridge Parkway by William G. Lord

(8) The Blue Ridge Parkway, Dr. Harley E. Jolley, University of Tennessee Press

(9) Public Law 87-135, 87th Congress, August 10, 1961

(10) Public Law 90-555 of October 9, 1968, authorizing extension of Blue Ridge Parkway

Development of a Comprehensive Reconnaissance Survey Methodology Based on an Evaluation of the Roanoke River Parkway Survey

Gary W. Johnson and M. Wayne Colebank

ABSTRACT

The purpose of this paper is to present a reconnaissance survey methodology that can be used to determine the suitability of a river corridor for parkway development. The case study, the Roanoke River Reconnaissance Survey, assessed the parkway potential along the Roanoke River in Roanoke, Virginia. A team of National Park Service planners, Federal Highway Administration engineers and consultants conducted the assessment from March 1986 to February 1987. The assessment team combined approaches by McHarg (1969), Hornbeck and Okerlund (1973), and Jones and Jones (1973) to (1) select a parkway corridor based on environmental constraints and resource opportunities, (2) measure the magnitude of the resources, (3) determine landscape integrity along approximately 30 miles of the potentially affected river, and (4) identify potential parkway routes. For this paper, the Roanoke River Reconnaissance Survey methodology will be evaluated and necessary refinements proposed, leading to a comprehensive reconnaissance survey methodology applicable for surveying any river corridor and locating alternative parkway routes.

INTRODUCTION

The Roanoke River Parkway Reconnaissance Survey selected a parkway corridor based on environmental constraints and resource opportunities in the Roanoke River Valley. The Survey measured the magnitude of the resources within the corridor and suggested potential locations where a parkway could be developed to acceptable rural and urban road standards. This paper will be a concerted attempt to document the Roanoke Survey steps and to point out its difficulties and successes. It will also offer suggested means to overcome the shortcomings of the Survey, leading to a thorough and comprehensive survey methodology.

BACKGROUND

The concept of a public corridor or "greenway" to protect and enhance the course of the Roanoke River through the Roanoke Valley was first proposed in a 1928 Roanoke City master plan. The idea has since resurfaced in various ways, notably in comprehensive plans for Roanoke County and the adjacent Cities of Salem and Roanoke. The most recent revival

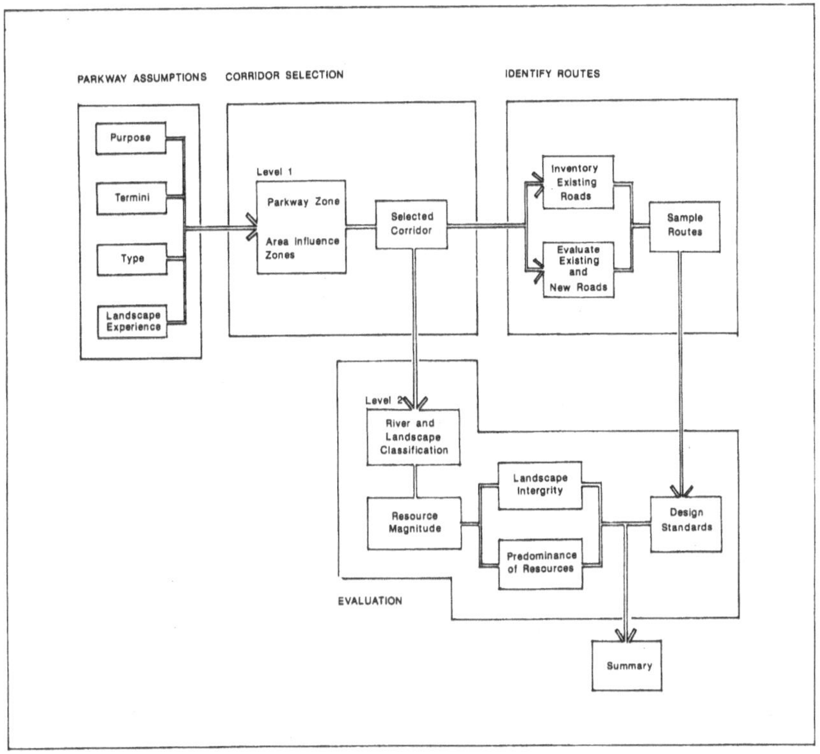

Fig. 1. Reconnaissance Survey Process.

has been associated with a regional project, EXPLORE, for providing extensive recreational, transportation and natural resource conservation opportunities in the Roanoke River Valley. Officials of The River Foundation, a non-profit corporation established to carry out this project, have envisioned a river parkway of over twenty-five miles connecting the central core of EXPLORE with the City of Roanoke and surrounding counties. While the corridor idea has survived in planning documents over the years, numerous questions remain for bringing the parkway concept to fruition. What type of road should it be? What should its purposes be? What route should it follow?

To provide some answers, The River Foundation turned to the National Park Service (NPS) and the Federal Highway Administration (FHWA), two Federal bureaus that have extensive experience in parkway location, design, construction, maintenance and operation. These agencies created a study team from both bureaus and began the Roanoke River Parkway Reconnaissance Survey in March 1986. Archaeologists, historians, landscape architects and transportation engineers were assembled as the survey team to assess the resources of the Roanoke River Valley. The NPS was responsible for preparation of the Survey document.

The work process that developed in the Survey is shown in Figure 1. Although each component was addressed by the survey team, this paper will concentrate on the procedures developed for the assumptions, corridor selection and resource evaluation portions. The authors' specific recommendations for improving the steps utilized in the Roanoke Survey have also been included in a separate section. References will be made to other components as necessary to demonstrate the interrelationships of the work efforts that were occurring concurrently to those expounded on in this paper.

ESTABLISHING PARKWAY ASSUMPTIONS

The initial investigative steps of the Roanoke Survey were undertaken with the knowledge that the parkway's purpose, termini, type and landscape experience would be refined during the course of several community involvement meetings sponsored by county governments. Because the reconnaissance survey was taking place separately from, and in advance of, most of the community meetings, the survey team — in association with The River Foundation — developed working assumptions about the purpose, termini, roadway type and landscape experiences desired for the parkway visitors. These assumptions were developed to facilitate corridor selection, resource evaluation and selection of sample route locations.

Another basic assumption centered around the definition of a parkway and what definition would be utilized in the Roanoke Survey. The term "parkway" is often defined in many different ways. As the term implies, technically a parkway must have some association with a "park" and a "(high)way". Since there are many types of highways, there is a corresponding variety in parkways.

Historically, parkways seemed to have four distinct purposes and functions. These were to encourage traffic movement between parks, provide access to the scenic character of the roadside, increase recreation opportunities and extend economic influences.

Most contemporary parkways restrict commercial traffic, limit access and have a high standard of design. The NPS defines its national parkways as Federally owned, elongated parks featuring a road designed for pleasure travel, utilizing scenic, recreational and/or historic resources of national significance. Two factors are integral to developing a parkway to acceptable standards — the presence of rural land use character and resources of interpretive value. These definitions and criteria formed the framework for the Roanoke Survey.

Three designs for roadway standards were developed based on these assumptions. The standards included a roadway for use in existing urban areas, one for along existing rural roads and another for new parkway construction. These standards reflect the optimum design characteristics for increasing user experience and traversing the land uses found in the Roanoke Valley. Sample routes selected in the Roanoke Survey incorporated one of these standards as its fundamental design.

CORRIDOR SELECTION

Because the Roanoke River would be the primary unifying element for the parkway experience, the survey team initially defined an area that included most of the drainage courses contributing to the river as the boundaries for the parkway corridor. Preliminary site visits, however, revealed that this ridgeline-to-ridgeline corridor included land too far removed from the river. Selecting a more appropriate corridor then became a matter of selectively reducing the width of the corridor, but not to the extent that the natural, cultural and scenic resources that contribute to the Roanoke Valley experience were excluded. Narrowing the corridor was accomplished by identifying two types of zones — a parkway zone and an area influence zone (Hornbeck and Okerlund 1973). By utilizing these steps, all physical and perceptual resources in proximity of the parkway termini with potential to affect the corridor boundaries were included. The major components of the two phases are explained in further detail below.

PARKWAY ZONE

The parkway zone encompassed the most feasible watersheds in which to locate and construct a road between the termini. This zone was physically located by excluding steep slopes, floodplains and wetlands, critical plant and/or animal habitats, high-density land use, and other areas protected by law. These factors were mapped at USGS 1:2000 map scale. The information was then transferred to a corridor scale map (1:6600) developed for the Survey. The resource factors were overlayed using a Rules of Combination logic (Hopkins 1977). The resulting composite suitability map showed areas either with or without construction constraints

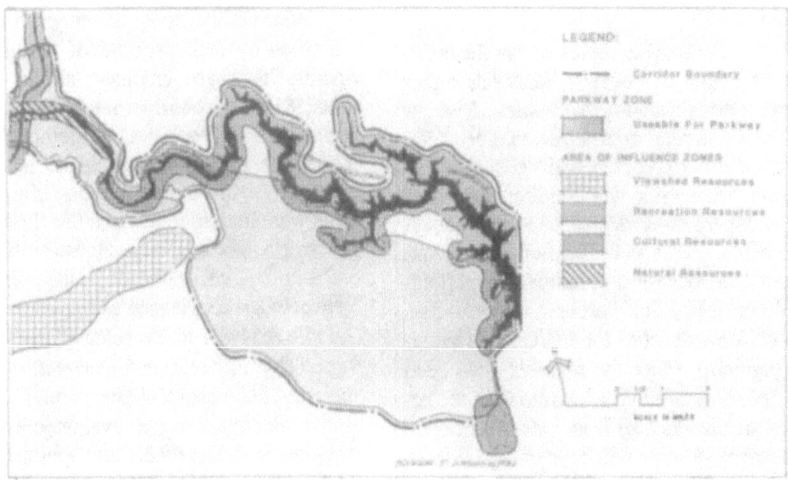

Fig. 2. Selected Corridor.

(McHarg 1969). The areas indicated on this map were smaller than the ridgeline-to-ridgeline area previously identified, primarily as a result of the steepness of terrain on both sides of the Roanoke Valley. The parkway zone was defined by drawing a boundary around the areas where construction was suitable. Large rural areas at each end of the corridor were rated by this procedure as suitable for roadway development. To connect the suitable rural areas at either end of the parkway corridor, the parkway zone boundary was also drawn through the urban areas of the Cities of Roanoke and Salem. The parkway zone boundary included existing roadways that could be modified to meet one of the development standards for the Roanoke Parkway.

AREA INFLUENCE ZONE

The location of area influence zones (resource opportunities outside the parkway zone) were then identified. Area influence zones contain opportunities that would improve the driving and educational experience of parkway visitors and be, consequently, an important influence on the location of corridor boundaries. The area influence zones included the spatial limits of the visual domain (viewshed) of the river and roadway and all natural, cultural, recreation and scenic resources that could contribute to a river parkway experience.

Information available from existing reports, documents and field observations were utilized to create an overlay of these resources indicating their location within the parkway corridor. Where historical resources were clustered, a hand-drawn polygon was prepared to delineate this resources group. The same was done for recreation resources where urban recreation parks were too numerous to identify individually. Visual resources identified were within the seen areas from the selected roadway routes. No distinctions were made on the integrity or significance of the recreational or visual resources in this step. These area influence zone locations were then overlayed with the parkway zone map to compare their alignments. The influence zones were evaluated in a subjective manner based on their difficulty for access, proximity to the parkway corridor and potential value to the parkway user. The parkway zone boundaries were then adjusted to include the appropriate area influence zones. The adjusted parkway zone was considered as the selected corridor for the Roanoke River Parkway (Figure 2).

EVALUATION

Potential roadway routes within the corridor were found to occur in locations either adjacent to and following the Roanoke River or away from it in rural or urban areas. Therefore, the implementation of river and landscape classification framework was required for a detailed study of river-related and nonriver-related routes. This classification framework facilitated the location and comparison of road-related constraints and resource opportunities by subdividing the corridor into discrete evaluation segments. Once the segments had been identified, a qualitative assessment of the resources within the segments was undertaken. The assessment steps will be identified later in this section. Maps utilized for this procedure were enlarged to a reach scale of 1:1600 to provide more detail of the existing landscape to the survey team and aid delineation of the unit boundaries developed below.

The classification of river segments in the corridor was based on a methodology pioneered by Jones and Jones (1973). In their methodology, a river corridor is classified by patterns of physiography and geology as well as the characteristics of the river. Six reaches were identified in the corridor based on the orientation of the river channel, stream gradient and topographic features. The Roanoke River was classified into thirteen runs. Since river runs were identifiable as perceptually different from each other, they were typified in perspective sketches (Figure 3). These sketches were utilized in community meetings to understand the nature of the existing corridor. Projections could then be made about the types of potential experiences available to the parkway user.

The smallest level of classification, the unit, is the essential segment of river creating the distinctive "sense of place". Twenty-nine river units were identified in the selected corridor. During the identification of units, a correlation between the physical limits of the units and the perceptual limits of neighborhoods and communities in urban areas was discovered. Hence, numerous units were named after the "places" associated with certain parts of the cities.

Nonriver portions of the corridor were classified by defining units of minimum distinctive landscape character similar to river units. Since the nonriver landscapes were less related to river processes, the method for defining segments involved the identification of a single level of landscape units. Forty-seven units were identified through the classification procedure. The majority of these units were located in the eastern portion of the corridor and were homogeneous in nature and resource content. Sample roadway routes selected in these units were driven by auto and analyzed to identify their overall spatial character and viewshed limits. Each unit as was evaluated as visually separate from the others and spatially unique because of the presence of vegetation, landform, slope, etc.

Each unit's character was defined by the magnitude of occurrence for 28 categories of characteristics. A sample inventory form (Figure 4) shows the characteristic categories measured for each unit. The majority of the unit's characteristics were measured in the field. Other category evaluations were made from historic, archaeological, recreation, land use, slope, hydrology, watershed and viewshed maps prepared by the survey team. An extensive collection of color print photographs, color slides and aerial photographs were also used to determine category measures.

To assess the corridor resources, a qualitative evaluation of each river and landscape unit was conducted by ordinally rating three indicators of a unit's landscape integrity. Definitions of the integrity indicators were as follows:

Uniqueness: A measure of the relative availability or rarity of natural, cultural and recreation resources, measured by the frequency with which they are expressed in any river or landscape unit.

Diversity: A measure of the variety, complexity and contrast of the visual impressions derived from measuring the prominence of landform, waterform, vegetation and man-made form within each unit.

Encroachment: A measure of the degree of landscape modification by man and the

Fig. 3. Run Perspective Sketches.

degree of visual disruption measured by relative presence or absence of development or visually intrusive elements.

Indicators on the positive side were uniqueness and diversity of the resource and on the negative side, encroachment by urbanization. The combination of these three qualitative dimensions resulted in an ordinal rating of each of the 28 resources categories found within each unit (Hopkins 1977). The ordinal rating (from 0-3) was placed on the inventory form and the chart which was used to graphically display the measure of each unit's resources. The relative presence or absence of the resource categories according to these dimensions were equated to the quality of landscape experience for the potential parkway user.

RIVER UNIT INVENTORY
ROANOKE RIVER PARKWAY
FOR: THE RIVER FOUNDATION
BY: NATIONAL PARK SERVICE - DSC

ZONE:
REACH:
RUN:
UNIT:

DATE: SURVEYED BY:
WEATHER: FILM, ROLL NO(S)
FRAME(S)

MAGNITUDE OF RIVER CHARACTERISTICS / RIVER CHARACTERISTIC CATEGORIES		UNIQUENESS	DIVERSITY	ENCROACHMENT
NATURAL — **PHYSICAL ELEMENTS**				
POOLS AND RIFFLES				
DEEP WATER HOLES				
RAPIDS				
TRIBUTARIES				
BANKS				
EXPOSED SUNNY AREAS				
BIOLOGICAL - AQUATIC				
CRITICAL HABITAT				
BIOLOGICAL - VEGET.				
VEGETATION VARIETY				
% FOREST COVER				

MAGNITUDE OF RIVER CHARACTERISTICS / RIVER CHARACTERISTIC CATEGORIES		UNIQUENESS	DIVERSITY	ENCROACHMENT
CULTURAL — **PHYSICAL ELEMENTS**				
ARCHEOLOGICAL SITES				
HISTORICAL SITES				
SIGNIFICANT STRUCTURES				
HISTORIC LAND ROUTES				
SETTLEMENT				
LAND USE				
URBAN				
RURAL RESIDENTIAL				
WOODED				
OPEN FIELDS				
SCENIC — **IMAGEABILITY**				
PROMINENT NATURAL LANDMARK				
COMPLEXITY OF NATURAL LANDMARKS				
PROMINENT LANDFORMS				
COMPLEXITY OF PROFILE				
SENSE OF PLACE				
VISUAL CONTRAST IN VEGETATION				
ENCLOSURE				
LANDFORM				
VEGETATION				
INTEGRITY				
RIVER				
LANDSCAPE				

Fig. 4. Sample Inventory Form.

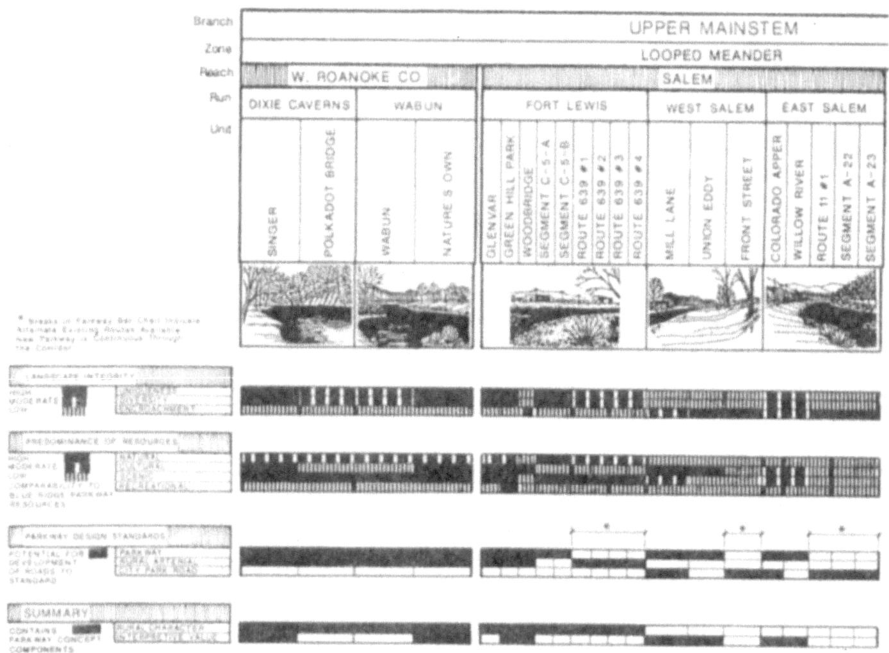

Fig. 5. Partial Evaluation Findings Chart.

The summary of the resource evaluation steps was contained in a chart titled the Evaluation Findings (Figure 5). This chart was utilized to: (1) capsulize the integrity of the units within the corridor; (2) make some comparative judgements about the parity of resources within the Roanoke Valley and the Blue Ridge Parkway; (3) delineate the units' compatibility for each of the highway design standards assumed for the parkway; and (4) to state the units' standing relative to the criteria utilized by the NPS for parkway development.

ASSESSMENT OF THE SURVEY STEPS

Having described the Survey's methodology, it is appropriate to address the assets and deficiencies in the procedures and make a few general comments. These comments are offered in the effort of developing a more comprehensive reconnaissance survey methodology.

Reaches, runs and units proved to be the most utilitarian classification levels for survey purposes. The graphic representation of corridor units at a reach scale was very effective in the Survey and served two important purposes. First, classification of corridor units provided the framework for comparing the relative presence (magnitude) of resources in the Evaluation Findings. The reach classification provided segments large enough to handle resource and sample road routes in a comprehensive manner without presenting too much information. Run segments coincided with varying land uses within the reach and provided a very convenient way for describing the corridor's landscape character. Second, classification allowed laymen and professionals to relate to the information being generated in the Survey. The graphic format utilized in the Survey permitted the development of composite overlays for the resources. These were used by interpretive specialists and the community to assess possible "themes" or interpretive potentials along the parkway length.

Data synthesis was the major problem in

the Roanoke Survey, as it is in many projects of this type. It occurred for three reasons: inconsistently applied criteria, unsupported evaluation findings and undocumented synthesis procedures. The following examples are representative of these problems.

First, the corridor selection process, although simple in concept, was inconsistent in the application of the stated criteria for the Roanoke Survey. Resources of local, regional and/or State importance were included as influences on the location of the corridor boundaries. Since, by definition, the parkway corridor was to be modified for incorporation of all significant resources, NPS significance criteria was not followed. This non-specific ranking of influence resources could have been itemized in the text or the appendix to the Survey report to document the level of significance of resources influencing the corridor's boundaries.

Second, the integrity of historic and significant structures was evaluated on the ratings for uniqueness, diversity and encroachment. In reality, the integrity of a historic structure is more likely determined by an assessment of its present physical condition than to its 'uniqueness' or 'diversity'. These measures of integrity have no real meaning for this resource and are consequently of little substantive value for the evaluation of a historic resource.

The inventory form utilized to record the presence and magnitude of unit resources arrived at an ordinal rating of each of the 28 categories measured for each unit. This rating was the result of the combination of the three qualitative measures identified on the form. No indication of the arithmetic manipulations of these measures was provided primarily because the ratings and their resulting rankings in the Evaluation Findings were arrived at by "professional judgements" of the survey team members. The reader was left to infer the data synthesis operations employed.

Similarly, the Evaluation Findings stated that lands with 'rural character' was one of the criteria for development of a parkway to acceptable rural parkway standards. However, the inventory form did not contain a category or ratings for 'rural character'. The evaluation for this criteria was developed from the unspecified combination of ratings for the 'Rural Residential' and 'Landscape Integrity' categories.

The data synthesis problems did not constitute a "fatal flaw" for the Roanoke Survey, but clarification of these data assimilations would have strengthened the Survey's technical credibility and would be helpful for interested parties. These difficulties could have been resolved by restructuring the inventory form, applying consistent data synthesis steps and elaborating on the evaluation process. The following actions would have ameliorated the difficulties in the Roanoke survey procedures and are offered to eliminate similar problems in future surveys.

1. The inventory form should record the characteristics of the resources in a nominal scale (Anderson 1980). Characteristics should be chosen to be consistent with or comprehensive enough to support the eventual (evaluation) findings. For each of the resource types, the inventory should be modified to suit the evaluation procedure particular to that resource. For example, the characteristics required to evaluate a historic structure might include "structurally sound", "typical of the period" or "candidate for the National Register of Historic Places". As another example, numerical ratings for visual analysis components would be identified and recorded on the inventory form as required to complete the survey's visual analysis process. By utilizing this procedure, the inventory form would express the presence or absence of the resource characteristics. Evaluation of the resource would be made in a separate step. Therefore, multiple combinations of data would be an option to the survey team throughout the survey's duration.

2. The evaluation process should state the exact steps and procedures used to combine the data for each type of resource or individual characteristic.

Identification of the steps utilized in the synthesis has the potential to be a substantial work effort. This portion of the evaluation process would likely be located in the document appendix and not in the main text. An initial scoping process by the team members would reduce the required effort to accomplish this task and encourage more systematic procedures for data handling. The actual data manipulations would be completed in the evaluation process.

3. Evaluation findings would rank the products developed in the evaluation procedure based on specifically identified criteria for each resource or individual characteristic of the resource. This does not preclude the analysis of different forms of inventoried data. The criteria could include evaluations for multiple data types. For example, a ranking for a 'high' rural character might be described as an "area that contains a 'high' visual quality rating with greater than 90% rural land use and an encroachment score of less than 12%."
4. Documentation should record the above steps and their results for reference and scrutiny by individuals other than the survey team. Documentation of the data synthesis should be sufficiently clear as to allow replication of the survey results. The Roanoke Survey fell short of this objective. Even with an appendix to the project document, no information was presented on the data combinations used to develop the Evaluation Findings. Inclusion of this type of information in an appendix would bolster the reliability of the survey findings and provide information for replication of the results. Incorporation of these steps would insure that conclusions drawn in the findings would be defensible, based on an acceptable method of data synthesis. They would also force the survey team members to attend to data handling procedures with more rigor than was shown in the Roanoke Survey.

REFLECTIONS

The procedures utilized in the Roanoke Survey are an eclectic composite of steps borrowed from studies done for other land planning purposes. Because of the multiplicity of steps utilized in the survey components, difficulties in data manipulation and evaluation did occur. It was the intent of the authors to illuminate these difficulties even more so than the successes realized in the Roanoke Survey. We have suggested means to correct the deficiencies that occurred and with the suggestions offered, feel that a more comprehensive reconnaissance survey methodology has been developed. Hopefully more improvements can and will be made to this methodology after further utilization and discussion. If this paper has furthered the understanding and evolution of a reconnaissance survey methodology, then we have succeeded in our purpose.

BIBLIOGRAPHY

Hornbeck, Peter L. and Garland A. Okerlund Jr. 1973. Visual Values for the Highway User. For U.S. Department of Transportation, Federal Highway Administration. Washington, D. C.

Hopkins, Lewis D. 1977. "Methods for Generating Land Suitability Maps:A Comparative Evaluation." Journal of the American Institute of Planners. Volume 43, No. 4.

McHarg, Ian. 1969. Design With Nature. Natural History Press. Garden City, New York.

Jones and Jones. 1973. The Nooksack Plan. For Whatcom County Board of Commissioners and the Whatcom County Park Board. Seattle, Washington.

Anderson, Paul. 1980. Regional Landscape Analysis. Environmental Design Press. Reston, Virginia.

Development of a Management Information System for the Blue Ridge Parkway

Benjamin C. Johnson and William E. Shepherd, Virginia Polytechnic Institute & State University, Blacksburg

The parkway manager needs sound information to adequately manage and protect land resources and plan for their future use and enjoyment by the American people. This has proved to be a major problem to older parkway systems and poses a new challenge to to the planners for a future parkway system. The current complexity brought on by environmental, social, and economic issues in a climate of information dissemination poses unique difficulties to parkway planners and mangers. It seems as if conflict, confrontation, and often contradiction become the order of the day causing delays or, occasionally, elimination of useful proposals. The public's right to know is paramount. The designers' and managers' need for more complete and detailed data is critical. The society's obligation to protect our national and cultural heritage is essential.

The need for detailed and complete information goes beyond the boundary of the park site and often covers large areas of adjacent land that is neither controlled nor managed by the parkway. Such a large assemblage of information is not collected for lack of a means for its collection, storage, and retrieval. The frustration and limitations on data due to its form, source, and character has been expressed by the planners and managers for the Blue Ridge Parkway. To date, mechanisms to collect, record, store, and access this very diverse data has proven to be unmanageable.

The data is represented in a variety of patterns which can be characterized in four basic forms:

1. Data from documented sources, such as books (written form), maps (graphic form), charts and reports (numerical form), photographs (visual record form), and plans (instructional and record form).
2. Data that is a product of the day to day management of the parkway such as safety and enforcement records (written and map), maintenance practice (map and written), observation (notes and impressions), collection - discovery (artifacts, written, notes), and management experience (impressions and practice).
3. Data from secondary sources such as eye witness accounts (verbal), oral histories (verbal), unpublished files (written), political policy and practice (oral, written, implied), memos and notes (written), drawings and art (graphic), tapes and films (oral and visual), and cultural practice (oral, written, graphic). (This data is often the least collected due to its form but frequently the most critical management decision making.)
4. Data that comes form research within the region of the parkway but not necessarily directed to the parkway. (This data usually is reliable for its region but is uneven as it is directed to the parkway objectives. Academic interest driven by other issues seldom is directly applicable to another use of application.)

Often data is not recorded or indexed in a way that it can be readily accessible to the parkway designer or manger. Even day to day data collected in a different context is unavailable to the decision makers. Engineering data on the existing conditions of the Blue Ridge Parkway is not usable due to its ungainly format and its inability to be updated. There are over 800 design drawings that detail the parkway's form. Still more data are unwritten and either lost altogether or existing only in the memories of individuals who have worked or participated in the development and management of the parkway over the past 50 years.

Therefore, there is a very special and unique need for a Management Information System to support the parkway as a total experience. The system would enable managers to benefit from historical information that currently is kept in a variety of places. Further, it would assist them in updating and acquiring previously unmanageable information.

There is a diverse array of users for the management information system:

1. Parkway or agency managers represent the largest user group for the information system. This group comprises the full range of personnel from the Ranger at the Ranger District to the Park Superintendent and his staff at the Parks central office and on to the National Park Service staff and ultimately to the Department of the Interior.
2. Municipal and public officials and planners comprise a second and critical user for the information system. This group must manage the parkway as it passes through its region and directly impacts its residents. Further, this group has the responsibility to manage and plan the adjacent land that is private and not in the parkway domain. By understanding the information base, plans, proposals, and policies, the State, regional, local, and municipal officials and planners can develop the context for the decision making in regard to the specific segment affecting their areas. The information system could provide the common denominator for negotiating conflicts as they arise within the region of influence.
3. Researchers and educators who see the parkway as a unique and approachable cross section of the landscape comprise the third group of users of the Management Information System. This group has the potential to mediate the differences between the previous groups. Care must be exercised that this group may have its own agenda that may vary in context from the two previous groups. Researchers generally represent the scientific community who have the discipline and experience to develop quantitative and qualitative issues associated with the region and the parkway.

The aforementioned users could benefit from such a system which would (in concept) abstract, sort, and classify important data in such a way that it is readily and rapidly available. Moreover, these are the players who have knowledge, talent, skill, and credibility to collect and continually update the data, to certify its accuracy, and to judge its usefulness to the parkway's future.

There are internal and external requirements for the information system.

The external requirements for the system include but are not limited to:

1. Flexibility is a principle requirement for the system. The users must have the capability to use, adjust, verify, update, clarify the data in order to test ideas, plans, and policies prior to implementation.
2. Accessibility is critical in establishing the common denominator for decision making and management.
3. A means for corporation and incorporation is important in order to keep the management system viable for the long as well as the short term future. Incorporation of new material as it is derived is essential, while corporation will improve the credibility of the management environment.

There are three basic internal requirements for the management information system:

1. A method is required for dealing with requests for information from intended users.
2. A capability is needed for acquiring, classifying, storing, and analyzing data about all aspects of the parkway.
3. A method of retrieving data from storage and translating it into the form required by the user also will be necessary.

First, getting the information to the user in a workable format in a timely fashion is critical. The system we envision provides three frameworks for providing information to users. The geo-relational framework focuses on information that is tied to physical location. This data would include mappable geophysical, ecological, and human cultural information most commonly found in a Geographic Information System. In addition, generic engineering data used in the construction of the facility along with day to day management data on maintenance, enforcement, and safety would be available. Linear, nodal, and point data, often not found in the traditional GIS would be stored. Information about the quality, extent, depth, and character of the data would be recorded.

The geo-relational framework should be based on a hierarchal classification of spatial units. This classification allows for the definition of point, line, and spatial elements in their appropriate scale. The system provides for the scale transfer of data by zooming in and out of a region based on the detail of information that will be required in decision making.This unique characteristic marks the variation in concept between this information system and the common GIS approaches. An example of this scale transfer is suggested when at one point the linear characteristic of a roadway may focus on a corridor, then move to a right of way alignment, then roadway design, then finally to a center line stripe. Most GIS approaches will only define the corridor. This potential for detail is necessary in management practice for each district where detailed plans are required. Another example of point data would be on the discovery of a rare and endangered species of plant material. Following a typical GIS the location of a rare plant would be indicated by its potential habitat. Our Management Information System will allow for recording the actual location of the rare plant as it relates to the roadway. Interestingly, then its habitat can be determined with certainty and a search for additional locations can be made. This further provides the opportunity for the Ranger Districts to share their findings with other districts and thereby creates a better means for managing the resource.

The data-relational framework includes the vast array of information that cannot be mapped or cannot specifically be tied to a site. This can best be described as library data and materials associated with the parkway or the region. This material may include bibliographic references, oral histories, cultural characteristics and implications, public interests, contemporary histories, plans and proposals for the parkway or the surrounding area, implemented or not. This non-traditional data plays by default an important role in decision making. In the past this data has not been catalogued for use in the management or design process. The only time that this type of information has been critical is when there is strong public sentiment against a design or management proposal. Often the agency users are miffed at the unforeseen public reaction to an issue. Resource information, design information, archival information, cultural surveys, public opinion on past issues, family histories, editorial comments, and eye witness accounts characterize the form of much of this data. Indexing, cross referencing and updating this information will be challenge but this may give rise to the technique for establishing the system in the first place.

The functional framework represents the administrative structure and the operational functions of the users. This framework describes the linkage between the different public elements in the design and management process and private user elements that affect the process. The name, addresses, and relationships will be established and maintained. As new connections arise, they will be added to the framework.

Secondly, there must be a capability for the acquisition, analysis, classification, storage, and updating the broad array of data envisioned in the system. Establishing the format for acquiring and storing the data requires accuracy and simplicity. Further, it requires knowledge of existing data. To date, all of the geo-relational data is in the form of maps and drawings. Scale is generally inconsistent; however there is a set of the original "as built" drawings from the late 1930's that have been preserved and are of a common scale. They locate the parkway on a reference point basis and are all in the same format. One problem is that these 800 maps have not been updated since the original parkway construction. They are the "official" maps and have been used by different management elements of the parkway for different tasks since that date. Currently there is no better and more detailed material available. To update these drawings has proved too time consuming and expensive. The plan is to scan these maps from the original and to store the data electronically in a format that will utilize computer aided design technology (CADT). This would minimize the laborious task of getting the data in useful format. From this point, the update procedure would commence using the Ranger District personnel (who know the most about their area of the Parkway) to unload the material. Micro-computers located in each District could accomplish the task as part of their ongoing management activity. The computer activity would be easy for the on-site personnel, and as a result, the staff would move a long way in terms of general computer literacy. We feel that with care and an adaptation of the CADT, the Geographic Information System (GIS) would be achieved. Satellite data, coupled with university related research programs, would facilitate the need.

Analyzing the data poses new questions and problems. The data storage technique, that is currently untested, provides the opportunity to manipulate the data. One major problem with the computer aided GIS technology is the errors caused by small overlapping data entries resulting from map scale, drawing error, or geo-coordination. This problem is solved by the computer aided design technology. Modeling, computation, quantification, and graphic presentation are all properties of the technology. Micro-programs will be required to make this system "friendly" to those with little experience.

The classification of the data will be established in one of the three categories of geo-relational, data-relational, or functional. Georelation will take the form of CADT templates. Data-relational will take the form of a library classification referenced to a computer generated map where possible. And, the functional framework will be described in a series of flow charts that will be CADT indexed where possible.

Information will be stored from each framework by placing it in one of three different interrelated environments. So the data can be quickly recovered, an electronic storage system will be developed. This should aid in making the mappable data readily usable, the indexed data findable from data-relational framework, and the key individuals updated from the functional framework. A working hard copy of the source information will be necessary so that users may know the form and quality of the data. This will allow users of the indexed information to preview parts of the information for potential use without engaging the computer in an overall search. Finally, it will be important to keep all of the original documents for archival review. The locations for each type of storage should logically follow the need. The electronic store should be kept at the District Ranger headquarters so that it can be easily updated. A hard copy should be at the Parkway Headquarters, and the Archival store should be kept at a university or state library that is equipped to care for such important documents.

Thirdly, a method of retrieving data from storage and translating it into the form required by the user will be necessary. Central to the design of the Information System will be the mechanism for the retrieval of data in a format that will be appropriate to the users' needs. The District Ranger will need mapping of his management units in order to provide the field personnel the necessary information to accomplish their work. The parkway superintendent will need the updated management plans for each of the Ranger Districts in order to manage policy. While one real benefit of the system will be the electronic mailing of information between management units, the virtue of the system will be that the Ranger Districts will have the capability to respond to changing situations in their management area on a timely and sound basis. Other users of the system will have the choices of map, report tabular, or graphic formats based upon their need and desire.

Finally, there are at least three broad criteria in which any information system can be measured:

1. The accuracy in determining the location and subject identification is essential. This system will be established following the ongoing means for the field measurement system. That is, for linear system the mile post reference system will be used. This is very closely tied to the station point system used in the roadway design. The nodal data will be referenced to the property identification reference system that has been used to establish property ownership. This will either be tied to longitude and latitude or the Universal Transverse Mercator system (UTM). Spatial systems will be referenced by UTM or a terrain classification system. Subject information will be accessed by title, topic, and key word reference. Planning and Design information (past or present) will be referenced by project number, location, or type of project. And, archival data will be found through catalog number, subject, location, personal name, date, or key word. Operations will be identified by project number, date, agency, or in some cases by issue identification
2. The establishment of reliability for the data is essential. The amount of related data will be uneven to a given location but the system will be able to establish the boundaries of the data, its initial scale and its reliability. The data will be linked to hierarchical levels for balance and detail. The data will be able to be linked to an established catalog or reference system.
3. The capability for the system is to handle all types of data. The system is designed to take all forms of data. There will be some limitations on the forms of data for direct manipulation. The system is designed to record, store, and maintain text, tabular information, graphic data, mapped information, photographic information, and artifacts.

We feel that there is increasing pressure for the parkway to meet new and greater demands than ever before. Therefore, it will be essential to develop a system that will provide the users adequate and up to date information to make better and more informed decisions. These decisions must be based on a diverse and informed cross section of input. We believe that a system, as outlined above (conceptualized), best meets the needs of the parkway now and in the future.

A Basic Approach to Classification of Natural Resource Information for the Blue Ridge Parkway

William E. Shepherd & Benjamin C. Johnson, Virginia Polytechnic Institute & State University, Blacksburg

In our previous paper (Johnson and Shepherd, 1987) we have reviewed the wide array of sources of information relative to the parkway and have discussed the need to organize it into a system of storage, such as computer-based, hard copy, and physical stores of artifacts, objects, etc.

We also have outlined our approach to fulfilling the requirements of a management information system through linked data frameworks for access to geographic location, thematic materials, and administrative function and, in some detail, have described the benefits of such a system to the management and operation of the parkway.

We turn now to the problems and prospects of gathering and storing the spatial related data of natural resources. As used here, natural resources refer to the full range of attributes of the physical environment or, in other words, the landscape. These resources include the rocks, water, soils, flora, vegetation, wildlife, and climate, as well as the many structures and improvements within the landscape of the parkway. The term we use to describe the aggregate of these natural resources is terrain.

While considerable information has been developed and is available on many aspects of terrain, much of it is fragmented, uneven in detail, and highly generalized. Some areas have relatively detailed sound resource information on, for example, ecological inventories of threatened plant communities or wildlife habitat conditions, while many other areas lack even the bareness of data on, for example, rock, soil, and water conditions.

These areas are then "unknown sites" relative to suitability for some use program or management prescription. As used here an unknown site refers to a site or larger tract of land about which very little is known except its location and the general geographic environment. Our investigations of published sources indicated that both fragmented sites and extensive tracts of land within the parkway have not been inventoried or evaluated for many natural resources, with the exception of topographic base maps. These unknown tracts are of particular concern in attempting to develop a comprehensive data base of information on parkway resources.

The problem is to devise a means of storing information on the terrain of the Blue Ridge Parkway with what information is currently available. In the planning, management, and administration of the parkway there is an increasing demand that existing information on terrain be more available and, in particular, more rapidly available.

In addition, the acquisition of new information should be organized more economically and efficiently.

We have approached this problem from a practical point of view. While it may be desirable to undertake terrain resource surveys for the entire parkway to develop a comprehensive natural resource data base, it is probably not feasible nor within the budgetary priorities of the National Park Service. Such a research program would require a team of natural scientists and support personnel years to complete and at considerable cost.

The question then is threefold:

1. How can we make best use of the information which is available to meet current needs?
2. How can we organize this limited information to get the most out of it?
3. How can we plan for future acquisitions of information on the basis of need priority?

Our approach is to first look at the problem of fragmented information relative to unknown sites, and how to organize a system which can properly transfer information between known and unknown sites or tracts for purposes of planning, design, and management of the larger landscape.

We start from the observation that some level of information on terrain is required in order to base predictions about unknown sites upon previous studies and investigations of known areas.

We also believe that there will be an economy of effort if results of management practices for known areas may be transferred to other known areas in which improvements and practices have not been made.

There is also a need to provide the planner and designer with information on the distribution and areal extent of terrain conditions which may impose special design problems or hazards in the use of existing facilities or for improvements to be made in the future.

In addition there will be a further economy if the features by which soils, microclimate, vegetative resources, etc. in one site are recognized, recorded, and stored to be available for similar projects in other similar sites.

This approach is essentially the transfer of pertinent information between analogous sites, i.e., known and unknown areas which share similar attributes. How then can we determine what site attributes to look for to determine if a site is analogous to another site? Or, more importantly, which of the many attributes of a site need we know to make this transfer of information with some certainty?

Most of us share the common perception that every expanse of country can be divided into a finite number of physical regions each with a characteristic landscape of similar broad attributes or pattern of attributes. Such regions are clearly distinct from their neighbors and usually recognizable both on the ground and from the air. We all recognize and have named these regions as, for example, the Ridge and Valley, Blue Ridge, Piedmont, and Coastal Plain provinces of Virginia. Even within these regions we recognize the recurrence of patterns in landform, soils, and vegetation in smaller and smaller areas. For example, certain ridges, knolls, hollows, valley floors, bottomlands, etc. of the Ridge and Valley province are common geographic names (labels) given to distinct places in our landscape. The unity or distinguishing character of such regions and places can be attributed to a common genesis of rock, landform, soil, etc., over periods of time.

More formally this observation has been expressed in a State Factor expression which stated that each part of the land surface is the end product of an evolution governed by parent geologic material, geomorphic processes, past and present climates, and time (Davis, 1899). And further that a change in any factor (or variable) results in a change in character of the landscape and the pattern of attributes thus formed.

Therefore at a larger scale the landscape can be subdivided into natural (recognizable) units on factors which control the formation of these regions. This "genetic" classification would produce units which are unique (non-recurring), although similarities would exist between large units of similar origin, material, and climatic history.

At smaller scales the landscape could further be divided into a hierarchy of units on more subtle variables which directly influence landform, water, and soil characteristics. This "physiographic" classification would produce small recurring "site types" which could be aggregated into larger types which could be described and mapped within the larger genetic framework.

We have found that the characters used to define these various land types are surprisingly small and, for the most part, both recognizable in the field and accessible within the emerging research literature on terrain classification and evaluation (Shepherd, 1984).

In general, we see a need to abstract available terrain information into readily usable form and to sort and classify it according to the type of terrain to which each item refers.

A reconnaissance survey of the parkway then could provide a broad framework for ascertaining in what areas terrain information is available and accessible, and what areas require more detailed research and investigation.

We visualize a series of pigeon-holes, one for each terrain type, so that all information on one terrain type may be stored in the same pigeon-hole, regardless of which part of the parkway it comes from. We believe considerable economies would follow. Such a system would allow one to use information gained in one area to guide the planning of operations, or the location of improvements in another area. There would be less need to carry out identical preliminary surveys in these similar areas. Also when one known area had been worked over in some detail, a knowledge of the way its attributes varied spatially, and with the seasons, would guide the choice of type of facility or management practice in another analogous but unvisited (unknown) area. Better understanding of the results of management would allow for a reduction in the number of trial and error procedures.

Once set up, the pigeon-holes could conveniently contain information not only about the effects on structures, improvements, and land use activities on the attributes of each terrain type, but also on how to recognize each class, e.g., information on rock types, soils, vegetation, annotated areal photography, etc. Once in existence a storage system would attract information both on terrain and on how to recognize terrain types. However a system of pigeon-holes depends upon a prior classification of terrain that groups together within each class all terrain of analogous attributes, whenever it occurs.

Therefore we need to know:

1. How to recognize different kinds of terrain; and
2. The properties of each type of terrain once it has been recognized.

At present, the solution of the first problem, by means of geological or soil maps, airphotos, remote sensing data, etc., is often easier than the second. However, there are situations in which it is possible to recognize the terrain but, having done so, there is no readily available information on the suitability of that unit for a particular purpose or practice. As we've stated before, the necessary information may either not have been collected or it may have been lying unabstracted, and possibly forgotten, in old files or reports.

The usefulness of statements based upon stored information will depend both upon how accurately the terrain types at unknown sites may be recognized or matched, and also upon how much information is available about the terrain type represented at an unknown site. In order to ascertain the probable attributes of a new site, we must first match that site with a site of which we know the attributes. This is no more than a semi-mechanized and formal parallel to the mental processes of any experienced designer, planner or manager who applies experience from situation to another new situation.

Formally we may set about this in one of two ways:

1. We can match an unknown site with the known site to which it is most closely similar, and then assume that the unknown properties of the former are the same as the known properties of the latter. In this case we are using the terrain classification as an aid in the matching of particular individual known and unknown sites, and as a repository for information about individual known sites.
2. We may identify the type of terrain encountered at an unknown site and then apply to it all the information present in the pigeon-hole for that terrain type. Here we are predicting the properties of the unknown case from a generalization of the properties of all known examples of the same terrain type.

These two examples represent extremes. They both bring us back to the point that if information on terrain is to be made most readily available, and in particular, if we are to be able to achieve economy of using information from one area to manage and guide operations, etc., in a different but similar area, then there is a need for a storage system based upon a terrain classification.

As we've stated, we believe that such a storage system should be a computer-based data store to handle the complexity and volume of material to be stored. In our previous paper we discussed at length our approach to this problem for the entire management information system. I will briefly review the criteria for such a data store relative to geographic data and, in particular, the current approaches to data acquisition in the landscape.

As you may recall, there are three criteria by which a computer based data storage capability can be measured; 1) the degree of refinement of location identification; 2) the volume of related data at each location; and 3) the manipulation facilities or the capability to receive, edit, display, file, and retrieve data. The value of any system can be judged by the extent to which all three of these measures are satisfied (Tomlinson, 1971).

The first criterion represents the fineness of landscape stratification and the degree of precision of the referencing system in identifying geographic location. This ranges from crude grid squares through polygonal shapes to a nested hierarchy of natural units of increasing detail.

The second criterion represents the amount of scientific, technical, cultural, and practical data available for each location or pigeon-hole in our system. It can range from a minimum of one item of data to thousands of pieces of information.

The third criterion represents the capability of the storage system to handle data. This increases from simple input and retrieval through a sequence of operations of increasing complexity and sophistication, such as sorting and overlaying procedures to rigorous methods of ecological and systems analysis.

However, we see a direct linkage between the basic approach to location identification, the information content to be developed at that location, and a system of terrain classification. This linkage is somewhat dependent upon the basic approaches to resource data acquisition and/or transfer from one site to another site in the landscape.

We have found that there are two basic (alternative) approaches to classifying data from the landscape for a data store or "geographic information system". These alternatives may be termed the parametric approach and the landscape approach (Mabbutt, 1968).

The parametric approach tends to consider the landscape from the point of view of land uses envisioned. It inventories and/or evaluates the landscape for those use requirements (variables) which limit, control, or optimize a particular use or group of related land uses. For example, the simplest form of parametric map is one which divides a single variable into acceptable and not acceptable classes, such as a flood prone area map or active fault zone map. Such parameters are of considerable importance in locating structures for human occupancy.

Ideally the parametric approach seeks to devise a list of relevant land attributes, measure their values, and then map each variable. These maps then may be overlaid to evaluate the composite aggregation of attribute values. This overlay approach may be characterized as a layering of horizontal arrays which are typically mapped at a single scale or level of discrimination. In computer based systems these variables are mapped in single two dimensional arrays of either grid cells or area polygons which can be superimposed to produce new (composite) maps. Data abstracted from secondary sources, such as maps published for other purposes, can present problems of integration into a new mapping scale and format.

The parametric approach tends to emphasize precise measurements and is most useful when only a few land uses are being considered. As the number of uses and their requirements increase, the operation becomes more complex not only from the standpoint of evaluation but also from difficulties and problems of data gathering either from secondary sources or, perhaps more significantly, directly from field measurements. In addition, many variables are difficult to express in a parametric overlay system, such as variables of natural process, ecological relationship, and time.

As the need for a range of attributes increases, the approach tends to lose its utility because of the requirement for parametric data which is often difficult to obtain or measure.

When parametric classifications are used to inventory and evaluate land resources certain inherent problems must be considered, such as the choice of attributes to be mapped, their subdivision into classes, and recognition of these classes on the ground. This is especially difficult because of their essentially arbitrary nature relative to natural processes (Mitchell, 1973).

In addition, the parametric approach presents significant problems and difficulties in the situation where data is fragmented or does not exist. Under the parametric approach there is no mechanism to transfer data from a known site to an unknown site, in other words there are no analogous sites or terrain types. Variables are not organized and classified into a natural unit framework, nor, in most cases, could they serve as terrain or site type analogues.

On the other hand, the landscape approach seeks to classify land into natural units, measure and describe their attributes, and relate them to land use. This approach views the landscape as an aggregation of materials, forms, and processes which, in their interaction, provide patterns of landforms, water regimes, climatic influences, plant communities, wildlife habitat, and sites for human settlements and activities. Under this approach, all biological activity, including human uses and structures, is viewed as land use (Foreman and Godron, 1985).

Landscape ecology, as well as other natural sciences, recognizes that the landscape can be viewed as a mosaic of natural units which vary in size, shape, and scale. These natural units are the building blocks of a landscape region, expanse of country or continent and have been variously described by numerous researchers in the natural sciences and related disciplines (Bailey, 1978).

The landscape approach is dependent upon a system of classification to serve as a practical referencing system for natural units, i.e., the object of study. The purposes of this classification are to organize knowledge and simplify interrelationships by identifying similar units for inventory, evaluation, and management of the terrain resource base. The underlying principle of this approach is to identify and describe units with similar attributes which provide similar contexts for use and respond to a defined set of planning, design, and management strategies.

In this context, classification plays an important role in organizing knowledge and experience, extrapolating research, transferring experience, effectively allocating resources, and evaluating planning and design alternatives and management outcomes.

To this end, we suggest that two classifications be developed; a genetic scheme for large nonrecurring units, such as the distinct geomorphic regions within the Blue Ridge Mountain Complex, and a physiographic scheme for smaller recurring units within the regional landscape.

In the genetic classification, large scale natural units will be defined by logical subdivision of the landscape on the basis of origin, process, and resultant pattern of terrain, as outlined earlier in this paper.

In the physiographic classification, smaller scale landscape units will be identified on the basis of their distinct forms, materials, and processes. This system recognizes a hierarchy of recurring land types from, for example, larger erosional and depositional landscape units, to smaller physiographic and landform subdivisions of more localized experience.

In the literature, these units have been identified by a range of terms, such as land systems, land types, habitat types, terrain types, site types, etc., by numerous researchers in the scientific disciplines in many agencies and regions. Since 1978 considerable effort has been made to coordinate systems, especially in Federal agencies concerned with land resource planning and management. Efforts are currently being made to develop a comprehensive National Land Classification Framework for use on public lands (Smalley, 1985).

The classification system we propose consists of a three level hierarchy of nested physiographic units termed terrain types, site types, and elements, as shown on Table 1. This system appears to be compatible with other taxonomic approaches being developed by the Federal Interagency Team of the Resources Evaluation Techniques Program (Driscoll, 1980). There are however, slight differences in terms, structures, and characters used to define classes primarily because of the more detailed scope and purposes of resource management information in the Blue Ridge Parkway.

The upper level of the classification system we call the terrain type, whose members are termed terrain units. These units are a logical subdivision of land type associations as mapped in the Cumberland Plateau and Highland Rim

PHYSIOGRAPHIC SYSTEM

Classes	Mapping Scales	Survey Scales
Terrain Type	1:12,000 to 1:24,000	Reconnaissance
Site Type	1:1,200 to 1:12,000	Semi-detailed
Element	not usually mapped	Detailed

Table 1. Nested Hierarchy of Physiographic Classes.

physiographic provinces by Smalley (1984) and as generally defined by Weltz and Arnold (1975).

A terrain unit is a mosaic of landforms resulting from a common lithologic origin or close association of different but related lithologic units that have collectively undergone similar geomorphic and climatic evolution. It represents a reasonable range of lithologic, soil, and drainage conditions significant for prediction of, for example, habitat character or engineering performance.

A terrain unit, as described here, is similar to Beckett and Webster's (1962) recurrent landscape pattern, Grant's (1968) terrain unit, and Christian's (1953) simple land unit. However, a terrain unit is more rigorously defined than other units and is mapped at a considerably more intensive scale.

A terrain unit is essentially a relief unit formed from a specific rock type with distinct stratigraphic orientation and characterized by morphologic and lithologic characters which can be recognized and delineated on aerial photographs and topographic maps with the aid of supplementary geologic information.

Terrain units are typically contiguous, although isolated units may occur in close proximity. These units may be quite extensive and irregular in shape.

Site types are the subordinate class within each terrain unit and members within this class are termed site units. A site is a physiographic unit, relatively homogeneous in external attributes, internal properties, and variations significant to land use. It is defined by attributes of lithology, structure, slope morphology, surficial materials, including soil and water regime.

A site, as described here, is similar to Bourne's (1931) site, Webster's (1963) facet, and the land unit of Christian (1953).

A site is typically a pattern of simple slopes of similar material and water regime formed by a dominant geomorphic process on a distinct rock type of the terrain unit. A change in material, configuration, water regime, or process signals a change from one site to another. Sites within a terrain unit exhibit an internal consistency based upon a common lithologic origin and evolution.

A site represents a reasonably uniform set of terrain conditions, such that a single assessment of inherent constraint or opportunity can typically be made throughout.

An element is a small relief unit of simple slope surface, not susceptible to practical division on the basis of observable features or properties significant to land use. It is typically a small area of uniform terrain described by a small set of characters, such as micro-relief, soil texture, depth of regolith, runoff, drainage, or groundwater regime. Elements tend to be associated with site types, such that they occur in a pattern unique to that type.

An element, as described here, is similar to Grant's (1968) terrain component, Woolridge's (1932) flats and slopes, and Brink's (1965) land element.

Typically, elements are not mapped but are generally described as a variation within a site unit. Elements can be used to structure the sense of character variability and to ensure logical consistency within a site-type.

We have found that physiographic systems produce highly visible units which can be directly observed in the field, primarily because they are partially defined on morphologic characters. Recognizable units allow users to "see terrain" and conceptualize conditions within a spatial context, which is a familiar and real part of their everyday working domain. This, we believe, provides two important advantages of such a system. It bridges the gap between producers of information and user, such as park ranger, interested property owner, community officials, or the public at large, who have a special interest in their parkway. Physiographic units are, for the most part, easily recognized in the field by those interested enough to inquiry. It also allows parkway personnel and interested users to assist in gathering data, i.e., documentation, in a relatively simple and systematic manner, such as through checklists, observations, samplings, photographs, etc. Such activity could greatly assist in filling some of the many voids in resource data which currently exist throughout the parkway.

The physiographic system we've outlined,

while relatively simple to construct and easy to use, is also conceptually sound and a powerful tool in organizing and systematizing information on natural resources for management of the parkway.

In conclusion, we believe that the concepts, principles, and informational frameworks we've outlined for a management information system, most nearly meets the current needs of the parkway and would provide a firm and practical foundation to build upon for the future.

Line Creek Parkway Corridor Study

Allan B. Cooksey, A.S.L.A. and Peter A. Oppermann, A.S.L.A.[1]

Kansas City, Missouri, has one of the largest park and boulevard systems in the nation. A primary reason for the outstanding system is that it is a priority—citizens and community leaders see its worth and work not only to maintain it but to improve it. The Line Creek Parkway Corridor Study is another example of Kansas City's commitment to its parks.

The Board of Park and Recreation Commissioners believes the parkway is essential to development in the Line Creek and Second Creek watersheds. It will open currently inaccessible land and will provide a badly needed major north-south connector to the area.

Line Creek Parkway will generally parallel I-29 and US-169 highways in the northwest quadrant of the Kansas City metropolitan area (Figure 1) and be a major north-south connection from Northeast 68th Street to Northwest 108th Street. The developed parkway will provide vehicular access to areas that currently have little or none. Extension of east-west connector streets will enhance development adjacent to the corridor. The parkway will intersect with Tiffany Springs Parkway, which is currently under construction, will continue north to Northwest 108th Street, and will turn east to become the proposed Shoal Creek Parkway.

Our firm, Tuttle-Ayers-Woodward Co., a division of Shafer, Kline & Warren, P.A., studied the Line Creek watershed and suggested a system for developing and building a parkway. Four major objectives were to:

- identify existing development areas as well as areas that may develop following parkway construction,
- evaluate east-west transportation links to promote development adjacent to the corridor,
- allocate land for an 80-acre community park in the corridor, and
- recommend phased construction to coincide with adjacent development.

METHOD AND DATA

We began our data gathering by examining influences on the location and alignment of the proposed Line Creek Parkway. We analyzed slope limitations, hydrology, soil types, vegetation, utilities, land ownership, existing and proposed developments, zoning classifications, and existing and potential land uses.

We assumed the current and proposed transportation systems within and adjacent to the study area would remain with parkway development. We used Kansas City topographic maps to delineate site data, routes most desirable for the parkway, and development of adjoining land.

RESULTS OF FINDINGS

Following are summaries of information we collected.

Slope limitations and hydrology

The area's topography includes some slopes of more than 12 percent, which will require substantial quantities of cuts and fills to reach acceptable road grades. Slopes in the project area could limit development and construction.

The study area contains several ponds and two major drainage patterns. The northern portion of the area flows north and drains into the Second Creek watershed; the Line Creek watershed drains the southern portion and flows south. Major drainage patterns, the 100-year flood plain, and the floodway are obstacles to development.

On the other hand, study area hydrology offers opportunities for the parkway. First, drainage patterns in or near the parkway right-of-way could be modified to become assets to development. Second, we can greatly enhance the area by establishing the parkway in conjunction with or close to the drainage patterns.

Soils

Most of the northern portion of the study area is the Sharpsburg-Higginsville-Sibley Association. Ridges are generally Sharpsburg silt loam, slopes and most drainageways are Higginsville silt loam, and creek beds and flood plains are Kennebec silt loam. (Figure 3)

The southern portion of the site consists mainly of the KnoxSnead Association with Basehor loam, Snead-rock outcrop, Knox silt loam, Knox silty clay loam, Nodaway silt loam, Wiota silt loam, and Knox-urban land complex.

Vegetation

Vegetation in the corridor consists of scattered woodlands, cropland, and pasture. (Figure 4) The southern half of the site has heavily wooded swales, upland areas, and scattered woodlands. Most of the northern half is active cropland with existing vegetation comparable to woodlands that dominated the area before it became agricultural.

Wooded areas are primarily oak, hickory, and maple; developed areas have various ornamental plantings.

Utilities

The study area north of Barry Road has neither water mains nor sanitary sewers. (Figure 5) A sanitary sewer trunk is proposed for the extreme northwest corner of the area in conjunction with a treatment plant in the Second Creek watershed. The treatment plant will serve the study area north of proposed Missouri Highway 152.

The southern portion has water mains from 15 inches to 24 inches in diameter, generally along the west perimeter of the study area. A major sanitary sewer trunk is in the center of the study area.

Land ownership

Three primary land owners within the study area have development plans for their holdings. Several parcels, particularly in the southern half of the study area, have single-family residences and multi-family residential developments. (Figure 6) A small park at the south end is part of the Kansas City parks system. The northern portion includes scattered farmsteads with numerous owners.

Line Creek Parkway development will require acquisition of properties within the proposed right-of-way through purchase or dedication.

Existing and proposed developments

The study area north of proposed Missouri Highway 152 includes scattered farmsteads and single-family homes but is primarily cropland and pasture. The area south of the proposed highway has single-family developments, multi-family developments, and a restaurant. (Figure 7)

Most of the southern portion of the study area is undeveloped and heavily wooded. It has little cropland or pasture.

Proposed projects include two commercial developments along Barry Road and several multi-family and single-family subdivisions in the southern portion. A single-family development on Tiffany Springs Parkway nears the west side of the study area.

Existing zoning

Zoning varies throughout the study area. (Figure 8) It ranges from general transient retail business (GP2) to agricultural and low-density residential (GP7) in the "general planned" dis-

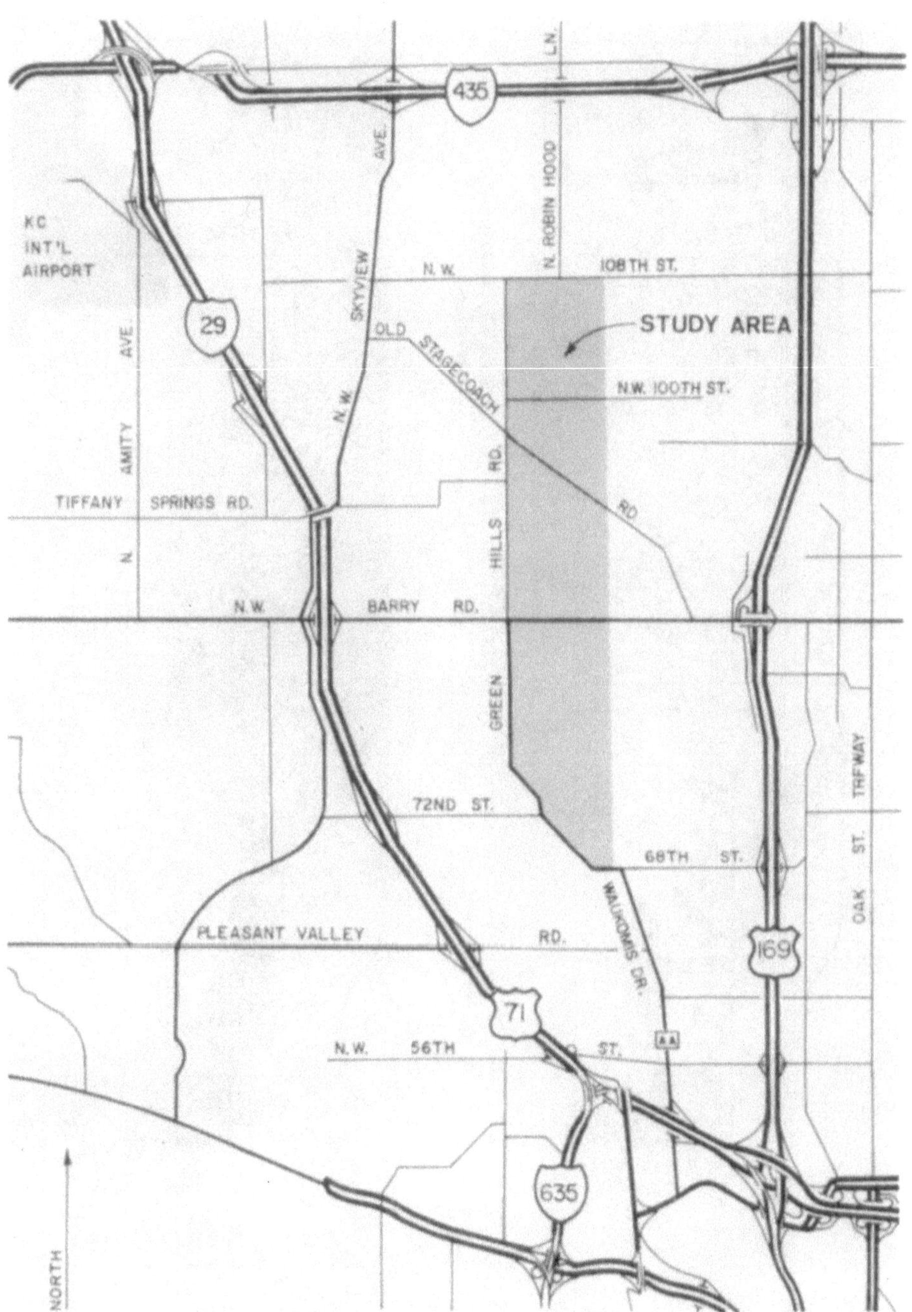

LINE CREEK PARKWAY LOCATION MAP

Figure 1

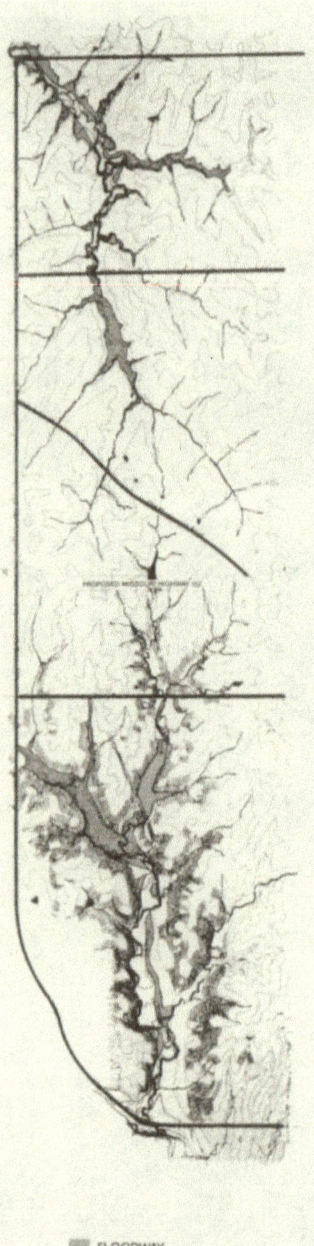

Figure 2 **SLOPE LIMITATIONS & HYDROLOGY**

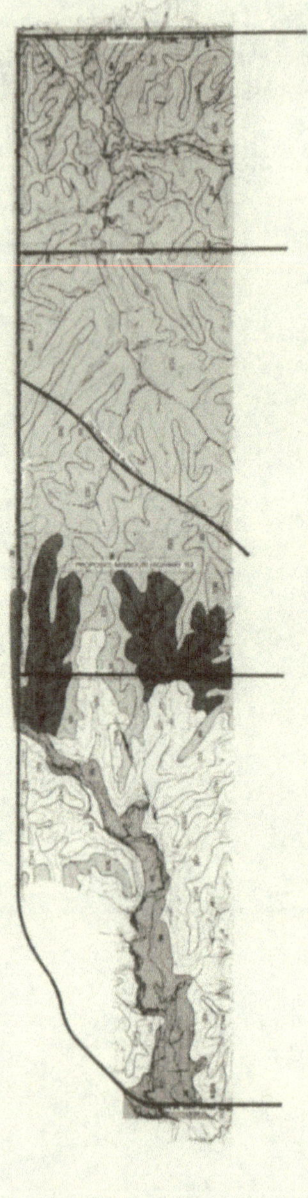

Figure 3 **SOILS**

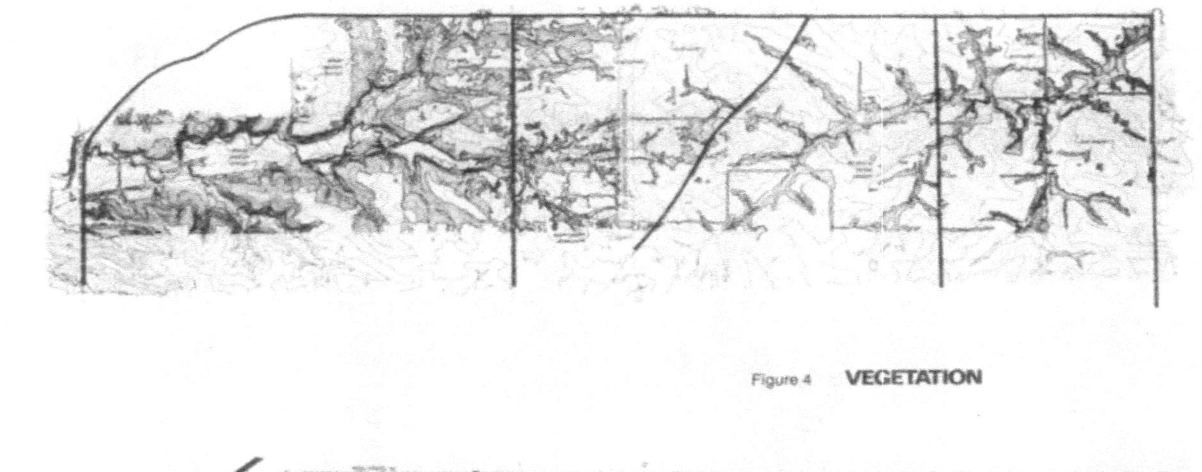

Figure 4 **VEGETATION**

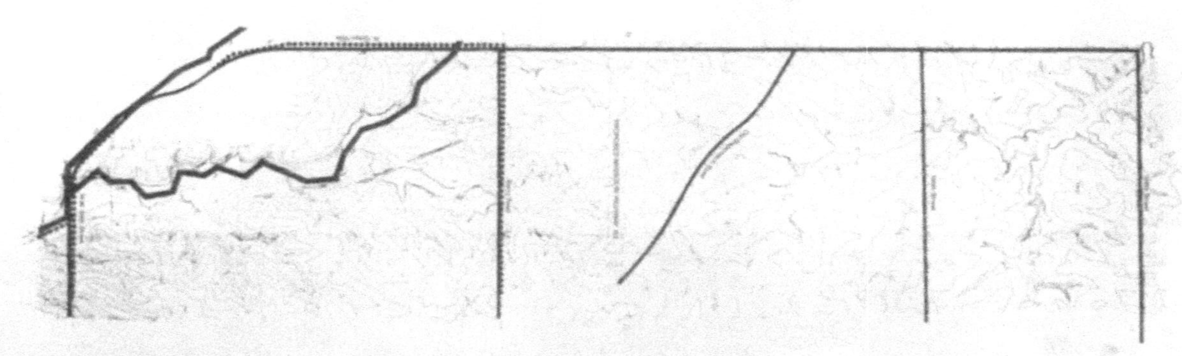

Figure 5 **UTILITIES**

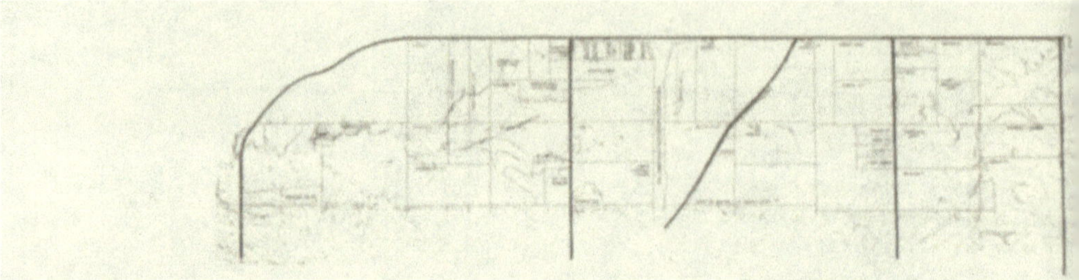

Figure 6 **LAND OWNERSHIP**

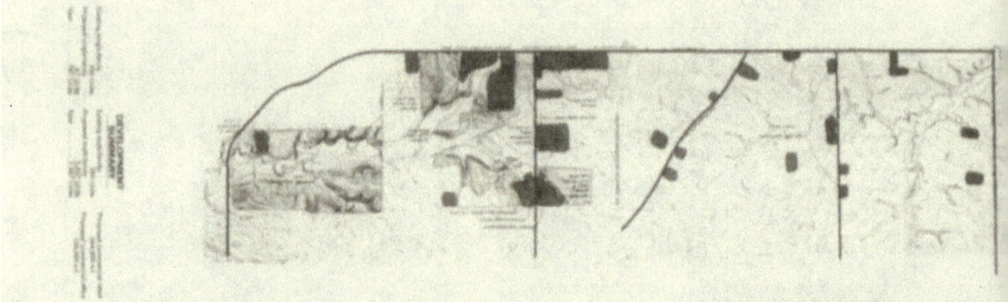

Figure 7 **EXISTING AND PROPOSED DEVELOPMENT**

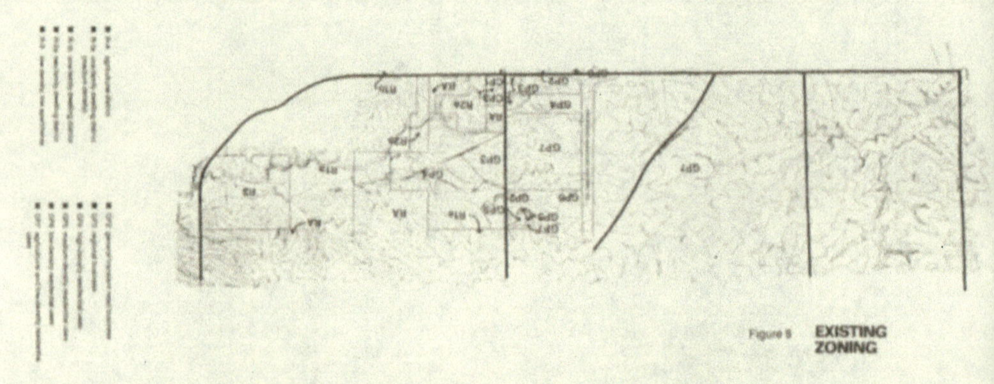

Figure 8 **EXISTING ZONING**

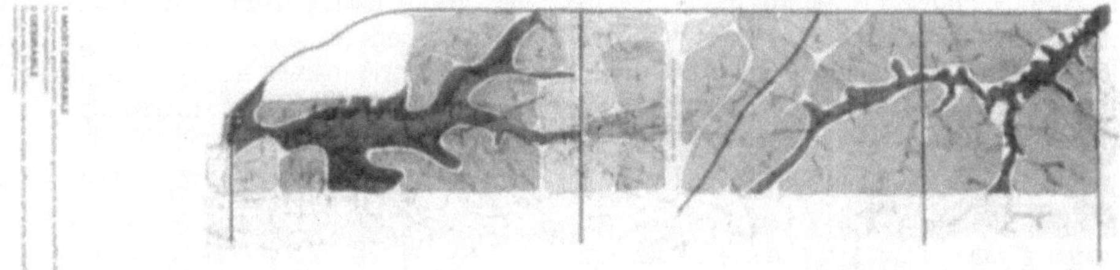

Figure 9 COMPOSITE EXISTING LAND-USE POTENTIAL

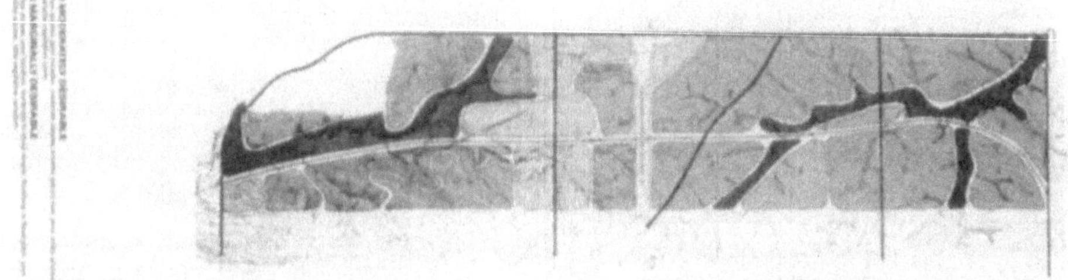

Figure 10 COMPOSITE PROPOSED LAND-USE POTENTIAL

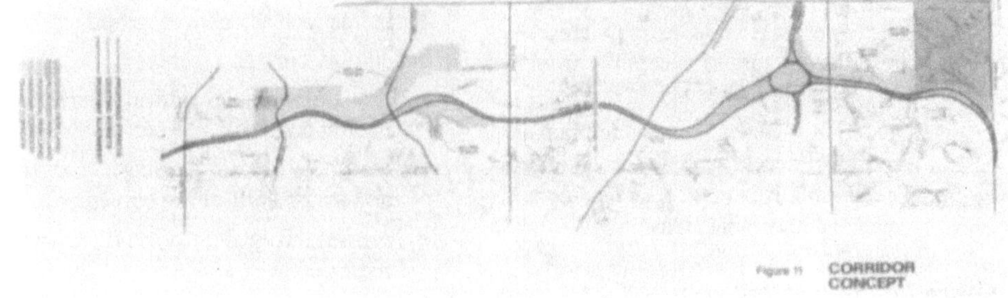

Figure 11 CORRIDOR CONCEPT

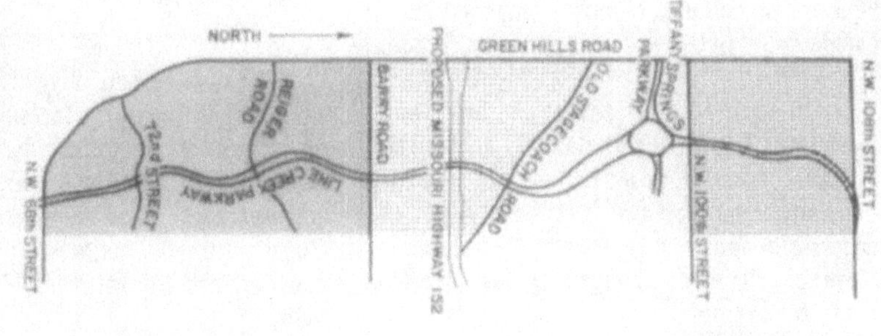

Figure 12 PHASED DEVELOPMENT

tricts in the northern two-thirds of the area. It ranges from agricultural (RA) to low density, low apartments (R3) in the southern one-third.

Composite existing land-use potential

Developing a composite analysis map to evaluate the existing land-use potential, we assigned values from 1 to 4 to site influences. We determined 1 to be Most Desirable, 2 to be Desirable, 3 to be Moderately Desirable, and 4 to be Marginally Desirable. (Figure 9)

Development potential decreases in the higher ranges. For example, Most Desirable (1) areas have good access and location, gentle slopes, good parcel size, favorable utility access, and variable vegetative cover. Marginally Desirable (4) areas have poor access, relatively poor location, moderate to steep slopes, location in or adjacent to flood plain or floodway, poor utility access, and linear parcel shapes.

Based on the map, we made assumptions about the potential for development in each area. We concluded that:

- areas with the most potential (Most Desirable areas and Desirable areas) are adjacent to and accessible from Barry Road and Green Hills Road and
- Moderately Desirable areas are buffered from access to Barry Road and Green Hills Road by Most Desirable areas and Desirable areas.

Composite proposed land-use potential

We placed a theoretical alignment on the base map and mapped changes in the existing land-use potential to compare proposed land-use potential of a developed parkway. (Figure 10)

Although Most Desirable (1) areas and Desirable (2) areas were relatively unchanged as a result of the proposed parkway, other areas generally improved one step as a result of accessibility and relative location. Moderately Desirable (3) areas changed to Desirable (2) areas, for example.

Line Creek Parkway, we determined, will have a significant, positive effect on the potential for development of private properties along the corridor. It will provide greater access to the major portions of the study area, increase land values, and encourage development of land currently less than desirable to develop.

CONCEPT ALTERNATIVES

In developing concept alternatives, we considered the objectives established by the Board of Park and Recreation Commissioners, our own predesign goals, and the design requirements of the parkway within the study area.

Commissioners' objectives were to:

- identify existing development areas as well as areas that may develop following parkway construction,
- evaluate east-west transportation links to promote development adjacent to the corridor,
- allocate land for an 80-acre community park in the corridor, and
- recommend phased construction to coincide with adjacent development.

In addition, our goals were to:

- provide a variable-width median using natural features of the corridor,
- minimize stream crossings, bridges, and major storm sewer culverts,
- maintain acceptable cut-and-fill requirements,
- preserve and enhance vegetation,
- limit penetration into the 100-year flood plain/floodway, and
- develop an aesthetic parkway.

Because certain physical aspects of the study area influence the location and alignment of the parkway significantly, we established design criteria based on discussions with Parks and Recreation staff members, various other City departments, major land owners within the corridor, and the Missouri Highway Department.

Once we established the design requirements, we evaluated our data, analyzed existing and proposed land uses, and combined our conclusions with the objectives and corridor requirements to develop initial alignments we could review and modify.

The major differences in the alternatives were north of Barry Road. We could explore alternative configurations there because it is an area of gentle, rolling terrain with no major developments. Existing and proposed developments, steep slopes, a lake, the flood plain and floodway, and the proposed transit corridor restricted our alignment alternatives south of proposed Missouri Highway 152.

After discussing the most desirable aspects of each alternative with Parks and Recreation representatives and with private land owners, we settled on the alternative that became the corridor concept plan.

CORRIDOR CONCEPT PLAN

The concept we adopted relates well with the existing environment and with future land uses. (Figure 11)

The parkway runs north from the intersection of AA Highway and Northwest 68th Street and parallels the proposed transit corridor that will parallel Line Creek Parkway from Northwest 68th Street to the proposed Reiger Road intersection. The transit corridor will be a maximum 75 feet wide; Line Creek Parkway right-of-way adjacent to the transit corridor is 150 feet. The flood plain and steep slopes on both sides of the Line Creek drainage pattern are important reasons for locating the alignment parallel to the transit corridor.

North of the Northwest 72nd Street intersection, the parkway widens, and northbound lanes follow the abandoned railroad grade across the dam south of Barry Road. Southbound lanes align below the dam, turn northeast, and parallel the northbound lanes to intersect with Barry Road. Widening the right-of-way at the lake not only creates a smooth transition out of the Line Creek flood plain, it also takes advantage of the panoramic view of the Line Creek valley.

The intersections of Northwest 72nd Street and Reiger Road with the parkway maintain acceptable vertical and horizontal limits.

The steep slopes of the Line Creek watershed influenced alignment location. The major parkway intersection at Barry Road is located in the sag curve of the proposed Barry Road improvements.

Line Creek Parkway proceeds north from Barry Road to where proposed Missouri Highway 152 will bridge the parkway. At the top of the Line Creek watershed, the parkway intersects with Old Stagecoach Road, important because its diagonal alignment through the study area eases vehicular access to the west and northwest.

North of Old Stagecoach Road, the right-of-way widens as it descends into the Second Creek watershed and straddles the Second Creek drainage pattern. Aesthetic design merges smoothly with the intersection at Tiffany Springs Parkway.

The intersection of Tiffany Springs and Line Creek parkways will be a large traffic circle that will allow a pleasant downhill approach from all directions and a smooth transition for various routes. Locating the traffic circle in the drainage pattern takes advantage of the downhill approach, provides high visibility near the circle, preserves existing vegetation, and maintains large areas of land suitable for development.

As the parkway continues north of the traffic circle, it intersects with Northwest 100th Street, aligns close to the Second Creek drainage pattern, and descends farther into the Second Creek valley. Approximately one-half mile north of Northwest 100th Street, the parkway moves out of the Second Creek watershed and turns east to merge with Northwest 108th Street (proposed Shoal Creek Parkway), the northern boundary of the study area.

In addition to considering a community park for the area, we considered including land along the Line Creek Parkway flood plain and floodway as park land. For example, the area that begins at existing Robinhood Park west of the parkway and south of proposed Northwest 72nd Street and extends north nearly a mile within the Line Creek watershed flood plain and floodway is unsuitable for development. Its shape and proximity to the parkway, however, make it suitable for either active or passive recreational uses. A small lake—approximately ten acres—on the east side of the parkway could be a passive-use buffer.

Some 3,500 feet of frontage adjacent to the west side of the parkway extends 1,000 feet west from Tiffany Springs Parkway north to the south line of the proposed community park and could be park land. The area is unsuitable for development because it is in the flood plain and floodway. Including this land will provide a continuous park along the west side of the parkway from Tiffany Springs Parkway north to Northwest 108th Street.

The variable-width median of Line Creek Parkway from Northwest 68th Street to Northwest 108th Street creates a linear park that can be used for active and passive recreation as well as for north-south transportation. It will have a positive effect on development and economic growth along and adjacent to the parkway.

With the addition of a community park and the inclusion of additional land in the Kansas City, Missouri, park system, Line Creek Parkway can become a catalyst for development along the corridor as well as in adjacent areas.

PHASED DEVELOPMENT

While we suggest that engineering design for the parkway alignment be completed as a single project, we know that construction will take more than one season. We believe development could occur in four phases (Figure 12) to allow access to the major east-west transportation links at the beginning and end of each phase.

The four phases are:

- Northwest 68th Street to Barry Road,
- Barry Road to Old Stagecoach Road,
- Old Stagecoach Road to Tiffany Springs Parkway, and
- Tiffany Springs Parkway to Northwest 108th Street.

Three projects proposed for the area could affect the priority of the four phases. The projects are:

- improvements to Barry Road,
- construction of proposed Missouri Highway 152, and
- continued construction of Tiffany Springs Parkway from the west. Other projects could also affect construction phasing. East-west transportation links, however, are adequate to accommodate combinations of phased parkway development.

CONCLUSION

The Board of Park and Recreation Commissioners has accepted our study and retained our firm to develop right-of-way plans from Barry Road north to Old Stagecoach Road during 1987. We anticipate beginning right-of-way plans in late 1987 for the remaining parkway, which now includes one and one-half miles that were not part of the corridor study. If a March 1988 bond issue is successful, we will begin final engineering plans and acquisition of right-of-way.

Development of Line Creek Parkway is a high priority for Board of Park and Recreation Commissioners, who expect the $20-million project to be completed over the next four to six years.

NOTES

1. Peter A. Oppermann, A.S.L.A., is land planning director for Shafer, Kline & Warren, P.A., Overland Park, Kansas; Allan B. Cooksey, A.S.L.A., is land planning director for the firm's division, Tuttle-Ayers-Woodward Co., Kansas City, Missouri.

BIBLIOGRAPHY

City Assessor's Office, City of Kansas City, Missouri

Department of Parks and Recreation, Kansas City, Missouri

Mike Burke, council member, representative for Northland Industries

Richard Erickson for R & E Properties

Harold Hamil, council member, representative for Northland Industries

Everett Hedeen, AIA, planning consultant to Hudson Oil Co. properties

Walker La Brunerie for W. Kimpton properties

Mike Rice, P.E., consultant to Executive Hills, Inc.

Flood Insurance Rate Map, National Flood Insurance Program, U.S. Department of Housing and Urban Development

Planning and Development Department, City of Kansas City, Missouri

Public Works Department, City of Kansas City, Missouri

Soil Survey of Platte County, Missouri, United States Department of Agriculture, Soil Conservation Service, 1985

State of Missouri Highway Department, Kansas City District, City of Kansas City, Missouri

Perceptions and Attitudes of Parkway Rangers Regarding Law Enforcement and Natural Resource Management: Multiple Duties as Sources of Conflict

Worth H. Hester and Dennis L. Soden, University of West Florida, and Robert J. Meadows Glendale College *

* Worth H. Hester is an MPA Candidate at The University of West Florida; Dennis L. Soden is Director of Coastal Zone Studies and Assistant Professor of Political Science at The University of West Florida, Pensacola, FL. Robert J. Meadows is Associate Professor and Head, Department of Criminal Justice at Glendale College, Glendale, CA.

INTRODUCTION

This paper addresses an issue of growing concern within our National Parks system which has direct relevance for Parkway operations and management, namely the increased need for law enforcement activities and how the growth in these activities in turn affects natural resource management. Parkways are an excellent example wherein there is a need for an increased number of personnel in non-traditional Ranger roles. Within the National Park Service, operators of such Parkways as The Blue Ridge and Natchez Trace, this has become an issue of growing concern to management (RANGERS, 1986; Shankland, 1970), as well as students of the Park Service (Meadows and Soden, forthcoming).

This study looks at how the increase in law enforcement activities has effected Parkway Rangers assigned to The Blue Ridge Parkway, a 470 mile ribbon of highway starting at Shenandoah National Park in Virginia and running south through North Carolina to its terminus at Great Smoky National Park in Tennessee. In particular, the findings reported here summarize how the role of law enforcement activities is perceived among rangers and view law enforcement in comparison to natural resource activities. In addition, how rangers feel about the decisions which the National Park Service makes in regard to both natural resource management and law enforcement activities is addressed. More importantly for planners and managers of Parkways in the future, how Rangers perceive the nature of their work provides insight into how well multiple duties may be assumed by Parkway operations personnel. In this regard, whether the role of the Parkway Ranger should be that of a "generalist" or "multispecialist" or if, in fact, Parkway Rangers specially trained in law enforcement should monitor the many law enforcement related activities associated with Parkway operation are issues considered in this paper.

Part of the rise in law enforcement needs stems from the increase in visitations to Parkways. In the case of the Blue Ridge Parkway annual visitation has risen from less than twelve million in 1975 (National Park Service, 1976) to greater than 21 million in 1985 (National Park Service, 1985). From another perspective, Parkways as alternative roadways maintain many of the attributes of traditional highways and the law enforcement activities which are associated with them, including among others, speed control, traffic control, etc.

THE STUDY

The results reported in this paper are based on survey questionnaires completed in the Fall of 1986 by 19 Park Rangers assigned to the Blue Ridge Parkway. Through the cooperation of the management of the Blue Ridge Parkway, surveys were distributed on a one-time basis to the 38 rangers then assigned to the unit. Nineteen surveys representing a 50 percent response on a single administration were returned. The survey[1] was designed to address concerns about the degree to which generalists' activities rather than specialists' activities hallmark Ranger work on the Parkway and what attitudes individual Rangers hold regarding a range of law enforcement and natural resource issues. The summary of those findings are reported elsewhere (Hester, Soden, Meadows, 1987) and the particulars of the findings regarding law enforcement attitudes are also considered in other work (Meadows and Soden, forthcoming). These findings show a remarkably high degree of professionalism among the Rangers surveyed and a dedication to their work regardless of the amount of time spent on either law enforcement or natural resource-related work. This study is more limited in scope and restricted in the findings reported. Yet, it will provide insight into an issue of major concern in the development of an effective Parkway operation.

FINDINGS

Crime in national parks is not uncommon. In 1979 alone, there were 8,600 felony crimes committed in National Parks including, in the worst cases, murder, rape, and armed robbery (Everhart, 1983: 56). Major crime is the exception, rather than the rule, with the majority of crimes involving petty theft of property valued at less than fifty dollars (Everhart, 1983: 56). As visitations to The Blue Ridge Parkway, the focus of this study, have increased over the years the rate of crime has also grown. This being the case, it is most probable that the National Park Service will continue to make many decisions pertaining to law enforcement issues as part of all its operations. The decisions they make will be of considerable value for those involved in Parkways management whenever operational changes come about because of increased usage. In light of the increased amount of time spent on law enforcement issues, Blue Ridge Parkway Rangers were asked to indicate the degree to which they agree with decisions made about law enforcement by the National Park Service.

Respondents were asked: "How would you describe the degree to which you agree with decisions which are made about law enforcement issues by the National Park Service?" Table 1 reports that more than 50 percent of the respondents are almost always in agreement with National Park Service decisions regarding law enforcement issues. (Based on the sum of response categories "4" and "5"). However, over 30 percent responded that they are seldom in agreement with law enforcement decisions (based on the sum of response categories "1" and "2"). While earlier research suggests a high degree of professionalization about law enforcement issues (Meadows and Soden, forthcoming), it would appear that law enforcement issues may be a source of professional concern among the Ranger force, especially when considered as part of the larger National Park Service organizational setting. And, while not all Parkways are associated with agencies as large as The Department of the Interior and the National Park Service, they do and will typically be part of larger bureaucratic structures. As such, they may be faced with similar personnel concerns as decisions come down from the "top" to the operative Parkway employee.

In contrast, in the area of natural resource decision making, the respondents are more supportive of National Park Service decisions and see it as less of an overall organizational problem. When asked "How would you describe the degree to which you agree with decisions which are made about natural resource management issues by the National Park Service," 52.6% of the respondents stated that they are almost always in agreement with the National Park Service about natural resource management issues (based on the sum of response categories "4" and "5"), as shown in Table 2. No appreciable percentage registers total disagreement (based on the sum of response categories "1" and "2"). Overall, Blue Ridge Parkway Rangers appear to agree with both law enforcement and natural resource management decisions made by the National Park Service indicating a sizeable degree of satisfaction among respondents about these two issues which impact on Parkway operation. In a historically natural resource oriented agency such as the National Park Service, it is not

TABLE 1
Park Ranger Perceptions Of National Park Services Decisions On Law Enforcement Issues

ITEM: How would you describe the degree to which you agree with decisions which are made about law enforcement issues by the National Park Service?

N = 19

Response Categories		Frequency	%
Never Agree with NPS Decisions	1	2	10.5
	2	4	21.1
	3	3	15.8
	4	9	47.3
Always Agree with NPS Decisions	5	1	5.3
No Answer		0	0
TOTALS		19	100

Mean Results = 3.16

TABLE 2
Park Ranger Perceptions Of National Park Services Decisions About Natural Resource Management Issues

ITEM: How would you describe the degree to which you agree with decisions which are made about natural resource management issues by the National Park Service?

N = 19

Response Categories		Frequency	%
Never Agree with NPS Decisions	1	1	5.3
	2	0	0
	3	8	42.1
	4	9	47.3
Always Agree with NPS Decisions	5	1	5.3
No Answer		0	0
TOTALS		19	100

Mean Results = 3.47

surprising that the decisions made regarding the newer role of law enforcement do appear to be of more concern to operative employees than decisions pertaining to their traditional roles as natural resource managers.

In sum, there is agreement that there is an increasing need for law enforcement within the National Park Service (RANGER, 1986). Historically, however, the majority of the work of the National Park Service has focused on the stewardship of our nation's most prized natural resources. The bifurcation produced within the National Park Service when both law enforcement and resource management must be undertaken is of great concern to the study at hand, but is not an entirely new issue of concern (Bonanno, 1986). Many feel that where the need for law enforcement in our nation's parks has increased, natural resource management has, as a result, suffered. In this regard, it has been argued that this growth in Park Service duties leads to a need for trained law enforcement specialists within the National Park Service, separate and distinct from traditional Park Rangers who focus on natural resource management, interpretation, etc.

In this regard, survey respondents were asked to respond to the statement that "Many contend that there is a need for trained law enforcement specialists within the National Park Service, as well as for natural resource management." Among five response categories exhibited in Table 3, 73.7% of those surveyed believed that there is an equal need for both specialists in both law enforcement and natural resource management, an important concern of which Parkway operators should be aware. However, when asked whether the "Park Ranger should be a 'specialist' or a 'multispecialist' with skills in resource protection, resource management, law enforcement or other skills required to do one's job," Park Rangers responding to the survey do not appear to advocate pure specialization. As Table 4 shows a majority of the Blue Ridge Parkway Rangers (73.7%) record views that the role of the Park Ranger should be that of a "generalist" or "multispecialist". These respondents essentially agree with the idea that a Park Ranger should hold multiple skills in resource protection, resource management, law enforcement and any other skills necessary to perform one's job. In conjunction with Table 3, this reflects a view that while law enforcement specialists may be important and worthwhile components of the Ranger force, each Ranger feels that they should maintain a certain degree of generalization, or multispecialist approach as a way of enhancing the overall operation of the Parkway.

CONCLUSION

This paper addresses an issue which must be of concern to any Parkway operator. The tensions which occur between careerists content in working in a natural resource setting who are now faced with completing many non-natural resource activities such as law enforcement, cannot be discounted. Yet, among members of the National Park Service assigned to the Blue Ridge Parkway, the evidence discussed here suggests that the issue cannot be simply addressed by providing for a cadre of law enforcement specialists who would contend with issues of typical roadway law enforcement and a separate cadre for administration of natural resources duties. At least within the setting of the National Park Service, while a clear need for specialists is seen, Rangers believe that they should indeed also be able to conduct themselves in the multiple settings which occur as part of day-to-day operations. What appears most problematic based on the survey findings, is the agreement and disagreement with decisions made by the larger organizations ultimately responsible for Parkway operations. The typical concern that management is unaware of the realities of the employee on the frontline presents what may become a point of tension if decisions regarding Parkway operations are made without proper concern for the experience and practical needs of operative employees.

Unfortunately these findings do not provide clear-cut lines from which Parkway managers can simply draw organizational charts depicting separate roles for stewards of the land and law enforcement officers. The findings do

TABLE 3
Park Rangers Perceptions Of The Need For Different Types Of Personnel For Law Enforcement And Natural Resource Management Within The Park Service

ITEM: Many contend that there is a need for trained law enforcement specialists within the Park Service, as well as natural resource management. I believe there is:

N = 19

Response Categories	**Frequency**	**%**
Equal need for both.	14	73.7
The Park Service mission should emphasize Natural Resource management whenever possible.	3	15.8
The Park Service must recognize law enforcement as a priority over natural resource management.	2	10.5
Not sure	0	0
No Answer	0	0
TOTALS	19	100

TABLE 4
Park Ranger Perceptions Of Their Role As Generalists Or Multispecialists Within The Park Service

ITEM: I believe a Park Ranger should be a "generalist" or "multispecialist" with skills in resource protection, resource management, law enforcement or other skills required to do one's job.

N = 19

Response Categories	**Frequency**	**%**
Strongly Agree	8	42.1
Agree	6	31.5
Not sure	1	5.3
Disagree	3	15.8
Strongly Disagree	1	5.3
No Answer	0	0
TOTALS	19	100

suggest, however, that while some specialists are seen as necessary by experienced Parkways personnel, a large portion may be generalists or multispecialists, who can address the multiple values, goals and job requirements attendant to Parkways.

NOTES

1. A copy of the survey is available from the authors upon request.

BIBLIOGRAPHY

Bonanno, Tony (1986), "Multi-Specialist Rangers: A New Look at An Old Idea," in RANGER: The Journal of the Association of National Park Rangers, II, 3 (Summer).

Everhart, William C. (1983), The National Park Service, Boulder, CO: Westview Press.

Hester, Worth and Soden, Dennis L. and Meadows, Robert (1987), "Ranger Attitudes and Perceptions of Law Enforcement and Natural Resource Issues; Summary of Findings from The Blue Ridge Parkway, Occasional Paper in Coastal Zone Studies, Pensacola, FL: University of West Florida.

Meadows, Robert and Soden, Dennis L. (forthcoming), "National Park Ranger Attitudes and Perceptions Regarding Law Enforcement Issues," in The Justice Professional.

National Park Service (1975), Public use of the National Park System calendar year report. Denver, CO: United States Department of the Interior.

National Park Service (1985), National Park Statistical Abstract of 1985. Denver, CO: United States Department of the Interior.

RANGER (1986), "Keynote Speakers—Director Mott's Comments in RANGER: The Journal of the Association of National Park Rangers, II, 1 (Winter).

Shankland, Robert (1970), Steven Mather of the National Parks, 3rd ed., New York: Alfred A. Knopf.

Initial New River Parkway Study: Citizen Involvement Plan

C. Allen Beatty, Concord College, and Joseph T. Manzo, Concord College

INTRODUCTION

The West Virginia Legislature, in 1985, passed a bill establishing the New River Parkway Authority. This agency was created to coordinate with counties, municipalities, state and federal agencies, public nonprofit corporations, private corporations, associations, partnerships and individuals with planning, assisting and establishing recreational, tourism, industrial, economic and community development of the New River Parkway for the benefit of West Virginians.[1]

The initial leg of the New River Parkway is to be 27 miles of a north and southbound scenic two-lane highway connecting Pipestem State Park at its southern end with Sandstone National Park at its northern end, and all points between with an entrance and/or exit onto I-64 at Sandstone, WV. The Parkway is to be patterned after the Blue Ridge Parkway in Virginia. The highway will feature scenic pull-off areas, day use recreational facilities, and other tourist attractions. Besides the aforementioned state and national parks, these tourist attractions include Bluestone State Park, The Bluestone Dam and its Lake, Historic Downtown Hinton, WV, Brooks Falls, Sandstone Falls, and the magnificent cliffs adjacent to the I-64 interchange.

The New River Parkway Authority, with input form the West Virginia Department of Highways and the National Park Service, selected three alternate interchanges to provide ingress and egress to the proposed Parkway at its northern end. These alternates are as follows (see pages 284-286):

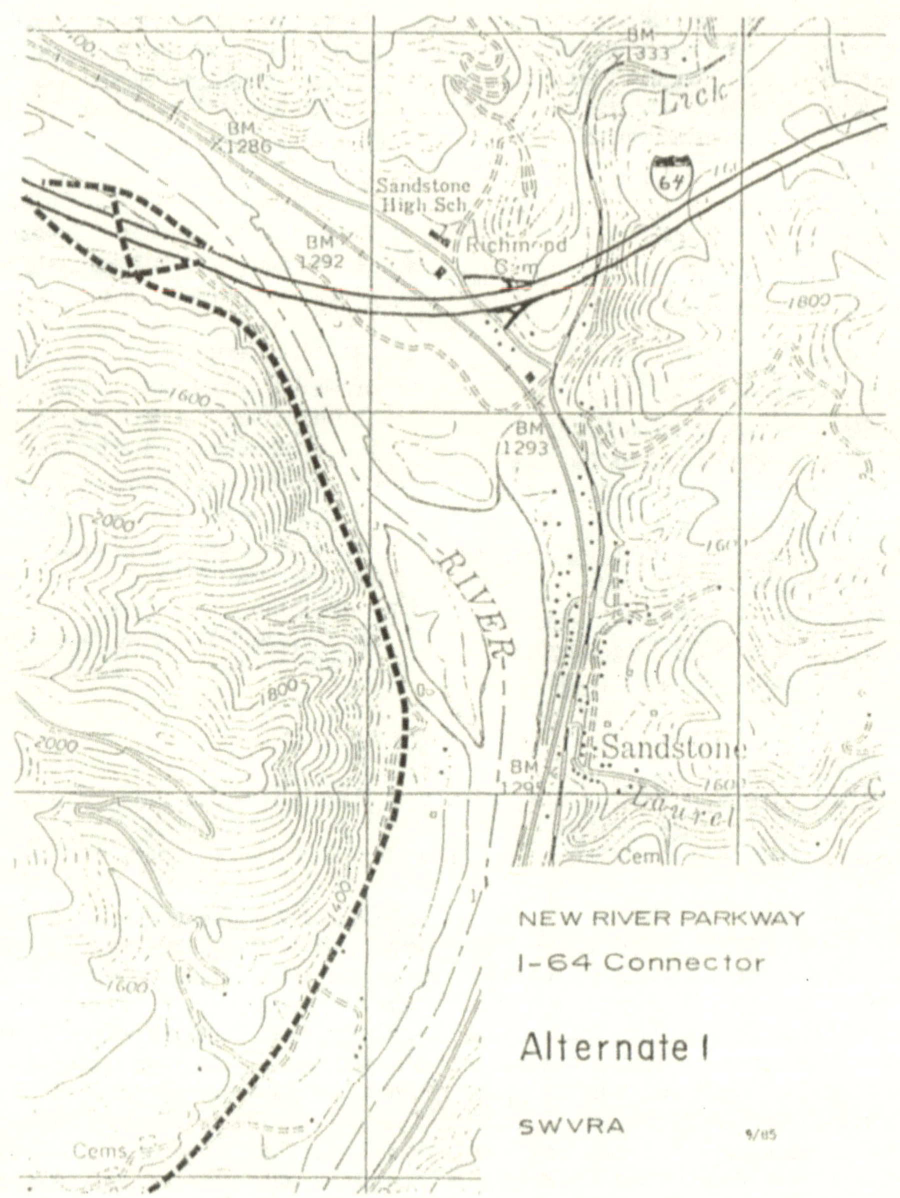
BM
1333
Lick
BM
1286
64
Sandstone
High Sch
BM
1292
Richmond
1800
1600
BM
1293
2000
RIVER
1800
2000
Sandstone
BM
Laurel
Cem
1600
Cems
NEW RIVER PARKWAY
I-64 Connector
Alternate I
SWVRA
9/85

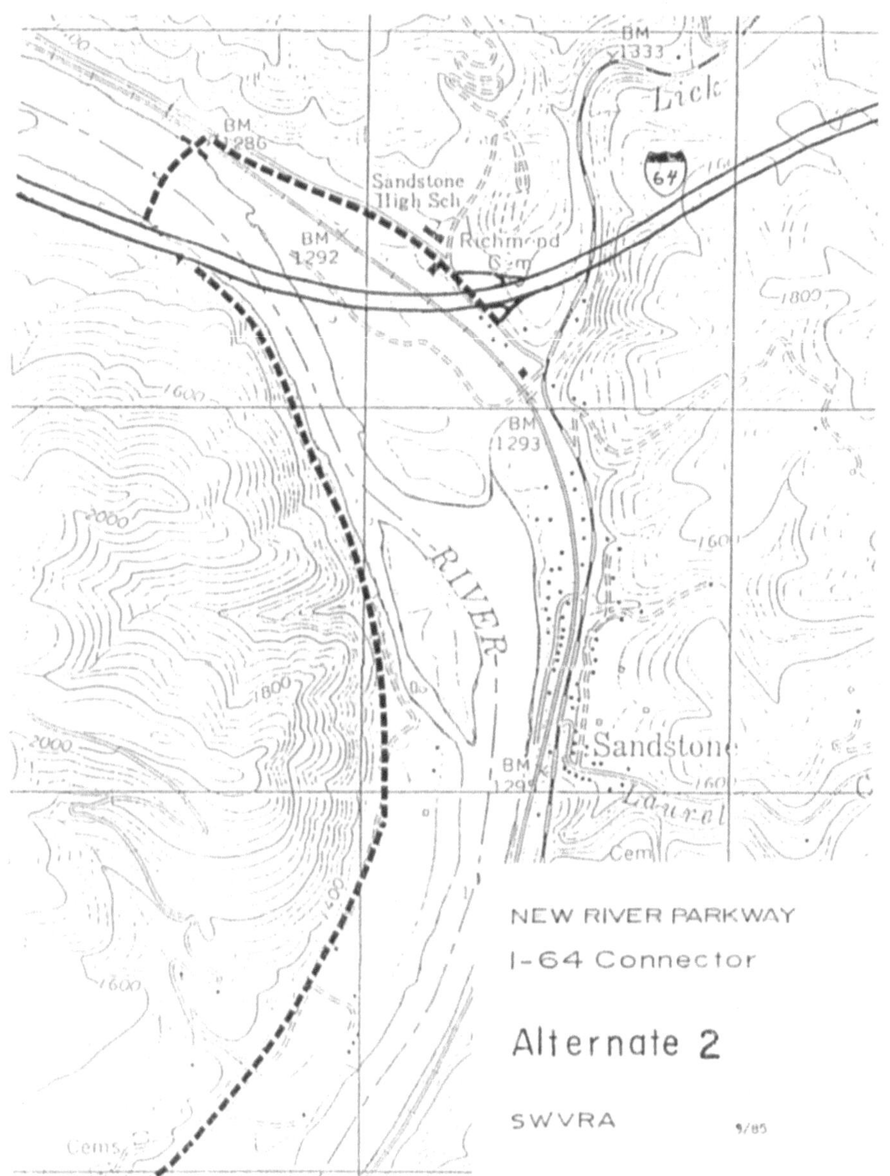
BM
1333
Lick
BM
1286
64
Sandstone
High Sch
BM
1292
Richmond
1800
1600
BM
1293
2000
RIVER
1600
1800
2000
Sandstone
BM
1295
Laurel
Cem
1600
Cems
NEW RIVER PARKWAY
I-64 Connector
Alternate 2
SWVRA
9/85

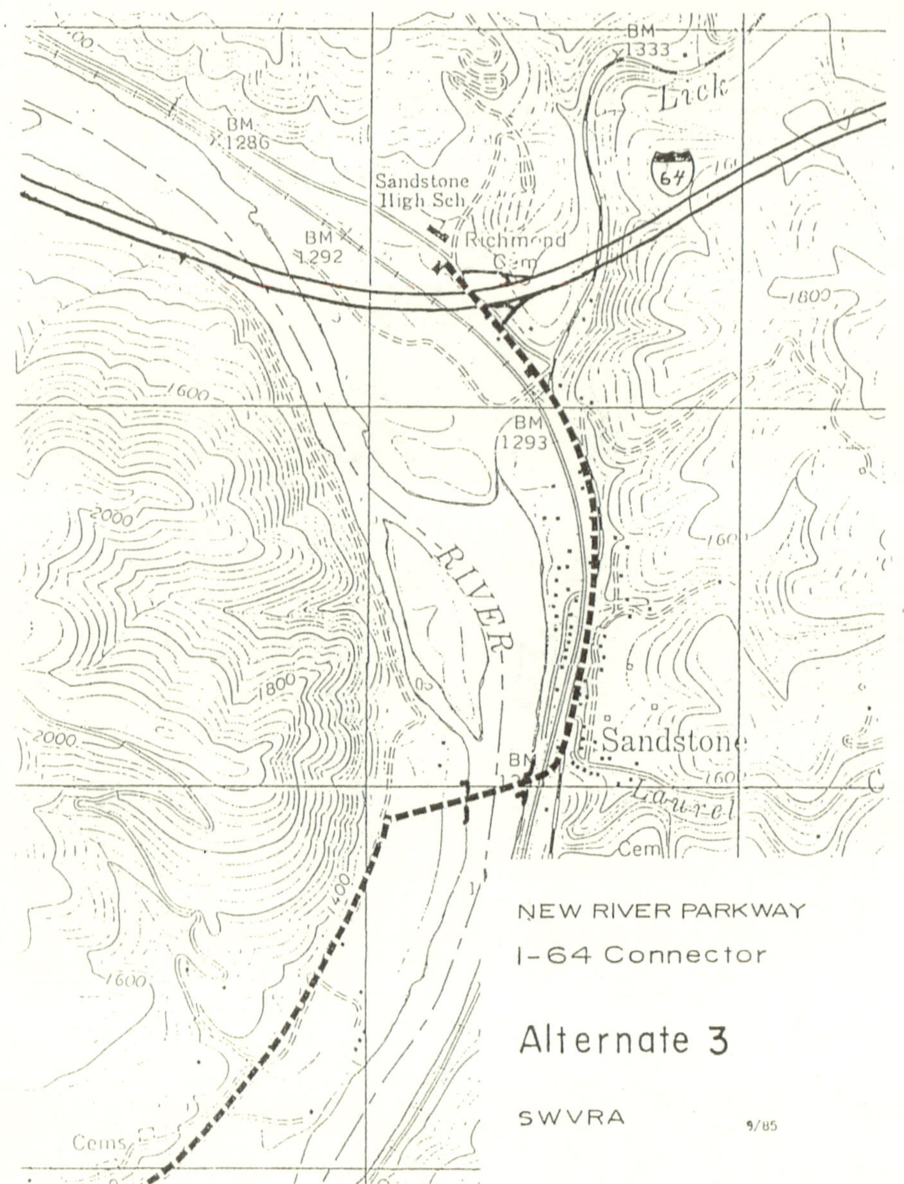
BM 1333
Lick
BM 1286
64
Sandstone High Sch
BM 1292
Richmond Cem
1800
1600
BM 1293
2000
RIVER
1800
2000
Sandstone
Laurel
Cem
1600
Cems
NEW RIVER PARKWAY
I-64 Connector
Alternate 3
SWVRA
9/85

Alternate #1

1. Construct an interchange on I-64 on the West side of New River.
2. Construct a new roadway on Raleigh County Route 27/2 and Raleigh County Route 26 from the vicinity of the proposed interchange to approximately milepost 8.83 on Raleigh County Route 26.

Alternate #2

1. Construct a new roadway along Summers County Route 7 from the I-64 interchange on the East side of New River to a proposed bridge approximately 2000' North of I-64 bridge.
2. Construct a new bridge across New River approximately 2000' North of the I-64 bridge.

Alternative #3

1. Construct New Roadway on a short segment of Summers County Route 7 form the I-64 interchange on the East side of New River to the intersection of Summers County Route 7 and W.V. Route 20.
2. Construct base and pavement widening approximately 0.62 miles of Summers County Route 7 that overlaps with W.V. Route 20.

INITIAL AND SECONDARY SCOPE OF THE CITIZENS INVOLVEMENT PLAN

Initial Scope

As private consultants with our own firm, Southern West Virginia Research Associates, we contracted with the primary and secondary funding agencies, The New River Parkway Authority and The National Park Service, to ascertain, using a survey technique, the attitudes of property owners whose land might be directly affected by the proposed Parkway's alternate entrance and exit interchanges, and subsequently, its initial southbound route. Included within this scope were the following: (1) a measurement of residence longevity of the property owner/resident within the immediately affected impact areas, (2) a survey of familiarity with the New River Parkway Authority, (3) and assessment of the scenic qualities within the area, (4) an inspection of attitudes relating to possible economic benefits that might accrue from increased tourism, (5) an appraisment of the impact that the proposed parkway will have on local transportation needs, (6) an estimation of using local people on the project wherever possible, (7) an evaluation of attitudes favorable or unfavorable for the proposed Parkway, and (8) a selection of one of the proposed alternate interchange sites and subsequent Parkway route.

Secondary Scope

SWVRA increased, at no additional cost to the primary and secondary funding agencies, the scope of their original proposal to include, in the survey, two other categories of owner/residents in the Parkway's geographical area. These were either owner/residents in the immediate impact area, operationally defined as individuals that would <u>not</u> be personally affected by possible projected land use, or property owner/residents in the context area, operationally defined as individuals living in the Summers and Raleigh County geographical area that is in a <u>close proximity</u> to the proposed Parkway's northern alternate access and exit interchanges and routes. Essentially, SWVRA surveyed most of the citizens in the area who could possibly be affected, in some manner, by the proposed Parkway and who could provide meaningful input into the final decision regarding the location of the Parkway's northern entrance/exit interchange and its initial southbound route. Hence the Citizen Involvement Plan.

STRATEGY

The Citizen Involvement Plan entailed producing an instrument with its concomitant methodological philosophy that would elicit attitudes from landowners, renters, and local business people for whom data would not otherwise be available.

The Instrument

The strategy, based on the above, was to design an unscheduled (unstructured) survey instrument to measure, statistically, the citizens' responses in the aforementioned seven (7) scope areas. Several revisions of the survey questions were required before the instrument was ready for application. The revisions were based on the following: (1) validity, (2) appropriateness, (3) language, and (4) length. Effort was made in each instance to avoid "loaded" questions. The revised survey items were then submitted to local individuals in close proximity to the survey area for their feedback regarding the aforementioned revision basis. It needs to be mentioned that SWRVA took great care in not using property/owner residents in the immediate survey area for this purpose. This was based on the feature of contamination. SWRVA did not want to contaminate any attitudes of possible respondents, therefore destroying the instrument's validity and reliability. After field testing the instrument in the above manner, and gaining valuable information, a survey form consisting of a personal data section for identifying property owner or resident status plus ten questions was finalized (see appendix). The finalized instrument was submitted to the New River Parkway Authority and the National Park Service for their respective approval, disapproval, or constructive criticism. Receiving both explicit and implicit approval SWRVA began the interviewer selection process.

Interviewer Selection

SWRVA recruited possible interviewers who were familiar with the geographical area to be surveyed. This was accomplished, in part by placing help wanted ads in the newspapers that service the study area and its immediate surroundings, and by personally contacting individuals we knew who possessed the requisite geographical knowledge of the area. Extreme care was taken not to recruit any possible interviewers that would be directly affected by the proposed Parkway.

The recruited individuals were then required to attend a training session that was twofold in nature. First, to familiarize them with the New River Parkway Authority and the scope of the project. Second, to school them in the techniques and methods that are needed to collect valid evidence when conducting an unscheduled (unstructured) interview.

To accomplish the first task, the legislative sponsors of the Legislative Bill 2073 that officially established the New River Parkway Authority gave a presentation explaining the philosophy underlying the creation of the Authority. They also included in their presentation the scope of the project and what desirable benefits such a Parkway would bring to the area.

The second portion of the training session began with a measurement of the interviewer's knowledge and expertise that would be needed in conducting field surveys, especially when using an unscheduled (unstructured) survey instrument. This apriori expertise and knowledge was ascertained by administering a pre-test. It was assumed that most of the possible interviewers would not possess the requisite knowledge and skills. This assumption, based on the pre-test scores was valid. To eliminate these deficiencies the interviewers were taught the necessary skills, techniques and knowledge that are salient to conducting field surveys. Their acquisition of these interviewing essentials was measured by a post-test. Their efficacy was determined by a score of seventy percent of above on the instrument Those who scored within this range were selected as interviewers.

Respondent Notification

Before the interviewers were sent out into the field to collect the information sought, SWVRA mailed to the property owners/residents in the immediate impact area a letter notifying them that the interviews would be conducted in a specified time frame. Additionally, the major newspapers in the counties of Raleigh and Summers were given press releases regarding the impending interviews. These releases and other pertinent information about the proposed Parkway were published one week before the interviewing was to commence. These notification procedures were to increase citizen awareness that the interviews would be conducted in the area, and to eliminate possible hostilities that might occur between the respondent and interviewer when an interviewer appears unannounced.

Interviewer Field Material and Assignments

Each interviewer was supplied by SWRVA with a packet of materials that included: (1) a copy of the notification letter previously mailed to property owners/residents in the immediate impact area, (2) a copy of the legislative bill establishing the New River Parkway Authority, (3) three maps, each indicating a proposed alternate northern Parkway access/exit interchange and subsequent Parkway route, (4) a short technical explanation concerning each proposed alternate, (5) interview format and survey questions, (6) field note forms, (7) additional paper for more copious notes if needed.

When the interviewers received their packets they were given specific interview assignments based on a geographical grid system. This was the pattern followed except for those who were assigned to conduct interview/surveys in the local post offices with context area property owner/residents. These interviews were conducted on Saturday mornings between 9:30 and 12:30 PM. These hours were selected after consultation with local postmasters. SWVRA was informed that most area residents visited their respective post offices on Saturday mornings to pick up their mail.

SURVEY ANALYSIS

It needs to be emphasized at this point that the instrument developed by SWVRA was, as previously mentioned, unscheduled (unstructured) in its design. An instrument of this type gives the respondent a wide latitude of responses to the probe questions. However, extensive note taking, or the use of field notes after the interview is required of the interviewer. It was from these notes, after several readings, that each survey was content analyzed and subsequently coded into specific categories, as they related to the scope of the survey. This coding was necessary so the information gathered could be subjected to statistical analysis.

The statistical analysis selected for investigating citizen responses to the survey instrument was the Statistical Analysis System, generally referred to as SAS. It is a computer software system for organizing and, of course, analyzing data. The portion of the system used by SWRVA was predominantly "descriptive." Essentially, the data was analyzed by frequencies, numerical counts and percentages. The system also, when requested, produced bar graphs and pie graphs to visibly depict the descriptive data.

The total number of individuals interviewed was 94. These respondents were categorized, as previously stated, based on the information they provided, as property owners (absentee), property owners/residents immediate impact area, and property owners/residents context area. These categories were computer transcribed for simplicity as owner=owner, owner=resident impact area, and owner=resident context area.

The numerical total and the percentages that each category constituted of total interviewed are seen in Table 1.

The residence longevity for N ranged from one year to eighty years. The average length of residency was 26.1 years. Given the length of longevity it was assumed that the individuals who participated in the survey had more than adequate knowledge and insights about the study area.

The content analysis of the survey items focusing upon citizen choice of interchange location, and their justification for selectivity disclosed that the justification responses could be categorized into five distinct reasons. These were scenery, local transportation benefit, economic benefit, cost, and privacy. There were some respondents who gave no reason. This response, for statistical analysis was labeled as such.

Using these six categories the collected data was cross-tabulated with each category of respondent. The cross-tabulations and respective bar graphs are presented in Tables 2 through 10.

The data presented in Tables 11, 12, and 13

TABLE 1

CATEGORIES OF RESPONDENTS AND THEIR PROPORTION TO THE TOTAL INTERVIEWED

CATEGORY	N	PERCENTAGE
Owner=Owner	28	29.8
Owner=Resident Impact Area	22	23.4
Owner=Resident Context Area	44	46.8
Total	94	100

TABLE 2

FREQUENCY CONTROLLING FOR OWNER=OWNER BY LOCATION AND WHY THAT LOCATION
(N 28)

	ALTERNATE LOCATION							
	ALT.#1	% of N	ALT.#2	% of N	ALT. #3	% of N	No Op.	% of N
Why Location								
Scenery	2	7.14	0	00.0	3	10.71	0	00.0
Local Transportation	5	17.06	0	0.00	1	3.57	0	00.0
Economic Benefit	2	7.14	1	3.57	2	7.14	0	00.0
Cost	6	21.43	1	3.57	2	7.14	1	3.57
Privacy	0	0.00	0	0.00	0	0.00	0	0.00
No Reason	1	3.57	0	0.00	0	0.00	1	3.57
Total	16	57.14	2	7.14	8	28.57	2	7.14

Table 3

OWNER=OWNER
CHOICE OF LOCATION FREQUENCY BAR GRAPH

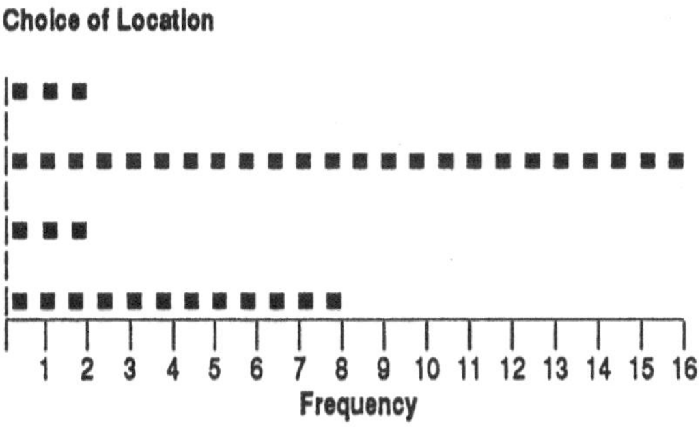

Location	Choice of Location	Freq.	Cum. Freq.	Percent	Cum. Percent
No Opinion	■ ■ ■	2	2	7.14	7.14
Alternate #1	■ ■	16	18	57.14	64.29
Alternate #2	■ ■ ■	2	20	7.14	71.43
Alternate #3	■ ■ ■ ■ ■ ■ ■ ■ ■ ■ ■ ■	8	28	28.57	100.00

1 2 3 4 5 6 7 8 9 10 11 12 13 14 15 16

Frequency

Table 3.

TABLE 4

OWNER=OWNER
WHY LOCATION FREQUENCY BAR GRAPH

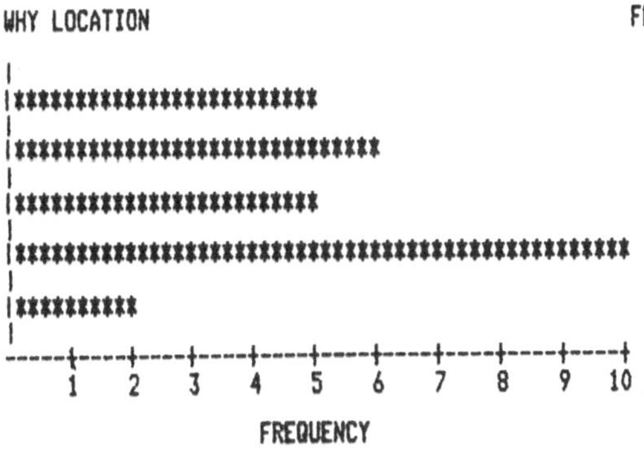

WHYLOCAT	WHY LOCATION	FREQ	CUM. FREQ	PERCENT	CUM. PERCENT
SCENERY	*************************	5	5	17.86	17.86
LOCAL TRANS.	******************************	6	11	21.43	39.29
ECON. BENEFIT	*************************	5	16	17.86	57.14
COST	**	10	26	35.71	92.86
NO REASON	**********	2	28	7.14	100.00

1 2 3 4 5 6 7 8 9 10

FREQUENCY

TABLE 5

FREQUENCY CONTROLLING FOR OWNER=RESIDENT IMPACT AREA AND WHY THAT LOCATON
(N 22)

ALTERNATE CHOICE								
	ALT.#1	% of N	ALT.#2	% of N	ALT.#3	% of N	No.Op.	% of N
Why Location								
Scenery	0	0.00	0	0.00	2	9.09	0	0.00
Local Transportation	1	4.55	0	0.00	0	0.00	0	0.00
Economic Benefit	1	4.55	0	0.00	3	13.64	0	0.00
Cost	7	31.82	0	0.00	1	4.55	1	4.55
Privacy	0	0.00	2	9.09	0	0.00	0	0.00
No Reason	1	0.00	0	0.00	0	0.00	3	13.64
Total	10	45.5	2	9.09	6	27.27	4	18.18

TABLE 6

OWNER=RESIDENT IMPACT AREA
CHOICE OF LOCATION FREQUENCY BAR GRAPH

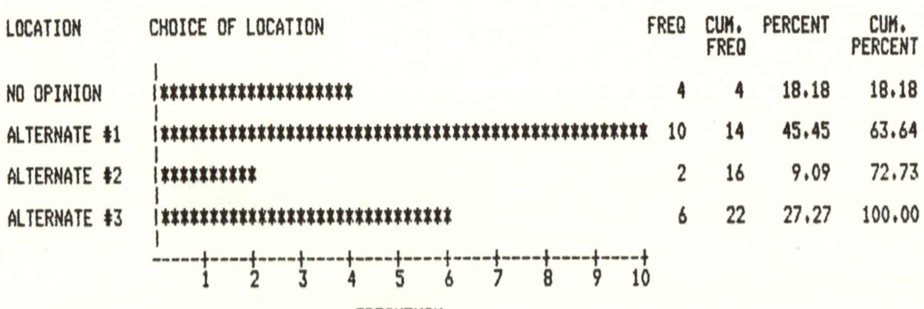

LOCATION	FREQ	CUM. FREQ	PERCENT	CUM. PERCENT
NO OPINION	4	4	18.18	18.18
ALTERNATE #1	10	14	45.45	63.64
ALTERNATE #2	2	16	9.09	72.73
ALTERNATE #3	6	22	27.27	100.00

TABLE 7

OWNER-RESIDENT IMPACT AREA
WHY LOCATION FREQUENCY BAR GRAPH

```
WHYLOCAT         WHY LOCATION                                               FREQ  CUM.  PERCENT    CUM.
                                                                                  FREQ           PERCENT
                 |
SCENERY          |**********                                                  2     2     9.09      9.09
                 |
LOCAL TRANS.     |*****                                                       1     3     4.55     13.64
                 |
ECON. BENEFIT    |********************                                        4     7    18.18     31.82
                 |
COST             |*********************************************               9    16    40.91     72.73
                 |
PRIVACY          |**********                                                  2    18     9.09     81.82
                 |
NO REASON        |********************                                        4    22    18.18    100.00
                 |
                 -----+----+----+----+----+----+----+----+----+
                      1    2    3    4    5    6    7    8    9
                                   FREQUENCY
```

TABLE 8

FREQUENCY CONTROLLING FOR OWNER-CONTEXT AREA AND WHY THAT LOCATION (N 44)

ALTERNATE CHOICE								
	ALT.#1	% of N	ALT.#2	% of N	ALT.#3	% of N	No Op.	% of N
Why Location								
Scenery	4	9.09	0	0.00	1	2.27	0	0.00
Local Transportation	4	9.09	1	2.27	3	6.82	0	0.00
Economic Benefit	3	6.82	0	0.00	1	2.27	0	0.00
Cost	14	31.82	1	2.27	3	6.82	2	4.55
Privacy	1	2.27	0	0.00	0	0.00	1	2.27
No Reason	1	2.27	1	2.27	0	0.00	3	6.82
Total	27	61.36	3	6.82	8	18.18	6	13.64

TABLE 9

OWNER=CONTEXT AREA
CHOICE OF LOCATION FREQUENCY BAR GRAPH

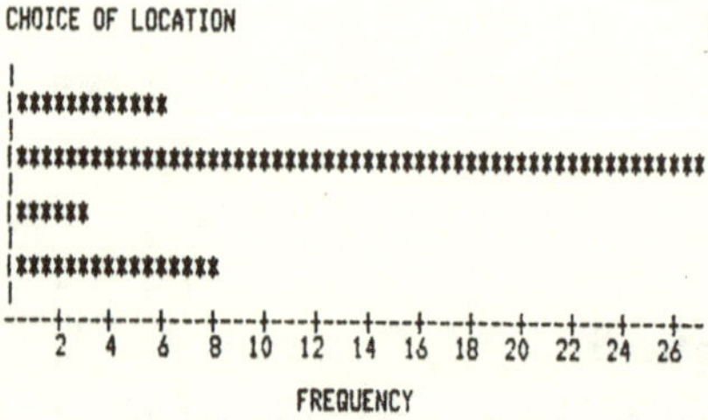

LOCATION	FREQ	CUM. FREQ	PERCENT	CUM. PERCENT
NO OPINION	6	6	13.64	13.64
ALTERNATE #1	27	33	61.36	75.00
ALTERNATE #2	3	36	6.82	81.82
ALTERNATE #3	8	44	18.18	100.00

CHOICE OF LOCATION — FREQUENCY (axis: 2 4 6 8 10 12 14 16 18 20 22 24 26)

TABLE 10

OWNER=CONTEXT AREA
WHY LOCATION FREQUENCY BAR GRAPH

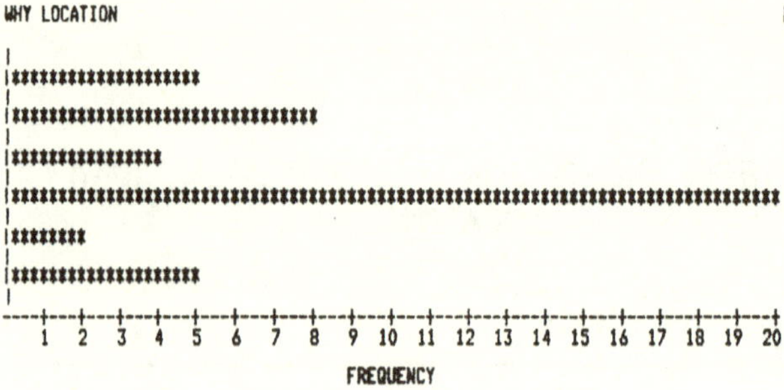

WHYLOCAT	FREQ	CUM. FREQ	PERCENT	CUM. PERCENT
SCENERY	5	5	11.36	11.36
LOCAL TRANS.	8	13	18.18	29.55
ECON. BENEFIT	4	17	9.09	38.64
COST	20	37	45.45	84.09
PRIVACY	2	39	4.55	88.64
NO REASON	5	44	11.36	100.00

WHY LOCATION — FREQUENCY (axis: 1 2 3 4 5 6 7 8 9 10 11 12 13 14 15 16 17 18 19 20)

TABLE 11

COMBINED CATEGORY CHOICE OF LOCATION ALTERNATIVES FREQUENCY BAR GRAPH

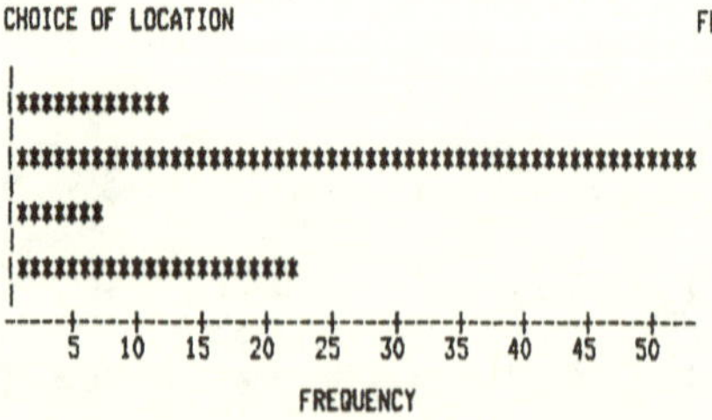

LOCATION	FREQ	CUM. FREQ	PERCENT	CUM. PERCENT
NO OPINION	12	12	12.77	12.77
ALTERNATE #1	53	65	56.38	69.15
ALTERNATE #2	7	72	7.45	76.60
ALTERNATE #3	22	94	23.40	100.00

CHOICE OF LOCATION — FREQUENCY (axis: 5 10 15 20 25 30 35 40 45 50)

TABLE 12

PIE GRAPH OF COMBINED RESPONDENTS CATEGORIES BY CHOICE OF LOCATION CHOSEN

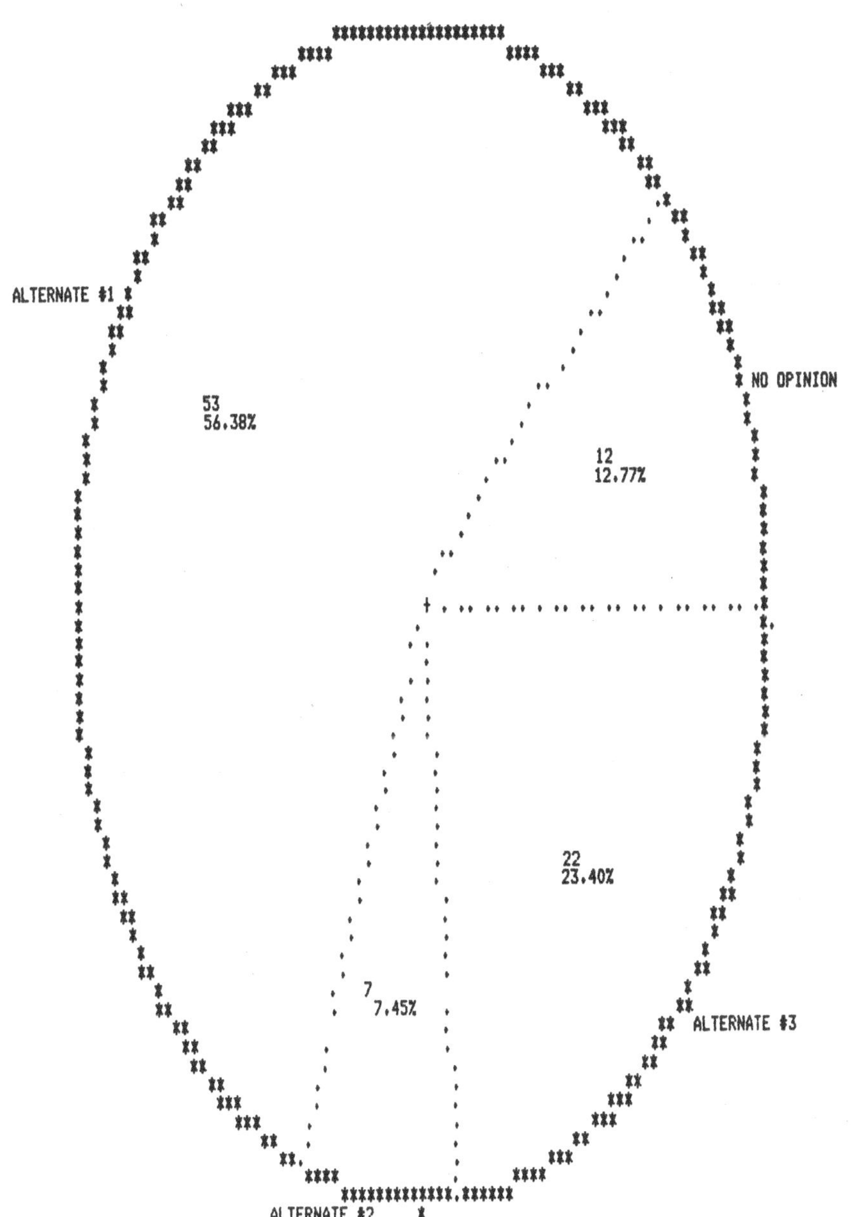

TABLE 13

WHY WAS ALTERNATIVE CHOSEN
FREQUENCY BAR GRAPH

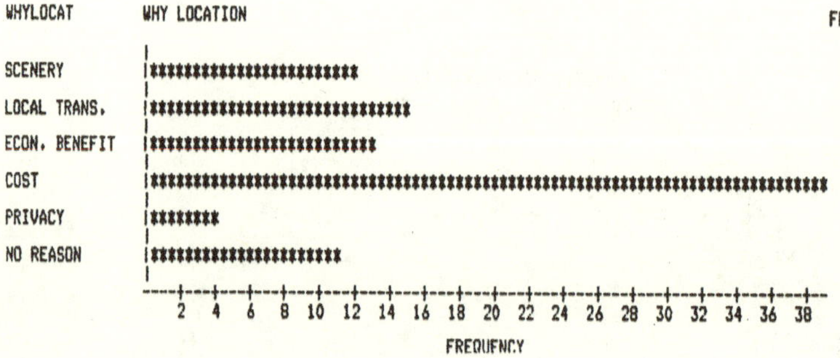

WHYLOCAT	WHY LOCATION	FREQ	CUM. FREQ	PERCENT	CUM. PERCENT
SCENERY		12	12	12.77	12.77
LOCAL TRANS.		15	27	15.96	28.72
ECON. BENEFIT		13	40	13.83	42.55
COST		39	79	41.49	84.04
PRIVACY		4	83	4.26	88.30
NO REASON		11	94	11.70	100.00

FREQUENCY

TABLE 14

Visitors to the area	Frequency	%
Yes	84	89.4
No	6	6.4
No opinon	4	4.3
Total	94	100.0

TABLE 15

Why visit	Frequency	%
Transportation	41	43.6
Scenery	25	26.6
No opinion	28	29.8
Total	94	100.0

TABLE 16
How Will Visitors Help Local Economy

Why economy	N	%
Jobs	15	15.96
Tourism	57	60.64
Access	4	4.26
No opinion	18	19.15
Total	94	100.00

TABLE 17
Overall Opinion of Parkway

Opinion	Frequency	%
For Parkway	76	80.85
Against	11	11.70
No opinion	7	7.45
Total	94	100.00

statistically summarize, and graphically indicate, alternate interchange access choice and why selection for that location, when the three categories of respondents were collapsed into a single entity representing the ninety-four respondents.

The frequency of responses for all categories of respondents as whether or not the interchange will bring more visitors to the area are presented in Table 14. Table 15 indicates their perceptions as why visitation would increase.

The content analysis of the survey item "how will visitors help the local economy" resulted in four categories of responses. These responses were 1) Jobs, 2) Tourism, 3) Accessibility to Area 4)No Opinion. The breakdown of the responses for the entire population surveyed are exhibited in Table 16.

The information regarding interviewer questions about the surveyed population's perceptions about the interchange improving local needs indicated that 32, or 34. 04 percent stated that it would improve transportation by reducing travel time to nearby areas for recreation, shopping, and to places of employment. Additionally, 36 or 38.30 percent perceived better roads in the area as a spin-off effect of the proposed parkway. When these two categories of responses were combined into a single category labeled transportation and better roads, the cumulative numbers 68, or 72.34 percent of the surveyed population felt that local transportation needs would be improved. Those individuals stating no opinion numbered 26, or 27.66 percent of the people surveyed.

A very careful assessment of each survey instrument for opinions favorable or unfavorable to the proposed New River Parkway and an access interchange in the Sandstone, WV area produced the statistical distribution that appears in Table 17.

SUMMARY, CONCLUSIONS AND RECOMMENDATIONS

This project was undertaken to investigate the attitudes of property owners whose land, and usage thereof, might be directly affected by the construction of a New River Parkway access interchange and its subsequent southbound route from Sandstone, WV.

Southern West Virginia Research Associates developed an unstructured (unscheduled) instrument to measure these attitudes. A design of this type was utilized to gain and provide the widest possible latitude of responses. The initial survey items, for the purpose of measurement, were subjected to a field test in an area within a close geographical proximity to the area to be canvassed to determine their appropriateness for the sake of enhancing validity. The original items, based on the results of the field test, were then modified to enhance their validity. The final instrument consisted of ten items. Additionally, there was no one item designed to collect personal data as it related to the property owner/resident status of the individual interviewed.

SWVRA expanded upon the initial scope of the survey regarding the population to be surveyed. Included in the survey were property owners/residence in the impact area, but who would not be personally affected by any land acquisition for the Parkway. The study population also included property owners/residents in the context area. Basically, this was operationalized as the area that would receive any possible economic benefits from such a proposed Parkway.

Interviewers were carefully selected from a local population that had some knowledge of the survey area. These individuals participated in a training session covering the salient techniques and skills needed to conduct a valid unstructured survey. Those interviewers who scored high (seventy percent, or more) on an instrument designed to measure these acquired skills and techniques were selected to field the survey.

The field work was conducted during the third week of September, 1985. The data collected was then content analyzed and transcribed into computer language for the purpose of statistical analysis. The computer analysis produced substantive evidence for SWVRA's conclusions and recommendations.

The range and average of property owner/resident longevity, which far exceeds the national average residency change of approximately once every three years, coupled with the previously unreported rate of three-fourths of the surveyed population having some familiarity with the New River Parkway Authority, led to the conclusion that the individuals surveyed were knowledgeable about the geographical area and the proposed Parkway. It was SWVRA's stance that the citizen input into any decisions, based on an assessment of all evidence regarding the actual location of a Parkway access interchange and its subsequent roadway corridor be valued.

It was concluded, based on a reporting rate of 84.9%, that the geographical area under consideration by the New River Parkway Authority was perceived as being scenic and should be exploited to attract visitors to the area. It was recommended that a Parkway access interchange be located in the study area. This recommendation was further substantiated by other evidence.

The respondents' choice of a Parkway access interchange location, no matter how the property owner/resident status was controlled, was overwhelmingly for alternate #1. The greatest variance in choice of location occurred between the owner=resident impact area and owner=resident context area. However, when compared to the distribution for the other two choices, alternates #2, and #3, between these two groups, alternate #1 exceeded all other choices by a vide margin. The greatest similarity in choice for alternate #1 occurred between owner=owner and owner=resident context area. When all three categories of respondents were combined, the majority, 56.38%, selected alternate #1.

The alternate choice that was perceived as being the least desirable by any category of respondents was alternate choice #2. It appeared, based on the data, and this was SWRVA's recommendation, that alternate #2 is not a viable option. Conversely, when all category of respondents were combined, alternate #3, when compared to the low response rate for alternate #2, could be considered as an alternative. The distribution of choices for these two alternatives were 23.40% for alternate #3, 7.45% for alternate #2. It was also to be noted that 12.77% of all respondents had no opinion choice. These individuals could possibly be perceived as supporting alternate #3. When the no opinion choice was combined with the alternate #3 choice then the effective rate was 46.17%. This was only a 10.21 percentage difference between alternate #1 and #3. Additionally, when examining the alternate choice for the property owner/resident controlled situation, better than one-fourth of the owner=owner and owner= resident impact area selected alternate #3. These are precisely the two groups that would be most affected by any decision to make alternate #3 a viable option.

This viability becomes more apparent when the reasons cited for alternate choice are scrutinized. Every category of respondents who selected alternate #1 indicated most often that their choice was predicated upon what they perceived as being less expensive to construct. All other variables, except local transportation needs, were not emphasized by the respondents in any degree of significance when compared to the economic factor of construction cost. However, when based on cost estimates for the interchange construction in this immediate area by the West Virginia Department of Highways, alternate #1 would be approximately 3.3 million dollars more costly to build than alternate #3. It was SWVRA's recommendation that the cost factor be weighed heavily, based on the evidence for alternate choice selectivity, by the New River Parkway Authority in any decisions regarding interchange selectivity. It was also the contention of the organization that construction cost figures relating to three proposed access interchanges and the factors used in the determinations be heavily publicized in the area. This should increase cognizance of cost and how it is determined among those individuals who will be most affected by any interchange site location. This recommendation and contention was also premised on the fact, reiterating the point, that alternate #3 received some significant consideration as a possible choice.

Most of those interviewed perceive a Parkway interchange in the area as increasing outside visitation. Better transportation was the primary reason for this perception. The secondary perception was the scenic beauty of the area. These perceptions receive more credence because the evidence assimilated also indicated that most of the respondents discerned that increased visitation vis-a-vis tourism, would help the local economy. These inferences were not without justification. There is overwhelming information that increased tourism can be a boon to a local economy i.e., the Smoky Mountain area especially Gatlinburg and Pigeons Ford Tenn., or Florida, a classic example where a large portion of the income in the state is generated through tourism. It was this organization's <u>recommendation</u> that the concept of tourism be pursued as a salient feature in creating a New River Parkway in an area that definitely, based on most economic indicators, is economically deprived.

This recommendation was further buttressed by the fact that most of the respondents see the creation of a Parkway as a mechanism to provide employment for local people. This includes both employment in the actual construction of such a planned Parkway and subsidiary employment opportunities long after construction is completed.

The evidence also indicates that most of the respondents perceive the Parkway and its access interchange as improving local transportation needs. This feature was especially important to those who are employed in adjacent areas. It was also important to many who want a greater access to goods and services beyond what the local area is now providing. The aspect of improving local transportation should merit increased attention when considering local support needed to bring a project of this nature to fruition.

The final assessment, based on the content analysis of the survey instrument, was that a significant majority of the surveyed population were favorably predisposed toward the construction of a New River Parkway and its concomitant access interchange. The overall favorable opinion, as previously reported elsewhere in this document, was 80.9%. Opinions unfavorable were 11.7%, the remaining 7.4% were unsure. Given this overwhelming support it was SWVRA's stance that construction of the Parkway and an access interchange, in the area under consideration, be undertaken.

Caution should be exercised, however. Opposition did exist from some property owners in two of the property owner/resident categories. Most exists in the owner=owner category, with some opposition existing in the owner=resident impact area. The opposition centers around alternate #3 as an access interchange. The opposition focused on a perception, right or wrong, that alternate #3 and its proposed roadway would infringe on the "Old Richmond Home Place." According to information gathered through the content analysis of the survey items, this homeplace was deeded to the above family on a sheepskin deed in 1789. Also, according to some respondents in this particular area, there is a graveyard on Richmond Island that contains two graves that are about 200 years old. These are supposedly the graves of two early Richmond sisters who lived and died on the island. If this is the case, it is suggested that this area of the "Old Home Place" be designated an historical site, but provide owner access to land. It also might be considered for preservation as Cade's Cove has been in the Smoky Mountains.

NOTES

1. House Bill 273, Committee on Political Subdivisions, April, 1985

APPENDIX: INTERVIEW FORMAT AND QUESTIONS TO BE ASKED DURING THE SURVEY

As interviewers, your initial contact with the respondent will probably occur at the door of the house. It might occur elsewhere on the property; whatever the situation, introduce yourself by name and where you are from. Be explicit about your task, and emphasize that you are representing Southern West Virginia Research Associates. You might begin the interview as follows:

Hello. My name is ________. I am from

________. I would like to talk to you about the new interchange and proposed connectors for the New River Parkway. This survey is being conducted by Southern West Virginia Research Associates who will forward your responses and input to the New River Parkway Authority so they can make the best decisions regarding the construction of the Parkway in relationship to the benefits it will bring to the local area.

During each interview with a property owner, (keeping in mind that this is an unstructured interview, therefore no sequential order is required) the following questions *must* be asked inthe context of the interview.

1. Are you the owner of this property? (If no, try and get the name of the property owner. If yes, please identify. Continue interview.)
2. Are you familiar with the proposed interchange and the Parkway Authority? (Interviewer will be prepared to discuss the development of the Parkway Authority, the enabling legislation, and its role in the project.)
3. How long have you lived here?
4. How many people in your household?
5. Do you feel the area is scenic enough to be of interest to a majority of non-residents who may pass through?
6. Where do you think the best location would be for the proposed interchange? (Interviewer will have maps displaying alternatives.)
7. Why there?
8. Will the interchange bring more visitors to the area? Why?
9. Would it be good to hire local people wherever possible on this project?
10. Will more visitors to the area help the local economy?
11. Will the interchange improve local transportation needs? Why?

The Blue Ridge Parkway: Can It Survive as a Park Without a Science-Research Program?

Garrett A. Smathers, Senior Research Scientist, National Park Service, Retired

The Blue Ridge Parkway is an elongated park that runs along the high crests of the southern Appalachians, connecting Shenandoah National Park with the Great Smoky Mountain National Park. Because of its national outstanding natural, cultural, and scenic features, the area was placed under the administration of the National Park Service (NPS). This regional jewel was to take its place along with the nation's national parks and monuments in preserving America's wonderlands.

PROTECTION AND PRESERVATION

As a member of the National Park System, the Parkway is administered under the codes and policies of the 1916 NPS Act. The founders of the 1916 Act made sure that the law was explicit in its purpose and content. Every knowledgeable NPS employee can recite its basic charge: "conserve the scenery, and the natural and historic objects, and the wildlife therein and provide for the enjoyment of the same in such a manner and by such means as will leave them unimpaired for the enjoyment of future generations."

To provide for the enjoyment of the parks' outstanding features requires public access to these resources in a manner that does not adversely impair them. Regardless whether man intrudes, there are always natural changes taking place in park ecosystems. Some natural perturbations take place abruptly, such as a volcanic eruption in Hawaii Volcanoes National Park that can destroy thousands of acres of forest. Other changes may be subtle and take thousands of years, such as plant succession following a retreating glacier in Glacier Bay National Monument in Alaska. These are not the changes or impairments the 1916 Act referenced, but they and other ecological and historical conditions of the park must be understood to protect, preserve, and provide for its enjoyment for generations to come.

FIRST SCIENCE PROGRAM—ITS PURPOSE AND SUPPORT

The first implementation of the 1916 Act was to establish a naturalist-educational program in the national parks. Its purpose was to provide visitors information about the parks' plants, animals, geology, and cultural history. It was reasoned that the more visitors understood about the park, the more they would appreciate and protect their natural and historical heritage.

Along with the naturalist-educational program there developed a wildlife biologist organizational unit that provided expert research-resources management of the parks' biological and physical resources. Also this unit was responsible in guiding the planning and developments of parks to prevent adverse impacts that would impair the unique features. Such names as Dr. Harold C. Bryant, Adolph Murie, and George Wright were the first scientists and resources management leaders of the new agency. (Smathers 1975)

In the first few years of the new agency it needed expert research-resources management personnel to guide park development, maintenance, and interpretation. Early park managers assumed this need was implied in the 1916 Act, wherein it stated that enjoyment of the parks' resources must be done in a manner that will not impair them for future generations. To do this would require an expert knowledge of the area's resources. Unfortunately, because of this omission in the 1916 legislation, in later years some parks' values were adversely impaired or destroyed.

A PROGRAM WITHOUT ROOTS

The science-research program is not a line item in the NPS budget. It exists solely at the desire of park management. In a manner, the science program serves at the pleasure of the park manager and Director of the NPS. Authority and funding of its existence flow from the Director to the Regional Director to the park Superintendent. They can give and they can take.

At times in some parks conflicts may develop between the superintendent and the scientist. Opinions may differ on project funding, importance of the research needs, planned developments, resources management activities or just plain personality conflict that can plague any organization. The scientist is usually supervised by the superintendent. His recommendations can be ignored, delayed, or not considered worthwhile. If he persists in his contentions the scientist can find himself being transferred to another job or worse. In reality, the park scientist has no recourse to a higher scientist-supervisor in settling professional matters on park problems.

In some parks the scientists and park managers work exceedingly well together. Conflicts are rare. If they do occur they are readily and mutually resolved. But historic records show that even in these good situations the condition can deteriorate. When normal transfer of personnel takes place, and a "new team" is reassembled, a different mix of personalities may not be as compatible as the old combination.

UPS AND DOWNS

The foregoing conditions, good or bad, can prevail in any park at any time. The greatest impact, good or bad, on the service-wide science-research program occurs in changes of the national administration. The new Secretary of the Interior and his appointed National Park Service Director set the service-wide policies and missions for the management of the parks. If the science-research program is favored, it generally has service-wide support and prospers. If not, it suffers and so do the parks.

The periods of service-wide support and non-support of the science-research program have been described by one observer as the "uppers" and "downers". Historic records show that four (4) major "downers" have occurred since the 1916 NPS Act. During "downers" park values suffer. Citizens visiting parks become alarmed and incensed over the degradation of resources. They readily file their complaints with Congress, conservation organizations, and the administration in office. The response is generally quick and effective and an "upper" follows.

A classical example of the "upper" and "downer" syndrome can best be described by an NPS program called Mission 66 and the development of the Blue Ridge Parkway.

PARKWAY AND MISSION 66

The Parkway's first planning and development activities were guided by a well disciplined and highly dedicated team of scientists and managers. The multidisciplinary group consisted of a naturalist, historian, landscape architect, and engineer. The superintendent, a highly respected leader, used the recommendations of the group in the decision making process. A full inventory and evaluation of every known natural and historical feature of the park corridor was made for its preservation, interpretation, and scenic value. Once these features and conditions were determined, the roadway and needed facilities were designed to be superimposed upon them with minimum impact. The roadway was designed as a window for viewing the outstanding resources without adversely affecting them with further human contact. Nature trails, side roads, parking areas, and visitor centers were strategically located to tell the story of an area.

In 1955, the Director of the NPS launched his Mission 66 program, a 10-year period from 1956 to 1966, to bring national parks up to standards. Shortage of funds to maintain and expand park facilities and visitor services, as well as an exponential increase in visitor use, were creating a crisis in national parks. With the full support of President Eisenhower, NPS Director, Conrad Wirth, moved forward with the Mission 66 program with wide support and great hopes for the national parks. Many fine accomplishments were made.

The Mission 66 program was a boon to the developing Parkway. New funding meant that roadway construction, facilities, and personnel staffing could move ahead at a faster pace than previously planned. Unlike most parks the Parkway already had safeguards in place to assure that accelerated planning and developments did not destroy park values.

Some other parks did not fare as well as the Parkway, because they did not have a science-research program to evaluate and advise planning activities. Adverse development impacts began to occur. Trails were built over shallow-rooted giant redwoods, and in one park a swampland was filled to expand a campground. Seeing park resources destroyed, and feeling the NPS Director was not supporting his science-research program, the Chief Scientist of the National Parks, Victor C. Culhane, resigned his position (Sumner 1967). Immediately the science-research program went into a "downer".

By the early 1960's concerned public, scientific community, and conservationist organizations became alarmed at the destruction of park resources values. Dr. Stanley A. Cain, a world renowned scientist, charged that the National Park Service did not have a basic ecological-research program to meet its resources management and planning needs (Cain 1959). The early 1960's was a period of great public awareness of environmental degradations by pollution and landscape destruction. The new Secretary of the Interior, Stewart L. Udall, became the articulate voice of environmental conservation (Everhart 1972). Because of his concern about the conditions of the national parks, the Secretary had two surveys made to analyze the problems and make recommendations. Both of the reports presented in 1963 were prepared by some of the most renowned natural scientists and conservationists of the time. The first of the reports, chaired by the famous ecologist Starker Leopold, emphasizes the importance of habitat preservation in the national parks, and the elimination of management interferences that prevented the ecological processes that gave rise and characterized it. It was also emphasized that no restorations of extirpated species were to be undertaken unless based upon sound ecological study and evaluation. This report was titled: Wildlife Management in the National Parks.

The second report, A Report of the Advisory Committee to the National Park Service on Research, was prepared by a select committee of scientists from the prestigious National Academy of Sciences. The committee was chaired by William J. Robbins, and consisted of national outstanding scientists, such as Stanley A. Cain, a world renowned plant ecologist. The Robbins report emphasized that parks were unique ecosystems, often only relics left of once great natural systems that characterized our national heritage. Among the report's many recommendations, it charged park managers to undertake no planning or development or resources management activities without a thorough study of the impact it would have upon the park ecosystem and those contiguous to the park. Further it recommended that there be an Assistant Director for Research in the National Parks, and that he have a staff of research scientists to work with managers in seeing that park values were protected and maintained. Unfortunately, both reports failed to recommend that the science-research program be established by legislation and with its own Director and funding.

The two reports had an immediate impact on the management of the national parks.In October 1965, the NPS Director's office issued guidelines that stated that no development or habitat management was to be undertaken in national parks without a thorough research study of its impact on the parks' natural and cultural resources.

OUT OF CONTROL

Before the close of Mission 66, the Parkway began to lose its highly respected research-planning team, because of personnel transfers and new directives from the NPS Washington office. Eventually, planning development became the sole responsibility of the landscape architect and superintendent, coordinated with the NPS Denver Service Center. Parkway naturalists and historians had only subordinate roles in the over all planning process. In spite of the Director's 1965 guidelines requiring research study before planning, Parkway officials moved ahead to develop high-density visitor use areas and facilities without ecological studies. This uncontrolled momentum resulted in devastation of one of the area's most outstanding scenic, scientific, and cultural features in the Mount Pisgah area between mileposts 406-409.

The entire Mt. Pisgah area is covered with an outstanding vegetation type called an Oak Orchard, because of the trees' grotesque growth form caused by severe microclimatic conditions. Studies have shown that these trees have evolved into a unique genetic type, probably as a result of the harsh environment (McGee 1970). Scientists have classified the Mt. Pisgah Oak Orchard vegetation as the best representative in the southern Appalachians (DeLapp 1978). The area contains several unique species of plant and animal life. For example, it is the potential habitat for the national endangered Northern Flying Squirrel.

The Flat Laurel Gap section of the Oak Orchard forest contains one of the southern Appalachian's outstanding peat bogs. This site reveals records of late Pleistocene glaciation-climate and its impact on the vegetation of the high mountain summits. 3,000 years of vegetation dynamics for this area can be determined from core-sampling the bog (Shafer 1986).

In addition to its natural history, the area abounds in Cherokee Indian mythology and events of European man's settlements. Here is also the story of George Vanderbilt, the great American capitalist and conservationist who started the first school of forestry in the United States in the nearby Pink Beds.

In 1966, Parkway officials began to develop the area and award concession contracts to provide food, lodging, and campground operations. Either Parkway officials did not know or ignored the 1965 Washington office directive requiring approval of such developments. Some environmentalists questioned if such services should be provided at this site, because all could be obtained in nearby localities off the Parkway, and there were no hardships on visitors at this location.

In 1966 a 40-room inn was constructed to replace an older and smaller facility used in the area before the Parkway acquired the land. At the same time a 140-unit campground with five (5) comfort stations was constructed in a segment of the Oak Orchard forest that contained the unique paleoecological bog. Later a picnic area with forty-five (45) tables and fireplaces and one (1) comfort station were added to the forested site. Within this complex a service station and camper-supply store that contained a 13,000 gallon gasoline underground storage tank were constructed. To handle wastes from these operations, a primary sewage treatment facility that discharges partially-treated effluent into a sand filtration-drainage system, was constructed. This facility is located upon seeps and springs of the headwaters of Pisgah Creek, which is part of the drinking water supply for eastern Haywood County. The sewage treatment facility handles an average of 22,000 gallons of sewage each day with peak periods approaching 31,000. The location and potential failure of this system in contaminating the drinking water supply is a constant concern of Haywood County officials.

A NEW PROMISE

In 1974 the National Park Service Science Center (NPSC) established a Cooperative Park Studies Unit (CPSU) at Western Carolina University (WCU) to provide research assistance to the Great Smoky Mountain National Park and the Blue Ridge Parkway. NPSC had a cooperative program with the National Aeronautical Space Administration (NASA) to provide space-age technology and ecological services to these Parks for the planning process. The NPS/WCU/CPSU, with minimal support funds from NPS, directed and completed student theses on park projects. This agreement provided the parks with highly definitive research information at a much reduced cost. One thesis project was directed to study heath lands of Mt. Pisgah and Flat Laurel Gap bog and the impacts of developments there. Regrettably, between 1976-1977, the NPSC program was abolished by the new Director of the NPS. The rationale for this action was that the NPSC service-wide program could be better carried out by the individual parks and the NPS Denver Service Center. After some maneuvering in 1977, the NPSC Chief Scientist was reassigned to the WCU/CPSU as a Senior Research Scientist to continue and expand the research program on the Blue Ridge Parkway. In 1978, with a change in the national administration, the former NPS Director was reassigned as superintendent of the Blue Ridge Parkway.

The NPS/WCU/CPSU research program, even with meager funding, began to bring great benefits to Parkway planning, resources management and interpretive activities. One highlight of its presence was preventing the construction of a large maintenance facility in the Frying Pan Gap area (mile post 410), a site in the outstanding Oak Orchard forest near the Mount Pisgah complex.

LAST DOWNER

On June 25, 1983, a preliminary "downer" occurred at the NPS/WCU/CPSU that was later to spread throughout the research program in the NPS. On that date, and without any prior warning, the Senior Research Scientist and his staff received notice from the NPS Southeast Regional Office that his position and the CPSU were being abolished by reduction in force (RIF). He was given 10 days to decide on transfer to a new assignment in Florida or take mandatory retirement. On contacting WCU and Parkway officials he was told they knew nothing about the notice. Upon writing to the Regional Office asking for clarification that the people he worked for knew nothing of the RIF, and that he had over $75,000 worth of research data that only he and his thesis students and University colleagues could process, he was told that he had not answered the RIF notice properly, therefore he was retired. In addition he was told that his concerns over the research data did not matter.

Since abolishment of the NPS/WCU/CPSU, many Parkway values have declined or been destroyed. For example: an endangered species of plant was mowed down; a primitive road built through a North Carolina Natural Heritage site to lay a waterline; mixing isolated endemic Fraser fir gene pools by transplanting seedings near Richland Balsam; using alkaline base materials to make a trail surface in acid soil of the spruce-fir forest zone; and asphalting nature trails. The most flagrant violation was planned construction of an employee's quarters in the already impaired Flat Laurel Gap bog. This proposed action, which drew the wrath of area scientists and conservationists, was defeated. However, the alternative is to build the facility near the present inn, which will destroy another large segment of the Oak Orchard vegetation.

The present research "downer" on the Parkway is correlated with increasing commercialization of the area. Aside from business activity at sites like the Mt. Pisgah complex and the Folk Arts Center at Oteen (milepost 382)—where a large green space has been sacrificed for a business venture that could well have been located off the Parkway—nodes of commercial characterization seemed to be proliferating. For example, it has been reported that the popular historic Mabry Mill site, (milepost 176) is now under plans for large expansion. Recently the NPS payed $660,000 for 82 acres of land on Hemphill Knob (milepost 368) to build a headquarters building. The land and facility will be separated from the large River Ridge Mall by the busy Interstate 40. Some visitors centers, that once displayed exhibits and artifacts telling the story of the natural and cultural history of the site, are now more like commercial operations. At the Craggy Gardens Visitor Center (milepost 365) practically all the exhibits that once revealed the outstanding ecology of the area have been replaced with book-sale racks, postcards, and similar materials. The information counter is now more like a sales counter.

Scientists have barely begun to inventory and study the unique ecological resources of the Parkway. Passing through five (5) degrees of longitude and nearly three (3) degrees latitude, and reaching to 6,050 feet elevation, the roadway corridor contains one of the most diversified plant and animal life habitats in North America. Much of this great national heritage will be lost or adversely impaired if the research program is not restored with park scientists. Thousands of dollars worth of the WCU/CPSU dormant data is being overlooked by management. It needs to be analyzed and applied. Only a concerned citizenry can accomplish this through legislation that will establish the science-research program as a permanent organizational unit not only on the Parkway, but in every park of the NPS.

REFERENCES

Cain, S. A. 1959. Ecological islands as natural laboratories, in the Meaning of Wilderness to Science. Sixth Biennial Wilderness Conference, Sierra Club, San Francisco, California.

DeLapp, J. A. 1978. Gradient analyses and classification of the high elevation red oak community of the southern Appalachians. MS thesis. North Carolina State University. Raleigh. 483 p.

Everhart, W. C. 1972. The National Park Service. Praeger, New York. 276 p.

McGee, C. E. 1973. Is variation in budbreak of red oak the result of heredity or environment? Twelfth South. For. Tree Improv. Proc. 1973: 185-189.

Shafer, D. S. 1986. Flat Laurel Gap Bog, Pisgah Ridge, North Carolina: Late Holocene development of a high-elevation heath bald. Castanea 51: 1-9.

Sumner, L. 1967. Biological research and management in the National Park Service, a history. Natural Resources Vol. 1 (4). National Park Service, Washington, D.C.

Smathers, G. A. 1975. Historical overview of resources management planning in the National Park Service. Proceedings: 26th Annual American Institute of Biological Meeting, Oregon State University. Symposium: Natural Resources Planning in the National Park Service II. Natural Resources Plan. National Park Service Science Center, Bay St. Louis, Mississippi. 16 p.

The Blue Ridge Parkway Study: Landscape Management; History, Classification, Simulation and Evaluation

Richard C. Smardon, Ph.D., Senior Research Associate, and James F. Palmer, Ph.D., Senior Research Associate, Faculties of Environmental Studies & Landscape Architecture, SUNY, ESF, Syracuse, New York; and Timothy R. Day, Assistant Professor, California Polytechnic State University, Department of Landscape Architecture, Pomona, California

BACKGROUND

In 1984, the School of Landscape Architecture of the State University of New York in cooperation with the University of Tennessee undertook a research project to study viewer reactions to certain vegetative management techniques used by the National Park Service in the Blue Ridge Parkway, North Carolina. The aims of the State University of New York were twofold. The first was to generate a series of photographic simulations depicting the visual effect produced by the control of vegetation immediately surrounding the Parkway's scenic overlooks. Ultimately, the simulations were incorporated into a visitor questionnaire (Day, 1984 and Palmer et al., 1986). The second aim and the purpose of this article involved the investigation and documentation of alternative methods of vegetation management to those currently used by the Park Service.

PURPOSE

In 1936, governance of the Blue Ridge Parkway became part of the National Park Service (see the Land Tenure Chronology in Table 1). The initial idea of a Blue Ridge Parkway began prior to World War I, but the concept of a scenic road connecting the Shenandoah to the north and the Great Smoky Mountains National Park to the south developed mostly during the Depression years.

One of the prime goals then and today was to provide the users with a living museum of natural and man-made form. The problem in pursuing this goal lies in the difficulty in maintaining the open quality which gives the Blue Ridge the character that the visiting public prefers. Rapid vegetation growth produced from highly conducive environmental conditions can eventually block the visitors' view from the road.

Most vegetation management techniques used by the park Service in the Blue Ridge are very expensive and time-consuming and perhaps more importantly, inconsistent with the living museum goal. Our approach then was to investigate alternative methods that might be more consistent with this goal by presenting the following:

- a clear picture of the most historically significant cultures of the Blue Ridge Settlement;
- the kinds of land management techniques utilized by native Americans and settlers; and
- the relationship between these techniques, where applicable, and the kinds of management practice problems faced by the National Park Service today.

BLUE RIDGE CULTURE AND MANAGEMENT PRACTICES

The first known party to have explored the Blue Ridge Mountain area was DeSoto in 1560 followed by the Bickell Party in the 1730's (Smathers, 1982). In addition to finding Indians inhabiting the area, they found a pristine virgin landscape described as "beautiful valleys covered with woods, pastures and savannahs". The trail system developed by the Indians was extensive, particularly on the slopes and summits where they set up summer camps. Some evidence indicates that these camp sites referred to as balds are still identifiable because of the intense use by the Indians and later

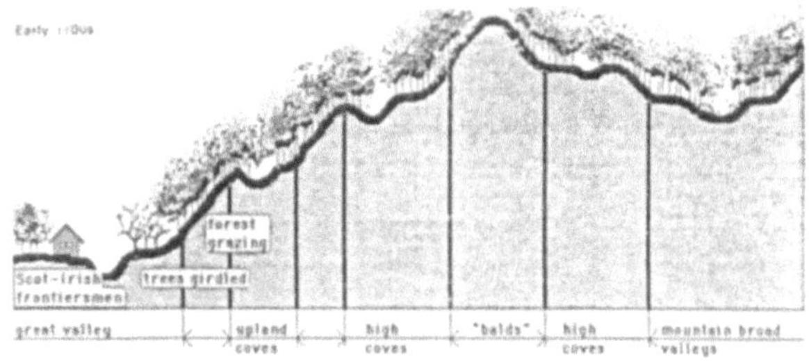

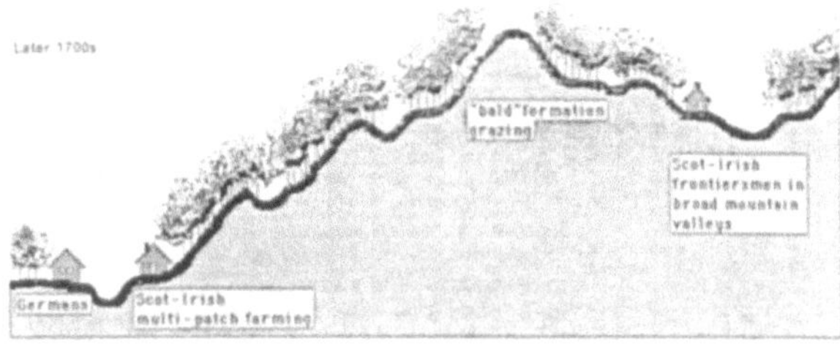

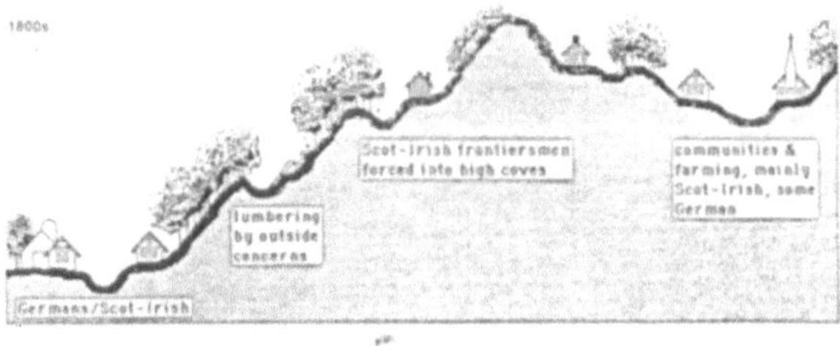

Fig. 1. Management practices of the different cultures settling in the Blue Ridge Mountains. (Source: Smardon, Day, Redway, and Reichardt, 1985.)

settlers (Mitchell, 1938; see Fig. 1).

By 1950, the Blue Ridge was sparsely settled in isolated family farming units (see Fig. 1). The land, like most of the south at this time, was managed as garden rather than field. Once suitable farm and pasture land was found by analyzing vegetation cover, hillsides were cleared by burning and girdling (Stilgoe, 1982).

Among the early mountaineers, the Scot-Irish rapidly adopted the Indian ways of cultivation (see the Land Tenure Chronology, Table 1). They used the simple technique of slash and burn but with no replenishment of the soil (Riddel, 1984). Following the Germans, they settled first in the bottom lands where soil and game were best. But, as they moved into the smaller coves where the soil was shallower, widespread erosion led the U.S. Department of Agriculture to proclaim that 100,000 farms were unfit for agriculture (Jolley, 1969).

Unlike the Scot-Irish, the German goal was to own the land and manage it more efficiently. They chose land heavily timbered in hardwoods, in valleys composed of limestone soils similar to their homeland (Long, 1972). They planted small gardens on the warm side of their homes on which several types of exotic and domestic vegetables were grown. In addi-

PERIOD	LOCATION	LAND TENURE PRACTICE	CULTURE	SOURCE
Late 1600s	*Virginia and Carolinas*	Plantation settlement, extensive agricultural practice, free-range of livestock, crude structures, cash cropping.	English with Scot Irish servants	Stilgoe (1982)
Pre-1716	*Shenandoah Valley*	Timber burned to increase game habitats.	Native Americans	Kerchevan (1902)
Early 1700s	*Appalachia*	Tree girdling, rough ploughing between dead stands.	Scot Irish	Kerchevan (1902)
1718	*Pennsylvania, Great Valley North Carolina Piedmont* and *Blue Ridge*	Small patch farming, trees girdled, left standing or burned, corn and tobacco crops.	Scot Irish	Stilgoe (1982) Graeff (1941) Opie (1980) Kerchevan (1902)
1775	*North Carolina*	German movement continues from Pennsylvania into western counties and highlands of North Carolina.	Germans	Bittenger (1901)
1776	*Blue Ridge North Carolina*	Blue Ridge and Alleghenys opened up for settlement by continental congress.		
1700s	*Pennsylvania*	Permanent meadows were ploughed; pasturing occurred 1 May - 1 Nov.; vegetable gardening on warm side of house; neatly fenced; efficient farm practices; tilled intensively, rotated crops, manured; farmstead kept orderly and clean; frequently cattle and sheep turned out into newly cut-over land to subdue it for cultivation; prevailing practice was to pasture livestock on worn-out field reverting to succession; fewer farmers laid down land in grass after taking two to four grain crops; upland meadows pastured several years before reverting to crop rotation; apple orchards common; fences symbolise good farming.	Germans	Long (1972)
1700s	*Pennsylvania*	German farm distinguished from Scot Irish by superior size of barns, plain compact form of houses, height of enclosures, extent of orchards, fertility of fields, luxuriousness of meadows, appearance of plenty and order.	German	Long (1972)
1700-1800	*Blue Ridge*	Bottom lands settled first, most fertile soil and game; future settlers moved into hills and coves.	Scot Irish	Kercheval (1902) and Weller (1965)
1700-1800	*Appalachia*	Houses built on bottom lands near streams; slopes farmed (perpendicular farming).	Scot Irish	Weller (1965)
1700-1800	*Appalachia*	Unfamiliar with manuring or soil conditioning; hillside patches cleared as lower fields depleted.	Scot Irish	Kollmorgen (1942)
1700-1800	*Appalachia*	Principal crops, corn and tobacco.	Scot Irish	Weller (1965) Stilgoe (1982)
Mid-late 1800	*Blue Ridge North Carolina*	Exploitation by lumber and mining companies result in large tracts of cut out, burned out, washed out lands; feldspar and mica; primarily small operations.	Scot Irish	Sheppard (1935)
19 present	*Blue Ridge North Carolina*	Governance by National Park Service.	National Park Service	Smathers (1982)

tion, they usually planted orchards of fruit trees in the first cleared field.

The Germans consolidated some of the abandoned patches left by the Scot-Irish and following their European traditions allowed cattle and sheep to graze and subdue the land for several years prior to cultivation. After a period of intense tilling, crops were planted and rotated followed by more manuring to increase fertility. Cattle were routinely allowed to free-range (unmanaged grazing) after the fields became permanent.

MANAGEMENT TECHNIQUES UTILIZED

The land management 'mind-set' carried into the Blue Ridge by these cultures largely determined how the Blue Ridge looks today. Our research indicates four major categories of use and management. They were sometimes used singly but most often in combination with other techniques.

Girdling

During the mid 1800's to early 1900's, a form of vegetation management called girdling was used primarily by the Scot-Irish. The technique involves simply removing a band or belt of a tree's bark and cambium layer thus inhibiting the flow of moisture and nutrients to the upper stems. Eliminating the tree canopy encouraged understory growth for forage or cultivation.

Slash Burning

This management technique, most closely associated with the German culture and known as slash burning, had as its goal the super-enrichment of the soil. Tree limbs and slabs were piled evenly across the ground and fired, singeing the soil. Then, rye was planted and harvested, after which more limbs were spread and fired, followed by a planting of grains. The process was repeated every 5 or 6 years.

A by-product of this technique was the resumption of successional growth. Large areas called colicks were formed after the fields became derelict and are composed even today of a dominant cover of compact heath shrubs.

Grazing

The settlers raised a variety of domestic animals including sheep, cattle and mules. Due to the thinness of the upland soils, evidence indicates that many of the so-called grassy balds referred to earlier were maintained and extended by the constant trampling. The succeeding grasses, mostly mountain oat grass (Danthonia ompressa and Rumex acetosella) were too competitive and choked most tree and shrub volunteers (Smathers, 1982).

Natural Succession

The natural succession process is exhibited by the ongoing emergence of plant species and is seen most dramatically following catastrophic phenomena like cutting and burning by man or by natural processes like high winds or soil erosion. The result is usually associated with deep erosion to less fertile subsoil in the margins of old fields and includes heath or broomsedge and asters which can compete with other grasses and which usually replace them quickly.

Growing in sparse stands, broomsedge (Andropogon spp.) for example, survives as a monoculture until enough ground litter is produced to support other forms of grass and woody vegetation (Bake, 1972). At the time of writing, the authors have not found enough reference material to indicate the length of time before other pioneering plants out-compete broomsedge on abandoned farmland. However, it appears that the plant has potential applications in a vegetation management policy for the Parkway. Broomsedge is particularly suitable because it does not pose the same entangling and overgrown characteristics of kudzu or woody pioneering plants which it out-competes. It presents to the viewer a fine-textured, uniform mass of vegetation for an apparently extended period of time; and its maintenance needs are minimal.

Opposite: ***Table 1.*** (Source: Smardon, Day, Redway, and Reichardt, 1985)

LANDSCAPE CLASSIFICATION

Along the 469 miles of the Blue Ridge Parkway, over 250 scenic overlooks have been established. Due to logistical and financial constraints, as well as the tolerance levels of questionnaire respondents (Zeisel, 1981), simulation of vegetation management techniques at every overlook was beyond the scope of this project. Therefore, it became necessary to select several overlook scenes representative of the range of visual experiences encountered along the entire Parkway.

In order to initiate this selection process, a library of Ektachrome slides was obtained from the University of Tennessee. The photographic library of 298 slides contained a shot from each of the established Parkway overlooks plus a number of duplicate photographs made to compensate for poor lighting conditions or technical problems.

The slide selection process involved four sequential steps:

1. Formulation of a landscape classification system.
2. Classification of each of the slides in the photographic library.
3. Grouping of overlook scenes based on similar landscape components.
4. Selection of 1-2 representative slides from each of the established groups of overlook scenes based upon degree of photographic quality and suitability for simulation purposes.

The classification system used to denote the representativeness of all the images and assist in selection of images for management prescription and simulation included land use, landform pattern and landform spatial configuration, distance zones seen and landscape compositional types (see Figure 2) and see Smardon et al. (1986) for further detail.

Selection of Images for Vegetative Management Simulations

Determining what slides (views) were suitable for simulation purposes was based largely on foreground vegetation. In order to simulate the results of possible management techniques for vegetation, it was important to choose views (slides) that contained as much foreground plant material as possible. By using views that show vegetation from the ground to the crown (top), a more accurate simulation could be produced than by using the views that just show the tops of plants. For example, if one option for management of vegetation was controlled burning of shrubs, and the original view contained just the crowns of the plant material, then the simulation of burning would not portray the total effect of the burning. The effect on surrounding grass and plants and the appearance of the ground could not be simulated. Views (slides) showing vegetation that could be viewed from base to crown were of more value than views showing only crowns when deciding what views would be simulated.

Foreground Vegetation Suitability. The first phase in determining foreground vegetation suitability for simulation was an area measurement of all slides. The foreground vegetation in each slide was measured as a percentage of the entire scene. The slides were projected onto a grid. The number of grid sectors with foreground vegetation in them were then counted. If less than 1/3 of the sectors were filled with foreground vegetation, the view (slide) was eliminated from further consideration for simulation. The 1/3 rule was used for several reasons. First, if less than 1/3 of the slide showed foreground vegetation, the view could be overpowered by the emergent background scenery during a simulation of vegetation removal. The view might then be judged on the quality of the background and not on the management technique that was simulated. Second, in order to start eliminating some of the 298 slides from consideration, the 1/3 rule proved to be an effective means of getting the number of possible slides for simulation to a manageable number. The slides that contained more than 1/3 foreground vegetation were then classified according to our foreground vegetation suitability index (Fig. 3).

The foreground vegetation suitability index accomplished several things. It was a means to identify the amount of vegetation that

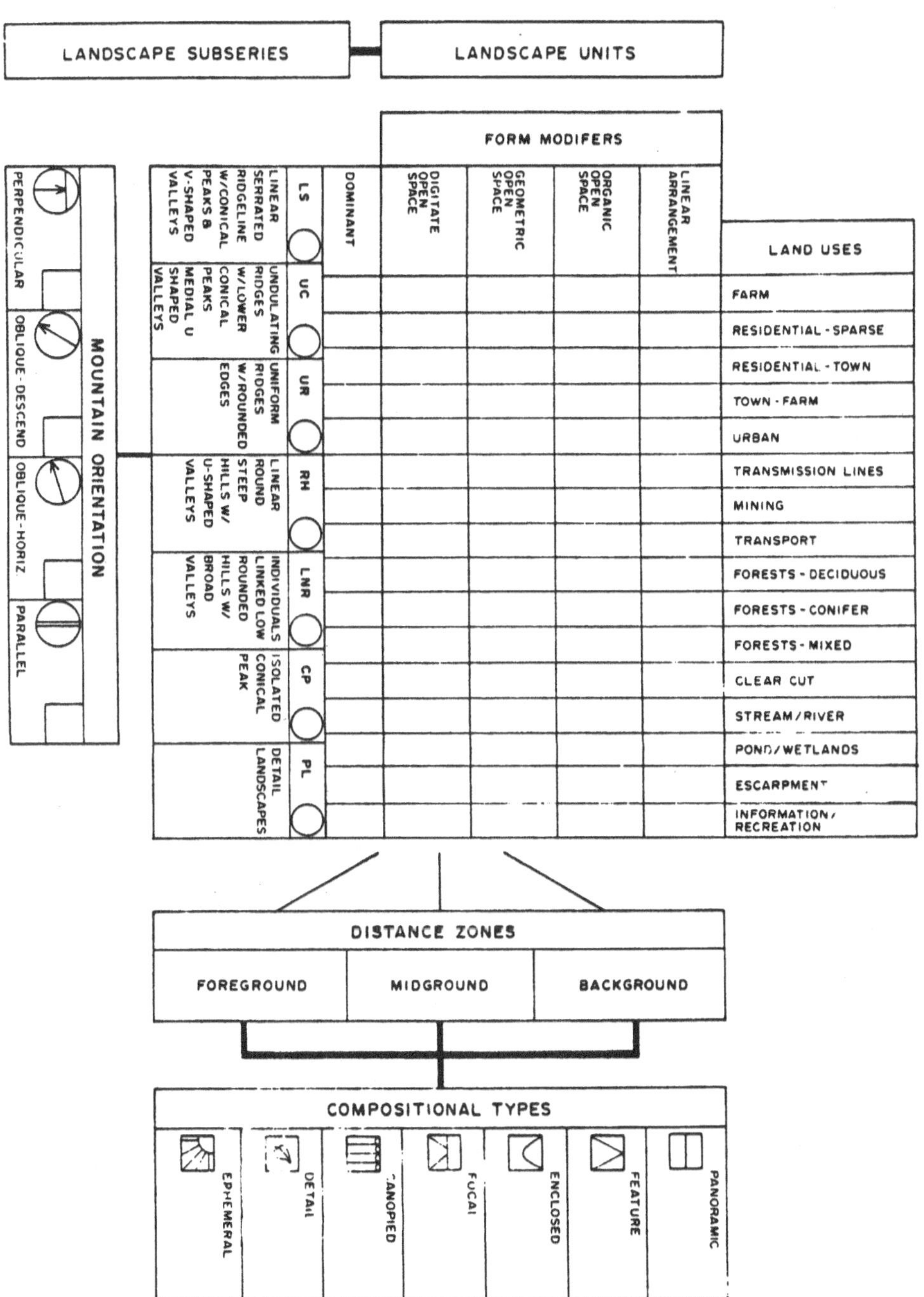

Fig. 2. Matrix for slide classification.

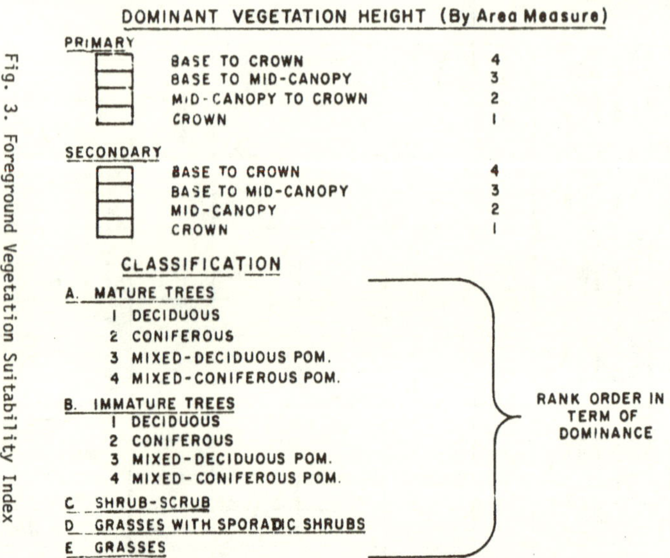

Fig. 3. Foreground Vegetation Stability Index.

could be seen from base to crown alone, in the primary and secondary vegetation. A grid system was used to determine the dominant vegetation. The vegetation was then classified in order of dominance for easy reference and comparison of vegetation without viewing the grass as the dominant foreground vegetative feature, shrubs or shrub grown as secondary foreground vegetation and mature deciduous trees as the third most dominant. (See Figure 3).

As stated before, views that showed the vegetation from base to crown were determined to be most applicable for simulation. The final phase for foreground vegetation suitability was the grouping of slides in two final categories. The first category included all the slides that had base to crown in both the primary and secondary foreground vegetation. This category was the most suitable for simulation according to foreground vegetation. The second category contained the slides with base to crown in either the primary or secondary foreground vegetation and base to mid-canopy in either or both the primary and secondary foreground vegetation. This category was marginal for simulation. In the final analysis, ten slides were determined suitable for simulation according to foreground vegetation, and twenty-one slides (views) were marginal.

After the final product was determined, the next step was to determine what images would be required to produce the final product. In this project, two factors were of prime concern: (1) the visual impact of roadside vegetation on the visitor to the parkway, and (2) the impact of management techniques utilized by the Park Service along the Parkway.

Data Treatment

After the 298 color slides were taken along the Parkway by University of Tennessee investigators, the slides were coded and classified, as previously described, to determine representative scenes from parkway overlooks. Once the sampling stage was completed, the next step was to apply appropriate management techniques to each scene. To accomplish this task, advice from Park Service managers was needed. Each of the 10 representative scenes was printed, inserted into an acetate envelope and was sent, together with an acetate marker, to the Blue Ridge Parkway Management Supervisor in Asheville, North Carolina. Comments and graphic delineation from the Park Service managers were drawn directly on the acetate overlay and returned. The managers identified three major management techniques common to the 10 representative scenes: first, mowing either by bush hog on accessible sites or by hand cutting; second, selective cutting of brush or trees to allow for significant views; and third, controlled burning in places inaccessible to machines.

In order to do the simulation, three pieces of information were needed: U.S.G.S. quadrangle maps for background topological data, photographs behind the vegetation to be removed or modified, and photographs in front of the scene for contextual information. Photographs behind vegetation are crucial because the three management techniques supplied by the Park Service involved eliminating vegetation in one form or another which would reveal new vegetation, topography or man-made form.

Another concern to be addressed is seasonal variation. Some management techniques might have a significant impact on views in summer, but the impact on views in winter might be quite different. Possible procedures might be to consider proposed changes with different seasonal impacts or to choose the season with the highest visitation frequency, such as summer with vegetation in full leaf. In this case, the latter procedure was used. It is important that simulations be made for the same season in which subjects will be responding to a photo questionnaire.

SPECIFIC VISUAL SIMULATION TECHNIQUES

Prototypical Scene Development

As stated before, the purpose of the project was to solicit visitor responses to certain NPS vegetation management techniques. After the representative scenes were chosen and comments were received from the National Park Service, each scene was analyzed to determine the appropriate montage technique. This was accomplished by overlaying the original 8-by-10 inch print with acetate and with the U.S.G.S. quads to determine hidden topographic features. Ideas were tested using markers.

It was decided that two pages with eight images per page would be prepared. Each page would contain the before and after images of four scenes, and each photograph would be 2-by-3 inches to allow for a rating scale beneath the images. Consequently, each montage was created at the 8-by-10 inch size and then photographically reduced.

Actual Simulation Development Techniques

In developing the simulations themselves, several ideas and media were tried. The first and most commonly used technique was "cut and paste." Depending on the amount of change required, two approaches can be utilized. First, in relatively small areas, for example, a bank of large shrubs that has to be eliminated and replaced with smaller shrubs or grass while providing appropriate background material, a technique called "windowing" can be performed (Figure 4).

When relatively large areas of the image, such as a tree mass, mountains or sky, have to be altered, a technique we called "layering" which is similar to the "windowing" technique described above can be used (Figure 5). Again, simply trim away the material to be changed, strip the backing from the edge to be retained, and cement new material in place. Experimentation proved to be equally successful in both front and back applications.

The next most common technique used we called "coloring." In this instance, a variety of

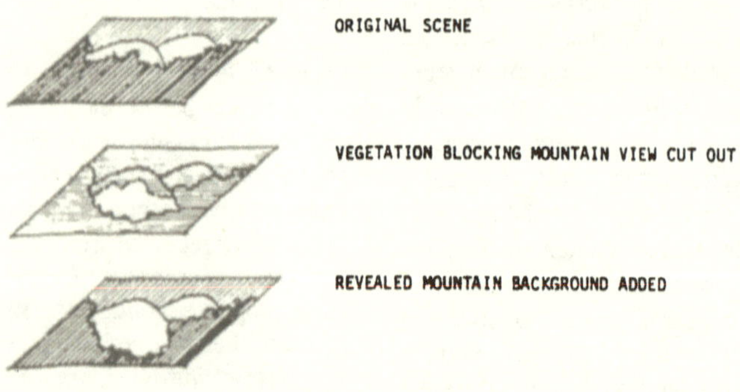

Fig. 4.

LAYERING

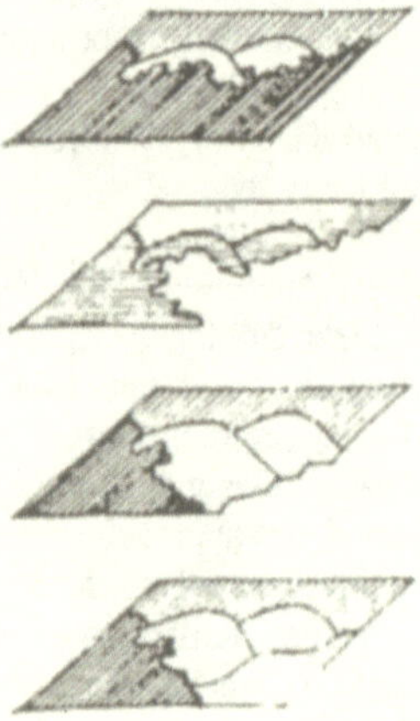

ORIGINAL SCENE

VEGETATION BLOCKING MOUNTAINS CUT AWAY

REVEALED MOUNTAIN BACKGROUND ADDED

REVEALED MOUNTAIN MIDDLE GROUND ADDED

Fig. 5.

Top: ***Fig. 4. Windowing.***
Bottom: ***Fig. 5. Layering.***

materials was used ranging from color dyes to air brush techniques. In our project, use of coloring was confined to "touch-up." Color dyes matched to the Cibachrome print material seemed to work best for touch-up in most instances (Ilford 1983 and undated).

The last type of montage application involves the techniques of "dodging" and "burning-in" commonly utilized in a darkroom (Time-Life, 1981). These procedures have been documented in a number of professional darkroom manuals. Basically, in slide printing, "dodging" means masking an area so that after development, the area appears black or dark, while "burning-in" produces the opposite effect. Experimentation with this approach did not equal the "cut and paste" technique. The various techniques are summarized in Table 2.

Specific Technique	Simulation Condition	Materials Needed	Skills Needed
windowing	small areas minor modifications	new materials to substitute and blend removed areas.	cut & paste no special skills
layering	major modif.	same as above	same as above
feathering	to blend veg.	new material	same as above
coloring	touch-up to hide cut edges	color dyes felt markers	artistic skills
dodging and burning-in	blending homogeneous zones - sky, etc.	darkroom equipment	trial and error

Table 2. Summary Matrix.

VISUAL SURVEY APPROACH TO EVALUATE VEGETATION MANAGEMENT ALTERNATIVES

Introduction

These simulations were used by the University of Tennessee team in the preparation of a questionnaire to assess vegetation management alternatives for the Blue Ridge Parkway. Each questionnaire was divided into five response sections: visual preference evaluations of photographic simulation pairs; ratings of vegetation management alternatives; reported participation in outdoor activities; rating of leisure attitude statements; and respondent characteristics. In addition, half the questionnaires included a page which indicated that ecological and economic benefits could be derived from reduced roadside mowing. Approximately 500 questionnaires were distributed between Tuesday, August 9 and Sunday, August 21, 1983. Questionnaire booklists were handed out and retrieved at pullouts along the full length of the Parkway.

This section investigates the visual preferences and attitudes toward vegetation management alternatives It also considers the potential of an informational leaflet to influence these responses. The primary methods used in this investigation are analyses of variance and t-tests. The following description of the three relevant portions of the questionnaire will establish the context needed to interpret the results of the analyses.

Information Leaflet

One-half of the questionnaires contained an "information leaflet" at the beginning of the visual preference section. Three photographs were arranged on the page in a diagonal tier, cutting down from left to right. Two of these photographs were also used to represent two sites in the questionnaire (sites 3 and 8). The third photograph was only used on this page. In the upper right hand corner was the following "ecological" message:

> *There are idle spots on every farm - and every highway is bordered by an idle strip as long as it is. Keep cow, plow, and mower out of these idle spots, and the full native*

flora, plus dozens of interesting stowaways could be part of the normal environment of every citizen. (Alda Leopold, Pioneer Ecologist from A Sand County Almanac).

In the lower left corner was the following "economic" message: "Just a 50% reduction in mowing on the Blue Ridge Parkway will save taxpayers $71,000 per year."

Visual Preference Evaluations

The general instructions in the questionnaire are:

Vegetation management along the Blue Ridge Parkway can be conducted at various levels of intensity. For example, the roadside grass can be mowed weekly, monthly, bimonthly, etc. We would like your opinion of some possible levels of grass mowing and tree-clearing that might be practiced on the Parkway. By rating the vegetation management examples in our photo, we can determine what Parkway visitors prefer.

There is a collection of photographs presented as three (3) pairs per page. Each picture has a short description under it. Please pay particular attention to the described feature as you rate each photograph. First, look through them quickly to get a general feeling for the photographs. Then, go back and carefully read the description. Rate EACH photo (compared to its pair) for HOW MUCH YOU LIKE IT. Simply circle the number of your choice below each photograph.

1 = not at all
2 = a little
3 = somewhat
4 = quite a bit
5 = very much

There are eighteen photograph pairs, each representing an alternative intensity of management. In most cases, both photographs appear to be of the same site. However, the photographs in two pairs (2a/b and 7a/b) are obviously of different sites; in several other pairs (1a/b, 10a/b, 11a/b, 16a/b and 18a/b), the montage process causes slightly noticeable differences between the photograph pairs that might be interpreted as site differences.

These photograph pairs represent two general types of management activity: eight simulate roadside mowing and ten vista maintenance. Among the mowing comparisons, three compare cutting from a single mower width from the roadside to complete mowing to the treeline (sites 2, 6 and 7). Three more present other mowing width comparisons (sites 1, 3 and 9). One pair addresses the frequency of mowing (site B) and the eighth pair mowing around a road sign (site 4). Among these photo pairs, two are the same but with different captions (sites 3 and 8) and two other pairs have one photograph in common (2a and 7b) and use the same captions.

Three management alternatives are represented among the ten vista management comparisons. Two sites (5 and 15) represent the effects of controlled burning as a vista management tool. Intensive cutting of woody vegetation is represented at four sites (10, 12, 13 and 16) while four more represent moderate or selective cutting (11, 14, 17 and 18). Of particular interest among these photographs are the reuse of one photograph (10a and I7a) to create a three sequence comparison (10a, 10b and 17a, 17b), and the removal of a single foreground tree to reduce vista enframement (sites 14 and 18). The management treatment is generally "tree removal" at these sites, however, at one, it is specifically removal of hardwoods to emphasize conifers (site 18). At two other sites (13 and 17), the treatment results in a mown foreground crest rather than residual wood vegetation.

Vegetation Management Alternatives

Respondents were also asked to indicate their support or non-support statements describing "various levels at which the grass and shrubs along the Blue Ridge Parkway could be maintained." Responses were recorded on a seven point bipolar scale: (1) strongly support, (2) support, (3) probably support, (4) don't know, (5) probably don't know, (6) don't support, (7) definitely don't support. A total of twelve management alternatives were described in all: four of these alternatives concerned the frequency of mowing; four described the width of the mowed area; one posed safety as the sole criterion for mowing; and three addressed intensity of cutting or trimming of woody vegetation to maintain vistas at roadside pull-offs.

MANAGEMENT FINDINGS

Vegetation Management Alternatives

The overall statistical analysis for each alternative management statement shows, in general, less intensive management practices receive greater support (see Table 3). An average or typical evaluation supports mowing every three or four weeks when the grass becomes about 8 inches tall. Mowing should extend to some natural break close (within a couple mower widths) to the road's edge. Moderate tree thinning is preferred, but the pull-off vistas should be maintained in any case. Overall, respondents are more supportive of vista maintenance than mowing activities.

The mean ratings for both those respondents who did and those who did not receive the leaflet about the ecological and economic benefits of reduced mowing are also compared in this table. In general, those provided with this information tend to be more supportive of reduced mowing and less supportive of intensive mowing. This is the direction of influence one would expect, however, the differences are only statistically significant for most intensive mowing practices and the restriction of mowing to reasons of safety. The mowing leaflet did not seem to influence ratings of vista maintenance alternatives in any significant way.

The relationship between the intensity of management and the influence of leaflet was further investigated using two-way analysis of variance models. The management alternatives are grouped for these analyses according to mowing frequency (statements 1 through 4), mowing width (statements 5 through 8), and vista maintenance (statements 10 through 12). The results in Table 4 indicate that the variation in ratings attributable to management intensity is significant in all three models. These differences were further investigated through multiple comparison mean separation tests. Tukey's honestly significant differences (HSD) procedure with a significance level of .05 was used. These results indicate that there is not significantly different support for monthly or fall mowings. However, both practices are preferred to bi-weekly mowings, which is preferred to weekly mowings. A similar situation exists for alternative mowing widths. A single mower width is preferred above mowing to the swale; both are preferable to double width mowing or mowing to the treeline. No difference is evident between these latter, more intensive alternatives. In the case of vista maintenance, waiting 5 to 7 years, before much of the distant view is blocked, is preferred. The other two alternatives, annual maintenance and maintaining at least 66 percent openness, are equally preferred. It is important to remember that overall, there is greater support for vista management than intensive mowing.

The information leaflet also had a significant effect on the ratings associated with grass management. However, it did not cause any difference in vista management preferences between the two groups. The influence of the leaflet was not even among all the statements. Rather, it had a significantly greater effect on opinions about more intensive mowing activities, as previously indicated by the t-tests in Table 3. In addition, those without the leaflet supported mowing to the treeline over double width mowing while the reverse is true for those who received the information leaflet.

Visual Preference Evaluations

The ratings of how much respondents like the simulated effects of management alternatives are summarized in Table 5. The sites have been grouped according to the general management practice they represent, as previously described. The mean values (x) represent the difference between the ratings for the less managed or control condition and the more managed or treatment condition. Therefore, a negative value represents visual improvement and a value of zero indicates no change in visual quality. A t-test is used to identify those cases where the mean change is significantly differ-

Vegetation Management Alternatives	Information Leaflet With	Information Leaflet Without	t
The roadside grass should be mowed:			
1. weekly, like a lawn	6.15	5.64	3.47***
2. every two weeks, when 3 to 6 inches tall.	4.50	3.88	3.21***
3. once per month, when at least 10 inches tall.	3.79	3.86	-.41n.s.
4. once in the Fall after the wildflowers are through blooming.	3.65	3.57	.42n.s.
5. only one mower width (7 feet) from the edge of the road surface	3.22	3.41	-1.04n.s.
6. two mower widths (14 feet) from the road's edge	4.43	4.23	1.20n.s.
7. from the road's edge to the ditch or swale.	3.92	3.73	1.14n.s.
8. from the road's edge to the treeline	4.90	4.18	3.67***
9. as little as possible, only when necessary to maintain driver safety and help prevent grass fires.	3.76	4.21	-2.11*
Shrubs and trees at pull-off vistas should be cut or trimmed:			
10. annually to maintain a completely clear view	3.70	3.46	1.19n.s.
11. every 5 to 7 years, before the shrubs in the foreground block much of the distant view	3.32	3.21	.63n.s.
12. just often envough so that no more than 1/3 of the view is blocked	3.53	3.57	-.22n.s.
Mean Sample Size	241	222	

Note: [1]On a seven-point bi-polar scale: (1) strongly suport, (4) don't know, (7) definitely don't support.
***p</=.001 **p</=.01 *p</=.05 n.s.p>/=.05

Table 3. Mean ratings of vegetation management alternatives and the effect of an information pamphlet.

Management Action	Effects	df	F-value
Mowing Frequency	Intensity	3	130.0***
	Information	1	9.7**
	Interaction	3	3.4*
Mowing Width	Intensity	3	38.9***
	Information	1	6.0*
	Interaction	3	4.4**
Cutting Woody Vegetation	Intensity	2	3.5*
	Information	1	.9n.s.
	Interaction	2	.6n.s.

***p< .001 **p< .01 *p< .05 n.s.p≥ 0.5

Condition	Site	With Leaflet x [1]	With Leaflet t	Without Leaflet x	Without Leaflet t	Paired t
Mowing width	1	1.57	10.4***	1.72	11.7***	-.7n.s.
	2	1.32	9.0***	.95	5.9***	1.7n.s.
	3	.21	1.2n.s.	-.29	-1.7n.s.	2.1*
	6	1.03	6.4***	.47	2.7**	2.4*
	7	-1.50	-10.1***	-1.19	-7.3***	-1.4n.s.
	9	1.00	5.8***	.64	3.4***	1.4n.s.
Mowing frequency	8	.13	.8n.s.	-.45	-3.0***	2.6**
Sign mowing	4	-1.71	-10.7***	-2.36	-18.1***	3.1**
Major clearing	10	-1.89	-14.5***	-2.13	-17.7***	1.4n.s.
	12	-.30	-1.8n.s.	-.16	-1.0n.s.	-.6n.s.
	13	-.06	-.4n.s.	-.23	-1.3n.s.	.7n.s.
	16	-2.57	-23.4**	-2.55	-24.7***	-.1n.s.
Moderate clearing	11	-.32	2.1*	-.31	-1.9n.s.	-.1n.s.
	14	1.53	11.2***	1.36	9.8***	.9n.s.
	17	1.35	9.6***	1.18	7.9***	.8n.s.
	18	.35	2.5*	.25	1.7n.s.	.5n.s.
Controlled burning	5	1.35	9.1***	1.19	7.7***	.8n.s.
	15	-.19	-1.1n.s.	-.17	-1.0n.s.	-.1n.s.

***p< .001 **p< .01 *p< .05 n.s.p≥ .05

1

Notes: The mean difference is a less managed or control condition rating, minus a more managed or treatment condition. Negative values indicate visual improvement.

Top: ***Table 4. Effects of management intensity and information on ratings of vegetation management alternatives.***

Bottom: ***Table 5. Mean change in visual preference ratings for simulated management situations.***

Management Action	Effects	df	F-value
Mowing width	Activity	1	595.4***
	Information	1	6.2*
	Site	5	10.1***
	Info * Activity	1	23.5***
	Info * Site	5	.4n.s.
	Activity * Site	5	40.5***
Controlled burning	Activity	1	69.6***
	Information	1	.2n.s.
	Site	1	2.4n.s.
	Info * Activity	1	.5n.s.
	Info * Site	1	.1n.s.
	Activity * Site	1	140.8***
Vista clearing	Activity	1	92.8***
	Information	1	.1n.s.
	Site	7	13.2**
	Info * Activity	1	1.2n.s.
	Info * Site	7	.2n.s.
	Activity * Site	7	295.5***

***p< .001 **p< .01 *p< .05 n.s.p≥ .05

Note: Among the effects incorporated into these analyses of variance models, Activity refers to control (photo a) and treatment (photo b) conditions. Information refers to those who did or did not receive the information leaflet. Site refers to those sites simulating the activity; in a sense these are simulation repetitions or repeated measures of the management activity. Intensity regroups the vista clearing sites into major and moderate clearings. The two way interactions are also indicated.

Table 6. Effects of management activity, information and site on ratings of visual preference.

ent from zero. The mean differences and t-tests are reported for both those who received the information leaflet and those who did not. A paired comparison t-test is used to identify significant differences between the mean change in ratings for these two groups.

Analysis of variance models reported in Table 6 are used to investigate the effects of these factors. Among the effects incorporated into these models is "activity" or the significance of the change in rating from the control (photo a) to a treatment (photo b) condition. The "information" effect refers to the difference between those who did or did not receive the information leaflet. In a sense, each of the simulated sites are a repetition or repeated measure of a particular management activity. Collectively, they represent the visual variation of using these practices in the landscape. This variation is represented by a "site" effect. For the analysis of vista clearing, a second model grouped the sites into clearing activity of major and moderate "intensity." All possible two-way interactions were also included in these models.

The pattern of visual preference for mowing alternatives is very similar between the two groups. Overall, respondents preferred the control or less mown condition. The major exception is a preference for mowing vegetation around a low road sign (site 8). The treatment in site 7 also received a very positive rating. However, this may be because the two photographs were of distinctly different sites.

There are significant differences between the mean change for these two groups at half the sites, which is similar to the influence among the mowing management statements. This result is supported by a significant effect in the analysis of variance model for mowing width, as well as the t-tests for mowing frequency (site 8) and mowing around road signs (site 4). In all these analyses, the information leaflet is associated with preference for reduced mowing activity. This effect is accentuated among those who received the leaflet, accounting for the significant interactive term.

The most significant effect in the analysis of variance model for mowing width concerns the change at each site from a more intensive management practice. As has already been described, respondents generally support less intensive mowing. The actual variation among the sites is also very highly significant, possibly indicating the relative difference in treatment intensity between photos at a particular site, as well as the visual sensitivity of different sites to management practices. The significant interaction between activity and site is attributable to the essential lack of difference between the photographs at site 3.

The overall preference for the visual effects of vista management practices is clearer, though different, than it was for mowing practices. Cutting activity that removes large amounts of woody vegetation from an overgrown vista to establish an open view are preferred. However, respondents do not appear to support cutting when the vista is only slightly blocked, or when a significant residual is left that still blocks the view. This result is more accentuated but seems to support responses to the management statements, where cutting has supported every 5 to 7 years (seemingly a long time), over annual clearing or clearing before one-third of the view is blocked. Controlled burning also received poor ratings, particularly in the case where there was little change in the vista's extent. Finally, there are no significant differences between the two groups, indicating that the information leaflet had no effect. This may be because the leaflet focused on mowing and the effect failed to carry over to tree clearing. Alternately, it may be because respondents already had a clear position on vista management that is based on a cultural reticence to cut down trees but a strong visual preference for vistas.

These results are supported by the analysis of variance results. The actual change in evaluation from the pre- to post-activity is very highly significant. There is also a very highly significant effect, which is strengthened when they are collapsed into major and moderate intensity groups. There is also a very highly significant interaction effect between the activity and site or intensity factors. Essentially, this represents the strong preference for major clearing and the perceived undesirability of only modest clearing. The controlled burning analysis exhibits a similar pattern for activity and the interactive term.

SUMMARY AND MANAGEMENT RECOMMENDATIONS

Bio-Physical and Historical Management Recommendations

Any vegetative management technique utilized should be preceded by a thorough analysis of the goals and objectives to be accomplished. Since the primary object of this research has been the human cultural aspect of viewing from the Blue Ridge Parkway, a number of physical parameters should be considered. Basically, viewing from the Blue Ridge Parkway involves two major components; the position of the viewer and the scene to be viewed. The viewer position generally means either viewing at a scenic overlook while standing or sitting, or viewing along the road while in a moving car. The speed of the car and the road configuration are also important because an impressive view is more likely to be seen while on a straight road at a low speed than on a curve except by a passenger. The amount of vegetation to be removed should be determined not only by what is viewed but whether the viewer is moving or standing still.

The major management constraint on the scene to be viewed is not only vegetation but also the underlying topography. Most of the Blue Ridge Parkway is located on relatively steep slopes or on a ridge top, which means that major long views contain foreground sloping away from the viewer. The management technique utilized, controlled burning and cutting or mowing, are effective especially in preventing severe erosion on steep slopes and in soils that are largely thin, well-drained and sterile. However, because of a climate highly conducive to plant growth, sites of prime viewing require constant care. Basically, plant material to be considered should be self-maintaining, physically and microclimatically appropriate to the area and the surrounding vegetable context of the view and the slope on which it is placed.

Environmentally, perennial vegetation to be introduced should contain the following characteristics. First, since most soils on steep slopes and ridge lines are thin and deplete of nutrients, plants should be shallow rooted, fibrous and have the ability to absorb and hold nutrients for extended periods of time. Second, since the climate is humid, temperate and rainfall is abundant, plants should be able to withstand the potential erosive effects of heavy rainfall, snow and sedimentation.

Physically, plants should be complimentary in terms of form, size and texture to the surrounding site context; but even more importantly, the height of the plant should be self-maintaining and predictable since placement on a given slope with respect to the viewer position is crucial in maintaining the desired view. Grasses such as broomsedge could be used in near foreground areas; but if the slope falls away sharply, shrubs could be used. Again, consideration should be given to the first two basic elements - the viewer position and the scene to be viewed.

Perceptually Based Management Recommendations

Perceptually based results from above support roadside mowing every three or four weeks when the grass becomes about 8 inches tall. Mowing should extend to some natural break close (within a couple mower widths) to the road's edge. Annual maintenance and maintaining 66 percent openness of vistas are equally preferred, so it would make sense to wait 5 to 7 years before trimming or cutting shrubs which would block distant views. Cutting which removes large amounts of woody vegetation from an overgrown vista are supported, but cutting is not supported when the vista is only partially blocked, or when significant residual woody material is left which partially blocks the view. In other words, do not cut unless there is potential for creating substantial increased visual access or open views! Controlled burning is also not supported unless there is substantial improvement in vista quality and extent.

Synthesis

The above summarized perceptual results regarding roadside mowing and vistas maintenance speak for themselves. In addition, our analysis shows greater support for vista maintenance than roadside mowing. The major syn thesis would be the combination of periodic mowing of roadsides and brush clearing of vistas combined with introduction of plant species that either (1) maintain low height and uniform texture and (2) are historically representative of past vegetative management practices; at suitable locations. The latter would be especially appropriate near interpretive areas and facilities.

The question of the total mix of vegetative management over the length of the Parkway is more difficult. Since the investigators dealt primarily with static images and simulations, we would propose that questions involving spatial sequences of visual experience need sequential or dynamic simulation. A future agenda item for research would be to simulate moving sequences of vegetative management changes along the Blue Ridge Parkway utilizing video with different simulation media such as scale models, computer assisted graphics or electronic photomontage (computer and video) to illustrate different management alternatives in "real time" sequence.

BIBLIOGRAPHY

Bake, W.A. 1972. The Blue Ridge. Viking Press, New York.

Bailey, R.G. 1978. Description of the Eco-Regions of the United States. U.S. Department of Agriculture. Forest Service.

Bittenger. L.F. 1901, republished 1968. The Germans in Colonial Times. Russel & Russel, New York.

Bolton, C.K. 1967. Scotch-Irish Pioneers in Ulster and America. Genealogical Publishing Co., Baltimore, MD.

Day, T.R. 1984. "Simulating Vegetation Management Techniques Utilizing Color Photographic Montage." School of Landscape Architecture. State University of New York, Syracuse.

Ford. H.J. 1966. The Scotch-Irish in America. Archon Books Camden. CT.

Graeff, A.D. et al. 1942. The Pennsylvania Germans. Princeton University Press. Princeton. N.J.

Jolley, H. 1969. The Blue Ridge Parkway. University of Tennessee, Knoxville, TN.

Ilford, Inc. 1983. "Retouching Cibachrome II Materials." Technical Brochure TB34EN, Ilford, Inc.

Ilford, Inc. undated. "Retouching Cibachrome Tips and Hints," Ilford, Inc.

Kercheval, S. 1902. History of the Valley of Virginia. W.N. Grabil.

Kollmorgen, W.M. 1942. "The Pennsylvania German farmer." In A.D. Graeff (et.al), The Pennsylvania Germans. Princeton University Press, Princeton, N.J.

Long, A., Jr. 1972. "The Pennsylvania German Family Farm." Publications of the Pennsylvania German Society, Vol. VI. The Pennsylvania German Society, Breinigsville, PA.

Opie, J. 1981. "Where American history began: Appalachia and the small independent family farm." In W. Somerville (ed.), Appalachia/America. Proceedings of the Appalachian Studies Conference, East Tennessee State University, The Appalachian Consortium Press.

Palmer, J.F., T.R. Day, R.C. Smardon, A. Redway III and L. Reichardt. 1986. "Simulating and evaluating management practices." In F.R. Noe (ed.), Visual Methods and Perceptions: Approaches to a National Parkway. National Park Service Scientific Series, Washington, D.C. (in press).

Riddel, F.S. (ed.) 1974. Appalachia: Its People, Heritage and Problems. Kendall Hunt Publishing Co., DuBuque, IA.

Sheppard, M.E. 1935. Cabins in the Laurel. University of North Carolina Press, Chapel Hill, N.C.

Simpkins, O.N. 1974. "The Celtic roots of Appalachian culture." In F.S. Biddle. (ed.), Appalachia: Its People, Heritage and Problems. Kendall Hunt Publishing Co., DuBuque, IA.

Smardon, R.C., T.R. Day, A. Redway III and L. Reichardt. 1986. "Historical overview and landscape classification." In F.R. Noe (ed.), Visual Methods and Perceptions: Approaches to A National Parkway. National Park Service Scientific Series, Washington, D.C. (in press).

Smardon, R. C., T.R. Day, T. Redway and L. Reichardt. 1985. "Vegetation management techniques: past and present." In Landscape Research, Vol. 10, No. 5, pp. 9-13.

Smathers, G.A. 1982. "Man as a Factor in Southern Appalachia: Bald Formation and Illustrations of Selected Sites along the Blue Ridge Parkway in North Carolina." U.S. Dept. of Interior, Interior Park Service.

Stilgoe, J.R. 1982. Common Landscape of America 1580 to 1845. Yale University Press, New Haven, CT.

Time-Life, Inc. 1981. "Photographer's Handbook Revised Edition." Life Library of Photography. Time-Life Books, Inc., New York.

Weller, J.E. 1965. Yesterday's People: Life in a Contemporary Appalachia. University Press of Kentucky, Frankfurt, KY.

Zeisel, J. 1981. Inquiry by Design: Tools for Environmental-Behavior Research. Brooks/Cole Publishing Co., Monterey, CA.

Alternatives to Land Acquisition for Parkway Development: The Conservation Easement Option

Dennis L. Soden, Director, Coastal Zone Studies, Department of Political Science, The University of West Florida, Pensacola

INTRODUCTION

The development of Parkways requires the purchase of large parcels of land so that the multiple parkway roles of being an alternative means of transportation while, at the same time, providing for full enjoyment of the surrounding scenery are achieved (Burggraf, 1986: 26). Purchase of the required properties fee-simple is obviously the most direct means of acquiring the necessary land required for road construction. Unless the agency involved in the development of a parkway has eminent domain authority, acquisitions are, however, limited to the property available on the market and, of course, the available funds. These two factors are complicated by the fact that funds available to government units, typically the developers of parkways, are increasingly becoming scarce, and the "budget crisis" does not seem to be going away. In addition, when government does enter into the land market, its competition is likely to inflate market prices. This was the situation which was occasioned when the development of the Santa Monica Mountains National Recreation Area was undertaken (The Conservation Foundation, 1985: 225-226). Thus, the purchase of fee-simple, while necessary to obtain in order to provide a roadway, may be an expensive way of fulfilling the second goal of Parkways—providing enjoyment of the surrounding scenery. What alternatives exist to full fee-simple acquisition?

As an alternative to fee-simple, this paper briefly addresses the concept of the conservation easement and its potential in Parkway planning and development. The issue of conservation easements is complex and has been the focus of a considerable literature in the last decade (see for example: Barrett and Livermore, 1983; Champion and Soden, 1987).

The extant literature addresses a full range of topics which reflect the complexity and various dimensions of the conservative easement subject, including financial and tax considerations (Daugherty, 1978; Kinnamon, 1980); legislative features at federal, state and local levels (U.S. Department of Commerce, 1978; Thomas, 1975); legal components (Conservation Law Foundation, 1976); and, urban versus rural considerations (Schroeder, 1971; Roe, 1976; Knight and Dye, 1981). This paper does not address these specific issues in detail. Rather the issues of legal, tax and legislative processes are left to to lawyers, accountants and lawmakers within their respective domains. Instead, the general idea of a conservation easement is put forth as one option among the set of instruments available in fulfilling Parkway goals. It does so by suggesting that the acquisition of property through conservation easements may be an approach which can be more heavily relied upon than previously considered for accomplishing Parkway needs.

THE EASEMENT STRATEGY

In its simplest form, the obtainment of an easement provides use of a property without eliminating its taxable status as property, or markedly decreasing local government tax revenues (Christie, 1985: 147); an issue of importance in an era of fiscal constraint among most government entities. Easements are categorized as either affirmative or negative. An affirmative easement, in general, provides public access or right-of-use to properties. A negative easement precludes some use as a way of protecting areas from development or unsound use. In doing so, a negative easement acts as a means of restricting activity on the land. Conservation easements fall into this latter category, restricting use of land by placing limits on the activities which may occur in order to prevent incompatible activities on adjacent lands. Of concern here is the use of conservation easements to prevent activities which are incompatible with Parkway goals (Jarvis, 1982: 97; Reitze, 1974: 77).

"Conservation Easements" is a generic term which includes several less-than-fee-simple options including: (1) natural ecosystem easements; (2) scenic easements; and, (3) open space easements. While most are aware of common easements such as a right-of-way given for road or utilities access, the conservation easement and its derivatives are adapted to provide economy, flexibility and specificity. The latter limits the development rights of the landowner on his property (Barrett and Livermore, 1983: 4).

The three basic types of conservation easements can be summarized as:

(1) Natural Ecosystem Easements. Very detailed easements with restrictions and prohibitions carefully designed in consideration of sensitive ecological values. (Barrett and Livermore, 1983: 88)

(2) Scenic Easements. Generally involves regulating scenic qualities of the land, including limitations on development density, structure design (i.e., height), and are designed to actively preserve the view. (Barrett and Livermore, 1983: 89)

(3) Open Space Easements. Easements which allow for land to be kept in productive uses such as agriculture, grazing and forestry. They are designed to insure conservation standards and land use mixes and require consultation before any change in land use may occur. (Barrett and Livermore, 1983: 90)

These easement categories are not all inclusive, nor are they mutually exclusive, they do, however, illustrate a set of techniques by which Parkway planners may obtain rights to additional lands in order to insure Parkway values.

DEVELOPING THE CONSERVATION EASEMENT: GOALS AND PROBLEMS

The use of conservation easements is not new to Parkways; early scenic easements were used to preserve the view along the Blue Ridge Parkway and Natchez Trace Parkway in the 1930s and 1940s, and the Great River Road in Wisconsin in the 1950s. More recently, however, the concept has become more fully developed, studied and researched. In their book designed to aid groups and individuals in securing conservation easements, Thomas S. Barrett and Putnam Livermore (1983) provide a basic guide for the development of conservation easements. They propose that seven basic factors come into play in conservation easement development. These are:

(1) A generalized statement of the purpose of the easement;

(2) Reference to the specific conservation values of the land involved;

(3) A list of specific rights given the grantee which will enable enforcement of the easement;

(4) A list of specific restrictions pertaining to the undesirable activities which might be reasonably anticipated;

(5) A general statement on restriction of uses inconsistent with the intent and purpose of the easement;

(6) A list of specific uses or rights to be permitted or retained by the grantor;

(7) A general reservation in the easement regarding rights which are not inconsistent with the intent and purpose of the easement. (Barrett and Livermore, 1983: 82-83).

In developing a conservation easement, the proper mix of restriction and latitude must be achieved. Early use of conservation easements are indicative of the problems which may be encountered in trying to achieve this mix.

For example, easement violations are particularly noted where property has changed ownership since the easement was granted or acquired (Jarvis, 1982: 104). Other instances show that landowners are not always fully informed of what rights they are relinquishing when they grant an easement (The Conservation Foundation, 1985: 258-259), while at other times grantors simply have not abided by the easement leading to legal battle lines being drawn between the grantor and grantee (Champion and Soden, 1987). We might next ask, how can a safe middle ground be achieved, including both specific provisions necessary for protection and more general provisions necessary for flexibility? Barrett and Livermore again provide a useful tool for conservation easement construction by providing a seventeen point Conservation Easement Checklist as shown in Table 1.

The checklist in Table I includes the seventeen elements most commonly found in conservation easements. Since conservation easements range across a wide range of purposes—protection of wetland ecosystems (Kundell and Woolf, 1986), perpetuation of farming along Parkways like the Blue Ridge Parkway (Champion and Soden, 1987), or preserving scenic vistas (Vinesett and Soden, 1987)—the content will obviously vary according to the unique characteristics obtaining in each instance. The conservation easement will also vary according to federal, state and local tax laws relevant to it, as well as whether it is a natural ecosystem easement, a scenic easement or an open space easement. Perhaps most important, however, is insuring that the easement conforms to the characteristics of the land it is designed to protect (Barrett and Livermore, 1983: 82).

SUMMARY AND CONCLUSION

Conservation easements are but one of many measures available to Parkway developers and planners to protect the values of the Parkway. The list of alternatives appear to go on ad infinitum, including partial ownership to restrict certain uses, lease acquisition, land exchange, zoning, private stewardship or gift of individual interest to name just a few (The Conservation Foundation , 1985: 259-260; Barrett and Livermore, 1983: 95-118). Conservation easements may emerge as the "most efficient and flexible device" available for land acquisition and conservation today. Coupled with the budget crisis which characterizes much of public activity today, it would seem logical that public agencies involved in Parkway development would see conservation easements as a cost effective means of monitoring and enforcing Parkway values at costs far less than fee-simple acquisition. Conservation easements provide Parkways the benefit of control over the land as it regards values important for their success, while at the same time landowners benefit by having the assurance that their lands are included in future protection. In addition, landowners almost always benefit from reduction in property taxes or tax deductions (Barrett and Livermore, 1983).

Although conservation easements are receiving more attention in recent years as the cost of fee-simple acquisition rises, they are not novel ideas without a tradition in law and planning. Conservation easements suggest that land use involves not only rights to development but rights to intangible uses (i.e., preservation), and that these rights can be transferred to others for uses including preservation, esthetics and conservation. They are not, however, a "cure-all" for Parkway planning and development. Clearly it must be understood that conservation easements are simply one alternative to fee-simple. By all means, if you can own all the land necessary to ensure the values of the parkway under development without bearing an excessive financial burden, then do so.

This paper only briefly presents the idea of conservation easements as a viable alternative which planners and developers of Parkways should be aware. The specificity of legal and tax ramifications tied to conservation easement is left to others, but a full-scale commitment to the concept is suggested as a way of providing an opportunity for most fully developing Parkways today and in the future.

TABLE 1: CONSERVATION EASEMENT CHECKLIST

	Element	Description
1.	Parties	Identify grantor and grantee including rights to transfer property.
2.	Legal and Qualitative Description of the Property	Legal description and a "story" of the land identifying conservation values.
3.	Type and Purpose of Easement	Statement about type of easement involved (i.e., open space, etc.) and purpose (i.e., to protect local watershed, scenic values, etc.) Also includes a reference to governing statute(s).
4.	Statement of Intent	Intention of easement (i.e., conservation) and goals of both grantor and grantee.
5.	Documentation of Conservation Values to be Preserved	Includes resource inventories, maps, reports, photographs, and scientific documentation, to be used as supporting evidence of conservation values intended for preservation.
6.	Grant of Easement	Contains the actual conveyance of easement interest, the length and terms.
7.	Rights, Restrictions, Permitted Uses and Reservations	Determines rights, permitted uses, reservations and restrictions which govern use of land; a negotiated section which is the force and substance of the easement.
8.	Allocation of Costs	Costs of maintenance, insurance, taxes, assessments and liabilities to be assumed by grantor and grantee.
9.	Subsequent Deeds	Statement on the incorporation of the easement in subsequent deeds wherein title is transferred.
10.	Executory Limitation	Provision for forfeit of easement by grantee to another qualified holder.
11.	Assignment	States that grantee will hold easement exclusively for conservation purposes and will only transfer for the same purposes.
12.	Integration	Statement that easement is culmination of complete agreement among the parties of all oral and written discussions.
13.	Severability	Statement that if any of the provisions are declared invalid the remaining provisions remain in "full force".
14.	Costs of Enforcement	Statement pertaining to liability for costs related to easement enforcement.
15.	Habendum Clause	Statement that grantee has easements for use for stated term and that grantor plus all successors shall be bound for stated term.
16.	Date, Signatures, and Acknowledgement	Signatures, date and supporting evidence (i.e., witness, notary, approval of governing body).
17.	Exhibits	Any support documents, maps, photos, scientific reports should be attached as numbered exhibits.

Adapted from: Thomas S. Barrett and Putnam Livermore (1983) THE CONSERVATION EASEMENT IN CALIFORNIA., Covelo, CA: Island Press.

BIBLIOGRAPHY

Barrett, Thomas S. and Putnam Livermore (1983) The Conservation Easement in California, Covelo, CA: Island Press.

Burggraf, Frank (1986) "The Parkway — A Uniquely American Construct — Is It Obsolete?" in Barry M. Buxton and Steven M. Beatty (eds.) Blue Ridge Parkway: Agent of Transition, Boone, NC: Appalachian Consortium Press.

Champion, Richard II. and Dennis L. Soden (1987) "Planning Process and the National Park Services: Boundary Review of The Blue Ridge Parkway," Working Papers in Public Administration, No. 87-1, Boone, NC: Appalachian State University.

Christie, Donna R. (1985) Florida Coastal Law and Policy: Cases and Readings, Gainesville, FL: Florida Sea Grant College.

Conservation Law Foundation (1976) Conservation Restrictions, Conservation Law Foundation of New England.

Daugherty, Arthur (1978) Open Space Preservation: Federal Tax Policies Encouraging Donation of Conservation Easements, Washington, D.C.: United States Department of Agriculture, Economics, Statistics, and Cooperative Services.

Jarvis, T. Destry (1982) "Adjacent Lands and Intermingled Ownership Problems" in Eugenia H. Connally (ed.) National Parks In Crisis, Washington, D.C.: National Parks and Conservation Association.

Kinnamon, David (1980) "Tax Incentives for Sensible Land. Use Through Gifts of Conservation Easements", in Real Property Problems and Trial Journal, 15

Knight, Robert and Nancy Dye (1981) "Attorney's Guide to Montana Conservation Easements" in Montana Law Review, 42: 21.

Kundell, James E. and S. Wesley Woolf (1986) Georgia Wetlands: Trends and Policy Options, Athens, GA: Carl Vinson Institute of Government.

Reitze Jr., Arnold W. (1974) Environmental Planning: Law of Land and Resources, Washington, D.C.: North American International.

Roe, Charles (1976) "Innovative Techniques to Preserve Rural Land Resources" in Environmental Affairs, 5:419.

Schroeder, William (1971) "Preservation and Control of Open Space in Metropolitan Areas," in Indiana Legal Forum, 345.

The Conservation Foundation (1985) National Parks for a New Generation: Visions, Realities and Prospects, Washington, D.C.: The Conservation Foundation.

Thomas, Alexander (1975) "Transfers of Land to the State for Conservation Purposes: Methods, Guarantees and Tax Analysis for Prospective Donors: in Ohio State Law Journal, 36: 545.

U.S. Department of Commerce, National Oceanic and Atmospheric Administration, Office of Coastal Management (1978) The Use of Less-Than-Fee-Simple Acquisition as a Land Management Tool for Coastal Programs, Summary Review, Washington, D.C.: U.S. Department of Commerce.

The Problem of Regulating Development in the N.C. Mountains Along the Blue Ridge Parkway

William G. Smith, N.C. Dept. of Natural Resources and Community Development, Division of Community Assistance, Winston-Salem, N.C.

Western North Carolina today is faced with a major irony: The beauty that makes the mountains so attractive is in danger of being destroyed by that attractiveness.

These mountains — through which the Blue Ridge Parkway runs — have long been a favorite vacation spot and are rapidly becoming a place for people to spend their retirement years. Therein lies the irony. What makes the mountains so popular is, in large part, their vast unspoiled scenic beauty. Inevitably, however, as more people are attracted to the mountains, they become less attractive. People do not want to move to the mountains so that they can look out the window at a neighboring high-rise condominium.

The consequence of this was underscored several years ago when high-rise condominiums were built atop Sugar Mountain in Avery County. The project ultimately led to a statewide Ridge Law but not until after the project was built. The condominiums have no doubt brought in some additional tourist dollars by providing luxurious accommodations with an unsurpassed — and now unique — view, but they have left a permanent mark on the landscape. (The condos enjoy a monopoly due to their status as the only such ridge top development in North Carolina.)

BLUE RIDGE PARKWAY PRESERVATION

The Blue Ridge Parkway is perhaps the best example of mountain preservation. Thanks to the foresight of our fathers' generation, the unspoiled beauty and natural areas along the Parkway will hopefully be protected for generations to come.

The Parkway is protected in a variety of ways. The federal government owns about 87,000 acres in Virginia and North Carolina. Within this property, some 4,500 acres are in an agricultural special-use program which allows former owners to continue the agricultural usage of land through a permit system. This program is intended to maintain pastoral scenes along the highway.

Another 2,062 acres along the Parkway (1,115 in Virginia and 947 in North Carolina) are in scenic easements which restrict the use of land, but allow individuals to maintain ownership. In North Carolina, Parkway ownership by the federal government or easements average about 115 acres per mile. In Virginia the average is about 100 acres. (A recently published long-range plan for the Parkway recommends that the average acreage per mile in both states be increased to 125.)[1]

But what about the land around the Parkway? Obviously it would never be practical or economically healthy for all mountain land to be controlled to the extent the Parkway lands are. Most communities must grow to survive. Too many people have had to leave their native mountains in search of employment.

Second-home development and tourism have provided a much needed boost to the mountain economy. According to the State Division of Travel and Tourism, 21 percent of the local labor force in Watauga County work in tourist-related jobs, 5 percent in Ashe and 10 Percent in Alleghany.[2] Construction and other related industries as well as service industries have also grown with the increase in development.

But, in my opinion, local officials must look more seriously at the need for some controls. Nearby mountain land is generally uncontrolled and poor development standards are creating many problems directly affecting mountain life. The unregulated development may lead to serious economic and environmental consequences in the future.

As community planner with the Division

of Community Assistance in the Department of Natural Resources and Community Development, I have worked for the past 14 years with the planning programs in Watauga, Ashe, Alleghany and Wilkes counties — the counties in Northwest North Carolina through which the Blue Ridge Parkway runs.

In the past three years, I have been specifically involved in Ashe and Alleghany counties with subdivision regulations. I have seen the changes — both good and bad — that development is bringing to the mountains and at the same time heard the arguments against environmental regulations.

STATE & LOCAL REGULATIONS IN WESTERN N.C.

The State of North Carolina has taken steps to protect development in the past. In 1973 the state adopted a Sedimentation Pollution Control Act that requires control of sediment runoff from all land disturbing activities on sites of more than one acre. Sedimentation from streams, lakes and other waters constitutes a major pollution problem. This act provides for the "creation, administration, and enforcement of a program for the adoption of minimal mandatory standards that will permit development of this State to continue with the least detrimental effects from pollution by sedimentation."[3]

In 1983 in response to the high-rise condominium project on Sugar Mountain in Avery County, the State of North Carolina adopted its Ridge Law to regulate developments on mountain ridges over 3,000 ft. high. Specifically, the law allows counties and towns to regulate the construction of tall buildings or structures (over 40 ft. high) on protected mountain ridges.[4]

In many of the counties through which the Parkway passes in Western North Carolina, the state regulations provide the only control of development. The incorporated towns within the region have zoning ordinances, but few land-use controls exist in the less populated county areas - the land where large future developments will most likely be built. Most of the counties do not enforce comprehensive land-use regulations. None have county-wide zoning and only two have subdivision regulations.

Controlling development is particularly important to protect the Parkway in the Northwest corner of the western mountains because most of the lands adjoining the Parkway are in private ownership while in the other far western counties national forest lands serve as a buffer. Also, development has been more difficult in the far western counties because the terrain is steeper.

The problems with mountain development have been apparent for many years. One of my first assignments in 1973 was to meet with the Ashe County Planning Board to discuss the benefits and limitations of the proposed Mountain Area Management Act (MAMA) which was being considered by the N.C. General Assembly. It was written out of concern for the type of development that was occurring in the mountains. It failed to pass, but a similar program on the coast (the Coastal Area Management Act) was enacted.

With funds from the U.S. Department of Housing and Urban Development's 701 planning grant program, land-use studies were prepared for Watauga, Ashe, Alleghany, and Wilkes counties. Implementation of these reports' recommendations have varied among the northwest counties.

Watauga and Wilkes counties have done the most toward implementing these recommendations. Both enforce subdivision regulations and floodplain ordinances. Watauga enforces its own sedimentation ordinance. Wilkes enforces a limited area zoning ordinance around North Wilkesboro and Wilkesboro and the Kerr Scott Dam Reservoir.

Ashe County adopted a mobile home ordinance in 1973 and a floodplain ordinance in 1977, but does not enforce either zoning or subdivision regulations. Alleghany does not enforce any of the traditional land-use controls such as subdivision regulations or zoning.

TRENDS IN MOUNTAIN DEVELOPMENT

Not surprisingly while local controls have been slow in receiving approval, development has been increasing. Watauga was the first of the counties to experience the affects of second-home and tourist-related development. Although Blowing Rock in Watauga and Linville in Avery County had been popular second-home communities for many years, it was not until the 1960s and early 1970s that the market began to expand throughout the counties.

Although the gas shortage of the mid-1970s slowed development temporarily, the demand for mountain property today is as great as it ever was with development spreading into Ashe, Alleghany and Wilkes counties.

In Ashe County alone, between 1982 and 1986, 190 new subdivisions were recorded in the register of deeds office. Most were in the townships near the New River and the Parkway.[5]

In Alleghany County the scale of development has not been as great as in Ashe or Watauga. The Roaring Gap development near the Parkway and Stone Mountain State Park has prospered for many years and several new developments have occurred along the New River. Recently the Fred Willard family property on the New River and the Glade School site near the Parkway were subdivided and sold at auction; both properties contained several hundred acres each.

Wilkes is also experiencing new second-home development in its northeast corner near Stone Mountain State Park and in the northwest corner near Elk Creek. Both areas are near the Parkway.

PROBLEMS WITH MOUNTAIN DEVELOPMENT

Uncontrolled development has, in many cases, contributed to turning dreams of a mountain home into nightmares. The mountain environment is very delicate. When excavation and construction are not done properly, many problems can occur.

An elderly Greensboro couple, for example, purchased a lot in a development near the Creston Community in Ashe County in 1979 for $4,000 but sold it a few years later for one hundred dollars just to get rid of it because of numerous problems with access roads.

The steep dirt roads up the mountain were rutted by erosion and the developer did not repair them. In 1982 a new road was cut because the original was too steep. The new road cut off a large portion of the couple's lot and made it too small to build on. For them it was easier to quit than fight the matter in court.[6]

POORLY DESIGNED SUBDIVISIONS

Mountain people call the rocky mountain terrain that is almost too steep to walk on "mule-faced property." But people who do not know the dangers in mountain development have been attracted to this land because of the scenic view.

Unfortunately, much mountain property is not acceptable for development. Or, if the property is usable, site preparation may cost three, four or more times that of normal development.

According to Gerald Elliot, Ashe County's sanitarian, some developments have been built on steep hillsides that do not have enough topsoil to support septic tank systems. Others have been built or planned on expensive river-bottom land in floodplains with high-water tables. Still other developments have lots that are too small or in the wrong configuration. Although there is no perfect lot size or shape, certain principles need to be followed.[7]

In one 20-acre subdivision near Crumpler in Ashe County, only three building sites were found to be suitable for a septic tank system.[8]

SUBSTANDARD ROADS

Another major problem occurs when roads are not properly built. Many developers of new subdivisions in the mountain counties prefer private roads rather than public ones that must be built to state standards. Although minimizing the impact on the environment is given most often as the reason for private roads, the primary reason is often money.

The N.C. Department of Transportation requires 50 foot rights-of-way, paved surfaces at least 18-feet wide with grades not exceeding 12 percent. A typical private road is built of 2 or 3 inches of crushed stone, is about 12-feet wide and has a grade often exceeding the state limit.[9]

Many are so narrow that only one car can pass at a time. Under normal circumstances, these roads are bad enough, but when an emergency occurs and fire trucks or ambulances can not get through, life and property are threatened.

Last winter a family living in Daniel's Daughter development in Ashe County faced this problem firsthand. Their home was destroyed by fire when pumper trucks could not get to their property because access roads were impassable. The West Jefferson fire chief expressing the frustration of the firefighters, was quoted as saying, "That's a perfect example of what they're saying about subdivision regulations. You can't get in; you can't get out; you can't do anything." Ironically this house was only 75 feet from the New River.[10]

Because roads deteriorate quickly in the mountains, maintenance is critical. But private roads are not maintained by the Department of Transportation. Although the North Carolina General Statutes require developers to warn buyers through disclosure statements that they are responsible for road maintenance, the property owners are the ones who are left with the cost of upkeep.

If a homeowners' association is formed and all the property owners are required to pay an annual maintenance fee, funds may be available to cover maintenance costs. But in many cases, these associations do not exist.

At a planning board meeting in Ashe County, a resident of one of the older subdivisions told a story that is representative of many others. He and his wife bought a lot in a subdivision several years ago. Initially, the house was planned as a summer home, but when he retired, the house became a permanent residence. As the development gets older, road maintenance has become more expensive. There is no home owners' association requiring a maintenance fee.[11]

For many who only visit occasionally, this is not a major problem. As a result, only about 30 percent of the property owners pay for road maintenance. Since this generates only enough funds to keep the roads passable, no significant upgrading of the road systems has occurred. Often residents will pave the part of a road in front of their home, while other sections are left graveled.

By far the worst situation is when no roads are provided by the subdivider. Land in Ashe and Alleghany can be divided into lots with 50 ft. rights-of-way drawn on the plat and sold to individuals. Except for the survey work, no improvements have to be done to the property. The subdivider takes his money and leaves the site improvements to the property owners.

Roads should be installed before lots are sold. Often during construction, roads have to be shifted to avoid problems such as underground rock. When this happens lot lines may need to be shifted. Re-platting lots that have been sold is very difficult once control of the entire tract has been given up.

ENVIRONMENTAL PROBLEMS

The uncontrolled development that has already taken place in North Carolina's mountains has left its mark and will have a significant impact on the natural environment for generations to come.

Roads and home sites that are not properly stabilized will allow soils to be washed into streams and rivers and destroy much of the aquatic life.

A 1985 study by the N.C. Division of Environmental Management stated that sedi ment is the major pollutant of the New River. While overall, the River has one of the better biological ratings in the state, the study says that the growing development of vacation and retirement homes will impact on water quality.[12]

ECONOMIC LOSS

Another problem with improper development is the economic loss. Poorly designed subdivisions are generally not successful. Not only do the subdivider and property owners lose, but less successful subdivisions also cost the counties money in both tourist and tax dollars.

The natural beauty of the mountains is their greatest asset. If the countryside is scarred with poor development, people will not come to visit or live. This economic benefit will be diverted elsewhere.This is important since tourism is important to these mountain counties.

In unsuccessful subdivisions new homes are not built and put on county tax rolls or units are abandoned, reducing their tax value.

Then, too, with current land development practices, many subdivisions are not taxed according to their true value. Without subdivision regulations in Ashe and Alleghany counties, there is no control of how the property is listed for taxes. This is how it works:

When a subdivision plat or individual lots are recorded, the register of deeds office changes the property's designation from acreage to lots. A tax assessor examines the property, and it is almost always taxed at a higher rate. Since there are no legal restrictions, a subdivider will begin selling lots before any plats are recorded. If he uses land-purchase agreements, no plat needs to be recorded until all the payments have been made.

The result is that the improved property is not taxed as lots for several years and the county suffers a large tax loss.

OBSTACLES TO LAND-USE CONTROLS

With all of the problems of uncontrolled development, why are there so few regulations? Don't the elected officials see the inherent problems?

Elected officials are aware of the problems, but implementing local ordinances is a very difficult political decision. Several issues are involved:

- Mountain people have a long tradition of self-reliance and distrust for government intervention. The Scot-Irish ancestry has produced an independent people who are accustomed to handling their own problems.
- Another obstacle to local regulations is a concern over limiting the division of property among family members. Mountain farms are often passed down from generation to generation. Subdivision ordinances would require family divisions to meet the same standards as any other subdivision.

  A farmer with a 100-acre tract can give a son or daughter an acre or two lot without creating a legal subdivision. However, a division of more than two lots would fall under subdivision regulations. Many people do not believe that this is right.
- Often expressed among critics of subdivision regulations is a need to exempt smaller projects of 10 lots or less. They argue that following procedures for development as required by subdivision ordinances is too costly for small developers and eliminates many local developers who have land but little capital.
- Any new development standard will mean additional costs to the developer. A realtor speaking against proposed subdivision regulations in Ashe County calculated that to meet the proposed development standards the development cost of a typical subdivision would triple.[13]
- Administrative costs to the county are also a concern, particularly to local elected officials. In a time of cutbacks in federal funding and increased financial demands on local government, counties are reluctant to take on new responsibilities.

  Larry South, Ashe County manager, has estimated that it costs the county approximately $20,000 to support an administrative officer. Even if a fee schedule is established, it would be difficult for a subdivision regulation program to generate enough income to be self-supporting.[14]
- Critics of subdivision regulations contend that enough environmental programs are already in existence: The government would be better off enforcing the programs it already has on the books.

REASONS FOR REGULATIONS

These arguments have merit and have been used successfully for years to block regulations in the mountains. But the public needs to be more aware of the total picture.

Mountain Ethics

County zoning and subdivision regulations ensure local control in the truest sense. While based on state statutes, the ordinances that have been proposed were designed by planning boards of local citizens. These ordinances would be administered by local people who are directly responsible to their elected officials.

On the other hand, if the development problem becomes too severe or is ignored, the N.C. General Assembly may step in and mandate that certain regulations be passed. This sentiment was expressed by former state representative Margaret "Pinky" Hayden, who sponsored the Ridge Law several years ago. At a meeting of the Blue Ridge Environmental Defense League in Glendale Springs (Ashe County), she said:

> *Local government can handle it (land-use regulations) less expensively and local folks will take care of their own problems if they are motivated to do it. Often a move in Raleigh provides the motivation.*[15]

Family Exclusion

There are many problems with excluding land divided within a family. First, what is a family? Would an exclusion be limited to parents and their children? Or would it include second cousins? Should there be a cap on the number of lots that can be created?

Within the past year a "family subdivision" with more than 50 lots was reported in Ashe County. An elderly woman divided her farm among nine children and their children. Since some of the heirs live out of state, they will probably sell their lots to non-family members, so in the future many unrelated families will probably live there.[16]

The subdivision of land must follow the same rules, whether or not the dividers are relatives.

Exemption for Small Subdivisions

The General Statutes of North Carolina define a subdivision and provide for certain exclusions. When small subdivisions are excluded under all circumstances, a major loophole is created in the ordinance.

For example, if 10-lot subdivisions are regulated, a subdivider can create a 9-lot subdivision and then sell the remaining land to someone else to create another subdivision the same size or smaller.

An example of circumventing regulations can be seen in Ashe County where several adjoining subdivisions have been built containing 49 lots or less. This was apparently done to avoid requirements imposed by the State of Florida on any subdivision marketed to Florida residents whether the land is in Florida or not. Since their regulations only apply to subdivisions with 50 lots or more, the developers in Ashe County have avoided the regulations.

Fragmenting the development process undermines the basic intent of subdivision regulations, which is to develop land in a comprehensive and coordinated fashion.

Adding Cost to New Development

New standards will impose a short-term increase in costs on the developer and ultimately to the property owner. But the costs will be less in the long-term. Redoing mistakes is more expensive than doing it right the first time.

Then too, quality developments do sell. Subdivisions with well designed roadways and lots with approved septic tank systems are in great demand. River Mountain Subdivision on the New River in Alleghany County is a good illustration. The owners built a quality subdivision. Although each lot costs several thousand dollars more than the average county lot, they have sold quickly. Except in a few cases local enforcement programs are not self-supporting operations and neither is the local educational system. Protecting local resources is a responsibility of local governments.

Other Regulatory Programs

The state Land Quality Division does enforce a number of regulatory programs affecting subdivisions, including the N.C. Sedimentation Pollution Control Act. Any land disturbing activities on more than one acre must get an approved sedimentation plan from this division. In order to stabilize the disturbed land, the Land Quality staff recommends development standards, but these are not mandatory.

Douglas Miller, regional engineer in the Winston-Salem Field Office whose jurisdiction includes Ashe and Alleghany counties, explained, "The guidelines (Sedimentation Pollution Control Act) address control of runoff when one or more acres are graded. They do not address paving, road width, road grading, lot sizes, or accessibility of emergency vehicles, or anything like that."[17]

CONCLUSLON

Mountain residents are faced with a major dilemma. Do they continue living as they have for generations holding to the apparent belief that land-use should not be regulated? Or do they realize their roles as stewards of the land and look to protecting their property for future generations? Hugh Morton, the developer of Grandfather Mountain, gave a warning recently that should be considered carefully. "There are people who don't care about the mountains the same way we do and unless we make some rules and regulations, we're in trouble."[18]

There is some evidence that the public is becoming more aware. A recent study conducted for Ashe County by the Appalachian State University School of Business indicated that county residents are concerned about growth and were willing to accept some types of land-use controls, such as zoning.[19]

Maybe this is a sign that some of the obstacles to good planning can be overcome. The mountain counties must take the responsibility to ensure that future problems due to poor development do not occur. This decision will affect generations to come along the Blue Ridge Parkway.

NOTES

1. Land Protection Plan Virginia and North Carolina, Blue Ridge Parkway, The National Park Service, p.18.
2. N.C. Department of Commerce, Division of Travel and Tourism.
3. "Sedimentation Pollution Control Act of 1973," North Carolina General Statutes, Chapter 113A, Article 4.
4. "Mountain Ridge Protection Act of 1983," North Carolina General Statutes, Chapter 113A, Article 14.
5. Ashe County Register of Deeds Office, Jefferson, N.C.
6. Bill McIlwain, "Mountain Getaway A Horror," Winston-Salem Journal, February, 1986.
7. Charles Peek, "Mule-Faced Projects Cost All," Jefferson Times, May 22,1986, p.1.
8. Ibid.
9. Subdivision Roads Minimum Construction Standards, N.C. Department of Transportation, Division of Highways, (1983).
10. "Frustrated Firefighters Watch House Burn." Jefferson Times, March 5, 1987.
11. Ashe County Planning Board Meeting, Jefferson, N.C. (June 1986).
12. Assessment of Surface Water Quality in North Carolina, N.C. Department of Natural Resources and Community Development, Division of Environmental Management, (May 1985), p.133.
13. Susan Van Wyk, "Subdivision Regulations Will Stop Development," The Skyland Post, April 30, 1986, p.1.
14. Interview with Larry South, September 1986.
15. D. Smith, "Hayden Opposes Nuke Waste, Erosion Issues," Mountain Times, July 19, 1984, p.8.
16. Files of North Carolina Department of Natural Resources and Community Development, Division of Land Quality, Winston-Salem Field Office.

17. Lynn Worth, "Group Risks Compromise on Subdivision Rules," Jefferson Times, April 28, 1986. p.1.
18. "We Must Protect Mountains," The Skyland Post, June 4, 1986, p.1.
19. Dr. Rickey C. Kirkpatrick and Dr. B.J. Dunlap, Land-Use Planning in Ashe County: A Statistical Study of Residents' Attitudes, Appalachian State University, Boone, N.C.

BIBLIOGRAPHY

Ashe County Planning Board Meeting. Jefferson, N.C. (June 1986).

Ashe County Register of Deeds Office. Jefferson, N.C.

Assessment of Surface Water Quality in North Carolina. N.C. Department of Natural Resources and Community Development, Division of Environmental Management. (May 1985), 133.

"Frustrated Firefighters Watch House Burn." Jefferson Times. (March 5, 1987).

Kirkpatrick, Rickey C. and Dunlap, B.J. Land-Use Planning in Ashe County: A Statistical Study of Residents' Attitudes. Appalachian State University, Boone, N.C.

Land Protection Plan Virginia and North Carolina. Blue Ridge Parkway. The National Park Service, 18.

McIlwain, Bill. "Mountain Getaway A Horror." Winston-Salem Journal. (February, 1986).

Miller, Douglas, regional engineer with the Department of Natural Resources and Community Development, Division of Land Quality. Interview. (March 23, 1986).

"Mountain Ridge Protection Act of 1983." North Carolina General Statutes. Chapter 113A. Article 14.

N.C. Department of Commerce. Division of Travel and Tourism.

N.C. Department of Natural Resources and Community Development, Division of Land Quality. Winston-Salem Field Office. Files.

Peek, Charles. "Mule-Faced Projects Cost All." Jefferson Times. (May 22, 1986), 1.

"Sedimentation and Pollution Control Act of 1873." N.C. General Statutes, Chapter 113A. Article 4.

Smith, D. "Hayden Opposes Nuke Waste, Erosion Issues." Mountain Times, (July 19, 1984), 6.

South, Larry. Interview. (September 1986).

Subdivision Roads Minimum Construction Standards. N.C. Department of Transportation. Division of Highways. (1983)

Van Wyk, Susan. "Subdivision Regulations Will Stop Development." The Skyland Post (April 30, 1986), 1.

"We Must Protect Mountains." The Skyland Post. (June 4, 1986), 1.

Worth, Lynn. "Group Risks Compromise on Subdivision Rules." Jefferson Times. (April 28, 1986), 1.

www.ingramcontent.com/pod-product-compliance
Lightning Source LLC
LaVergne TN
LVHW050928080826
845145LV00001B/257

* 9 7 8 1 4 6 9 6 4 2 0 2 4 *